Microsoft SQL Server 6.5 Programming

*Peter DeBetta, John Papa,
Dave Martin, Marc Israel, et al.*

SAMS
PUBLISHING

201 West 103rd Street
Indianapolis, IN 46290

Unleashed

Microsoft SQL Server 6.5 Programming Unleashed

Copyright © 1998 by Sams

International Standard Book Number: 0-672-31244-1

Library of Congress Catalog Card Number: 97-80855

Printed in the United States of America

First Printing: May 1998

00 99 98   4 3 2 1

Trademarks

Publisher: *Joe Wikert*

Executive Editor: *Rosemarie Graham*

Managing Editor: *Patrick Kanouse*

Acquisitions Editor
Corrine Wire

Development Editor
Marla Reece-Hall

Project Editor
Rebecca Mounts

Copy Editors
Tonya Maddox
Sean Medlock

Technical Editors
Trevor Dwyer
Ray Rankins
Jeff Steinmetz
Kevin Thompson

Cover Designer
Jason Grisham

Book Designer
Gary Adair

Indexer
Christine Nelsen

Production
Marcia Deboy
Michael Dietsch
Jennifer Earhart
Cynthia Fields
Maureen West

Contents

28 Data Warehousing and Online Transaction Processing (OLTP) 711

Dedication

This book is dedicated to my mom (and my friend), Jeanette. —Peter DeBetta

This book is dedicated to my family, those who have passed away or are about to pass away—I wish I could have spent more time with you. May God take you under His wing until we meet again.—Timothy Atwood

Acknowledgments

When it finally came time to write this acknowledgment, I was at a loss for words. After many hours of writing and editing, on top of teaching, consulting, and developing more than full time, I realized that a once small notion I had last year has become a reality.

I first and foremost want to thank my mom and dad, Jeanette and Dick. I did not become the doctor that they wanted me to be; despite this fact, they have always encouraged and inspired me to be the best that I could be. I also want to thank my little (albeit taller) brother, Bob, for the talks and for teaching me some new songs to play on my guitar—which provided some down time from all the hustle and bustle.

I would like to thank, over and over again, both Carol Bohn and Carol van den Boom for believing in and putting up with me. Two friends (and colleagues) also deserve much gratitude: Mark Hunter and Byer Hill. They always stood behind me and supported me through the entire process. Many, many thanks to John and Caroline Ellison and their two daughters, Morgan and Reagan, for providing some warm meals when I didn't have the time, and a warm place when I did. Thanks to Terry Decker for making me realize that I am not so much an author as I am a teacher—and I hope this shows in my presentation of the material. Thanks to Johnny Papa for staying on and writing for this book and for being a good friend. Dave Martin gets a special thank you for everything from helping write this book to helping me rewire my home phone lines—but especially for just being there.

From Macmillan, I want to thank Marla Reece-Hall and Corrine Wire for the pivotal roles they played in making this book a success. Without them, this would have been nothing but an ongoing dream for me. Many thanks also for Katie Wise and Kevin Thompson for making all of the authors' jobs a lot easier. I also want to thank Rebekah Darksmith; I especially want to thank Brad Jones for all he did. Of course, thank you to all the authors who participated in the writing of this book.

I am quite sure that there are many others I have not mentioned here. To each of you, I say thanks.

Finally, a tremendous thank you to every teacher who has inspired a young mind—not always an easy task.—Peter DeBetta

> "Two roads diverged in a wood, and I —
> I took the one less travelled by,
> And that has made all the difference."
>
> *-Robert Frost*

About the Authors

Timothy Atwood

Timothy Atwood, a degreed professional in business administration and computer science, currently works as both a consultant and an instructor of Devry Institute of Technology. He has worked in database development, local and wide area networking, Web development, and UNIX/PC programming for various companies, ranging in size from small to Fortune 50. Throughout his 17 years in the field, Tim has used his auditing and business skills, as well as his computer expertise, to save his clients several million dollars, with the implementation of efficient automation.

Peter DeBetta

A graduate of Bucknell University, Peter DeBetta has been programming for 18 years. As this book went to press, he began his role as Vice President of Technology at Securities Education Institute Incorporated (www.seiinc.com) in Chapel Hill, NC. He has developed numerous multi-tier client/server and Web-based applications using tools such as Visual Basic, SQL Server, Access, Visual Interdev (Active Server Pages), and even Excel. Peter is an MCT for Visual Basic 4 and 5, SQL Server 6.5 Administration and Database Implementation. In addition, Peter continues to run his own development and consulting company, Milori Software (www.milori.com), based in Cary, NC. You can reach Peter via email at peter@milori.com.

Stephen Garrett

Stephen Garrett is a senior consultant with Magenic Technologies, a Microsoft Solution Provider Partner located in Minneapolis, Minnesota. He has more than five years of client/server programming experience, primarily with Visual Basic and SQL Server and Oracle. He is currently trying to cut back on Mountain Dew. Stephen can be reached via email at stepheng@magenic.com.

Dave Hamilton

Dave Hamilton is a Visual C++ database programmer working for Professional Business Services in Lincoln, NE. He is also the author of Sams' *Programming NT 4.0 Unleashed* and writes reviews for the C/C++ Journal. He can be reached at hamilton@soapnotes.com.

Greg Haselmann

Greg Haselmann is a senior consultant at Magenic Technologies, a Microsoft Solution Provider Partner located in Minnesota. He is a Microsoft Certified Systems Engineer who specializes in systems analysis and database design administration and development, with most of his efforts focused on SQL Server. Besides his computer addiction, his interests include tennis, reading, raising orchids, and obeying his cats' commands. He can be reached via Internet email at gregh@magenic.com.

Marc Israel

Marc Israel is the president of EFII, a Paris-based Microsoft Solution Provider. He has been working in the database area for 10 years, and became specialized in SQL Server in 1992. As a Microsoft Certified System Engineer (MCSE), Microsoft Certified Solution Developer (MCSD), and Microsoft Certified Trainer (MCT), he gives SQL Server courses for Microsoft France, Microsoft Northern and Western Africa, and for the Authorized Technical Education Center (ATEC). Working closely with Microsoft, Marc is doing frequent roadshows to demonstrate the power and usefulness of SQL Server. Mark gets involved in project-based development on SQL Server technologies for major French and international companies. Marc also wrote a book on the SQL Server administration, published in French for the Editions Eyrolles, Paris, 1997. Marc can be reached on CompuServe at 100302,1144 or on the Internet at misrael@efii.com.

Dave Martin

Dave Martin received his BEng(Hons) in manufacturing systems engineering at the University of Hertforshire, England. He has developed many client/server solutions for shop floor automation and manufacturing resource management, using Visual Basic, Access, and SQL Server. He is now an information systems auditor with a large manufacturing company.

Bennett McEwan

Bennett McEwan is president of Geist, LLC, a company in scenic upstate New York, specializing in explaining SQL Server. The work Ben enjoys most is mentoring, where he helps programmers or database administrators through the tough spots in mission-critical applications.

Ben also teaches SQL Server training classes, writes and designs Visual Basic client/server applications, and consults on difficult SQL Server performance and replication issues. You can catch him on comp.databases.ms-sqlserver. Email Ben at bmcewan@global2000.net, visit his page at http://www.metis.com/~geist, or call him directly at (518) 784-3045. He has been known to give foolishly discounted rates if you send him a box of cigars.

John Papa

John Papa is employed as a technical lead for DB Basics, a software development company, in Raleigh, North Carolina. A 1995 graduate of Siena College near his hometown of Albany, New York, John has been developing applications on SQL Server databases for three years. In that short time he has a become a Microsoft Certified Solution Developer certified in SQL Server 6.x, Visual Basic 4 & 5, and Windows Operating System and Services Architecture I & II.

John prides himself on his closely knit family and attributes all that he has become and all that he will achieve to God, his parents John and Peggy, and his loving wife, Colleen. You can reach John at JohnP@DBBasics.com.

Jeff Steinmetz

Jeff Steinmetz is a managing consultant with Magenic Technologies, a Microsoft Certified Solution Provider Partner. He is both a Microsoft Certified Solution Developer (MCSD) and a Microsoft Certified Systems Engineer (MCSE). He specializes in enterprises-wide client/server information systems, involving SQL Server, Internet/intranet Technologies, and all of the Microsoft BackOffice Technologies. Jeff also contributed to two previous Sams publications: *Office 95 Unleashed* and *Microsoft SQL Server 6.5 Unleashed*. If you have been in the Minneapolis area, you may have seen him speaking at various users groups and can usually run into him at most locally sponsored Microsoft seminars. His exposure to computer programming spans from the TRS-80, to the ill-fated Next Computer. After dabbling in music and theater for a few years, the programming bug returned in the form of Visual C++ 1.0 under Windows 3.1, and stuck from then. In his spare time, Jeff enjoys working on music in his home studio, dabbling in graphics design, and watching a ton of movies with his wife, Kat. He can be reached at jeffst@cyberdude.com or http://staff.magenic.com/jeffs. Jeff also served as a technical editor for this book.

Steven Waldner

Steven Waldner is a Microsoft Certified Solutions Developer with certifications in SQL Server implementation, Visual Basic and Windows Architecture. A veteran developer with over 10 years' experience, he has consulted internationally with companies such as American Express and Dayton-Hudson Corporation. Currently, he is a senior consultant with Magenic Technologies International of St. Louis Park, Minnesota. Steven lives in Minneapolis with his wife and two children.

About the Technical Editors

Trevor Dwyer

Trevor Dwyer is currently working for the UK's largest provider of computer hardware and services. Trevor is developing data warehousing and analysis solutions for the internal business. He has been involved with data migration projects using Oracle, AS/400, and Microsoft SQL Server for the past five years. Passionate about developing with SQL, Trevor has been involved with discussion forums on CompuServe and is active with various Microsoft beta programs. He has also been recognized for a MVP, a program that Microsoft uses to highlight the technical contribution provided through their online forums.

Ray Rankins

Ray Rankins is currently owner and president of Gotham Consulting Services in upstate New York. Ray is a nationally recognized consultant and instructor with over 10 years' experience in client/server and has been working with Sybase and Microsoft SQL Server since 1987 as a DBA, application developer, database designer, project manger, consultant, and instructor. He has worked in a variety of industries, including financial, manufacturing, healthcare, retail, insurance, communications, public utilities, and government. His areas of expertise include SQL Server performance and tuning, SQL Server application and database design and development, client/server architecture, and very large database design and implementation; he teaches and speaks on these topics from the local to the international level. He is also coauthor of *Sybase SQL Server 11 Unleashed*, *Microsoft SQL Server 6.5 Unleashed*, and the *Sybase SQL Server 11 DBA Survival Guide*, all published by Sams. Ray can be reached via the Internet at rrankins@nycap.rr.com.

Kevin Thompson

Kevin Thompson is a 1988 graduate of Purdue University with a bachelor's degree in computer science. He works as a consultant for Client Server Associates, Inc. in Indianapolis, IN. He is a Microsoft Certified Solutions Developer as well as a Certified PowerBuilder Developer. He has developed enterprisewide systems with SQL Server since 1993. Kevin and his wife, Lisa, live in Indianapolis with their three children.

Introduction

Last year, while teaching a SQL Server database programming class, I was presented with a question to which I had no answer. I returned later in the day to state that it could indeed be done, I'm just not sure how. It seemed that this question was really part of a much bigger question: Where can I find the answers to the real-world problems?

As I began researching the topic, I found that the amount of reference on advanced Transact-SQL topics was minimal, especially when compared to the amount available on all the other Microsoft programming and systems administration topics. I turned to Macmillan and presented the idea; it was well-received. What resulted was this book, *Microsoft SQL Server 6.5 Programming Unleashed*—the product of many people's time, effort, and knowledge, all from a diversity of backgrounds and experiences.

This book is meant to be both a learning tool and a solid reference for all aspects of programming with SQL Server. It is modular by design, consisting of 28 chapters in five major sections; this design allows you the freedom to read individual chapters as the topics becomes pertinent to your work or interest.

What Will I Learn from This Book?

Microsoft SQL Server 6.5 Programming Unleashed jumps right into intermediate and advanced concepts of database programming with SQL Server. This book is designed to be a in-depth reference for anyone who programs against a Microsoft SQL Server back-end, going beyond what other books and classroom instruction might teach. It does assume that you have some introductory database experience. A wide array of topics are covered in this book:

- Advanced Transact-SQL programming topics, including query optimization, cursors, dynamic execution, and string manipulation, are all covered in detail. Abundant code examples help illustrate the concepts.
- Writing effective code for multiple tier client/server applications is extensively explored.
- Database migration and data conversion and integration from legacy databases, Access, Oracle, and Sybase SQL Server are thoughtfully presented and discussed.
- Connectivity to SQL Server using DAO, RDO, ADO, ODBC, and DBLibrary are thoroughly explained in concept and via sample applications.
- Database application development using Visual Basic and Visual C++ is presented to provide understanding for both client and business server application logic from a variety of development environments.
- Real-world implementations, including data warehousing and online transaction processing (OLTP), complete the book not only physically, but conceptually.

As you can see, all the bases have been covered.

Conventions Used in This Book

The following conventions are used in this book:

- Code lines, commands, statements, variables, and any text you type or see on the screen appears in a `computer` typeface.

- Placeholders in syntax descriptions appear in an *`italic computer`* typeface. Replace the placeholder with the actual filename, parameter, or whatever element it represents.

- *Italics* highlight technical terms when they first appear in the text and are being defined.

- A special icon ➡ is used before a line of code that is really a continuation of the preceding line. Sometimes a line of code is too long to fit as a single line in the book, given the book's limited width. If you see ➡ before a line of code, remember that you should interpret that "line" as part of the line immediately before it.

IN THIS PART

I

PART

Advanced Programming Techniques

Beyond the Basics of Data Manipulation Language

CHAPTER 1

When I first starting working with Structured Query Language (SQL), I thought it was rather simple in comparison to other programming languages. How far can you take a statement (SELECT) that has approximately a dozen clauses to specify everything you need? As I delved deeper, I found that the syntax grew more complicated quickly. Nesting statements, dynamic execution, and advanced functions and expressions all gave SQL the additional power and capability to complete even the most difficult tasks.

And as I investigated even further, I found that with all its complexity, there were no standard naming conventions. Apparently, Structured Query Language was lacking some structure. I even noticed a lack of consistency within many procedures. Without such standards or consistency, debugging someone else's code can be a nightmare.

Thus the purpose of this chapter is two-fold: to establish a standard convention for naming objects and to explore some of the more advanced features of Transact-SQL.

Naming Conventions—A Little Review

As a programmer, it seems that everywhere you look, someone has established naming conventions for one thing or another. When it comes to database servers and various flavors of Structured Query Language, no one has taken the plunge and stated: "This is the way one should name their variables, and so on." And still to this date, I have yet to see an established set of naming conventions used in Microsoft's SQL Server's Transact-SQL (T-SQL) language.

What's Good for the Goose—Microsoft's Own Discrepancies

Even Microsoft does not use a standard naming syntax in its system stored procedures. Examine the code snippets in Listings 1.1 and 1.2 from the sp_help and sp_rename system stored procedures:

Listing 1.1. Sample code from the sp_help system stored procedure.

```
create procedure sp_help   -- 1995/09/13 18:23
    @objname varchar(92) = NULL     /* object name we're after */
as

declare @objid int          /* id of the object */
declare @sysstat smallint     /* the type of the object */
declare @dbname varchar(30)
declare @colname varchar(30)
```

Listing 1.2. Sample code from the sp_rename system stored procedure.

```
CREATE PROCEDURE sp_rename   --1996/05/13 10:28
    @objname    varchar(150)           -- Could be highly qualified.
   ,@newname         varchar( 30)
   ,@objtype  varchar( 13)   = null
```

```
as
--Some code and comments have been removed for readability
Declare
        @OrigParm1ItemType  varchar(13)   -- max length + 1
        ,@WorkParm1ItemType  varchar(13)

Declare
        @RetCode            integer
        ,@ExecRC            integer
        ,@CurrentDb         varchar(30)
        ,@Int1             integer
        ,@Int2             integer
        ,@SetQIStatus       integer
        ,@CountNumNodes     integer
        ,@BitsQuoted        integer
```

In the sp_help procedure, both the @objname parameter and @objid variable start with "obj," yet they are of different datatypes. In the sp_rename procedure, @objname, @newname, and @objtype are all of varchar datatype. Some of the variables use a title case type of naming as well: @CurrentDb and @CountNumNodes. And some even use a datatype indication: @Int1 and @Int2.

Perhaps it would be wiser to name all these items so that their names reflect the type of data they can hold as shown in the Listing 1.3.

Listing 1.3. Modified sample of sp_help stored procedure.

```
CREATE PROCEDURE sp_help  -- 1995/09/13 18:23
    @chvObjName varchar(92) = NULL      /* object name we're after */
as

DECLARE @intObjId int        /* id of the object */
DECLARE @insSysStat smallint     /* the type of the object */
DECLARE @chvDbName varchar(30)
DECLARE @chvColName varchar(30)
```

For the same reasons that intCounter and strName are easier to read when programming in Microsoft's Visual Basic, coding @chvObjName and @intObjId can assist you when programming in T-SQL. But the original question still begs an answer: What are the naming conventions in SQL Server T-SQL? Microsoft has mentioned certain elements when naming indexes and the like: Use the table name and field name(s), for example. You can take the rules one step further.

The Name of the Game

Naming conventions for both datatypes and objects need to be established. First and foremost, there needs to be a syntax for the names. Title case has always been a popular feature used in naming objects, and so the tradition will be carried on. A set of standard prefixes is necessary so that items can be easily identified in code. Keep in mind that some restrictions apply when you name variables and objects in SQL Server.

■ First, identifier (object and variable) names cannot exceed 30 characters. Although this seems like a lot, it can be restricting at times (especially when you are accurately trying to describe the role an object plays in the database). Because the prefixes use two or three characters, you are left with that many less to name your objects and variables.

■ Second, an item's name might begin only with a letter or the following characters: _ (underscore), # (pound or hash), or @ (at). Furthermore, the @ and # symbols have special meanings. The @ symbol represents a local variable in T-SQL. So you might not use it when naming a database object. The # symbol represents a temporary object. A local variable cannot use an initial # in its name.

■ Next, an identifier might contain alphanumeric characters or any of the following symbols: # (pound or hash), $ (dollar), or _ (underscore). You have no restrictions on placement within the name, as long as the initial character follows the rule previously mentioned.

■ Finally, spaces and other characters are not allowed in identifier names. Also, you cannot use keywords, such as table, as an object name.

NOTE

It wouldn't be programming unless there was some exception to the rule. And of course, there is: quoted identifiers. By using quoted identifiers in T-SQL, you can create table names such as "This Is My Table", "This&That", or even "table". Quoted identifiers allow for nonstandard names in an environment that prefers standard names. And although SQL Server supports quoted identifiers, I strongly do not recommended this practice.

The Conventions

Here's an introduction to the naming conventions for T-SQL. You must still adhere to the rules for identifiers as described by Microsoft. The conventions listed here describe conventions that are in accordance with those rules.

Local variables use a lowercase, three-letter prefix with all remaining words in title case. Table 1.1 gives you a listing of conventions for datatypes and some examples.

Table 1.1. The datatype naming conventions for T-SQL.

Datatype	Prefix	Example
int	int	@intObjectId
smallint	ins	@insCounter
tinyint	iny	@inyQuantity

Datatype	Prefix	Example
float	flt	@fltValue
real	rel	@relInterest
numeric	num	@numMass
decimal	dec	@decVolume
money	mny	@mnyTotal
smallmoney	mns	@mnsSalary
bit	bit	@bitTerminated
datetime	dtm	@dtmBirth
smalldatetime	dts	@dtsBeginAccount
char	chr	@chrLastName
varchar	chv	@chvAddress1
binary	bny	@bnyFlags
varbinary	bnv	@bnvData
text*	txt	@txtMemo
image*	img	@imgPicture

Although text and image are valid datatypes, they might not be declared as local variables. Keep in mind that local variables must begin with a single @ (at) symbol.

Objects use a lowercase, two-letter prefix with all remaining words in title case. The exceptions are tables and columns, neither of which use a prefix, although the title case rule still applies. Table 1.2 lists the object naming conventions.

Table 1.2. The object naming conventions for T-SQL.

Object	Prefix	Example
Table	–	SalesReps
Column	–	AuthorId
View	vw	vwContractAuthors
Stored Procedure	pr	prDeleteTerminatedReps
Rules	rl	rlZipCheck
Defaults	df	dfStandardQuantity
User Defined Datatypes	dt	dtAddressLine
Index (Clustered)	ic	icAuthorFullName

continues

Table 1.2. continued

Object	Prefix	Example
Index (Non-Clustered)	in	inClientStateCity
Primary Key (Clustered)	pc	pcCustomerId
Primary Key (Non-Clustered)	pn	pnStateLookupId
Foreign Key	fk	fkRepCompanyId
Trigger	tr	trStoreDelete
Cursor	cr	crTables

Some Additional Notes

Microsoft does use some standard naming conventions for its objects in SQL Server. System and extended stored procedures use sp_ and xp_ prefixes, respectively (with a few exceptions, of course). Systems tables start with a sys prefix. Try to stay away from naming your objects in a like manner. If you create a system stored procedure, however, sp_ is the most appropriate way to name it.

Keep in mind that, like the Reddick naming conventions used in Visual Basic for Applications, the objective here is to provide an industry standard for naming identifiers in SQL Server. So when you do change someone else's code, or even your own code, six months down the road, your task will be much easier if you can quickly identify the type of each object and variable.

Using Subqueries and In-Line Views

Now that naming conventions are under control, it's time to do a little programming. You will be learning to do some more advanced queries in T-SQL using both subqueries and in-line views (also known as derived tables). Both techniques provide a means of embedding SELECT statements within other T-SQL statements. You will examine examples of both in order to better understand how they work and when they are appropriate to use.

> **NOTE**
>
> Throughout this chapter, you will use the pubs database in SQL Server for the example code.

Subqueries in T-SQL

Subqueries come in two varieties: simple and correlated. Subqueries are SELECT statements that are nested within another T-SQL statement. Generally, subqueries are used within the WHERE or HAVING clause of another SELECT, INSERT, UPDATE, or DELETE statement, another subquery, or even as an expression.

Simple Subqueries

Start off by examining a SELECT statement with a simple subquery as shown in Listing 1.4.

Listing 1.4. Example of a simple subquery.

```
SELECT     title, price
FROM       titles
WHERE      title_id IN
           (SELECT  title_id
           FROM     sales
           WHERE    qty > 30)
```

This statement returns a list of books that have had more than 30 copies sold. Using the pubs database, you get a total of four rows affected (returned). Only those titles whose title_id exists in the sales table and had more than 30 copies sold are returned by the subquery. This list is used as the criteria for the list of titles that will be returned. You have another way to achieve the same results, and although the next statement in Listing 1.5 is indeed different, it is semantically the same.

Listing 1.5. A simple subquery using the EXISTS clause.

```
SELECT     title, price
FROM       titles
WHERE      EXISTS
           (SELECT  *
           FROM     sales
           WHERE    sales.title_id = titles.title_id
           AND      qty > 30)
```

Again, if a title_id *exists* in the sales table with more than 30 copies sold, only then will it be listed by the main SELECT statement. To better understand the semantics, take a look at the results with a few query options turned on. Figure 1.1 demonstrates the Query Options dialog box and shows two options that have been set: Show Query Plan and Show Stats I/O.

FIGURE 1.1.

The Query Options dialog box.

After turning these options on, you can execute the two SELECT statements to get the following results (Listing 1.6 and Listing 1.7) for Listings 1.4 and 1.5 respectively:

Listing 1.6. Results from executing Listing 1.4.

```
STEP 1
The type of query is SELECT
FROM TABLE
titles
Nested iteration
Table Scan
EXISTS : nested iteration
  FROM TABLE
  sales
  Nested iteration
  Table Scan
title                                                           price
----------------------------------------------------------------- ----
You Can Combat Computer Stress!                                 2.99
Secrets of Silicon Valley                                       20.00
Is Anger the Enemy?                                             10.95
Onions, Leeks, and Garlic: Cooking Secrets of the Mediterranean 20.95

(4 row(s) affected)

Table: titles  scan count 1,  logical reads: 3,  physical reads: 0,
➡  read ahead reads: 0
Table: sales  scan count 18,  logical reads: 18,  physical reads: 0,
➡  read ahead reads: 0
```

Listing 1.7. Results from executing Listing 1.5.

```
STEP 1
The type of query is SELECT
FROM TABLE
titles
Nested iteration
Table Scan
EXISTS : nested iteration
  FROM TABLE
  sales
  Nested iteration
  Table Scan
title                                                           price
----------------------------------------------------------------- ----
You Can Combat Computer Stress!                                 2.99
Secrets of Silicon Valley                                       20.00
Is Anger the Enemy?                                             10.95
Onions, Leeks, and Garlic: Cooking Secrets of the Mediterranean 20.95

(4 row(s) affected)

Table: titles  scan count 1,  logical reads: 3,  physical reads: 0,
➡  read ahead reads: 0
Table: sales  scan count 18,  logical reads: 18,  physical reads: 0,
➡  read ahead reads: 0
```

As you examine the results of these two statements, you will notice that both look remarkably the same. And for good reason, for behind the scenes, SQL Server processes both the same. You can, however, achieve the same results in yet another manner. By using table joins instead of subqueries, you can not only get the same set of data returned, but you will most likely keep processing down on your server.

Joins and Subqueries

Examine the following SELECT statement (Listing 1.8) and its results (Listing 1.9):

Listing 1.8. Selecting titles based on sales via a join.

```
SELECT    titles.title, titles.price
FROM      titles JOIN sales ON sales.title_id = titles.title_id
WHERE     sales.qty > 30
```

Listing 1.9. Results of executing Listing 1.8.

```
STEP 1
The type of query is SELECT
FROM TABLE
sales
Nested iteration
Table Scan
FROM TABLE
titles
Nested iteration
Using Clustered Index
title                                                         price
---------------------------------------------------------    ----
Secrets of Silicon Valley                                    20.00
Is Anger the Enemy?                                           10.95
Onions, Leeks, and Garlic: Cooking Secrets of the Mediterranean    20.95
You Can Combat Computer Stress!                              2.99

(4 row(s) affected)

Table: titles  scan count 4,  logical reads: 8,  physical reads: 1,
➡  read ahead reads: 0
Table: sales  scan count 1,  logical reads: 1,  physical reads: 0,
➡  read ahead reads: 0
```

Sure, SQL Server returns the rows in a different order, but the results are the same. The semantics are quite different, however, and beg further discussion.

Notice in the Query Plan section that an EXISTS is not being performed. Rather, the SELECT finds the data from the sales table and then uses the clustered index from the titles table to find the matching titles. Looking at the Stats I/O information, you notice that this SELECT statement actually had lower scan count and logical reads values.

In most cases, a join in the SELECT statement is easier and more efficient than an equivalent subquery. My recommendation: Use joins when possible over subqueries for better results.

NOTE

Use of indexes can greatly affect the Stats I/O of a T-SQL statement. Be sure that key fields (the columns being joined) in both tables are indexed for better lookup performance.

Further Subquery Considerations

Based on what you have read so far, there doesn't seem to be a good time to use subqueries. So why use them at all? Well, situations do exist where (no pun intended) a subquery can do the job that a join just cannot do. Say that you want to get a list of titles that sold more than the average sales quantity. A SELECT statement with a join alone cannot accomplish this task. You also need to use a subquery to get the job done, as shown in Listing 1.10.

Listing 1.10. Selecting titles that sell more than the average.

```
SELECT      titles.title, titles.price
FROM        titles JOIN sales ON sales.title_id = titles.title_id
WHERE       sales.qty >
            (SELECT AVG(qty)
            FROM sales)
```

Why must you use the subquery? Simply put, you cannot compare aggregate values, in this case, AVG(qty) —with non-aggregate values—qty. When performing a SELECT statement, if you select the average quantity and the quantity, you must use GROUP BY on the second quantity (because it is not being aggregated), which in turn prevents you from finding the average quantity. Look at the following statement in Listing 1.11 and its results.

Listing 1.11. Selecting qty and AVG(qty) from the sales table.

```
SELECT      qty, AVG(qty) AS avgqty
FROM        sales
GROUP BY    qty

qty     avgqty
------  ----------
3       3
5       5
10      10
15      15
20      20
25      25
30      30
35      35
40      40
50      50
75      75

(11 row(s) affected)
```

Notice how the avgqty column and the qty column are always equal. Because you need to group by the qty column, you will only see the average quantity for each unique quantity. The average of 3 is 3, the average of 3 and 3 is 3, and so on.

Correlated Subqueries

A correlated subquery relies on the main query for its processing. In essence, a correlated subquery cannot exist on its own. If you were to compare simple and correlated subqueries to English syntax, a simple subquery would be an independent clause, and a correlated subquery would be a dependent clause. Correlated subqueries rely on a value from the main query to retrieve its rows—so you will always see a column from the main query being referenced by the subquery. Listing 1.12 demonstrates an example of a correlated subquery.

Listing 1.12. A correlated subquery (from SQL Server Books Online).

```
SELECT     DISTINCT au_lname, au_fname
FROM       authors
WHERE      100 IN
           (SELECT royaltyper
           FROM titleauthor
            WHERE titleauthor.au_id = authors.au_id)
```

Observe how the subquery references a column from the main query; the subquery could not exist on its own. And, as usual, most cases of correlated subqueries can be replaced with a join. In many cases, the join is easier to read and more efficient behind the scenes. So why use a correlated subquery? Just like the example shown in Listing 1.11, occasions occur when the job can be done only via a subquery. My advice, however, is to use a join when possible. You usually gain speed and they tend to be easier to decipher when you look back on your code.

In-Line Views (Derived Tables)

New to SQL Server 6.5, ANSI in-line views (derived tables in SQL Server) enable you to create a temporary view on demand without the physical storage for the view. Derived tables are just another form of an embedded SELECT statement. Instead of performing complicated joins, a derived table presents an alternative to the SELECT statement with no change to the performance of the query. Examine Listing 1.13 and Listing 1.14 to see the difference.

Listing 1.13. Selecting authors and titles using only joins.

```
SELECT     au_lname, title
FROM       authors a JOIN titleauthor ta ON a.au_id = ta.au_id
           JOIN titles t ON t.title_id = ta.title_id
```

Listing 1.14. Select authors and titles using derived tables.

```
SELECT     a.au_lname, tt.title
FROM       authors a JOIN
           (SELECT title, au_id FROM titleauthor ta
           JOIN titles t ON t.title_id = ta.title_id) tt
           ON a.au_id = tt.au_id
```

They work the same but look very different. The SELECT statement in Listing 1.13 joins authors to titleauthor to titles. Behind the scenes, two are initially joined and then the third is joined to those results. The SELECT statement in Listing 1.14 shows the work that is happening behind the scenes in the query itself. First titleauthor is joined to titles, and then authors is joined to those results.

> **NOTE**
>
> The parentheses and the table alias following the derived table are both required when performing query with derived tables.

In most cases, there is no net benefit to using derived tables in your T-SQL code. You will encounter, on occasion, queries that have too many joins to be readable. In these cases, using several in-line views can help make reading the query easier on the eyes and the mind without sacrificing performance.

Just recently, however, I came across a situation where a query I was writing could not be done without either a derived table in the syntax or the creation of a view. I wanted to insert rows of data from a table in a particular order, but because I was converting the column data from numeric to character data, the order was incorrect. Instead of the desired results of 1, 2, 3, 4, 5, 6, 7, 8, 9, 10, 11, I was getting 1, 10, 11, 2, 3, 4 ,5 ,6 ,7 ,8 ,9.

The following two features were at work when I came across the problem:

- The INSERT statement requires that only the fields being inserted can be present in the SELECT clause.

- If DISTINCT is specified in the column list of a SELECT statement, and ORDER BY clause is used, all columns in the ORDER BY clause must appear in the column list.

Listing 1.15 shows a sample of the situation with both the incorrect and correct query. I have commented out the erroneous query in the code.

Listing 1.15. A query that required a derived table.

```
CREATE TABLE #MyTempTable
(
    ThisCol varchar(10)
)

/* This INSERT causes an error
INSERT #MyTempTable
    SELECT    DISTINCT CONVERT(varchar(10), qty)
    FROM      sales
    ORDER BY  qty
*/

--This INSERT works
```

```
INSERT #MyTempTable
    SELECT    Col1
    FROM      (SELECT DISTINCT Col1 = CONVERT(varchar(10), qty),
                      Col2 = qty
              FROM    sales) xyz
    ORDER BY  Col2


SELECT * FROM #MyTempTable

DROP TABLE #MyTempTable
```

The first INSERT causes an error because the qty column in the ORDER BY clause is not in the column list. The INSERT statement would fail if I added the additional column to the list because it requires its input to be exact (just one column). So, I retrieved the distinct set of data in the derived table, allowing me to use the ORDER BY on the numeric column. The main SELECT is a simple query, with no DISTINCT clause, so this action is perfectly valid.

The derived table could have been made into a view, but it would have been no more efficient. If this in-line view is unique to this operation in the database, you have no need to add the storage overhead (albeit a small amount). A derived table in this situation is exactly what is needed.

Outer Joins, Cross Joins, and Self Joins

For most queries that are performed, the standard inner join suffices when trying to retrieve data from more than one table. Situations do arise, however, when you need to retrieve information that is not common to both tables. This is where outer and cross joins come in handy. Or perhaps you need to select information from more than one instance of the same table. Self joins will do the job nicely.

Outer Joins

Outer joins come in three varieties: left, right, and full. Left and right outer joins vary only in the order of the tables listed in the FROM clause. A full outer join is the combination of both a left and right outer join being performed at the same time (which, by the way, is not possible— hence the need for the full outer join). Keep reading to find out more.

Left and Right Outer Joins

You can start off with an example of a left outer join. In Listing 1.16, you want to retrieve all titles and their associated quantity of sales. If the title had no sales, you still want to see it listed.

Listing 1.16. Selecting all titles and associated sales using a left outer join.

```
SELECT    sales.qty, titles.title
FROM      titles LEFT OUTER JOIN sales
          ON titles.title_id = sales.title_id
```

> **NOTE**
>
> You'll notice in Listing 1.16 that I avoid using the older syntax for joins, that is, =, *=, =*, and so on. That is because this syntax is not ANSI SQL compliant, and it has been my experience that using the symbols occasionally produces undesired results when trying to exclude data. Although you might have to do a little more typing, you don't have to worry about having problems like this arise.

Unlike an inner join, all rows from the outer table will be included in the results plus any matching rows in the other table. So, all titles will be listed, regardless of whether they have been sold. By inspecting the results of Listing 1.16 in the following output, you see that two titles in particular have a (null) value in the qty column. Because neither of these books have their title_id as an entry in the sales table, there is no qty value to display—so a (null) is displayed instead. If an inner join had been used instead, neither of these titles would appear in the result list, as shown by the following output.

```
qty     title
------  -----------------------------------------------------------------
5       The Busy Executive's Database Guide
10      The Busy Executive's Database Guide
25      Cooking with Computers: Surreptitious Balance Sheets
35      You Can Combat Computer Stress!
15      Straight Talk About Computers
10      Silicon Valley Gastronomic Treats
25      The Gourmet Microwave
15      The Gourmet Microwave
(null)  The Psychology of Computer Cooking
30      But Is It User Friendly?
50      Secrets of Silicon Valley
(null)  Net Etiquette
20      Computer Phobic AND Non-Phobic Individuals: Behavior Variations
3       Is Anger the Enemy?
75      Is Anger the Enemy?
10      Is Anger the Enemy?
20      Is Anger the Enemy?
25      Life Without Fear
15      Prolonged Data Deprivation: Four Case Studies
25      Emotional Security: A New Algorithm
40      Onions, Leeks, and Garlic: Cooking Secrets of the Mediterranean
20      Fifty Years in Buckingham Palace Kitchens
20      Sushi, Anyone?

(23 row(s) affected)
```

> **NOTE**
>
> Other rows are listed multiple times; these titles have more than one entry in the sales table and will be displayed for each sale of that particular title.

NOTE

You can use the ISNULL function to change the null values to a zero numeric value. You will find more information about ISNULL later in this chapter.

By the way, you can achieve the same results by using a right outer join. The only difference is the order of the tables in the FROM clause. The relative position of the table to the outer join clause determines whether you choose left or right. In the previous example, you wanted all results from the table to the left of the clause, so a left outer join was used. Left and right outer joins are processed in the same fashion by SQL Server. Listing 1.17 shows the same query using a right outer join, and Listings 1.18 and 1.19 show the Query Plan results from each. Notice how they are indeed parsed exactly the same.

Listing 1.17. Selecting all titles and associated sales using a Right Outer Join.

```
SELECT      sales.qty, titles.title
FROM        sales RIGHT OUTER JOIN titles
            ON titles.title_id = sales.title_id
```

Listing 1.18. The Query Plan from Listing 1.16.

```
STEP 1
The type of query is SELECT
FROM TABLE
titles
Nested iteration
Table Scan
LEFT OUTER JOIN : nested iteration
  FROM TABLE
  sales
  Nested iteration
  Table Scan
```

Listing 1.19. The Query Plan from Listing 1.17.

```
STEP 1
The type of query is SELECT
FROM TABLE
titles
Nested iteration
Table Scan
LEFT OUTER JOIN : nested iteration
  FROM TABLE
  sales
  Nested iteration
  Table Scan
```

Let's take this one step further by listing only those books that have not been sold (see Listing 1.20). The query only needs a minor adjustment to return the desired results.

Listing 1.20. Selecting titles that have not been sold.

```
SELECT     sales.qty, titles.title
FROM       titles LEFT OUTER JOIN sales
           ON titles.title_id = sales.title_id
WHERE      sales.title_id IS NULL
```

The addition of the WHERE clause makes all the difference. But why check if the title_id is null in the sales table? Well, if the title_id in the titles table has no entry in the sales table, there will be no matching title_id in the sales table. This query will only return the two titles that had no sales, as shown in the following output.

```
qty    title
------ -------------------------------------------------------
(null) The Psychology of Computer Cooking
(null) Net Etiquette

(2 row(s) affected)
```

> **NOTE**
>
> Actually, all column values for that title in the sales table will be null, so any column in the sales table can be used to check for the existence—or lack thereof. It is best to compare related columns, however, for the sake of consistency.

Full Outer Joins

Full outer joins combine the technology of left and right outer joins into one statement. The example presented in Listing 1.21 shows a full outer join in conjunction with a derived table that uses a right outer join. Although it is more complicated, it gives the desired results: Show authors with no matching titles and titles with no matching authors. Keep in mind that you can always create a view to replace the in-line view of this query.

Listing 1.21. Selecting orphaned authors and titles.

```
SELECT     a.au_lname, tt.title
FROM       authors a FULL OUTER JOIN
           (SELECT au_id, title FROM titleauthor ta
           RIGHT OUTER JOIN titles t ON t.title_id = ta.title_id) tt
           ON a.au_id = tt.au_id
WHERE      a.au_lname is null or tt.title is null
```

The results are a list of author's last names (au_lname) with a null value in the title column and titles with a null value in the au_lname column.

Cross Joins

The least common type of join, a cross join, is not a join at all; it is the Cartesian product of all the rows from all tables participating in the SELECT statement. For example, if you want to generate a list of the combination all authors with all titles, you can create a SELECT statement as in Listing 1.22.

Listing 1.22. A cross join of authors and titles.

```
SELECT    au_lname, title
FROM      authors CROSS JOIN titles
```

The result of this query, too long to show here—414 rows to be exact—is the combination of each author with each title. This is an impractical means of selecting data. Normally, you would not want all items from both tables as a set of results. Sometimes, however, a cross join can be advantageous.

A colleague of mine, for example, wrote a client-server application using a cross join in this scenario: An inventory table needs to be cleared each month and populated with each warehouse. For each warehouse, each product must be listed. So, my colleague used a stored procedure that truncates the inventory table and then performs a cross join between the products and warehouses tables to repopulate the inventory table.

Another practical example occurs when you need to create sample data for, say, an authors table. You can create a table with a list of first and last names and then do a cross join on itself to create a larger list of names in order to perform tests on your database. Listing 1.23 demonstrates this using the authors table to create a testauthors table.

Listing 1.23. Creating a testauthors table using a cross join.

```
SELECT    a1.au_fname, a2.au_lname
INTO      testauthors
FROM      authors a1 CROSS JOIN authors a2
```

Self Joins

Self joins are not a special kind of join. In fact, a self join is really an inner or outer join on the same table. For example, imagine you want to get a list of titles that have the same price. You can write a SELECT statement as follows in Listing 1.24.

Listing 1.24. Selecting books that have the same price.

```
SELECT    DISTINCT t1.price, t1.title
FROM      titles t1
          JOIN titles t2 ON t1.price = t2.price
          AND t1.title_id <> t2.title_id
```

The process involves using the titles table twice in the join. Notice how the table aliasing is used to create the join of titles with itself. This query also uses two expressions in the ON clause of the join. The first matches the prices in the first instance of the titles table with the second instance. The second part makes sure that a title in the first instance does not match with a title in the second instance, thus preventing a title from being displayed if it finds itself as a match (which will happen because the price of the same title is the same). The results of this query appear as follows:

```
price                        title
- - - - - - - - - - - - - - -  - - - - - - - - - - - - - - - - - - - - - - - - - - - - - - - - - - - - - - -
- - - - - - - -
2.99                         The Gourmet Microwave
2.99                         You Can Combat Computer Stress!
11.95                        Cooking with Computers: Surreptitious Balance Sheets
11.95                        Fifty Years in Buckingham Palace Kitchens
19.99                        Prolonged Data Deprivation: Four Case Studies
19.99                        Silicon Valley Gastronomic Treats
19.99                        Straight Talk About Computers
19.99                        The Busy Executive's Database Guide

(8 row(s) affected)
```

The systypes system table provides you with another example of a self join. User Defined Datatypes might, on occasion, need to be resolved to their base datatype. You will see this used in several other chapters of this book. In order to do this, you must perform a self join on systypes as shown in Listing 1.25.

Listing 1.25. Resolving base datatypes from User Defined Datatypes.

```
SELECT     t1.name, t2.name
FROM       systypes t1 JOIN systypes t2
           ON t1.type = t2.type
WHERE      t1.usertype >= 100
AND        t2.usertype < 100
AND        t2.usertype NOT IN (18,80)
```

This query joins systypes to itself based on the type column of each table. The first line of the WHERE clause makes sure that only User Defined Datatypes are listed from the first instance of systypes (t1). The next two lines exclude User Defined Datatypes and the timestamp and sysname datatypes from the second instance of systypes (t2), preventing a datatype from t1 from matching to itself or a System User Defined Datatype in t2. The 100 value is the lowest value that a User Defined Datatype will be in the usertype column. The values of 18 and 80 represent the sysname and timestamp datatypes respectively.

If you join the results of this query with syscolumns, you can generate a list of column names and base datatypes. This can then be used to generate the same table in another database that does not have the same User Defined Datatypes of the original database as shown in the following output.

```
name                                  name
------------------------------------  -------------------------------
id                                    varchar
tid                                   varchar
empid                                 char
```

(3 row(s) affected)

The nature of any relational database brings the need for performing joins between the tables. Most joins you create will be relatively simple; but occasions do happen that require more complex joins of data on more than just two or three tables. You can sleep soundly knowing that SQL Server can do the job—and do it well.

More Advanced DELETE and UPDATE Statements

The DELETE and UPDATE statements tend to be used in their simple forms: delete or update a row based on a particular column's value. But just like a SELECT statement, DELETE and UPDATE can use joins and subqueries when evaluating what data should be deleted or updated. This less-often used feature allows for some powerful capabilities when modifying or deleting data.

> **TIP**
>
> While you practice using DELETE and UPDATE, be sure to place your DELETE and UPDATE statements between a BEGIN TRAN and ROLLBACK TRAN so the changes will not be permanent.

The DELETE Statement—A Second Look

Let's examine a simple DELETE statement that removes rows from the sales table based on the supplied title_id (see Listing 1.26).

Listing 1.26. Deleting rows from the sales table.

```
DELETE      sales
WHERE       title_id = 'BU1032'
```

This statement removes two rows from the sales table based on the title_id of 'BU1032'. But what if you want to remove all sales for a particular publisher. You need to find the titles associated with that particular publisher and then remove those from the sales table. Here is where a join will help. Why not perform a join to the titles and publishers table (as shown in Listing 1.27) to find those sales associated with that publisher?

Listing 1.27. Deleting sales for a particular publisher by id.

```
DELETE    sales
FROM      sales
          JOIN titles t ON sales.title_id = t.title_id
WHERE     t.pub_id = '1389'
```

Or use Listing 1.28 if you want to delete based on the name of the publisher.

Listing 1.28. Deleting sales for a publisher by name.

```
DELETE    sales
FROM      sales
          JOIN titles t ON sales.title_id = t.title_id
          JOIN publishers p ON t.pub_id = p.pub_id
WHERE     p.pub_name = 'Algodata Infosystems'
```

As you can see, a join can be performed in the DELETE statement to find and delete only those rows that match with data in other tables. The join does its comparison and limits the number of rows in the sales table that will be deleted. In other words, only delete sales records when you find a matching title (by some publisher).

Subqueries Revisited

You can also use subqueries to restrict what rows in a table will be deleted. The example in Listing 1.28 has the same results as Listing 1.29 but uses a subquery in place of a join.

Listing 1.29. Deleting sales for a publisher using a subquery.

```
DELETE    sales
WHERE     title_id IN
          (SELECT    title_id from titles
          WHERE      pub_id = '1389')
```

Although this query is less efficient, it is easier to read. As usual, I recommend sticking to joins whenever possible. And again, you have exceptions to this rule, as shown in Listing 1.30.

Listing 1.30. Deleting sales based on the average quantity of sales.

```
DELETE    sales
WHERE     qty <
          (SELECT AVG(qty) from sales)
```

This query deletes all sales whose quantity is less than the average quantity in the sales table. There is no equivalent DELETE statement that uses a join to perform the same task. A subquery is not only useful in this situation, but necessary.

The New and Improved UPDATE Statement

Actually, this is nothing new to T-SQL. But just like a DELETE statement, an UPDATE statement can use joins and subqueries to limit the data needing to be updated. Not only can UPDATE statements use joins or subqueries to limit the rows that will be updated, but they can also use a subquery as an expression for the update value.

Limiting Rows to Be Updated

This should be old hat by now (see Listing 1.31).

Listing 1.31. Updating royalties for books that sell well.

```
UPDATE    titleauthor
SET       royaltyper = royaltyper * 1.1
WHERE     title_id IN
          (SELECT   title_id
          FROM      sales
          GROUP BY  title_id
          HAVING    sum(qty) >=30)
```

As you can see, the royaltyper is being increased by 10% for all titles that have a total sales quantity of 30 or more. The subquery is again the only solution because the comparison involves using an aggregate to determine what titles have sold well.

Assigning Update Values Using Subqueries

What about using the results of a subquery as the update value for a column? The UPDATE statement in Listing 1.32 does just that. Using a correlated subquery, it updates the royaltyper column of titleauthor to be the sum of all sales for the particular book. Perhaps not practical in the real world, it does demonstrate the ability to use subqueries with a new twist.

Listing 1.32. Updating royaltyper based on total sales.

```
UPDATE    titleauthor
SET       royaltyper = (SELECT   SUM(qty)
                        FROM      sales
                        WHERE     sales.title_id = titleauthor.title_id)
```

And how about one step further: Updating the royaltyper to be 10% greater than the total sales quantity for those titles that have sold a total of 30 or more copies. Take a look at Listing 1.33 for the answer. It is simply a compilation of the two UPDATE statements used in Listings 1.31 and 1.32.

Listing 1.33. Updating royaltyper using two subqueries.

```
UPDATE      titleauthor
SET         royaltyper = 1.1 * (SELECT     SUM(qty)
                                FROM       sales
                                WHERE      sales.title_id = titleauthor.title_id)
WHERE       title_id IN
            (SELECT    title_id
            FROM       sales
            GROUP BY   title_id
            HAVING     sum(qty) >=30)
```

TIP

If you do decide to run these data modification statements without a BEGIN TRAN and ROLLBACK TRAN, you always have the option of running the instpubs.sql script located in the \MSSQL\INSTALL\ directory of SQL Server. This script file recreates the origianl pubs database. Just be sure to log in as sa, or you might get unwanted results.

Advanced Functions

Some of my most favorite functions are those that seem to be often forgotten by SQL Server developers. I am, of course, being a little overdramatic, but some of the slickest functions are the system functions of SQL Server. These functions can return information about the current SQL Server login, database user, database, and user workstation. Information on indexes and statistics can be retrieved. And to top it off, the ability to convert nulls to real data and back is present here as well.

User, Login, and Workstation Information

SQL Server has six system functions that enable you to find out about who is logged on to SQL Server, who is actually manipulating data, and where this person came from.

Dealing with the User

The USER_NAME system function can return the name of the current user if no argument is specified, or if the user's ID is included, the name of the user with that ID. USER_ID performs a similar task, returning the ID for the current user or for the specified user name.

An example table called SomeTable contains three columns: Id of type int, Description of type varchar(50), and DBUser of type varchar(30). A sample stored procedure that performs an insert on SomeTable can use the USER_NAME function to put the name of the current database user into the third column of the table, as shown in Listing 1.34.

Listing 1.34. Inserting data with the USER_NAME function.

```
CREATE PROCEDURE prInsertSomeTable
@ColA int, @ColB varchar(50)
AS
Insert     SomeTable
VALUES     (@ColA, @ColB, USER_NAME())
```

Which Login?

The SUSER_NAME and SUSER_ID functions return the Login name and ID respectively. Although these two functions are not used as often as the USER_NAME and USER_ID functions, they can be handy when you need to know who is modifying data when aliases have been used for the database users. Because all aliased users will return the same user name in a database, you can still query for that person's login name to find out who is actually doing what. The syntax of SUSER_NAME and SUSER_ID is exactly the same as that of USER_NAME and USER_ID.

Workstation Alert

The HOST_NAME and HOST_ID functions give information about which workstation a particular login has come from. Try the following line of code in the SQL Query Tool window:

```
SELECT HOST_NAME()
```

What you will see returned is the name of the computer that you are currently on while connected to SQL Server. So not only can you find out who is in your database, but also *where* they are.

TIP

You can use these identifier functions in an update trigger so you can record who last made a change to the data. Just be sure that the table being modified has the additional columns to hold this information.

WARNING

Not all applications that can connect to SQL Server send the workstation name. Among products written by Microsoft, this is uncommon, but other software vendors might not send this data. Do not rely on this information always being there. If you write custom applications, however, you can send this information to SQL Server if so desired, but the application must be coded to do so.

Finding Object Information

It is often useful to find out more information about the data that you are manipulating. The COL_LENGTH and COL_NAME functions enable you to derive a column's length and name, whereas DATALENGTH returns the length of any type of data.

Column Information

SQL Server contains two system functions that return information about a column: COL_LENGTH and COL_NAME. And as you can tell, their names are self-explanatory.

COL_LENGTH takes two arguments, the table name and the column name. What it returns is the defined length of the particular column. So for example, the following line of code

```
SELECT COL_LENGTH('publishers', 'pub_id')
```

will return the defined length of the pub_id column in the publishers table—which in this case is 4. This can be replaced by a more complicated query as shown in Listing 1.35. But as you will see, this can be a bit more tedious to perform on a regular basis.

Listing 1.35. Selecting the length of a column from syscolumns.

```
SELECT     length
FROM       syscolumns
WHERE      id = OBJECT_ID('publishers')
AND        name = 'pub_id'
```

This query introduces another pair of identifying functions: OBJECT_ID and its counterpart, OBJECT_NAME. Both of these functions require an argument and can also be replaced by querying the system tables. The point is that these functions make light of the work that normally requires querying system tables.

COL_NAME works a little differently, requiring the ID of the table and the column ID (position) of the column whose name you are after, as such:

```
SELECT COL_NAME(OBJECT_ID('publishers'), 1)
```

This SELECT statement returns a value of 'pub_id' when executed.

A Different Length

In addition, SQL Server's DATALENGTH system function enables you to find the length of an expression, as opposed to a table's column. You can use this function with variables in stored procedures to determine the length of the data in that variable. You need to be aware of a few rules when using this function:

- varchar, varbinary, text, and image datatypes can store variable length data—so they return their actual length.
- Null returns Null.
- All other datatypes return their defined length.

To help demonstrate this function, the code in Listing 1.36 selects the length of the name of the pub_id column in the publishers table. After executing this query, a value of 6 would be returned. Although the name column of syscolumns has a defined length of 30, it is of type varchar and thus, the actual length of the data in the column is returned instead. If the column were defined as char, then 30 would always be returned (because the data would contain padded spaces to fill the 30 character width).

Listing 1.36. Selecting the length of a varchar column.

```
SELECT      DATALENGTH(name)
FROM        syscolumns
WHERE       id = OBJECT_ID('publishers')
AND         name = 'pub_id'
```

Working with Null

Actually, we're talking about null. Three system functions enable you to replace a null value, compare values (and return null if they are indeed the same), and find the first non-null value. This is a good suite of functions to do what is normally difficult or tedious in T-SQL.

The ISNULL Function

The ISNULL system function enables you to replace a null value with an alternate value. If the first argument contains a non-null value, that value is returned. If the first argument is indeed null, the second argument is returned from the function instead (see Listing 1.37).

Listing 1.37. Testing the ISNULL function.

```
DECLARE     @intTest int
SELECT      ISNULL(@intTest,5)
SELECT      @intTest = 37
SELECT      ISNULL(@intTest,5)
```

The first ISNULL in the code returns a value of 5 because the variable @intTest has an initial value of null. After assigning the number 37 to @intTest, however, a 37 is returned by the second ISNULL in the code. This is particularly useful when you need to compare a variable's value and you are not sure if it contains a null. If the variable being compared does contain a null, the comparison always fails. ISNULL enables you to specify an alternate value if the variable does contain a null.

Another use is to format a column's null data to something more acceptable. Earlier on, you saw an example of selecting all titles and their associated sales quantity. There were two titles, however, that had no sales, so the qty column contained a null. The code shown in Listing 1.38 demonstrates how to return a value of 0 in those cases.

Listing 1.38. Replacing null values with zero values.

```
SELECT    ISNULL(qty,0) AS qty, title
FROM      titles t
          LEFT OUTER JOIN sales s ON t.title_id = s.title_id
```

The NULLIF Function

NULLIF is a comparison function. It compares the values of its two arguments and returns either a null if they are the same, or if the arguments are different, it returns the value of the first argument. Normally, you will avoid returning a null value from an expression, but on those special occasions, when a null would be most appropriate, you have the NULLIF function.

The COALESCE Function

My favorite of these three, COALESCE, enables you to supply a variable number of arguments and returns the value of the first non-null argument in the list. I use this function quite often in updating stored procedures. Examine the code in Listing 1.39.

Listing 1.39. An update code snippet using COALESCE.

```
IF COALESCE(@chrNewColValue, '') <> COALESCE(@chrOldColValue)
    UPDATE MyTable
    SET MyCol = @chrNewColValue
    WHERE IdCol = @chrRecordId
```

You have the ability to compare the new value for the column with its current value. If the column definition supports nulls, this comparison would potentially fail, even if the old and new values differed. If either one contained a null, a comparison between the two would always fail, so the data would not get updated. COALESCE enables you to change the null value to an empty string (' ') for both the old and new values, thus allowing a comparison that works.

Summary

You have come to the end of a chapter on programming with T-SQL. And as you have seen, T-SQL has some more advanced capabilities that give you better flexibility when retrieving, modifying, and deleting data. Using these features allows the SQL Server to do work that might have otherwise been done by a business server or client application. Try to take advantage of SQL Server's capability to manipulate and modify data—that's what it was designed for.

Furthermore, if these advanced statements can be encapsulated in stored procedures, you have gained even better performance. By placing these more complicated T-SQL statements in stored procedures, they are parsed and compiled ahead of time, cutting down on the amount of time it takes to do the job.

Finally, no rule states you cannot go further than what is shown here or in any other references on T-SQL. Experiment with new combinations of T-SQL statements to create procedures that do what you never expected. You will see plenty of examples of this throughout the book. Just close your eyes and take the plunge.

> **WARNING**
>
> In regards to the final statement in this chapter: Under no circumstances do I ever recommend trying out code on a production server. Always use a test server to do this. I do my experimenting on one of my home computers, never at the client site. Be sure to perform backups on a regular basis, as well. I cannot imagine anyone enjoying spending hours just to rebuild test databases.

Using Advanced Data Manipulation Language

CHAPTER 2

One of the main advantages of the Data Manipulation Language is the capability to mine data from a data warehouse. You can make important decisions on the basis of historical and current data. This chapter delves into some advanced concepts using a relational database with multiple linked tables.

Starting with the AVG function later in this chapter, you also see many examples of advanced DML used to extract information from a data warehouse. A data warehouse stores potentially many decades of records in a similar format. Using Advanced DML, you can now write queries for data mining to spot trends, anomalies, and so on in order to make more meaningful business decisions. It is the data mining, not the data warehouse, that is the most critical application. Using knowledge of your own industry to query data brings more meaningful information than using a prebuilt data mining package.

Understanding Aggregate Functions

An aggregate function returns a single summary value computed on any number of rows from a given table.

> **WARNING**
>
> The value returned is the same as the datatype being summarized. For instance, if you calculate the average number of units sold, which is defined as an integer, your summary average value returns as an integer.

Although aggregate functions perform well on summarizing table data, if you want to present data in a spreadsheet-type format for analyzing data, go to Chapter 13, "Crosstabulation." Crosstabulation enables you to summarize data in a spreadsheet-type format in one step. To achieve this on other database products, this easily takes several queries and temporary tables to achieve the same effect. Chapter 5, "Effective Use of Built-In Functions" covers additional T-SQL functions. Table 2.1, a review of aggregate functions, summarizes the available aggregate functions.

> **NOTE**
>
> In reference to Table 2.1, selected records means records selected by the query. This can be all records or records matching the criteria of a WHERE statement.

Table 2.1. Review of aggregate functions.

Function Name	Function Description
AVG	Calculates the average for selected records of numeric data in a column or the average for DISTINCT (unique) values of the selected records. All NULL values are ignored in the computation for the total and the record count.
COUNT	Returns the total count of records in a column or the count for DISTINCT (unique) values selected by the query. All NULL values are ignored in the total count.
COUNT(*)	Returns the total count of all records (rows) in the column, including NULL values of selected records by the query. DISTINCT is not allowed with this function.
MAX	Returns the largest value in a column of all selected records by the query of any char, number, or datetime datatype.
MIN	Returns the smallest value in a column of all selected records by the query of any char, number, or datetime datatype.
SUM	Returns the total value in a column of all selected records or all the DISTINCT (unique) values selected by the query. This function is used for only number datatypes. All NULL values are ignored.

Creating the Tables

Before you can practice complex queries, you need to create several tables and enter some data. This set of relational tables is a basic sales and inventory tracking system for a retailer of musical CDs (compact discs). Refer to Figure 2.1 for the ER diagram (Entity Relationship).

TIP

If you hate to document, you can create an Entity Relationship diagram in seconds using Crystal Reports, Microsoft Query, or any other product that shows the relationships between tables. This diagram was made using Crystal Reports with Adobe Photoshop.

Execute the code in Listing 2.1 to create the tables needed for this and other chapters.

FIGURE 2.1.

Entity Relationship diagram for Retailer CD database.

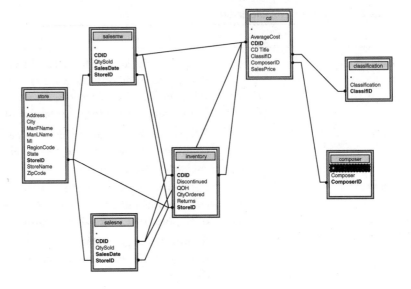

Listing 2.1. Create Retailer CD tables.

```
CREATE TABLE Store(
    StoreID    integer NOT NULL PRIMARY KEY,
    StoreName    varchar(30) NOT NULL
        CONSTRAINT stname UNIQUE (StoreName,Address,City,State),
    Address    varchar(40),
    City    varchar(20),
    State    varchar(2),
    ZipCode    varchar(10),
    ManFName    varchar(25),
    MI        varchar(1) NULL,
    ManLName    varchar(30),
    RegionCode    char(2) NOT NULL )

CREATE TABLE Composer (
    ComposerID    integer  NOT NULL PRIMARY KEY,
    Composer    varchar(40)
        CONSTRAINT author UNIQUE (Composer) )

CREATE TABLE Classification (
    ClassifID    integer  NOT NULL PRIMARY KEY,
    Classification    varchar(25)
        CONSTRAINT class UNIQUE (Classification),)

CREATE TABLE CD (
    CDID        integer  NOT NULL PRIMARY KEY,
    CDTitle        varchar(40),
    ComposerID        integer  NOT NULL
        REFERENCES Composer(ComposerID),
    ClassifID    integer  NOT NULL
        REFERENCES Classification(ClassifID),
    SalesPrice        money,
    AverageCost    money)
```

```
CREATE TABLE Inventory(
     CDID        integer  NOT NULL
         REFERENCES CD(CDID),
     StoreID        integer NOT NULL
         REFERENCES Store(StoreID),
              CONSTRAINT inv PRIMARY KEY(CDID,StoreID),
     QOH         integer NULL,
     Returns        integer NULL,
     QtyOrdered    integer NULL,
     Discontinued  char(1) NOT NULL)

CREATE TABLE SalesMw (
    StoreID    integer NOT NULL
        REFERENCES Store(StoreID),
    CDID    integer  NOT NULL
        REFERENCES CD(CDID),
             CONSTRAINT smw PRIMARY KEY(CDID,StoreID,SalesDate),
    QtySold    integer,
    SalesDate    datetime)

CREATE TABLE SalesNe (
    StoreID    integer NOT NULL
        REFERENCES Store(StoreID),
    CDID    integer NOT NULL
        REFERENCES CD(CDID),
             CONSTRAINT sne PRIMARY KEY(CDID,StoreID,SalesDate),
    QtySold    integer,
    SalesDate    datetime)
```

The Composer table holds the names of the recording artists. The Classification table stores the method of classifying music. The Store table holds the information about the firm's retail stores. The CD table stores the information regarding each musical compact disc. The company tracks inventory with the Inventory table. Finally, sales for the midwest and northeast are tracked in the SalesMw and SalesNe tables, respectively.

The tables make use of some features not commonly written about. You notice for the Inventory, SalesMw, and SalesNe tables that the primary key uses more than one column as indicated by the PRIMARY KEY CONSTRAINT. When needed, foreign keys were created by using the REFERENCE statement. Because you have several lookup tables that you do not want to replicate the descriptions, the UNIQUE CONSTRAINT was used to eliminate this problem.

TIP

Use Front End systems such as Visual Basic for datatype and content editing to reduce the time spent at the server. However, always try to reduce errors at the server by using several techniques such as UNIQUE CONSTRAINTS to reduce the possibility of error. Remember, garbage in, garbage out!

Adding Data to the Tables

Now execute the code in Listing 2.2 to insert data into each of the tables.

Listing 2.2. Data for CD Retailer database.

```
/*  Add records to database Classification */

INSERT into Classification
    VALUES(    1,"Pop Rock")
INSERT into Classification
    VALUES( 2,"Country & Western")
INSERT into Classification
    VALUES( 3,"Alternative")
INSERT into Classification
    VALUES( 4,"Heavy Metal")

/*  Add records to database Composer  */
INSERT into Composer
    VALUES(    100,"John Denver")
INSERT into Composer
    VALUES(    101,"Psychedelic Furs")
INSERT into Composer
    VALUES(    102,"Queensryche")
INSERT into Composer
    VALUES(    103,"Def Leppard")
INSERT into Composer
    VALUES(    104,"Garth Brooks")
INSERT into Composer
    VALUES(    105,"Colin Raye")
INSERT into Composer
    VALUES(    106,"Styx")
INSERT into Composer
    VALUES(    107,"Chicago")
INSERT into Composer
    VALUES(    108,"Outfield")
INSERT into Composer
    VALUES(    109,"REO Speedwagon")
INSERT into Composer
    VALUES(    110,"Cars")
INSERT into Composer
    VALUES(    111,"Rick Springfield")
INSERT into Composer
    VALUES(    112,"Genesis")
INSERT into Composer
    VALUES(    113,"Pat Benetar")
INSERT into Composer
    VALUES(    114,"Tears for Fears")
INSERT into Composer
    VALUES(    115,"Depeche Mode")
INSERT into Composer
    VALUES(    116,"Eagles")

/* Add records to Store */
INSERT into Store
    VALUES(    1040,"CD Review","1099 IRS Way","Kansas City","MO",
        "55555-1212","George","H","Bush","MW")
```

```
INSERT into Store
    VALUES(    1099,"CD Cash Exchange","5 Expensive Consultants",
"Chicago","IL","60655","Hillary",NULL,"Clinton","MW")
INSERT into Store
    VALUES(    1200,"CD National Warehouse","122 Washington",
        "New York","NY","10048","Greg",NULL,"Hodgson","NE")
INSERT into Store
    VALUES(    1210,"CD National Warehouse","16 Wall Street Way",
        "New York","NY","10048","Greg", NULL,"Hodgson","NE")
INSERT into Store
    VALUES(    1220,"CD National Warehouse","155 Commercial Ave,",
        "New York","NY","10048","Greg", NULL,"Hodgson","NE")
INSERT into Store
    VALUES(    1300,"CD National Warehouse","99 Congress,",
        "Chicago","IL","60504","Sam","P","Johnson","MW")
INSERT into Store
    VALUES(    1310,"CD National Warehouse","625 Clark St.",
        "Chicago","IL","60511","Sam", "P","Johnson","MW")
INSERT into Store
    VALUES(    1320,"CD National Warehouse","66 Jackson St.",
        "Chicago","IL","60504","Sam", "P","Johnson","MW")
INSERT into Store
    VALUES(    1330,"Fantastic CD's","88 Jefferson St.",
        "Indianapolis","IN","32768","Marla", NULL,"Reece","MW")

/* Add records to CD table */

INSERT into CD
    VALUES(2000,"John Denver's Greatest Hits",100,1,16.99,6.99)
INSERT into CD
    VALUES(2001,"Chicago 16",107,1,14.99,5.99)
INSERT into CD
    VALUES(2002,"Chicago 17",107,1,14.99,5.99)
INSERT into CD
    VALUES(2003,"Chicago 18",107,1,14.99,5.99)
INSERT into CD
    VALUES(2004,"Chicago's Greatest Hits",107,1,16.99,7.99)
INSERT into CD
    VALUES(2005,"Midnight to Midnight",101,3,14.99,5.99)
INSERT into CD
    VALUES(2006,"Catching Up With Depeche Mode",115,3,14.99,5.99)
INSERT into CD
    VALUES(2007,"Ultra",115,3,15.99,5.99)
INSERT into CD
    VALUES(2008,"Operation Mindcrime",102,4,14.99,5.99)
INSERT into CD
    VALUES(2009,"Empire",102,4,14.99,5.99)
INSERT into CD
    VALUES(2010,"Promised Land",102,4,12.99,4.99)
INSERT into CD
    VALUES(2011,"On Through the Night",103,4,11.99,3.99)
INSERT into CD
    VALUES(2012,"Pyromania",103,4,14.99,5.99)
INSERT into CD
    VALUES(2013,"Hysteria",103,4,14.99,5.99)
INSERT into CD
    VALUES(2014,"Vault - Greatest Hits",103,4,13.99,4.99)
```

2

USING ADVANCED
DATA MANIPULA-
TION LANGUAGE

continues

Listing 2.2. continued

```
INSERT into CD
    VALUES(2015,"Garth Brooks Greatest Hits",104,2,15.99,6.99)
INSERT into CD
    VALUES(2016,"Colin Raye's Greatest Hits",105,2,14.99,5.99)
INSERT into CD
    VALUES(2017,"Styx Greatest Hits",106,1,13.99,5.99)
INSERT into CD
    VALUES(2018,"Play Deep",108,1,12.99,2.99)
INSERT into CD
    VALUES(2019,"Wheels are Turning",109,1,14.99,5.99)
INSERT into CD
    VALUES(2020,"REO Speedwagon - The Hits",109,1,16.99,7.99)
INSERT into CD
    VALUES(2021,"The Cars",110,1,9.99,3.99)
INSERT into CD
    VALUES(2022,"Cars Anthology",110,1,25.99,11.99)
INSERT into CD
    VALUES(2023,"Heartbeat City",110,1,14.99,5.99)
INSERT into CD
    VALUES(2024,"Rick Springfield Greatest Hits",111,1,11.99,2.99)
INSERT into CD
    VALUES(2025,"Genesis Live",112,1,19.99,8.99)
INSERT into CD
    VALUES(2026,"Pat Benetar Greatest Hits",113,1,16.99,6.99)
INSERT into CD
    VALUES(2027,"Songs from the Big Chair",114,1,14.99,5.99)
INSERT into CD
    VALUES(2028,"The Hurting",114,1,11.99,3.99)
INSERT into CD
    VALUES(2029,"Eagles Greatest Hits Vol 1",116,1,9.99,2.99)
INSERT into CD
    VALUES(2030,"Eagles Greatest Hits Vol 2",116,1,9.99,2.99)

/*  Add records to Inventory  */

INSERT into Inventory
    VALUES(2000,1330,10,0,0,"N")
INSERT into Inventory
    VALUES(2015,1330,5,0,3,"N")
INSERT into Inventory
    VALUES(2016,1330,6,0,11,"N")
INSERT into Inventory
    VALUES(2017,1330,5,2,0,"N")
INSERT into Inventory
    VALUES(2000,1040,3,0,9,"N")
INSERT into Inventory
    VALUES(2015,1040,1,0,10,"N")
INSERT into Inventory
    VALUES(2016,1040,4,0,11,"N")
INSERT into Inventory
    VALUES(2018,1040,15,8,0,"N")
INSERT into Inventory
    VALUES(2019,1040,22,3,0,"N")
INSERT into Inventory
    VALUES(2020,1040,10,0,0,"N")
```

```
INSERT into Inventory
    VALUES(2021,1040,19,0,NULL,"N")
INSERT into Inventory
    VALUES(2008,1200,11,0,NULL,"N")
INSERT into Inventory
    VALUES(2009,1200,5,0,9,"N")
INSERT into Inventory
    VALUES(2011,1210,18,0,NULL,"N")
INSERT into Inventory
    VALUES(2012,1210,5,0,NULL,"N")
INSERT into Inventory
    VALUES(2013,1210,1,0,6,"N")
INSERT into Inventory
    VALUES(2025,1220,3,0,8,"N")
INSERT into Inventory
    VALUES(2026,1220,3,0,7,"N")
INSERT into Inventory
    VALUES(2019,1300,2,0,8,"N")
INSERT into Inventory
    VALUES(2020,1300,9,0,0,"N")
INSERT into Inventory
    VALUES(2027,1310,2,0,8,"N")
INSERT into Inventory
    VALUES(2028,1310,4,0,4,"N")
INSERT into Inventory
    VALUES(2029,1320,2,0,8,"N")
INSERT into Inventory
    VALUES(2030,1320,6,0,0,"N")
INSERT into Inventory
    VALUES(2001,1099,6,0,0,"N")
INSERT into Inventory
    VALUES(2002,1099,2,0,3,"N")
INSERT into Inventory
    VALUES(2003,1099,7,0,0,"N")

/*  Add records to Midwest Sales Table  */
INSERT into SalesMw
    VALUES(1300,2001,10,"Oct 31,1997")
INSERT into SalesMw
    VALUES(1300,2002,15,"Oct 31,1997")
INSERT into SalesMw
    VALUES(1300,2001,5,"Nov 30,1997")
INSERT into SalesMw
    VALUES(1300,2003,16,"Nov 30,1997")
INSERT into SalesMw
    VALUES(1300,2017,9,"Nov 30,1997")
INSERT into SalesMw
    VALUES(1330,2000,2,"Oct 31,1997")
INSERT into SalesMw
    VALUES(1330,2000,109,"Nov 30,1997")
INSERT into SalesMw
    VALUES(1330,2029,5,"Nov 30,1997")
INSERT into SalesMw
    VALUES(1330,2030,5,"Nov 30,1997")
INSERT into SalesMw
    VALUES(1330,2015,20,"Nov 30,1997")
INSERT into SalesMw
    VALUES(1330,2016,66,"Nov 30,1997")
```

2

USING ADVANCED
DATA MANIPULA-
TION LANGUAGE

continues

Listing 2.2. continued

```
INSERT into SalesMw
    VALUES(1310,2005,11,"Nov 30,1997")
INSERT into SalesMw
    VALUES(1320,2022,14,"Nov 30,1997")


/*  Add records to Northeast Sales Table  */
INSERT into SalesNe
    VALUES(1200,2006,10,"Oct 31,1997")
INSERT into SalesNe
    VALUES(1200,2007,15,"Oct 31,1997")
INSERT into SalesNe
    VALUES(1200,2007,8,"Nov 30,1997")
INSERT into SalesNe
    VALUES(1200,2008,12,"Nov 30,1997")
INSERT into SalesNe
    VALUES(1200,2009,19,"Nov 30,1997")
INSERT into SalesNe
    VALUES(1210,2008,7,"Oct 31,1997")
INSERT into SalesNe
    VALUES(1210,2009,55,"Nov 30,1997")
INSERT into SalesNe
    VALUES(1210,2010,18,"Nov 30,1997")
INSERT into SalesNe
    VALUES(1210,2022,11,"Nov 30,1997")
INSERT into SalesNe
    VALUES(1210,2023,20,"Nov 30,1997")
INSERT into SalesNe
    VALUES(1210,2020,15,"Nov 30,1997")
INSERT into SalesNe
    VALUES(1220,2018,6,"Nov 30,1997")
INSERT into SalesNe
    VALUES(1220,2005,3,"Nov 30,1997")
```

You see several rows created without any error messages after executing this SQL code.

Using the AVG Function

The average function computes the average on the rows selected by the query, or the DISTINCT rows. All NULL values are not used in the computation. The return datatype is the same datatype as the column being averaged. Only the numeric datatypes can be used with the AVG function. The first test of AVG is to average the selling price and the cost of all CDs in the CD table. Execute the code in Listing 2.3.

Listing 2.3. Calculating AVG for all data.

```
SELECT AVG(SalesPrice),AVG(AverageCost) from CD
```

Your output should be as follows:

```
.........................   ........................
14.86                       5.86
(1 row(s) affected)
```

Because all the aggregate functions can calculate on a segment of the entire population of records, the next example adds the WHERE statement to calculate the average selling price and cost for only those CDs with a classification of type POP ROCK (which is ClassifID = 1). Execute the code in Listing 2.4.

Listing 2.4. Calculating AVG for part of the data.

```
SELECT AVG(SalesPrice),AVG(AverageCost) from CD
    WHERE ClassifID = 1
```

Your output should be as follows:

```
.........................   ........................
14.99                       5.94
(1 row(s) affected)
```

You can now test the impact of using the AVG function on an INTEGER datatype by executing the code in Listing 2.5.

Listing 2.5. Using AVG on INTEGER values.

```
SELECT AVG(CDID) from CD
    WHERE ClassifID = 2
```

Your output should appear as follows:

```
..........
2015
(1 row(s) affected)
```

By selecting records with a classification of 2, only two records were averaged with values of 2015 and 2016, respectively. Although you expect an answer of 2015.5, the actual output of 2015 is the result of returning a datatype the same as the column you are averaging.

TIP

You can convert the return datatype from INTEGER to FLOAT by multiplying the data in the INTEGER column by 1.0 to convert to FLOAT. In this case, you multiply the integer column by 1.0 and take the AVG of the result.

Execute the code in Listing 2.6 to see the expected average.

Listing 2.6. Converting INTEGER to FLOAT using AVG.

```
SELECT AVG(CDID * -1.0) from CD
    WHERE ClassifID = 2
```

Your output should appear as follows:

```
- - - - - - - - - - - - - - - - - - - - - - - - - - - - - - - - - - - - - - - - -
2015.500000
(1 row(s) affected
```

Using the COUNT Function

The COUNT function counts the number of records selected or the number of DISTINCT records. All NULL values are ignored.

To see the difference regarding DISTINCT, execute the code in Listing 2.7 to see a count of all records with a Classification ID not NULL.

Listing 2.7. Counting all non-NULL values.

```
SELECT COUNT(ClassifID) from CD
```

Your output appear as follows:

```
- - - - - - - - - -
31

(1 row(s) affected)
```

Because you entered 31 records with no ClassifID values set to NULL, the expected output occurred. You can now test DISTINCT by executing the code in Listing 2.8.

Listing 2.8. Counting unique values.

```
SELECT COUNT(DISTINCT ClassifID) from CD
```

Your output should appear as follows:

```
- - - - - - - - - -
4
(1 row(s) affected)
```

As you can see, DISTINCT only selects those records that have unique values. In this case, you entered records that contained only one of four possible values; therefore, the return value of 4 was as expected. You can reduce the count to 1 by adding a WHERE clause, such as WHERE ClassifID = 1.

> **WARNING**
>
> A common mistake with DISTINCT is to code the DISTINCT statement before the COUNT statement. Because each row counted is already unique, DISTINCT will have no impact. A sample miscoded SQL statement follows:
>
> ```
> SELECT DISTINCT COUNT(ClassifID) from CD
> ```
>
> Make sure the DISTINCT statement follows the COUNT to avoid all problems.

Microsoft provides a way to count all records including NULL values, which is useful if you want to write a query to monitor the actual number of records in a database. This is accomplished by using * as the parameter of the COUNT function. The Store table has records with NULL values for the middle initial (field MI). First, execute the code in Listing 2.9 to see the results of a count on the field MI.

Listing 2.9. Counting values except NULL values.

```
SELECT COUNT(MI) from Store
```

Your output should appear as follows:

```
- - - - - - - - - -
4
(1 row(s) affected)
```

Only four records had value other than NULL. To count all records regardless if NULL, execute the code in Listing 2.10.

Listing 2.10. Counting values including NULL values.

```
SELECT COUNT(*) from Store
```

Your output should appear as follows:

```
- - - - - - - - - -
9
(1 row(s) affected)
```

As you can see, changing the COUNT parameter to * does count all records, even NULL values.

> **TIP**
>
> You have an additional undocumented method to count all records, even those that have NULL values by using the ISNULL function. This function checks to see if the value is NULL. If TRUE, then the second parameter is assigned to the field. Refer to the section, "The ISNULL Function," in Chapter 1, "Beyond the Basics of Data Manipulation Language.' for more information.

You can practice this tip by executing the code in Listing 2.11.

Listing 2.11. Using ISNULL to count all values including NULLs.

```
SELECT COUNT(ISNULL(MI,"")) from Store
```

Your output should appear as follows:

```
- - - - - - - - - -
9
(1 row(s) affected)
```

By using the ISNULL function, the same results were obtained as when the parameter (*) was used. Obviously, this is extra work for the COUNT statement; however, this can have desirable impact when using AVG or SUM on NULL values, because all records are averaged.

Using the MIN and MAX Functions

The MIN function outputs the smallest value of a column, and the MAX function outputs the largest value. Although you can still use DISTINCT with these functions, you have no apparent need to do so. Execute the code in Listing 2.12 to see a demonstration of these two functions.

Listing 2.12. Finding the smallest and largest selling prices.

```
SELECT MAX(SalesPrice),MIN(SalesPrice) from CD
```

Your output should appear as follows:

```
- - - - - - - - - - - - - - - - - - - 25.99                    9.99
(1 row(s) affected)
```

Using SUM to Add a Column

The SUM function adds up all non-NULL values and returns the same datatype as the column's datatype. Again, as in an earlier tip, you can always convert the datatype, but this is probably not necessary. Also, although DISTINCT does apply, you have very few circumstances that warrant using it. To add up all the selling prices in your CD table, execute Listing 2.13 for a simple grand total.

Listing 2.13. Adding non-NULL values in a column.

```
SELECT SUM(SalesPrice) from CD
```

Your output should appear as follows:

```
- - - - - - - - - - - - - - - - - - - - - - - - -
460.69
(1 row(s) affected)
```

Again, this is another useless query. However, Microsoft does provide a way to make your queries more meaningful by allowing calculations within the aggregate functions. Consider how you might determine the actual value of inventory, the highest cost product in inventory, and the lowest cost product in inventory. Execute Listing 2.14 to see the results.

Listing 2.14. Using calculations within aggregate functions.

```
SELECT SUM(CD.AverageCost*Inventory.QOH),
    MAX(CD.AverageCost*Inventory.QOH),      MIN(CD.AverageCost*Inventory.QOH)
FROM CD,Inventory
    WHERE CD.CDID = Inventory.CDID
```

Your output should appear as follows:

```
------------- 1,032.14                 131.78                  5.98

(1 row(s) affected)
```

By adding the calculations as parameters inside the aggregate functions, you can get meaningful results.

> **NOTE**
>
> If you reduce the population to NULL values when using aggregate functions, a NULL value will be returned, except for count, which will return a zero value.

Using the GROUP BY Clause

As you probably noticed, you have a severe limitation by producing only one row of summary data. The resulting output will not be as meaningful as it should. If you try to select more than one column for output as additional clarification and the additional column is not using an aggregate function, you get an error message. The GROUP BY statement enables you to sort (group) by a field not being aggregated. You can have several nested levels of these GROUP BY statements. Execute the SQL in Listing 2.15 to see how many titles are offered by classification.

Listing 2.15. Grouping CDs by classification.

```
SELECT CD.ClassifID,Classification.Classification,
    Count(CD.CDID) "Total Offerings"
FROM CD,Classification
    WHERE CD.ClassifID = Classification.ClassifID
        GROUP BY CD.Classifid,Classification.Classification
```

Your output should appear as follows:

```
ClassifID   Classification            Total Offerings ----------
1           Pop Rock                  19
2           Country & Western         2
3           Alternative               3
4           Heavy Metal               7
```

(4 row(s) affected)

Although you could have just used the CD table and grouped by ClassifID, it was more meaningful to join the CD table to the Classification table and print both the ClassifID as well as the Classification. You now know that you offer mostly pop rock to your customers. Your country and western selections can use some improvements! You can also further define this query by seeing all offerings with a selling price over $12.00 generated by executing Listing 2.16.

Listing 2.16. Extracting partial records using GROUP BY.

```
SELECT CD.ClassifID,Classification.Classification,
    Count(CD.CDID) "Total Offerings"FROM CD,Classification
WHERE CD.ClassifID = Classification.ClassifID and
        CD.SalesPrice >= 12.00
        GROUP BY CD.Classifid,Classification.Classification
```

Your output should appear as follows:

```
ClassifID   Classification            Total Offerings -
1           Pop Rock                  14
2           Country & Western         2
3           Alternative               3
4           Heavy Metal               6
```

(4 row(s) affected)

It appears that your more profitable CDs over $12.00 are mostly catering to pop rock. Finally, how about sorting your classification types alphabetically? You can do this by utilizing the ORDER BY clause. Execute the code in Listing 2.17 to see this sorting in action.

Listing 2.17. Sorting your grouped results with ORDER BY clause.

```
SELECT CD.ClassifID,Classification.Classification,
    Count(CD.CDID) "Total Offerings"FROM CD,Classification
WHERE CD.ClassifID = Classification.ClassifID
        GROUP BY CD.Classifid,Classification.Classification
        ORDER BY Classification.Classification
```

Your output should appear as follows:

```
ClassifID   Classification            Total Offerings ----------
3           Alternative               3
2           Country & Western         2
```

```
4           Heavy Metal          7
1           Pop Rock             19
```

(4 row(s) affected)

Only use the ORDER BY clause with columns you intend to output to the screen. Any other use generates an error.

> **TIP**
>
> You can use the ORDER BY clause on values output other than columns from a table. For instance, you can sort on aggregate values, provided you have coded an alias (column heading) for the aggregate.

To sort on aggregates, execute the code in Listing 2.18.

Listing 2.18. Sorting your grouped results by an aggregate.

```
SELECT CD.ClassifID,Classification.Classification,
    Count(CD.CDID) "Total Offerings"FROM CD,Classification
WHERE CD.ClassifID = Classification.ClassifID
        GROUP BY CD.Classifid,Classification.Classification
        ORDER BY "Total Offerings"
```

Your output should appear as follows:

```
ClassifID   Classification       Total Offerings ----------
2           Country & Western    2
3           Alternative          3
4           Heavy Metal          7
1           Pop Rock             19
```

(4 row(s) affected)

Selecting Output with the HAVING Clause

The HAVING clause enables you to perform calculations on aggregates to limit what data is output. You can think of this similar to the WHERE clause, but the WHERE clause does not enable you to perform calculations on aggregates. The HAVING clause only works if you have a GROUP BY clause. In addition, it must directly follow the GROUP BY clause. Any ORDER BY clauses should follow the HAVING clause. You can now see how using the HAVING clause affects results by executing the code in Listing 2.19 by displaying those CD titles with an average selling price over $15.

Listing 2.19. Changing Output with the HAVING clause.

```
SELECT CD.ClassifID,Classification.Classification,
    Count(CD.CDID) "Total Offerings"
```

continues

Listing 2.19. continued

```
FROM CD,Classification
    WHERE CD.ClassifID = Classification.ClassifID
        GROUP BY CD.Classifid,Classification.Classification
    HAVING AVG(CD.SalesPrice) > 15
        ORDER BY Classification.Classification
```

Your output should appear as follows:

```
ClassifID   Classification              Total Offerings
----------  --------------------------  --------------
3           Alternative                 3
2           Country & Western           2

(2 row(s) affected)
```

If you have any doubts about the results, go back and write a query to calculate the average sales price by classification. You will get the same results.

Using the CUBE Operator

The CUBE operator in conjunction with the GROUP BY clause calculates whatever aggregate function you use on all records and appends this to the last row (unless you sort otherwise). This operator is contained on the same line with the GROUP BY clause, and if you are grouping on more than one item, it computes subtotals for each grouping. Listing 2.20 demonstrates how this operator works. This is excellent to have a summary of all groupings.

Listing 2.20. Working with the CUBE operator.

```
SELECT Classification.Classification,
    Count(CD.CDID) "Total Offerings"
FROM CD,Classification
    WHERE CD.ClassifID = Classification.ClassifID
        GROUP BY Classification.Classification with CUBE
```

Your output should appear as follows:

```
Classification            Total Offerings
------------------------  --------------
Alternative               3
Country & Western         2
Heavy Metal               7
Pop Rock                  19
(null)                    31

(5 row(s) affected)
```

Using the ROLLUP Operator

The ROLLUP operator in conjunction with the GROUP BY clause produces results similar to the CUBE operator, but calculates all possible subtotals and totals in the GROUP BY clause from left to right. Listing 2.21 shows an example of the ROLLUP operator.

Listing 2.21. Working with the ROLLUP operator.

```
SELECT CD.ClassifID,Classification.Classification,
    Count(CD.CDID) "Total Offerings"
FROM CD,Classification
    WHERE CD.ClassifID = Classification.ClassifID
        GROUP BY Classification.Classification, CD.ClassifID with ROLLUP
```

Your output should appear as follows:

```
ClassifID   Classification            Total Offerings
----------  ------------------------  ---------------
3           Alternative               3
(null)      Alternative               3
2           Country & Western         2
(null)      Country & Western         2
4           Heavy Metal               7
(null)      Heavy Metal               7
1           Pop Rock                  19
(null)      Pop Rock                  19
(null)      (null)                    31

(9 row(s) affected)
```

As you can see, the output adds subtotals and totals by the groupings in the GROUP BY clause. You should use the CUBE operator to provide a summary row at the end. Use the ROLLUP operator to provide totals and subtotals if you have more than one column you are grouping together.

Computing Results with COMPUTE and COMPUTE...BY

You can use COMPUTE with aggregate functions or with normal SELECT queries. With aggregate functions, SQL Server does not allow multiple aggregate functions. For instance, if you wanted to calculate lowest average selling price, using MIN(AVG(SalesPrice)) produces an error in the SELECT statement. The COMPUTE clause enables you to produce these results.

Before you start coding with COMPUTE, here are some rules for this statement:

- You cannot use DISTINCT with row aggregates.
- You cannot use SELECT INTO with COMPUTE.
- The columns in the COMPUTE clause must appear in the SELECT list.

Execute the code in Listing 2.22 to see an example of using COMPUTE.

Listing 2.22. Using COMPUTE with aggregate functions.

```
SELECT CD.ClassifID,Classification.Classification,
    AVG(CD.SalesPrice) "Average Selling Price"
FROM CD,Classification
    WHERE CD.ClassifID = Classification.ClassifID
        GROUP BY CD.Classifid,Classification.Classification
        ORDER BY Classification.Classification
        COMPUTE MIN(AVG(CD.SalesPrice))
```

Your output should appear as follows:

```
ClassifID   Classification            Average Selling Price
---------   ----------------------    -------------------------
3           Alternative               15.32
2           Country & Western         15.49
4           Heavy Metal               14.13
1           Pop Rock                  14.99

                                      min
                                      ============================
                                      14.13
```

```
(5 row(s) affected)
```

As you can see, the lowest average selling price is $14.13 from the Heavy Metal classification. This also proves the results from Listing 2.19. If you want to add more subtotals, SQL Server provides the COMPUTE...BY clause.

When using the COMPUTE...BY clause to provide subtotals, you must also use the ORDER BY clause, and all columns in the COMPUTE...BY clause must appear in the ORDER BY clause. Execute the code in Listing 2.23 to see how COMPUTE...BY works.

Listing 2.23. Using COMPUTE...BY.

```
SELECT CD.ClassifID,Classification.Classification,
    CD.SalesPrice
FROM CD,Classification
    WHERE CD.ClassifID = Classification.ClassifID
        ORDER BY Classification.Classification
        COMPUTE MIN(CD.SalesPrice) BY Classification.Classification
```

Your output should appear as follows:

```
ClassifID   Classification            SalesPrice
---------   ----------------------    -------------------------
3           Alternative               14.99
3           Alternative               14.99
3           Alternative               15.99

                                      min
```

```
                                 ============================
                                 14.99

ClassifID    Classification      SalesPrice
----------   -------------------  -----------------------
2            Country & Western    15.99
2            Country & Western    14.99

                                 min
                                 ============================
                                 14.99

ClassifID    Classification      SalesPrice
----------   -------------------  -----------------------
4            Heavy Metal          14.99
4            Heavy Metal          14.99
4            Heavy Metal          12.99
4            Heavy Metal          11.99
4            Heavy Metal          14.99
4            Heavy Metal          14.99
4            Heavy Metal          13.99

                                 min
                                 ============================
                                 11.99

ClassifID    Classification      SalesPrice
----------   -------------------  -----------------------
1            Pop Rock             16.99
1            Pop Rock             14.99
1            Pop Rock             14.99
1            Pop Rock             14.99
1            Pop Rock             16.99
1            Pop Rock             13.99
1            Pop Rock             12.99
1            Pop Rock             14.99
1            Pop Rock             16.99
1            Pop Rock             9.99
1            Pop Rock             25.99
1            Pop Rock             14.99
1            Pop Rock             11.99
1            Pop Rock             19.99
1            Pop Rock             16.99
1            Pop Rock             14.99
1            Pop Rock             11.99
1            Pop Rock             9.99
1            Pop Rock             9.99

                                 min
                                 ============================
                                 9.99

(35 row(s) affected)
```

The interesting aspect of COMPUTE...BY is that it does not necessarily have to be used with aggregate functions. In fact, the example from Listing 2.23 is the more common usage of this clause. You can now look down the list of all offerings and immediately see the smallest price; however, you can also sort by price to see the same results.

Using Unions to Display Data from Multiple Queries

The UNION operator enables you to display output from multiple queries. Because it is a binary operator, all queries are executed from left to right. You can override this with the use of parentheses. When combining output from more than one query, you must make sure that the total number of columns to output is the same in all queries; otherwise you will get an error message. Each of the datatypes in each column from left to right must match. If not, you need to use the CONVERT function. In addition, you cannot use the UNION operator within a CREATE VIEW statement or with the FOR BROWSE option. You can create an output table with the INSERT INTO statement from the result of two or more queries. The first example in Listing 2.24 demonstrates pulling two columns from two tables.

Listing 2.24. A simple UNION.

```
SELECT CONVERT(varchar(30),SalesPrice) from CD

UNION

Select Classification from Classification
```

Your output should be as follows:

```
-----------------------------
11.99
12.99
13.99
14.99
15.99
16.99
19.99
25.99
9.99
Alternative
Country & Western
Heavy Metal
Pop Rock

(13 row(s) affected)
```

As you can see, the output of the second SELECT statement follows the output of the first SELECT statement. Because the output contained datatypes of Money and VARCHAR, it was necessary to change one of the datatypes to match the other by using the CONVERT function. You can also change order using the GROUP BY clause or any other SQL used with aggregate functions to alter the output to meet your needs.

In the set of tables, you will notice two sales tables. This was meant to be stored as a distributed database—the sales table for the Midwest region would be located on a server in the Midwest, and the same for the Northeast sales table. However, to get results, all data must be combined and then summarized. You will now practice combining the data of both of these tables into one report by executing the code from Listing 2.25.

Listing 2.25. Listing the output from two identical tables.

```
SELECT * from SalesMw
UNION
SELECT * from SalesNe
```

Your output should appear as follows:

```
StoreID     CDID        QtySold     SalesDate
----------  ----------  ----------  ---------------------
1200        2006        10          Oct 31 1997 12:00AM
1200        2007        8           Nov 30 1997 12:00AM
1200        2007        15          Oct 31 1997 12:00AM
1200        2008        12          Nov 30 1997 12:00AM
1200        2009        19          Nov 30 1997 12:00AM
1210        2008        7           Oct 31 1997 12:00AM
1210        2009        55          Nov 30 1997 12:00AM
1210        2010        18          Nov 30 1997 12:00AM
1210        2020        15          Nov 30 1997 12:00AM
1210        2022        11          Nov 30 1997 12:00AM
1210        2023        20          Nov 30 1997 12:00AM
1220        2005        3           Nov 30 1997 12:00AM
1220        2018        6           Nov 30 1997 12:00AM
1300        2001        5           Nov 30 1997 12:00AM
1300        2001        10          Oct 31 1997 12:00AM
1300        2002        15          Oct 31 1997 12:00AM
1300        2003        16          Nov 30 1997 12:00AM
1300        2017        9           Nov 30 1997 12:00AM
1310        2005        11          Nov 30 1997 12:00AM
1320        2022        14          Nov 30 1997 12:00AM
1330        2000        2           Oct 31 1997 12:00AM
1330        2000        109         Nov 30 1997 12:00AM
1330        2015        20          Nov 30 1997 12:00AM
1330        2016        66          Nov 30 1997 12:00AM
1330        2029        5           Nov 30 1997 12:00AM
1330        2030        5           Nov 30 1997 12:00AM

(26 row(s) affected)
```

Although you can sort in a more meaningful manner, you can always use the INSERT INTO statement to combine both tables into one. However, this is not the fastest method to combine both tables. The SELECT...INTO process can combine multiple tables into one table; because transactions are not logged, this process will run much faster. However, if the server went down, you would have to start over, which is one of the risks of SELECT...INTO.

Summary

Aggregate functions enable you to provide one row of summary data for such purposes as decision making. These queries are fast to write and produce immediate results. If you need more detail-level summary data, you can use the GROUP BY clause. By grouping data together with summary results, you can easily spot trends such as which store is the most profitable, or which store has the highest sales.

To provide more flexibility, the HAVING clause enables you to perform calculations before sending output to the screen. This enables you to filter the data when the WHERE clause cannot be used with computing aggregate functions. If you want to see additional totals and subtotals, you can also use the CUBE operator, the ROLLUP operator, the COMPUTE clause and the COMPUTE..BY clause.

Finally, the UNION operator enables you to combine the results of two or more queries. Because it is a binary operator, the order of operations is from left to right unless overridden with parentheses. In addition, by using DML queries, you can extract meaningful information stored in a data warehouse by performing data mining. By using DML to look for trends, you can make more informed strategic decisions, which will provide a definite edge over the competition. At this stage, prebuilt data mining packages are not sophisticated enough to spot trends for every possible industry.

Optimizing Queries

IN THIS CHAPTER

CHAPTER 3

Indexes can make or break (or even brake) the performance of SQL Server if implemented without much thought. Most programmers know to put an index on the primary key field(s) of a table and even the foreign key field(s) of related tables. But what type of index should you use? Do you need to put indexes on other fields within a particular table? When should you use a composite index?

Locks and transaction isolation levels are another necessary part of optimizing performance and selecting the types of queries to use. For example, you might eventually need to know whether using read uncommitted isolation levels is better than using read committed isolation levels. A better understanding of locks and isolation levels will help you, the programmer, make better choices about indexes and table structure.

We will answer these and other questions in the following section. But to understand when to use indexes, you must understand index structures themselves.

A Closer Look at Index Structures

SQL Server provides for two types of indexes: clustered and non-clustered. Although the role of any index is to speed data retrieval and updates, each type of index is tuned to do certain jobs more effectively than the other. In some cases either type of index will provide similarly quick data retrieval, but the performance from those same indexes may differ greatly when there's a minor change to the query.

Non-Clustered Indexes

Most people are familiar with the concept of non-clustered indexes, although they might not be aware of it. This type of index is similar to an index of a book or labels on a file cabinet's drawers. You use the index to find out where an item is located, and then you use the information presented in the index to go to that item (be it a page or a drawer—or a row of data).

Examine Figure 3.1 to see a better picture of a non-clustered index.

This figure is abridged for readability. It shows the index root with its first two entries: Alvin and Marti. The index root is a page of data that contains evenly dispersed entries from the entire set of data from the indexed column. The number of entries that will fit in this initial page will depend upon the size of the column being indexed.

Next, each entry points to another page in the index node level. The first page of data will contain evenly dispersed entries from the first item in the index root to the second item in the index root. Depending on how many rows are in the table being indexed, the number of levels in the index nodes will vary. This figure shows just one level, but larger tables with larger indexed columns could increase the number of levels of index nodes.

FIGURE 3.1.

The structure of a non-clustered index.

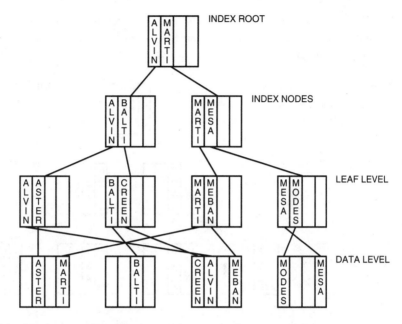

Imagine you were trying to find an order number that ranged from 1 to 1048576. If each index page could only hold four entries, the index root would contain 1, 262144, 524288, and 786432. The first page in the first index node level would contain 1, 65536, 131072, and 196608. The first page in the next index node level would contain 1, 16384, 32768, and 49152. The first page in the next index node level would contain 1, 4096, 8192, and 12288. This would continue until the eighth level, known as the leaf level, where the first page would contain 1, 2, 3 and 4; the second page would contain 5, 6, 7 and 8; and so on.

This leaf level points to the actual data (in the data level) being sought, and is not necessarily in any particular order. Hence the crossing of the lines in Figure 3.1. The name "Marti" was entered before the name "Alvin," and thus comes before that entry in the table's data pages. Information in a book (such as this one) is not presented in alphabetical order, but rather by topic. The last names in a customer table are not necessarily in alphabetical order, but rather ordered based on when they were entered into the table.

Clustered Indexes

Clustered indexes are a little different than their non-clustered counterparts. Whereas a textbook uses the equivalent of a non-clustered index, a dictionary or encyclopedia uses a mechanism like that of a clustered index. Encyclopedias are often separated into volumes based on the letter of the topic you want to investigate (index nodes). Then, the topics are listed alphabetically and the pages are marked to reveal the topic that starts on that page and the one that ends on that page (leaf level). However, the data itself is already in order. There is no need to find the topic in the index and then look it up based on some page number reference.

This is how a clustered index functions. The data itself is actually reorganized to match with the index nodes and, therefore, is combined with the leaf level. Examine Figure 3.2 for a better view of this phenomenon.

FIGURE 3.2.

The structure of a clustered index.

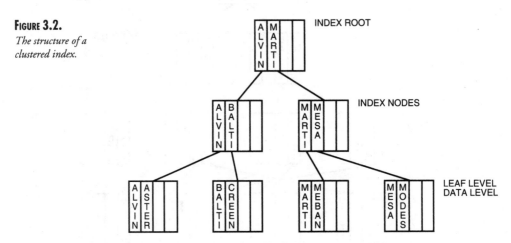

This structure has the potential to both increase and decrease performance when manipulating data. You will read more about this in the coming sections.

Because the data and leaf levels are now one, clustered indexes require less space than an equivalent non-clustered index. And because the data is reorganized with the clustered index, you can only create one clustered index per table, as opposed to non-clustered indexes, of which there may be up to 254.

Clustered Versus Non-Clustered Indexes

So when should you use a clustered index and when should you use a non-clustered index? Let's look at some examples and determine which index would be a better choice.

ORDER BY and GROUP BY Clauses

If you are often selecting data and using the ORDER BY and/or the GROUP BY clause, either type of index will help with SELECT performance. If you typically select customers and sort by last and first name, either index will provide a quick means of retrieving that data. Some of the following factors may sway you to use one type or the other, however.

Returning a Range of Values

For example, if you are returning all names between 'Smith' and 'Talbert', or orders for dates between '11/1/97' and '11/30/97', and you do this sort of thing often, you are better off using a clustered index on the particular column on which the range is based. Because clustered indexes already contain the data in a sorted order, it is more efficient for retrieving data that is in a particular range. It only needs to find the start and end of the data to retrieve all of it, unlike a non-clustered index, which needs to look up each entry from the leaf level in the data level.

One or Few Unique Values in Columns

Some columns in your table will contain few, if any, unique values. An example is a status column that contains only the values 'Inactive', 'Active', or 'Terminated'. In such a case, it is not wise to use any type of index on that column. The justification is simple: If you have a table with 15,000 rows, approximately 1/3 (or 5,000) of the rows will contain 'Active' in the status column. It is just as efficient, if not more so, to scan the entire table than to look up each entry in the index pages (the index root and node) and then find the actual data page on which each row with an 'Active' status resides. Listing 3.1 is an example script that will create a simple table with few unique values and an index on the column containing those highly duplicated values. This script can be found in the file SCR0301.SQL from Sams' Web site for this book. Don't be alarmed when this script takes a few minutes to run (you will be inserting 15,000 rows).

Listing 3.1. Creating a table with few unique values.

```
CREATE TABLE FewUniques
(
        Id       int      IDENTITY(1,1) NOT NULL,
        Status   char(10) NULL
)
GO

SET IDENTITY_INSERT FewUniques ON
DECLARE   @intCounter int
BEGIN TRAN
SELECT    @intCounter = 1

WHILE     @intCounter <= 15000
BEGIN
        INSERT FewUniques (Id, Status) VALUES (@intCOunter, 'Active')
        SELECT @intCounter = @intCounter + 3
END

SELECT    @intCounter = 2
WHILE     @intCounter <= 15000
BEGIN
        INSERT FewUniques (Id, Status) VALUES (@intCOunter, 'Inactive')
        SELECT @intCounter = @intCounter + 3
END

SELECT    @intCounter = 3
WHILE     @intCounter <= 15000
BEGIN
        INSERT FewUniques (Id, Status) VALUES (@intCOunter, 'Terminated')
        SELECT @intCounter = @intCounter + 3
END
COMMIT TRAN

SET IDENTITY_INSERT FewUniques OFF
GO

DUMP TRANSACTION pubs WITH NO_LOG, TRUNCATE_ONLY
```

continues

Listing 3.1. continued

```
GO

CREATE INDEX inFewUniquesStatus
ON FewUniques (Status)
GO
```

Next, you can run the two SELECT statements shown in Listing 3.2. Be sure to turn on the Query options "Show Query Plan" and "Show Stats I/O." The results will amaze you.

Listing 3.2. Selecting table data with and without an index.

```
--Force the Query Optimizer to use a table scan
SELECT     *
FROM       FewUniques (index=0)
WHERE      Status = 'Inactive'

--Force a particular index to be used by the Query Optimizer
SELECT     *
FROM       FewUniques (index=inFewUniquesStatus)
WHERE      Status = 'Inactive'
```

You may notice the extra code in parentheses after the table name in each query. This feature (known as an optimizer hint) will be discussed in the "Using Index Optimizer Hints" section later in this chapter. The Stats I/O information shows two very different results (see Listing 3.3). The first SELECT statement forced a table scan and only needed to perform 157 reads from memory (all the data was in memory because it was just inserted, so no disk or physical reads needed to be done). The second SELECT statement required 5,053 reads.

Listing 3.3. The Stats I/O results from Listing 3.2.

```
--Stats I/O from table scan access (comment was added)
Table: FewUniques  scan count 1,  logical reads: 157,  physical reads: 0,
➥   read ahead reads: 0
--Stats I/O from indexed access (comment was added)
Table: FewUniques  scan count 1,  logical reads: 5053,  physical reads: 0,
➥   read ahead reads: 0
```

The statistics page, the index root, the index nodes, and the data pages all must be read when selecting data via an index. This normally will decrease the number of reads required, but when the number of records being returned is high, more reads are required.

Low Number of Unique Values

What if the number of unique values increases? And what if the table is larger? As the number of rows in of the table and the number of unique values in a column grow, the index becomes more beneficial. Examine and run the code in Listing 3.4.

Listing 3.4. Creating a table with a low number of unique values.

```
DROP TABLE FewUniques
GO

CREATE TABLE FewUniques
(
        Id       int      IDENTITY(1,1) NOT NULL,
        Status   char(10) NULL,
        Col3     char(20) NOT NULL,
        Col4     char(50) NOT NULL
)
GO

DECLARE    @intNum int
SELECT     @intNum = 0

BEGIN TRAN

WHILE      @intNum <= 1300
BEGIN
    INSERT FewUniques VALUES (CHAR(@intNum % 26 + 65), 'test3', 'test4')
    SELECT @intNum = @intNum + 1
END

COMMIT TRAN
GO

CREATE INDEX inFewUniquesStatus
ON FewUniques (Status)
GO
```

This script will create, drop, and re-create the FewUniques table (with some modifications to increase the row size). It then inserts data into rows so that the status column will contain 'A', 'B', ..., 'Z', 'A', and so on. Next, it creates an index (once again) on the status column. When the two SELECT statements in Listing 3.5 are executed, the results are quite different (see Listing 3.6).

Listing 3.5. Selecting data with and without an index.

```
--Force the Query Optimizer to use a table scan
SELECT     *
FROM       FewUniques (index=0)
WHERE      Status = 'A'

--Force a particular index to be used by the Query Optimizer
SELECT     *
FROM       FewUniques (index=inFewUniquesStatus)
WHERE      Status = 'A'
```

Listing 3.6. Stats I/O from Listing 3.5.

```
--Stats I/O from table scan access (comment was added)
Table: FewUniques  scan count 1,  logical reads: 55,  physical reads: 0,
➥ read ahead reads: 0
--Stats I/O from non-clustered indexed access (comment was added)
Table: FewUniques  scan count 1,  logical reads: 53,  physical reads: 0,
➥ read ahead reads: 0
```

The end results show that by using the index, two fewer pages needed to be read. The index has now become efficient. As the table grows in size (either number of rows or size of rows), this difference will increase and make the index the preferable method of accessing the data. Thus, a clustered index will do even more for the performance of this query by requiring fewer comparative reads than an equivalent non-clustered index.

Listing 3.7 shows another version of our table FewUniques where a clustered index is being created instead of a non-clustered one. This will drastically increase performance when you're selecting data from the table based on the status column.

Listing 3.7. Creating a table with a low number of unique values.

```
DROP TABLE FewUniques
GO

CREATE TABLE FewUniques
(
        Id        int       IDENTITY(1,1) NOT NULL,
        Status    char(10)  NULL,
        Col3      char(20)  NOT NULL,
        Col4      char(50)  NOT NULL
)
GO

DECLARE    @intNum int
SELECT     @intNum = 0

BEGIN TRAN

WHILE      @intNum <= 1300
BEGIN
    INSERT FewUniques VALUES (CHAR(@intNum % 26 + 65), 'test3', 'test4')
    SELECT @intNum = @intNum + 1
END

COMMIT TRAN
GO

CREATE CLUSTERED INDEX icFewUniquesStatus
ON FewUniques (Status)
GO
```

Listing 3.8 shows the results of querying this table, which looks like Listing 3.5 with one change—the index name is inFewUniquesStatus instead of icFewUniquesStatus. Note that the clustered index was much more efficient at retrieving the data. Because the data resides on the leaf level of the index, no additional jump to the data pages was necessary to read the data. Thus, fewer page reads needed to be performed.

Listing 3.8. Stats I/O from Listing 3.5.

```
--Stats I/O from table scan access (comment was added)
Table: FewUniques  scan count 1,  logical reads: 78,  physical reads: 0,
➥  read ahead reads: 0
--Stats I/O from clustered indexed access (comment was added)
Table: FewUniques  scan count 1,  logical reads: 5,  physical reads: 0,
➥  read ahead reads: 0
```

High Number of Unique Values and Updating Indexed Column Data

As you have seen, clustered indexes help when there are some unique values on the column being examined, but a non-clustered index is the preferred method of data access when the number of unique values increases to the number of rows in the table. Although the number of pages read will not vary much from non-clustered to clustered index access, the write performance of the table is now in question.

Whenever you make a change to the column that is indexed, SQL Server has to make modifications to the index using that column. When using a clustered index, this requires possible changes to the index root, changes to the index nodes, and the insertion of the entire row in the data/leaf level, potentially requiring a shift of rows.

When you modify a column that has a non-clustered index, the index root may change, index nodes will change, and the leaf level will change. But the data level (separate from the leaf level) will not need to be shifted around because rows will be appended if needed. Because the data pages are handled separately from the index pages, less movement of entire rows of data will be required. This allows for quicker modifications to the data.

> **TIP**
>
> Remember to update the statistics (UPDATE STATISTICS) and rebuild your indexes (DBCC DBREINDEX) on a regular basis. Over time, indexes become, well, fragmented, in a similar fashion to a hard drive. Rebuilding an index is really a kind of index defragmentation. Updating statistical information helps the Query Optimizer make better decisions about how it should process the query. Statistics are always updated when you rebuild an index.

Frequently Updated Columns

If you are instead using the indexed column to find the row that needs to be updated, a clustered index will get to the data faster. If you never update the column(s) on which the clustered index is built, you will not hurt performance when updating data because the index's data isn't involved. We will see more about this in the "Using Indexes for Retrieving and Updating Data" section later in this chapter.

Returning a Range of Values

The winner—most of the time—is the clustered index. The exception to the rule appears in a later section. But for most cases, the clustered index will do a much better job of retrieving a range of data. Listings 3.9 through 3.11 show the table and index creation, the two SELECT statements (using non-clustered and clustered indexes), and the Stats I/O results from both.

Listing 3.9. Creating a table with many unique values.

```
DROP TABLE FewUniques
GO

CREATE TABLE FewUniques
(
        Id        int       IDENTITY(1,1) NOT NULL,
        status char(20) not null
)
GO

DECLARE    @intNum int
SELECT     @intNum = 0

BEGIN TRAN

WHILE      @intNum <= 5000
BEGIN
    INSERT FewUniques VALUES ('test' + convert(char(6),@intNum))
    SELECT @intNum = @intNum + 1
END

COMMIT TRAN
GO

CREATE CLUSTERED INDEX icFewUniquesId
ON FewUniques (Id)
GO

CREATE INDEX inFewUniquesId
ON FewUniques (Id)
GO
```

Listing 3.10. Retrieving a range of rows.

```
SELECT    Status
FROM      FewUniques (index=0)
WHERE     Id BETWEEN 1000 and 1500

SELECT    Status
FROM      FewUniques (index=inFewUniquesId)
WHERE     Id BETWEEN 1000 and 1500

SELECT    Status
FROM      FewUniques (index=icFewUniquesId)
WHERE     Id BETWEEN 1000 and 1500
```

Listing 3.11. Stats I/O results from Listing 3.10.

```
--Stats I/O from table scan access (comment was added)
Table: FewUniques  scan count 1,  logical reads: 71,  physical reads: 8,
➥  read ahead reads: 54
--Stats I/O from non-clustered indexed access (comment was added)
Table: FewUniques  scan count 1,  logical reads: 506,  physical reads: 0,
➥  read ahead reads: 0
--Stats I/O from clustered indexed access (comment was added)
Table: FewUniques  scan count 1,  logical reads: 9,  physical reads: 0,
➥  read ahead reads: 0
```

Even the table scan was more efficient than the non-clustered index. As I stated earlier, if more than a few rows are being returned, using a non-clustered index is usually a poor choice. The clustered index requires the least number of reads to get the job done. SQL Server searches for only the first and last values in the index node pages and finds the first and last page on which the data resides. Then the data/leaf pages are read sequentially to get the requested information.

Primary and Foreign Keys

The decision to create a clustered index on a primary key will really depend on if another index would better benefit by being clustered. It isn't necessary to make the primary key a clustered index. Another index, one that has frequent range retrievals, for example, might be a better candidate for the clustered index. If this situation exists, use your good judgment and make the primary key a non-clustered index.

As for foreign keys, the same rule applies. Keep in mind, however, that foreign keys often contain repeated values (being the "many" side of a one-to-many relationship) and thus often fit the criteria for becoming a clustered index. Again, you are not obliged to make a foreign key a clustered index, but if it is the best candidate, there should be no question in your mind. If the table contains both a primary and foreign key, the decision becomes a little more involved.

3

OPTIMIZING
QUERIES

For example, the `titles` table in the `pubs` database could have been designed to have a clustered index on the `pub_id` field and a non-clustered index on the `title_id` (primary key) field. The `pub_id` of `titles` will not have a unique set of data (most publishers produce more than one book). A clustered index on the `pub_id` column would be wiser than one on the `title_id` column because the latter has no duplicates. Thus, you would see a better overall performance when retrieving data from `titles` and `publishers`. If the `publishers` table is rarely joined to the `titles` table, or only a few titles are ever selected when joining to the `publishers` table, the present scenario of a clustered index on the `title_id` field and no index on the `pub_id` field is better.

The key is to know what types of queries will be performed. The more you know about what the users will be retrieving from the database, the easier the decisions about what types of indexes to use will be.

The following table contains a summary of when to use clustered and non-clustered indexes.

Table 3.1. Comparing clustered and non-clustered indexes.

Action/Description	Use Clustered	Use Non-Clustered
Columns often grouped/ordered by	Yes	Yes
Return a range of values	Yes	No
Low number of unique values	Yes	No
High number of unique values	No	Yes
One or a few unique values	No	No
Low number of returned rows	No	Yes
Frequently updated columns	No	Yes
Foreign key columns	Yes	Yes
Primary key columns	Yes	Yes
Frequent indexed column modifications	No	Yes

Of course, on a regular basis you will encounter situations that really are a combination of these conditions. Test out each type of index and see which will best do the job for you.

The Do's and Don'ts of Composite Indexes

When creating composite (multi-column) indexes, it is important to keep a few rules in mind. The order of the columns plays a very important role in the efficiency of the index and even the Query Optimizer's decision to use the index. Too many columns can also dramatically increase the size of the index, taking up more space and requiring more time to find the information being sought.

■ Rule 1: Don't include columns that no longer result in a unique set of data.

For example, if the index on the `lastname` and `firstname` columns contains very few duplicates, don't add the `middlename` column. You are only increasing the number of pages that need to be searched to find the same information.

TIP

The following `SELECT` statement (replace column and table information as needed) will find duplicate items within `Col1` and `Col2` (and their count) in `Table1`.

```
SELECT    Col1, Col2, COUNT(*) as Total
FROM      Table1
GROUP BY  Col1, Col2
HAVING    COUNT(*) > 1.
```

■ Rule 2: Columns that will not be individually searched on should never be listed first in the index.

For example, if you often search by `lastname` and `firstname` or just `lastname`, then `firstname` should not appear as the initial column of the composite index of `lastname` and `firstname`. If it does come before `lastname`, the search for just the `lastname` will never use the index, and if you force the use of that index, it will be very inefficient.

■ Rule 3: If you often retrieve data from only one or just a few fields of the table, a non-clustered index can cut down on the number of reads required if it contains all the fields being retrieved.

This is known as a *covered query*. If the index contains all the data that needs to be retrieved, there is no need to go to the data pages to get the data because the index already can supply all the requested information. Covered queries should only be used if the same few columns are very frequently requested. In addition, do not forget about performance when modifying data. If some of these fields are updated frequently, the index will need more maintenance from you and SQL Server. If the speeding up of the `SELECT` statement will not make up for the slowing down of these updates, a covered query is not recommended.

For example, let's say you create an index on the `authors` table that contains the following columns: `au_lname`, `city`, `state`, and `phone`. You are requesting the information (for a directory listing) from these four columns on a regular basis. However, you find that the authors tend to move a lot (we're funny that way), requiring changes to the `city`, `state`, and `phone` columns as frequently as you look up the information. The index is causing the updates to move much more slowly because three of the four columns get updated often, and the retrieval increase does not make up for that lost time. Thus, it's time to lose the index.

Listing 3.12 creates some more sample data in order to test the covered query scenario. Listing 3.13 selects data using both a clustered and non-clustered index. Listing 3.14 shows that the non-clustered index requires fewer reads to get the same data, even though a range of values is being retrieved.

Listing 3.12. Creating a table with many unique values.

```
DROP TABLE FewUniques
GO

CREATE TABLE FewUniques
(
        Id      int       IDENTITY(1,1) NOT NULL,
        status char(20) not null
)
GO

DECLARE    @intNum int
SELECT     @intNum = 0

BEGIN TRAN

WHILE      @intNum <= 5000
BEGIN
    INSERT FewUniques VALUES ('test' + convert(char(6),@intNum))
    SELECT @intNum = @intNum + 1
END

COMMIT TRAN
GO

CREATE CLUSTERED INDEX icFewUniquesId
ON FewUniques (Id)
GO

CREATE INDEX inFewUniquesId
ON FewUniques (Id)
GO
```

Listing 3.13. Selecting data via a covered query.

```
SELECT     Id
FROM       FewUniques (index=inFewUniquesId)
WHERE      Id BETWEEN 1000 and 1500

SELECT     Id
FROM       FewUniques (index=icFewUniquesId)
WHERE      Id BETWEEN 1000 and 1500
```

Listing 3.14. Stats I/O results from Listing 3.13.

```
--Stats I/O from non-clustered indexed access (comment was added)
Table: FewUniques  scan count 1,  logical reads: 5,  physical reads: 0,  read ahead
➥reads: 0
--Stats I/O from clustered indexed access (comment was added)
Table: FewUniques  scan count 1,  logical reads: 9,  physical reads: 0,  read ahead
➥reads: 0
```

The results show that no data pages were required to be read by the non-clustered index because it contained all the data being retrieved. It even beat the clustered index on range retrieval (because the data/leaf level pages take up more room). If the table had a larger row size, the non-clustered index would be that much more efficient than its clustered counterpart.

Can I Have Too Many Indexes?

Yes, Virginia, you can have too many indexes. Indexes can certainly help with data retrieval performance, but too many indexes can lead to inefficiency. With each index that you add to a table, that much more work must be done to maintain the set of indexes. Standard maintenance tasks, like updating table statistics and rebuilding indexes, will take longer with each new index you create. If an index is based on a column that gets updated, that is also additional work for SQL Server to perform every time you update that column.

If you are creating a data warehouse and few updates will be performed on the data, have at it. Create all the indexes you need to help speed up data retrieval. If, on the other hand, you are creating an *online transaction processing (OLTP)* database, you probably should keep the number of indexes to a minimum so that the data modifications will be faster.

Part of the standard database testing should include trying various combinations of clustered and non-clustered indexes. Some scenarios would reveal that several indexes fit in both the clustered and non-clustered index categories. The only way to find out which is best is to give each a try. Test out queries with each type and see which is more beneficial. Then let each test run for a few days or so and check with the users to see if they notice any difference in performance.

> **TIP**
>
> Try varying the order of clustered and non-clustered indexes when you're asking the users about performance. You may find that they always see an increase on the second go-around, for example. If you vary the order of your index type when testing with users and see a pattern like this, you know they are being primed to see better (or worse) performance the second time around. You must then rely on your own tests to see what works best.

Using Indexes for Retrieving and Updating Data

When is an index good for both data retrieval and modification? The answer: When the field of the index is used to locate data for retrieval and modification but is not modified itself and when data is more frequently updated than inserted or deleted from the table. For example, the authors table in the pubs database has a key column au_id, which is used to find the author for retrieval and updates but is never modified itself.

All indexes cause a decrease in performance when inserting data. Because there is new information being introduced to the table, the index must react accordingly. If a new author is inserted into the authors table, a new entry in all indexes must also be added, adding time to the process.

The performance can increase when deleting data from a table if the field of the index is used to locate the row(s) to be deleted. Although some maintenance by SQL Server is required when removing a row from a table, the increased speed in finding the record to be deleted will normally outweigh the decreased speed of that maintenance. If you delete an author with an au_id of '123-45-6789' by using an index that has a key of only au_id, this index speeds the search for said author. Although an entry must be removed from the index (because the row is no longer in the table), the amount of time it takes to do this is much less than the amount of time saved by using the index to find the author in the first place.

Updating data always results in a performance increase if the field in the index is used to locate the row and if that field is not changed by any of the updates. If you update the field within an index, you cause the same maintenance by SQL Server that results in a performance decrease. If you were to update the author whose au_id was '111-22-3333' and an index using just au_id was present, using it would decrease the amount of time needed to find the record and make the change. Without it, SQL Server would have to search the entire table to make sure it found all records that needed updating.

Retrieving data will usually result in a speed boost if the indexes' field is used to locate the data. Keep in mind the information already presented to you in this chapter. If you select all rows of a table, it's best to use no index because the additional page reads of the index will just be added onto the number of data pages in the table, resulting in more work for SQL Server.

Indexes, Transactions, and Data Manipulation

This section aims to fill in a few gaps before going on to the discussion of locking and query optimization. The topic of transaction isolation levels introduces the four basic locking schemes in SQL Server.

Transaction Isolation Levels

SQL Server syntactically provides for the four transaction isolation levels as prescribed in the ANSI-SQL standard. The four transaction isolation levels are

- Read uncommitted
- Read committed
- Repeatable read
- Serializable

Two of these, repeatable read and serializable, are functionally the same in SQL Server and are provided for compatibility with ANSI SQL. (So it's actually only three isolation levels.) Read committed is the default isolation level for SQL Server connections. Transaction isolation levels can be set as follows:

```
SET TRANSACTION ISOLATION LEVEL READ COMMITTED
```

This setting is on a per-connection basis and lasts until the connection is dropped or the transaction isolation level is changed. You can temporarily override the setting by influencing the query optimizer (see "Using Locking Optimizer Hints" later in this chapter).

Read Uncommitted

Potentially, read uncommitted will give you the greatest increase in performance because it will read data regardless of its current locking state. Locking concurrency does not exist as far as this level is concerned. But this also provides for the least data integrity, allowing you to read data that has not yet been committed (mid-transaction). Imagine if a user was running a long update on some book prices, and at the same time another user was retrieving title prices with read uncommitted in effect. If the first update was rolled back, the second user's data would be incorrect, reflecting whatever values were in the table at the time it was read.

Read Committed

Read committed is the default setting for SQL Server. When data is being modified, a request to read that data will wait until the modifier's transaction has finished. This prevents data from being read until it has been committed, which provides better data integrity but slows down performance.

Repeatable Read and Serializable

When SQL Server reads data, normally the lock is released as soon as SQL Server is done. However, repeatable read and serializable cause locks to be held on data being read until the transaction in which the read exists has completed. This prevents what is known as the *phantom phenomenon*—reading different values from the same data within a single transaction. Although these two transaction isolation levels provide for the best data integrity, they also have the biggest potential for performance decrease because they hold locks on data that is being read. Unless it is vital to have consistent reads within the same transaction, these two should be avoided.

3

OPTIMIZING QUERIES

> **NOTE**
>
> SQL Server treats both repeatable read and serializable the same, even though standard ANSI SQL differentiates between the two (although it's a subtle differentiation). Because they work the same in SQL Server, you can use either one when coding.

How Transactions and Indexes Affect Locking

Now to the heart of the matter. We have only mentioned locking in passing up until this point. We will now examine SQL Server's locking mechanism and how indexes and transaction isolation levels affect it. We will first examine the types of locks available in SQL Server. Next, we will investigate how you can use indexes to decrease locking concurrency. Finally, we will take a look at transaction scopes and the locking mechanism.

The Spectrum of Locks

There are two basic categories of locks in SQL Server: *table* and *page*. Table locks affect the entire table on which the data resides. If a table is locked for a read, no data modifications may occur anywhere in the table until that read is finished. If only a page is locked for a read within the table, other pages may be modified at will.

Based on this information, it is preferable to use page locks over table locks. But what are the differences and what are all of the actual locks? Table 3.2 shows the available page locks in SQL Server and their compatibility with each other.

Table 3.2. Page lock compatibility.

Current Lock	Requested Locks				
	Exclusive	Shared	Update	Insert_Page	Link_Page
Exclusive	No	No	No	No	No
Shared	No	Yes	Yes	No	No
Update	No	Yes	No	No	No
Insert_Page*	No	No	No	Yes	Yes
Link_Page*	No	No	No	No	No

An Update lock is a special type of shared lock that is not compatible with itself. It is used to indicate that an update will be performed next, and its incompatibility with itself prevents more than one process from scaling up to an exclusive lock.

Denoted by asterisks in Table 3.2, Insert_Page and Link_Page are the two locks used in Insert Row-Level Locking, which allows more than one row to be inserted at the same time on the same (last) page of a table. Insert_Page allows for compatibility with itself and is the lock that allows for multiple inserts on the same page of data. Link_Page is used to go from a full page to the next page of data. An Insert_Page lock automatically escalates to a Link_Page lock when the data page is full.

Table locks are all-encompassing, as if you were locking all pages at the same time. Examine Table 3.3 for a list of table locks and their compatibility with each other.

Table 3.3. Table lock compatibility.

Current Lock	Requested Lock			
	Exclusive	Shared	Exclusive Intent	Shared Intent
Exclusive	No	No	No	No
Shared	No	Yes	No	Yes
Exclusive Intent	No	No	Yes	Yes
Shared Intent	No	Yes	Yes	Yes

Intent locks are actually a reflection of the page locks that are occurring in the table. Consider the following scenario: A user runs a query that causes a Shared page lock, and another user runs a query that needs to place a Shared lock on the entire table. This is acceptable because a Shared Intent table lock allows for a Shared table lock. If another user runs a query that needs to place an Exclusive table lock while a page has a Shared lock, the request has to wait until the page lock is released (pending no other Shared page locks occur during the interim).

If more than four Shared lock requests occur while an Exclusive lock is waiting, the Exclusive lock will be next in line and additional Shared locks will wait until the previous Shared and Exclusive locks have completed. This is known as a *demand* lock and is automatically performed by SQL Server.

A third category of locks, *extent* locks, are automatically allocated by SQL Server when needed. An extent (8 pages) can be locked by the CREATE and DROP statements and by the INSERT and UPDATE statements if new pages for data or indexes are being added to the table.

Using Indexes to Decrease Locking Concurrency

So why all the talk about locking? Well, it just so happens that if you can lock as few pages as possible when manipulating data, you will potentially increase the performance of SQL Server by not making processes wait for locked data to be freed. If 200 users are modifying different customers' data, it is more beneficial to lock only the page on which the individual customer's information resides than to lock the entire table. Although several customers may reside on the same page, thus making some requests wait until each has completed, this is preferable to making all requests wait in a queue while each modification locks the entire table.

So how do you request page locks instead of table locks? By using indexes, of course. As mentioned earlier, an index on a field that locates the data to be modified will increase performance by going right to the page where the data resides, rather than wading through all the data pages to find the particular row. Well, if you only go to the row's page in the table, you only need to lock that page, rather than the entire table, when updating the data.

This helps increase performance yet again. Not only are fewer pages read when making the change to the row, but fewer pages are locked, potentially preventing others from having to wait until your modification has finished.

Transaction Scope, Transaction Isolation Levels, and Locking

Certain locking rules apply within a transaction, depending on what type of transaction isolation level is currently in effect. Table 3.4 helps describe those differences.

Table 3.4. Transaction isolation levels and locking effects.

Isolation Level	Lock Type and Length	
	Shared	Exclusive
Read uncommitted	As Needed	Length of Transaction
Read committed	As Needed	Length of Transaction
Repeatable read	Length of Transaction	Length of Transaction

As you can see, Shared locks are normally held only while data is actually being retrieved. The Shared lock is released once that process is completed, even if the transaction has not yet completed. This is why the phantom phenomenon can happen. If the transaction isolation level is set to repeatable read (or serializable), the Shared lock is held for the length of the transaction. Exclusive locks are always held for the length of the transaction, regardless of the isolation level.

What does this mean? It means your transactions should be only as long as needed to maintain data integrity. Lengthy transactions that modify data (that use Exclusive locks, in other words) can slow down SQL Server by making other processes wait for those transactions to complete. The longer a transaction that contains data modification statements takes to execute, the greater the potential for locking concurrency.

Listing 3.15 shows a sample script that will hold onto a Shared lock in the authors table. It also has a delay that lasts two minutes to give you time to check the current server activity.

Listing 3.15. Testing transaction isolation levels.

```
SET TRANSACTION ISOLATION LEVEL REPEATABLE READ
GO

BEGIN TRAN

SELECT    *
FROM      authors
WHERE     au_lname = 'Green'

WAITFOR DELAY '00:02:00'

ROLLBACK TRAN
GO
```

Once you execute this script, you can go to the Server menu and select Current Activity in Enterprise Manager to see what is happening in the server. Your results should look something like Figure 3.3.

FIGURE 3.3.

Current Activity window while shared page locks are in effect.

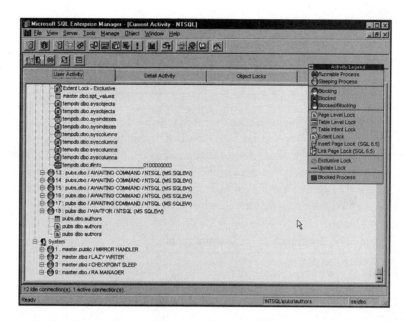

The Activity Legend reveals that page table intent locks are being taken out by SQL Server when retrieving the data. The Current Activity Window shows that the Shared locks are held until the transaction is completed (in other words, until the WAITFOR and ROLLBACK TRAN statements are completed).

Optimizing the Query Optimizer

Now we get to the good stuff: Telling SQL Server how to perform its queries. SQL Server has excellent decision-making capabilities when it comes to figuring out which index, if any at all, would get the job done most efficiently. Sometimes, however, complicated queries with many joins and elaborate WHERE clauses can be interpreted incorrectly. SQL Server provides a mechanism to override the Query Optimizer's decision and specify exactly what indexes, locking, and table order should be used to get or change the data.

Using Index Optimizer Hints

You have already seen this feature in action in previous sections of this chapter. The following code listing demonstrates two examples of data retrieval with index optimizer hints from the authors table.

Listing 3.16. Index optimizer hints.

```
SELECT     au_lname, au_fname
FROM       authors (index = 0)

SELECT     au_lname, au_fname
FROM       authors (index = 1)
WHERE      au_id = '213-46-8915'

SELECT     au_lname, au_fname
FROM       authors (index = aunmind)
WHERE      au_lname = 'Green'
```

The first SELECT statement uses the hint (index = 0) to force a table scan (no index) when retrieving the data. The second SELECT statement uses the hint (index = 1) to force the use of the
clustered index. The third SELECT statement forces the use of the non-clustered index aunmind
with the hint (index = aunmind). The index number and name are interchangeable (except for
table scans, where a 0 will need to be used). Therefore, if you preferred, the third SELECT statement could have very well been as shown in Listing 3.17.

Listing 3.17. A variation on index optimizer hints.

```
SELECT     au_lname, au_fname
FROM       authors (index = 2)
WHERE      au_lname = 'Green'
```

Because the aunmind index in the authors table has an ID of 2, either value can be used by the
query optimizer.

> **TIP**
>
> The index ID can be found in the sysindexes table of the database in which the index
> resides. An ID of 0 means no index, and an ID of 1 always represents the clustered index.
> And IDs 2 through 255 represent non-clustered indexes.

Listing 3.18 is a variation on Listing 3.15, and shows how a table lock can be used instead of
page locks by forcing a table scan.

Listing 3.18. Testing index optimizer hints.

```
SET TRANSACTION ISOLATION LEVEL REPEATABLE READ
GO

BEGIN TRAN

SELECT     *
FROM       authors (index=0)
WHERE      au_lname = 'Green'
```

```
WAITFOR DELAY '00:02:00'

ROLLBACK TRAN
GO
```

Once again, you need to go to the Current Activity window to see the results shown in Figure 3.4. If the Current Activity window is already open, you will need to refresh the displayed data by clicking the Refresh button.

FIGURE 3.4.

The Current Activity window while a table lock is in effect.

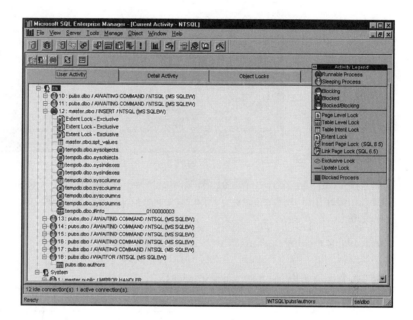

Using Locking Optimizer Hints

Let's take the example in Listing 3.18 one step further. By changing the optimizer hint, we can make SQL Server do an `Exclusive` table lock on the `authors` table (as shown in Listing 3.19 and Figure 3.5).

Listing 3.19. Forcing an exclusive table lock.

```
BEGIN TRAN

SELECT    *
FROM      authors (tablockx)
WHERE     au_lname = 'Green'

WAITFOR DELAY '00:02:00'

ROLLBACK TRAN
GO
```

FIGURE 3.5.

*The Current Activity
window while an*
Exclusive *table lock is
in effect.*

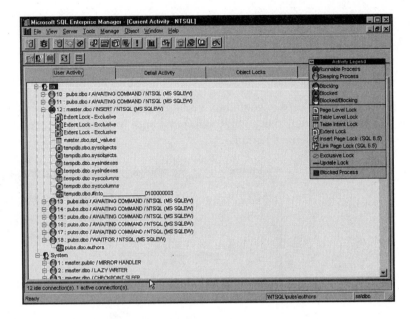

This script will give activity results like those shown in Figure 3.5. The SELECT statement uses the optimizer hint of tablockx to keep exclusive table locks in place until the transaction has completed.

The available locking optimizer hints are shown in Table 3.5.

Table 3.5. Locking optimizer hints and descriptions.

Optimizer Hint	Description
holdlock	Hold the lock until the end of the transaction.
nolock	Do not use locks when retrieving data.
paglock	Use page locks.
tablock	Use a table lock.
tablockx	Use an exclusive table lock.
updlock	Use an update lock.

holdlock can be used to hold shared locks for the duration of the transaction. This should already sound familiar to you in the form of serializable and repeatable read transaction isolation levels. If you would prefer to occasionally hold Shared locks, you would be better off keeping the default transaction isolation level of read committed and using the holdlock optimizer hint as needed.

`nolock` has the same functionality as the read uncommitted transaction isolation level. It forces the reading of uncommitted data by not requiring any locks while reading the data (thus bypassing the blocking by any exclusive locks).

One final note regarding index and locking optimizer hints: You can combine both types, but it is important to list the index hint last. The code in Listing 3.20 shows an example of a valid set of optimizer hints.

Listing 3.20. Mixing optimizer hints.

```
SELECT    *
FROM      authors (paglock holdlock index=aunmind)
```

Optimizing Table Order in Queries

There is no optimizer hint to place in the SELECT statement that will force tables to be selected in the order in which they appear. Rather, SQL Server will decide which table would be the better choice to select from first, based on what data is being requested and what is in the WHERE clause. So when tables are joined, SQL Server decides which one it uses first.

Well, not exactly. You see, there is a way to force the optimizer to use the tables in the order they are presented. It's just not part of the SELECT statement itself. Rather, you use the SET FORCEPLAN statement to tell SQL Server to use the table order as it appears or to decide on its own. Examine Listing 3.21 and its query plan in Listing 3.22.

Listing 3.21. Joining three tables.

```
SELECT    au_lname, title
FROM      titles t
          JOIN titleauthor ta ON ta.title_id = t.title_id
          JOIN authors a ON a.au_id = ta.au_id
WHERE     au_lname = 'Green'
```

Listing 3.22. Query plan from Listing 3.21.

```
STEP 1
The type of query is SELECT
FROM TABLE
authors a
Nested iteration
Index : aunmind
FROM TABLE
titleauthor ta
Nested iteration
Table Scan
FROM TABLE
titles t
Nested iteration
Using Clustered Index
```

Although the titles table is listed first, then titleauthor, and finally authors in the FROM clause, authors is used first by the query optimizer because its data is being preselected. We can force SQL Server to use the tables as they appear, as shown in Listings 3.23 and 3.24.

Listing 3.23. Using the SET FORCEPLAN statement.

```
SET FORCEPLAN ON

SELECT    au_lname, title
FROM      titles t
          JOIN titleauthor ta ON ta.title_id = t.title_id
          JOIN authors a ON a.au_id = ta.au_id
WHERE     au_lname = 'Green'
SET FORCEPLAN OFF
```

Listing 3.24. Query plan from Listing 3.23.

```
STEP 1
The type of query is SELECT
FROM TABLE
titles t
Nested iteration
Table Scan
FROM TABLE
titleauthor ta
Nested iteration
Table Scan
FROM TABLE
authors a
Nested iteration
Table Scan
```

Now SQL Server is using titles first, then titleauthor, and finally authors, just as they are listed in the FROM clause. In this case, however, examination of the Stats I/O would reveal that the latter is much more inefficient than the former. SQL Server decided to use authors first because it would cut down on the number of lookups in the other tables by limiting the authors table to a single or few rows. In most cases, SQL Server will make the best decision. But if you find a complex join query that's running more slowly than you think it should, you may want to play around with table order and the SET FORCEPLAN statement.

Summary

In all honesty, the information provided here provides only some of the SQL Server optimization techniques. Network performance, NT Server performance, application design, and so on will all have an effect on how well your SQL Server will do its job.

Great queries and indexes mean nothing if there is not enough memory on the NT Server on which SQL Server resides. What may appear to the users to be poor performance could be alleviated not by playing with indexes but by installing faster network cards or using switches on the network. Applications that issue client-based transaction statements and hold them open can slow down a server to a crawl.

Be sure to check all possibilities when you need to increase performance. Work with the network administrators and application programmers. Make sure that everyone is doing their part to make SQL Server perform to the best of its ability.

For more information on other optimization techniques, see Chapter 14, "Writing Effective Code," or see the book *Microsoft SQL Server 6.5 Unleashed.*

Advanced Transact-SQL Statements

CHAPTER 4

IN THIS CHAPTER

This chapter will look at:

- The functions required to return information, errors, and messages to the user.
- How the CASE expression is used to augment the DML introduced in Chapter 2, "Using Advanced Data Manipulation Language."
- The transactions covered in Chapter 3, "Optimizing Queries," will be extended to cover data distributed over several servers while still maintaining data consistency.

You will find yourself using the advanced coding techniques found in this chapter again and again in your applications.

Printing Information

The PRINT statement allows you to display a custom message to the user. The message may have up to 255 ASCII characters, and may include variables. The variables can be local or global, but if they are not of the CHAR or VARCHAR datatype their type must be changed using the CONVERT statement.

Listing 4.1 shows an example of a PRINT statement that shows how variables are used to concatenate data and then print it. Notice the way CONVERT functions are used to change the datatypes from INT to VARCHAR.

Listing 4.1. Printing with variables.

```
DECLARE @intMinQty INT, @intNumOrders INT, @chrOutputText CHAR(60)

/* define the variables                                        */
SELECT @intMinQty = 15
SELECT @intNumOrders = COUNT(*) FROM sales WHERE qty > @intMinQty

/* Concatenate the string using convert to format the variables */
SELECT @chrOutputText = 'There are '
                    + CONVERT(VARCHAR,@intNumOrders)
                    + ' orders with a quantity greater than '
                    + CONVERT(VARCHAR, @intMinQty)

PRINT @chrOutputText

/*  CODE RESULTS   -   DO NOT RUN CODE AFTER THIS LINE          */

(1 row(s) affected)


(1 row(s) affected)


(1 row(s) affected)

There are 5 orders with a quantity greater than 25
```

Each SELECT statement in Listing 4.1 returns a count message. These messages can be suppressed by preceding the first SELECT statement with the SET NOCOUNT ON statement and placing a SET NOCOUNT OFF statement after the last statement. Listing 4.2 shows Listing 4.1 after it's been modified to suppress the additional messages. Always remember to include SET NOCOUNT OFF or the counts will continue to be suppressed.

Listing 4.2. Using SET NOCOUNT OFF to suppress count messages.

```
SET NOCOUNT ON
DECLARE @intMinQty INT, @intNumOrders INT, @chrOutputText CHAR(60)

/* define the variables                                        */
SELECT @intMinQty = 15
SELECT @intNumOrders = COUNT(*) FROM sales WHERE qty > @intMinQty

/* Concatenate the string using convert to format the variables */
SELECT @chrOutputText = 'There are '
                        + CONVERT(VARCHAR,@intNumOrders)
                        + ' orders with a quantity greater than '
                        + convert(VARCHAR, @intMinQty)

PRINT @chrOutputText
SET NOCOUNT OFF

/*   CODE RESULTS   -   DO NOT RUN CODE AFTER THIS LINE         */

There are 5 orders with a quantity greater than 25
```

When returning messages from procedures, you should always use a PRINT statement rather than a SELECT statement. SELECT statements should be reserved for data processing or output. The PRINT statement is useful for communicating the status or outcome of a procedure to the user (not the programmer). PRINT statements should not be used to send critical messages. For this you should use the RAISERROR statement, which is covered in the section "Purposely Causing Errors" later in this chapter.

The sysmessages System Table

All the messages that can be returned by SQL Server are stored in the sysmessages table in the master database. There are around 2,200 predefined messages, to which you can add your own messages (see the section "Adding Entries to sysmessages" later in this chapter). The structure of the sysmessages table is shown in Table 4.1.

4

ADVANCED TRANSACT-SQL STATEMENTS

Table 4.1. The structure of the sysmessages table.

Column	Datatype	Description
Error	INT	Unique message identifier.
Severity	SMALLINT	Severity level of the error.
Dlevel	SMALLINT	Gives descriptive level of message.
Description	VARCHAR(255)	Error description with placeholders for parameters.
Langid	SMALLINT	Language. (Default is NULL)

TIP

You can list all the defined messages in sysmessages by running the following statements.

```
SELECT error, severity, description
FROM master..sysmessages
ORDER BY error
```

Explaining Severity Levels in sysmessages

Each of the messages in the sysmessages table has a severity value, which is used to control how the message is treated. Table 4.2 is a summary of the severity levels, giving some idea of how they will affect you as a programmer and your users.

Table 4.2. Error message severity levels.

Error Range	Notes
0–10	These are informational messages (not errors), a way of reporting additional information after a command has executed. Example error: 15343 New message added.
11-16	These are basic errors. Example error: 504 Stored procedure '%.*s' not found.
17	Caused by reaching the limit of a configurable system parameter. These cannot always be solved by a user and require either the DBO or SA to change a setting for the database. Example error: 7111 Can't log text value because log is out of space.

Error Range	Notes
18	A software-based error. The statement can finish and the SQL Server connection is maintained. Example error: `516 - Attempt to get system date/time failed.`
19	Some physical resource limit has been reached. The SA may be able to help resolve these errors, or the transaction may have to performed in a different manner. Example error: `701 There is insufficient system memory to run this query.`
20	Fatal error in the current process. The current process will be terminated, but the database integrity will be unaffected. Example error: `2806 Stored procedure '%.*s' is corrupted. Must re-create procedure.`
21	Fatal error in database process. Any active process in the current database is terminated to protect the database integrity.
22-23	Fatal error. Database or table integrity suspect. Database or table integrity has been affected by a system failure.
24	Hardware error.
25	Internal system error.

WARNING

For errors 0 through 18, the user's session normally isn't interrupted. All errors in the range of 19-25 are fatal errors that cause at least the current process to be terminated. For errors over 20, the current process is terminated—other processes in the database are terminated and the connection to SQL Server is lost.

4

Defining Your Own Messages

You can add, change, and delete user-defined messages in the `sysmessages` table by using the system stored procedures `sp_addmessage()`, `sp_altermessage()`, and `sp_dropmessage()`.

Adding Entries to `sysmessages`

By using the system stored procedure `sp_addmessage()`, you can add your own user-defined messages to the `sysmessages` table. You can choose a message identification number between 50,001 and 2,147,483,647, which leaves just a little room for growth! The description can be up to 255 characters in length. If you decide to include variables in the error, remember to leave space for them. Listing 4.3 shows the code for adding a message and the successful return from the server.

Listing 4.3. Adding a message to the sysmessages table.

```
sp_addmessage 50001, 12, 'A number greater than 0 was
                                    expected. Please retry'

/*   CODE RESULTS   -   DO NOT RUN CODE AFTER THIS LINE      */

New message added.
```

If you try to add a message with an existing message_id, the code will fail, as shown in Listing 4.4.

Listing 4.4. Adding a message to the sysmessages table with an existing message_id.

```
sp_addmessage 50001, 12, 'The specified value for %s was invalid.'

/*   CODE RESULTS   -   DO NOT RUN CODE AFTER THIS LINE      */

Msg 15043, Level 16, State 1
You must specify 'REPLACE' to overwrite an existing message.
```

If you really want to overwrite the error, add the REPLACE option to the end of the line. Notice that there are two more options added to the line. The first sets the language for the message (this defaults to U.S. English), and the second determines whether the message will be recorded in the Windows NT event log.

Listing 4.5. Adding a message to the sysmessages table using the REPLACE option.

```
sp_addmessage 50001, 12, 'The specified value for %s was invalid.'
                                    , US_English, TRUE, REPLACE

/*   CODE RESULTS   -   DO NOT RUN CODE AFTER THIS LINE      */

Replacing message.
New message added.
```

TIP

Before adding error messages to the sysmessages table, you should contact the system administrator to ensure that you use an acceptable message_id and to determine what the severity of the error should be.

Changing the State of Entries in sysmessages

If you need to alter the state of a message you have placed in sysmessages, you can use the sp_altermessage() system stored procedure. This procedure allows you to change whether a particular message is written to the Windows NT Event Log by default.

Listing 4.6. Altering the state of a message in the sysmessages table.

```
sp_altermessage 50001, WITH_LOG, FALSE

/*  CODE RESULTS   -   DO NOT RUN CODE AFTER THIS LINE        */

Message altered.
```

Deleting Entries in sysmessages

Any of the user-defined messages in the sysmessages table can be deleted by using the sp_dropmessage() stored procedure. Listing 4.7 shows an example of the stored procedure call and the results returned.

Listing 4.7. Deleting a message in the sysmessages table.

```
sp_dropmessage 50001

/*  CODE RESULTS   -   DO NOT RUN CODE AFTER THIS LINE        */

Message dropped.
```

Purposely Causing Errors

You saw in the "Printing Information" section how to notify the user of progress and status. Now you'll learn how to notify the user or the programmer when things are not going to plan.

You can use the RAISERROR statement to return an error that is handled by the system in the same way as the standard errors. The RAISERROR statement can also set a system flag using the WITH LOG option so that the error will be recorded into the Windows NT Event Log. Any error written to the Windows NT Event Log is also written to the SQL Server Error Log.

> **WARNING**
>
> To issue a RAISERROR with a severity level of 19 or higher requires system administrator privileges.

Listing 4.8 returns a message that is already in the sysmessages table. If the message_id exists in sysmessages and the SETERROR option is used, @@error is set to the message_id. If the SETERROR option is not used and the severity of the message is less than 10, @@error is set to 0.

4

ADVANCED TRANSACT-SQL STATEMENTS

Listing 4.8. Returning a sysmessages entry that requires a parameter.

```
DECLARE @chrPrintMsg CHAR(255), @chrErr CHAR(20)
SELECT @chrErr = '='

/*  Raise error 105 with a severity of 15,                  */
/*  passing the = for inclusion in the message              */
RAISERROR(105,15,2, 1, @chrErr)

/*  Build a string to display the current value of the global  */
/*  variable @@error. You do not normally have to do this, this */
/*  step is for the purposes of this example                   */
SELECT @chrPrintMsg = 'The value of @@error is ' +
                                        CONVERT(char,@@error)
PRINT   @chrPrintMsg

/*  CODE RESULTS    -   DO NOT RUN CODE AFTER THIS LINE       */


(1 row(s) affected)

Msg 105, Level 15, State 2
Unclosed quote before the character string '='.

(1 row(s) affected)

The value of @@error is 105
```

TIP

If you look in the sysmessages table, you will see that many entries have parameters. For example, in Listing 4.7 the error contains '%.*s'. This example requires two parameters—the first is the length of the string, and the second is the string value.

Listing 4.9 returns an error that is not already defined in the sysmessages table. For errors that do not exist in the sysmessages table, but that are generated using RAISERROR, set @@error to the message_id number 50,000 unless the severity is less than 10. If the severity is less than ten and you want to set @@error to an actual value, you need to use the WITH SETERROR option.

Listing 4.9. Raising a message not defined in sysmessages.

```
DECLARE @chrPrintMsg CHAR(255)

/*  Raise the error, giving the error text, severity and state  */
RAISERROR('Undefined error raised using the WITH SETERROR option'
                                        ,1,2) WITH SETERROR

/*  Build a string to display the current value of the global  */
/*  variable @@error. You do not normally have to do this, this */
/*  step is for the purposes of this example                   */
```

```
SELECT @chrPrintMsg = 'Using WITH SETERROR sets the error number
                        generated to ' + CONVERT(char,@@error)
PRINT @chrPrintMsg

/*  CODE RESULTS   -   DO NOT RUN CODE AFTER THIS LINE            */

Undefined error raised using the WITH SETERROR option

(1 row(s) affected)

Using WITH SETERROR sets the error number
                        generated to 50000
```

The CASE Expression

The CASE expression is an extremely powerful tool. In its simplest form, it allows only equality comparisons to be made. By using the more advanced CASE expression syntax, multiple Boolean comparisons can be made to determine the action to be taken.

The Simple CASE Expression

One of the uses of the simple CASE statement is to expand values to provide more meaningful output for the user. For the purposes of this example, assume that the titles table does not have a type field, and that this information can be found in the first two characters of the title_id. Each line in the CASE statement looks for equality between the substring function that isolates the first two characters of the title_id. When it finds equality, it assigns the text string to the output field BookType.

Listing 4.10. Using the case expression to expand a list.

```
SELECT  title_id,
        CASE SUBSTRING(title_id,1,2)
                WHEN 'BU' THEN 'Business'
                WHEN 'MC' THEN 'Modern Cooking'
                WHEN 'PC' THEN 'Popular Computing'
                WHEN 'PS' THEN 'Psychology'
                WHEN 'TC' THEN 'Traditional Cooking'
        END AS BookType
FROM titles
```

The following shows the output from the query:

```
title_id BookType
-------- -----------------
BU1032   Business
BU1111   Business
BU2075   Business
BU7832   Business
MC2222   Modern Cooking
MC3021   Modern Cooking
```

4

ADVANCED
TRANSACT-SQL
STATEMENTS

```
MC3026    Modern Cooking
PC1035    Popular Computing
PC8888    Popular Computing
PC9999    Popular Computing
PS1372    Psychology
PS2091    Psychology
PS2106    Psychology
PS3333    Psychology
PS7777    Psychology
TC3218    Traditional Cooking
TC4203    Traditional Cooking
TC7777    Traditional Cooking

(18 row(s) affected)
```

AUTOMATIC CODE GENERATION FOR CASE EXPRESSIONS

When you're creating these types of queries, you can save a lot of typing and the associated mistakes by using a query to build the main parts of the code. For example, the main section of Listing 4.10 could be generated by the code in Listing 4.11. After running the query, just cut and paste the code back into the query window and complete the statements. This will become a great help if the list is much longer than the one used in the example.

Listing 4.11. Auto-generating the code for Listing 4.9.

```
select distinct 'WHEN '''
              + SUBSTRING(title_id,1,2)
              + ''' THEN' from titles

/*  CODE RESULTS   -    DO NOT RUN CODE AFTER THIS LINE          */

--------------
WHEN 'BU' THEN
WHEN 'MC' THEN
WHEN 'PC' THEN
WHEN 'PS' THEN
WHEN 'TC' THEN

(5 row(s) affected)
```

Advanced CASE Expressions

The simple CASE expressions used in the last section are only a fraction of the power that CASE can bring to your code. In this section the full power of CASE expression will be unleashed.

Summarizing Data Using the CASE Expression

The CASE expression can be a great way to get more control when summarizing data. In this example, a report is required to return the total sales for each day of the week. At first it seems simple, but a CASE-based solution provides a more elegant result.

In Listing 4.12 and Listing 4.13, both queries return the correct totals for the sales on that day. At first glance, the code in Listing 4.12 appears to be superior because it performs the task in fewer statements.

Listing 4.12. Selecting the total sales by weekday–simple query.

```
SELECT   sum(qty) AS Total,
         datename(weekday, ord_date) AS Weekday
FROM     sales
GROUP BY datename(weekday, ord_date)
```

Listing 4.13. Using a CASE expression to sum sales by weekday.

```
SELECT   sum(qty) AS Total,
         CASE datepart(weekday, ord_date)
                 WHEN 1 THEN 'Sunday'
                 WHEN 2 THEN 'Monday'
                 WHEN 3 THEN 'Tuesday'
                 WHEN 4 THEN 'Wednesday'
                 WHEN 5 THEN 'Thursday'
                 WHEN 6 THEN 'Friday'
                 WHEN 7 THEN 'Saturday'
         END AS Weekday
FROM sales
GROUP BY datepart(weekday, ord_date)
```

But look at the output from Listing 4.12:

```
Total        Weekday
----------   ------------------------------
130          Monday
115          Saturday
45           Sunday
40           Thursday
78           Tuesday
1090         Wednesday

(6 row(s) affected)
```

You can see that the days of the week are all present and the totals are listed correctly, but the days of the week are not in order. The incorrect order cannot be fixed by using an ORDER BY statement because it cannot be added to the GROUP BY clause. A different solution is required.

```
Total        Weekday
-----------  --------
45           Sunday
130          Monday
78           Tuesday
1090         Wednesday
40           Thursday
115          Saturday

(6 row(s) affected)
```

Using the CASE Expression with Complex Conditions

In the last section you were using simple equalities to establish which part of the CASE statement would be executed. This section shows how the CASE expression allows Boolean expressions to be used. In Listing 4.14, you can compare the value in ytd_sales and then discount the book based on that value. In addition to the Boolean logic at the end of the WHEN expressions, there is an ELSE expression. If none of the Boolean logic is true, the code in the ELSE expression is executed.

Listing 4.14. A CASE expression with complex conditional terms.

```
SELECT
title_id, price, ytd_sales,
"DiscountPrice" =
          CASE
                WHEN ytd_sales < 1000 THEN
                              CONVERT (SMALLMONEY, price * .50)
                WHEN ytd_sales < 3000 THEN
                              CONVERT (SMALLMONEY, price * .85)
                ELSE price
          END

FROM titles
```

The following is the output from Listing 4.14:

```
title_id price                    ytd_sales   DiscountPrice
-------- ------------------------ ----------- -------------------------
BU1032   19.99                    4095        19.99
BU1111   11.95                    3876        11.95
BU2075   2.99                     18722       2.99
BU7832   19.99                    4095        19.99
MC2222   19.99                    2032        16.99
MC3021   2.99                     22246       2.99
MC3026   (null)                   (null)      (null)
PC1035   22.95                    8780        22.95
PC8888   20.00                    4095        20.00
PC9999   (null)                   (null)      (null)
PS1372   21.59                    375         10.80
PS2091   10.95                    2045        9.31
PS2106   7.00                     111         3.50
PS3333   19.99                    4072        19.99
```

```
PS7777    7.99                 3336      7.99
TC3218   20.95                  375     10.48
TC4203   11.95                15096     11.95
TC7777   14.99                 4095     14.99

(18 row(s) affected)
```

Look at this output and use the ytd_sales column to compare the values in the price column to those in the DiscountPrice column. See how the values were affected depending on which part of the CASE statement was executed.

Summarizing Data Using the Searched CASE Expression

You can further extend the power of the CASE expression by basing the expression on the results of a SELECT statement. The SELECT statement is placed in parentheses and replaces the field name in the Boolean expression of the standard CASE expression.

Listing 4.15 shows a query where an output field is created based on the value of the SELECT statement, summing the sales quantity of each store in the stores table. If the output field does not meet any of the conditions of the WHEN expression, it is placed in the last category of the ELSE expression. The output demonstrates how useful the CASE expression can be when there is data to be summarized or sorted.

Listing 4.15. Using a SELECT-based CASE Expression.

```
SELECT DISTINCT st.stor_name,

'Sales Rating' =
    CASE
      WHEN (SELECT SUM(sa.qty) FROM sales sa
                              WHERE st.stor_id = sa.stor_id) < 10
          THEN 'Poor'
      WHEN (SELECT SUM(sa.qty) FROM sales sa
                              WHERE st.stor_id = sa.stor_id) < 80
          THEN 'Average'
      WHEN (SELECT SUM(sa.qty) FROM sales sa
                              WHERE st.stor_id = sa.stor_id) < 100
          THEN 'Good'
      ELSE 'Excellent'
    END,

'Sales Total' = (SELECT SUM(sa.qty) FROM sales sa
                              WHERE st.stor_id = sa.stor_id)

FROM stores st, sales sa

ORDER BY 'Sales Total'

stor_name                                 Sales Rating Sales Total
----------------------------------------- ------------ -----------
```

4

ADVANCED
TRANSACT-SQL
STATEMENTS

continues

Listing 4.15. continued

Eric the Read Books	Poor	8
Fricative Bookshop	Average	60
Bookbeat	Good	80
News & Brews	Good	90
Barnum's	Excellent	125
Doc-U-Mat: Quality Laundry and Books	Excellent	130

```
(6 row(s) affected)
```

Updating Data Using the CASE Expression

The CASE expression is not limited to selecting and summarizing data. It can also be used to update tables. Listing 4.16 shows how to use a CASE expression with the UPDATE statement to update the payterms field in the sales table, based on the sales performance of that store. In this case you need to use a correlated subquery (see Chapter 1, "Beyond the Basics of Data Manipulation Language") to enable a summation of the qty field to be made. Based on the outcome of the selection, the value of payterms is updated to a new value. When you use a CASE expression with an update statement, large amounts of data can quickly be updated to new values based on a series of conditional expressions.

Listing 4.16. Using CASE to update data.

```
UPDATE sales

SET payterms =
    CASE
        WHEN (SELECT SUM(qty) FROM sales s1
            WHERE sales.stor_id = s1.stor_id) < 10
            THEN 'On Invoice'
        WHEN (SELECT SUM(qty) FROM sales s1
            WHERE sales.stor_id = s1.stor_id) < 100
            THEN 'Net 30'
        ELSE 'Net 60'
    END
GO
SELECT stor_id, SUBSTRING(ord_num,1,5) ord_num,
        ord_date, qty, payterms, title_id FROM sales
GO
```

The result set from this query is as follows:

```
(21 row(s) affected)

stor_id ord_num ord_date                     qty    payterms     title_id
------- ------- ---------------------------- ------ ------------ --------
6380    6871    Sep 14 1994 12:00AM          5      On Invoice   BU1032
6380    722a    Sep 13 1994 12:00AM          3      On Invoice   PS2091
7066    A2976   May 24 1993 12:00AM          50     Net 60       PC8888
7066    QA744   Sep 13 1994 12:00AM          75     Net 60       PS2091
7067    D4482   Sep 14 1994 12:00AM          10     Net 30       PS2091
7067    P2121   Jun 15 1992 12:00AM          40     Net 30       TC3218
```

```
7067   P2121   Jun 15 1992 12:00AM       20      Net 30      TC4203
7067   P2121   Jun 15 1992 12:00AM       20      Net 30      TC7777
7131   N9140   Sep 14 1994 12:00AM       20      Net 60      PS2091
7131   N9140   Sep 14 1994 12:00AM       25      Net 60      MC3021
7131   P3087   May 29 1993 12:00AM       20      Net 60      PS1372
7131   P3087   May 29 1993 12:00AM       25      Net 60      PS2106
7131   P3087   May 29 1993 12:00AM       15      Net 60      PS3333
7131   P3087   May 29 1993 12:00AM       25      Net 60      PS7777
7896   QQ229   Oct 28 1993 12:00AM       15      Net 30      BU7832
7896   TQ456   Dec 12 1993 12:00AM       10      Net 30      MC2222
7896   X999    Feb 21 1993 12:00AM       35      Net 30      BU2075
8042   423LL   Sep 14 1994 12:00AM       15      Net 30      MC3021
8042   423LL   Sep 14 1994 12:00AM       10      Net 30      BU1032
8042   P723    Mar 11 1993 12:00AM       25      Net 30      BU1111
8042   QA879   May 22 1993 12:00AM       30      Net 30      PC1035

(21 row(s) affected)
```

Distributed Transactions

When you're dealing with data found on two servers, data that's modified on one server also needs to be updated on the other. This requires a *distributed transaction*. For example, let's say you're selling books. Before you can sell a book, you have to verify that you have copies in stock. When the sale is agreed, you must remove the correct quantity from the stocklist. If all the tables were based in one database, or even in several databases on one server, you could use a series of the transactions that were discussed in Chapter 3, "Optimizing Queries." In our example, the store of books is kept on a remote database. To ensure consistency, a distributed transaction is used.

Why Use the DTC?

The DTC provides a mechanism for ensuring data consistency when data is manipulated across more than one server. In Chapter 3, "Optimizing Queries," you saw how to handle data consistency using transactions when the data was based on a single server. When you need to update data in several locations, a more complex system is required to prevent the data inconsistency that occurs if one of the other servers cannot complete its transactions. The DTC provides a simple method of controlling the transactions across several servers, managing the process.

Behind the Scenes in the DTC

Each computer involved in a distributed transaction has a local transaction manager. All application and resource managers work through their local transaction managers, which work together to manage transactions that span more than one system. Each distributed transaction consists of a two-phase commit protocol.

When the application first generates the distributed transaction, in this case using the BEGIN DISTRIBUTED TRANSACTION statement, the Distributed Transaction Coordinator (DTC) on the local machine (known as the *commit coordinator*) sends a message to the remote computer and sets up a relationship (Figure 4.1, step 1). Each system informs its transaction manager that this transaction is connected to the local transaction manager on the other system. The remote system sends an agree message to the local system (Figure 4.1, step 2). These incoming and outgoing relationships between the systems and their local transaction managers form a tree called a *commit tree.* Any member of the commit tree has the right to abort its local transaction at any time, which in turn aborts the transaction on all of the systems involved.

FIGURE 4.1.

Sequence of operations for distributed transactions.

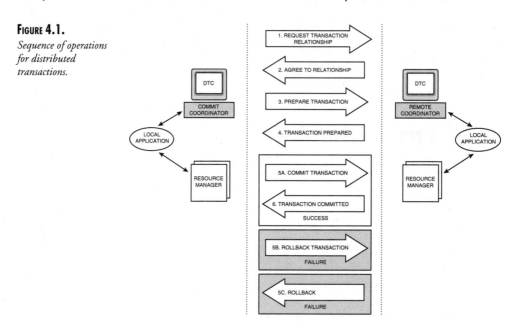

After the relationship is set up, the local DTC sends a prepare request to each of the remote systems involved in the transaction (Figure 4.1, step 3). Each remote prepares the transaction and reports back to the commit coordinator that it is prepared (Figure 4.1, step 4). Until it receives a commit or abort from the commit coordinator, the transaction remains in doubt on that system. The commit coordinator maintains an entry in its distributed transaction log until all remote systems have confirmed that they have completed the transaction. The transaction can be completed by any of the steps 5A, 6, 5B, or 5C in Figure 4.1.

In steps 5A and 6, the transaction succeeds at the local computer and the remote is told to commit. The cycle is completed when the remote computer responds to the commit coordinator that its commit was successful.

In steps 5B and 5C, the transaction fails and is rolled back. The difference between the two is that in step 5B, the remote system initiates the rollback, and in step 5C, the local system calls for the rollback.

If one of the systems fails at any time while the query is still in doubt, the local transaction manager on that computer will determine the fate of the transaction when the computer restarts. It will use the information stored in its log file to decide whether it had been informed of the outcome of any incoming transactions. If any incoming transactions remain in doubt after the computer checks the log file, the commit coordinator for that transaction is queried to determine the outcome. The local transaction manager also determines the outcomes of any transactions for which it was the commit coordinator. It also responds to the requests from the other servers involved in the transaction, who are waiting to complete the transaction.

> **WARNING**
>
> One of the biggest problems with distributed transactions is that anytime the transaction is in doubt, any resources modified by the transaction remain locked until a commit or abort is received. In order to minimize this problem, it is especially important to use small, fast-executing transactions.

Transactions that remain in doubt for a long period can be a real problem, and the DTC gives you a graphical tool to resolve these stalled transactions. This tool can be used on either the commit coordinator or on the remote system to force the outcome of transactions in doubt. To show the current transactions, right-click on the DTC in the Server Manager window of SQL Enterprise Manager and select the Transactions option. Right-click again on entries in the log to commit, abort, or forget the transactions. The Forget option is sometimes required to remove transactions that have been manually completed from the event logs of other servers that have already committed the transaction.

> **NOTE**
>
> Only transactions that are in doubt can be forced using the DTC Transactions Manager in SQL Enterprise Manager.

Using the DTC to Maintain Consistency Across Systems

One reason to use the DTC is that you may need to update several tables across two or more servers. If you need to update a large amount of complex data on many servers, you should also consider using *replication* (see Chapter 17, "Replication").

There are several key elements to consider when you're setting up the transactions. First, you initialize the DTC with the BEGIN DISTRIBUTED TRAN statement. There will be at least two stored procedures. One will be based locally at the server initiating the transaction to update the local data. The other is on the remote server and will handle the update of the remote data. Once all the data manipulation is complete and successful, the COMMIT TRAN is issued by the local procedure. If the remote procedure tries to abort the procedure by using a ROLLBACK statement, an error is generated because the transaction only has scope on the commit coordinator. If the remote procedure doesn't complete and an error is generated, the distributed transaction will be rolled back.

> **NOTE**
>
> If you want two servers to use distributed transactions, they must be connected by running the system stored procedures sp_addserver() and sp_addremotelogin(), or connected to each other using the Manage Remote Servers dialog box, accessed from the Server | Remote Servers menu in Enterprise Manager.

Listing 4.17 shows the stored procedure that's used to update the remote server. It takes the job_id passed from the local jobs table and updates the remote jobs table with the new job description.

Listing 4.17. Stored procedure to update remote database using the DTC.

```
CREATE PROCEDURE prUpdateJobs(@insJob_Id smallint,
                             @chvJob_Desc varchar(50)) AS
UPDATE jobs SET job_desc = @chvJob_Desc WHERE job_id = @insJob_Id
```

Listing 4.18 is the stored procedure on the local machine that updates the local table and then calls the remote stored procedure passing the same information. After calling the remote procedure, the two updates are committed to the databases. If either of the queries fails, the changes made within the scope of the transaction are rolled back.

Listing 4.18. Local stored procedure to update the local table.

```
CREATE PROCEDURE prUpdateJobs(@insJob_Id     smallint,
                             @chvJob_Desc    varchar(50),
                             @chvServerName  varchar(30)) AS

declare @chvExecStr varchar(255)

/* Start a Transaction */
BEGIN DISTRIBUTED TRANSACTION UpdateJobs

/* Change Local Jobs Table */
UPDATE jobs SET job_desc = @chvJob_Desc where job_id = @insJob_Id

/* Make a string with the remote server name and                    */
```

```
/* stored procedure to execute                              */
/* Syntax for remote procedure call is NTSQL2.pubs..prUpdateJobs*/
select @chvExecStr = @chvServerName + '.pubs..prUpdateJobs '

/* Update remote server.                                     */
exec @chvExecStr @insJob_id, @chvJob_Desc

/* Commit the MS DTC transaction */
COMMIT TRANSACTION
```

The EXECUTE statement for the stored procedure is shown in Listing 4.19. Note that the only return is that no rows were returned. In this case, no news is good news. If you examine the jobs table on each server, both should have changed the job_desc field to 'CEO' for the job_id 5.

Listing 4.19. Executing the procedures with successful results.

```
exec prUpdateJobs 5,'CEO', NTSQL2

This command did not return data, and it did not return any rows
```

To simulate a failure, you can prevent the remote code from running by stopping the DTC on NTSQL2. Now, when you execute the query as shown in Listing 4.20, the update fails on the remote server because the DTC cannot establish a link. The DTC returns an error and rolls back the query. If you now re-query the jobs on the two servers, the job_desc for job_id will remain at 'CEO', unaffected by the query.

Listing 4.20. Executing the procedures with failed results.

```
EXEC prUpdateJobs 5,'Chief Executive Officer', NTSQL2

Msg 8501, Level 16, State 1
DTC on server 'NTSQL' is unavailable
Msg 8524, Level 16, State 1
The current transaction couldn't be exported to remote site.
                            It has been rolled back.
```

Using the DTC for Paired Transactions

Another use of the DTC is to update two different tables that must remain synchronized across two different servers. In our example, whenever a sale is entered, the same quantity of books must be deducted from the remote database table bookinv. The bookinv table contains an inventory list. Listing 4.21 contains the code for creating a table of book inventory and populating it with some sample data. The table should be created in the pubs database of the remote machine.

Listing 4.21. Creating a book inventory table with sample data.

```
CREATE TABLE bookinv
(
        title_id        tid
                CONSTRAINT p1_constraint PRIMARY KEY NONCLUSTERED,
        quantity        integer,
        location        char(2),
        lastaudit       datetime
)

INSERT INTO bookinv
SELECT DISTINCT title_id,
                COALESCE(CONVERT(int,RAND(ytd_sales)*100),10),
                SUBSTRING(type,1,2),
                pubdate
FROM titles
```

Listing 4.22 shows the remote server's stored procedure for checking and updating the remote table. It is called by sending the `title_id` and the quantity requested. At line 7, the available quantity for the `book_id` is found from the `bookinv` table. At line 10, a check is made to ensure that there are enough books available to be removed from stock.

If there are not enough books, lines 11 through 17 are executed. These lines build a error message and then raise an error stating that the transaction cannot be completed.

If there are enough books, lines 19 through 28 are executed. Line 22 updates the table with the correct amount of books removed from the stock number. Lines 24 through 27 build and print a message that states the successful transfer of the books from inventory.

Listing 4.22. Creating a remote stored procedure for checking and updating the book inventory table.

```
 1: CREATE PROCEDURE prUpdatebookinv(@tidTitles tid,
 2:                                 @intQty int) AS
 3:
 4: Declare @intAvailQty int, @chvOutputMsg varchar(255)
 5:
 6: /* Get Quantity of available books in inventory   */
 7: SELECT @intAvailQty = (SELECT quantity FROM bookinv
 8:                                 WHERE title_id = @tidTitles)
 9:
10: IF @intAvailQty - @intQty < 0
11:      BEGIN
12: /* If available quantity is less than zero then raise error */
13:         SELECT @chvOutputMsg = 'There are only '
14:                 + CONVERT(varchar(10),@intAvailQty)
15:                 + ' available, remote transaction denied'
16:         RAISERROR (@chvOutputMsg, 16, -1)
17:      END
18: ELSE
19:      BEGIN
20: /* If available quantity is greater than zero,            */
21: /* update the inventory table                             */
```

```
22:            UPDATE bookinv SET quantity = quantity - @intQty
23:                               WHERE title_id = @tidTitles
24:            SELECT @chvOutputMsg = 'There were '
25:                   + CONVERT(varchar(10),@intAvailQty)
26:                   + ' available, remote transaction succeeds'
27:            PRINT @chvOutputMsg
28:      END
```

Listing 4.23 is the local stored procedure. It requires a `title_id`, quantity of books, the `StorID`, and the remote server name. At line 11, the remote procedure call is built, and at line 15, an order number is generated. At line 18, the distributed transaction `UpdateJobs` is started. The first action in the distributed transaction, in lines 21 and 22, is to update the local `titles` table, increasing the sales quantity in the `ytd_sales` field. Then an entry is added to the sales table in lines 25 through 28, recording the sale. After the local changes are made, the remote stored procedure is called in line 31. The final statement block in lines 33 through 42 decides if there has been an error generated in either of the procedures. If there has been an error, the distributed transaction is rolled back, restoring the tables. If there is no error, the database changes are committed. This strategy is possible because if the value of `@@error` is set in the remote stored procedure, the value of `@@error` is still visible to the calling procedure.

Listing 4.23. Creates the local stored procedure that controls the distributed transaction.

```
 1: CREATE PROCEDURE prCreateSale (@tidTitleid tid,
 2:                                @intQty int,
 3:                                @chrStorId char(4),
 4:                                @chvServerName varchar(30)) AS
 5:
 6: DECLARE @chvExecStr varchar(255),
 7:         @chvOrdNum varchar(20)
 8:
 9: /* Make a string with the remote server name and     */
10: /* stored procedure to execute                        */
11: SELECT @chvExecStr = @chvServerName
12:                      + '.pubs..prUpdatebookinv '
13:
14: /* Generate a order number */
15: SELECT @chvOrdNum = @chrStorId + SUBSTRING(@tidTitleId,1,2)
16:
17: /* Start a Transaction */
18: BEGIN DISTRIBUTED TRANSACTION UpdateJobs
19:
20: /* Update local titles table */
21: UPDATE titles SET ytd_sales = ytd_sales + @intQty
22:               WHERE title_id = @tidtitleid
23:
24: /* Add entry to local sales table  */
25: INSERT sales(stor_id, ord_num, ord_date, qty
26:                                  , payterms, title_id)
27:    VALUES (@chrStorId, @chvOrdNum, GETDATE(), @intQty
28:                                  , 'Net 60', @tidtitleid)
29:
30: /* Update remote server.                              */
```

continues

Listing 4.23. continued

```
31: EXEC @chvExecStr @tidtitleid, @intQty
32:
33: IF @@error > 0
34:      BEGIN
35:          ROLLBACK TRAN
36:          PRINT 'TRANSACTION WAS ROLLED BACK'
37:      END
38: ELSE
39:      BEGIN
40:          COMMIT TRAN
41:          PRINT 'TRANSACTION WAS COMMITTED'
42:      END
```

When the EXECUTE command shown in Listing 4.24 is issued, the procedure tries to remove 100 books of the book type 'BU1032' from the remote bookinv table, update the year-to-date sales in the titles table, and enter a sales record in the sales table. In this case the procedure fails because there are only 40 books available. The distributed transaction is rolled back, leaving the database in its original state. You can check the states of the tables involved and confirm that this happens by running a query against each of the tables.

Listing 4.24. Executing the stored procedure, with an unsuccessful outcome.

```
EXEC prCreateSale 'BU1032',100,'6380','NTSQL2'

/*  Enter only the EXEC statement - sample output follows  */

Msg 50000, Level 16, State 1
There are only 40 available, remote transaction denied
TRANSACTION WAS ROLLED BACK
```

In Listing 4.25, the sales demand is only 20 books, which is an amount that the available inventory can support. In this case the remote query is successful, the distributed transaction is successful, and the updates are written to the tables in both the remote and local databases. Listings 4.26 and 4.27 show sample data, with the queries used to create them. Run them before and after the queries are executed to help show what is happening in the database tables.

Listing 4.25. Executing the stored procedure, with a successful outcome.

```
EXEC prCreateSale 'BU1032',20,'6380','NTSQL2'

/*  Enter only the EXEC statement - sample output follows  */

There were 40 available, remote transaction succeeds
TRANSACTION WAS COMMITTED
```

Listing 4.26. Checking queries and sample data for the local database.

```
/* run these two queries against the local database */

SELECT stor_id, convert(char(10),ord_num), ord_date, qty, title_id
                                                         FROM SALES
GO

SELECT title_id, ytd_sales FROM titles
GO

/* Sample data for local database after a fresh install of pubs */
```

stor_id		ord_date	qty	title_id
6380	6871	Sep 14 1994 12:00AM	5	BU1032
6380	722a	Sep 13 1994 12:00AM	3	PS2091
7066	A2976	May 24 1993 12:00AM	50	PC8888
7066	QA7442.3	Sep 13 1994 12:00AM	75	PS2091
7067	D4482	Sep 14 1994 12:00AM	10	PS2091
7067	P2121	Jun 15 1992 12:00AM	40	TC3218
7067	P2121	Jun 15 1992 12:00AM	20	TC4203
7067	P2121	Jun 15 1992 12:00AM	20	TC7777
7131	N914008	Sep 14 1994 12:00AM	20	PS2091
7131	N914014	Sep 14 1994 12:00AM	25	MC3021
7131	P3087a	May 29 1993 12:00AM	20	PS1372
7131	P3087a	May 29 1993 12:00AM	25	PS2106
7131	P3087a	May 29 1993 12:00AM	15	PS3333
7131	P3087a	May 29 1993 12:00AM	25	PS7777
7896	QQ2299	Oct 28 1993 12:00AM	15	BU7832
7896	TQ456	Dec 12 1993 12:00AM	10	MC2222
7896	X999	Feb 21 1993 12:00AM	35	BU2075
8042	423LL922	Sep 14 1994 12:00AM	15	MC3021
8042	423LL930	Sep 14 1994 12:00AM	10	BU1032
8042	P723	Mar 11 1993 12:00AM	25	BU1111
8042	QA879.1	May 22 1993 12:00AM	30	PC1035

```
(21 row(s) affected)
```

title_id	ytd_sales
BU1032	4095
BU1111	3876
BU2075	18722
BU7832	4095
MC2222	2032
MC3021	22246
MC3026	(null)
PC1035	8780
PC8888	4095
PC9999	(null)
PS1372	375
PS2091	2045
PS2106	111
PS3333	4072
PS7777	3336

4

ADVANCED
TRANSACT-SQL
STATEMENTS

continues

Listing 4.26. continued

```
TC3218    375
TC4203    15096
TC7777    4095

(18 row(s) affected)
```

Listing 4.27. Checking queries and sample data for the remote database.

```
/* Run this query against the remote database */

SELECT * FROM bookinv

/* Results for a bookinv created against a fresh install of pubs*/

title_id quantity     location lastaudit
-------- -----------  -------- ------------------------
BU1032   40           bu       Jun 12 1991 12:00AM
BU1111   38           bu       Jun 9 1991 12:00AM
BU2075   86           bu       Jun 30 1991 12:00AM
BU7832   40           bu       Jun 22 1991 12:00AM
MC2222   20           mo       Jun 9 1991 12:00AM
MC3021   21           mo       Jun 18 1991 12:00AM
MC3026   10           UN       Dec 11 1997  1:35AM
PC1035   87           po       Jun 30 1991 12:00AM
PC8888   40           po       Jun 12 1994 12:00AM
PC9999   10           po       Dec 11 1997  1:35AM
PS1372   3            ps       Oct 21 1991 12:00AM
PS2091   20           ps       Jun 15 1991 12:00AM
PS2106   1            ps       Oct 5 1991 12:00AM
PS3333   40           ps       Jun 12 1991 12:00AM
PS7777   33           ps       Jun 12 1991 12:00AM
TC3218   3            tr       Oct 21 1991 12:00AM
TC4203   50           tr       Jun 12 1991 12:00AM
TC7777   40           tr       Jun 12 1991 12:00AM

(18 row(s) affected)
```

WARNING

MS DTC doesn't support the PREPARE TRAN or SAVE TRAN statements that can be used in standard transactions. If a PREPARE TRAN is issued within the scope of the distributed transaction, an error is returned. If a SAVE TRAN is used within a distributed transaction, it is ignored with no error. If the transaction is subsequently rolled back or aborted, the entire transaction is rolled back to the BEGIN DISTRIBUTED TRANSACTION.

Troubleshooting DTC Procedures

One issue with using the DTC is that transactions spread across more than one node can be difficult to troubleshoot. There are several things that you can do to minimize problems. First, keep your transactions short and simple. A large transaction is difficult to debug and maintains a large number of page locks for a significant period during its processing. You can refer to Chapter 14, "Writing Effective Code," for many useful techniques for writing simple code.

Debugging DTC Procedures

If you encounter a problem with a distributed transaction, first try to run the code piece by piece using the Query Manager. If no problems are found when the code is run locally, place a number of extra commands in the transaction that either return the values being used or use a temporary table to store the variables as they change in the procedures. When you use a table, remember that any changes made within the transaction will be rolled back if the transaction fails. If this is the case, record all the values just before the BEGIN DISTRIBUTED TRANSACTION statement. If you are still unable to find the bug, try separating the transaction into several smaller ones. This will probably produce a better-written procedure with many shorter transactions.

Summary

This chapter has shown you a number of ways to use T-SQL statements to improve your applications and manage distributed transactions. As you have seen, CASE expressions are a very helpful way to label, organize, and summarize your output and sift through complex conditions. You've also seen reusable code that uses the PRINT statement, messages you define in the sysmessages system table, and the RAISERROR command to provide your application's user with easy-to-understand, informative error messages.

Of course, you might be working on a system that requires multiple servers and distributed transactions. This chapter has also shown you how to create a remote stored procedure for checking and updating data on a remote server as well as code for checking queries and sample data for the local database. These examples should help you keep data on multiple servers concurrent by monitoring these distributed transactions.

Effective Use of Built-in Functions

IN THIS CHAPTER

Functions are a very important, powerful feature that allows you to accomplish tasks without having to write a lot of code. Just imaging trying to use SQL to compute the tangent of a line to the circle without using the built-in functions. This chapter not only reviews all of SQL Server's functions, but it also provides some effective methods for implementing these functions. If you need assistance on summary-level functions, please review Chapter 2, "Using Advanced Data Manipulation Language."

Making Computations Work With Mathematical Functions

Mathematical functions provide a means to perform operations on numeric data. While this book assumes you are familiar with the order of operations, it is imperative that you know the order of mathematical computations. Many decisions have been made based upon erroneous reports in which the order of operations was misunderstood. Table 5.1 shows a complete list of mathematical functions available in SQL Server.

Table 5.1. Mathematical functions.

Function	Description
ABS	Returns the absolute value of numeric data.
ACOS	Returns the arc cosine in radians of any number passed to the function. The input range is from –1 to 1, and the output range is 0 to pi.
ASIN	Returns the arc sine in radians of any number passed to the function. The input range is from –1 to 1, and the output range is –pi/2 to pi/2.
ATAN	Returns the arc tangent in radians of any number passed to the function. The input range is infinity, meaning unbounded at both ends, and the output range is –pi/2 to pi/2.
ATN2	Returns the arc tangent in radians of the two numbers (y/x) passed to the function. The input range is infinity, meaning unbounded at both ends, and the output range is –pi to pi.
CEILING	Returns the value representing the smallest integer that is greater-than or equal to the *input_number*.
COS	Returns the cosine of any number passed as an angle in radians to the function.
COT	Returns the cotangent of any number passed as an angle in radians to the function.

Function	Description
DEGREES	Converts radians to degrees.
EXP	Returns *e* raised to the nth power, where *e* = 2.71828183.
FLOOR	Returns the value representing the largest integer that is less-than or equal to the *input_number*.
LOG	Returns the natural logarithm of some *input_number*, which is greater than zero.
LOG10	Returns the logarithm of some *input_number* calculated upon the *input_base*. The base must be a positive value greater than 1, and the *input_number* must be a positive number greater than 0.
PI	Constant value of pi = 3.141592653589793.
POWER	Returns a number (*input_x*) raised to the power of a number (*input_y*). *Input_x* and *input_y* can be any number, except that if *input_x* is negative, *input_y* must be an integer.
RADIANS	Converts from degrees to radians.
RAND	Returns random number from 0 to 1.
ROUND	Rounds the *input_x* number to the number of places specified. If the number of places specified is positive, it rounds to the right of the decimal. If the number of places specified is negative, it rounds to the left of the decimal. If no places are specified, the default is 0, which rounds to the nearest integer.
SIGN	Returns a value of 1 if the number is greater than zero, 0 if the number is zero, or -1 if the number is less than zero.
SIN	Returns the sine of any number, which is passed as an angle in radians, to the function.
SQRT	Returns the square root of an *input_number*. The value of the *input_number* must not be negative.
TAN	Returns the tangent of any number, which is passed as an angle in radians, to the function.

Out of all the mathematical functions, the most useful are ABS, CEILING, FLOOR, POWER, RAND, ROUND, and SQRT. If you are an engineer, implementing the trigonometric functions should be second nature. In business applications, these seven functions prove their worth. Their practical business uses are discussed in the following sections.

ABS

The ABS function returns the absolute value of any number passed to it. Regardless of whether the number passed is negative or positive, the ABS function always returns the number as positive. The syntax for the ABS function is as follows:

```
ABS(input_number)
```

The next several examples discussed should theoretically never happen if there is strong control over the quality of data input whether from a file, keyboard, or from EDI processing. However, in reality, data inputs cannot be fully trusted, so the ABS function provides some security at the processing end. While integrating and mechanizing many business environments, very few database packages provide financial functions. The first sample calculates the economic ordering quantity.

Implementing ABS to Reduce Input Errors

The ABS function can come in handy in management's never-ending efforts to reduce costs. For example, when analyzing trends, management attempts to reduce purchase and inventory costs by using the economic ordering quantity (EOQ) formula. This formula is as follows:

```
EOQ = SqrRt(2 * Abs(S) * Abs(O) / Abs(C))
```

Where S is the total sales in units, O is the ordering cost for each order, and C is the carrying cost for each order. While the formula could be calculated using the square root function only, negative input can occur, resulting in attempting to take the square root of a negative (imaginary) number. To avoid this condition, you can implement the ABS function as it's shown in Listing 5.1. For this example assume that S = 2,000 units, O = $8.00, and C = $0.20.

Listing 5.1. The EOQ formula in action.

```
SELECT SQRT(2.0*ABS(2000.0)*ABS(-8.0)/ABS(0.20))
```

Your output should look similar to the following:

```
--------------------
400.0
(1 row(s) affected)
```

TIP

When using the SQRT function, all datatypes must be the same. If you alter the data to be integers and real values, you receive an arithmetic overflow error.

One of the most exciting features of functions and formulas is that you can now store this value. As your input parameters change, you can store the updated value and use EDI to automatically figure your purchasing requirements. The next example is also taken from real code used for tracking claim payments for an insurance company.

Using ABS as an Audit Tool

When a claim is made, a claims adjuster sets up a loss reserve and an expense reserve before any payments are made on the claim. Eventually, if the claim is valid, the insurer makes loss and expense payments to process the claim. The total of these four fields is called the *total incurred*. Logically, the reserve dollars, which are used to set aside anticipated funds for settling claims, should be reduced to $0.00 once the claim is paid.

When you're auditing a firm's data, instead of checking to see if loss reserve plus expense reserve equals zero, use absolutes: ABS(loss reserve) and ABS(expense reserve) to see if the sum is zero. Running both queries should have resulted in the same returned count of selected records, but did not. Ultimately, a bug was discovered in the system, which reports loss reserve as negative and expense reserve as positive for the same amount only under specific conditions, resulting in these discrepancies. As you can see, a simple function can have many uses!

CEILING

The CEILING function returns the value representing the smallest integer that is greater-than or equal to the *input_number*. The syntax for the CEILING function is as follows:

```
CEILING(input_number)
```

Have you ever wondered how the average family has 2.35 kids? How you can order 1.3 cars for your sales lot? By replacing the ABS function (shown previously as the EOQ calculation in Listing 5.1) with the CEILING function, you no longer need to worry about placing an order with a non-integer quantity. The CEILING function always rounds up to the next integer. Listing 5.2 demonstrates the use of the CEILING function with the EOQ calculation.

Listing 5.2. Ordering whole units.

```
SELECT CEILING(SQRT(2.0*ABS(1985.0)*ABS(-8.0)/ABS(0.20)))
```

Your output should look similar to the following:

```
- - - - - - - - - - - - - - - - - - - - -
399.0
(1 row(s) affected)
```

This function could also be used to round up dollars to the next integer without using the ROUND function.

FLOOR

This function returns the value that represents the largest integer that is less-than or equal to the *input_number*. The syntax for the FLOOR function is as follows:

```
FLOOR(input_number)
```

The FLOOR function can be used to compute the modulus, as shown in the following section. It can also be used to retrieve the decimal portion of a number relatively fast.

Using FLOOR to Calculate the Modulus

Surprisingly, SQL Server does build the MOD function into its function library. However, using the FLOOR function as your basis, you can create a modulus function. The modulus returns the remainder of one number divided into another number. Listing 5.3 shows the SQL Server code necessary to return the modulus using sample data. 5 divided by 2 returns a remainder of 1. The formula to return the modulus is x-y*FLOOR(x/y).

Listing 5.3. Computing the modulus with FLOOR.

```
SELECT 5-2*FLOOR(5/2)
```

Your output should look similar to the following:

```
- - - - - - - - - - - - - - - - - - - - - -
1
(1 row(s) affected)
```

The T-SQL in Listing 5.3 is equivalent to the mathematical equation 5 Mod 2. You can even use this function with floating numbers. Another use for FLOOR is to produce the decimal portion of a float value.

Using FLOOR to Make Some Cents

Again, Microsoft does not provide a TRUNC function. To mimic part of this function, you can use FLOOR to determine the decimal portion of any number. While you could use string functions to accomplish this task, FLOOR provides a faster and more elegant solution. The formula to compute the decimal value of any number is x - FLOOR(x). Listing 5.4 demonstrates this concept.

Listing 5.4. Returning the decimal portion using FLOOR.

```
SELECT 1.22-FLOOR(1.22)
```

Your output should look similar to the following:

```
- - - - - - - - - - - - - - - - - - - - - -
0.22
(1 row(s) affected)
```

SQL Server also lets you integrate two functions in this manner. For example, you could obtain the decimal portion of the value of pi by integrating the PI function with the FLOOR function in a query similar to Listing 5.4.

POWER

The POWER function returns a number (*input_x*) raised to the power of a number (*input_y*). *input_x* and *input_y* can be any number, but if *input_x* is negative then *input_y* must be an integer. Almost every business implements the POWER function to some extent.

Calculating the Present Value with the POWER Function

The formula to compute the present value is FV*(1/(1+i)n), where FV is the future value, i is the interest rate, and n is the number of periods. Listing 5.5 calculates the present value using SQL Server functions. For this example you assume that the future value is 1464, the interest rate is 10%, and the number of periods is 4.

Listing 5.5. Calculating present value with POWER.

```
SELECT 1464*(1/POWER((1+.10),4))
```

Your output should look similar to the following:

```
--------------------------------
1002.7397260273972602739726027397
(1 row(s) affected)
```

The length of this result is fixed under the ROUND section, discussed later in this chapter.

RAND

RAND is another specialty function. One of the most common complaints in the information technology field is the lack of testing of potential candidates. SQL Server, Oracle, Dataease, Informix, and the like have been used to generate tests used by businesses as well as schools. One database holds the actual questions (in text format) with a unique key on a QuestionNumber column from 1 to *n* (the highest number of your questions). This database cannot be accessed by the end-user. When the end-user takes an exam, the system automatically copies all 100 exam questions into the true test database randomly with the RAND function. Everyone should have the same questions, but in a different sequence. Once the end-user has finished the exam, the exam is then graded automatically. This process disables the login ID used to take the exam, so the user can't change his or her answers.

While the code is too long to present in this book, the logic can easily be implemented. You code a WHILE loop to create a RAND number multiplied by the total number of test questions. Use the CEILING function on the result to make it an integer from 1 to your highest test question number, and then attempt to enter the question if it does not exist. Repeat this process until the number of records stored in the exam database is the same count as the total questions on the exam. This process takes under 20 seconds even on a 486 with 100 total exam questions. The actual RAND coding looks similar to the following:

```
CEILING(RAND()*100)
```

This produces random numbers from 1 to 100 (remember that CEILING goes to the next highest integer number). Other uses for RAND include for statistics and probabilities.

ROUND

The ROUND function rounds the *input_x* number to the number of places specified. If the number of places specified is positive, it rounds to the right of the decimal. If the number of places specified is negative, it rounds to the left of the decimal. If no places are specified, the default is 0, which rounds to the nearest integer. The syntax for the ROUND function is as follows:

```
ROUND(input_x,<places_to_round>)
```

In this chapter's POWER function section, Listing 5.5 calculates the present value via the POWER function. The result is calculated to 32 decimal places. Since the output should be in monetary format, there are two options. The first option is to convert the datatype to money using the CONVERT function. The SQL coding required to accomplish this follows:

```
SELECT CONVERT(money,1002.7397260273972602739726602739726)
```

This option is adequate for most situations. However, if you have just run this T-SQL, you notice that it results in an error. There are too many decimal places for the code to translate the number into a MONEY datatype. What's the other solution?

The second means is to use the ROUND function, which computes faster than the first option. Listing 5.6 applies the ROUND function to the present value calculation.

Listing 5.6. Rounding present value to two decimal places.

```
SELECT ROUND(1464*(1/POWER((1+.10),4)),2)
```

Your output should look similar to the following:

```
---------------------------------
1002.740000000000000000000000000000000
 (1 row(s) affected)
```

The only disadvantage with ROUND is that the function uses zeros for placeholders in order to retain the datatype.

TIP

Most of you have seen reports that display money values and a total dollar amount at the end of the report. Sometimes the dollar amounts do not sum to the exact dollar amount shown in the total. Most often, this occurs because the aggregates carry the computations out to 32 decimal places. The output however only displays 2 decimal places, rounding when conditions are met. This usually occurs when complex calculations are performed on columns.

One way to address this problem is to avoid printing the report first, and enter the data into a table. You can then track the fraction remaining from the third decimal place to the thirty-second decimal place. Every time the fraction adds to a penny, add (or subtract, if necessary) the penny to the amount for the next record.

SQRT

The SQRT function returns the square root of a value 0 or greater. The syntax of SQRT is as follows:

```
SQRT(input_number)
```

Again, the `input_number` can't be negative or an error will result. Refer to Listing 5.1 for an example using the SQRT function.

Calculating Dates with Date Functions

Date calculations are frequently used in most business applications. Many examples include due dates, interest computations, aging reports, loan calculations, birthdays, and the number of days left in a pregnancy. SQL Server date functions perform CHAR (or VARCHAR) to DATETIME (or SMALLDATETIME) conversions automatically. Before you can even work with the date functions, you need to understand the components of the date, which are listed in Table 5.2.

Table 5.2. Parts of the date.

Date Part	Description	Value Range
YY	Year	1753 to 9999
QQ	Quarter	1 to 4
MM	Month	1 to 12
DY	Day of year	1 to 366
DD	Day of month	1 to 31

continues

Table 5.2. continued

Date Part	Description	Value Range
WK	Week of year	1 to 53
DW	Weekday	1 to 7 or Sun. to Sat.
HH	Hour	0 to 23 (military time)
MI	Minute	0 to 59
SS	Second	0 to 59
MS	Millisecond	0 to 999

NOTE

SQL Server treats any dates with the last two digits of the year less than 50 as the next century and any dates with the last two digits greater-than or equal to 50 as the current century. Therefore, 01/01/70 is treated as 1970, while 01/01/36 is treated as 2036. As a general rule, always try to use the four digits of the year whenever possible.

For example, assume you are trying to calculate a 30-year mortgage that started in 1940 and ended in 1970. You enter 40 to 70 as the year range. SQL Server translates that year range into 2040 to 1970, which would yield a starting date 70 years following the ending date of the loan! In addition, consider that some countries have 100 year loans. This obviously causes problems if the year is not expressed as all four digits.

Table 5.3 lists all of SQL Server's available Date functions.

Table 5.3. Date functions.

Function	Description
DATEADD	Returns the result of adding a time interval to a date.
DATEDIFF	Returns the time interval between two dates in the format specified for the *datepart* parameter.
DATENAME	Returns the text representation of the date as specified by *datepart*.
DATEPART	Returns an integer of the *datepart* specified from a date.
GETDATE	Returns the current system date and time.

The DATEADD Function

This function allows you to add a time interval to a date in order to arrive at the new date. This is used all the time in business for calculating due dates, aged dates, and shipping and delivery dates. The syntax for the DATEADD function is as follows:

```
DATEADD(datepart,number,date)
```

While the *datepart* could be any of the values listed in Table 5.2, it is unlikely you will often add seconds or milliseconds to a date. Listing 5.7 calculates the due date of an invoice with a net term of 30.

Listing 5.7. Calculating the due date using DATEADD.

```
SELECT DATEADD(DY,30,"10/01/97")
```

Your output should look similar to the following:

```
- - - - - - - - - - - - - - - - - -
Oct 31 1997 12:00AM
 (1 row(s) affected)
```

Notice that the date function completes all string conversions and returns the output in the SQL Server standard date format. All of these date functions perform this conversion automatically.

The DATEDIFF Function

DATEDIFF returns the difference between two dates as specified by *datepart*. The syntax for the DATEDIFF function is as follows:

```
DATEDIFF(datepart,date1,date2)
```

Listing 5.8 calculates the number of days past due of an invoice.

Listing 5.8. Calculating the number of days past due with DATEDIFF.

```
SELECT DATEDIFF(DY,"08/30/97","10/01/97")
```

Your output should look similar to the following:

```
- - - - - - - - - - - - - - - - - -
32
 (1 row(s) affected)
```

In reality, the first date would be a field called DueDate, and the second date would be a field called CurrentDate (or a specified period ending date). The system automatically calculates the number of days past due and ages the invoices accordingly. From here, you can automatically send out different types of notices based upon the number of days past due. This could also be used to determine whether a customer gets a discount with terms 2%/10 net 30. If the customer pays within ten days, the invoice would be discounted 2%. As you can see, date functions play an important role in all businesses.

> **NOTE**
>
> Keep in mind that the function returns an INTEGER value. While you probably won't exceed this when computing the difference for days, weeks, and months, you could potentially exceed an INTEGER's value range when taking the difference on times, especially with milliseconds. For example, the difference in milliseconds between September 1, 1973 and September 1, 1975 is approximately 3.8 billion milliseconds (60ms×60sec×60min×24hr×365dy×2yr). If you calculate this and try setting the result to an INTEGER value, you receive an arithmetic overflow error.

The DATENAME Function

This function returns date's character string representation. The syntax for the DATENAME function is as follows:

```
DATENAME(datepart,date)
```

Listing 5.9 shows the day of the week.

Listing 5.9. Displaying the day of the week with DATENAME.

```
SELECT DATENAME(DW,"10/01/97")
```

Your output should look similar to the following:

```
------------------
WEDNESDAY
 (1 row(s) affected)
```

You can use this function in a letter that states you will call the customer on Monday, August 12. Keep in mind that the only *datepart* values that return a character string are the day of the week (DW) and the month (MM).

The DATEPART Function

This function returns the integer value of the *datepart* specified. (Note that the DATEPART function is different than the *datepart* parameter.) For example, the DATEPART function can be used to return the numerical representation of the current month of the year. The syntax for the DATEPART function is as follows:

```
DATEPART(datepart,date)
```

Listing 5.10 extracts the month from a date.

Listing 5.10. Displaying the numeric month with DATEPART.

```
SELECT DATEPART(MM,"Oct 31 1997")
```

Your output should look similar to the following:

```
- - - - - - - - - - - - - - - - -
10
(1 row(s) affected)
```

Some practical uses would be to search for all sales within the month of October. Maybe you stored the month in an INTEGER column separated from the rest of the date. If so, the T-SQL in Listing 5.10 could be embedded in a WHERE clause to retrieve all sales for October.

The GETDATE Function

The GETDATE function returns the current system date and time of the server. GETDATE accepts no parameters, yet it is one of the most useful functions. You can use this value to update an audit field in triggers. (Refer to Chapter 11, "Specialized Triggers," for a detailed example of using triggers to audit data manipulation.) Listing 5.11 displays the current date and time.

Listing 5.11. Displaying the current date and time with GETDATE.

```
SELECT GETDATE()
```

Your output should look similar to the following:

```
- - - - - - - - - - - - - - - - -
Aug 12 1998 5:30PM
(1 row(s) affected)
```

A great GETDATE implementation is to stamp the name of the user who ran the report and the date the report was generated. This makes an excellent audit trail, since the user can't change the server date and time. My report endings always show these two lines with the actual values filled in:

> Report Generated By: ...
>
> Report Generated On: ...

The first line displays the system username, and the second uses GetDate to display current date and time. Your auditors will thank you for adding these two items.

Using String Functions to Manipulate Strings

A good portion of data stored in a database is composed of string data. SQL Server provides several powerful functions that can be used to manipulate strings. Table 5.4 is a summary of all available string functions.

Table 5.4. String functions.

Function	Description
+	Concatenates two or more strings.
ASCII	Returns the decimal equivalent of a single ASCII character. If a string is passed, only the first character is translated.
CHAR	Returns the corresponding ASCII character represented by the decimal number passed in this function. The decimal equivalent must be passed in an INTEGER format. This function has the opposite effect of ASCII. If a value other than 0-255 is used, NULL is returned.
CHARINDEX	Returns the starting position of a string pattern found within a string.
DIFFERENCE	Used to compare two strings. A value from 0–4 is returned, with 4 being the best match, which means the two strings are identical.
LOWER	Converts all characters to lowercase.
LTRIM	Removes leading blank spaces from a string.
PATINDEX	Returns the starting position of the first occurrence of a pattern found in a string. The difference between this and CHARINDEX is that if the string can be found anywhere, you need to use wildcards with PATINDEX.
REPLICATE	Repeats one or more characters a specified number of times.
REVERSE	Returns a character string in reverse order.
RIGHT	Returns part of a character string starting from the right to as many characters specified.
RTRIM	Removes trailing blank spaces.
SOUNDEX	Returns a four-character SOUNDEX code to compare the similarity between two strings.
SPACE	Returns a string of spaces repeated a number of times specified.
STR	Converts numeric data to string data.
STUFF	Deletes a specified number of characters at a starting position in the first string, and inserts all the characters from the second string at the deletion point from the first string.
SUBSTRING	Returns all or part of a string as specified.
UPPER	Converts all letters to uppercase.

The most commonly used string functions listed in Table 5.4 are CHARINDEX, DIFFERENCE, LOWER, LTRIM, RTRIM, REVERSE, STR, SUBSTRING, and UPPER. This section first provides a description and syntax of each of these. Several examples using a combination of these functions follow.

The CHARINDEX Function

This function returns the starting position of a pattern specified in a string value. The syntax for the CHARINDEX function is as follows:

```
CHARINDEX(pattern,string_value)
```

The pattern can be one or more characters. One possible use is to eliminate commas within string values. This only finds the first occurrence—if a string has more than one comma, you have to locate the comma, write out the new string without the comma, and repeat the search for the comma until no more values are found (when the function returns a value of 0).

The DIFFERENCE Function

This function returns a value between 0–4 to compare the similarities between strings using SOUNDEX. The higher the value, the closer the match. A value of 0 means no match, while a value of 4 reflects an exact string match. The syntax for the DIFFERENCE function is as follows:

```
DIFFERENCE(string1,string2)
```

You can use this function when searching for names or addresses. For instance, if you need the name Kathy Ward and are not sure if it is spelled Cathy, Kathy, Kathie, or some other way, selecting all values of 3 or greater should locate the record desired. Since this feature is not case sensitive, you do not need to worry about having to convert to all upper- or all lowercase and performing a match based upon case.

Soundex values are very useful in situations where an operator is taking an order from a customer over the phone. For example, a customer named Colleen Hogan calls to place an order for 100 widgets. The operator searches for Colene Hogan and finds the match almost instantly. The customer does not have to worry about spelling his name because the DIFFERENCE function found all logical matches.

The LOWER Function

This function converts all alphabetic characters to lowercase. All non-alphabetic characters remain unchanged. The syntax for the LOWER function is as follows:

```
LOWER(input_string)
```

This can be used in conjunction with other functions to correct data-entry mistakes. Some people could input all characters in uppercase, some all in lowercase, and some in proper case.

The LTRIM Function

This function removes all leading spaces in a string. The syntax for the LTRIM function is as follows:

LTRIM(*input_string*)

This is commonly used to correct data-entry mistakes, or to correct data during data migration, data conversion, EDI, or some other data importing. You can combine this function with RTRIM to remove all leading and trailing spaces from a string.

The REVERSE Function

This function reverses all characters in a string. The syntax for the REVERSE function is as follows:

REVERSE(*input_string*)

The REVERSE function also accepts a column as input. You can use this embedded within a SQL query, possibly to set default passwords. For example, you can place a trigger on a table that holds a list of users. When a new user is inserted into the table, the trigger updates the Password field to be the reverse of the username.

The RTRIM Function

This function removes trailing blank spaces on the right side of the string. The syntax for the RTRIM function is as follows:

RTRIM(*input_string*)

This is commonly used to correct data-entry mistakes, or to correct data during data migration, data conversion, EDI, or some other data importing. Another use for this function is to apply it on a CHAR column in a SELECT statement. Sometimes the data in a CHAR column does not completely fill the column, so it is padded with spaces.

The STR Function

This function converts numeric-type data to string data. The syntax for the STR function is as follows:

STR(*input_number*,*total_length*,*decimal*)

The *input_number* is the numeric data to be converted to string. Optionally, the *total_length* can be used to specify the total length of the string including sign, spaces, digits, and the decimal point. The *decimal* parameter is also optional, and specifies the number of places to the right of the decimal (the default length is 10). The results from this function are often used to concatenate string data for output.

The SUBSTR Function

The SUBSTR function returns all or part of a character string. The syntax for the SUBSTR function is as follows:

SUBSTR(*input_string,starting_position,length*)

The *input_string* is the string or column name that you want to retrieve a subset of. The *starting_position* is the location in the *input_string* where your subset begins. The *length* is the number of characters to extract from the *input_string* beginning at the *starting_position*. Some practical uses of the SUBSTR function are to parse a phone number column for the area code, to retrieve the last name from a name column, or to get the final six digits from a UPC code.

Examples Using String Functions

SQL Server provides a limited set of string manipulation functions. However, by using these built-in functions, you can manufacture your own custom string functions. Several examples are provided so that you can see many different, actual cases where advanced string manipulation was required. Keep in mind that while the following examples use a SELECT statement with fixed data, they could be altered to use columns from a table. You may even want to consider creating your own custom stored procedures with output parameters returning the outcome of complex string manipulations. Refer to Chapter 6, "Effective Use of Stored Procedures as an Administrative Tool," which uses some of these examples in stored procedures.

Using Strings to Reverse the Order of a Name

There have been many instances in database conversion projects in which names have been stored in a single field. This sample takes a name stored in one field in the format First Name, Last Name, and converts it to Last Name, First Name. In reality, you can use this in a stored procedure to actually split the data into two separate fields. In cases where a middle initial or suffix is involved, the concept is the same, but a slightly more complex method is used. Refer to Listing 5.12 for sample T-SQL that changes the order of the first and last name.

Listing 5.12. Changing the order of a name.

```
DECLARE @chvFullName CHAR(30),
        @chvReorderedName VARCHAR(30)
SELECT @chvFullName = 'Julie Ely'
SELECT @chvReorderedName =
  SUBSTRING(@chvFullName, -- create Last Name
        (CHARINDEX(" ",@chvFullName) + 1 ) ,
        30))) +
        ', ' + -- Comma and Space Separator
        SUBSTRING(@chvFullName, -- Create First Name
        1 ,
        (CHARINDEX(" ",@chvFullName) - 1 )
```

5

EFFECTIVE USE OF
BUILT-IN
FUNCTIONS

Your output should look similar to the following:

```
- - - - - - - - - - - - - - - - - - - - - - - - - - - - - - - - - - -
Ely, Julie
(1 row(s) affected)
```

The first three lines are used to extract the last name. You use the SUBSTRING function to do this. While the string data is a name, this could easily be a column from a table. To arrive at the starting position, CHARINDEX is used to locate the space between the first name and the last name, and adds 1 to the value of the space's position to calculate the starting position of the last name. There is no need to determine the length; you only get the remainder of the string if you supply a length longer than the string. The concatenation function is used and adds the comma and space separator to the last name. Finally, the first name is concatenated again using the SUBSTRING function. The first string parameter is the fixed name. The starting position should always be 1 as specified in the listing, and the ending position uses the CHARINDEX function to locate the space separator and subtract 1 to arrive at the length.

> **NOTE**
>
> If you plan on using either name part independently, it is better database design to create two separate columns, one for the first name and another for the last name. This also allows you to perform faster searches by first or last name using indexes.

Again, this assumes a few items:

- The name is always first name, space, last name.
- The field length and type is set to char(30).
- No spaces preceding the first name.
- No middle initial or suffix has been entered.

Any of these limitations could be worked out with SQL Server, such as using LTRIM in the computation to eliminate spaces before the name even begins. The REVERSE function can be used, by looking at the location of the first space, to see if there is a suffix or middle initial. The field length can be assigned by using the DATALENGTH function, which is discussed later in this chapter.

Changing Strings to Sentence Case

As robust as SQL Server's functions are, one feature not provided is the capability to convert a line of data to sentence case. *Sentence case* refers to initializing the first character of a string and lowercasing the remaining characters. Listing 5.13 is an example that converts a sentence to sentence case.

Listing 5.13. Changing a line to sentence case.

```
SELECT UPPER(SUBSTRING("this Is a tEst.",1,1)) +
    LOWER(SUBSTRING("this Is a tEst.",2,20))
```

Your output should look similar to the following:

```
--------------------
This is a test.
(1 row(s) affected)
```

This process extracts the first character with the SUBSTRING function in line 1 and converts it to uppercase with the UPPER function, regardless of the case when selected. The rest of the line is selected again by the SUBSTRING function and converted to lowercase with the LOWER function in line 2. To improve this, you could look for instances of the period and automatically capitalize the first character after the period. You also have to factor out abbreviations, such as Mr. and Dr., as well as numbers with decimals, such as "You've just won $9,999.99". This method could be applied similarly to capitalize the first letter in every word.

Using Strings to Extract the Decimal Portion of a Real Number

Since SQL Server does not provide any type of TRUNCATE function, a second method to extract the decimal portion of a real number is demonstrated in Listing 5.14. The first method is described in this chapter's "Using FLOOR to Make Some Cents."

Listing 5.14. Extracting the decimal portion of a real number.

```
SELECT SUBSTRING(STR(4.1313,20,6),
        CHARINDEX(".",STR(4.1313,20,6)),7)
```

Your output should look similar to the following:

```
--------
0.131300
(1 row(s) affected)
```

You could now apply the CONVERT function to change the data back to a real number. The SUBSTRING function is used in line 1 to extract the decimal portion of the real number. The first parameter uses the STR function to convert from number to string datatype. The starting position is determined by locating the decimal place with the CHARINDEX function in line 2. Since a length of six decimal places is desired, SUBSTRING's last parameter in line 2 is set to a value of 7 to include the decimal point and six significant digits. As you can see, you can make use of SQL Server functions to accomplish the same task many different ways.

Using String Functions to Search for Phonetically Similar Data

One continuing problem with customer service is attempting to look up a customer name and not finding it. This could be caused by a typing mistake or the service agent could be entering the name incorrectly. The DIFFERENCE function allows you to extract close or exact matches from a string. Listing 5.15 is an example of how to locate the name Kathy Ward.

Listing 5.15. Locating a customer name.

```
SELECT DIFFERENCE("Kathy Ward","kathy WARD"),
        DIFFERENCE("KATHY Ward","Cathy Ward"),
    DIFFERENCE("KATHY Ward","Cathie Ward")
```

Your output should similar to

```
---------- ---------- ----------
4          3          3
(1 row(s) affected)
```

This example reflects two things. As you can see in lines 1 or 2, case does not matter with the DIFFERENCE function. The second item you should notice is the output results. An exact match is always a value of 4, and a very close match is a value of 3. You could do a SELECT statement from a table that only selects records with a difference value of 3 or greater. This should locate the information desired.

Using Text Functions in SQL

SQL Server permits the storage of text and image data with the TEXT and IMAGE datatypes. Functions are provided so that you can work with these datatypes in a table. Table 5.5 lists the available TEXT functions.

Table 5.5. Text functions.

Function	Description
TEXTPTR	Points to the starting location of the text stored in the column.
TEXTVALID	Checks to make sure the TEXTPTR is valid.

These functions can be combined with several other functions, such as PATINDEX to find a matching pattern in the text, or DATALENGTH to get the size of the text or image stored.

Using SQL Functions to Retrieve System Information

SQL Server provides functions that return information about the database and server. These functions can retrieve system data such as user names, database names, and column names. Other functions such as NULLIF and COALESCE can be used to embed logic into SQL queries. A list of the system functions is listed in Table 5.6.

Table 5.6. System functions.

Function	Description
COALESCE	Returns the first non-NULL expression. Very similar to the CASE statement, but looks for non-NULL versus Boolean values TRUE or FALSE.
COL_LENGTH	Returns the defined length of the column.
COL_NAME	Returns the column name.
DATALENGTH	Returns the actual length of the data. Very useful only for CHARACTER, BINARY, TEXT, and IMAGE datatypes. All other datatypes are fixed.
DB_ID	Returns the database identification number.
DB_NAME	Returns the name of the database.
GETANSINULL	Returns a value of 1 if the database supports the rules of ANSI NULL.
HOST_ID	Returns the workstation ID number.
HOST_NAME	Returns the name of the workstation.
IDENT_INCR	The increment value as specified when creating an identity column.
IDENT_SEED	The SEED value, or starting value, used for an identity column. (It does not, however, tell you what the current or next incremental value is; this can be retrieved from system tables.)
INDEX_COL	Returns the name of the column indexed.
ISNULL	Replaces NULL entries with a specified expression.
NULLIF	If expression1 is equivalent to expression2, the expression is NULL. Similar to the way a CASE statement works.
OBJECT_ID	Database object ID number.
OBJECT_NAME	Database object name.
STATS_DATE	Returns the date when the specified index was last updated.
SUSER_ID	Returns the login user ID number.
SUSER_NAME	Returns the login user's name.
USER_ID	Returns the user's database ID number.
USER_NAME	Returns the user's database ID name.

The most commonly used system functions are the COL_LENGTH, DATALENGTH, ISNULL, HOST_NAME, SUSER_NAME, and USER_NAME.

The COL_LENGTH Function

This function returns the defined length of a column. The syntax for the COL_LENGTH function is as follows:

```
COL_LENGTH(table_name,column_name)
```

The *table_name* is the name of the table specified, and the *column_name* is the name of the column specified. This has been used to pass values to stored procedures for columns defined with any character-based datatype.

The DATALENGTH Function

This function returns the actual length of data specified in an expression or column. If the data passed to the DATALENGTH function is NULL, NULL is returned. Keep in mind that when used with a CHAR datatype, this function always returns the defined length of the variable or column.

> **TIP**
>
> If you do get a NULL value when one is not desired, you could use the ISNULL function to replace the NULL value with one or more spaces (or some other default value desired). The ISNULL function is discussed in the next section.

The syntax for the DATALENGTH function is as follows:

```
DATALENGTH(input_data)
```

The *input_data* can be a column, an expression, or data. This function is extremely useful only for CHARACTER, BINARY, TEXT, and IMAGE datatypes. All other datatypes are returned as fixed values whether data exists or not. This function counts all values, including spaces.

> **TIP**
>
> While Microsoft states that this is useless for fixed-width character columns because trailing spaces are stored to the end of the column, all you have to do is use the RTRIM function before the DATALENGTH function to return the actual length of meaningful data.

This function might be classified as a string function because it's used so often in conjunction with string functions. Most of the time this function is used to determine the length of a string variable or column.

Using the DATALENGTH Function with String Functions

You saw an example of using string functions to convert a line of text to sentence case earlier in this chapter. However, the length of the data was hard-coded. Listing 5.16 adds the function DATALENGTH to work with any scenario.

Listing 5.16. Using DATALENGTH to determine length of a string value.

```
SELECT UPPER(SUBSTRING("this Is a tEst.",1,1)) +
    LOWER(SUBSTRING("this Is a tEst.",2,
        (DATALENGTH("this Is a tEst.")-1)))
```

Your output should look similar to the following:

```
- - - - - - - - - - - - - -
This is a test.
(1 row(s) affected)
```

One noticeable difference is that the number of characters output is no longer 20 but the actual string you want. By adding line 3, you now subtract one from the actual length of the data since the first letter of the sentence has already been counted.

Using DATALENGTH and COL_LENGTH Functions on a Table

What's the difference between the DATALENGTH and COL_LENGTH functions? This section answers that question by applying those functions to the table Composer. (This table was created in Chapter 2, "Using Advanced Data Manipulation Language.") Listing 5.17 demonstrates these differences.

Listing 5.17. DATALENGTH Versus COL_LENGTH to determine length of a string value.

```
SELECT Composer,DATALENGTH(Composer) "Actual_Width",
        COL_LENGTH('Composer','Composer')"Defined_Width"
    FROM composer
        ORDER BY DATALENGTH(Composer)
```

Your output should look like the following:

Composer	Actual_Width	Defined_Width
Styx	4	40
Cars	4	40
Eagles	6	40
Chicago	7	40
Genesis	7	40
Outfield	8	40
Colin Raye	10	40
John Denver	11	40
Queensryche	11	40
Def Leppard	11	40
Pat Benetar	11	40
Garth Brooks	12	40
Depeche Mode	12	40
REO Speedwagon	14	40
Tears for Fears	15	40
Psychedelic Furs	16	40
Rick Springfield	16	40

```
(17 row(s) affected)
```

The `Actual_Width` column used the `DATALENGTH` function in line 1 to compute the actual length stored in the column. The `COL_LENGTH` function returns the defined length of the column, which was defined as a maximum length of 40. In addition, you can see from line 4 that you can use `ORDER BY` with an expression using the `DATALENGTH` function.

The ISNULL Function

This function allows you to replace `NULL` values with a specified value. The syntax for the `ISNULL` function is as follows:

```
ISNULL(expression,replacement_value)
```

The *expression* can be any column, data, or calculated data. The *replacement_value* is substituted whenever a `NULL` value is selected. This function is very useful in changing `NULL` values in a column to default values. This function can also be used in conjunction with aggregate functions to count values including `NULL` values.

A common situation in which to use the `ISNULL` function is when selecting data for a sales report. Imagine that the `Standard Cost` column in a query could contain `NULL` values. When a query is run containing this field in the select list, you may want to see 0 in lieu of `NULL` values.

The HOST_NAME Function

This function returns the name of the workstation on which you are working. The syntax for the `HOST_NAME` function is as follows:

```
HOST_NAME()
```

No parameters are required. This function is most often used when implementing database security.

WARNING

This function's return value is determined by the front-end application on the connected workstation. If the front-end application supplied SQL Server with this value, then that is what is returned from `HOST_NAME`. The ISQL program is an example of an application that fits this description. However, if a front-end application does not supply the information to SQL Server, `HOST_NAME` returns blank. In short, it is the front-end application that is connected to SQL Server that determines if the `HOST_NAME` function will return the name of the host application.

The SUSER_NAME Function

This function returns the name of the user logged into the server. The syntax for the SUSER_NAME function is as follows:

```
SUSER_NAME()
```

No parameters are required. This function is most often used when implementing database security. For example, you can refer to this function in a trigger when you want only certain users to be able to increase the price of a title. You can use this function in update and delete triggers when you want to store the name of the user who made the change. Chapter 11 discusses how to use the SUSER_NAME function in triggers to audit data changes and to implement business-rules security.

The USER_NAME Function

This function returns the name of user logged into the database. The syntax for the USER_NAME function is as follows:

```
USER_NAME()
```

No parameters are required. This function is most often used when implementing database security. As opposed to the SUSER_NAME function, this function returns the name of the user logged into the database. Keep in mind that if you alias yourself as DBO, USER_NAME returns DBO as the user logged into the database. In contrast, SUSER_NAME returns the name of the user logged into the server. Logged in as SA, USER_NAME returns DBO and SUSER_NAME returns SA.

Summary

SQL Server provides many powerful functions. This chapter teaches you different methods for manipulating data with math functions, string functions, system functions, text functions, date functions, and the CONVERT function. While the examples showed some varied and complex use of functions, the examples only reflect a small portion of what you can really do with these built-in functions, including making your own functions using stored procedures.

Effective Use of Stored Procedures as an Administrative Tool

CHAPTER 6

IN THIS CHAPTER

Stored procedures offer many advanced features not available in the standard SQL language. The ability to pass parameters and perform logic allows the application designer to automate complex tasks. In addition, the fact that these procedures are stored at the local server reduces the amount of bandwidth and time required to execute the procedure. Besides the ability to create your own procedures, Microsoft provides you with several stored procedures that are ideal for manipulating data at the system and administrative levels. The only way you can change data in a systems table is by using systems stored procedures, or by changing a parameter to allow any query to update a systems table, which is never recommended. By providing these stored procedures, the SQL Server prevents you from needing to write thousands of lines of code, as well as preventing the accidental modification of data in a systems table.

This chapter assumes you already know how to create a stored procedure and how to pass parameters. It provides a wealth of examples to apply these concepts, focusing on reducing administrative tasks using stored procedures, systems stored procedures, and extended stored procedures. As an applications programmer, you can automate tasks to reduce or eliminate the need for a systems administrator, which coincides with Microsoft's plans towards reducing the role of the DBA.

I've included several definitions and examples of the various procedures directly in this chapter. However, many more procedures are described in detail either by procedure in Appendix C, "System Stored and Extended Stored Procedures Quick Reference," or by the system tables they relate to in Appendix A, "The System Tables of the Master Database."

> **NOTE**
>
> This chapter requires you to have the same access as a systems administrator. Either sign on as the systems administrator or contact your systems administrator for the appropriate user access.

Using Administrative Stored Procedures

The most commonly used system stored procedures can be grouped into administrative, assistance, configuration, and monitoring categories.

An actual sample of user-based administration can be found in the section "Advanced Uses of Stored Procedures." The administrative stored procedures for users include `sp_addgroup`, `sp_addlogin`, `sp_adduser`, `sp_changegroup`, `sp_dropgroup`, `sp_droplogin`, `sp_dropuser`, `sp_password`, and `sp_who`. Database administrative stored procedures use `sp_certify_removable`, `sp_create_removable`, `sp_dbinstall`, and `sp_dboption`. These are described in detail in Appendix C.

Some smaller companies may distribute their databases for use by customers, suppliers, and so on, through the use of removable media. In planning for this requirement, you should create the database with `sp_create_removable`. You can then verify that all objects in the database can be removed with `sp_certify_removable`. After copying the data to a backup device, you can install at any location on the database by using `sp_dbinstall`. Before you can use the database, you need to use `sp_dboption` to place the database back online. I have used this for many small applications at branch offices to track sales. A procedure exports the data on a daily basis and sends it to the main office, utilizing IBM's ADVANTIS network, for merging with the master database. This keeps all of the branch offices' numbers and information confidential.

The syntax of these four procedures is discussed in the following sections.

sp_create_removable

```
sp_create_removable databasename,syslogical,sysstorage,
    sysdsize,loglogical,logphysical,logsize,datalogical,dataphysical,datasize
```

The `databasename` is the name of the database to create. The `syslogical` parameter is a logical name associated with where the system tables will be stored at the `sysstorage` location, requiring `sysdsize` megabytes of storage. The `loglogical` parameter is a logical name associated with where the system logs will be stored at the `logphysical` location, requiring `logsize` megabytes of storage. Finally, the `datalogical` parameter is a logical name associated with where the data will be stored at the `dataphysical` location, requiring `datasize` megabytes of storage.

An example of creating a removable database is

```
sp_create_removable sales, salessys, 'c:\sales\data\salessys.dat',3,
    saleslog,'c:\sales\data\saleslog.dat',6,
    salesdata,'c:\sales\data\salesdata.dat',20
```

You can try the preceding sample code only after you have created the `c:\sales` and `c:\sales\data` subdirectories on the SQL Server. This is usually a hard concept to grasp without an illustration, so try following these steps and creating the database to see this in action. In this case, you could install this database even over a network with `sp_dbinstall`.

sp_certify_removable

```
sp_certify_removable databasename,[AUTO]
```

The `databasename` is the name of the database to certify. The optional *AUTO* parameter will attempt to give all ownership of the objects in the database to the systems administrator. Otherwise, you will have to perform this with a variety of SQL scripts. You could now certify the database created earlier by entering

```
sp_certify_removable sales
```

This will take the database offline and add any comments to the certify log for review.

sp_dbinstall

```
sp_dbinstall databasename,logicalname,physicalname,size,devicetype,[destination]
```

All of this information is provided to you when the `sp_certify_removable` stored procedure is executed. However, you now need to specify a device type of SYSTEM or DATA for installation, and optionally the location (*destination* parameter) where you want to place the database.

```
sp_dbinstall sales,salessys,'l:\salessys.dat',3,'SYSTEM',
   'c:\sales\data\salessys.dat'
```

Then execute

```
sp_dbinstall sales,salesdata,'l:\salesdata.dat',3,'DATA',
   'c:\sales\data\salesdata.dat'
```

In this case, I assumed the location was from the logical network L drive. Now all you need to do is set the database online with sp_dboption.

sp_dboption

sp_dboption *[databasename,option,{TRUE¦FALSE}]*

To get a list of options, type sp_dboption at the SQL prompt. Each of these options can be turned on or off by using the values TRUE or FALSE. To set your database online, enter the sample code:

```
sp_dboption sales,'offline',FALSE
```

This sets the database offline value to FALSE; thereby bringing the database back online. This is a great way to segregate and back up databases for quick and easy distribution. Ideally, you would write SQL scripts to load these databases at other locations automatically.

Using Stored Procedures for Assistance Acquiring Information

The following procedures will provide you with help when dealing with the SQL Server: sp_help, sp_helpconstraint, sp_helpdb, sp_helpgroup, sp_helprotect, sp_helpserver, sp_helpsort, sp_helpsql, sp_helpstartup, sp_helptext, and sp_helpuser. These are all very powerful features built into the SQL Server, putting data at your fingertips that would require many large queries to write. Each of these is defined, including actual examples and advanced usage, in Appendix C.

Using Stored Procedures for Configuration and Fine-Tuning

The following stored procedures are the most common when used in configuring information on the SQL Server: sp_addtype, sp_configure, sp_droptype, sp_makestartup, sp_recompile, sp_serveroption, and sp_unmakestartup. While you could configure the SQL Server to change system values with your own stored procedures, this is not recommended.

The syntaxes and uses of these stored procedures are discussed in the next few sections.

sp_addtype

This stored procedure allows you to create your own specific datatypes, including how the SQL Server will handle NULL values. You could define such fields as Hire Date, Pay Rate, SS#, or other common fields. The syntax for sp_addtype is

```
sp_addtype typename, SQLtype[,NULLhandler]
```

The *typename* parameter is the name you will use to identify the new datatype. The *SQLtype* parameter is a valid SQL Server datatype. The optional *NULLhandler* allows you to specify how to handle NULL values—you can either accept them or reject them. However, you can override how NULLs are handled when creating tables. An example of creating your own datatype is

```
sp_addtype HireDate,datetime,"NOT NULL"
```

Once executed, you can run a query against the systypes table to validate the existence of the new datatype.

sp_droptype

If you no longer need a user-defined datatype, this stored procedure removes it from the database permanently. The syntax for sp_droptype is

```
sp_droptype typename
```

The user-defined datatype cannot be dropped if existing tables reference the datatype. Make sure all references have been removed before dropping this datatype.

sp_configure

This is the most dangerous system stored procedure available. Improperly using this could cause problems in the SQL Server. The syntax for sp_configure is

```
sp_configure [configname[,configvalue]]
```

Running this procedure with no parameters provides you with the current configuration. If you have altered some of the configuration values, you may need to shut down and restart the server before the update takes effect. You can get configuration information for a specific item by specifying the configuration name, and you can change the configured value by specifying the new value. A common usage is to increase the number of connections that can be made to the server. The default is 15, and the following example will increase this to 300:

```
sp_configure "user connections",300
```

In order to make this change work, you need to execute RECONFIGURE and then shut down and restart the SQL Server database.

> **NOTE**
>
> Be cautious when changing values. One configuration value of "allow updates", which allows a user to change values within all system tables, should ideally never be allowed. This means that you could write your own stored procedures and ad_hoc queries to directly modify system variables if you set the value to TRUE.

sp_recompile

This stored procedure forces all triggers and stored procedures to recompile the next time the table is accessed. The syntax for this stored procedure is

```
sp_recompile tablename
```

These processes are only compiled when created, so if you make any changes to the table (such as adding indexes), this could cause sluggish performance from the trigger or stored procedure (because the procedure will not use the index). You should always run this process after altering a table to keep your system optimized.

sp_serveroption

This stored procedure allows you to configure the type of SQL Server. The syntax for this stored procedure is

```
sp_serveroption [servername.option,{true¦false}]
```

Using no parameters returns the available server options that can be set for any server. If you want to change a server to a distribution server, you would code the following:

```
sp_serveroption SQL,DIST,TRUE
```

sp_makestartup

This stored procedure configures which stored procedures will be executed when the SQL Server is started. The syntax for this stored procedure is

```
sp_makestartup procedurename
```

Each procedure uses one connection. If you limit the number of connections, all other stored procedures should be referenced by the first procedure, auto-executed. Regardless, I highly recommend you use this approach.

NOTE

Although creating auto-executing stored procedures is a time-saving feature, these processes only execute when a server is started. Some excellent uses include maintenance of the database, reviewing database statistics, or checking the database for errors. However, don't use the auto-executing stored procedures to schedule daily jobs unless you bring down the server each night.

sp_unmakestartup

This system stored procedure allows you to disable the auto-execution of the stored procedures specified. The syntax for this stored procedure is

```
sp_unmakestartup procedurename
```

Using Stored Procedures to Monitor the System

The more common stored procedures used in monitoring the SQL Server are `sp_monitor` and `sp_spaceused`.

sp_monitor

You can use this stored procedure to monitor the performance of your SQL Server. The syntax is

```
sp_monitor
```

If you start seeing large amounts of dropped packets, you need to look for network congestion and try to solve the problem. If there are a lot of read/write errors, there could be an I/O bottleneck at the server or problems with the storage device. If the CPU is busy more than 80 percent of the time, you might want to add CPUs. This process ideally should be run every day. If you bring down the server once per week, you may wish to make this an auto-executing procedure.

sp_spaceused

Another method for monitoring your system is to review the space used by a table in a database. You can also displace the disk space reserved and used by an entire database. The syntax is

```
sp_spaceused [tablename[,@updateusage={TRUE¦FALSE}]]
```

The `tablename` is the name of the table you want to review. If no parameters are specified, information is displayed on the current database. If an index is removed or added, this stored procedure could produce invalid information. If you suspect the output is wrong, add `@updateusage=TRUE` to correct this problem. This process should be done during off-peak hours, because it could take a long time to run.

Extended Stored Procedures

Extended stored procedures allow you to access the SQL Server as if the procedure were local by using DLLs (Dynamic Link Libraries). If the DLL causes an error, the SQL Server will remove the problem thread and won't stop running. If you want to create your own external procedures, you can use a language such as C or C++. This topic in itself would require several chapters. Refer to Appendix C for the format and explanation of all extended stored procedures.

Using External Procedures for Messaging

Messaging should be an integral part of your SQL Server. Here are some benefits of using messaging with the SQL Server and a mail client:

- If a procedure fails, you could email the end user responsible for maintaining the server. Better yet, page him.
- You can attach output from a query to an email message and then forward it to the appropriate parties. Imagine creating a DSS (Decision Support System) that sends critical daily reports to management.
- You can send mail if performance hits a critical point.
- It can be integrated with Alerts.

Setting up mail can be a daunting task. I have found that even though MAPI is supported, Microsoft Exchange seems to integrate better with the SQL Server than with Windows NT mail or any other mail system. The steps to set up messaging are

1. Make sure the post office is installed.
2. Make sure the clients attached to the post office are installed.
3. Set up a user named something like SQLSERVER to send mail to and receive mail from the SQL Server.
4. Run SQL setup and set up services to make sure that the Mail Client automatically starts when the SQL Server starts. The login name should be the same name that was set up in step 3.
5. You can now send and receive mail, using sp_processmail to process all incoming mail.

Once the mail client is installed and running, you can now use the external procedures xp_deletemail, xp_readmail, xp_sendmail, xp_findnextmessage, and sp_processmail to send and receive mail.

Some samples of sending mail include

```
xp_sendmail 'tatwood', @query = 'sp_monitor'
```

This sends the output from this stored procedure to the user tatwood. Here's another example:

```
xp_sendmail @recipients = 'tatwood;cwire',
@message = 'Server crash from 10/10 due to power failure.',
@copy_recipients = 'jsule',
@subject = 'Server Status'
```

This uses actual variables to specify how the message is formatted. Using email can automate many mundane tasks, especially if you use a stored procedure to automatically email several users with meaningful output.

> **TIP**
>
> Each line can store a maximum of 255 characters. If your output exceeds this, there is an elegant solution to the problem. Simply create a table with two or more columns that can store each line of text, but make sure the length of each variable is under 255 characters and that the total of all the columns equals the line length. You can now run a SELECT statement extracting all columns and send this information through email with no problems. If the line length is 455 characters, you could create one column of 255 characters and another of 200 characters. Each row is now broken into two columns, but the combined total matches the output of 455 characters.

Accessing the Operating System with External Procedures

One nice feature is the ability to access operating system commands on the SQL Server using xp_cmdshell. You should only grant this access to system administrators. Granting PUBLIC permissions will cause you grief. The syntax of this stored procedure is

```
xp_cmdshell "command"[,no_output]
```

The *command* parameter is any operating system command, surrounded by quotation marks. You can optionally add *no_output* if you do not want to display output. Some examples include

```
xp_cmdshell "dir c:\"
```

This will output the contents of the root directory of the server to the console. A better use is in the next example:

```
DECLARE @myresult int
EXEC @myresult = xp_cmdshell "dir c:\tim.txt"
IF (@myresult = 0)
    PRINT "Success"
ELSE
    PRINT "Failure"
```

Instead of looking at output, why not use a procedure to test for the existence of a file? Other uses include executing programs on the server, or even shutting the server down. Again, be very careful about who has access to this external procedure.

Using RETURN for More Meaningful Error Messages

The RETURN statement can be used to return a numerical value after exiting a stored procedure. However, if you add a number after the RETURN statement, the number will be returned. This number can be any non-zero number except for the reserved range of –1 to –99. If you intend to create your own message errors using RETURN, you should be consistent about the meaning and range of the integer values used. For instance, you could reserve return codes 100–199 for problems with the sales database. This concept is demonstrated in the next section.

Advanced Uses of Stored Procedures

This section will demonstrate advanced DML, cursors, stored procedures, system stored procedures, the RETURN statement, and using advanced parameters.

Let's use an example. Your firm specializes in the finance sector. To maintain your competitive edge utilizing technology, you hire contractors. These contractors, which comprise over 70 percent of your staff, bring critical knowledge and expertise on current and existing technology. In a recent audit, it was discovered that login IDs still existed for contractors and regular employees who were terminated by the company. Your job is to devise a method to handle this administrative mess.

The solution, which is one of many methods possible, involves many concepts discussed throughout this book. You will create two tables and several stored procedures to handle the administrative tasks. The two tables, which will be identical copies of one another, will store information about each user.

Creating the First Administrative Table

The first table will store information on all current users of the system. Execute the code in Listing 6.1 to create the first table.

Listing 6.1. Creating the user-tracking table.

```
-- This sets up a table called myusers to store data on employees
CREATE TABLE myusers(
    UserID        varchar(30)NOT NULL PRIMARY KEY,
       FirstName     varchar(30),
    LastName     varchar(30),
    EmployeeType    char(1) NOT NULL, -- C-Contractor, P-Permanent
    DBAccess        varchar(30), -- Default database to access
    StartDate       datetime,   -- Employee Start Date
    ExpDate         datetime -- Employee Expiration Date
    )
```

The UserID and DBAccess fields are identical to the syslogins table, which stores the entire set of login IDs for the SQL Server. To obtain the field attributes, I used sp_help syslogins to display this information to the screen. The FirstName and LastName fields are sixty characters combined, which should be adequate for virtually 99 percent of the end users. To track the employee type, the EmployeeType field stores a value of C for a contract programmer and a value of P for a permanent employee. The hire date and expiration date information is stored in this database for your automatic removal process. Your output, if successful, will be

```
This command did not return data, and it did not return any rows
```

Creating the Archive Administrative Table

Before an employee is removed from the `myuser` table and the `syslogins` table, it is a good idea to archive the information to a backup table. This process not only protects you from complaints by an accidentally deleted user, but it also helps track administrative costs and management abuse of the system. Execute the code in Listing 6.2 to create the second archive table.

Listing 6.2. Creating the second archive table.

```
-- This sets up a table called oldusers to store data on terminated
employees
CREATE TABLE oldusers(
    UserID          varchar(30),
        FirstName     varchar(30),
    LastName      varchar(30),
    EmployeeType    char(1) NOT NULL, -- C-Contractor, P-Permanent
    DBAccess        varchar(30), -- Default database to access
    StartDate       datetime,  -- Employee Start Date
    ExpDate         datetime -- Employee Expiration Date
    )
```

Your output should appear as

```
This command did not return data, and it did not return any rows
```

Now that the tables have been created, you can start creating the procedures necessary to add a user, update the user's expiration date, and delete the user. One more notable difference—the `UserID` is no longer a primary key. This `UserID` field will keep track of how often managers forget to remind the administrators to update the expiration date by extracting the count of records in the `oldusers` table greater than one.

Adding a User Login ID

The challenge in adding a login ID is to first add it to the `myusers` table and then add some of the same information to the `syslogins` table. However, as in any good system, input parameters should be checked for validity before any users are added. Because the overall procedure references an additional stored procedure that checks for the existence of the default database assigned to the user, you will need to create this stored procedure first. Execute the code in Listing 6.3 to create the `pr_verifydb` stored procedure.

Listing 6.3. Verifying the existence of the default database.

```
/*  This procedure verifies that the database exists before adding
    the new user to any of the tables    */
CREATE PROC pr_verifydb (@dbname varchar(30))
AS
DECLARE @dbid int
SELECT @dbid = dbid from sysdatabases -- Suppresses output, other uses
    where name = @dbname
IF @@rowcount = 0 -- No records match, create our own error codes!
    RETURN 50
RETURN 0 -- Everything is perfect!!!
```

Your output should appear as

```
This command did not return data, and it did not return any rows
```

This stored procedure accepts the parameter @dbname, which holds the value passed by the pr_adduser stored procedure to test for the existence of the default database. The local variable @dbid will store the database ID associated with the default database in the sysdatabases table, if found. Not only does this suppress output to the screen, but it can be used to expand the procedure for other possibilities. The system variable @@rowcount tracks the number of rows selected. If any matches are found by using the SELECT statement, @@rowcount should be greater than 0. In fact, there should be only one database name stored, so the value should either be a 0 if the database name is not found or 1 if the database name is found.

Instead of a simple RETURN statement, I decided to assign return codes to create my own meanings. A value of 0 is assigned if the database is found. A value of 50 is assigned if the database is not found. Creating your own RETURN codes is discussed in detail in the sections "Using Return for More Meaningful Error Messages" and "Advanced Uses of Stored Procedures." You are now ready to create the stored procedure to add the user by executing the code in Listing 6.4.

Listing 6.4. Giving a user access to the SQL Server.

```
/*  This procedure adds users to the mytable database, and then
    adds the user to the login table.  */
DROP PROC pr_adduser
GO

CREATE PROC pr_adduser (@UID varchar(30),@FN varchar(30),
    @LN varchar(30),@PW varchar(30),@EmpT char(1),
    @DB varchar(30),@SD datetime, @ED datetime)
AS
DECLARE @returnstat int -- Used to verify existence of assigned database
BEGIN
/*  The next several blocks of code test the parameters to make sure the
    parameters are as close to accurate as possible.  Every effort to
    errorcheck data should be made.  */

    SELECT @UID = LTRIM(RTRIM(@UID))
    SELECT @FN = LTRIM(RTRIM(@FN))
    SELECT @LN = LTRIM(RTRIM(@LN))
    SELECT @PW = LTRIM(RTRIM(@PW))
    SELECT @DB = LTRIM(RTRIM(@DB))


--Check UserID for valid first character
    IF DATALENGTH(@UID) < 3 or DATALENGTH(@UID)>=30 or @UID = ""
        BEGIN
            RAISERROR ("User ID Lengths Must be from 3 to 30
            ➥characters"
                ,16,1)
            RETURN
        END

--Check UserID Length
```

```
        IF UPPER(SUBSTRING(@UID,1,1)) < "A" or UPPER(SUBSTRING(@UID,1,1)) >
        ➥"Z"
            BEGIN
                RAISERROR ("User ID Must begin with an alphabetic
                ➥character"
                    ,16,1)
                RETURN
            END
-- Check First Name Length
        IF DATALENGTH(@FN) <= 1 or DATALENGTH(@FN) >= 31 or @FN = ""
            BEGIN
                RAISERROR ("The First name must be range from 2 to 30
                ➥characters"
                    ,16,1)
                RETURN
            END
-- Check Last Name Length
        IF DATALENGTH(@LN) <= 1 or DATALENGTH(@LN) > =31 or @LN = ""
            BEGIN
                RAISERROR ("The Last name must be range from 2 to 30
                ➥characters"
                    ,16,1)
                RETURN
            END

-- Check Password Length
        IF DATALENGTH(@PW) < 8 or DATALENGTH(@PW) > 31 or @PW = ""
            BEGIN
                RAISERROR ("Password Lengths Must be from 8 to 30
                ➥characters"
                    ,16,1)
                RETURN
            END

-- Check for valid Employee Type
        IF UPPER(@EmpT)<>"C" and UPPER(@EmpT)<>"P"
            BEGIN
                RAISERROR ("Employee Type must be a value of 'C' or
                ➥'P'",16,1)
                RETURN
            END

-- Check to make sure the end date is not prior to the start date
        IF @SD >= @ED
            BEGIN
                RAISERROR ("The Start Date must be prior to Ending
                ➥Date",16,1)
                RETURN
            END

-- Verify existence of assigned database
        EXEC @returnstat = pr_verifydb @DB
        IF @returnstat =50 — Compare custom-made return value
            BEGIN
            RAISERROR("Assigned Database Does Not Exist!",16,1)
            RETURN
        END
```

continues

Listing 6.4. continued

```
/* Used to make sure no extra spaces are entered.  Better to do this
   at one spot than to repeat this for entering the same data in two
   separate tables  */


-- Add user to myusers table
    INSERT myusers(UserID,FirstName,LastName,EmployeeType,
        DBAccess,StartDate,ExpDate)
    VALUES (@UID,@FN,@LN,@EMPT,@DB,@SD,@ED)
-- Use system stored procedure to add users to system stored table
    EXECUTE sp_addlogin @UID,@PW,@DB
END
```

Your output should appear as

```
This command did not return data, and it did not return any rows
```

As you can see, a lot of code was used to add eight parameters in some combination to two tables. The input parameters to the stored procedure are: @UID to hold the user ID, @FN to store the first name, @LN to store the last name, @PW to store the password, @EmpT to store the employee type, @DB to store the default database name, @SD to store the start date, and @ED to store the expiration date.

The extra code checks for potential input errors, reducing possible input error by the administrator. However, before the data is checked for errors, all leading and trailing spaces are removed with RTRIM and LTRIM. The most obvious item to check is the length of the character input parameters. The user ID is tested for a length between 3 to 30 characters using the DATALENGTH function. The additional test, where @UID = " ", tests for NULL or blank values that are not evaluated as integers. You will notice a consistent use of the functions LTRIM and RTRIM, which remove all leading and ending blank spaces to correct for input errors.

The second check on the user ID is to make sure that the first letter is a valid character, which should be an alphabetic character—the type allowed for creating the user ID in the syslogins table. You will notice that SUBSTRING extracts the first character and UPPER converts the result to uppercase for comparison. This way, if the sort order does not treat uppercase and lowercase the same, this procedure will not require alteration. The first name and last name are tested for a length between two and 30 characters. The additional test, where @FN = " ", is used to check for NULL values that are not evaluated as integers.

The password length is similarly checked for a length between eight to 30 characters. Next, the employee type is checked for valid values of C or P. The expiration date is checked to make sure that it is not prior to, or equal to, the hire date.

The last check verifies the existence of the default database, which uses the stored procedure pr_verifydb that you created in Listing 6.3. If the value of 0 is returned, there is a match. If 50 is returned, the database does not exist. If any of these parameters are invalid, you do not add the user to either table. This is accomplished through the use of the BEGIN and END statements, which encapsulate the entire procedure. If any error is found, the RAISERROR statement displays the error message, and the RETURN statement that directly follows causes you to exit the stored procedure completely.

If all input is valid, the user is then added to the myusers table with the INSERT statement. The system stored procedure sp_addlogin is called to add the user to the system database.

> **NOTE**
>
> Although you could have stored the password in the myusers table, the password would not be encrypted and would be a potential security risk.

To verify these processes, enter the next several users. If you do this all in one batch, make sure you have the keyword EXEC in front of each call to the stored procedure:

```
pr_adduser "jsule","john","sule","test1233","C","master","12/
10/97"
pr_adduser "matwood","michelle","atwood","test1233","C","master",
    "12/10/96","12/10/98"
pr_adduser "tatwood","tim","atwood","test1233","C","master",
    "12/10/96","12/10/97"
pr_adduser "ghodgson","greg","hodgson","test1233","C","master"
    ,"12/10/96","12/10/99"
pr_adduser "grerick","glen","rerick","test1233","C","master",
    "12/10/96","12/10/99"
pr_adduser "ahudson","ann","hudson","test1233","C","master",

    "12/10/96","12/10/97"
```

Modifying the End Date of the End User

Instead of continually writing a script to update the expiration date of an end user, enter the code in Listing 6.5 to automate this process.

Listing 6.5. Updating an end user's expiration date.

```
/*  This procedure updates employee Expiration Date in case the
    employee will continue employment after the original
    Expiration Date  */

CREATE PROC pr_updateuser(@UserID varchar(30), @NewExpDate datetime)
AS
UPDATE myusers -- Changes Expiration Date in the myusers table
    SET ExpDate = @NewExpDate
    Where UserID = @UserID
IF @@rowcount = 1 -- Checks to make sure process completed properly
    PRINT "User Updated"
ELSE
    PRINT "Invalid UserID entered"
```

Your output should appear as

```
This command did not return data, and it did not return any rows
```

This stored procedure demonstrates updating data effectively with input parameters. The parameters passed are the user ID and the new expiration date. The procedure searches the data until a match is made and sets the original expiration date to the new expiration date. To improve on possible errors, whether an update occurred or not, the output was always the same. By adding the last IF statement to make sure that one row was output (User Updated), you could tell the administrator if he or she was successful or not.

Why is this stored procedure necessary? Most contract workers' dates are usually extended. On several of my personal contracts, I have seen the date changed seven times. This is usually because corporate policy dictates that renewals last three months. To test this process, execute the following code:

```
pr_updateuser tatwood,"01/10/99"
```

Your output should be

```
User Updated
```

Removing an End User

You can now see two different methods for deleting an end user. Execute the code in Listing 6.6.

Listing 6.6. First method for deleting user.

```
CREATE PROC pr_deluser (@TD datetime )
AS
DELETE syslogins WHERE name IN(
     SELECT UserID FROM myusers
          WHERE EmployeeType = "C" and ExpDate <= @TD)
```

When you execute the code, the output is

```
sg 259, Level 16, State 2
Ad-hoc updates to system catalogs not enabled.
System Administrator must reconfigure system to allow this.
```

Although your immediate thought may be to use sp_configure to allow for direct updates to system tables, followed by RECONFIGURE to save the changes, this is never a good idea. Any query could update a system table, easily causing database corruption. There has to be a better way. Before you can create the stored procedure to delete a user, you need to create one more stored procedure to copy the user into the archive oldusers database by executing the code in Listing 6.7.

Listing 6.7. Archiving end user data.

```
/*  The purpose of this procedure is to copy a user's information
    into a permanent archive database before wiping the user from
    the system completely  */
CREATE PROC pr_copyuser (@UID varchar(30) )
AS
INSERT INTO oldusers -- Database archiving the data
    SELECT *
        FROM myusers
        WHERE UserID = @UID
DELETE myusers — Remove user from myusers table
    WHERE UserID = @UID
```

Your output should be

```
This command did not return data, and it did not return any rows
```

This procedure accepts the UserId provided by the cursor, selects the data from the myusers table, copies all data into the oldusers table, and then deletes the row from the myusers table. You can now create the proper procedure to delete an end user by executing the code in Listing 6.8.

Listing 6.8. Proper method for deleting an end user.

```
/*  This procedure deletes a login ID in the system tables and
    deletes the employee from myusers table after the employee
    data has been copied to the oldusers table */
CREATE PROC pr_deluser (@TD datetime )
AS
-- Cursor used to fetch employees who have expired
DECLARE getuser_curs CURSOR
    FOR
        SELECT UserID
        FROM myusers
        WHERE ExpDate <= @TD
-- Stores UserID's that matched into temp variable
DECLARE @HoldID varchar(30)
-- Tracks number of users deleted instead of @@ROWCOUNT
DECLARE @MyCount int
-- Assigns initial count value to 0
SELECT @MyCount = 0
OPEN getuser_curs
FETCH NEXT FROM getuser_curs into @HoldID
-- Test myusers database for expired employees
WHILE @@FETCH_STATUS = 0 BEGIN
    EXEC sp_droplogin @HoldID
    EXEC pr_copyuser @HoldID
-- If match, increments count of users deleted
    SELECT @MyCount = @MyCount + 1
    FETCH NEXT FROM getuser_curs into @HoldID
END
DECLARE @MyDisp varchar(50)
-- Displays text total of number of users deleted
```

continues

Listing 6.8. continued

```
SELECT @MyDisp = "Number of Users Deleted is " + ltrim(str(@MyCount))
PRINT @MyDisp
— Cleanup of cursor work
CLOSE getuser_curs
DEALLOCATE getuser_curs
```

This process uses cursors within a stored procedure. The only parameter passed is the date you want to test against the expiration date. Two variables are declared—@HoldID stores the match of each user ID, and @MyCount stores the total number of matches. In this case, @@rowcount does not return a valid value. If a match occurs, a call is made to the system stored procedure sp_droplogin to remove the login from the system tables. The pr_copyuser procedure is called to archive the data and delete the user from the myusers table. A PRINT statement reflects the number of people deleted. For good memory management, all space used by the cursor is deallocated. To try this stored procedure, use the following example:

```
pr_deluser "04/10/98"
```

Your output should be

```
(0 row(s) affected)
Login dropped.
(0 row(s) affected)
Login dropped.
(0 row(s) affected)
Number of Users Deleted is 2
```

However, this process should be automated to run daily, getting the system date from the SQL Server. You can use the code in Listing 6.9 to create a stored procedure to further automate this process.

Listing 6.9. Using the system date as a default parameter.

```
DECLARE @myvalue varchar(12)
SELECT @myvalue=CONVERT(varchar(12), getdate())
EXEC pr_deluser @myvalue
```

If you run the stored procedure with GETDATE() as the parameter, you will immediately receive an error message 170. You can't place functions on the same line as an EXEC statement. To work around this problem, you can create a temporary string value that holds the converted date using the CONVERT function. This string is used as the parameter, which contains the current date.

Suggestions for Improving This Process

With these few procedures, the benefits for the administration of users are great. These procedures met the goals of the business case. In addition, if managers forget to notify the administrators to change the expiration date and the user is deleted, this is tracked in the oldusers database. You could conceivably charge the department for the added administrative costs! However, there is room for improvement:

- I would add the fields in the myusers table to the Employee table and add a field to store the group, username, department, and manager name. This would waste less space, and would allow you to use external stored procedures to send a list of employees about to be deleted within two weeks to the managers via email.

- Because users can have a group name and username in the system and you can't remove the login ID if these items exist, you could use the added fields discussed previously to automate the removal from a group and the removal of the username to the database.

- I would add the ability to change a user from C (Contract) to P (Permanent).

- I would create a stored procedure to verify that a process creates the intended object successfully. You can do this by calling a systems stored procedure (after a process runs) to test for the validity of the object created and return a more meaningful message.

- I would create a procedure to test for birthdays, names, and words in the password and disallow them.

- I would create a stored procedure to remove any non-alphabetic characters (except 0–9) from the user ID, first name, and last name.

Summary

This chapter focuses heavily on built-in stored procedures. System stored procedures allow you to access and modify system components with a greater degree of security. You also learned how to create a removable media database. External procedures provide you with a way to access the server, using DLLs to perform such tasks as setting up users, sending and receiving email, and accessing the operating system. The RETURN statement also provides a method for generating custom error messages besides using the standard messages provided by the SQL Server. An example using advanced DML, cursors, stored procedures, system stored procedures, the RETURN statement, and advanced parameters demonstrates these advanced concepts, including potential pitfalls. Stored procedures, whether built in or created, provide you with some of the most powerful means of performing data manipulation or administrative tasks.

Employing Cursors

IN THIS CHAPTER

CHAPTER 7

A *cursor* is a mechanism that allows you to access individual rows of data rather than working against the entire set of rows (as is done with a SELECT, UPDATE, or DELETE statement). By dealing with each row separately, you can gather information piece by piece and perform actions against the data on a row-by-row basis. You can also use the data to generate T-SQL code and immediately execute or print it for later use.

Cursor Declaration

You are probably familiar with the basics of cursor usage, including declarations, so this section is short. A cursor's definition, as well as all the rules that apply to cursor usage, are covered in this chapter.

Defining a Cursor

The DECLARE statement is not only used to define variables that are used in code, but also to create a cursor's definition. The syntax appears in Listing 7.1:

Listing 7.1. Cursor declaration syntax.

```
DECLARE name_of_cursor [INSENSITIVE] [SCROLL] CURSOR
FOR select_statement
[FOR {READ ONLY ¦ UPDATE [OF columns]}]
```

The required portions consist of the key items: DECLARE, the cursor variable, CURSOR, FOR, and the SELECT statement. The *name_of_cursor* variable is the name that you later use to refer to the cursor and must adhere to the standard naming conventions of SQL Server. The keyword CURSOR states that this variable is of type cursor. The FOR keyword and the SELECT statement define the cursor contents.

The INSENSITIVE option causes a copy of the cursor data to be put in tempdb. Because of that, the cursor sees no changes to the data. This is known as a *Snapshot* or *Static* cursor. This option does not allow updates to the data.

The SCROLL option allows you to move around the cursor at will. Without this option, you may only move forward and only one row at a time. Although this seems limiting, you do not usually need to do anything but run through and either collect or update the data.

FOR READ ONLY specifies that the cursor is just that. By default, cursors are updatable, and this option overrides the default. FOR UPDATE states that the cursor is updatable, which you now know is the default—why use it? Because the optional column list allows you to specify which columns are updatable. Without it, all columns are, by default, updatable (as if you never used the FOR UPDATE option in the first place). The other reason to use this option is that scrollable cursors and cursors that use an ORDER BY clause in the SELECT statement are read-only and not sensitive by default; now you need to use the FOR UPDATE option in order to update underlying data.

You see several examples of cursor declarations throughout this chapter, but one simple declaration is shown in Listing 7.2 for kicks. This cursor lets you manipulate titles and quantities where the qty is currently greater than 10. Notice the use of the naming syntax discussed in the first chapter.

Listing 7.2. Example of a cursor declaration.

```
DECLARE crTitleSales CURSOR FOR
        SELECT    title, qty
        FROM      titles t
                  JOIN sales s ON t.title_id = s.title_id
        WHERE     qty > 10
```

Rules of Cursor Use

There are two aspects of cursors discussed here: Scope of a cursor and how its declaration affects its final form. The latter will be discussed first, showing how various types of SELECT statements can have different affects on the actual cursor created. You also see how various types of cursors affect performance and some other rules for use. The former shows how cursors maintain their existence even after a procedure has completed and returned to the client.

Cursor Facts

The facts about cursors

- Forward-Only (non-scrollable) cursors are better for performance if used on large tables.

- Forward-Only cursors are dynamic (not insensitive) by default. This makes the cursor quicker to open and allows it to update row data.

- You may not declare a cursor on a table that is made within the same batch or stored procedure.

- You may create a cursor on a temporary table that was made in the same batch or stored procedure.

- You may create a cursor on a table that is made in the same batch or stored procedure if you create the cursor via dynamic execution.

- The keywords COMPUTE, FOR BROWSE, and INTO are not allowed within the SELECT statement of a cursor declaration.

- If UNION, DISTINCT, GROUP BY, or HAVING are used, if an outer join is used, or if a constant expression is included in the SELECT list of the SELECT statement, the cursor will be insensitive.

- Cursors declared as insensitive are also always read-only.

Listing 7.3 demonstrates the last fact:

Listing 7.3. Attempt to declare an insensitive, updatable cursor.

```
DECLARE crAuthors INSENSITIVE CURSOR FOR
        SELECT * FROM authors
        FOR UPDATE
```

This statement fails and returns the following error:

```
Msg 16929, Level 16, State 1
Cursor is read only
```

The cursor never gets created because of conflicting credentials. You may not update the data if you are no longer browsing the original data. Even though this is a forward-only cursor, it is read-only by default and may not be made updatable.

There you have it. The rules are straightforward and all exceptions have been listed. There is another aspect of cursors—scope—which is discussed next.

Cursor Scope

Cursors exist throughout the life of a connection. A cursor declared earlier during a connection's existence is available until either the connection is closed or the cursor is destroyed. How do you destroy a cursor? Simply deallocate it, as shown Listing 7.4.

Listing 7.4. Declaring and deallocating a cursor.

```
DECLARE crAuthors INSENSITIVE CURSOR FOR
        SELECT * FROM authors

/*Other code that uses the cursor*/

DEALLOCATE crAuthors
```

Unless you deallocate a cursor, it will not only remain available for use, but can even be left open and fetched from as needed while the connection is maintained. For example, you can declare a cursor in one batch. You can open the cursor later. Still later you can fetch data from the cursor and continue to do this on a periodic basis. The cursor remains open until you close it and remains available until it is destroyed.

Opening, Closing, and Moving Through Cursors

This has been introduced in the prior section. Continue on and read further about the mechanism of opening and closing a cursor.

The OPEN and CLOSE Statements

The OPEN and CLOSE statements allow you to open the cursor for use and close it when you're finished. Although you must always explicitly open a cursor, there are a couple of ways to close it without explicitly stating so.

The first is the Set Statement option, which causes a cursor to close when a transaction (implicit or explicit) completes. By using the statement in Listing 7.5, you can ensure that a cursor closes at the end of a stored procedure or batch:

Listing 7.5. Forcing a cursor to close.

```
SET CURSOR_CLOSE_ON_COMMIT ON
```

If you want to ensure that a cursor is closed each time you make a call to the server, you can turn on this option and sleep soundly.

> **NOTE**
>
> Keep in mind that the cursor is still allocated, even if you explicitly close it with the CLOSE statement or force its closure with SET CURSOR_CLOSE_ON_COMMIT ON. Be sure to deallocate it if you do not plan on using it again, but want to keep the connection open.

Another method is to simply close the current connection. Not only does this close the cursor, it deallocates it as well. If you want to maintain the current connection, this method obviously is not the preferred one.

Recycling a Cursor

You know that recycling helps save the environment and is a good thing to do. Just because you can keep a cursor open for the lifetime of a connection does not mean you should—particularly if you either hold the lock via optimizer hints or via the Repeatable Read or Serializable transaction isolation level. The end result is that you can tie up data pages and prevent modifications from occurring, thus creating more concurrency issues and dropping performance. In essence, this sort of recycling potentially has only bad effects on the SQL Server environment. Listing 7.6. shows an example of how to declare a cursor that blocks modifications:

Listing 7.6. Declaring a cursor that blocks modifications.

```
/*Either use the holdlock optimizer hint...*/
DECLARE crAuthors CURSOR FOR
        SELECT * FROM authors (holdlock)

/*...or set the transaction isolation level*/

SET TRANSACTION ISOLATION LEVEL REPEATABLE READ

DECLARE crAuthors CURSOR FOR
        SELECT * FROM authors (holdlock)
```

If either section in Listing 7.6 is used to declare the cursor, opening without closing the cursor leaves a page and table intent lock on the authors table. The only real advantage might be that you alone may make changes to the data via the UPDATE statement for the particular row in which the cursor is located.

> **WARNING**
>
> This method of holding locks will hold a lock on remaining rows of that data page where the cursor is located. If you are going to hold the lock, keep the time frame as short as possible; otherwise, you may start negatively affecting performance by increasing locking concurrency.

In general, a cursor is declared, opened, closed, and deallocated all within the same procedure or batch. You usually do everything that you want to do and have no need to keep the cursor hanging around.

> **WARNING**
>
> If your batch or procedure fails part of the way through or if you execute a RETURN statement before deallocating or closing the cursor, you may accidentally leave the cursor open or allocated.

The FETCH Statement

You can declare, open, close, and deallocate a cursor. The last bit is fetching data. This is where the fun begins. For starters, the name itself begs for some sort of dog joke.

The FETCH statement is the key to using cursors. You are going to take a look its standard use and then dig a little deeper to find some interesting methods and uses of cursors in general.

Standard Use of FETCH

The FETCH statement has the most complicated syntax of all the cursor statements, as shown in Listing 7.7:

Listing 7.7. FETCH syntax.

```
FETCH
[[NEXT ¦ PRIOR ¦ FIRST ¦ LAST ¦ ABSOLUTE {n ¦ @n} ¦ RELATIVE {n ¦ @n}] FROM]
name_of_cursor
[INTO @variable1, @variable2, ...]
```

The only required elements are the actual word FETCH and the name of the cursor from which you are fetching data. The power of using cursors does not come from this simple use. Before exploring further, however, examine the rest of the syntax. First, there are several options that allow control regarding what you fetch. They are listed in Table 7.1:

Table 7.1. FETCH directives.

Directive	Description
NEXT	Retrieves the next row in the cursor.
PRIOR	Retrieves the previous row in the cursor.
FIRST	Retrieves the first row in the cursor.
LAST	Retrieves the last row in the cursor.
ABSOLUTE	Using either a literal int, smallint, tinyint, or a variable of said datatypes, retrieves the nth physical row in the cursor. For negative values of n or @n, the cursor counts backward from the last row of the cursor.
RELATIVE	Using either a literal int, smallint, tinyint, or a variable of said datatypes, retrieves the nth relative row from the current row position of the cursor. For negative values of n or @n, the cursor counts backward from the current row of the cursor.

If you do use any of the FETCH directives, you must also use the FROM clause—no exceptions. The last part of the syntax deals with storing retrieved row data into variables. The number of variables must match the number of columns, and each variable must fit in size and match in type the datatype of the corresponding column from the selected column list.

Take a look at the example in Listing 7.8:

Listing 7.8. Fetching cursor data into variables.

```
DECLARE crTitleSales CURSOR FOR
        SELECT   title, qty
        FROM     titles t
                 JOIN sales s ON t.title_id = s.title_id
        WHERE    qty > 10

DECLARE   @chvTitle varchar(100),
          @intQty smallint

OPEN crTitleSales

FETCH NEXT FROM crTitleSales INTO @chvTitle, @intQty

CLOSE crTitleSales

DEALLOCATE crTitleSales

PRINT 'First Title with sales quantity over 10'

SELECT    @chvTitle AS 'Title',
          @intQty AS 'Quantity'
```

The results of Listing 7.8 should look like this:

```
First Title with sales quantity over 10
Title                                                      Quantity
------------------------------------------------------    --------
Secrets of Silicon Valley                                  50
```

If @intQty were declared as int rather than smallint, an error would occur and SQL Server would not allow the fetch. The varchar datatype of @chvTitle, however, is actually 20 bytes bigger than the defined datatype of the title column. This is allowed, since it is the same base datatype of the column and it is equal to or larger than the defined length.

Cursor Thresholds

How do you know if you're finished moving through a cursor? SQL Server supplies a global variable—@@fetch_status—to help you find the answer. If @@fetch_status contains a value of 0, then everything is all right. If it contain another value, you have a situation on your hands. The next two sections explain these in more detail.

Moving Past the End of the Cursor Set

Moving past the beginning or end of the cursor row set results in @@FETCH_STATUS containing a value of -1. You can use a WHILE statement and check the value of @@FETCH_STATUS so that fetching stops when there are no longer any rows to retrieve. Examine the code snippet in Listing 7.9:

Listing 7.9. Checking @@FETCH_STATUS with a WHILE statement.

```
FETCH NEXT FROM crColumnTypes INTO @chvName, @chvNameType
WHILE (@@FETCH_STATUS <> -1)
BEGIN
        SELECT @chvPrint = '          @' + @chvName + ' ' + @chvNameType
        PRINT @chvPrint
        FETCH NEXT FROM crColumnTypes INTO @chvName, @chvNameType
END
```

As long as the cursor has not moved past the end of the row set, @@FETCH_STATUS will not contain a value of -1. You keep fetching the rows until that point. Notice how a FETCH is performed prior to entering the WHILE construct. This prevents you from entering the loop if there are no rows at all in the cursor. Another FETCH (at the end) is performed within the loop after processing the data, so that the loop will not be executed any further if you have again moved past the end of the cursor.

Dealing with Deleted Rows

What if the row itself has been deleted since opening the cursor? The cursor will look for it and can position itself on it—even if it has been deleted. Again, your friend @@FETCH_STATUS provides a way to take care of the situation. A value of -2 indicates that you have moved onto what once was a row in the underlying data.

> **TIP**
>
> If the cursor is declared INSENSITIVE, there is no need to check for missing rows in the cursor (@@FETCH_STATUS = -2). Since the cursor is actually a copy of the underlying data, rows cannot be deleted from the cursor's row set.

You do not want the WHILE construct to check for a missing row; this causes an exit from the loop as soon as a deleted row is encountered. Rather, you need to check within the looping structure as shown in Listing 7.10, which is an enhancement of Listing 7.9:

Listing 7.10. Checking for row existence in a cursor.

```
FETCH NEXT FROM crColumnTypes INTO @chvName, @chvNameType
WHILE (@@FETCH_STATUS <> -1)
BEGIN
        IF (@@FETCH_STATUS <> -2)
        BEGIN
                SELECT @chvPrint = '    @' + @chvName + ' ' + @chvNameType
                PRINT @chvPrint
        END
        FETCH NEXT FROM crColumnTypes INTO @chvName, @chvNameType
END
```

As you can see, the check for the row's existence occurs within the loop. If the row is present, the data is used to print information. If not, the loop carries on and fetches the next row of data. What if the row has been deleted? All the variables contain NULL values and are therefore not of much use to you.

> **WARNING**
>
> If @@FETCH_STATUS returns -2, the variables into which the data was retrieved all contain NULL values. If the selected columns of a present row all support and actually contain NULL values, however, the variables also all contain NULL values. Existence of NULL values in these variables does not ensure that the row has been deleted. You must use @@FETCH_STATUS to verify whether a row has been deleted.

Some Advanced Cursor Uses

You are going to take a big leap in this section. Cursors can definitely be used to help perform many productive tasks. This section wraps up by discussing a stored procedure that is currently used to help generate a stored procedure that updates a table. There is a lot of code, as well as some fairly complicated cursors and SELECT statements. Take your time while all the details are explained.

Generating Stored Procedure Code from a Stored Procedure

The lines of this code have been numbered for easier reference and ease of explanation. You can find the entire code listing in the file SCR0701.SQL if you want to open it in SQL Server Enterprise Manager.

Look through the code in Listing 7.11 and see if you understand what is being done. The more difficult items involve some complex CASE expression, including nested ones, within SELECT statements that are part of cursor declarations.

Listing 7.11. Generating new procedure code from a stored procedure.

```
 1: CREATE PROC prGenerateUpdateProc
 2: @chvTable varchar(30),
 3: @chvKey varchar(30)
 4: AS
 5:
 6: SET NOCOUNT ON
 7: DECLARE
 8:      @chvName varchar(30),
 9:      @intType int,
10:      @chvNameType varchar(255),
11:      @chvPrint varchar(255),
12:      @chvName2 varchar(30),
13:      @chvNameType2 varchar(255),
14:      @chvMessage varchar(255),
15:      @intReturnVal int,
16:      @chvDBName varchar(30)
17:
18: IF NOT EXISTS
19:      (SELECT   *
20:       FROM     sysobjects so
21:       JOIN     syscolumns sc
22:                ON so.id = sc.id
23:       WHERE    so.name = @chvTable
24:       AND      sc.name = @chvKey)
25: BEGIN
26:      SELECT @intReturnVal = 1
27:      SELECT @chvMessage = 'Either table ''%s'' or column ''%s''' +
                ➥' does not exist in the database ''%s''.'
28:      SELECT @chvDBName = DB_NAME()
29:      RAISERROR (@chvMessage, 10, -1, @chvTable, @chvKey, @chvDBName)
30:      RETURN @intReturnVal
31: END
32:
33: DECLARE crColumnTypes SCROLL CURSOR FOR
34:      SELECT sc.name AS name,
35:             st2.name +
36:             CASE
37:             WHEN st2.type IN (37,45,39,47)
38:                  THEN '(' + RTRIM(CONVERT(varchar(10),sc.length)) + ') '
39:             WHEN st2.type IN (55, 63)
40:                  THEN '(' + RTRIM(CONVERT(varchar(10),sc.prec)) + ', '
41:                  + RTRIM(CONVERT(varchar(10),sc.scale)) + ') '
42:             ELSE ' '
43:             END +
```

```
44:                 CASE sc.status & 8
45:                 WHEN 0 THEN 'NOT NULL'
46:                 WHEN 8 THEN 'NULL'
47:                 END AS type
48:         FROM    syscolumns sc
49:                 JOIN systypes st ON sc.usertype = st.usertype
50:                 JOIN systypes st2 ON st.type = st2.type
51:         WHERE   id = OBJECT_ID(@chvTable)
52:         AND     st2.usertype < 100
53:         AND     st2.name NOT IN ('sysname','timestamp')
54:         ORDER BY  sc.colid
55:
56: DECLARE crColumns SCROLL CURSOR FOR
57:         SELECT  sc.name AS name,
58:                 CASE
59:                 WHEN st2.type IN (37,45) THEN
60:                     CASE
61:                     WHEN sc.status & 8 = 8 THEN 1
62:                     WHEN sc.status & 8 = 0 THEN 8
63:                     END
64:                 WHEN st2.type IN (39,47) THEN
65:                     CASE
66:                     WHEN sc.status & 8 = 8 THEN 2
67:                     WHEN sc.status & 8 = 0 THEN 9
68:                     END
69:                 WHEN st2.type IN (38, 106, 108, 109, 110) THEN 3
70:                 WHEN st2.type = 111 THEN 4
71:                 WHEN st2.type IN (48, 52, 55, 56, 59, 60, 62, 63, 122) THEN 5
72:                 WHEN st2.type = 50 THEN 6
73:                 WHEN st2.type IN (58, 61) THEN 7
74:                 END AS type
75:         FROM    syscolumns sc
76:                 JOIN systypes st2 ON sc.type=st2.type
77:         WHERE   id = OBJECT_ID(@chvTable)
78:         AND     st2.usertype < 100
79:         AND     st2.name NOT IN ('sysname','timestamp')
80:         ORDER BY  sc.colid
81:
82: SELECT @chvPrint='CREATE PROC prUpdate' + @chvTable
83:
84: PRINT @chvPrint
85:
86: OPEN crColumnTypes
87:
88: FETCH NEXT FROM crColumnTypes INTO @chvName, @chvNameType
89: IF (@@fetch_status <> -1)
90: BEGIN
91:     WHILE 1 = 1
92:     BEGIN
93:         FETCH RELATIVE 0 FROM crColumnTypes INTO @chvName, @chvNameType
94:         FETCH RELATIVE 1 FROM crColumnTypes INTO @chvName2, @chvNameType2
95:         SELECT    @chvName2 = @chvName,
96:                   @chvNameType2 = @chvNameType
97:         SELECT @chvPrint = '        @' + @chvName2 +
                        ➥SPACE(34-DATALENGTH(@chvName2)) + @chvNameType2
98:         IF (@@fetch_status <> -1)
99:         BEGIN
```

continues

Listing 7.11. continued

```
100:            SELECT @chvPrint = @chvPrint + ', '
101:            PRINT @chvPrint
102:        END
103:        ELSE
104:        BEGIN
105:            PRINT @chvPrint
106:            BREAK
107:        END
108:    END
109: END
110:
111: CLOSE crColumnTypes
112:
113: PRINT 'AS'
114: PRINT ''
115: PRINT 'DECLARE '
116:
117: OPEN crColumnTypes
118:
119: FETCH NEXT FROM crColumnTypes INTO @chvName, @chvNameType
120:
121: WHILE (@@fetch_status <> -1)
122: BEGIN
123:    IF (@@fetch_status <> -2)
124:    BEGIN
125:        SELECT @chvPrint = '        @' + @chvName + '2' +
126:                SPACE(33-DATALENGTH(@chvName)) + @chvNameType + ','
127:        PRINT @chvPrint
128:    END
129:    FETCH NEXT FROM crColumnTypes INTO @chvName, @chvNameType
130: END
131:
132: CLOSE     crColumnTypes
133:
134: PRINT '      @intReturnVal                    int,'
135: PRINT '      @chvMessage                      varchar(255),'
136: PRINT '      @inyCount                        tinyint'
137: PRINT ''
138: PRINT 'SELECT @intReturnVal = 0'
139: PRINT 'SELECT '
140:
141: OPEN crColumnTypes
142:
143: FETCH NEXT FROM crColumnTypes INTO @chvName, @chvNameType
144: IF (@@fetch_status <> -1)
145: BEGIN
146:    WHILE 1 = 1
147:    BEGIN
148:        FETCH RELATIVE 0 FROM crColumnTypes INTO @chvName, @chvNameType
149:        FETCH RELATIVE 1 FROM crColumnTypes INTO @chvName2, @chvNameType2
150:        SELECT    @chvName2 = @chvName,
151:                @chvNameType2 = @chvNameType
152:        SELECT @chvPrint = '        @' + @chvName2 + '2 = ' + @chvName2
153:        IF (@@fetch_status <> -1)
154:        BEGIN
155:            SELECT @chvPrint = @chvPrint + ','
```

```
156:            PRINT @chvPrint
157:        END
158:        ELSE
159:        BEGIN
160:            PRINT @chvPrint
161:            BREAK
162:        END
163:    END
164: END
165:
166: CLOSE crColumnTypes
167:
168: SELECT @chvPrint = 'FROM        ' + @chvTable
169: PRINT @chvPrint
170: SELECT @chvPrint = 'WHERE        ' + @chvKey + ' = @' + @chvKey
171: PRINT @chvPrint
172: PRINT ''
173: PRINT 'IF @@ROWCOUNT = 0'
174: PRINT 'BEGIN'
175: PRINT '    SELECT @intReturnVal = -1'
176: SELECT @chvPrint= '    SELECT @cvrMessage = ''' + @chvTable +
         ➥' with Id of '' + '
177: PRINT @chvPrint
178: SELECT @chvPrint= '    RTRIM(CONVERT(varchar(10), @' + @chvKey + ')) + '
179: PRINT @chvPrint
180: PRINT '    '' was not found.'''
181: PRINT '    PRINT @cvrMessage'
182: PRINT '    RETURN @intReturnVal'
183: PRINT 'END'
184: PRINT ''
185: PRINT 'SELECT    @inyCount = 0'
186: PRINT ''
187: PRINT 'BEGIN TRAN'
188:
189: OPEN crColumns
190:
191: FETCH NEXT FROM crColumns INTO @chvName, @intType
192:
193: WHILE (@@fetch_status <> -1)
194: BEGIN
195:     IF (@@fetch_status <> -2)
196:     BEGIN
197:         IF @chvName <> @chvKey
198:         BEGIN
199:             IF @intType = 1
200:                 SELECT @chvPrint = 'IF COALESCE(@' + @chvName +
201:                     '2, 0x0) <> COALESCE(@' + @chvName + ', 0x0)'
202:             ELSE IF @intType = 2
203                 SELECT @chvPrint = 'IF COALESCE(@' + @chvName +
204:                     '2, '''') <> COALESCE(@' + @chvName + ', '''')'
205:             ELSE IF @intType = 3
206:                 SELECT @chvPrint = 'IF COALESCE(@' + @chvName +
207:                     '2, 0) <> COALESCE(@' + @chvName + ', 0)'
208:             ELSE IF @intType = 4
209:                 SELECT @chvPrint = 'IF COALESCE(@' + @chvName +
210:                     '2, ''1/1/1900'') <> COALESCE(@' +
```

continues

Listing 7.11. continued

```
211:                          @chvName + ', ''1/1/1900'')'
212:            ELSE
213:                SELECT @chvPrint = 'IF @' + @chvName + '2 <> @' + @chvName
214:                PRINT @chvPrint
215:                PRINT 'BEGIN'
216:                PRINT '        SELECT @inyCount = @inyCount + 1'
217:                SELECT @chvPrint = '        UPDATE ' + @chvTable +
218:                    ' SET ' + @chvName + ' = @' + @chvName
219:                PRINT @chvPrint
220:                SELECT @chvPrint = '        WHERE ' + @chvKey +
221:                    ' = @' + @chvKey
222:                PRINT @chvPrint
223:                PRINT 'END'
224:                PRINT ''
225:            END
226:        END
227:        FETCH NEXT FROM crColumns INTO @chvName, @intType
228: END
229:
230: CLOSE crColumns
231: DEALLOCATE crColumns
232: DEALLOCATE crColumnTypes
233:
234: PRINT 'IF @inyCount = 0'
235: PRINT 'BEGIN'
236: PRINT '    ROLLBACK TRAN'
237: PRINT '    SELECT @intReturnVal = 1'
238: PRINT '    SELECT @chvMessage =    ''No changes were detected. '' + '
239: PRINT '                        ''No changes were made.'''
240: PRINT '    PRINT @chvMessage'
241: PRINT '    RETURN @intReturnVal'
242: PRINT 'END'
243: PRINT 'ELSE'
244: PRINT 'BEGIN'
245: PRINT '    COMMIT TRAN'
246: PRINT '    RETURN @intReturnVal'
247: PRINT 'END'
248:
249: SET NOCOUNT OFF
250:
251: GO
```

Declaring the Procedure and Some Variables

Lines 1 through 17 are simply the CREATE for the stored procedure and some variable declarations used in the code. The procedure takes two arguments: The table name and the key field (this procedure only works with tables that use a single column to uniquely identify the row data). Lines 18 through 32 check to make sure that the table and column passed into the procedure do exist and if not, return an error.

The Cursors

Lines 32 through 55 declare one of two cursors that are used in this procedure. This cursor is used three times in the procedure. It selects two columns: the name column from the syscolumns table (which holds all the column names for every table), and a second value, which evaluates out to the actual datatype (and size or precision and scale, if necessary).

Lines 37 through 38 handle `char` and `binary` datatypes and add the column length in a pair of parentheses after the datatype name. Lines 39 through 41 handle decimal and numeric datatypes and add the precision and scale values in a set of parentheses. Instead of just getting `varchar` or `numeric` as the datatype, you get `varchar(10)` or `numeric(5, 3)` instead. Line 42 adds nothing and is for all other datatypes (since they don't require any size information). Lines 44 through 47 add the phrase `NULL` or `NOT NULL` to the end of the string to reflect the column's nullability.

The join in lines 48 through 50, from `syscolumns` to `systypes` to `systypes`, is required to get the base datatype of each column. The `WHERE` clause eliminates system datatypes and user-defined datatypes from the list returned, so you are assured of getting only base datatypes for the `name` column from the second copy of `systypes`. The `ORDER BY` clause provides the original column order.

Lines 56 through 80 define a second cursor. Again, two columns are selected: the column name and an `int` value, which evaluates out to reflect the category of the datatype, including its nullability. The return values from the nested case expression are shown in Table 7.2.

Table 7.2. Datatype categories from Listing 7.11.

Value	Description
1	Nullable `binary` and `varbinary`
2	Nullable `char` and `varchar`
3	Nullable numerics (`money`, `int`, `real`, `decimal`, and so on)
4	Nullable `datetime` and `smalldatetime`
5	Not nullable numerics (`money`, `int`, `real`, `decimal`, and so on)
6	Bit (not nullable by definition)
7	Not nullable `datetime` and `smalldatetime`
8	Not nullable `binary` and `varbinary`
9	Not nullable `char` and `varchar`

You see these values crop up in a later portion of the code, when the cursor is actually created and data is fetched. Although the values `5` through `9` are distinguished from one another later in the code, this always supplies a base category of datatypes and can be used for other procedures.

Printing Information

This procedure prints all the information to the Results pane of the SQL Query Tool window. The `Set Nocount On` statement located on line 6 prevents the dreaded `"Rows Affected"` message from appearing among the printed information. The variable @chvPrint is used to print all pertinent information. You see it used in a SELECT statement, often immediately followed by a PRINT statement. In addition, many lines contain static information being printed (32 lines, to be exact). Look at the results to see how the static lines being printed fit into the scheme.

Using the Cursors

The heart of the procedure is most definitely the use of the two defined cursors. The first cursor, crColumnTypes, is used to generate the parameters for the stored procedure. One little problem, however, is that you do not want a comma on the last item in the list. See Listing 7.12 to better understand (this example was generated from the sales table):

Listing 7.12. A sample procedure and its parameters.

```
CREATE PROC prUpdatesales
        @stor_id                char(4) NOT NULL,
        @ord_num                varchar(20) NOT NULL,
        @ord_date               datetime NOT NULL,
        @qty                    smallint NOT NULL,
        @payterms               varchar(12) NOT NULL,
        @title_id               varchar(6) NOT NULL
AS
```

Notice how the last item, @title_id, does not have a comma at the end. This presents a problem from a code-generation standpoint: how to avoid putting the comma on the last item. This is a little trick that indicates the last row of the cursor is used, so the comma could not be appended on the last item.

Generating the Parameters

Line 88 performs the initial row data FETCH. The IF statement in line 89 checks to see whether you have gone past the end of the cursor, as does line 98. Then you execute a WHILE statement with an expression that is always true. You use a BREAK statement to get out of the loop.

The two FETCH statements on lines 93 through 94 are the key to finding out if you are on the last row. The first selects the cursor row data from the current row (no row movement) into @chvName and @chvNameType by using the Relative 0 clause. The second fetches the next row of data into @chvName2 and @chvNameType2. These values are immediately replaced in line 95 with those in @chvName and @chvNameType.

Why bother doing this? You now have the current row data in @chvName2 and @chvNameType2 and have also moved forward a row. If you were on the last row of the cursor, the first FETCH would get the data and the second FETCH would move you past the end of the cursor. You now store the initial value to print in line 97 and then check to see if you have moved too far. Again, if you were not on the last row before the loop began, the comma would be appended to the variable @chvPrint and printed (lines 100 and 101). If you were on the last row, the second

FETCH would put you past the end, and lines 105 and 106 would execute, simply printing the last item with no comma and breaking from the loop.

Generating the Variable Declarations

This first cursor is closed on line 111 and opened for a second run in lines 117 through 132 to generate most of the declared variables (shown in Listing 7.13). Why isn't the second loop through the data concerned with the final comma? You are appending additional DECLAREs to the end, so the comma has to be on all the generated rows and the PRINT statement can take care of the final comma's lack of appearance (line 136).

Listing 7.13. The DECLARE statement section results.

```
DECLARE
        @stor_id2                  char(4) NOT NULL,
        @ord_num2                  varchar(20) NOT NULL,
        @ord_date2                 datetime NOT NULL,
        @qty2                      smallint NOT NULL,
        @payterms2                 varchar(12) NOT NULL,
        @title_id2                 varchar(6) NOT NULL,
        @intReturnVal              int,
        @chvMessage                varchar(255),
        @inyCount                  tinyint
```

Creating the SELECT Statement

The cursor is used for a third time in lines 141 through 166. Using the same mechanism as the first instance of this cursor, it creates the column list portion of the SELECT statement that retrieves the current values based on the key field in @chvKey. Once again, the comma is left off the last item printed. Listing 7.14 shows the final results of lines 141 through 172. Lines 167 through 172 add the FROM and WHERE clause portions.

Listing 7.14. The SELECT statement section results.

```
SELECT
        @stor_id2 = stor_id,
        @ord_num2 = ord_num,
        @ord_date2 = ord_date,
        @qty2 = qty,
        @payterms2 = payterms,
        @title_id2 = title_id
FROM    sales
WHERE   ord_num = @ord_num
```

Second Cursor, Only Use

After lines 173 through 188 add some error-trapping code in the results, lines 189 through 228 add the bulk of the code in the results. Using the datatype category from the second cursor, it generates the appropriate check to see if the existing data has changed. If the field is not nullable, it prints a simple check (the second part of Listing 7.15). If the field is nullable, it creates a check using the COALESCE function and the appropriate default data for the column's datatype. Since the notes column is of varchar datatype, it uses a default of ' '. However, because orig_price is of money datatype, it uses a default of 0.

Listing 7.15. A portion of the results from the second cursor.

```
IF COALESCE(@notes2, '') <> COALESCE(@notes, '')
BEGIN
        SELECT @inyCount = @inyCount + 1
        UPDATE titles SET notes = @notes
        WHERE title_id = @title_id
END

IF @pubdate2 <> @pubdate
BEGIN
        SELECT @inyCount = @inyCount + 1
        UPDATE titles SET pubdate = @pubdate
        WHERE title_id = @title_id
END

IF COALESCE(@orig_price2, 0) <> COALESCE(@orig_price, 0)
BEGIN
        SELECT @inyCount = @inyCount + 1
        UPDATE titles SET orig_price = @orig_price
        WHERE title_id = @title_id
END
```

Cleaning Up

The remaining lines of code destroy the cursors, print some final code in the Results pane, and turn the Nocount setting back to its start value of off.

There you have it. All in all, this procedure should be digestible. There are some complicated constructs in the procedure, but nothing that you cannot figure out or learn by examining in detail. Use this as an example or even as part of other procedures that you need or want to create. Take a good look at the system stored procedures in the master database. You find lots of great code from which you can learn quite a lot.

Using Cursors to Modify Data

Now take a deep breath. You have just absorbed a lot of information. This last section covers the concept of modifying data based on the cursor position. First, you see how to update and delete rows via a cursor. You then examine a procedure that randomly selects a title and reduces its price by 50 percent—something your standard UPDATE statement cannot do.

A Cursor Cannot UPDATE or DELETE (By Itself)

A cursor does not actually update or delete row data on its own. Rather, it is used in conjunction with an UPDATE or DELETE statement to get the job done. The WHERE clause of either statement can contain the phrase Where Current Of and the name of the cursor. Look at the following example in Listing 7.16:

Listing 7.16. Deleting an author via a cursor.

```
DECLARE crAuthors SCROLL CURSOR FOR
        SELECT    *
        FROM      authors
        FOR UPDATE

OPEN crAuthors

FETCH NEXT FROM crAuthors
FETCH NEXT FROM crAuthors
FETCH NEXT FROM crAuthors
FETCH NEXT FROM crAuthors
FETCH NEXT FROM crAuthors
FETCH NEXT FROM crAuthors

BEGIN TRAN --Start transaction

DELETE authors WHERE CURRENT OF crAuthors

ROLLBACK TRAN --Undo the delete so we don't have to re-add the row

CLOSE crAuthors

DEALLOCATE crAuthors
```

After opening the cursor, you fetch six consecutive rows (this particular row won't break any referential integrity rules) and then delete the row using the DELETE statement and the Where Current Of clause. The cursor provides the position; the DELETE provides the action.

Advanced Updating Using a Cursor

This last code example alters the titles table and creates a stored procedure to randomly change one title's price to be 50 percent of its original value. The additional column is used to store the original price, and the procedure resets all entries before choosing a new title to reduce in price. Seems like a simple task, and with this procedure it is. This could not be done, however, with a conventional T-SQL UPDATE statement. Once again, look through the code in Listing 7.17.

Listing 7.17. Randomly selecting a title to update.

```
 1: ALTER TABLE titles
 2: ADD orig_price money NULL
 3:
 4: GO
 5:
 6: CREATE PROC prHalfPriceTitle
 7: AS
 8:
 9: DECLARE    @intCount int,
10:            @intRow int,
11:            @chvDiscard varchar(6),
12:            @chvPrint varchar(255)
13:
14: BEGIN TRAN
15:
16: SELECT @intCount = COUNT(*) FROM titles (holdlock)
17: WHERE  orig_price IS NULL AND price IS NOT NULL
18: SELECT @intRow = CONVERT(int, RAND() * @intCount) + 1
19:
20: DECLARE crTitles SCROLL CURSOR FOR
21: SELECT title_id FROM TITLES
22: WHERE  orig_price IS NULL and price IS NOT NULL
23:
24: OPEN crTitles
25:
26: FETCH ABSOLUTE @intRow FROM crTitles INTO @chvDiscard
27:
28: IF @@fetch_status >=0
29: BEGIN
30:         UPDATE titles SET price = orig_price WHERE orig_price IS NOT NULL
31:         UPDATE titles SET orig_price = NULL WHERE orig_price IS NOT NULL
32:         UPDATE titles SET orig_price = price WHERE CURRENT OF crTitles
33:         UPDATE titles SET price = price * .5 WHERE CURRENT OF crTitles
34: END
35: ELSE
36:         PRINT 'No titles to update.'
37:
38: CLOSE crTitles
39: DEALLOCATE crTitles
40:
41: SELECT     title_id,
42:            price,
43:            orig_price,
44:            title
45: FROM       titles
46: WHERE      orig_price IS NOT NULL
47:
48: COMMIT TRAN
49:
50: GO
```

Lines 1 through 5 perform the alter to the `titles` table and add the `orig_price` column for storing the original price of the discounted book. Lines 6 through 13 take care of the procedure creation and variable declarations. Line 14 starts a transaction, and it is completed on line 48. Why have a transaction at all? You are going to find the current number of titles and use that value to pick one at random. If titles are added or deleted after the count is taken, but before the discount is applied, you may get an error (choosing a book that doesn't exist) or not give a new title a chance for discount.

The key to making a shared table lock stick around while you make your discount changes is in lines 16 and 17, which also returns the count. The holdlock optimizer hint directs SQL Server to hold the lock for the duration of the transaction. Everyone will be able to read the `titles` table data, but only you can update it now.

Line 18 generates a random number from 1 to the number of titles. Lines 20 through 22 define the scrollable cursor, which you use to choose the row to be updated. Lines 16, 17, and 22 use a condition where `orig_price` contains a `NULL` value and price does not contain a `NULL` value. This prevents books with a `NULL` price from being updated—50 percent of `NULL` is `NULL`—no need to try changing a `NULL` price.

Lines 24 through 38 use the cursor to pick the row to be updated. The random value is used in conjunction with the `FETCH ABSOLUTE` statement to move to the randomly selected row. As long as your `@@fetch_status` is not -1 or -2, you perform four updates.

The first update resets all prices to their original value. The second sets every row's `orig_price` value to `NULL`. The third stores the value in the `price` column of the current cursor row into the `orig_price` column. The fourth sets the price of the current cursor row to 50 percent of its value.

Line 39 destroys the cursor—you have no further need for it. Lines 41 through 46 select the changed row back to the client. Finally, lines 48 through 50 commit the transaction and end the procedure.

Summary

You have seen some simple and some very complicated uses of cursors. Cursors can definitely make life easier in regard to tasks that are repetitive or normally impossible within T-SQL. Try to experiment with them, for it is the only way to know what really can be done. In addition, get familiar with the `system` tables. They hold a lot of very useful information. Listing 7.11 relies entirely on them.

7

EMPLOYING CURSORS

Advanced String Manipulation and Bitwise Operators

CHAPTER 8

IN THIS CHAPTER

In conjunction with stored procedures, character string functions provide unlimited possibilities for manipulating alphanumeric data. Chapter 5, "Effective Use of Built-in Functions," provides several examples of combining character string functions as well as a function summary. You may look to Chapter 6, "Effective Use of Stored Procedures as an Administrative Tool," to see examples of how to reverse a name, extract the decimal portion of a real number, and change the case of a sentence to proper case. SQL Server also allows the use of bitwise operators. Using bitwise operators instead of regular operators improves the database's performance. This chapter discusses:

- Advanced string manipulation to spell currency
- Binary operators
- Comparing values with bitwise operators
- EBCDIC conversion with binary operators

Advanced String Manipulation to Spell Currency

When you write a check or draft, you normally spell out the currency in the amount space. Most databases do not come with a built-in function to do this, with the notable exception of Dataease. However, each database supports the ability to create a series of functions or stored procedures to accomplish this task. To create this process with SQL Server, the values are broken down into components. The first main component was spelling single digits, and the next component was to spell the tens column. Listing 8.1 is the stored procedure that creates the single digits.

Listing 8.1. Spelling single digits.

```
DROP PROC pr_single
GO
CREATE PROC pr_single @chrDigit CHAR(1), @chrSd VARCHAR(6) OUTPUT
AS
IF @chrDigit = '1'
    BEGIN
        SELECT @chrSd = "One"
    RETURN
    END
ELSE
IF @chrDigit = '2'
    BEGIN
        SELECT @chrSd = "Two"
    RETURN
    END
ELSE
IF @chrDigit = '3'
    BEGIN
```

```
                SELECT @chrSd = "Three"
         RETURN
         END
ELSE
IF @chrDigit = '4'
      BEGIN
                SELECT @chrSd = "Four"
         RETURN
         END
ELSE
IF @chrDigit = '5'
      BEGIN
                SELECT @chrSd = "Five"
         RETURN
         END
ELSE
IF @chrDigit = '6'
      BEGIN
                SELECT @chrSd = "Six"
         RETURN
         END
ELSE
IF @chrDigit = '7'
      BEGIN
                SELECT @chrSd = "Seven"
         RETURN
         END
ELSE
IF @chrDigit = '8'
      BEGIN
                SELECT @chrSd = "Eight"
         RETURN
         END
ELSE
IF @chrDigit = '9'
      BEGIN
                SELECT @chrSd = "Nine"
         RETURN
         END
ELSE
      SELECT @chrSd = ""
```

This stored procedure receives one character, which was converted to a character string before passing, and then returns a converted string number. This stored procedure works for the ones place and the hundreds place of any number. However, the pr_SpellCur (spell currency) stored procedure is limited to numbers of up to 999,000,000,000 dollars, which can easily be altered to an even higher number. This stored procedure simply tests for the values 0 through 9. When a match is made, @chrSd is assigned the appropriate string value, which is returned to the calling stored procedure.

> **TIP**
>
> When using nested IF statements, you should consider adding a RETURN statement when the appropriate match has been made. This keeps SQL Server from having to execute all of the IF statements.

The next stored procedure, in Listing 8.2, handles the tens column.

Listing 8.2. Spelling the tens column.

```
DROP PROC pr_twonum
GO
CREATE PROC pr_twonum @chrDigit CHAR(2), @chvDD VARCHAR(10) OUTPUT
AS
IF SUBSTRING(@chrDigit,1,1) = '1'
    BEGIN
     IF @chrDigit = '10'
         BEGIN
             SELECT @chvDD = "Ten"
             RETURN
         END
    ELSE
    IF @chrDigit = '11'
         BEGIN
             SELECT @chvDD = "Eleven"
           RETURN
     END
    ELSE
    IF @chrDigit = '12'
         BEGIN
             SELECT @chvDD = "Twelve"
           RETURN
     END
    ELSE
    IF @chrDigit = '13'
         BEGIN
             SELECT @chvDD = "Thirteen"
           RETURN
     END
    ELSE
    IF @chrDigit = '14'
         BEGIN
             SELECT @chvDD = "Fourteen"
           RETURN
     END
    ELSE
    IF @chrDigit = '15'
         BEGIN
             SELECT @chvDD = "Fifteen"
           RETURN
     END
    ELSE
    IF @chrDigit = '16'
```

```
            BEGIN
                SELECT @chvDD = "Sixteen"
            RETURN
      END
      ELSE
      IF @chrDigit = '17'
            BEGIN
                SELECT @chvDD = "Seventeen"
            RETURN
      END
      ELSE
      IF @chrDigit = '18'
            BEGIN
                SELECT @chvDD = "Eighteen"
            RETURN
      END
      ELSE
      IF @chrDigit = '19'
            BEGIN
                SELECT @chvDD = "Nineteen"
            RETURN
      END
END

IF SUBSTRING(@chrDigit,1,1) = '2'
      BEGIN
            SELECT @chvDD = "Twenty"
            RETURN
      END
ELSE
IF SUBSTRING(@chrDigit,1,1) = '3'
      BEGIN
            SELECT @chvDD = "Thirty"
       RETURN
      END
ELSE
IF SUBSTRING(@chrDigit,1,1) = '4'
      BEGIN
            SELECT @chvDD = "Forty"
            RETURN
      END
ELSE
IF SUBSTRING(@chrDigit,1,1) = '5'
      BEGIN
            SELECT @chvDD = "Fifty"
            RETURN
      END
ELSE
IF SUBSTRING(@chrDigit,1,1) = '6'
      BEGIN
            SELECT @chvDD = "Sixty"
            RETURN
      END
ELSE
IF SUBSTRING(@chrDigit,1,1) = '7'
```

8

STRINGS/BITWISE
OPERATORS

continues

Listing 8.2. continued

```
        BEGIN
                SELECT @chvDD = "Seventy"
                RETURN
        END
ELSE
IF SUBSTRING(@chrDigit,1,1) = '8'
        BEGIN
                SELECT @chvDD = "Eighty"
                RETURN
        END
ELSE
IF SUBSTRING(@chrDigit,1,1) = '9'
        BEGIN
                SELECT @chvDD = "Ninety"
                RETURN
        END
ELSE
        SELECT @chvDD = ""
```

This stored procedure accepts two values and outputs the converted character string to the calling stored procedure. Because the teen values require different handling, you need two characters if the tens place has a value of 1. The first check uses the SUBSTRING function to determine whether the first character is a value of 1. If the value of the first character is 1, the teen value is returned. If the value is not 1, then the procedure returns the appropriate tens place value. The procedure that puts the conversion together is the pr_SpellCur procedure, shown in Listing 8.3.

Listing 8.3. The spell currency stored procedure.

```
DROP PROC pr_SpellCur
GO
CREATE PROC pr_SpellCur @mnyMonCon MONEY
        AS
DECLARE @intHoldlen INTEGER
DECLARE @chvDollout VARCHAR(255)
DECLARE @intCountdown INTEGER
DECLARE @@intRemLen INTEGER
DECLARE @intPosition INTEGER
DECLARE @chvHoldCHAR VARCHAR(100)
DECLARE @chvCompare VARCHAR(2)
DECLARE @chrWordChk CHAR(1)
DECLARE @chrCents CHAR(2)
SELECT @intHoldlen = CONVERT(INTEGER,DATALENGTH(LTRIM(STR(FLOOR(@mnyMonCon)))))
SELECT @chvHoldChar = LTRIM(STR(FLOOR(@mnyMonCon)))
SELECT @@intRemLen = @chvHoldlen
SELECT @chrCents = LTRIM(STR((@mnyMonCon-floor(@mnyMonCon))* 100))


WHILE @@intRemLen != 0
BEGIN

IF @chvHoldlen = 1 AND @chvHoldChar = '0'
        SELECT @chvDollout = @chvDollout + "Zero"
```

```
IF @@intRemLen % 3 = 0
    SELECT @intCountdown = 3
    IF SUBSTRING(@chvHoldCHAR,@chvHoldlen-@intRemLen+1,3) != "000"
        SELECT @chrWordChk = "Y"
    ELSE
        SELECT @chrWordChk = "N"
IF @@intRemLen % 3 = 1
    BEGIN
        SELECT @intCountdown = 1
        SELECT @chrWordChk = "Y"
    END
IF @@intRemLen % 3 = 2
    BEGIN
        SELECT @intCountdown = 2
        SELECT @chrWordChk = "Y"
    END

WHILE @intCountdown != 0
BEGIN
    DECLARE @chvSpellIt VARCHAR(10)
    SELECT @@intRemLen = @@intRemLen - 1
    SELECT @intPosition = @chvHoldlen - @intRemLen

    IF @intCountdown = 3
        BEGIN
            SELECT @chvCompare = SUBSTRING(@chvHoldCHAR,@intPosition,1)
            EXEC pr_single @chvCompare,@chvSpellIt OUTPUT
            IF SUBSTRING(@chvHoldChar,@intPosition,1) != '0'
            SELECT @chvDollout = @chvDollout + @chvSpellIt + " Hundred"
            SELECT @chvDollout = RTRIM(@chvDollout) + " "
        END
    IF @intCountdown = 2
        BEGIN
            SELECT @chvCompare = SUBSTRING(@chvHoldChar,@intPosition,2)
            EXEC pr_twonum @chvCompare,@chvSpellIt OUTPUT
            SELECT @chvDollout = @chvDollout + @chvSpellIt
            SELECT @chvDollout = RTRIM(@chvDollout) + " "
        END

    IF @intCountdown = 1 AND ((@intPosition != 1 AND SUBSTRING(@chvHoldChar,
        (@intPosition-1),1) != '1') OR @intPosition = 1)
        BEGIN
            SELECT @chvCompare = SUBSTRING(@chvHoldChar,@intPosition,1)
            EXEC pr_single @chvCompare,@chvSpellIt OUTPUT
            SELECT @chvDollout = @chvDollout + @chvSpellIt
            SELECT @chvDollout = RTRIM(@chvDollout) + " "
        END
    IF @@intRemLen = 9 AND @chrWordChk = "Y"
        SELECT @chvDollout = @chvDollout + "Billion "

    IF @@intRemLen = 6 AND @chrWordChk = "Y"
        SELECT @chvDollout = @chvDollout + "Million "

    IF @@intRemLen = 3 AND @chrWordChk = "Y"
        SELECT @chvDollout = @chvDollout + "Thousand "
```

8

STRINGS/BITWISE
OPERATORS

continues

Listing 8.3. continued

```
    IF @@intRemLen = 0
        SELECT @chvDollout = @chvDollout + "Dollars "
        SELECT @intCountdown = @intCountdown - 1
    END
END

SELECT @chvDollout = RTRIM(@chvDollout) + " And " + RTRIM(@chrCents) + " Cents"
PRINT @chvDollout
```

The hardest part of this stored procedure is accounting for spaces between the spelling of numbers. If you have a value of 100, you cannot add an automatic space for tens and ones, because you have two extra spaces in the spelling of the currency. To account for this, as well as the other placeholders, several variables are declared; those variables are summarized in Table 8.1.

Table 8.1. Variables used in the spell currency stored procedure.

Operator	Description
@mnyMonCon	Input parameter passed when calling the stored procedure. This holds the monetary value you'll convert to a spelled character string.
@chvHoldlen	Holds the total length of the number being converted, excluding the decimal portion. A number, 1234.56, would store a value of 4.
@@intRemLen	Holds the remaining length to be converted. As the numbers are converted from left to right, this variable retains the remaining length to convert.
@chvDollout	Holds the character string of the converted monetary amount.
@intCountdown	The process breaks the integer portion of the monetary number into groups of three digits, if available. @intCountdown is assigned the value if the length MOD 3 has a remainder other than 0; otherwise, @intCountdown is assigned a value of 3. This value then tracks the location of the hundreds, tens, and ones place when converting numbers into words.
@intPosition	Stores the position for the location in the integer portion of the monetary value. Calculated by taking @chvHoldlen - @intRemLen; used as a parameter with the SUBSTRING function to extract one or more characters.
@chvHoldChar	Stores integer portion of the monetary value to convert.
@chvCompare	Stores one or two characters, which are passed to the stored procedures to calculate hundreds, tens, and ones places.
@chrWordChk	Variable used to let the procedure know when to add the suffix, such as billion, million, and so on.
@chrCents	Stores the decimal part of the monetary value.

After the variables are declared, the procedure assigns values to several of these variables. The @chvHoldlen variable is assigned the total length by taking the FLOOR value, converting it to a character value with the STR function, then using the LTRIM function to remove leading spaces. It then uses the DATALENGTH function to return the total length and uses the CONVERT function to convert the length of the string to an integer value.

As you can see, this makes use of several functions to manipulate one character string. You need to use FLOOR, because STR rounds up if the cents portion is over 50 cents. LTRIM is necessary to remove leading spaces, since these are not valid parts of the monetary value. Finally, the CONVERT function is used to convert the returned value of DATALENGTH, which is not an integer value, into an integer value. The @chvHoldChar variable stores the integer portion of the monetary value using the same process of extraction, with the exception of using CONVERT and DATALENGTH. @@intRemLen is set equal to the value of @chvHoldlen. Both values are needed to locate the position in the conversion process to extract the required characters. The @chrCents variable stores the cents by taking the monetary value minus the FLOOR of the monetary value (which is now an integer) and calculates the cents. This value is multiplied by 100 to change the decimal value to a whole number, and the STR function then converts the integer values to characters. Finally, LTRIM finishes cleaning up the data by removing leading spaces.

At this point, you know that the total length of the integer portion, the character value of the integer value, and the decimal portion are all stored. You are now ready to begin the conversion process. A WHILE loop controls converting the integer portion by checking that the value of @@intRemLen is not equal to zero. This means that you have not yet converted all the numbers into words. Since a monetary value of 0.56 cents will catch the zero portion, the procedure checks for this occurrence and stores the word Zero (for zero dollars) to the output string @chvDollout.

To determine the remainder, the procedure takes the MOD of the remaining length and divides it by three. For modularity purposes, this procedure breaks the monetary value up into groups of threes to hold the hundreds, tens, and ones places. Any remainder other than zero is always the first one or two digits when the number does not have a hundreds or even a tens place. This remainder value is assigned to the @intCountdown variable to both extract this block of character(s) and to track the location within this block. One extra check (to see if the value is 000) with this remainder process occurs if there are characters in all three positions. If this case does occur, the @chrWordChk value is assigned a value of N, and the suffix does not print. If this check is not done, a value of 1000000, would yield an error string of "one million thousand dollars".

The second WHILE loop tracks the value of @intCountdown and continues until this value reaches 0. The remaining length is decremented by 1. The @intPosition variable is then calculated by taking the total length minus the remaining length. A local variable @chvSpellIt is declared to store the results when calling the stored procedures pr_single or pr_twonum. The result (@chvSpellIt) is concatenated to the @chvDollout variable. Three comparisons are made in this loop to check for a value of 1, 2, or 3 with the @intCountdown variable. If this value is 3, this indicates a value in the hundreds place and calls the stored procedure pr_single. To pass the single character parameter required, SUBSTRING is used to extract the single character within the @chvHoldChar variable. The output, as long as this value is not 0, is concatenated to the @chvDollout variable including the suffix hundred. The @chvDollout value has any undesirable trailing spaces removed by using RTRIM on the @chvDollout variable.

When @intCountdown has a value of 2, two characters are extracted. This is necessary to return the spelling of any teen values. Thus, if 17 is passed, the procedure returns 17 instead of the word Ten. All values greater than 1 return the corresponding tens value such as twenty, thirty, and so on. When @intCountdown is 1, the procedure makes sure the tens place did not have a value of 1. If it did, there is no need to call the stored procedure pr_single, since the ones place has already been accounted. If the value can be converted, it follows the same procedure as the hundreds and tens place and concatenates the spelled words to the @chvDollout variable.

After the inner WHILE loop has completed, the procedure now checks to see if a suffix such as billion, million, or the like is required. If the @chrWordChk value is set to Y and the remaining length is 9, 6, or 3, the appropriate suffix of Billion, Million, or Thousand is added. It is at this point that you could add a check for 12 or 15, and add the appropriate suffix for numbers larger than 999,000,000,000 dollars. If the remaining length is zero, the word Dollars is appended to the @chvDollout variable and the outer WHILE loop exits. The decimal part, along with the word Cents, is now appended to the @chvDollout variable and this value is output to the screen. You could also return this value if you need to store it in a table (or for any other purpose). While this currency-spelling project could be done many different ways, it does demonstrate that you can combine functions seamlessly. It also demonstrates how you can use the functions in solving a business problem and how you can put them to use right away in your business.

Using the Procedure to Spell Currency

Before you can test this process, execute the code in Listing 8.4 to create a table and insert some data.

Listing 8.4. Creating test data for the spell currency procedure.

```
DROP TABLE tim
    GO
CREATE TABLE tim (
    SPELL   money)
    GO

INSERT INTO tim (Spell) VALUES (123.22)
INSERT INTO tim (Spell) VALUES (1234.22)
INSERT INTO tim (Spell) VALUES (12345.22)
INSERT INTO tim (Spell) VALUES (123456.22)
INSERT INTO tim (Spell) VALUES (1234567.22)
INSERT INTO tim (Spell) VALUES (12345678.22)
INSERT INTO tim (Spell) VALUES (123456789.22)
```

```
INSERT INTO tim (Spell) VALUES (1234567890.22)
INSERT INTO tim (Spell) VALUES (1000000000.22)
INSERT INTO tim (Spell) VALUES (0.22)
```

After you have created the table and data, execute the code in Listing 8.5 to test the process to see if it will spell the currency.

Listing 8.5. Testing the spell currency procedure.

```
DECLARE @mnyHoldID MONEY
-- Holds the dollar amount for money

-- Declare a cursor for the money values
DECLARE cuMoney CURSOR
FOR
SELECT SPELL FROM tim

OPEN cuMoney
FETCH NEXT FROM cuMoney into @mnyHoldID
-- Retrieves first row
WHILE @@FETCH_STATUS = 0 BEGIN
    EXEC pr_SpellCur @mnyHoldID
-- Calls procedure spell currency
    FETCH NEXT FROM cuMoney into @mnyHoldID
END
CLOSE cuMoney
DEALLOCATE cuMoney
```

This batch process uses cursors to fetch one row at a time and then calls the pr_SpellCur procedure to output the data in words instead of numbers. Your output should look like the following:

```
One Hundred Twenty Three Dollars And 22 Cents
One Thousand Two Hundred Thirty Four Dollars And 22 Cents
Twelve Thousand Three Hundred Forty Five Dollars And 22 Cents
One Hundred Twenty Three Thousand Four Hundred Fifty Six Dollars And 22 Cents
One Million Two Hundred Thirty Four Thousand Five Hundred Sixty Seven Dollars
And 22 Cents
Twelve Million Three Hundred Forty Five Thousand Six Hundred Seventy Eight
Dollars And 22 Cents
One Hundred Twenty Three Million Four Hundred Fifty Six Thousand
Seven Hundred Eighty Nine Dollars And 22 Cents
One Billion Two Hundred Thirty Four Million Five Hundred Sixty Seven Thousand
Eight Hundred Ninety Dollars And 22 Cents
One Billion Dollars And 22 Cents
Zero Dollars And 22 Cents
```

You can continue to add data to the table to test the procedure or incorporate this process into your current business needs. The final code in Listing 8.6 adds the capability to output the spelled currency and pass it back to the calling process, rather than just display the words to the screen.

Listing 8.6. Passing spelled currency as a parameter.

```
DROP PROC pr_SpellCur
GO
CREATE PROC pr_SpellCur @mnyMonCon money, @chvDollout VARCHAR(255) OUTPUT
    AS
DECLARE @chvHoldlen INTEGER
DECLARE @intCountdown INTEGER
DECLARE @@intRemLen INTEGER
DECLARE @intPosition INTEGER
DECLARE @chvHoldChar VARCHAR(100)
DECLARE @chvCompare VARCHAR(2)
DECLARE @chrWordChk CHAR(1)
DECLARE @chrCents CHAR(2)
SELECT @chvHoldlen = CONVERT(integer,DATALENGTH(LTRIM(STR(FLOOR(@mnyMonCon)))))
SELECT @chvHoldCHAR = LTRIM(STR(FLOOR(@mnyMonCon)))
SELECT @@intRemLen = @chvHoldlen
SELECT @chrCents = LTRIM(STR((@mnyMonCon-floor(@mnyMonCon))* 100))


WHILE @@intRemLen != 0
BEGIN

IF @chvHoldlen = 1 AND @chvHoldChar = '0'
    SELECT @chvDollout = @chvDollout + "Zero"

IF @@intRemLen % 3 = 0
    SELECT @intCountdown = 3
    IF SUBSTRING(@chvHoldChar,@chvHoldlen-@intRemLen+1,3) != "000"
        SELECT @chrWordChk = "Y"
    ELSE
        SELECT @chrWordChk = "N"
IF @@intRemLen % 3 = 1
    BEGIN
        SELECT @intCountdown = 1
        SELECT @chrWordChk = "Y"
    END
IF @@intRemLen % 3 = 2
    BEGIN
        SELECT @intCountdown = 2
        SELECT @chrWordChk = "Y"
    END

WHILE @intCountdown != 0
BEGIN
    DECLARE @chvSpellIt VARCHAR(10)
    SELECT @@intRemLen = @@intRemLen - 1
    SELECT @intPosition = @chvHoldlen - @intRemLen

    IF @intCountdown = 3
        BEGIN
            SELECT @chvCompare = SUBSTRING(@chvHoldCHAR,@intPosition,1)
            EXEC pr_single @chvCompare,@chvSpellIt OUTPUT
            IF SUBSTRING(@chvHoldCHAR,@intPosition,1) != '0'
            SELECT @chvDollout = @chvDollout + @chvSpellIt + " Hundred"
            SELECT @chvDollout = RTRIM(@chvDollout) + " "
        END
    IF @intCountdown = 2
        BEGIN
            SELECT @chvCompare = SUBSTRING(@chvHoldCHAR,@intPosition,2)
            EXEC pr_twonum @chvCompare,@chvSpellIt OUTPUT
```

```
            SELECT @chvDollout = @chvDollout + @chvSpellIt
            SELECT @chvDollout = RTRIM(@chvDollout) + " "
        END

    IF @intCountdown = 1 AND ((@intPosition != 1 AND SUBSTRING(@chvHoldCHAR,
        (@intPosition-1),1) != '1') OR @intPosition = 1)
        BEGIN
            SELECT @chvCompare = SUBSTRING(@chvHoldCHAR,@intPosition,1)
            EXEC pr_single @chvCompare,@chvSpellIt OUTPUT
            SELECT @chvDollout = @chvDollout + @chvSpellIt
            SELECT @chvDollout = RTRIM(@chvDollout) + " "
        END
    IF @@intRemLen = 9 AND @chrWordChk = "Y"
        SELECT @chvDollout = @chvDollout + "Billion "

    IF @@intRemLen = 6 AND @chrWordChk = "Y"
        SELECT @chvDollout = @chvDollout + "Million "

    IF @@intRemLen = 3 AND @chrWordChk = "Y"
        SELECT @chvDollout = @chvDollout + "Thousand "

    IF @@intRemLen = 0
        SELECT @chvDollout = @chvDollout + "Dollars "
        SELECT @intCountdown = @intCountdown - 1
    END
END

SELECT @chvDollout = @chvDollout + "And " + @chrCents + " Cents"
```

The only difference here is the addition of @chvDollout as an OUTPUT parameter. When calling this procedure, you need to add a second parameter to store the output. The following code provides a demonstration on how to call the stored procedure with parameters:

```
DECLARE @chvSpellIt VARCHAR(255)
EXEC pr_SpellCur 1100111553.66,@chvSpellIt OUTPUT
PRINT @chvSpellIt
```

Binary Operators

The four binary operators, which work on integer or binary datatypes only, are summarized in Table 8.2. Speed is the main advantage of using binary operators, since you are now talking in the native language of the computer. In addition, you can use bitwise operators to convert binary or compressed data.

NOTE

When using binary operators, it is important to remember the order of operations. In this case, the bitwise operators are below the arithmetic operators such as + and -. If you want to add a value after the binary operation takes place, you need to add the appropriate parentheses, such as (8 & 1) + 100. Forgetting the order of operations could result in corrupt data or reports.

Table 8.2. Binary operators.

Operator	Description
&	Bitwise, logical AND
¦	Bitwise, logical OR
^	Bitwise, logical EXCLUSIVE OR
~	Bitwise NOT

These operators work on a bit-level basis. Each bit is compared against the next. Each return bit result depends upon the bitwise operator.

Bitwise AND

The results of bitwise AND (&) follow:

```
1 & 1 = 1
1 & 0 = 0
0 & 0 = 0
0 & 1 = 0
```

Bitwise OR

The results of bitwise OR (¦) follow:

```
1 ¦ 1 = 1
1 ¦ 0 = 1
0 ¦ 0 = 0
0 ¦ 1 = 1
```

Bitwise EXCLUSIVE OR

The results of bitwise EXCLUSIVE OR (^) follow:

```
1 ^ 1 = 0
1 ^ 0 = 1
0 ^ 0 = 0
0 ^ 1 = 1
```

Bitwise NOT

The result of bitwise NOT (~) returns the opposite bit stream. For example, ~00001111 returns 11110000.

Comparing Values with Bitwise Operators

In any database language, users are allowed to enter data, whether it is from a menu or a data-entry screen. The first example, in Listing 8.7, selects numeric values from a menu and shows how you can use bitwise operators to evaluate the data.

Listing 8.7. Testing numeric values with bitwise operators.

```
DROP PROC pr_bitwise
     GO
CREATE PROC pr_bitwise
     AS
DECLARE @chvHold INTEGER
SELECT @chvHold = 2
IF ( @chvHold & 1) = 1
     BEGIN
         PRINT 'One Selected'
         RETURN
     END
IF ( @chvHold & 2) = 2
     BEGIN
         PRINT 'Two Selected'
         RETURN
     END

IF ( @chvHold & 3) = 3
     BEGIN
         PRINT 'Three Selected'
         RETURN
     END

IF ( @chvHold & 4) = 4
     BEGIN
         PRINT 'Four Selected'
         RETURN
     END
```

8

STRINGS/BITWISE
OPERATORS

Notice that the @chvHold variable has been hard coded to a value of 2. You could simply change this to a parameter for your own use. The decimal values are converted implicitly to binary values and compared with the & operator. If a match occurs, it prints out the option selected. Execute the following code to test this stored procedure:

```
EXEC pr_bitwise
```

Your output should look like the following:

```
Two Selected
```

This same process is tested for alphanumeric choices. Execute the code in Listing 8.8.

Listing 8.8. Testing alphanumeric values with bitwise operators.

```
DROP PROC pr_bitalpha
     GO
CREATE PROC pr_bitalpha
     AS
DECLARE @chvHold INTEGER
SELECT @chvHold = ASCII('A')
IF ( @chvHold & 65) = 65
    BEGIN
        PRINT 'A Selected'
        RETURN
    END
IF ( @chvHold & 66) = 66
    BEGIN
        PRINT 'B Selected'
        RETURN
    END

IF ( @chvHold & 67) = 67
    BEGIN
        PRINT 'C Selected'
        RETURN
    END

IF ( @chvHold & 68) = 68
    BEGIN
        PRINT 'D Selected'
        RETURN
    END
```

The only difference here is that the character value needs to be converted to decimal for the binary operation to take place. The CONVERT function only converts characters 0–9, and no implicit conversion takes place in this database package. The only means is to use the ASCII function to return the ASCII value and compare this decimal result to see if a match exists. Execute the following code to test this process:

```
EXEC pr_bitalpha
```

Your output should look like the following:

```
A Selected
```

The value A is selected because it was hard-coded, but again, you could easily pass parameters to this stored procedure. This is meant to demonstrate some of the nuances of bitwise operators. Another practical example follows with EBCDIC conversion.

EBCDIC Conversion with Binary Operators

I have worked in several small and large shops and have found ways to manipulate software packages to perform tasks never originally intended, due in part to a lack of programming tools. One case involved receiving EBCDIC data, including binary and packed fields from an IBM shop for proprietary EDI, which wasn't converted to ASCII. The source would not translate the file to ASCII, and Visual Basic was not yet implemented. If none of the fields were binary or compressed, you could easily import the binary data with SQL Server's BCP (Bulk Copy Program) and convert the EBCDIC text characters to ASCII characters with a simple translation table. However, most shops store number fields with COMP-3. This means that two numbers are stored in each byte, and the very last byte stores one number and the sign.

Since two numbers are stored in one byte, the first four bits compose one number, and the last four bits compose the second number. As you can see, 2^4 provides 16 possible values of 0 through 15, more than adequate for values of 0 through 9 to be stored in this field. To extract the two numbers, you simply declare a variable of type integer to store the value of the first byte & 11110000 and to store the first byte & 00001111. By using masking, the first number stored contains a replica of the first four bits, because 0 AND any number always produces 0. The same goes for the last four bits. To implement this, you need to know the beginning and ending locations. You can store the values in a string, concatenating each value as extracted. Then when you extract the sign, you can convert this string to an integer value, divide by 100 to add the decimal point, and then multiply by a -1 if the number is negative.

Again, this section provides you with guidelines if you want to use SQL Server to convert from EBCDIC to ASCII. The ideal method is for the source file to be translated into an ASCII comma-separated value or to use tools such as Visual C++ or Visual Basic to complete this task.

Another practical use for the bitwise operators is to evaluate bit data that is stored in tables. For example, assume that a table has four-bit columns that represent the stages of an order. Each column represents whether the order has been credit-checked, priced, shipped, and closed. You could then write a query requesting all orders that have been credit-checked or priced, but not both. Execute the T-SQL in Listing 8.9 to create a sample table that contains the columns previously listed. This listing also inserts sample data into the table.

Listing 8.9. Creating a table that stores bit data.

```
DROP TABLE tableX
GO

CREATE TABLE tableX
(
bitPriced BIT,
bitCredit_checked BIT,
bitAllocated BIT,
bitShipped BIT
)
GO

INSERT tableX (bitPriced, bitCredit_checked, bitAllocated, bitShipped)
VALUES (1,1,0,0)
INSERT tableX (bitPriced, bitCredit_checked, bitAllocated, bitShipped)
VALUES (1,0,1,0)
INSERT tableX (bitPriced, bitCredit_checked, bitAllocated, bitShipped)
VALUES (0,0,0,0)
INSERT tableX (bitPriced, bitCredit_checked, bitAllocated, bitShipped)
VALUES (1,1,1,0)
GO
```

You can test this example by selecting all orders that have been priced or allocated, but not both. Listing 8.10 uses the EXCLUSIVE OR bitwise operator to resolve the search condition.

Listing 8.10. Selecting data using bitwise operators.

```
SELECT *
FROM tableX
WHERE bitAllocated ^ bitPriced = 1
```

Using bit columns not only saves space in the database, but also makes logic much cleaner and quicker, since only the bits need to be compared. This final example of selecting orders by their stage of completion is a common business use. For example, you can also use bitwise operators to compare all survey applicants that fit a specific category of yes/no answers. As you can see, there are many uses for bitwise operators in business applications.

Summary

This chapter demonstrates various methods of combining string functions, as well as other functions, for creating a procedure to spell currency. While this procedure could spell values up to 999,000,000,000, the procedure is flexible enough to handle larger numbers. Bitwise operators are discussed and demonstrated for menu options. The CONVERT function does not convert alphabetic characters to integer values; therefore, CONVERT could not be used. Since bitwise operators require integer or binary values, the best method is to use the ASCII function to return the character's integer value and use this result with the bitwise operator. Finally, if you are importing binary data and want to convert packed fields, the only method is to use these bitwise operators.

Dynamic Execution

IN THIS CHAPTER

This chapter focuses on understanding, developing, and executing dynamic T-SQL statements. First, you'll learn what dynamic execution is and how it can help you. Then you'll learn how to create and run a dynamically executable T-SQL string and how cursors can provide more flexibility. Finally, dynamic execution is wrapped up with an outline of its pros and cons.

What Is Dynamic Execution?

Have you ever written several stored procedures that select fields from the same table using the same criteria and they only differ by the fields they select? Wouldn't it be great to replace them with one stored procedure that accepts variables to represent the selected fields? (See Chapter 6, "Effective Use of Stored Procedures as an Administrative Tool," for more information regarding stored procedures.) It might sound like a pipe dream, but with *dynamic execution* of T-SQL, this dream becomes a reality.

Dynamic execution enables you to use the same T-SQL statement to execute different queries. How do you do this? By using variables and the T-SQL EXEC (EXECUTE) statement, you can create scaleable and reusable T-SQL.

> **TIP**
>
> You can use the EXEC keyword instead of using the EXECUTE keyword to achieve the same results. I prefer to use EXEC because there is less to type.

Valid Syntax of Dynamic Execution

You might have only used the EXEC statement to invoke standard, remote, and extended stored procedures. However, the EXEC statement can unleash much more power. The EXEC statement can execute valid T-SQL statements contained within single quotation marks, a string variable, or a concatenation of both. Whether you want to run a SELECT statement or an action query, dynamic execution gives you the flexibility to use the same SQL statement for several queries. See Listing 9.1 for the syntax to execute a SQL string with the EXEC statement.

Listing 9.1. Syntax of the dynamic execution of T-SQL.

```
EXEC ({@chvTSQLString ¦ 'T-SQL String'}
[ + {@chvTSQLString ¦ 'T-SQL String'}...])
```

@chvTSQLString represents the name of a string variable. This variable can be of the VARCHAR, CHAR, or TEXT datatypes and can contain multiple strings that, when concatenated, represent a valid T-SQL statement.

> **WARNING**
>
> The TEXT datatype can be used only as a parameter to a stored procedure. Even then, it must be converted to a VARCHAR using the CONVERT function before it can be used in the EXEC statement. TEXT variables cannot be used as a local variable in a batch.

T-SQL String represents a string containing valid T-SQL statements. The string passed to the EXEC statement must be enclosed with single quotation marks. If more than one string is passed, then they must be separated by spaces and concatenated with the + operator.

Further, both types of parameters, strings enclosed within single quotation marks and string variables, can be concatenated together and passed to the EXEC statement.

> **NOTE**
>
> The argument(s) used in the EXEC string must contain character data. All numeric data must be converted either prior to using the EXEC statement or in the EXEC statement itself using the CONVERT function. In addition, any functions can be passed within the T-SQL string, on the condition that the arguments used in the EXEC string can be resolved to character data. Listing 9.18 shows frequent use of embedded functions in the sp_lockinfo system stored procedure.

Usage

When used in conjunction with a stored procedure, execution of dynamic SQL allows the stored procedure to perform a different SQL statement based upon the parameters passed to the stored procedure. For example, you can use dynamic execution to select all fields from any table in the pubs database simply by changing the value of the argument you pass in to the stored procedure. In the same manner, you can also change which fields you want to select, which criteria you want to specify, the order in which you want the result set to be returned, along with many other variations of any T-SQL statement.

Dynamic execution of T-SQL is a rarely documented feature of SQL Server used frequently by DBAs and advanced users. It does provide the flexibility to manipulate T-SQL statements, but it also comes with limitations. However, if you learn to work within its constraints, dynamic execution can prove to be a valuable tool in developing enterprise applications.

Creating the Executable String

Whether you are retrieving data from a table or writing data to the database, dynamic execution can help you get more use (or reuse) out of your T-SQL. Because dynamic execution can be used with any T-SQL statement, it is a great tool for writing database maintenance T-SQL. For example, there is no reason why you cannot change a table's schema using dynamic execution.

The next few sections explain how you can use dynamic execution with data retrieval queries, followed by creating dynamic action queries and dynamic database altering scripts. Most of the examples use stored procedures to demonstrate the usefulness of dynamic execution.

> **TIP**
>
> Consider using stored procedures to contain your dynamic T-SQL. They have the capability to accept parameters and encapsulate the T-SQL, thus making your stored procedure appear as a black box to outside calling programs.

Dynamic Selects

A simple query such as retrieving the names of the authors in the authors table can be written in T-SQL with or without the EXEC statement. To rewrite this SQL statement in an EXEC string, precede it with the EXEC keyword and enclose the T-SQL within quotation marks and parentheses. Both methods are shown in Listing 9.2.

Listing 9.2. Simple SELECT query written in two ways.

```
SELECT au_fname, au_lname FROM authors


EXEC ('SELECT au_fname, au_lname FROM authors')
```

Listing 9.2 shows how easy it is to rewrite a T-SQL statement using the EXEC statement. Both of these queries return the same set of data. You can modify this same query further to include variables for the fields. This requires that you define two variables in the batch to be used in the query and that you set the names of the au_fname and au_lname fields to these two variables, respectively. Examine Listing 9.3 to see how to code and execute this query.

Listing 9.3. Simple SELECT query written using variables for field names.

```
DECLARE @chvField1 VARCHAR(30),
        @chvField2 VARCHAR(30),
        @chvSQL VARCHAR(255)
SELECT @chvField1 = 'au_fname'
SELECT @chvField2 = 'au_lname'
SELECT @chvSQL = 'SELECT ' + @chvField1 + ', ' + @chvField2 + ' FROM authors'
EXEC (@chvSQL)
GO
```

Notice that the variable @chvSQL was set equal to a concatenation of several literal strings and variables. Dynamic execution does not limit you to using one or the other. This query retrieves the same results as the queries in Listing 9.2. However, due to the variables, this query offers more flexibility than the other queries offer. For example, by changing the values of the field name variables to phone and address, you can reuse the rest of the code to retrieve different data fields for the same table.

> **NOTE**
>
> The variables declared in Listing 9.3 were defined as VARCHAR(30) because SQL Server limits the length of field names and table names to 30 characters. This convention is used throughout this chapter. You might also notice that Listing 9.3 uses a VARCHAR(255) variable. This is the largest T-SQL length that allows for its variable.

You can use this same idea to retrieve data in different sequences. By putting a variable after the ORDER BY statement, you can specify the field that you want to order the data. The query in Listing 9.4 returns all fields in the authors table ordered by the authors' last name.

Listing 9.4. Simple SELECT query that uses a variable for the field to sequence the result set.

```
DECLARE @chvOrderBy VARCHAR(30),
        @chvSQL VARCHAR(255)
SELECT @chvOrderBy = 'au_lname'
SELECT @chvSQL = 'SELECT * FROM authors ORDER BY ' + @chvOrderBy
EXEC (@chvSQL)
GO
```

Using dynamic execution, you have the option of replacing any part of a T-SQL statement with a variable. There might be a situation where you want to retrieve all data from one table on one condition or another table on another condition. As the previous listings show, you can simply replace the dynamic part of the query with a variable. For this scenario, you replace the table name with a variable. Listing 9.5 shows a variation of this situation where the table name of a query is substituted with a variable.

Listing 9.5. SELECT query with a variable for the table name so that condition determines which table the result set is based on.

```
DECLARE @chvTable VARCHAR(30),
        @chvSQL VARCHAR(255)
IF getdate() > '7/1/1997'
SELECT @chvTable = 'sales'
ELSE
SELECT @chvTable = 'authors'

SELECT @chvSQL = 'SELECT * FROM ' + @chvTable
EXEC (@chvSQL)
GO
```

9

DYNAMIC
EXECUTION

Using Stored Procedures

After you create your dynamic T-SQL, it might be to your advantage to encapsulate the functionality inside a stored procedure. To truly reap the benefits of using dynamic execution, you might want to call the dynamic T-SQL from several different batches or programs. You cannot do this if the dynamic execution is contained within a standard batch; this is where stored procedures step in.

For example, what if you want to retrieve sales data ordered by one field in some cases and ordered by another field in other cases? Suppose further that you need to specify whether the data is sorted in ascending order or in descending order. As shown previously in Listing 9.3, it is a simple task to do this in a batch. Using a stored procedure, as shown in Listing 9.6, for this task provides a tremendous amount of flexibility at the cost of slightly more effort.

Listing 9.6. Stored procedure that returns sales data ordered by a dynamic field in either descending or ascending order.

```
CREATE PROCEDURE SalesQtys
    @chvOrderBy VARCHAR(30) = 'qty',
    @chvSortType VARCHAR(4) = 'ASC'
AS
DECLARE @chvSQL VARCHAR(255)
SELECT @chvSQL = 'SELECT stor_id, ord_num, title_id, qty'
SELECT @chvSQL = @chvSQL + ' FROM Sales'
SELECT @chvSQL = @chvSQL + ' ORDER BY ' + @chvOrderBy + ' ' + @chvSortType
EXEC (@chvSQL)
GO
```

The SalesQtys stored procedure, shown in Listing 9.6, accomplishes this task. You can now call this stored procedure, passing to it the field name to sort by and a sort type, which returns the sales data in a dynamic order. Further, stored procedures enable you to specify default values for arguments. You can call this stored procedure without passing it any arguments, thus making it appear like static T-SQL.

> **TIP**
>
> Use default values for stored procedures containing dynamic T-SQL when you can identify the most likely values you will pass to the stored procedure. This way, you will not have to pass any values for your majority cases.

You can now call the SalesQtys stored procedure from any batch or stored procedure. To return the result sets in different orders, just pass the stored procedure the appropriate values for its arguments. Listing 9.7 shows how you can call the SalesQtys stored procedure from Listing 9.6 from different batches.

Listing 9.7. Calling the `SalesQtys` stored procedure from three different batches, with different arguments.

```
SalesQtys @chvOrderBy = 'stor_id', @chvSortType = 'DESC'
GO
SalesQtys
GO
SalesQtys @chvOrderBy = 'title_id'
GO
```

The first batch in Listing 9.7 will return the sales data sorted by the store in descending order. This batch passes both values into the `SalesQtys` stored procedure, thus overriding the default values for the arguments. The second batch does not pass any arguments to the stored procedure. In this batch, the data will be returned according to the default values of the `SalesQtys` stored procedure, by ascending quantity order. The last batch uses the title for the sort column and the default sort type, ascending order.

Dynamic Deletes

Deleting data from tables is a relatively simple and common task. There might be several business rules in an application that warrant deleting rows from a table. You can create separate distinct stored procedures for each `DELETE` query or you can use dynamic execution, as shown in Listing 9.8, to create one stored procedure that can handle all these business rules.

Listing 9.8. Creating a stored procedure that removes all rows from whichever table is passed to it.

```
CREATE PROCEDURE prDeleteData
    @chvTable VARCHAR(30)
AS
DECLARE @chvSQL VARCHAR(255)
SELECT @chvSQL = 'DELETE ' + @chvTable
EXEC (@chvSQL)
GO
```

The `prDeleteData` stored procedure accepts the name of a table and creates a valid T-SQL query that removes all rows from that table. Notice that there is no default value for the table in Listing 9.8. There are two reasons for this: There might not be any one table that you most often delete from and even if there were, you would be better off specifically asking for a table to be deleted than blindly accepting a default table.

> **WARNING**
>
> Most developers have been burned once by forgetting to include a WHERE clause on their DELETE statement, thus losing all the data in that table. It needs to happen only once before you vow never again to execute a DELETE without cautious consideration.

The prDeleteData stored procedure is certainly powerful and reusable. However, most of the time you want to limit your deletions to a subset of the data in a table. For example, the News & Brews store might have closed and needs to be removed from the database. Another scenario might require you to remove the data from the sales table for those sales of less than 10 products. The prDeleteData stored procedure shown in Listing 9.9 can certainly be modified to handle both of these cases and still delete all rows, if necessary.

Listing 9.9. The prDeleteData stored procedure modified to remove data based upon criteria specified through arguments.

```
CREATE PROCEDURE prDeleteData      @chvTable VARCHAR(30),
                                   @chvWhereField VARCHAR(30) = NULL,
                                   @chvWhereFieldDataType VARCHAR(30) = 'CHAR',
                                   @chvOperator VARCHAR(2) = '=',
                                   @chvValue VARCHAR(30) = NULL
AS
DECLARE @chvSQL VARCHAR(255), @chvQuotes CHAR(1)
SELECT @chvSQL = 'DELETE ' + @chvTable
-----------------------------------------------------------------------
--If the WHERE clause field is specified, then create the WHERE clause.
--Otherwise, do not specify a WHERE clause.
-----------------------------------------------------------------------
IF NOT @chvWhereField IS NULL
        BEGIN
            SELECT @chvSQL = @chvSQL + ' WHERE ' + @chvWhereField + ' ' +
@chvOperator + ' '
            SELECT @chvWhereFieldDataType = LOWER(RTRIM(@chvWhereFieldDataType))
-----------------------------------------------------------------------
-------
            -- If the datatype requires quotation marks, then enclose it within them.
-----------------------------------------------------------------------
-------
            SELECT @chvQuotes = CASE @chvWhereFieldDataType
                    WHEN 'char' THEN 'y'
                    WHEN 'datetime' THEN 'y'
                    WHEN 'datetimn' THEN 'y'
                    WHEN 'smalldatetime' THEN 'y'
                    WHEN 'text' THEN 'y'
                    WHEN 'varchar' THEN 'y'
                    ELSE 'n'
            END
            IF @chvQuotes = 'y'
                    SELECT @chvSQL = @chvSQL + '''' + @chvValue + ''''
            ELSE
                    SELECT @chvSQL = @chvSQL + @chvValue
        END
EXEC (@chvSQL)
GO
```

> **NOTE**
>
> Keep in mind that you cannot delete data from a table if it is referenced by data from another table. If you execute the `prDeleteData` stored procedure, you might receive an error message that says `DELETE statement conflicted with COLUMN REFERENCE con-straint...`. This means that the data cannot be removed due to foreign key violations. This chapter assumes that you will design your deletes to avoid this scenario. If you want to remove data from a table and delete all the rows from other tables that reference it, then cascading delete triggers (which are discussed in Chapter 11, "Specialized Triggers") will do the trick.

You have a few options when executing the `prDeleteData` stored procedure shown in Listing 9.9. If you want to delete all data from a table, only specify the table name. If you want to delete only a subset of the data, specify the following: the table name (`@chvTable`), the field name for the criteria (`@chvWhereField`), the value to compare the field to (`@chvValue`), the datatype of the field (`@chvWhereFieldDataType`), and the operator to use for the comparison (`@chvOperator`). However, even the operator can be omitted. If you leave the operator out, it will assume that you want to check that the field and the value are equivalent. Otherwise, you can pass it whatever operator you need. Listing 9.10 shows the three options.

Listing 9.10. Three ways to call the `prDeleteData` stored procedure.

```
--Deletes all data from the stores table
prDeleteData    @chvTable = 'stores'
GO

--Deletes all 'News & Brews" stores from the stores table
prDeleteData    @chvTable = 'stores',
     @chvWhereField = 'stor_name',
     @chvWhereFieldDataType = 'CHAR',
     @chvOperator = '=',
     @chvValue = 'News & Brews'
GO

--Deletes all 'News & Brews" stores from the stores table
prDeleteData    @chvTable = 'stores',
     @chvWhereField = 'stor_name',
     @chvValue = 'News & Brews'
GO
```

The first call to `prDeleteData` in Listing 9.10 deletes all data in the stores table. The second and third calls to the `prDeleteData` stored procedure in Listing 9.10 have exactly the same effect. They both delete any rows from the stores table where the store's name is "News & Brews." The second batch explicitly specifies all the arguments to `prDeleteData`. However, because some of these arguments have default values, it is not necessary to pass values for them.

The `prDeleteData` stored procedure has a default value of = for the `@chvOperator` argument and a default value of CHAR for the `@chvWhereFieldDataType` argument. Thus, the second batch yields the same results as the third batch.

The code in Listing 9.11 shows how you can delete all sales where the quantity was fewer than 10 units. Notice how the value for the operator is passed in as <. Other possible operator values are listed in Table 9.1.

Listing 9.11. Using the `prDeleteData` stored procedure to remove all sales of fewer than 10 total items.

```
prDeleteData      @chvTable = 'sales',
      @chvWhereField = 'qty',
      @chvWhereFieldDataType = 'NUMERIC',
      @chvOperator = '<',
      @chvValue = '10'
GO
```

Table 9.1. Valid values for the `@chvOperator` argument of the `prDeleteData` stored procedure.

Operator	Description
<	Less than
>	Greater than
=	Equal to
<=	Less-than or equal to
>=	Greater-than or equal to
!= or <>	Not equal to

TIP

If you take a close look at the `prDeleteData` stored procedure in Listing 9.9, you might notice that it requires you to pass the datatype of the WHERE clause field. Otherwise, the stored procedure assumes that the datatype is a character field. `prDeleteData` uses this information to determine if the WHERE clause value needs to be enclosed in single quotation marks. If you are like me, you are probably thinking that this stored procedure should determine what the datatype of the field is without you explicitly telling it. It certainly can.

Listing 9.12 shows the stored procedure `prNeedsQuotes` that, using the table name and field name, queries the system tables sysobjects, syscolumns, and systypes to determine the datatype of a field. If the datatype requires that single quotation marks surround the field's value, `prNeedsQuotes` returns a value of y in its output argument; otherwise, it returns a value of n. This stored procedure resolves user-defined datatypes to their base datatypes, as well. For example, let's assume the field being checked was au_id in the authors table. It has a datatype of the user-defined datatype ID. Therefore, prNeedsQuotes determines the base datatype of the user-defined type ID to be VARCHAR.

The prNeedsQuotes stored procedure is quite practical. In fact, the final revised prDeleteData, shown in Listing 9.13, uses prNeedsQuotes, as do other stored procedures later in this chapter (such as Listing 9.14 and 9.17).

Listing 9.12. The prNeedsQuotes stored procedure uses system tables to determine the datatype of a field.

```
CREATE PROCEDURE prNeedsQuotes
    @chvTable VARCHAR(30),
    @chvField VARCHAR(30),
    @chvNeedsQuotes CHAR(1) OUTPUT
AS
    DECLARE @chvDataType VARCHAR(30),
        @intUserType INT

    ------------------------------------------------------------------
    --Determine the datatype of the WHERE clause field by looking in
    -- the system tables.
    ------------------------------------------------------------------
SELECT @chvDataType = LOWER(st.name), @intUserType = st.usertype
    FROM (sysObjects so INNER JOIN sysColumns sc ON so.id = sc.id)
        INNER JOIN sysTypes st ON sc.usertype = st.usertype
    WHERE so.type = 'U'
        AND so.name = @chvTable
        AND sc.name = @chvField
    ------------------------------------------------------------------
    -- If the usertype for this datatype is > 100, then it is a
    -- user defined datatype.
    -- In this case we must resolve it to its base datatype.
    ------------------------------------------------------------------
IF @intUserType > 100
        BEGIN
            SELECT @chvDataType = LOWER(st2.name)
            FROM sysTypes st1 INNER JOIN sysTypes st2 ON st1.Type = st2.Type
            WHERE st2.userType < 100
              AND st2.userType NOT IN (18, 80)
              AND st1.usertype = @intUserType
        END
    ------------------------------------------------------------------
    -- Based on the datatype, determine whether the WHERE clause field value
    -- needs to be enclosed within single quotations marks.
    ------------------------------------------------------------------
SELECT @chvNeedsQuotes =
        CASE @chvDataType
            WHEN 'char' THEN 'y'
            WHEN 'datetime' THEN 'y'
```

continues

Listing 9.12. continued

```
                WHEN 'datetimn' THEN 'y'
                WHEN 'smalldatetime' THEN 'y'
                WHEN 'text' THEN 'y'
                WHEN 'timestamp' THEN 'y'
                WHEN 'varchar' THEN 'y'
                ELSE 'n'
        END
GO
```

Listing 9.13. The final revision of the `prDeleteData` stored procedure, which uses `prNeedsQuotes` to determine whether the `WHERE` clause value needs to be enclosed in quotation marks.

```
CREATE PROCEDURE prDeleteData
    @chvTable VARCHAR(30),
    @chvWhereField VARCHAR(30) = NULL,
    @chvOperator VARCHAR(2) = '=',
    @chvWhereValue VARCHAR(30) = NULL
As

DECLARE @chvSQL VARCHAR(255),
    @chvNeedsQuotes CHAR(1)

SELECT @chvSQL = 'DELETE ' + @chvTable

------------------------------------------------------------------------
    -- If the WHERE clause field is specified, then create the WHERE clause.
    -- Otherwise, do not specify a WHERE clause.
------------------------------------------------------------------------
IF NOT @chvWhereField IS NULL
    BEGIN
        SELECT @chvSQL = @chvSQL + ' WHERE ' +
➡@chvWhereField + ' ' + @chvOperator + ' '
------------------------------------------------------------------------
    -- The stored procedure prNeedsQuotes determines the datatype of the
    -- field by looking in the system tables. It returns a value of
    -- 'y' or 'n' in the Output argument @chvNeedsQuotes. 'y' means
    -- that the field is a datatype that requires quotations marks around
    -- its value.
------------------------------------------------------------------------
EXEC prNeedsQuotes    @chvTable = @chvTable,
                @chvField = @chvWhereField,
                @chvNeedsQuotes = @chvNeedsQuotes OUTPUT
        ------------------------------------------------------------------
    -- If the datatype requires quotation marks, then use them.
        ------------------------------------------------------------------
        IF @chvNeedsQuotes = 'y'
            SELECT @chvSQL = @chvSQL + '''' + @chvWhereValue + ''''
        ELSE
            SELECT @chvSQL = @chvSQL + @chvWhereValue
    END
EXEC (@chvSQL)
GO
```

Dynamic Updates

What is probably more practical than using dynamic execution to perform deletes is using dynamic execution to perform updates. Listing 9.14 shows stored procedure prUpdateData, which updates an unspecified field with an unspecified value in an unspecified table where another unspecified field is compared against a value. That sure is a mouthful and certainly confusing, so you need to dissect this stored procedure.

The power in prUpdateData is the flexibility it has in allowing dynamic updates; what gives it that power are the stored procedure's arguments. So how do you use this stored procedure? First, determine which table's data you want to update and pass that table's name to the @chvTable argument. Then pass the name of the field you want to update and the value for this field to the @chvSetField and @chvSetValue arguments, respectively. Finally, if you want to update all rows in the table, then you are done. However, if you want to limit your update to a subset of rows, you need to specify your criteria. To do this, pass the name of the criteria's field, the operator for the comparison, and the value to be compared to the arguments @chvWhereField, @chvOperator, and @chvWhereValue, respectively.

Listing 9.14. The prUpdateData stored procedure using prNeedsQuotes to determine whether the WHERE clause value needs to be enclosed in quotation marks.

```
CREATE PROCEDURE prUpdateData
    @chvTable VARCHAR(30),
    @chvSetField VARCHAR(30),
    @chvSetValue VARCHAR(30),
    @chvWhereField VARCHAR(30) = NULL,
    @chvOperator VARCHAR(2) = '=',
    @chvWhereValue VARCHAR(30) = NULL
AS

DECLARE @chvSQL VARCHAR(255),
    @chvSetFieldQuotes CHAR(1),
    @chvWhereFieldQuotes CHAR(1)

SELECT @chvSQL = 'UPDATE ' + @chvTable + ' SET '

SELECT @chvSQL = @chvSQL + @chvSetField + ' = '
-------------------------------------------------------------------------
-- The stored procedure prNeedsQuotes determines the datatype of the field by
-- looking in the system tables. It returns a value of 'y' or 'n' in the Output
-- argument @chvNeedsQuotes. 'y' means that the field is a datatype
-- that requires
-- quotations marks around its value.
-------------------------------------------------------------------------
EXEC prNeedsQuotes      @chvTable = @chvTable,
            @chvField = @chvSetField,
            @chvNeedsQuotes = @chvSetFieldQuotes OUTPUT


-------------------------------------------------------------------------
-- If the datatype requires quotation marks, then enclose it within them.
-------------------------------------------------------------------------
```

continues

9

DYNAMIC
EXECUTION

Listing 9.14. continued

```
IF @chvSetFieldQuotes = 'y'
    SELECT @chvSQL = @chvSQL + '''' + @chvSetValue + ''''
ELSE
    SELECT @chvSQL = @chvSQL + @chvSetValue


--------------------------------------------------------------------
-- If the WHERE clause field is specified, then create the WHERE clause.
-- Otherwise, do not specify a WHERE clause.
--------------------------------------------------------------------
IF NOT @chvWhereField IS NULL
    BEGIN
        SELECT @chvSQL = @chvSQL + ' WHERE ' +
        ➥@chvWhereField + ' ' + @chvOperator + ' '
        --------------------------------------------------------------------
        -- The stored procedure prNeedsQuotes determines the datatype of the
        -- field by looking in the system tables. It returns a value of
        -- 'y' or 'n' in the Output argument @chvNeedsQuotes. 'y' means
        -- that the field is a datatype that requires quotations marks
        -- around its value.
        --------------------------------------------------------------------
        EXEC prNeedsQuotes      @chvTable = @chvTable,
                    @chvField = @chvWhereField,
                    @chvNeedsQuotes = @chvWhereFieldQuotes OUTPUT
        --------------------------------------------------------------------
        -- If the datatype requires quotation marks, then use them.
        --------------------------------------------------------------------
        IF @chvWhereFieldQuotes = 'y'
            SELECT @chvSQL = @chvSQL + '''' + @chvWhereValue + ''''
        ELSE
            SELECT @chvSQL = @chvSQL + @chvWhereValue
    END
EXEC (@chvSQL)
GO
```

Just as `prDeleteData` uses the `prNeedsQuotes` stored procedure to determine if field values need to be enclosed within quotation marks, so does `prUpdateData`. However, `prUpdateData` calls the `prNeedsQuotes` stored procedure twice: once for the `@chvSetField` argument and once for the `@chvWhereField` argument.

Using Cursors with Dynamic Execution

These stored procedures that use dynamic execution use it to an extreme and are probably not the answer to all your problems. However, they are practical templates that you can use to model your dynamic execution stored procedures. Your situations might call for a simpler version of one of these stored procedures; but then again, you might require a more complex use of dynamic execution.

Have you ever wanted to drop all foreign keys so you can perform structural changes on a table without having to drop all the tables that reference it? Or maybe you need to drop all the triggers in the database because they are no longer used. Normally, you must type the T-SQL to drop all these objects individually. However, using cursors with dynamic execution makes these tasks relatively simple.

Let's examine the problem of dropping all triggers in the database. You might have dozens of triggers in your database, so I won't even suggest that you type the T-SQL to drop them all individually. The task at hand becomes how to acquire a list of all the triggers. The name of all the objects in the database and what type of object they are, including triggers, is stored in the system table sysobjects. This is the logical place to start, so you'll query this table for the list of trigger names. The T-SQL in Listing 9.15 retrieves all triggers in the current database.

Listing 9.15. Retrieving all the triggers in the database from the sysobjects table.

```
SELECT name FROM sysobjects WHERE type = 'TR'
```

> **NOTE**
>
> The sysobjects table contains a row for every object in the database. To get a list of these objects by type, you can use the same query as shown in Listing 9.15 substituting the value of TR with one of the values shown in Table 9.2.

Table 9.2. Valid values for the type field in the sysobjects table.

Type	Description
C	Check constraint
D	Default
F	Foreign key
K	Primary key
P	Stored procedure
S	System table
TR	Trigger
U	User-defined table
V	View
X	Extended stored procedure
RF	Stored procedure for replication

The next step is to loop through the list of triggers using a cursor. Inside of the loop, you use dynamic execution to drop the triggers. Go over Listing 9.16, which begins by declaring a cursor called cuTriggers. You open this cursor on the list of triggers stored in the sysobjects table

9

DYNAMIC EXECUTION

using the T-SQL from Listing 9.15. Then loop through the cursor until you have no more triggers in the list. Each time through the loop, execute a T-SQL statement to drop the current trigger using dynamic execution. Next, get the subsequent trigger name from the cursor using the FETCH command. The loop needs an "out condition," so check the value of the @@fetch_status global variable. If it equals -1, then you stop looping because you have no more rows in the cursor. Finally, wrap up by releasing the memory reserved by the cursor using the DEALLOCATE command.

> **NOTE**
>
> Cursors are slow because they keep a connection open longer and require overhead to traverse themselves. Avoid cursors where possible. However, they are vital to some batch routines, such as when you want to create dynamic T-SQL using the system tables (see Listing 9.16).

Listing 9.16. Dropping all the triggers in the database using a cursor and dynamic execution.

```
DECLARE cuTriggers CURSOR
    FOR
    SELECT name FROM sysobjects WHERE type = 'TR'

OPEN cuTriggers

DECLARE @chvTrigger VARCHAR(30)

FETCH NEXT FROM cuTriggers INTO @chvTrigger
WHILE (@@fetch_status <> -1)
BEGIN
    -------------------------------------------------------------------
    -- A @@fetch_status of -1 means that there are no more rows in the cursor.
    -- Since we want to loop through all triggers, this will be our exit clause.
    -------------------------------------------------------------------
    EXEC ("DROP TRIGGER " + @chvTrigger)
    FETCH NEXT FROM cutriggers INTO @chvTrigger
END
DEALLOCATE cuTriggers
GO
```

The Benefits of Dynamic String Execution

Dynamic execution enables you to create scalable, reusable T-SQL code by combining the functionality of several batches of T-SQL into one flexible solution. You can also perform database schema T-SQL using dynamic execution, as is shown in Listing 9.16. You can drop, create, and alter objects just as you can through static T-SQL.

All on-the-fly, you can specify the names of tables, SELECT list fields, WHERE clause fields, ORDER BY fields, GROUP BY fields, HAVING clause fields, database names, and any other previously untouchable aspects of T-SQL. As displayed in Listing 9.17, you can also create an extremely generic SELECT statement. The stored procedure in this listing, prSelectData, uses the same basic code structure that the prDeleteData and prUpdateData stored procedures use. You can further modify prSelectData by adding more fields to the SELECT list or the ORDER BY list or even add a new clause to the query. Your choices are only limited by T-SQL; whatever it can do, so can you through dynamic execution.

Listing 9.17. Using dynamic execution you can create a generic data retrieval stored procedure.

```
CREATE PROCEDURE prSelectData
    @chvTable VARCHAR(30),
    @chvSelectField VARCHAR(30),
    @chvWhereField VARCHAR(30) = NULL,
    @chvOperator VARCHAR(2) = '=',
    @chvWhereValue VARCHAR(30) = NULL,
    @chvOrderByField VARCHAR(30) = NULL,
    @chvOrderByType VARCHAR(4) = 'ASC'
AS

DECLARE @chvSQL VARCHAR(255),
    @chvWhereFieldQuotes CHAR(1)

SELECT @chvSQL = 'SELECT ' + @chvSelectField + ' FROM ' + @chvTable

-------------------------------------------------------------------
-- If the WHERE clause field is specified, then create the WHERE clause.
-- Otherwise, do not specify a WHERE clause.
-------------------------------------------------------------------
IF NOT @chvWhereField IS NULL
    BEGIN
        SELECT @chvSQL = @chvSQL + ' WHERE ' + @chvWhereField +
➡' ' + @chvOperator + ' '
        -------------------------------------------------------------------
        -- The stored procedure prNeedsQuotes determines the datatype of the
        -- field by looking in the system tables. It returns a value of
        -- 'y' or 'n' in the Output argument @chvNeedsQuotes. 'y' means
        -- that the field is a datatype that requires quotations marks
        -- around its value.
        -------------------------------------------------------------------
        EXEC prNeedsQuotes    @chvTable = @chvTable,
                    @chvField = @chvWhereField,
                    @chvNeedsQuotes = @chvWhereFieldQuotes OUTPUT
        -------------------------------------------------------------------
        -- If the datatype requires quotation marks, then use them.
        -------------------------------------------------------------------
        IF @chvWhereFieldQuotes = 'y'
            SELECT @chvSQL = @chvSQL + '''' + @chvWhereValue + ''''
        ELSE
            SELECT @chvSQL = @chvSQL + @chvWhereValue
    END
```

continues

Listing 9.17. continued

```
--------------------------------------------------------------------
-- If the ORDER BY field is specified, then create the ORDER BY clause.
-- Otherwise, do not specify a ORDER BY clause.
--------------------------------------------------------------------
IF NOT @chvOrderByField IS NULL
    SELECT @chvSQL = @chvSQL + ' ORDER BY ' + @chvOrderByField +
➥' ' + @chvOrderByType
EXEC (@chvSQL)
GO
```

Dynamic execution is used in several system stored procedures in SQL Server 6.5. For example, examine the T-SQL code for the system stored procedure sp_lockinfo in Listing 9.18. (Chapter 6 discusses the details of this stored procedure.) The point is that SQL Server uses dynamic execution of T-SQL extensively.

Listing 9.18. System stored procedure sp_lockinfo using dynamic execution.

```
CREATE PROCEDURE sp_lockinfo
as
/* =====================================================*/
/* sp_lockinfo - returns detailed lock                 */
/* information for the server                          */
/* Microsoft SQL Server 6.5                     */
/* =====================================================*/

DECLARE @lkdbnm varchar(32),
    @lkdbid smallint,
    @lkobjid int,
    @UserDBID smallint,
    @usrdbnm varchar(32),
    @User_ID smallint,
    @grpid smallint,
    @stmt varchar(255)


/* =========================================================*/
/* build temp table with processes and their associated locks */
/* =========================================================*/

SELECT
    'FullName'   = case when p.spid > 9 then lo.name else 'System' end,
    'UserID'= p.uid,
    'UName'   = '                                    ',
    'ProcessID'= p.spid,
    'Status'= p.status,
    'DBID'        = p.dbid,
    'DbName'= d.name,
    'Command'= p.cmd,
    'Host'= p.hostname,
    'Application'= p.program_name,
    'Blocking'   = case when l.type >= 256 then 100 else 0 end,
    'Blockedby'= p.blocked,
    'LockType'   = l.type,
```

```
          'LKObjDBID'     = l.dbid,
          'LKObjDB'       = '                                        ',
          'LKObjID'       = l.id,
          'LKObj'         = case when l.id = 0 then
(select name from master..spt_values where number = l.type
➥and type = 'SFL')              else '
' end,
          'LockedPage'    = l.page,'GroupID'     = p.gid,
          'GName'      = '                         ','CPUUsage'    = p.cpu,
          'PhysicalIO'    = p.physical_io,'HostProcess'    = p.hostprocess
into #info from master..sysprocesses p,     master..syslocks l,
master..syslogins lo (nolock),master..sysdatabases d (nolock)
WHERE     p.spid    = l.spid and p.suid = lo.suid and p.dbid= d.dbid

/* ===================== */
/* flag blocking processes */
/* ===================== */

UPDATE #info set Blocking = 1 where ProcessID in
(select Blockedby from #info where Blockedby > 0)

/* ==========================================*/
/* get list of locked object IDs */
/* ==========================================*/

EXEC ('declare c1 cursor for select distinct LockedDBName = d.name,
➥LKObjID , LKObjDBID from #info, master..sysdatabases d
WHERE LKObjDBID = d.dbid   and LKObjID > 0 FOR READ ONLY')

open c1

fetch c1 into @lkdbnm, @lkobjid, @lkdbid

WHILE @@fetch_status >= 0
   begin
    /* set database.owner.name of locked objects in #info */
    select @stmt ='Update #info set LKObj=' + '''' + @lkdbnm +
➥'''' + '+ ''.'' + u.name + ''.'' + o.name' +
      ',LKObjDB=' + ''''+@lkdbnm + '''' + ' from '+
➥@lkdbnm+'..sysobjects o,'+@lkdbnm+'..sysusers u ' +
    'where o.id='+convert(char(10),@lkobjid)+
    ' and LKObjID=o.id' +
    ' and u.uid=o.uid and LKObjDBID=' + convert(char,@lkdbid)
    exec(@stmt )
    /* next please */
    fetch c1 into @lkdbnm, @lkobjid, @lkdbid
   end
deallocate c1

/* ==========================================*/
/* resolve UserID, GroupID for all processes    */
/* get a list of each database we need to visit */
/* ==========================================*/

exec ('declare c1 cursor for
➥select distinct DBID, DbName
➥from #info FOR READ ONLY')
```

continues

Listing 9.18. continued

```
open c1

fetch c1 into  @UserDBID, @usrdbnm

WHILE @@fetch_status >= 0
   BEGIN
   /* set user/group in #info */
   select @stmt = 'Update #info set GName=g.name,UName=u.name
   from '+@usrdbnm+'..sysusers u,'+
   @usrdbnm+'..sysusers g,#info '+
   'where u.uid=UserID and g.uid=GroupID and DBID=' + convert(char(10),@UserDBID)
   EXEC(@stmt )
   /* next please */
   fetch c1 into  @UserDBID, @usrdbnm
   end
deallocate c1

/* ====== return the #info table ===== */
SELECT
   FullName , ProcessID,     Status,     DName = DbName,
   Command,Host, Application, Blockedby,LockType,LKObj,
   GName = GName,CPUUsage, PhysicalIO, HostProcess,UName,Blocking
FROM #info (nolock) ORDER BY LKObj, ProcessID

return(0)

GO
```

Despite the power and flexibility that dynamic execution yields, it seems to be the least documented feature of SQL Server 6.5. Every time you need to find a definition or example of a SQL Server feature, all you have to do is open one of several SQL Server books or the online help utilities, and you will be flooded with pages of information. However, for whatever reason, dynamic execution documentation is a scarce commodity. It's bizarre that such a useful tool appears to have been overlooked by so many references.

One of the most useful stored procedures I have put together is also one of the most simple. It uses dynamic execution of T-SQL to retrieve the count of all objects in a given database. I'll bet that on several projects you have worked on, you had to establish a production and a test database. The structures start out identical and the struggle becomes keeping them in synch. It probably seems that no matter what you do, the databases always manage to get out of synch. This is where the prSysobjectsCount stored procedure makes your life a little bit easier. This stored procedure returns the count of all objects in a given database. You can run this stored procedure twice: once for the test database and once for the production database. You can then compare number of objects in both databases to see if they are still in synch. Now this stored procedure can definitely be made more robust. For example, you can make it tell you which objects are not in the other database or even have it schedule this to run every night and kick off an email to you with its results. Later chapters discuss these features.

Listing 9.19. prSysobjectsCount **returns the count of all objects in a given database.**

```
CREATE PROCEDURE prSysobjectsCount
    @chvDatabase VARCHAR(30),
    @chvOwner VARCHAR (30) ='DBO'
AS
    EXECUTE ("
    SELECT      CASE Type
        WHEN 'U'  THEN 'User table'
        WHEN 'S'  THEN 'System table'
        WHEN 'P'  THEN 'Stored procedure'
        WHEN 'V'  THEN 'View'
        WHEN 'TR' THEN 'Trigger'
        WHEN 'F'  THEN 'Foreign key'
        WHEN 'D'  THEN 'Default'
        WHEN 'K'  THEN 'Primary key or Unique'
        WHEN 'C'  THEN 'Check constraint'
        WHEN 'L'  THEN 'Log'
        WHEN 'R'  THEN 'Rule'
        WHEN 'X'  THEN 'Extended stored procedure'
        WHEN 'RF' THEN 'Stored procedure for replication'
        END
        AS 'Type',
        COUNT(*) AS Total
    FROM " + @chvDatabase + "." + @chvOwner + ".sysobjects
    GROUP BY Type")
GO
```

The Pitfalls of Dynamic String Execution

The prSysobjectsCount stored procedure does point out an interesting annoyance of dynamic execution: You must pass it a VARCHAR variable or character data. Because VARCHAR limits you to 255 characters, you must concatenate multiple variables to use long strings with the EXEC statement. You do have the option of using TEXT variables, but remember that they are limited in themselves because they cannot be local variables. This limitation does not stop you from coding useful dynamic execution T-SQL, it just frustrates you. However, unlike most deterrents, the results are often worth the frustration.

Another dynamic execution pitfall arises when you mix EXEC statements with non-EXEC statements. Now before you try this and see that it returns counts of all the objects, be aware that if you mix EXEC and non-EXEC statements, you risk getting unreliable results. What really occurs is the counts would reflect the total number of objects in the current database before the stored procedure was executed.

It is important to note that the statements inside the EXEC statement are not compiled until the statement is executed. Combining statements that change the current database can result in errors or worse, incorrect results.

9

DYNAMIC
EXECUTION

Listing 9.20. The incorrect and correct ways to use the EXEC statement.

```
--Correct:
USE pubs
SELECT stor_name FROM stores

--OR

EXEC("USE pubs")
EXEC("SELECT stor_name FROM stores")

--Incorrect:
EXEC ("USE pubs")
SELECT stor_name FROM stores
```

Summary

One of the biggest problems with dynamic execution is the lack of a dynamic array structure. Imagine how flexible your dynamic execution T-SQL can be if you can pass in an array of field names to the prSelectData stored procedure. Suddenly, the limitation of hard coding the number of fields in the SELECT list, the WHERE clause, or the ORDER BY clause would no longer hinder you. Nonetheless, this is a limitation and you must find alternative ways to work around it. One way to do this is to pass character delimited strings that can be parsed to reveal the fields. You have more creative ways to get around this T-SQL limitation. Another way is to create a table that holds all the data you need for your dynamic execution. You can just loop through the rows of the table, which would represent a different SELECT field. Whatever way you choose, the trick is to find the method that satisfies the situation.

Using dynamic execution in conjunction with stored procedures provides a great deal of flexibility; however, it does come at a slight cost. The first time a stored procedure is executed, it is compiled and its query plan is stored in memory. The query plan is used each subsequent time the stored procedure is executed, thus making it faster. You can compare this to the first time you drove your car to work for your job interview because you probably did not know where you were going (even if you did, just play along). But the next time you drove there, you remembered the way much more clearly. Stored procedures that use dynamic execution are compiled the first time they are executed, but the T-SQL can be different for each execution. Therefore, the query plan used the last time the stored procedure was executed cannot be re-used and must be re-created. Imagine if your office moved every day; you would have to plan a new route to work every morning!

The time it takes to re-create the query plan is negligible in most cases. So don't be concerned with this delay unless you are using dynamic execution in time-critical, business-critical situations. Then I perform some benchmarks on the dynamic execution stored procedure before implementing it in production applications.

Security Issues

CHAPTER 10

Before SQL Server's security issues are discussed, a brief introduction to security is in store. If you want to understand the inner workings of security, you need to understand the concepts behind SQL Server's security model.

Security Clearance

In order to gain access to any object in a given database, you must exist as two separate entities in SQL Server. The first is a *login*, which allows you to connect to the server. The second is a *user* within the database, which allows access to the objects within.

The Difference Between System and Database Users

A SQL Server login is also know as a *system user*. The login is the entry point to SQL Server: the gateway. When a request to connect to SQL Server occurs, it is validated by the server and if all is well, is directed to a database as a database user.

Security Models

There are three security models supported by SQL Server: Standard, Integrated, and Mixed. In actuality, only the first two are unique. The Standard model requires that each individual who needs access to SQL Server has a login defined within the server, and that each individual supply a name and password to gain access. SQL Server Enterprise Manager provides both GUI and T-SQL means of creating additional logins on the server.

> **NOTE**
>
> You must be logged in as the System Administrator (SA) in SQL Server in order to create additional logins. If you do not have an SA login, your database administrator can assist you.

Standard security provides for the highest level of security. Not only do the users have to log on to the Windows NT domain, but they must also log on to SQL Server to gain entry into any data that resides there.

The second model, Integrated security, allows access to SQL Server by any user who is both logged onto the domain in which the server resides and who is mapped in the SQL Server logins (a task most easily achieved via the SQL Server Security Manager). You cannot supply a login name or password to SQL Server; there is no manual login. The name of the model thus speaks for itself: It is truly *integrated.*

Integrated security is less secure, because any user who exists in SQL Server is automatically admitted by virtue of the fact that he or she has already been approved of by Windows NT. Users tend to like this feature, however, since they do not need to log on each time they run any applications that utilize that particular SQL Server.

The Mixed model provides for both of the previous types of access. If no name or password is supplied, Integrated authentication is used. If a name and password are supplied, SQL Server uses Standard security instead.

Logins and Users

No matter which security model is used, the admission process is the same. First, you are authenticated by SQL Server. Second, you are allowed access to certain databases. A server login name is serverwide and accessible via the SUSER_ID or SUSER_NAME system functions within SQL Server. A database user's scope is only within a database and can be found using the USER_ID and USER_NAME functions. Each user in a database must be mapped (or *aliased*) to a login.

Mapping a user is really just an association between a user and a login. When a user is created in a database, he or she must be associated in one of two ways with an existing login. The first is a direct correlation between the login and user, known as a *user*. The second method, aliasing, does not add a user to the database, but merely maps an existing login to an existing user in the database.

Imagine the current owner of a database needed to go out of town for some period of time. The technique of aliasing could be used to assign another login to the database owner (DBO) user in a database, allowing a second person to have administrative abilities within that database.

For example, Mary has a login on SQL Server MainServer. She is mapped as a user to two databases, Pubs and Accounting, as Mary. Once she has logged on to MainServer, she can access either of the two databases to which she is mapped. The Sales database contains no mapping for the login Mary, so she has no means of seeing anything in that database.

Joe also has a login on MainServer and is mapped to the Pubs database as Joe and the Sales database as DBO. Joe has no access to the Accounting database. Joe needs to go out on assignment for a few days, and has Mary aliased to the DBO user of the Sales database, allowing Mary to administrate Sales while he is away.

There are groups in databases as well.

Why so many features? SQL Server provides for more flexibility by implementing these features. Although this topic begs for further discussion, it is not the real reason you are here. Additional information can be found in the companion book *SQL Server 6.5 Unleashed.*

User Permissions on Database Objects

Once a user has been allowed access to a database, the user must then have permissions on the database objects in order to perform tasks such as selecting data or executing stored procedures. This is the final layer of security in SQL Server. Figure 10.1 shows the three levels of security implemented by SQL Server.

FIGURE 10.1.

Gaining access to data in SQL Server.

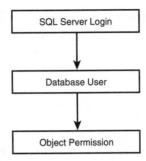

Each user or group that user is in must have permission to an object before using it. For example, Mary has execute permission on the stored procedure prAuthorPhoneList, but Joe does not. It comes to pass that Mary may execute this procedure, and Joe may not.

However, Mary may not be able to execute the procedure after all. It all depends upon who owns the procedure, who owns the objects referenced in the procedure, and what permissions Mary has on those objects themselves. This brings you to your next topic.

Understanding the "Chain of Ownership"

Just because you have permission on an object does not mean you have the ability to use the object. You must either have permission to all objects involved, or be given virtual permission. This virtual permission is achieved via a "chain of ownership."

Help Yourself to Anything in the Refrigerator

Examine Figure 10.2, where the owner and object are listed for six database objects.

FIGURE 10.2.

A sample chain of ownership.

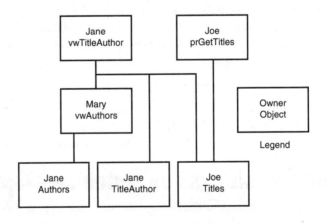

Joe is the owner of both the procedure prGetTitles and the table Titles. If Joe gives Bob permission to execute the procedure prGetTitles (which returns an alphabetic list of titles), Bob receives those titles with no problems. If, however, Mary gives Bob permission to select from her view vwAuthors, Bob will not be able to access those records unless Jane has also given Bob select permission on the Authors table itself.

NOTE

You may have noticed that it's not stated whether Mary has permission to select from Jane's Authors table. A user can create a view to another user's object without having permission to that object itself. Granted, Mary could not use her own view if Jane has not given her select permission to the Authors table. Regardless of this fact, Mary's permissions to the Authors table has no bearing on the chain of ownership relating to Bob's permissions to either object.

To illustrate this scenario, let's use an analogy. If you give someone the keys to your house and ask that person to check on your pet fish while you are away, you often tell that person to "help themselves to anything in the refrigerator." More often, this statement is even understood between the owner and the user. If Bob has your house keys, he can use anything in your house.

What if you are garaging a friend's motorcycle? The motorcycle is not yours, and you can't give Bob the keys to that anyway, because you cannot give permission to use something that is not yours. Even though Bob can see the motorcycle, he cannot use it.

The chain of ownership works in the same fashion. Although Mary may have permission to select from the Authors table, she cannot give Bob permission to use it, neither directly nor indirectly via a view or a stored procedure.

TIP

Although using different owners for different objects further enhances security, the administration can be a nightmare. Keep the number of database object owners (DBOO) to a minimum. You might consider using the DBO as the primary owner and rarely creating objects for individual users.

NOTE

Keep in mind that an object's uniqueness is not just its name, but its name and owner. You can have more than one Authors table, as long as each one is owned by a different user. This technique can be used to create what you can call personalized objects for users. For example, a table named Settings can be created for each user. When a user does a SELECT * FROM Settings, SQL Server first looks for the Settings object owned by the individual. If one is not found, it looks for one owned by DBO. You could use the DBO-owned Settings table to hold default values and create a user-owned Settings table if the user needs to hold custom parameters, information, and so on.

10

Worse yet, Jane gives Bob permission to the view vwTitleAuthor. Bob must also have permission to vwAuthors, Authors, and Titles. Since Jane already owns both vwAuthor and TitleAuthor, there is no need to assign Bob permission to this table, and even though Jane owns the Authors table, the view vwTitleAuthor uses the vwAuthors view to get to that data. Thus, the chain of ownership changes not only from vwTitleAuthor to vwAuthors, but also from vwAuthors to Authors itself. The moral of the story is that permission is needed for every change in object ownership, not just for objects owned by other people.

That motorcycle mentioned previously is now a car, and now Bob has permission to your house and your cell phone (which is locked in the car and is currently blocking outgoing calls via a passcode), but not the car itself. Bob needs the keys to the car and the passcode in order to use the cell phone.

If, however, DBO owned all of the objects as shown in Figure 10.3, life would be a lot easier. The DBO would only need to give Bob permission to the vwTitleAuthor view and Bob would be able to use it without any problems. The best part about this is that Bob cannot use any of the other objects unless given specific permission to do so.

FIGURE 10.3.

A better chain of ownership.

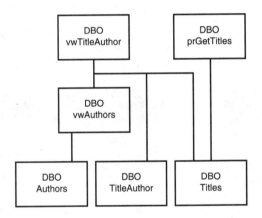

Permissions within Procedure Statements

Now you have seen the basics of the security mechanisms within SQL Server. Now get into the nitty gritty. The discussion of the chain of ownership and how this can be used to help tighten security without complicating administration continues.

With Permission Comes Trust and Responsibility

Keeping to the design of "DBO owns it all," you can block users from directly accessing any table object by using views and stored procedures to give access to only what is needed. You can use this technique in a three-tier client/server application in which no user has permission to access any table directly, but only through stored procedures.

This helps prevent potentially damaging results by restricting how and what a user may access in the database. If a user tries to connect to the tables in a program such as Microsoft Access or Excel, he or she will not be able to do so, since no permission has been given for the individual tables. Only the Visual Basic application (and each programmer) knows the procedure names that are called within your SQL Server database.

If it is necessary to give a user permission to a table (perhaps to clean up or just query and report data from within Access), it is understood that that user will not abuse that new authority. This user is being trusted not to damage or misuse the information in said table. If the trust is not there, you need to find another way to get the job done: Create additional reports for the user or clean the data yourself with help from the user.

The Rules of Stored Procedures Statement Permissions

This section brings together all the concepts mentioned up to this point.

Here are a few rules to keep in mind when creating database objects (particularly stored procedures):

- **Don't give users direct permission to tables.** Use views or stored procedures instead.
- **Avoid writing procedures that can eliminate or alter entire tables of data.** In most client/server applications, users only ever need to delete a few rows or one row at a time. Write stored procedures that reflect that fact.
- **Keep the number of database object owners (DBOO) to a minimum.** This not only helps prevent you from giving more permissions than you have to, but it keeps the administration to a minimum.

If you adhere to these rules, you save yourself a lot of grief later in the process. Unless there are pressing reasons to stray, you will only be asking for a potentially difficult time down the road in the development process.

Dynamic Execution and Permissions

This is where life can get interesting. As you have seen, if all objects are owned by the same user, giving permission to an object allows the user to access, albeit indirectly, all other objects referenced by that first object. This is normally advantageous, but when creating stored procedures that dynamically execute code, you can open a can of worms.

Examine a simple stored procedure that can have a very damaging effect on your database.

Listing 10.1. A stored procedure with dynamic execution.

```
CREATE PROC prExecute
@chvExec varchar(255)
AS

EXEC (@chvExec)

GO
```

10

SECURITY ISSUES

As simple as this procedure might be, a user can trash a lot of data in the database if he or she has permission to execute it. How? Imagine you gave Joe execute permission on prExecute and he made the following call (keep in mind that Joe must have delete permission on the Authors table):

Listing 10.2. Calling the stored procedure from Listing 10.1.

```
DECLARE @chvDoThis varchar(255)

SELECT @chvDoThis = 'DELETE AUTHORS'

EXEC prExecute @chvDoThis
```

Say good-bye to the Authors table, for it is now void of data. If Joe did not have delete permission on the Authors table, this procedure would fail. The chain of ownership does not apply to dynamic execution.

When does dynamic execution become dangerous? Whenever a user is allowed to specify the tables or columns to be manipulated via stored procedure parameters, that user also has permission to directly manipulate the table data. Chapter 13, "Crosstabulation," discusses a procedure that relies entirely on the supplied parameters to determine what data is retrieved. Unlike the procedure shown in Listing 10.1, you do not allow the user to specify any T-SQL statement as a parameter value. The stored procedure in Listing 10.1 is neither practical nor wise to implement; it merely demonstrates the power and possible destruction that can occur when using dynamic execution.

"The Rules of Stored Procedures Statement Permissions" states that you shouldn't give users direct permission to tables. Situations exist, however, where the present database has direct access to tables already in place. As you add to these databases, how do you prevent users from accessing data to which they shouldn't have access? One technique is to check for those permissions as needed in the stored procedure itself.

You can query several system tables to discover whether a user has permission to any object. The tables involved are sysobjects, syscolumns, sysobjects, sysprotects, and sysusers in the current database, and spt_values from the master database. The following system stored procedure is not a simple one with a query containing a five table join, but it gives you the full ability to determine a user's permissions on a column within a table. This procedure shown in Listing 10.3 can be found in the Microsoft SQL Server 6.5 master database.

Listing 10.3. The sp_column_privileges system stored procedure.

```
1: CREATE PROCEDURE sp_column_privileges (
  2:      @table_name         varchar(32),
  3:      @table_owner        varchar(32) = null,
  4:      @table_qualifier    varchar(32) = null,
  5:      @column_name        varchar(90) = null)
  6: as
```

```
 7:    8: declare @table_id int
 8:   10: if @column_name is null  /* If column name not supplied, match all */
 9:        select @column_name = '%'
10:   13: if @table_qualifier is not null
11: begin
12:        if db_name() <> @table_qualifier
13:        begin    /* If qualifier doesn't match current database */
14:           raiserror 20001 'Table qualifier must be name of current database'
15:           return
16:        end
17: end
18: if @table_owner is null
19:        begin            /* If unqualified table name */
20:            select @table_id = object_id(@table_name)
21:        end
22: else
23:        begin            /* Qualified table name */
24:            select @table_id = object_id(@table_owner + '.' + @table_name)
25:        end
26:   30: select    convert(varchar(32),db_name()) TABLE_QUALIFIER,
27:        convert(varchar(32),user_name(o.uid)) TABLE_OWNER,
28:        @table_name TABLE_NAME,
29:        convert(varchar(32),c.name) COLUMN_NAME,
30:        convert(varchar(32),user_name(p.grantor)) GRANTOR,
31:        convert(varchar(32),user_name(u.uid)) GRANTEE,
32:        convert (varchar(32),case p.action
33:            when 193 then 'SELECT'
34:            when 195 then 'INSERT'
35:            when 197 then 'UPDATE'
36:            else 'REFERENCES'
37:            end) PRIVILEGE,
38:        convert (varchar(3),case when p.protecttype = 205 then 'NO'
39:            else 'YES'
40:            end) IS_GRANTABLE
41: from sysprotects p, sysobjects o, sysusers u,
42:        master.dbo.spt_values v, syscolumns c
43: where    c.id = @table_id
44:        and c.name like @column_name
45:        and c.id = p.id
46:        and c.id = o.id
47:        and case substring(p.columns, 1, 1) & 1
48:            when NULL then 255  /* all columns have permission */
49:            when 0 then convert(tinyint, substring(p.columns, v.low, 1))
50:            else (~convert(tinyint, isnull(substring(p.columns, v.low, 1),0)))
51:            end    & v.high <> 0    /* permission applies to this column */
52:        and v.number <= (select count(*) from syscolumns
53:            where id = @table_id) /*ranges from 1 to # of columns in table*/
54:            and v.type = 'P'
55:            and v.number = c.colid
56:            /* expand groups */
57:            and ((p.uid = u.uid and u.uid <> u.gid) or
58:                 (p.uid = u.gid and u.uid <> u.gid))
59:            and p.protecttype <> 206      /* only grant rows */
60:            and p.action in (26,193,195,197)
61:            and o.uid <> u.uid            /* no rows for owner */
62:            and not exists (              /* exclude revoke'd privileges */
63:                select *
```

continues

Listing 10.3. continued

```
64:                    from sysprotects p1
65:                    where
66:                        p1.protecttype = 206
67:                        and p1.action = p.action
68:                        and p1.id = p.id
69:                        and p1.uid = u.uid
70:                        and case substring(p1.columns, 1, 1) & 1
71:                            when NULL then 255 /*all columns have permission*/
72:                            when 0 then convert(tinyint,
73:                                substring(p1.columns, v.low, 1))
74:                            else (~convert(tinyint,isnull(
75:                                substring(p.columns, v.low, 1),0)))
76:                            end & v.high <> 0) /*permission applies to column*/
77:        union all
78:        select           /* Add rows for table owner */
79:            convert(varchar(32),db_name()) TABLE_QUALIFIER,
80:            convert(varchar(32),user_name(o.uid)) TABLE_OWNER,
81:            @table_name TABLE_NAME,
82:            convert(varchar(32),col_name(@table_id, c.colid)) COLUMN_NAME,
83:            convert(varchar(32),user_name(u.uid)) grantor,
84:            convert(varchar(32),user_name(o.uid)) grantee,
85:            convert (varchar(32),case v.number
86:                when 193 then 'SELECT'
87:                when 195 then 'INSERT'
88:                when 197 then 'UPDATE'
89:                else 'REFERENCES'
90:                end) PRIVILEGE,
91:            convert(varchar(3),'YES') IS_GRANTABLE
92:        from sysobjects o, spt_values v, sysusers u, syscolumns c
93:        where
94:            c.id = @table_id
95:            and c.name like @column_name
96:            and c.id = o.id
97:            and u.suid = 1      /* grantor is dbo of database */
98:            and v.type = 'P'    /*cross product - all privileges*/
99:            and v.number in (26,193,195,197)
100:            and not exists (    /* exclude revoke'd privileges */
101:                select *
102:                from sysprotects p1
103:                where
104:                    p1.protecttype = 206
105:                    and p1.action = v.number
106:                    and p1.id = o.id
107:                    and p1.uid = o.uid)
108:        order by 4, 7
109: 111: GO
```

Now take a deep breath and dive in. Lines 1 through 8 are the CREATE for the procedure and one variable declaration. Lines 10 through 28 qualify the optional parameters @table_owner, @table_qualifier, and @column_name. If the argument @table_owner is NULL, the default owner (the current user or DBO) is assumed. The parameter @table_qualifier is the database name, which should only be the current database. @column_name can either specify a particular column, or all columns if nothing is passed into the argument.

Lines 30 through 79 and 81 through 111 perform similar tasks for two different categories of users—the DBOO and all other users. The first SELECT statement queries the tables for those users (and the groups to which they belong) for permissions. The second adds information about the DBOO's permissions.

The database name is returned as TABLE_QUALIFIER, the owner of the table is returned as TABLE_OWNER, the table name is returned as TABLE_NAME, and the column name is returned as COLUMN_NAME. So far, so good. The sysprotects's grantor column holds the user ID of the permission-giver. It is converted to the username via the USER_NAME function and is returned as GRANTOR. The uid column of sysprotects holds the user ID of the user who was granted permission. It is joined to the sysusers table and that value, once again converted to the username, is returned as GRANTEE. This covers lines 30 through 35.

Lines 36 through 41 translate the action column from sysprotects into a readable value and return it as PRIVILEGES. The action value is used in a CASE expression and resolved as follows:

Table 10.1. sysprotects action column values and meanings.

Action Value	Translated Permission
26	REFERENCES
193	SELECT
195	INSERT
196	DELETE
197	UPDATE
198	CREATE TABLE
203	CREATE DATABASE
207	CREATE VIEW
222	CREATE PROCEDURE
224	EXECUTE
228	DUMP DATABASE
233	CREATE DEFAULT
235	DUMP TRANSACTION
236	CREATE RULE

Only a portion of the permissions are used in the query, as only some apply to column and table permissions. The next few lines (42 through 44) return a Boolean as GRANTABLE based on the protecttype column of sysprotects. A value of 206 means the permission is revoked, 205 means permission is granted, and 204 means a user can grant permission to grant permission (although this value is not used by the query).

The join is standard fair, with two exceptions. First, it uses a subquery to find the revoked permissions separately from the granted permissions. Second, it does a bitwise operation against the low and high columns of spt_values to find the specific columns to which any permissions apply.

By checking the first bit of the binary column columns, it can determine if column- or table-level permissions are currently in effect. If column-level permissions are being used, the low and high columns of spt_values determine where in the binary value the column's permission is located. The column position equals the number value from spt_values, the low value is the location within the binary value, the high value is the comparison bit in the binary, and the type from spt_values is 'P'. You have to do a little more research by looking at the data in the spt_values table to get a better grasp of the fine details of that CASE statement on lines 51 through 57 and lines 74 through 79.

Lines 61 and 62 determine the user (uid) and any groups the user belongs to (gid) in the sysusers table against the user ID in sysprotects. Examine Listing 10.4 to see some details from the sysusers table.

Listing 10.4. Partial results from SELECT * FROM SYSUSERS.

```
suid    uid     gid     name
------  ------  ------  -----------------------------
-16384  16384   16384   test
-2      0       0       public
-1      2       0       guest
1       1       0       dbo
10      3       0       probe
11      4       16384   Peter
16383   16383   0       repl_subscriber
```

The suid column is the login to which the user is mapped. After looking over this output, you realize that both users and groups are indeed stored in the same table. Notice that the two groups always have the same value in the uid and gid columns. This is how SQL Server discerns a group from a user. Each user has a group's uid as its gid value. This is how SQL Server finds the group for the particular user. If the gid is 0, the user belongs only to the public group. If it is any other value (for example, Peter's gid is 16384), then the user belongs to the group whose uid matches that gid and also (always) to the public group.

Listing 10.5 shows a query that selects all users and their respective group or groups. It uses the same basic principals as the sp_column_privileges system stored procedure to find the users and groups.

Listing 10.5. Selecting a list of users and their groups.

```
SELECT    user_name(s1.uid) AS UserName,
          user_name(s2.uid) as GroupName
FROM      sysusers s1
          JOIN sysusers s2 ON s1.gid = s2.uid
```

```
WHERE      s1.uid <> s1.gid

UNION

SELECT     user_name(s1.uid) AS UserName,
           'public' as GroupName
FROM       sysusers s1
           JOIN sysusers s2 ON s1.gid = s2.uid
WHERE      s1.uid <> s1.gid
AND        s1.gid <> user_id('public')

ORDER BY   UserName, GroupName
```

The remaining portions of the query are either explained in comments or have been explained already. The key is to step through this code carefully, so that you may fully understand the process involved. It might take a while to fully grasp all the finer points of this stored procedure.

Summary

Your best bet in keeping tight security is to prevent the holes from appearing in the first place. Consistent object ownership and using views and stored procedures to give access to data helps increase security in most any database. Sometimes, however, you have to stray from the standards, and it is at that point you must take it upon yourself to make sure all is safe and secure.

When you do stray, keep it to a minimum. Stored procedures like the one in Listing 10.1 are not only in poor design, but are also very dangerous to data integrity.

If you decide it is your only route, make sure you parse and check that the user has permission to do what the user is trying to do. It is easier to check individual parameters than to parse through a T-SQL statement for potential problems. Force the user to pass supplied column and table information through parameters and you can then control exactly what will happen with those items.

The importance of going through all of the over one megabyte in length set of stored procedures cannot be stressed enough. Many procedures are very simple and easy to grasp. Others offer some phenomenal chances for learning in that they perform actions that you didn't even think were possible.

Specialized Triggers

CHAPTER 11

Triggers are wonderful tools, and this chapter discusses their features and how they can help you support an enterprise business solution. For example, a trigger on the `sales` table is executed whether a T-SQL statement was run via iSQL or a new sale was entered via an external application. This chapter, which assumes that you have at least a minimal working knowledge of triggers, concentrates on useful implementations of them. We'll begin the overview with a brief discussion of the components of triggers, such as the `inserted` and `deleted` tables and the `update()` function. Then we'll go over nesting triggers and the SQL statements that can't be performed by triggers. When triggers are created, information about them is stored in several system tables. We'll go through the system tables that are affected by triggers and what that information is used for.

After completing the overview, we'll jump straight into practical methods of enforcing business rules, such as preventing a price increase of 25 percent or more on any title that has sales of less than 100 units. Then we'll go over how triggers can be used to audit transactions and archive information. Triggers can be used to store system information regarding which SQL transactions are being executed most often. We'll discuss how this stored information can be used to improve database performance. We all know that foreign keys are faster at maintaining referential integrity (RI) than triggers are. However, triggers can maintain more complex relationships that foreign keys can't handle. We'll go over these relationships and how triggers can enforce them. Finally, we'll wrap up with more practical business uses for cascade deletes and updates.

What Can Triggers Do?

A trigger is executed when SQL performs an action query on the table the trigger is linked to. For example, if an `update` statement occurs on the `titles` table, the `titles` table's `update` trigger (if one exists) will be executed. Because triggers are performed when any of the three types of action queries are executed, there are three corresponding types of triggers:

- update triggers
- insert triggers
- delete triggers

If the same action must be performed by more than one trigger on the same table, you can combine these triggers into one trigger. For example, if you want an email sent to you whenever someone inserts or deletes records from the `discounts` table, you can create one trigger that handles both types of action queries. See Listing 11.1, which contains a trigger that will send email to the user "Colleen" by using the `xp_sendmail` extended stored procedure. (Extended stored procedures are discussed in detail in Chapter 6, "Effective Use of Stored Procedures as an Administrative Tool," and mail is discussed in Chapter 26, "Integrating SQL with Other Microsoft Products.")

NOTE

The xp_sendmail extended stored procedure requires that SQL Mail be configured properly and started. SQL Mail, in turn, requires a valid Microsoft Exchange profile name for the startup user account of the MSSQLServer Service.

Listing 11.1. The trigger trDiscounts_InsDel, which sends an email when an insert or delete occurs on the discounts table.

```
CREATE TRIGGER trDiscounts_InsDel ON discounts
FOR INSERT, DELETE
AS
DECLARE @intRowCount INTEGER,
    @chvMsg VARCHAR(255)

SELECT @intRowCount = @@RowCount
SELECT @chvMsg = CONVERT(VARCHAR(10), @intRowCount ) + ' record(s) were '
SELECT COUNT(*) FROM inserted
IF @@error <> 0
    SELECT @chvMsg = @chvMsg + ' deleted from the discounts table.'
ELSE
    SELECT @chvMsg = @chvMsg + ' inserted into the discounts table.'
EXEC master..xp_sendmail 'Colleen', @chvMsg
RETURN
```

TIP

Keep in mind that a trigger is only executed once per action query, regardless of the number of rows that are affected by the action query. For example, if you update 10 rows in the sales table, the update trigger on the sales table will only fire once. When you design your triggers, be sure to account for multiple rows, one row, or even zero rows being affected. Even if you execute an update statement that does not affect any rows in a table, the table's trigger fires. In this case, you should leave a clause that exits the trigger immediately to minimize the length of time the lock is kept open.

The inserted and deleted Tables

Depending on which type of action query is performed, the trigger that is subsequently executed will create either the inserted table, the deleted table, or both. Refer to Table 11.1 to find out which tables are created within a trigger for the corresponding action queries.

WARNING

You should be aware that the `inserted` and `deleted` tables can only be referenced by the trigger that created them. The scope of the `inserted` and `deleted` tables is limited to the trigger that caused their instantiation. If a trigger calls a stored procedure, that stored procedure will be able to reference neither the `inserted` nor the `deleted` tables that were created when the trigger fired.

Table 11.1. The tables that are created by the different types of triggers.

Trigger Type	Inserted Table	Deleted Table
Insert trigger	Yes	No
Update trigger	Yes	Yes
Delete trigger	No	Yes

NOTE

In the following discussion of `inserted` and `deleted` tables, please assume that the tables discussed have the appropriate triggers linked to them.

When a record is inserted into a table, the corresponding insert trigger creates an `inserted` table that mirrors the column structure of the table the trigger is linked to. For example, if you insert a row into the `titles` table, its trigger will create the `inserted` table using the same column structure as the `titles` table. For every row that was inserted into the `titles` table, a corresponding row is contained within the `inserted` table.

The `deleted` table also mirrors the column structure of the table it is linked to. When a `delete` statement is executed, every row that was removed from the table will be contained in the `deleted` table within the delete trigger.

A trigger fired by an UPDATE statement creates both an `inserted` and a `deleted` table. Both of these tables will have the same column structure as the table they are linked to. The `deleted` and `inserted` tables contain a "before and after" snapshot of the data in the linked table. For example, assume that you have executed the following T-SQL statement:

```
UPDATE titles SET advance = 5500 WHERE advance = 5000
```

The update trigger on the `titles` table will be fired when this T-SQL statement is executed. The trigger's `inserted` and `deleted` tables will contain a row for every data row that changed due to the T-SQL statement. The deleted table will contain the data values of the row as they appeared before the UPDATE statement. The inserted table will contain the data values of those same rows as they appear after the UPDATE statement.

The update( ) Function

Triggers can hamper the performance of T-SQL transactions and keep locks open while they execute. Therefore, if your trigger's logic only needs to run when certain columns' data is changed, you should check for those conditions. This is where the update( ) function steps in to make your life easier.

The update( ) function is only available within insert and update triggers. The update( ) function determines if the column you pass to it has been affected by the insert or update statement that caused the trigger to be fired. Listing 11.2 shows an update trigger on the titles table that prevents the advance column from being altered.

Listing 11.2. The trigger trTitles_Upd, which rolls back any T-SQL that changes the advance column.

```
CREATE TRIGGER trTitles_Upd ON titles
FOR UPDATE
AS

IF update(advance)
    ROLLBACK TRANSACTION

RETURN
```

The trTitles_Upd trigger checks if any data in the advance column has been changed. If so, the trigger rolls back the transaction in its entirety. It is vital to use the update( ) function in a trigger to avoid unnecessarily traversing the trigger's T-SQL logic. After all, why bother executing all of the code within a trigger for a case that does not require it? (Especially because triggers keep the locks open on the affected tables while the triggers are executing.) The revised trigger trTitles_Upd in Listing 11.3 shows a practical example of a trigger that has an "escape clause" to avoid unnecessary work.

Listing 11.3. The trigger trTitles_Upd, which exits quickly if the price column has not been updated.

```
1: CREATE TRIGGER trTitles_Upd ON titles
2: FOR UPDATE
3: AS
4:
5: DECLARE @chvMsg VARCHAR(255),
6:     @chvTitleID VARCHAR(6),
7:     @mnyOldPrice MONEY,
8:     @mnyNewPrice MONEY
9: DECLARE     cuPriceChange CURSOR
```

continues

Listing 11.3. continued

```
10:     FOR
11:     SELECT d.title_id, d.price, i.price
12:     FROM deleted d INNER JOIN inserted i ON d.title_id = i.title_id
13: IF update(price)
14:     BEGIN
15:         OPEN cuPriceChange
16:         FETCH NEXT FROM cuPriceChange INTO
17:             @chvTitleID, @mnyOldPrice, @mnyNewPrice
18:         WHILE (@@fetch_status <> -1)
19:         --------------------------------------------------------------
20:         -- @@fetch_status = -1 means no more rows in the cursor.
21:         --------------------------------------------------------------
22:             BEGIN
23:                 SELECT @chvMsg = 'The price of title ' + @chvTitleID
24:                         + ' has changed from'
25:                         + ' ' + CONVERT(VARCHAR(10), @mnyOldPrice)
26:                         + ' to ' + CONVERT(VARCHAR(10), @mnyNewPrice)
27:                         + ' on ' +
28: ➥CONVERT(VARCHAR(30), getdate()) + '.'EXEC master..xp_sendmail 'Colleen',
@chvMsg
29: FETCH NEXT FROM cuPriceChange
30:                 INTO @chvTitleID, @mnyOldPrice, @mnyNewPrice
31:                 SELECT @chvMsg = ''
32:             END
33:     DEALLOCATE cuPriceChange
34:     END
35: RETURN
```

The trTitles_Upd trigger in Listing 11.3 will email the user "Colleen" for every price change. Because this trigger uses a cursor to loop through the affected rows, it will degrade the performance of the original T-SQL statement that fired the trigger. That's why it's vital for the trigger to check if the data in the price column has changed before it opens the cursor and loops through each affected row. The trTitles_Upd trigger in Listing 11.3 is smart enough to quit when there is no work to do, thus releasing the table locks. You can test this trigger by executing any update on the titles table, such as the T-SQL in Listing 11.4.

Listing 11.4. T-SQL that will execute the trigger trTitles_Upd.

```
BEGIN TRANSACTION
UPDATE titles SET price = price * .5 WHERE price < 10
ROLLBACK TRANSACTION
```

Notice that this code will change the data in the titles table just long enough to execute the trigger (and the emails). Then the transaction is undone by the ROLLBACK command. If you execute an UPDATE statement against the titles table that does not affect the price column's data, the trigger trTitles_Upd will exit when line 15 of Listing 11.3 returns false.

Keep in mind that the update() function does not really tell you if a column's data has changed. Rather, it tells you if a change was attempted on the column. Specifically, here are the situations where the update() function returns a value of true:

- The column is on the left side of the SET clause of an UPDATE statement.
- The column is in the column-list of an INSERT statement.

Even if the data was not actually modified, the update() function will return true. For example, the following T-SQL will cause the update() function to return true if it is passed the advance column:

```
UPDATE titles SET advance = advance
```

Notice that the column is on the left side of the SET clause.

> **TIP**
>
> In addition to using the update() function to avoid traversing unneeded logic, you can count on the @@rowcount global variable. @@rowcount always contains the value of how many rows were affected by the most recent transaction on the current connection. To circumvent any further processing, check the value of @@rowcount at the beginning of the trigger and exit immediately if it equals 0.

Nesting Triggers

You might be wondering what happens when a trigger modifies another table that also has trigger. In this case, the second trigger is executed as well. This is referred to as *nested triggers*. SQL Server allows you to prevent nested triggers from being executed by changing the value of the configuration option nested triggers from 1 to 0 (1, or ON, is the default value for this option). By default, SQL Server limits the levels of nested triggers to 16 deep. (If this limit is exceeded, SQL Server raises an error.) If you turn trigger nesting off, a trigger that modifies another table will not fire the second table's trigger.

T-SQL Limitations in Triggers

As powerful as triggers are, they do have limitations. Some T-SQL statements can't be executed within the confines of a trigger. The following types of statements are restricted:

- All CREATE statements
- All DROP statements
- ALTER command (DATABASE nor TABLE)
- TRUNCATE table

- SELECT INTO
- Permission statements (GRANT nor REVOKE)
- RECONFIGURE
- LOAD statements (TRANSACTION nor DATABASE)
- All disk statements
- UPDATE STATISTICS

The Role of the System Tables with Triggers

There are several system tables that store varying information about triggers. Table 11.2 identifies and describes the role of the system tables that contain pertinent trigger information. (Chapter 6 discussed system stored procedures at length, while Appendix C, "System Stored and Extended Stored Quick Reference," lists most of the system stored procedures. Refer to Appendix A, "The System Tables of the Master Database," for a listing of the system tables.)

Table 11.2. The role of the system tables that store information about triggers.

System Table	Role
sysobjects	Stores a row per trigger. Each table row contains columns that reference the table's triggers.
sysdepends	Stores references between triggers and the tables they are linked to.
syscomments	Stores the T-SQL text of triggers.
sysprocedures	Stores a preparsed version of the trigger's query.

In addition, SQL Server provides the system stored procedures sp_helptext and sp_help to display information for SQL Server objects. Listing 11.5 shows the sp_helptext system stored procedure, which accepts a parameter of an object, in our case a trigger name, and returns the T-SQL code that comprises that object.

Listing 11.5. The sp_helptext system stored procedure.

```
CREATE PROCEDURE sp_helptext
@objname VARCHAR(92)
as
DECLARE @dbname VARCHAR(30)

SET NOCOUNT ON

/*
**  Make sure the @objname is local to the current database.
*/
IF (@objname LIKE '%.%.%' AND
        SUBSTRING(@objname, 1, charindex('.', @objname) - 1) <> db_name() )
```

```
            BEGIN
                    RAISERROR(15250,-1,-1)
                    RETURN (1)
            END
/*
**  See if @objname exists.
*/
IF (OBJECT_ID(@objname) IS NULL)
        BEGIN
        SELECT @dbname = db_name()
        RAISERROR(15009,-1,-1,@objname,@dbname)
                RETURN (1)
        END

/*
**  Find out how many lines of text are coming back,
**  and return if there are none.
*/
IF (SELECT COUNT(*) FROM syscomments WHERE id = OBJECT_ID(@objname)) = 0
        BEGIN
                RAISERROR(15197,-1,-1,@objname)
                RETURN (1)
        END

IF (SELECT COUNT(*) FROM syscomments WHERE id = OBJECT_ID(@objname)
    AND texttype & 4 = 0) = 0
        BEGIN
                PRINT 'The object''s comments have been encrypted.'
                RETURN(0)
        END

/*
**  Else get the text.
*/
SELECT text FROM syscomments WHERE id = OBJECT_ID(@objname)

RETURN (0)

GO
```

Let's take a closer look at this system stored procedure to see how it uses the system tables to retrieve information about the triggers (in this case). The first several lines of code verify that the object name that was passed to the stored procedure is valid. Then the object is checked to see if its creation script was encrypted. If it was, the stored procedure is aborted. Finally, a simple select statement retrieves the creation script for the object.

Listing 11.6 shows how a simple query can retrieve all user-defined tables and the names of the triggers that reference them. The sysobjects table has the instrig, updtrig, and deltrig columns, which contain the object IDs of the triggers that reference their respective tables. The object_name() and coalesce() functions are system functions inherent in SQL Server. The object_name() function returns the name of the object, given the object's ID. The coalesce() function accepts a variant amount of arguments and returns the first non-null argument.

Listing 11.6. Retrieving all of the triggers for each table.

```
SELECT name,
       COALESCE(OBJECT_NAME(instrig), 'N/A') AS InsertTrigger,
       COALESCE(OBJECT_NAME (updtrig), 'N/A') AS UpdateTrigger,
       COALESCE(OBJECT_NAME (deltrig), 'N/A') AS DeleteTrigger
FROM sysobjects
WHERE type = 'U'
ORDER BY name
```

How to Use Triggers to Enforce Business Rules

One of the best uses of a trigger is to enforce business-specific rules that can't be enforced through any other single SQL Server object. You could use an application development tool, such as Visual Basic, to enforce these more complex types of business rules. However, your users would have to go through this application for the business rules to be enforced. Otherwise, they could sidestep the rules completely. By placing these types of rules within triggers, you ensure that the rules will be enforced regardless of how the data is interfaced.

Let's assume that we do not want to allow anyone to increase the price of any title by 25 percent or more of the title's current price. Let's add the further restriction that this only applies to titles that have not yet sold 100 copies. A trigger is the perfect instrument to enforce this rule because any attempt to update this field will be caught by the trigger. Listing 11.7 shows a trigger that enforces this rule.

Listing 11.7. Preventing price increases of more than 25 percent, using a trigger.

```
CREATE TRIGGER trTitles_Upd ON titles
FOR UPDATE
AS

DECLARE @mnyOldPrice MONEY,
        @mnyNewPrice MONEY,
        @chvTitleID VARCHAR(6),
        @chvMsg VARCHAR(255),
        @intTotalQty INTEGER

IF UPDATE(price)
    -------------------------------------------------------------------
    -- There is no need to perform the following logic unless the
    -- price has been changed.
    -------------------------------------------------------------------
    BEGIN
        DECLARE cuPriceChange CURSOR
        FOR
        SELECT d.title_id, d.price, i.price
            FROM inserted i INNER JOIN deleted d
                ON i.title_id = d.title_id

        OPEN cuPriceChange

        FETCH NEXT FROM cuPriceChange INTO
```

```
              @chvTitleID, @mnyOldPrice, @mnyNewPrice

    WHILE (@@fetch_status <> -1)
    -------------------------------------------------------------------
    -- A @@fetch_status of -1 means there are no more rows in the cursor.
    -------------------------------------------------------------------
    BEGIN
              -------------------------------------------------------------
              -- Retrieve the total sales for this title.
              -------------------------------------------------------------
              SELECT @intTotalQty = SUM(qty)
                  FROM sales
                  WHERE title_id = @chvTitleID


              -------------------------------------------------------------
              -- If the total sales for this title is less than 100 units
              -- and the price has increased more than 25%, then reverse the
              -- changes and notify an operator.
              -------------------------------------------------------------
              IF @mnyNewPrice > @mnyOldPrice * 1.25 AND @intTotalQty < 100
                  BEGIN
                      SELECT @chvMsg = 'An attempt has been made to reduce'
                          + ' the price of title'
                          + ' ' + @chvTitleID + ' by more than 25% from'
                          + ' ' + CONVERT(VARCHAR(10), @mnyOldPrice) + ' to'
                          + ' ' + CONVERT(VARCHAR(10), @mnyNewPrice) + '.'
                          + ' This is transaction has been rolled back.'

                      PRINT @chvMsg
                      EXEC master..xp_sendmail 'Colleen', @chvMsg

                      ROLLBACK TRANSACTION

                      DEALLOCATE cuPriceChange

                      RETURN
                  END

              FETCH NEXT FROM cuPriceChange
                      INTO @chvTitleID, @mnyOldPrice, @mnyNewPrice
    END

        DEALLOCATE cuPriceChange
    END
GO
```

Notice that the update() function is used immediately upon entering the trigger so we can circumvent any unneeded logic if the price has not changed. The cursor does not even get declared if the price does not change. This is why we do not need to release the memory the cursor reserves on every update. Once the trigger's logic has determined that an attempt was made to change the price of 0 or more titles, the affected rows are traversed to examine the changes to the prices. If any price has increased by more than 25 percent, the trigger formats an email message to send to the user "Colleen", rolls back all of the changes, releases the cursor's memory, and exits the trigger.

TIP

This trigger in Listing 11.7 rolls back all changes caused by the UPDATE statement if the price increase rule is violated. However, you can reverse specific changes based upon business rules, too. Rather than rolling back the entire transaction and exiting, you can write an UPDATE statement inside of the trigger to affect the same table that the trigger references. The UPDATE should simply change the price back to the original price (@mnyOldPrice). The updated trigger is shown in Listing 11.8.

Listing 11.8. Reversing price increases of more than 25 percent, but allowing the changes to other fields in the table.

```
CREATE TRIGGER trTitles_Upd ON titles
FOR UPDATE
AS

DECLARE @mnyOldPrice MONEY,
        @mnyNewPrice MONEY,
        @chvTitleID VARCHAR(6),
        @chvMsg VARCHAR(255),
        @intTotalQty INTEGER

IF UPDATE(price)
    ------------------------------------------------------------------
    -- There is no need to perform the following logic unless the
    -- price has been changed.
    ------------------------------------------------------------------
    BEGIN
        DECLARE cuPriceChange CURSOR
        FOR
        SELECT d.title_id, d.price, i.price
            FROM inserted i INNER JOIN deleted d
                ON i.title_id = d.title_id

        OPEN cuPriceChange

        FETCH NEXT FROM cuPriceChange INTO
            @chvTitleID, @mnyOldPrice, @mnyNewPrice

        WHILE (@@fetch_status <> -1)
        ------------------------------------------------------------------
        -- A @@fetch_status of -1 means there are no more rows in the cursor.
        ------------------------------------------------------------------
        BEGIN
            ------------------------------------------------------------------
            -- Retrieve the total sales for this title.
            ------------------------------------------------------------------
            SELECT @intTotalQty = SUM(qty)
                FROM sales
                WHERE title_id = @chvTitleID
```

```
--------------------------------------------------------------
-- If the total sales for this title is less than 100 units
-- and the price has increased more than 25%, then reverse the
-- changes and notify an operator.
--------------------------------------------------------------
IF @mnyNewPrice > @mnyOldPrice * 1.25 AND @intTotalQty < 100
    BEGIN
        SELECT @chvMsg = 'An attempt has been made to reduce'
            + ' the price of title'
            + ' ' + @chvTitleID + ' by more than 25% from'
            + ' ' + CONVERT(VARCHAR(10), @mnyOldPrice) + ' to'
            + ' ' + CONVERT(VARCHAR(10), @mnyNewPrice) + '.'
            + ' This is transaction has been rolled back.'

        PRINT @chvMsg
        PRINT ''
        EXEC master..xp_sendmail 'Colleen', @chvMsg

        UPDATE titles
            SET price = @mnyOldPrice
            WHERE title_id = @chvTitleID
    END

    FETCH NEXT FROM cuPriceChange
            INTO @chvTitleID, @mnyOldPrice, @mnyNewPrice
END

    DEALLOCATE cuPriceChange
    END
GO
```

As shown in Listing 11.8, triggers can enforce rules that are more complex than can be defined using check constraints. The trigger trTitles_Upd references columns in an external table, sales. This can't be done using a check constraint, but can be accomplished using a trigger.

NOTE

An update of a table within that table's trigger does not cause the trigger to fire recursively.

Auditing Triggers

You can also use triggers to audit transactions. For example, you may not want deleted sales data to be permanently lost. Rather, you would prefer to move the purged sales data to an archival sales table. The first step in this archival process is to create an audit table for the archived sales data. This table should mirror the column structure of the sales table while omitting the foreign keys that the sales table has. For this discussion we'll assume that you have created this table and have called it SalesArchive. You can use the T-SQL script in Listing 11.9 to create SalesArchive.

Listing 11.9. The table creation script for table `SalesArchive`.

```
CREATE TABLE SalesArchive
(
    stor_id        CHAR(4)          NOT NULL,
    ord_num        VARCHAR(20)      NOT NULL,
    ord_date       DATETIME         NOT NULL,
    qty            SMALLINT         NOT NULL,
    payterms       VARCHAR(12)      NOT NULL,
    title_id       tid,
)
GO
```

Transferring the purged sales data to the `SalesArchive` table allows you to query this data in the future. For example, you may want to run sales reports on historical data to forecast future sales by store. A delete trigger on the `sales` table can provide you with the ammunition to present these types of historical reports rather easily. Listing 11.10 shows the trigger `trSales_Del`, which transfers deleted sales data to the `SalesArchive` table.

Listing 11.10. The delete trigger on the `sales` table that archives the purged sales data.

```
CREATE TRIGGER trSales_Del ON sales
FOR DELETE
AS

INSERT SalesArchive
    SELECT stor_id, ord_num, ord_date, qty, payterms, title_id
        FROM deleted
GO
```

The beauty of this trigger is that it is simple yet powerful. Once this trigger is in place, every sale that is deleted is subsequently transferred to the `SalesArchive` table. Regardless of how the sales data is purged (such as from an iSQL window or a client application), the data is archived.

> **TIP**
>
> You could use a scheduled task in conjunction with the `trSales_Del` trigger in Listing 11.10 to archive sales data. For example, you could schedule a task to run once a week that deletes all sales occurring on or before the same day on the previous year. This task would kick off the `sales` table's delete trigger, which would then archive the sales, all done automatically.

Storing System Information

Triggers can be used to automatically store system information that `defaults` just can't handle. For example, assume that you want every table to contain two columns that represent who the last user to modify a row was and what day and time the modification occurred. Let's call these columns `modify_date` and `modify_user`. If you place an insert and update trigger on all tables that sets the values of these columns, you can use this information to query who performed each change on the system.

> **NOTE**
>
> Even though you could combine the update and insert triggers, it allows for greater flexibility when you create them separately. You can add further logic to either trigger without affecting the existing logic.

Listing 11.11 shows an update and insert trigger on the `stores` table that sets the values of the user who modified the table and the date and time the modification occurred. For this discussion, we'll assume that you have altered the `stores` table to include these two new columns, `modify_date` and `modify_user`.

> **NOTE**
>
> Keep in mind that these two columns must allow `null` values because they will not be included in an `INSERT` statement, and because data already exists in this table. You can use the following T-SQL to add these two columns to the `stores` table.
>
> ```
> ALTER TABLE stores
> ADD modify_date DATETIME NULL
> GO
>
> ALTER TABLE stores
> ADD modify_user VARCHAR(30) NULL
> GO
> ```

Listing 11.11. A sample trigger on the `stores` table that updates the `modify_date` and `modify_user` columns.

```
CREATE TRIGGER trStores_InsUpd ON stores
FOR INSERT, UPDATE
AS

DECLARE @intRowCount int

SELECT @intRowCount = @@RowCount
IF @intRowCount > 0
    UPDATE stores
        SET modify_date = getdate(), modify_user = suser_name()
        WHERE stor_ID IN
        (
        SELECT stor_id FROM inserted
        )
GO
```

This trigger updates the `modify_date` and `modify_user` columns for all rows that have been affected by an `update` or an `insert` statement. Notice that this trigger handles all rows that are affected, as opposed to assuming that only one row was updated. This trigger also exits quietly if no rows were modified. You can execute the T-SQL from Listing 11.12 to test the newly created trigger's effects. This script will modify all California store names and roll the changes back. Then, the script queries the "before" and "after" results to demonstrate the update trigger's effect.

Listing 11.12. This script will test the trigger we created in Listing 11.11.

```
BEGIN TRANSACTION

UPDATE stores
    SET stor_name = 'Test'
        WHERE state = 'CA'

SELECT * FROM stores

ROLLBACK TRANSACTION

SELECT * FROM stores
GO
```

> **NOTE**
>
> By selecting the data after the UPDATE statement and then again after the changes were rolled back, you can see how the `modify_date` and `modify_user` data changed. I could have queried the data before and after the update, but I used a ROLLBACK here so that I wouldn't leave the data "dirty."

Storing System Information in Custom Tables

Another way that triggers store system information can help you determine what fields are most often modified. You can place an update trigger on a table that inserts a record into a storage table for every column that was affected by the original `update`. This information can then be used to analyze which users are most often changing which data. You can then adjust the permissions or the views accordingly.

For example, create a new table called `UpdateLog` as it appears in Listing 11.13. Then create an update trigger on the `authors` table (also in Listing 11.13) that inserts a record into the `UpdateLog` table for every column that was affected by the original `update` statement.

Listing 11.13. Creating the UpdateLog table and an update trigger on the `authors` table.

```
CREATE TABLE UpdateLog
(
    table_name VARCHAR(30) NOT NULL,
```

```
        column_name VARCHAR(30) NOT NULL,
        updated_by VARCHAR(30) NOT NULL,
        updated_when DATETIME NOT NULL
)
GO

CREATE TRIGGER trAuthors_Upd ON Authors
FOR UPDATE
AS

DECLARE @intRowCount int

SELECT @intRowCount = @@RowCount
IF @intRowCount > 0
    BEGIN
        IF UPDATE(au_id)
            INSERT UpdateLog
                VALUES ('authors', 'au_id', suser_name(), getdate())

        IF UPDATE(au_lname)
            INSERT UpdateLog
                VALUES ('authors', 'au_lname', suser_name(), getdate())

        IF UPDATE(au_fname)
            INSERT UpdateLog
                VALUES ('authors', 'au_fname', suser_name(), getdate())

        IF UPDATE(phone)
            INSERT UpdateLog
                VALUES ('authors', 'phone', suser_name(), getdate())

        IF UPDATE(address)
            INSERT UpdateLog
                VALUES ('authors', 'address', suser_name(), getdate())

        IF UPDATE(city)
            INSERT UpdateLog
                VALUES ('authors', 'city', suser_name(), getdate())

        IF UPDATE(state)
            INSERT UpdateLog
                VALUES ('authors', 'state', suser_name(), getdate())

        IF UPDATE(zip)
            INSERT UpdateLog
                VALUES ('authors', 'zip', suser_name(), getdate())

        IF UPDATE(contract)
            INSERT UpdateLog
                VALUES ('authors', 'contract', suser_name(), getdate())
    END

GO
```

This example uses the update() function to determine which columns were modified in the authors table. If the column's data was modified, the trigger inserts a record into the UpdateLog table. This information can then be used as a basis for designing views to data and permissions for data changes.

Maintaining RI with Triggers

A trigger can maintain RI between two tables in much the same way a foreign key can. Foreign keys perform the same task more efficiently because they are tested before any data is changed, as opposed to how triggers fire after the data changes. A simple analogy for the relationship between foreign keys and triggers is to compare two scenarios for buying tickets to a movie. If the movie is sold out, the ticket agent will notify you before you enter the theater. This scenario wastes no time, like a foreign key. However, imagine if the ticket agent sells you a ticket without checking if the show is sold out. You buy your popcorn and search for a seat in the theater, but you find there are none remaining. You then return to the ticket counter and get your refund. This scenario is less efficient, making you commit to purchasing your tickets without knowing if you'll be able to find a seat.

Now that I've made such a strong argument for using foreign keys over triggers, I'll justify why you should use triggers to enforce RI. Implementing triggers, in lieu of foreign keys, is vital to the success of cascading delete and update triggers. This will become evident later in this chapter when cascading triggers are discussed in detail.

There are other types of RI that can be enforced using triggers that foreign keys simply can't handle. A good example of this is a column that must contain a valid value from one of two other tables. Imagine that the authors table has a column that stores the account where the author has his/her royalties electronically transferred. This account could be either a bank account or a brokerage account, each of which has different related information. Listing 11.14 will help you establish this new column in the authors table, create the new bank and brokerage tables, and fill them with some starter data.

Listing 11.14. This script adds the account column to the authors table and creates the new bank and brokerage tables.

```
ALTER TABLE authors
    ADD account VARCHAR(10) NULL
GO

CREATE TABLE bank
(
    account VARCHAR(10) NOT NULL PRIMARY KEY,
    name VARCHAR(50) NOT NULL
)
GO

CREATE TABLE brokerage
(
    account VARCHAR(10) NOT NULL PRIMARY KEY,
    name   VARCHAR(50) NOT NULL
)
GO

INSERT bank VALUES ('ABC', 'First Bank')
INSERT bank VALUES ('DEF', 'Second Bank')
```

```
INSERT bank VALUES ('XYZ', 'Third Bank')
GO

INSERT brokerage VALUES ('123', 'First Broker')
INSERT brokerage VALUES ('456', 'Second Broker')
INSERT brokerage VALUES ('987', 'Third Broker')
GO

sp_addmessage 56000, 10, 'Attempt to insert or update an invalid account.'
GO
```

You may have noticed that I threw in a custom message at the end of the script in Listing 11.14. (Messages are discussed in Chapter 6 .) We could have skipped this step and just printed a text message to the query window, but in an enterprise application you'll want to raise an error in that case. So we'll raise an error using this new custom message if our trigger finds that the RI has been violated.

Enforcing Complex RI via Triggers

Now that we've set up the basics of this discussion, we can proceed to demonstrate how a trigger can enforce complex RI. Specifically, we will enforce the restriction that an account in the authors table must be a valid account from either the bank or brokerage table. To do this, we will place the triggers from Listing 11.15 on the authors table.

Listing 11.15. The trAuthors_InsUpd trigger maintains a complex RI rule.

```
CREATE TRIGGER trAuthors_InsUpd ON Authors
FOR UPDATE
AS

DECLARE @intRowCount int

SELECT @intRowCount = @@RowCount
IF @intRowCount > 0
    BEGIN
    IF (NOT EXISTS
            (
            SELECT account FROM bank WHERE account IN
                (SELECT account FROM inserted)
            UNION
            SELECT account FROM brokerage WHERE account IN
                (SELECT account FROM inserted)
            )
        )
        BEGIN
            RAISERROR(56000, 10, 1)
            ROLLBACK TRANSACTION
            RETURN
        END
    END
GO
```

Like the other triggers in this chapter, trAuthors_InsUpd exits immediately if no rows were affected. Then, using a UNION query, the trigger checks if all accounts in the inserted table are in either the bank or brokerage table. (Unions are discussed in Chapter 2, "Using Advanced Data Manipulation Language.") If any account that was either inserted or modified does not exist in the bank or the brokerage table, an error is raised and the transaction is undone. You can test this by executing the T-SQL script in Listing 11.16.

Listing 11.16. Two test scripts. The first script violates the RI, and the second script passes the RI check.

```
----------------------------------------
-- This batch violates the RI.
----------------------------------------
BEGIN TRANSACTION

PRINT '--------------------'
PRINT 'BEGIN FIRST TRANSACTION'
PRINT ''
PRINT 'Updating the accounts to "xyz123"...'
PRINT ''
UPDATE authors SET account = 'xyz123'
PRINT 'Finished.'

COMMIT TRANSACTION
GO


----------------------------------------
-- This batch passes the RI.
----------------------------------------
BEGIN TRANSACTION

PRINT ''
PRINT ''
PRINT '--------------------'
PRINT 'BEGIN SECOND TRANSACTION'
PRINT ''
PRINT 'Updating the accounts to "123"...'
PRINT ''
UPDATE authors SET account = '123'
PRINT 'Finished.'

COMMIT TRANSACTION
GO
```

Cascade Delete Triggers

As promised in the previous section, we'll now discuss the role that triggers play in cascading deletes and updates. Triggers can reciprocate deletions from one table through the related tables' records in the database. We'll use the stores table for our example and concentrate on its relationships with the discounts and sales tables. For instance, a delete trigger on the stor_id column of the `stores` table causes a corresponding deletion of matching rows in the `discounts` and `sales` tables. The trigger uses the `stor_id` column as a unique key to locate and purge matching rows in the related tables.

Before you begin, you must drop the foreign keys on the `discounts` and `sales` tables that reference the `stores` table. You can drop the foreign keys either through the SQL Server Enterprise Manager's Manage Tables window or by executing an `alter table` script. To drop foreign keys, you must first know the names of the constraints. If you did not name the foreign keys when you created them, SQL Server has given them unique names for you. To avoid having to figure out which foreign keys to drop and what their names are, create and use the `prDropForeignKeys` stored procedure shown in Listing 11.17. Simply pass the name of the table that you want all references dropped from, and the stored procedure does the dirty work.

Listing 11.17. The `prDropForeignKeys` stored procedure drops the foreign keys that reference a given table.

```
CREATE PROCEDURE prDropForeignKeys
    @chvReferencedTable VARCHAR(30)
AS

DECLARE @chvTableWithForeignKey VARCHAR(30),
        @chvForeignKey VARCHAR(30),
        @chvSQL VARCHAR(255)

DECLARE cuFKs CURSOR
    FOR
    SELECT tb.name,
           fk.name
    FROM ((sysobjects tb INNER JOIN sysreferences r ON tb.id = r.fkeyid)
        INNER JOIN sysobjects fk ON r.constid = fk.id)
        INNER JOIN sysobjects refd_tb ON refd_tb.id = r.rkeyid
    WHERE refd_tb.name = @chvReferencedTable

OPEN cuFKs

FETCH NEXT FROM cuFKs INTO
    @chvTableWithForeignKey, @chvForeignKey

WHILE (@@fetch_status <> -1)
    BEGIN
        SELECT @chvSQL = 'ALTER TABLE ' + @chvTableWithForeignKey
                        + ' DROP CONSTRAINT ' + @chvForeignKey

        EXEC (@chvSQL)

        FETCH NEXT FROM cuFKs INTO
            @chvTableWithForeignKey, @chvForeignKey
    END

DEALLOCATE cuFKs
GO
```

Execute the stored procedure prDropForeignKeys, passing it the stores table as its argument. Once you have dropped the DRI enforced by the foreign keys on the stores table, you can test a cascading delete trigger on the stores table. Listing 11.18 shows how the trigger trStores_Del cascades its deletions.

Listing 11.18. After its data has been deleted, the trigger trStores_Del deletes corresponding rows from the sales and discounts tables.

```
CREATE TRIGGER trStores_Del ON stores
FOR DELETE
AS

DECLARE @intRowCount int

SELECT @intRowCount = @@RowCount
IF @intRowCount > 0
    BEGIN
        DELETE sales
            WHERE stor_id IN
                (SELECT stor_id FROM deleted)

        DELETE discounts
            WHERE stor_id IN
                (SELECT stor_id FROM deleted)
END
GO
```

This trigger removes all sales and discounts for the stores that were deleted. You can test this trigger by executing the T-SQL script in Listing 11.19.

Listing 11.19. This script demonstrates the cascading effects of the trStores_Del trigger from Listing 11.18.

```
BEGIN TRANSACTION

DELETE stores WHERE stor_id = '8042'

SELECT COUNT(*) StoresAfterDelete FROM stores WHERE stor_id = '8042'
SELECT COUNT(*) SalesAfterDelete FROM sales WHERE stor_id = '8042'
SELECT COUNT(*) DiscountsAfterDelete FROM discounts WHERE stor_id = '8042'

ROLLBACK TRANSACTION

SELECT COUNT(*) StoresBeforeDelete FROM stores WHERE stor_id = '8042'
SELECT COUNT(*) SalesBeforeDelete FROM sales WHERE stor_id = '8042'
SELECT COUNT(*) DiscountsBeforeDelete FROM discounts WHERE stor_id = '8042'
GO
```

Cascade Update Triggers

Cascading updates throughout related tables offer even more flexibility than cascading deletes do. We'll walk through two examples that unleash the power behind cascading updates.

One example shows how you can update the value of the stor_id column in the stores table and have its related table references modified to reflect the change. The second example demonstrates how you can maintain derived data through a cascading update trigger. Both examples require that the foreign keys be removed from the stores table. (You can use the prDropForeignKeys stored procedure from Listing 11.17 to do this.)

> **WARNING**
>
> Because cascading deletes and updates require you to drop foreign key constraints on the respective tables, you must put logic in the triggers to enforce the RI that was previously implemented by the foreign keys. For example, after dropping the foreign keys in the discounts and sales tables that reference the stores table, you must create triggers on all of those tables to enforce the lost RI. Otherwise, you could accidentally change a stor_id in the sales table to an invalid value.

After dropping the foreign keys that referenced the stores table, create the trigger trStores_Upd, as shown in Listing 11.20. This trigger updates the sales and discounts tables after its unique key (stor_id) has been updated.

Listing 11.20. The trigger trStores_Upd updates corresponding rows from the sales and discounts tables.

```
CREATE TRIGGER trStores_Upd ON stores
FOR UPDATE
AS

DECLARE @intRowCount int

SELECT @intRowCount = @@RowCount
IF @intRowCount > 1
    BEGIN
        IF UPDATE(stor_id)
            ROLLBACK TRANSACTION
    END
ELSE
    IF @intRowCount = 1
        BEGIN
            IF UPDATE(stor_id)
                BEGIN
                    UPDATE sales
                        SET sales.stor_id = (SELECT stor_id FROM inserted)
                        FROM sales INNER JOIN deleted
                        ON sales.stor_id = deleted.stor_id
                    UPDATE discounts
                        SET discounts.stor_id =
                            (SELECT stor_id FROM inserted)
                        FROM discounts INNER JOIN deleted
                        ON discounts.stor_id = deleted.stor_id
                END
        END
    END
GO
```

WARNING

Notice that the trigger in Listing 11.20 only handles cases where just one row was updated. When you are cascading updates to primary keys, it is wise to restrict the updates to affect one value at a time.

You can test this trigger by executing a T-SQL UPDATE statement that changes the value of a data in the stor_id column of the stores table.

Maintaining Derived Data

The second example of utilizing cascading update triggers manages derived data. For example, let's assume the field title exists in the sales table, denormalizing the data slightly. This will speed up reporting for the sales department because they always require the title to be displayed on all of their sales reports. This way the sales reports do not have to hit both the sales table and the titles table on each report. Add the column titles to the sales table using the following script:

```
ALTER TABLE sales
ADD title VARCHAR(80) NULL
GO
```

Now create the trigger trTitles_Upd, as shown in Listing 11.21. This trigger will look for any changes to the names of any titles. If there are any changes, it will copy them to the sales table.

Listing 11.21. The trTitles_Upd trigger copies any changes of the titles.title column to the corresponding sales.title column.

```
CREATE TRIGGER trTitles_Upd ON titles
FOR UPDATE
AS

DECLARE @intRowCount int

SELECT @intRowCount = @@RowCount
IF @intRowCount > 0
    BEGIN
        IF UPDATE(title)
            BEGIN
                UPDATE sales SET sales.title = inserted.title
                    FROM inserted INNER JOIN sales
                    ON inserted.title_id = sales.title_id
            END
    END
GO
```

Now your sales department can write a query selecting data from only the `sales` table. You can test this new trigger using the following T-SQL script:

```
BEGIN TRANSACTION

SELECT title FROM titles  WHERE title_id = 'BU1111'
SELECT title FROM sales WHERE title_id = 'BU1111'

UPDATE titles
    SET title = 'My Title'
    WHERE title_id = 'BU1111'

SELECT title FROM titles  WHERE title_id = 'BU1111'
SELECT title FROM sales WHERE title_id = 'BU1111'

ROLLBACK TRANSACTION
GO
```

Summary

Triggers are powerful tools when used to support enterprise business solutions. We've shown how the `inserted` table, the `deleted` table, and the `update()` function can help enhance business applications. We've proven that triggers are an excellent means of enforcing business rules, and that they can audit transactions and archive system information with little effort. Also, we've shown that by using information gathered by triggers, we can improve database performance and determine which indexing schemes to implement. Triggers can even maintain complex RI when foreign keys just can't cut it. An integral part of any enterprise SQL Server application, triggers can make your application soar.

Updating Table Indexes and Statistics

CHAPTER

12

Two often-overlooked aspects of database design are performance and tuning. Too often, developers (and sometimes DBAs) run out of time on tight schedules, and optimization of the database is the casualty. SQL Server provides several built-in statements for optimizing and retrieving statistical information from a database. This chapter provides guidelines on how to implement these statements, with useful utilities for improving performance on your server.

This chapter begins by demonstrating two indexing techniques to improve database performance. These techniques show how planning index and table design, along with creating and indexing a manufactured column, improve the query time. Then the chapter moves into a discussion of UPDATE STATISTICS, which optimizes indexes after data has been added. Finally, you're shown how the DBCC statements provide performance statistics regarding SQL Server.

Index Performance and Fine-Tuning

All too often, very little analysis is given to implementing useful indexes. If built correctly, indexes can give your application the "adrenaline boost" that it needs. Begin by looking at the components of indexing. The first component is the actual design of the table and related indexes. Typically, for a data warehouse, you will create many indexes for the stored data to ensure fast retrieval by your Decision Support Systems. In an Online Transaction Processing Database, having too many indexes is detrimental to performance because you're not only writing the data to the record, but also updating each of the clustered and non-clustered indexes. In the design phase, especially for real-time transaction processing, two methods improve speed drastically.

Designing Indexes for Speed

The first method applies to tables where multiple columns make the primary *unique* key, also known as the *composite* key. In lieu of creating a composite key on a table, you can create a new column that contains the data values for the columns that define the composite key. You can create a VARCHAR column with a length that's the sum of the lengths of the composite key. Then, store the composite key values in this new column, making it a single-column primary key. If you index this new column, it will make your table updates much faster. For instance, if you have four fields that make up the primary key, you not only have to update four separate indexes, but as a record is added, all four indexes must be scanned for the combination you are attempting to write to a record. But because you've combined the four fields into a single column, only one index will need to be searched when you update or query a record. The extra hard drive space that is required to store the new column is somewhat (but not totally) offset by the space saved by creating a simpler indexing scheme. Remember, indexes are allocated hard drive space as well.

> **TIP**
>
> If you create a column to hold the concatenation of multiple fields, you run the risk of throwing your data out of synch. One way to prevent this from occurring is to place an update trigger on the table that updates the new column with the changes to the individual columns.

The second method allows for faster queries against data for real-time processing. Although creating multiple indexes decreases performance when you're adding records, having multiple indexes *increases* performance when you're running queries against the data. One solution to this difference in performance is to not create the additional indexes in the table, but rather create the indexes, run the query, and drop the indexes. This technique will probably slow down queries against tables with few records, but tables with a high volume of records will show a significant improvement.

Distribution Pages and Storing Data with Stepping

Distribution pages are the second component in optimizing tables and indexes. SQL Server internally searches indexes for matches when running queries. It then creates a distribution page for each index it finds. So what does a distribution page store?

- Sample data values from the first indexed column in steps
- The index density

What is *stepping*? Imagine you have a statistical grouping of sequential data, and the information for every x number of records is bookmarked for reference. This concept is similar to how distribution pages work. The x number of records translates into the number of steps, and the grouping of data refers to the indexed data being queried.

So how does it work? A page can hold 2KB with an overhead of a 32-byte header. This leaves 2,016 bytes available for the distribution page. Here's the formula to arrive at the number of steps for fixed column indexes:

(2,016 - 2 - (number of key columns $\times$ 2 bytes))/(column width + 2)

To arrive at the number of steps for variable column indexes, the formula is

(2,016 - 2 - (number of key columns $\times$ 2 bytes))/(max column width + 2)

To compute the number of steps for a CHAR(10) column:

(2,016 - 2 - (1$\times$2)/(10+2)

= 2,012/12

= 167 steps.

If you have one million records with a step value of 167, a sample would be stored every 5,988 rows:

(1,000,000 rows / 167 steps = 5,988 rows/step)

> **NOTE**
>
> The more you increase the maximum column width, the lower the step number becomes. This creates more room for samples to be stored. To reduce the indexing search time, you can increase the number of samples. This sounds strange, but it makes sense because when you index character columns, there is a high probability that the first several characters will be identical.

If you were searching for the product ID PSL123456 and SQL Server discovered PSL123444 at step 100 and PSL123466 at step 105, you would search five steps to locate the match in the index. As in the preceding example, if you had 5,988 rows/step/5 steps, you would search a total of 29,940 rows. Much faster than searching all 1,000,000 records. In fact, a similar approach is commonly used in the C programming language for searching indexes of a table.

Using Index Densities Instead of Step Values

Although the step method can extract data for a simple search on a single column, there are other types of queries that do not benefit from steps. Complex joins, advanced DML with totals, composite indexes, and queries with calculations are among those queries that do not take full advantage of steps. In these cases, *index densities* are used in place of steps to narrow down the rows to search for matching criteria. The formula for index densities is

1/number unique values

Therefore, if you have one million records with 10,000 unique values, the index density would be

1/10,000 = .0001

The number of rows to search for a match would be

1,000,000 × .0001 = 100 rows

However, if the index consists of multiple columns, densities are stored for each of the combinations in column order. If you had columns called Product ID, Store ID, and Sales Associate ID, you would have a density for

```
Product ID
Product ID and Store ID combined
Product ID, Store ID, and Sales Associate ID combined
```

The greater the number of columns, the lower the index density and the fewer rows that will need to be searched. The fastest query will generate searches on all three columns for the preceding case. Refer to the section "Using DBCC Statements to Monitor Your Database" for details on how to retrieve the steps and density for each index on a table.

Updating the Distribution Page

The distribution page is not updated every time a record is added. In a high-volume database, this would cause a huge performance loss. Therefore, when you initially create a table with no data, the distribution page remains empty. It's updated only when

- You create an index on a table with existing data.
- You run the UPDATE STATISTICS statement.

From a systems administration point of view, you should create a utility to automatically update the distribution page at least once per week, or even daily if the data volume increases more than 10 percent per day. Fortunately, this utility is provided in the next section.

Creating a Utility to Optimize Table Indexes

Because it is unlikely that indexes will be added daily, you will need to use the UPDATE STATISTICS statement to update the distribution page in order to optimize SQL Server. The syntax for the UPDATE STATISTICS statement is

```
UPDATE STATISTICS tablename [,index_name]
```

The tablename is the name of the table to optimize. If only the name of the table is specified, the distribution page for all indexes will be updated. Optionally, if you specify the index_name, only the distribution page for that index will be updated. Listing 12.1 is a utility to optimize all indexes for all tables within the database.

Listing 12.1. Optimizing tables with UPDATE STATISTICS.

```
DROP PROCEDURE pr_updateindex
GO
CREATE PROCEDURE pr_updateindex
    AS
SET NOCOUNT ON
DECLARE getindex_curs CURSOR
    FOR
        SELECT name   -- Table Name
        FROM sysobjects -- System Table
        WHERE type = 'U' -- User tables

-- hold name of table retrieved from sysobjects
DECLARE @holdtable varchar(30)
```

continues

Listing 12.1. continued

```
DECLARE @message varchar(40) -- Used to Display UPDATING message
-- Used to dynamically execute UPDATE STATISTICS statement
DECLARE @dynamic varchar(51)

OPEN getindex_curs
FETCH NEXT FROM getindex_curs into @holdtable
-- Test sysobjects database for user tables
WHILE @@FETCH_STATUS = 0 BEGIN
        SELECT @dynamic = "UPDATE STATISTICS " + @holdtable
        SELECT @message = "Updating " + @holdtable
        EXEC (@dynamic )
PRINT @message

    FETCH NEXT FROM getindex_curs into @holdtable
END
CLOSE getindex_curs
```

This stored procedure uses the UPDATE STATISTICS command to dynamically update the distribution page for all indexes on all user tables for the current database. The getindex_curs cursor retrieves each user table stored in the @holdtable variable, where type has a value of 'U'. A message is displayed with the word Updating concatenated with the name of the table. The UPDATE STATISTICS command, with the table name concatenated, is stored in the @dynamic variable. This variable is then executed to optimize all the indexes for the current table. The cursor is closed after all tables have been optimized. Type the following to execute this stored procedure:

```
EXEC pr_updateindex
```

Depending on the number of tables in the current database and whether you created the tables from Chapter 2, "Using Advanced Data Manipulation Language," your output could look similar to this:

```
Updating tim
Updating classification
Updating cd
Updating spt_datatype_info_ext
Updating inventory
Updating spt_datatype_info
Updating spt_server_info
Updating salesmw
Updating salesne
Updating salesall
Updating INC
Updating helpsql
Updating spt_committab
Updating spt_monitor
Updating spt_values
Updating spt_fallback_db
Updating spt_fallback_dev
```

```
Updating spt_fallback_usg
Updating oldusers
Updating myusers
Updating subt
Updating maint
Updating newcur
Updating store
Updating composer
```

> **TIP**
>
> It is always a good idea to search for corrupted tables with the DBCC statements CHECKDB or CHECKTABLE before attempting this operation. It is also a good idea to perform it when everyone is off the system.

Verifying When the Last Optimization Took Place

If you have never optimized the indexes of a table before, or want to see when the indexes of a table were last optimized, this can be accomplished with the DBCC SHOW_STATISTICS statement. The sysindexes table stores the location of the distribution page. The format for the DBCC SHOW_STATISTICS statement is

```
DBCC SHOW STATISTICS (tablename, index_name)
```

The *tablename* parameter is the name of the table, and the *index_name* is the index desired. The following example uses tables and indexes created in Chapter 2:

```
DBCC SHOW_STATISTICS (salesne, sne)
```

Your output should be similar to this:

```
Updated                Rows        Steps        Density
------------------     ----------  ----------   -----------------------
Dec 22 1997 11:26PM    13          12           0.0414201

(1 row(s) affected)

All density              Columns
----------------------   -----------------------------------
0.112426                 CDID
0.0887574                CDID, StoreID
0.0769231                CDID, StoreID, SalesDate

(3 row(s) affected)

Steps
----------
```

```
2005
2006
2007
2007
2008
2008
2009
2009
2010
2018
2020
2022
```

```
(12 row(s) affected)
```

```
DBCC execution completed. If DBCC printed error messages,
see your System Administrator.
```

As you can see from the output, this distribution page holds a total of 12 steps, in which the data elements are also listed. Also notice that for each of the columns in the index, the index density changes as more columns are added.

Using DBCC Statements to Monitor Your Database

The DBCC statements allow you to perform quite a few administrative tasks to fine-tune your database. They are summarized in Table 12.1.

Table 12.1. DBCC statements.

Statement	Description
CHECKALLOC	Checks database for proper page allocation. Replaced with NEWALLOC.
CHECKCATALOG	Checks for consistency in tables and between tables for links, indexes, and so on, and also displays defined segments.
CHECKTABLE	Checks specific table for errors.
CHECKDB	Checks all tables in the current database for errors.
CHECKIDENT	Compares current identity value with maximum identity value. If the current value is invalid, the maximum value is assigned.
DBREPAIR	Drops the specified database. Better method is DROP DATABASE or sp_dbremove.
INPUTBUFFER	Returns 255 bytes of the current input buffer of the user specified. The user ID can be obtained from sp_who.

Statement	Description
MEMUSAGE	Displays information on memory usage.
NEWALLOC	In addition to providing the same output as CHECKALLOC, this also provides detail on all tables.
OPENTRAN	Displays information on the oldest active transaction. Will display information only if there is at least one active transaction or if the database contains replication information.
OUTPUTBUFFER	Displays the information in both Hex and ASCII for the current buffer of the user ID specified.
PERFMON	Displays SQL performance statistics.
PINTABLE	Forces a table to be cached in RAM until UNPINTABLE is called.
SHOW_STATISTICS	Displays information concerning the distribution page for indexes of a table.
SHOWCONTIG	Checks to see if data is contiguous or fragmented. If fragmented, you will take a performance hit and should use FILLFACTOR or drop and recreate the index.
SHRINKDB	Specifies the smallest size to which the database could be reduced, and also displays objects utilizing the most space.
SQLPERF	Displays performance statistics.
TEXTALL	Runs TEXTALLOC on all columns in a table that contains text or image columns.
TEXTALLOC	Checks allocation of space for text and image columns in a table.
TRACEOFF	Stops tracing of flag number specified.
TRACEON	Starts tracing of flag number specified.
TRACESTATUS	Returns status of 1 if trace is set to ON or 0 if trace is set to OFF.
UNPINTABLE	Removes requirement for table to stay in RAM. Table is eventually flushed out to disk as it's accessed.
UPDATEUSAGE	Updates space usage in the sysindexes table, as reported by the sp_spaceused stored procedure.
USEROPTIONS	Displays SET options in place for the current connection.

12

UPDATING TABLE
INDEXES AND
STATISTICS

You have already seen a demonstration of SHOW_STATISTICS. The more commonly used DBCC statements are discussed in the following sections.

DBCC CHECKALLOC

This command remains in SQL Server for backward-compatibility. There is no guarantee that future releases of SQL Server will contain it. (The new command is NEWALLOC.) This command checks the allocation of pages within a database. The syntax is

```
CHECKALLOC(database[,noindex])
```

The database name can be specified. If not, the current database is used. The *noindex* parameter will exclude reporting on indexes in a table. Execute the following DBCC statement:

```
DBCC CHECKALLOC
```

Your output will appear similar to the following (although it's been shortened here):

```
Checking master
Database 'master' is not in single user mode - may find spurious
    allocation problems due to transactions in progress.
Alloc page 0 (# of extent=30 used pages=92 ref pages=92)
Alloc page 256 (# of extent=32 used pages=90 ref pages=90)
.
.
.
Total (# of extent=955 used pages=6855 ref pages=6848) in this database
DBCC execution completed. If DBCC printed error messages, see your System
Administrator.
```

DBCC CHECKCATALOG

The CHECKCATALOG statement ensures that all references in links of system tables for all tables in the database are valid. The syntax for the statement is

```
CHECKCATALOG([database])
```

The database name can be specified. If not, the current database is used. Execute the following DBCC statement:

```
DBCC CHECKCATALOG
```

Your output should be similar to the following:

```
Checking current database
The following segments have been defined for database 1(database name master).
virtual start addr      size     segments
------------------      ------   ------------------------
                   4    1536
                                 0
                                 1
                                 2
```

```
        3588     7168
                              0
                              1
                              2
DBCC execution completed. If DBCC printed error messages, see your
    System Administrator.
```

DBCC CHECKTABLE

The CHECKTABLE statement checks a specific table for consistency in data pages, indexes, pointers, and reasonableness of the data pages. The syntax for the statement is

```
CHECKTABLE(table_name)
```

The table_name is the name of the table to check. The database used was created in Chapter 2. Execute the following statement:

```
DBCC CHECKTABLE (cd)
```

Your output should be the following:

```
Checking cd
The total number of data pages in this table is 1.
Table has 31 data rows.
DBCC execution completed. If DBCC printed error messages,
see your System Administrator.
```

This statement can also find and repair indexing page problems. You may want to use the CHECKTABLE option periodically to keep your database in tune.

DBCC CHECKDB

CHECKDB performs the same function as CHECKTABLE, but for all tables in the database. The syntax for the statement is

```
CHECKTABLE([database][,NOINDEX})
```

The database name can be specified. If not, the current database is used. Execute the following statement:

```
DBCC CHECKDB
```

Notice the automatic correction of errors in the following output (which has been reduced in size):

```
Checking master
Checking 1
The total number of data pages in this table is 32.
Table has 408 data rows.
Checking 2
The total number of data pages in this table is 7.
Table has 82 data rows.
Checking 3
```

```
The total number of data pages in this table is 59.
The number of rows in Sysindexes for this table was 1203.
It has been corrected to 1202.
Table has 1202 data rows.
    .
    .
    .
Checking 2123154609
The total number of data pages in this table is 1.
Table has 17 data rows.
DBCC execution completed. If DBCC printed error messages,
see your System Administrator.
```

Like the CHECKTABLE statement, the CHECKDB statement can also find and repair indexing page problems. The first step in repairing a database is to run the CHECKDB option. This can help you diagnose what problems the database may be having.

DBCC INPUTBUFFER

INPUTBUFFER allows you to examine the most recent 255 bytes of the input buffer for the user ID specified. Use the stored procedure sp_who to obtain the user ID of the current users in the system. The syntax for the statement is

```
INPUTBUFFER(userid)
```

Execute the following statement:

```
DBCC INPUTBUFFER (19)
```

Your output will be similar to the following:

```
Input Buffer
sp_who
 (1 row(s) affected)
DBCC execution completed. If DBCC printed error messages,
see your System Administrator.
```

DBCC MEMUSAGE

MEMUSAGE provides information on three important facets of memory usage:

- Displays the server's memory allocation at the time of initialization
- Displays the memory usage of the 20 largest objects in the memory cache
- Displays the memory usage of the 12 largest objects in the procedure cache

The syntax for the statement is

```
MEMUSAGE
```

Execute the following statement:

```
DBCC MEMUSAGE
```

Your output, which has been shortened for display purposes, will appear similar to the following:

```
Memory Usage:
                           Meg.     2K Blks        Bytes
     Configured Memory: 16.0000        8192     16777216
            Code size:   1.7166         879      1800000
      Static Structures:  0.2640         136       276848
               Locks:    0.2861         147       300000
         Open Objects:   0.1144          59       120000
       Open Databases:   0.0041           3         4344
    User Context Areas:  8.1266        4161      8521332
           Page Cache:   3.7419        1916      3923712
         Proc Headers:   0.0899          47        94306
       Proc Cache Bufs:  1.5117         774      1585152
Buffer Cache, Top 20:
      DB Id     Object Id     Index Id     2K Buffers
         1             6            0            758
         1            36            0            102
         1     553053006           0             68
         1             3            0             59
         1     553053006           2             50
         1             1            0             32
         1            36            2             30
         1            99            0             29
         1             5            0             25
         1            12            0             22
         1             6            1             16
         1            45          255             16
         1     704005539           0             13
         1             2            0              7
         1     704005539           2              7
         1             1            2              4
         1             9            0              4
         1             5            1              2
         1            37            0              2
         1     137051524           0              2
Procedure Cache, Top 16:
Procedure Name: sp_helpconstraint
Database Id: 1
Object Id: 1913057851
Version: 1
Uid: 1
Type: stored procedure
Number of trees: 0
Size of trees: 0.000000 Mb, 0.000000 bytes, 0 pages
Number of plans: 1
Size of plans: 0.111712 Mb, 117138.000000 bytes, 58 pages
Procedure Name: sp_help
Database Id: 1
Object Id: 364528332
Version: 1
Uid: 1
Type: stored procedure
Number of trees: 0
Size of trees: 0.000000 Mb, 0.000000 bytes, 0 pages
Number of plans: 1
```

```
Size of plans: 0.062954 Mb, 66012.000000 bytes, 33 pages
  .
  .
  .
DBCC execution completed. If DBCC printed error messages,
see your System Administrator.
```

DBCC NEWALLOC

NEWALLOC provides the same information as CHECKALLOC, but additional reports detailed information about each table in the database. The syntax for the statement is

NEWALLOC(*database_name[,NOINDEX]*)

The *database_name* can be specified. If not, the current database will be used. You can also exclude indexes with the *NOINDEX* parameter. Execute the following statement:

DBCC NEWALLOC

Your output, which has been shortened for display purposes, should be similar to the following:

```
Checking master
Database 'master' is not in single user mode - may find spurious
    allocation problems due to transactions in progress.
*****************************************************************
TABLE: sysobjects        OBJID = 1
INDID=1    FIRST=1    ROOT=8    DPAGES=32    SORT=0
    Data level: 1.  32 Data  Pages in 5 extents.
    Indid      : 1.  1 Index Pages in 1 extents.
INDID=2    FIRST=560    ROOT=561    DPAGES=1    SORT=1
    Indid      : 2.  11 Index Pages in 2 extents.
TOTAL # of extents = 8
*****************************************************************
TABLE: sysindexes        OBJID = 2
INDID=1    FIRST=24    ROOT=32    DPAGES=7    SORT=0
    Data level: 1.  7 Data  Pages in 1 extents.
    Indid      : 1.  1 Index Pages in 1 extents.
TOTAL # of extents = 2
*****************************************************************
  .
  .
  .
*****************************************************************
Processed 79 entries in the Sysindexes for dbid 1.
Alloc page 0 (# of extent=30 used pages=92 ref pages=92)
Alloc page 256 (# of extent=32 used pages=90 ref pages=90)
Alloc page 512 (# of extent=30 used pages=88 ref pages=88)
Alloc page 768 (# of extent=32 used pages=249 ref pages=249)
Alloc page 1024 (# of extent=32 used pages=256 ref pages=256)
Alloc page 1280 (# of extent=32 used pages=256 ref pages=256)
Alloc page 1536 (# of extent=32 used pages=212 ref pages=212)
Alloc page 1792 (# of extent=32 used pages=105 ref pages=105)
```

```
Alloc page 2048 (# of extent=13 used pages=17 ref pages=17)
Alloc page 2304 (# of extent=32 used pages=256 ref pages=256)
Alloc page 2560 (# of extent=32 used pages=256 ref pages=256)
Alloc page 2816 (# of extent=32 used pages=256 ref pages=256)
Alloc page 3072 (# of extent=32 used pages=256 ref pages=256)
Alloc page 3328 (# of extent=32 used pages=256 ref pages=256)
Alloc page 3584 (# of extent=32 used pages=256 ref pages=256)
Alloc page 3840 (# of extent=32 used pages=256 ref pages=256)
Alloc page 4096 (# of extent=32 used pages=256 ref pages=256)
Alloc page 4352 (# of extent=32 used pages=256 ref pages=256)
Alloc page 4608 (# of extent=1 used pages=1 ref pages=1)
Alloc page 4864 (# of extent=32 used pages=256 ref pages=256)
Alloc page 5120 (# of extent=32 used pages=256 ref pages=256)
Alloc page 5376 (# of extent=32 used pages=256 ref pages=256)
Alloc page 5632 (# of extent=32 used pages=256 ref pages=256)
Alloc page 5888 (# of extent=32 used pages=256 ref pages=256)
Alloc page 6144 (# of extent=32 used pages=256 ref pages=256)
Alloc page 6400 (# of extent=32 used pages=256 ref pages=256)
Alloc page 6656 (# of extent=32 used pages=256 ref pages=256)
Alloc page 6912 (# of extent=32 used pages=256 ref pages=256)
Alloc page 7168 (# of extent=32 used pages=256 ref pages=256)
Alloc page 7424 (# of extent=32 used pages=256 ref pages=256)
Alloc page 7680 (# of extent=32 used pages=256 ref pages=256)
Alloc page 7936 (# of extent=14 used pages=106 ref pages=106)
Alloc page 8192 (# of extent=1 used pages=1 ref pages=1)
Alloc page 8448 (# of extent=2 used pages=9 ref pages=2)
Total (# of extent=955 used pages=6858 ref pages=6851) in this database
DBCC execution completed. If DBCC printed error messages,
see your System Administrator.
```

DBCC OUTPUTBUFFER

OUTPUTBUFFER allows you to examine the current contents of the output buffer in both Hex and ASCII for the user ID specified. Use the stored procedure sp_who to obtain the user ID of the current users in the system. The syntax for the statement is

```
OUTPUTBUFFER(userid)
```

Execute the following statement:

```
DBCC OUTPUTBUFFER (19)
```

Your output will appear similar to the following:

```
Output Buffer
-------------------------------------------------------------------
---
0016c6a0:  04 01 04 f5 00 00 00 00 ff 51 00 c1 00 01 00 00
.........Q......
0016c6b0:  00 ff 51 00 c1 00 01 00 00 00 ff 41 00 c0 00 00
..Q........A....
0016c6c0:  00 00 00 ff 41 00 c0 00 00 00 00 00 7c 25 ee 32
....A.......¦%.2
0016c6d0:  35 00 00 00 00 a0 2d 00 04 73 70 69 64 06 73 74  5......-
..spid.st
```

```
0016c6e0:  61 74 75 73 08 6c 6f 67 69 6e 61 6d 65 08 68 6f
atus.loginame.ho
0016c6f0:  73 74 6e 61 6d 65 03 62 6c 6b 06 64 62 6e 61 6d
stname.blk.dbnam
0016c700:  65 03 63 6d 64 a1 29 00 06 00 08 00 34 01 00 08
e.cmd.).....4...
0016c710:  00 2f 0a 02 00 09 00 27 0c 01 00 08 00 2f 1e 02   ./
.....'...../..
0016c720:  00 09 00 27 05 02 00 09 00 27 0a 01 00 08 00 2f
...'.....'...../
0016c730:  10 d1 01 00 0a 73 6c 65 65 70 69 6e 67 20 20 02   .....sleeping
0016c740:  73 61 1e 20 20 20 20 20 20 20 20 20 20 20 20 20  sa.
0016c750:  20 20 20 20 20 20 20 20 20 20 20 20 20 20 20 20
0016c760:  20 05 30 20 20 20 20 06 6d 61 73 74 65 72 10 4d   .0
.master.M
0016c770:  49 52 52 4f 52 20 48 41 4e 44 4c 45 52 20 20 d1  IRROR HANDLER
.
0016c780:  02 00 0a 73 6c 65 65 70 69 6e 67 20 20 02 73 61  ...sleeping
.sa
0016c790:  1e 20 20 20 20 20 20 20 20 20 20 20 20 20 20 20   .
0016c7a0:  20 20 20 20 20 20 20 20 20 20 20 20 20 20 20 05
.
0016c7b0:  30 20 20 20 20 06 6d 61 73 74 65 72 10 4c 41 5a  0
.master.LAZ
0016c7c0:  59 20 57 52 49 54 45 52 20 20 20 20 20 d1 03 00  Y WRITER
...
0016c7d0:  0a 73 6c 65 65 70 69 6e 67 20 20 02 73 61 1e 20  .sleeping
.sa.
0016c7e0:  20 20 20 20 20 20 20 20 20 20 20 20 20 20 20 20
0016c7f0:  20 20 20 20 20 20 20 20 20 20 20 20 20 05 30 20
.0
0016c800:  20 20 20 06 6d 61 73 74 65 72 10 43 48 45 43 4b
.master.CHECK
0016c810:  50 4f 49 4e 54 20 53 4c 45 45 50 d1 04 00 0a 73  POINT
SLEEP....s
0016c820:  6c 65 65 70 69 6e 67 20 20 02 73 61 1e 20 20 20  leeping  .sa.
0016c830:  20 20 20 20 20 20 20 20 20 20 20 20 20 20 20 20
0016c840:  20 20 20 20 20 20 20 20 20 20 20 05 30 20 20 20                 .0
0016c850:  20 06 6d 61 73 74 65 72 10 52 41 20 4d 41 4e 41   .master.RA
MANA
0016c860:  47 45 52 20 20 20 20 20 20 d1 0a 00 0a 73 6c 65  GER
....sle
0016c870:  65 70 69 6e 67 20 20 02 73 61 1e 53 51 4c 20 20  eping
.sa.SQL
0016c880:  20 20 20 20 20 20 20 20 20 20 20 20 20 20 20 20
0016c890:  20 20 20 20 20 20 20 20 20 05 30 20 20 20 20 06              .0
.
0016c8a0:  6d                                                m
(1 row(s) affected)
DBCC execution completed. If DBCC printed error messages,
see your System Administrator.
```

DBCC PERFMON

PERFMON allows you to examine all SQL performance stats of IOSTATS, LRUSTATS, and NETSTATS. The syntax for the statement is

PERFMON

Execute the following statement:

DBCC PERFMON

Your output should look similar to the following:

```
Statistic                      Value
-----------------------------  -----------------------
Log Flush Requests             462.0
Log Logical Page IO            567.0
Log Physical IO                439.0
Log Flush Average              1.05239
Log Logical IO Average         1.29157
Batch Writes                   210.0
Batch Average Size             5.67568
Batch Max Size                 8.0
Page Reads                     4280.0
Single Page Writes             191.0
Reads Outstanding              0.0
Writes Outstanding             0.0
Transactions                   886.0
Transactions/Log Write         2.01822

(14 row(s) affected)


Statistic                      Value
-----------------------------  -----------------------
Cache Hit Ratio                96.4771
Cache Flushes                  89.0
Free Page Scan (Avg)           0.988379
Free Page Scan (Max)           1.0
Min Free Buffers               409.0
Cache Size                     1830.0
Free Buffers                   422.0

(7 row(s) affected)


Statistic                      Value
-----------------------------  -----------------------
Network Reads                  0.0
Network Writes                 933.0
Command Queue Length           0.0
Max Command Queue Length       0.0
Worker Threads                 11.0
Max Worker Threads             11.0
Network Threads                0.0
Max Network Threads            0.0
```

```
(8 row(s) affected)

Statistic                        Value
------------------------------- ------------------------
RA Pages Found in Cache          20363.0
RA Pages Placed in Cache         25266.0
RA Physical IO                   3544.0
Used Slots                       0.0

(4 row(s) affected)

DBCC execution completed. If DBCC printed error messages, see your System
Administrator.
```

Summary

This chapter demonstrates several techniques to improve performance by unleashing the power of indexes. Two methods of improving performance are planning the indexes in the design phase and using SQL's built-in optimizer to update table indexes. In the planning stage, different types of tables warrant different considerations. If the table is used for data warehousing, it is always a good idea to index as many fields as possible. Updates to the data warehouse are usually made in batch mode, so performance issues in adding records are meaningless. If the table is used for online transaction processing, the fewer indexes the better.

If you create one field to store all the fields that would make the concatenated primary key, and make this single field the primary key, you will see a noticeable improvement in performance. Every time a record is added, all of the indexes have to be searched to make sure the record is unique. When you narrow the search to one index, this improves the processing time greatly. If you must query these tables and there is a large number of records, you may want to consider creating an index during processing time, running the query, and then dropping the index. The second method uses UPDATE STATISTICS, the statement that optimizes indexes after data has been added. This updates the distribution page to account for any new or deleted records.

Finally, you witnessed the power of the remaining DBCC statements to provide performance statistics regarding SQL Server, as well as learning about some powerful utilities.

Crosstabulation

IN THIS CHAPTER

Crosstabulation is one of those words with which users of Microsoft Access, Seagate Crystal Reports, and the like will be very familiar. *Crosstabulation* is the process of taking data and transforming it into column names, so that data can be arranged in a cross-section–style format. A list of salespeople, clients, and sales amounts is an example. Instead of listing the first salesperson, the first client, and the sales; then the same salesperson, the next client, and the sales; and so on, what if you could have each salesperson listed alongside the left column, have the clients appear as columns, and have the total sales located where the two meet in the table?

This chapter aims at showing you how to perform crosstabulation entirely within SQL Server Transact-SQL and, by doing so, it combines many of the topics discussed up to this point in the book. The real objective is to show you how to take the individual functions, statements, and expressions and make a very complex, yet practical, stored procedure.

A Description of Crosstabulation

Not so long ago, I was teaching a SQL Server class when one of the students (who also happened to be a colleague of mine) asked a question: "How do you crosstabulate data in SQL Server?"

My answers ranged from connecting to the SQL Server with Access and using a crosstab query to using a program like Seagate's Crystal Reports and creating a crosstab report. Not one of my responses mentioned SQL Server's capability to crosstabulate the data. I suppose I had always accepted this fact and never questioned it—until that day in class.

I did a little thinking over lunch, and that afternoon in class I spoke once again on the topic. I stated that there is no reason why SQL Server couldn't do it, but I just didn't know how—and so I began my quest.

Essential Crosstabulation Considerations

As I began to delve deeper into the subject, I found many things to keep in consideration: How do I return the data to the user? How do I create columns in this data structure that are actually row values? How do I validate a user's permissions on the requested data? Where do I start?

> **NOTE**
>
> I readily admit that I used my most favorite resource during the initial and intermediate stages of the development of these questions: friends, colleagues, and coworkers. The creative process played an important role in the entire development of this procedure; the human factor, not just reference books, helped solve the problem.

Before you get into the code, I would like to fill you in on the thought process that lead to it and a brief outline of its internals.

I decided to use a bottom-up approach, so I started by determining what I was going to return as the crosstabulated data results. A temporary table would be best, given the situation. However, it just couldn't be done. The temporary table required too much modification to structure and content, and T-SQL just couldn't do the job.

A permanent table is needed. What about all the users? Each user would need his or her own table. By using SQL Server's capability to have more than one table of the same name with different owners, this could be done. The only problem (to which I still haven't found a solution) is when a server login is aliased to an existing user in the database. This means that multiple logins use the same database username. Thus, they could potentially use the same table (which is named `Crosstable`) when crosstabulating data, a definite potential for conflict.

> **NOTE**
>
> More than one object may exist with the same name if the owner of those objects differ. Therefore, `dbo.Crosstable`, `joe.Crosstable`, and `mary.Crosstable` can coexist in a database. By having users own their crosstables, a simple `SELECT` statement (`SELECT * FROM Crosstable`) without the owner qualifier returns a given user his or her crosstabulated results. For example, if Mary ran that `SELECT` statement, she would get results from `mary.Crosstable` (as long as it existed) or `dbo.Crosstable` (if she didn't own an object named `Crosstable`).

Because of the nature of T-SQL, the crosstable could not be defined using dynamic execution. This ruled out using randomly generated names for the crosstable. I let this topic stew in my brain for a while, and even later found no better approach. I decided that I would not try to complicate matters further in this book by finding some contrived means of eliminating any chance of this conflict. If you happen to find an alternate solution, drop me a line and let me know. I will continue to update and place this procedure on my company's Web site, and will take all suggestions into account.

Once the means of returning data was established, I went to work on the actual process. The parameters would consist of a column for the row header, a column for the column header, a column for the values to be aggregated, and the source itself (a table or a view).

Next, I check for the existence of the columns and source object. If all is well, two temporary tables are created to hold the row data and the column data. I create the crosstable, populate the rows from the row temporary table, and alter it using the data from the column temporary table. The altering of the crosstable was also an issue. Data tends not to be usable as a column name, because it often doesn't follow the rules for SQL Server identifiers. I considered using Quoted Identifiers, but this would be non-standard; I resolved to parse through the data and remove illegal characters, as well as prefix the value with an underscore if the initial value is numeric.

Next, a cursor is created to hold all the data. As we iterate through the cursor rows, an EXECUTE statement is issued updating the contents of the crosstable. When all is done, the crosstable results are returned and all tables and cursors are dropped and deallocated. This is the crosstab stored procedure's basic process, but a few other issues that needed addressing remained.

Security

This topic didn't cross my mind at first; I figured it would be easy enough to handle when and if I needed to cross that bridge. When everything started falling into place, I came to a different realization.

Security knocked me for a loop, although it really was a very long SELECT statement contained within an IF statement that did the trick. The information was already stored in several system tables—I just needed to figure an efficient and graceful way to do the job. I'm not sure if my answer qualifies as either, but it gets the job done and is reliable. An entire section of this chapter is dedicated to explaining the security check process.

Aggregates

Another factor was the use of aggregates in the crosstabulated results. I was sure that a simple sum ability would not suffice, so an average, min, max, and count would also be needed. An additional parameter had to be added to handle this and some additional work, to determine which aggregate operation was good with which datatypes.

Date Grouping

True crosstab ability has to include date-range grouping such as year, quarter, month, week, and weekday. Matters became complicated very quickly when this factor was added to the process. Along with the additional parameter, which is needed to determine type, I had to create many additional checks using IF statements and CASE expressions. You should plainly notice the majority of them in the procedure, and all are explained as they appear in the code.

The Procedure

The stored procedure is broken into sections, so that it's easier to work through and explain. The entire procedure can be found in the file SCR1301.SQL, comments and all. The code, in actual order, is presented to you a portion at a time. Listing 13.1 shows the stored procedure declaration, as well as all the variable declaration used by the procedure.

Listing 13.1. The procedure and variable declarations.

```
1: CREATE PROCEDURE prCrosstab
2:     @chrRowHead char(30),
3:     @chrColHead char(30),
4:     @chrValue char(30),
5:     @chrSource char(30),
6:     @inyType tinyint = 1,
7:     @inyGrouping tinyint = 0
```

```
 8: AS
 9:
10: /*  Variables for the procedure  */
11: DECLARE
12:      @chvRow varchar(255),
13:      @chvCol varchar(255),
14:      @chvVal varchar(255),
15:      @chvType varchar(10),
16:      @chvRowType varchar(10),
17:      @chvColType varchar(255),
18:      @chvTemp varchar(255),
19:      @chvColTemp varchar(255),
20:      @chvRowTemp varchar(255),
21:      @intType int,
22:      @intRowType int,
23:      @intColType int,
24:      @chvExec varchar(255),
25:      @chvGroup varchar(255),
26:      @fltTemp float,
27:      @dtmTemp datetime,
28:      @insR smallint,
29:      @intColumn int,
30:      @intReturn int,
31:      @intTemp int,
32:      @intColNameLen int,
33:      @intMaxRowHead int
34:
35: SET NOCOUNT ON
```

This code is self-explanatory. The SET NOCOUNT ON statement isn't necessary, but makes debugging a lot simpler. You see a recurring PRINT statement throughout the code. It is commented out and I use it to help me debug. The statement always occurs just before an EXECUTE statement, allowing you to print the actual string that is executed, so you know where to look if a problem occurs. In addition, Table 13.1 contains information regarding the parameters and what values are expected to be passed into them.

Table 13.1. Stored procedure parameter descriptions.

Parameter	Description
@chrRowHead	Column that appears as the first column in the crosstabulated results
@chrColHead	Column whose data is transformed into new column names in the crosstabulated results
@chrValue	Column on which to perform aggregate function
@chrSource	Source table or view
@inyType	1-Sum, 2-Average, 3-Minimum, 4-Maximum, 5-Count
@inyGrouping	1-Weekday, 2-Week of Year, 3-Month, 4-Quarter, 5-Year

Verifying Object Existence

The next portion has to verify that all the parameters were valid. The first step was to check for the existence of the three column names and the source table or view. After that, you need to make sure that the aggregate is appropriate for the datatype of the value column. Finally, the date grouping parameter needed to be verified against the column header column.

Verifying the Parameters

You should instantly recognize the statements used in Listing 13.2. You always see a very similar statement when managing stored procedures and views in SQL Enterprise Manager. The source object's existence is verified by interrogating the sysobjects table. The three supplied columns are individually checked to see if they exist in the syscolumns table for the supplied source object.

Listing 13.2. Verifying parameter values.

```
 1: /*  Check if source exists  */
 2:
 3: IF NOT EXISTS
 4:     (SELECT *
 5:     FROM sysobjects
 6:     WHERE name = @chrSource
 7:     AND type IN ('v','u'))
 8: BEGIN
 9:     RAISERROR 51001 'Source does not exist.'
10:     RETURN -1
11: END
12:
13: /*  Check for column existence  */
14:
15: IF NOT EXISTS
16:     (SELECT sc.name
17:     FROM syscolumns sc
18:         JOIN sysobjects so ON sc.id = so.id
19:     WHERE so.name = @chrSource
20:     AND sc.name = @chrColHead)
21: BEGIN
22:     RAISERROR 51002 'Invalid @chrColHead name.'
23:     RETURN -1
24: END
25:
26: IF NOT EXISTS
27:     (SELECT sc.name
28:     FROM syscolumns sc
29:         JOIN sysobjects so ON sc.id = so.id
30:     WHERE so.name = @chrSource
31:     AND sc.name = @chrRowHead)
32: BEGIN
33:     RAISERROR 51002 'Invalid @chrRowHead name.'
34:     RETURN -1
35: END
```

```
36:
37: IF NOT EXISTS
38:     (SELECT sc.name
39:     FROM syscolumns sc
40:         JOIN sysobjects so ON sc.id = so.id
41:     WHERE so.name = @chrSource
42:     AND sc.name = @chrValue)
43: BEGIN
44:     RAISERROR 51002 'Invalid @chrValue name.'
45:     RETURN -1
46: END
47:
48: /* Verify type is valid (1 (sum), 2 (avg), etc...) */
49:
50: IF @inyType <1 OR @inyType >5
51: BEGIN
52:     RAISERROR 51000 'Invalid crosstab type.'
53:     RETURN -1
54: END
```

The last portion of Listing 13.2 checks to see that the aggregate parameter value is not between 1 and 5. You could just as easily coded it to read IF @inyType NOT BETWEEN 1 AND 5, or a variety of other ways. In any case, the first four parameters are simple to check. The fifth—the aggregate type—still needs additional verification, but this can only be done once you have found the base datatypes of the three columns.

Verifying the Datatypes and Aggregates

Now you need to find the value column's datatype and make sure it is valid for use with the requested aggregate type. Take a look at Listing 13.3.

Listing 13.3. Verifying valid datatypes and aggregate correlation.

```
 1: /*   Create typestr to hold aggregate name   */
 2:
 3: SELECT @chvType =
 4:     CASE @inyType
 5:     WHEN 1 THEN 'SUM'
 6:     WHEN 2 THEN 'AVG'
 7:     WHEN 3 THEN 'MAX'
 8:     WHEN 4 THEN 'MIN'
 9:     WHEN 5 THEN 'COUNT'
10:     ELSE 'SUM'
11:     END
12:
13: /*   Get standard datatype of @chrValue column   */
14:
15: SELECT @chvTemp = t2.name
16: FROM sysobjects o
17:     JOIN syscolumns c ON (o.id = c.id)
18:     JOIN systypes t1 ON (t1.usertype = c.usertype)
19:     JOIN systypes t2 ON (t1.type = t2.type)
```

continues

13

CROSSTABULATION

Listing 13.3. continued

```
20: WHERE t2.usertype < 100
21: AND t2.usertype <> 18
22: AND t2.usertype <> 80
23: AND o.type IN ('u','v')
24: AND o.name = @chrSource
25: AND c.name = @chrValue
26:
27: /*  Categorize types for aggregate check  */
28:
29: SELECT @intTemp =
30:       CASE
31:       WHEN @chvTemp IN ('int', 'smallint', 'tinyint', 'float', 'real',
32:            'decimal', 'numeric', 'money', 'smallmoney') THEN 1
33:       WHEN @chvTemp IN ('datetime', 'smalldatetime') THEN 3
34:       WHEN @chvTemp IN ('bit', 'char', 'varchar') THEN 5
35:       ELSE 100
36:       END
37:
38: /*  Validate existing datatype is consistent with selected aggregate  */
39:
40: IF @inyType < @intTemp
41: BEGIN
42:       RAISERROR 51020 'Crosstab type not valid with @chrValue definition.'
43:       RETURN -1
44: END
45:
46: /*  Hold the datatype for future use  */
47:
48: SELECT @chvColType = RTRIM(
49:       CASE @inyType
50:       WHEN 5 THEN 'int'
51:       ELSE CASE
52:            WHEN @chvTemp IN ('bit', 'char', 'varchar') THEN 'int'
53:            WHEN @chvTemp IN ('decimal', 'numeric') THEN 'float'
54:            ELSE @chvTemp
55:            END
56:       END)
57:
58: /*  Verify grouping is valid for colhead  */
59:
60: IF @inyGrouping <0 OR @inyGrouping > 5
61: BEGIN
62:       RAISERROR 51010 'Invalid crosstab grouping.'
63:       RETURN -1
64: END
```

Using a simple SELECT statement and a Case expression, lines 3 through 11 create the string equivalent for the aggregate type to be used later in the code. Lines 15 through 25 find the value column's base datatype.

> **NOTE**
>
> The base datatype are defined as the initial datatypes (except `sysname` and `timestamp`) supplied by SQL Server. `sysname` and `timestamp` (both system-defined) and user-defined datatypes are resolved to their base datatype by excluding them in the second instance of the systypes table. `sysname` has a usertype value of `18`, `timestamp` is `80`, and user-defined datatypes always have a usertype value greater-than or equal to `100`.

The datatypes are categorized into one of four values: `1`, `3`, `5`, and `100`. Lines 29 through 36 take care of this process. These values are not randomly chosen; lines 40 through 44 perform a check to see if the aggregate type is valid to use with the `value` column's datatype. If the aggregate type is less than the datatype category, the procedure raises an error and returns. Table 13.2 shows a list of datatypes, aggregates, and category values. Each datatype supports any aggregate at an equal or greater level. Since the aggregates were already assigned a value when passed into the procedure, the datatypes are grouped, as shown in Table 13.2, and compared the two values.

Table 13.2. Datatypes and aggregates.

Category	Datatype	Aggregate
1	All numerics	Sum
2		Avg
3	datetime	Min
4		Max
5	All others	Count

In lines 48 through 56 you convert the `value` column's datatype to `int`, if a count is requested. If not, `bit`, `char`, and `varchar` values are converted to `int` (since only a count can be performed on `bit`, `char`, and `varchar`), and `numerics` and `decimals` are converted into `float`. Finally, the last part of Listing 13.3 validates that the date grouping is indeed valid.

Column and Row Head Datatypes

Listing 13.4 retrieves the base datatype for both the column and row header columns.

Listing 13.4. Retrieving the column and row head datatypes.

```
1: /*  Get standard datatype of @chrColHead column   */
2:
3: SELECT @chvTemp = t2.name
```

continues

Listing 13.4. continued

```
 4: FROM sysobjects o
 5:     JOIN syscolumns c ON (o.id = c.id)
 6:     JOIN systypes t1 ON (t1.usertype = c.usertype)
 7:     JOIN systypes t2 ON (t1.type = t2.type)
 8: WHERE t2.usertype < 100
 9: AND t2.usertype <> 18
10: AND t2.usertype <> 80
11: AND o.type IN ('u','v')
12: AND o.name = @chrSource
13: AND c.name = @chrColHead
14:
15: IF UPPER(@chvTemp) NOT IN ('CHAR', 'VARCHAR')
16:     SELECT @intColtype = 1
17: ELSE
18:     SELECT @intColtype = 0
19:
20: /*  Get standard datatype of @chrRowHead */
21:
22: SELECT @chvRowType = t2.name
23: FROM sysobjects o
24:     JOIN syscolumns c ON (o.id = c.id)
25:     JOIN systypes t1 ON (t1.usertype = c.usertype)
26:     JOIN systypes t2 ON (t1.type = t2.type)
27: WHERE t2.usertype < 100
28: AND t2.usertype <> 18
29: AND t2.usertype <> 80
30: AND o.type IN ('u','v')
31: AND o.name = @chrSource
32: AND c.name = @chrRowHead
33:
34: IF UPPER(@chvRowType) NOT IN ('CHAR', 'VARCHAR')
35:     SELECT @intRowtype = 1
36: ELSE
37:     SELECT @intRowtype = 0
38:
39: /*  Categorize types for grouping check  */
40:
41: SELECT @intTemp =
42:     CASE
43:     WHEN @chvTemp IN ('int', 'smallint', 'tinyint', 'float', 'real',
44:         'decimal', 'numeric', 'money', 'smallmoney') THEN 1
45:     WHEN @chvTemp IN ('datetime', 'smalldatetime') THEN 3
46:     WHEN @chvTemp IN ('bit', 'char', 'varchar') THEN 5
47:     ELSE 100
48:     END
49:
50: /*  Validate existing datatype is consistant with selected grouping  */
51:
52: IF (@intTemp = 5 AND @inyGrouping > 0) OR (@intTemp = 1 AND @inyGrouping >0)
53:     OR (@intTemp = 3 AND @inyGrouping = 0)
54: BEGIN
55:     RAISERROR 51030 'Crosstab grouping not valid with @chrColHead definition.'
56:     RETURN -1
57: END
```

Lines 3 through 13 find the column head's datatype. The next four lines categorize it as either a character or non-character datatype. This information is later used to provide needed conversions. Lines 22 through 37 do the same for the row head datatype.

The last portion (lines 41 through 57) validates that the column's datatype is consistent with the date grouping parameter. If it is a date, the date grouping must be between 1 and 5, otherwise, the date grouping must be 0.

This procedure is designed so that future upgrades are as simple as possible. One thought was to add an alternate grouping for character data, so that results can be grouped on a certain number of initial characters. For example, group on the first character so that all items beginning with an A would be together, and so on. The date grouping parameter could then serve as two types of data grouping.

Checking Column Security

The next task was to check security. This was not part of the initial plan, but rather a later realization. I modeled the query on the one used in the `sp_column_privileges` system stored procedure. A rather complicated query, it checks to see if the number of columns with select permission equals 3. Each of the column parameters are checked in the query and a value of 1 is returned to each that the current user has select rights. If all three are accessible, the IF statement succeeds and the procedure continues. Otherwise, an error is raised and the procedure returns. Examine Listing 13.5.

13

CROSSTABULATION

Listing 13.5. Checking permissions.

```
 1: /*  Check for permission on source  */
 2:
 3: IF user_id() <> 1
 4: BEGIN
 5:        IF (SELECT COUNT(DISTINCT c.name)
 6:          FROM syscolumns c, sysobjects o, sysprotects p,
 7:              sysusers u, master..spt_values v
 8:            WHERE c.name IN (@chrColHead, @chrRowHead, @chrValue)
 9:          AND c.id = o.id
10:          AND p.id = c.id
11:          AND c.colid = v.number
12:            AND v.type = 'p'
13:             AND o.id = object_id(@chrSource)
14:             AND (u.uid = user_id() OR u.uid IN
15:               (SELECT u1.uid
16:                  FROM sysusers u1
17:               WHERE u1.gid = u1.uid
18:               AND u1.gid IN
19:                    (SELECT u2.gid
20:                  FROM sysusers u2
21:                    WHERE u2.uid = user_id()
22:                    OR u2.uid = user_id('public'))))
23:             AND p.uid = u.uid
```

continues

Listing 13.5. continued

```
24:                 AND p.action = 193
25:                 AND p.protecttype = 205
26:                 AND columns IS NOT NULL
27:             AND CASE SUBSTRING(p.columns, 1, 1) & 1
28:                     WHEN null THEN 255
29:                     WHEN 0 THEN CONVERT(tinyint,
30:                             SUBSTRING(p.columns, v.low, 1))
31:                 ELSE (~CONVERT(tinyint, ISNULL(
32:                     SUBSTRING(p.columns, v.low, 1), 0)))
33:                     END & v.high <> 0
34:             AND NOT EXISTS
35:                 (SELECT *
36:                 FROM syscolumns c5, sysobjects o5,
37:                         sysprotects p5, sysusers u5,
38:                     master..spt_values v5
39:                 WHERE c.name IN (@chrColHead, @chrRowHead, @chrValue)
40:                     AND c5.colid = c.colid
41:                     AND c5.id = o5.id
42:                     AND p5.id = c5.id
43:                     AND c5.colid = v5.number
44:                     AND v5.type = 'p'
45:                     AND o5.id = object_id(@chrSource)
46:                     AND (u5.uid = user_id() OR u5.uid IN
47:                      (SELECT u6.uid
48:                         FROM sysusers u6
49:                      WHERE u6.gid = u6.uid
50:                         AND u6.gid IN
51:                             (SELECT u7.gid
52:                             FROM sysusers u7
53:                                 WHERE u7.uid=user_id()
54:                                 OR u7.uid=user_id('public'))))
55:                     AND p5.uid = u5.uid
56:                     AND p5.action = 193
57:                     AND p5.protecttype = 206
58:                 AND p5.columns IS NOT NULL
59:                     AND CASE SUBSTRING(p5.columns, 1, 1) & 1
60:                     WHEN NULL THEN 255
61:                         WHEN 0 THEN CONVERT(tinyint,
62:                             SUBSTRING(p5.columns, v5.low, 1))
63:                         ELSE (~CONVERT(tinyint,
64:                             ISNULL(SUBSTRING(p5.columns, v5.low, 1), 0)))
65:                     END & v5.high <> 0)) <> 3
66:     BEGIN
67:         RAISERROR 51003 'Permission denied on column.'
68:         RETURN -1
69:     END
70: END
```

The first IF statement excludes the dbo from the search. There is no need to do extra processing for the owner of the database. The next IF statement spans from lines 5 through 65. It contains a rather long SELECT statement.

In that statement, a count of the number of column names is the return value. The tables being queried are `syscolumns`, `sysobjects`, `sysprotects` (contains the security information), `sysusers`, and `spt_values`, from the `master` database.

Most of the query is straightforward. The name from `syscolumns` must be in the three supplied column names (line 8). `Syscolumns` and `sysobjects` are joined on their `id` columns. `sysprotects` and `syscolumns` are joined on their `id` columns as well (lines 9 through 10). The `sysobjects id` must match the supplied table or view for the procedure (line 13).

The current user's `id` must match the `uid` in `sysusers`, or any group to which the current user belongs (lines 14 through 22). The `uid` from `sysprotects` needs to match the `uid` from `sysusers`, and you look for an action of `193` (select permission) and a `protecttype` of `205` (permission is granted).

> **WARNING**
>
> If a user is a member of a group other than `public`, the user is not listed as a member of `public` in the `sysusers` table when it is queried—even though all users are always a member of `public`. When checking for a user's permissions, it is necessary to check the `public` group as well.

The subquery checks the same information, but with a `NOT EXISTS` clause. It finds those columns to which the user has been denied permission (`sysprotects protecttype` equals `206`).

The `spt_values` table is used to find the bit positions for the `columns` column in the `sysprotects` table for which you are checking permissions. You primarily see it referenced in lines 27 through 33 and lines 59 through 65.

The first byte of data from the `columns` column (binary datatype) is used in a `CASE` expression. The low value from `spt_values` is used to find another byte from the binary data. This value and the high value have a bitwise `AND` performed against them. If the result is not `0`, the user has permission to the specified column. Notice (for example in lines 43 through 44), the `spt_values` table's `number` column is matched with the `colid` from `syscolumns` and that the type is `'p'` (permission). This ensures that the high and low column values pertain to that particular column in the table when checking permissions.

If all is well, the query returns a value of `3`, meaning that the user has select permission on all three columns. If not, the main `IF` statement fails and the procedure raises an error and returns.

> **TIP**
>
> You can find information regarding the column definitions of the `system` tables and stored procedures in the appendixes of this book. The more you know about the system tables, the more ability you have to write very robust stored procedures.

Generating the Column Header List

The next portion of the procedure creates the column and row header lists. It starts by simply defining two temporary tables, as shown in Listing 13.6.

Listing 13.6. Creating the temporary tables.

```
CREATE TABLE #colnames (colname varchar(255) NULL, colnumber int NULL)
CREATE TABLE #rownames (rowname varchar(255) NULL)
```

The next step is to generate the column names using data from the requested column head value.

Creating the `colnames` Table

Listing 13.6 creates an `INSERT` statement based on the data from the source table for the requested column. A few details needed to be handled in this code: date groupings, converting non-character data to `char`, and sorting according to original datatype. The first item deals with creating the appropriate date grouping value for the requested parameter. The second item is required to make the data usable as a column name in the crosstable. The latter item is necessary when, for example, numeric data is converted into character data; the order is dictionary based when sorting numbers as characters (for example, 1, 10, 11, 2, 3, 4, 5, 6, 7, 8, 9), whereas you want the proper numerical order (1, 2, 3, 4, 5, 6, 7, 8, 9, 10, 11). Take a look at the code in Listing 13.7.

Listing 13.7. Creating the `colnames` table.

```
 1: /*  Insert distinct column data into #colnames  */
 2:
 3: SELECT @chvExec = 'insert #colnames select col1, col2 from '
 4:      + '(select distinct col1 = ' +
 5:      CASE @intTemp
 6:      WHEN 3 THEN
 7:           CASE
 8:           WHEN @inyGrouping IN (1,3) THEN 'datename(' +
 9:                CASE @inyGrouping
10:                WHEN 1 THEN 'weekday'
11:                WHEN 3 THEN 'month'
12:                END + ', ' + RTRIM(@chrColHead) + ')'
```

```
13:                ELSE CASE @inyGrouping
14:                    WHEN 2 THEN '''Week'
15:                    WHEN 4 THEN '''Quarter'
16:                    WHEN 5 THEN '''Year'
17:                    END + '_'' + ' + 'datename(' +
18:                CASE @inyGrouping
19:                    WHEN 2 THEN 'week'
20:                    WHEN 4 THEN 'quarter'
21:                    WHEN 5 THEN 'year'
22:                    END + ', ' + RTRIM(@chrColHead) + ')'
23:                END
24:        ELSE CASE @intColType
25:            WHEN 1 THEN 'convert(varchar(255), ' + RTRIM(@chrColHead) + ')'
26:            ELSE RTRIM(@chrColHead)
27:            END
28:        END + ', col2 = ' +
29:        CASE @intTemp
30:        WHEN 3 THEN 'datepart(' +
31:            CASE @inyGrouping
32:            WHEN 1 THEN 'weekday'
33:            WHEN 2 THEN 'week'
34:            WHEN 3 THEN 'month'
35:            WHEN 4 THEN 'quarter'
36:            WHEN 5 THEN 'year'
37:            END + ', ' + RTRIM(@chrColHead) + ')'
38:        ELSE '0'
39:        END + ', col3 = ' +
40:        CASE @intTemp
41:        WHEN 3 THEN 'datepart(' +
42:            CASE @inyGrouping
43:            WHEN 1 THEN 'weekday'
44:            WHEN 3 THEN 'month'
45:            WHEN 2 THEN 'week'
46:            WHEN 4 THEN 'quarter'
47:            WHEN 5 THEN 'year'
48:            END + ', ' + RTRIM(@chrColHead) + ')'
49:        ELSE RTRIM(@chrColHead)
50:        END + ' from ' + RTRIM(@chrSource) + ') xyz order by col3'
51:
52: --PRINT @chvExec
53: EXEC(@chvExec)
```

The SELECT statement that is created within the INSERT statement has three columns (of which only two are actually inserted). In order to achieve this, derived tables are used to create a resultset with three columns; only two of them are selected for the actual insert. The first column is generated in lines 4 through 28. If the column head's datatype is a date (line 6), it is converted into the Datename for the particular date grouping type. If the Datename function were to return a numeric, the name of the date grouping and an underscore are prefixed to the number (for example, Quarter_4). The distinct clause used in line 4 causes a unique set of data to be returned (since one occurrence of each column header is desired). Listings 13.8 and 13.9 each show a sample execution of the prCrosstab procedure and what the generated insert would look like.

13

CROSSTABULATION

Listing 13.8. A Sample of generated code from `prCrosstab`.

```
exec prcrosstab 'stor_id', 'ord_date', 'qty', 'sales', 1, 1 --weekday

insert #colnames
    select col1, col2
    from (select distinct col1 = datename(weekday, ord_date),
                    col2 = datepart(weekday, ord_date),
                    col3 = datepart(weekday, ord_date)
            from sales) xyz
    order by col3
```

Listing 13.9. Another sample of generated code from `prCrosstab`.

```
exec prcrosstab 'stor_id', 'ord_date', 'qty', 'sales', 1, 4 --quarter

insert #colnames
    select col1, col2
    from (select distinct col1 = 'Quarter_' + datename(quarter, ord_date),
                    col2 = datepart(quarter, ord_date),
                    col3 = datepart(quarter, ord_date)
            from sales) xyz
    order by col3
```

> **NOTE**
>
> You may have noticed that all of the generated code is lowercase. I chose to do this so it is easier to distinguish the generated code from the code of the actual stored procedure. You can call this the exception to the rule of naming conventions.

The second column (Listing 13.7, lines 28 through 39) is a numeric used for dates only (0 otherwise), which is used for finding the column when the crosstable is updated later in the procedure. For non-dates, the value is simply converted to char and compared.

The third column (lines 39 through 50) is used to provide the proper sorting (as seen in the ORDER BY clause line 50). By sorting on the appropriate datatype, the columns are listed in proper order no matter what the original datatype.

Finally, the generated INSERT statement is executed in line 53. Now that the #colnames table has the list of new columns for the crosstable, you need to verify that the number and length of the columns is valid.

Checking the Column Count and Length and Adding Row Data

In addition to verifying the column count and length of the column names, you also fill the #rownames table, if all is well, with the columns. Listing 13.10 shows the code to do the former.

Listing 13.10. Checking column count and name length.

```
 1: /*  Check column count  */
 2: IF (SELECT COUNT(*) FROM #colnames) > 249
 3: BEGIN
 4:      DROP TABLE #colnames
 5:      RAISERROR 51004 'Distinct column count exceeded max of 249.'
 6:      RETURN -1
 7: END
 8:
 9: /*  Verify colnames do not exceed max length  */
10: IF (SELECT MAX(DATALENGTH(RTRIM(colname)) - 1) FROM #colnames) > 29
11: BEGIN
12:      DROP TABLE #colnames
13:      RAISERROR 51050 'Column data length exceeded max of 30.'
14:      RETURN -1
15: END
```

Lines 2 through 7 check that there are fewer than 250 columns. In addition to the row head column in the crosstable, there's room left for additional columns for summary data at a later upgrade. The check is a simple count of the number of rows in the #colnames table. Lines 10 through 15 check that the maximum length of data in colname is less than or equal to 29 characters (the limit for SQL Server column names is 30). One character is left for prefixing an underscore if a column begins with a number. This means that the title from the titles table could never work as the column head for the crosstable.

Next, you populate the #rownames table with character data (converted, if necessary) from the rowhead column of the source table or view. Again, dynamic execution performs the insert as shown in line 14 of Listing 13.11. Listing 13.12 shows a sample of the generated statement.

Listing 13.11. Populating the rowname table.

```
 1: /*  If all is OK, continue to add #rownames data  */
 2: SELECT @chvExec = 'insert #rownames select distinct ' +
 3:      CASE @intRowtype
 4:      WHEN 1 THEN 'convert(varchar(255), '
 5:      ELSE ''
 6:      END + RTRIM(@chrRowHead) +
 7:
 8:      CASE @intRowType
 9:      WHEN 1 THEN ') '
10:      ELSE ''
11:      END + 'from ' + @chrSource
12:
13: --PRINT @chvExec
14: EXEC(@chvExec)
```

Listing 13.12. A sample INSERT generated from prCrosstab.

```
insert #rownames
    select distinct title_id
    from sales
```

Now that the two temporary table have been populated, move on to the crosstable itself.

Creating and Modifying the crosstable

Due to limitations in T-SQL, the crosstable must be defined statically in the stored procedure. A statement (with comments) was left in, which defines the actual length needed for the varchar datatype of the rowhead column.

Listing 13.13 shows the creation and altering of the crosstable.

Listing 13.13. Creating and altering the crosstable.

```
 1: /*
 2:      Would be nice if we could use this value to define the crosstable
 3:      but this table must be created in a non-dynamic fashion.
 4: */
 5: SELECT @intMaxRowHead = (SELECT MAX(DATALENGTH(RTRIM(rowname))) FROM #rownames)
 6:
 7: /*  Create crosstable  */
 8: /*  Define crosstable with rowhead field  */
 9: CREATE TABLE crosstable (rowhead varchar(255) NULL)
10:
11: /*  Alter crosstable by adding columns based on #colnames data  */
12:
13: DECLARE colname_cursor2 CURSOR FOR
14:      SELECT colname FROM #colnames
15:
16: OPEN colname_cursor2
17:
18: FETCH colname_cursor2 INTO @chvCol
19: WHILE @@fetch_status >= 0
20: BEGIN
21:      SELECT @chvColTemp=''
22:      IF @chvCol LIKE '%[^A-Z0-9]%'
23:      BEGIN
24:          SELECT @insR = 1
25:          WHILE @insR <= DATALENGTH(RTRIM(@chvCol))
26:          BEGIN
27:              SELECT @chvColTemp = RTRIM(@chvColTemp) +
28:                  CASE
29:                  WHEN SUBSTRING(@chvCol, @insR, 1) LIKE '[A-Z0-9_]'
30:                      THEN SUBSTRING(@chvCol, @insR, 1)
31:                  ELSE ''
32:                  END
33:              SELECT @insR = @insR + 1
34:          END
35:          SELECT @chvCol = @chvColTemp
36:      END
37:      SELECT @chvExec = 'alter table ' + user_name() + '.crosstable add ' +
38:          CASE
39:          WHEN SUBSTRING(@chvCol,1,1) LIKE '[^1234567890]' THEN @chvCol
40:          ELSE '_' + LTRIM(@chvCol)
41:          END
42:          + ' ' + @chvColType + ' null default (0)'
43:
```

```
44:      --PRINT @chvExec
45:      EXEC(@chvExec)
46:      FETCH colname_cursor2 INTO @chvCol
47: END
48:
49: CLOSE colname_cursor2
50: DEALLOCATE colname_cursor2
```

Line 9 defines the crosstable with a single nullable column named rowhead of varchar datatype (length of 255). Next, a cursor is created based on the temporary table #colnames (lines 13 and 14). After opening the cursor, the column name is fetched into the variable @chvCol.

If all is well (data was fetched), then the column name is parsed. Line 22 checks to see if any illegal characters are in the name. If so, loop through the string and append only the valid characters onto the variable @chvColTemp. Lines 28 through 32 use a CASE expression and the SUBSTRING function to return the valid character and, if the character is invalid, to return an empty string.

After looping through the name of the column, you alter the crosstable with the new column name. If the first character is a number (lines 38 through 41), an underscore is prefixed onto the name to make it valid. The datatype that was determined earlier is used for the column datatype. Line 42 defines the column as nullable with a default of 0.

Then execute the ALTER TABLE statement (see Listing 13.14 for an example) and move on to the next column, repeating the process until all columns have been added to the crosstable.

Listing 13.14. A sample of Alter Table statements.

```
alter table dbo.crosstable add Year_1992 smallint null default (0)
alter table dbo.crosstable add Year_1993 smallint null default (0)
alter table dbo.crosstable add Year_1994 smallint null default (0)
```

Once all the columns have been appended to the table, the cursor is closed and deallocated (lines 49 and 50), finishing this portion of the procedure. You need to update all the values in the crosstable with the requested aggregate value column data from the source table or view.

Updating the crosstable Values

Updating the crosstable is a two-step process. First, you must append rows assigning only the first column (rowhead) with the row head data in the rownames temporary table. After placing this data in the crosstable, you can use it to perform updates on the table (you essentially have a chart to plot data against—see Listing 13.15 for an example).

Inserting the Initial Data into the crosstable

Listing 13.15 performs the insert that adds the initial data to the crosstable. It is a simple insert from the rownames table.

Listing 13.15. Adding the initial crosstable data.

```
/*  Add #rowhead data to crosstable  */
SELECT @chvExec = 'insert ' + user_name() + '.crosstable (rowhead) select
    rowname from #rownames'

--PRINT @chvExec
EXEC(@chvExec)
```

Listing 13.16. A sample of the crosstable to this point in time.

```
/* If you were to complete the procedure (close cursors, drop temp tables, etc. */
/* you could then test to see what results were in the crosstable */
/* Since the procedure is not yet complete, this next statement will not work
correctly */
/* It is provided to demonstrate where the results listed below it come from */
SELECT * FROM crosstable

/* These are only sample results */
rowhead  Year_1992 Year_1993 Year_1994
-------  --------- --------- ---------
6380     0         0         0
7066     0         0         0
7067     0         0         0
7131     0         0         0
7896     0         0         0
8042     0         0         0
```

Not much to look at, although it uses dynamic execution to do the job. You may not think it is a necessary step, but you find that the procedure won't work without it when you put the theory to practice. Listing 13.16 shows how the `crosstable` looks up to this point. It is primed and ready for updating.

> **NOTE**
>
> After dynamically altering the crosstable, I found that all future addressing of the table needed to be via dynamic execution as well. In theory, you cannot alter a table and add data to those columns in the same procedure or batch. The use of dynamic execution allows you to perform this act, however, by its very nature. Dynamically executed statements are considered part of their own batch, thus, in a different scope from the batch or procedure that executed it.

Now you iterate through a cursor to fill the rest of the data in the table.

Populating the Remainder of crosstable Via a Cursor

Listing 13.17 is actually only creating the cursor that's declared via dynamic execution. Listing 13.18 shows a sample cursor declaration and the prCrosstab call that created it. Take some time to examine both sets of code.

> **TIP**
>
> Since the scope of cursor declarations are connection-based and not batch- or procedure-based, declaring a cursor via dynamic execution allows it to be used by the calling procedure or batch.

Listing 13.17. Creating the cursor to populate the crosstable.

```
 1: /*
 2:      Create cursor with @chrRowHead and @chrColHead groupings and @chrValue
 3:      aggregate
 4: */
 5:
 6: SELECT @chvExec = 'declare colname_cursor3 cursor for select ' +
 7:      CASE @intRowType
 8:      WHEN 1 THEN 'convert(varchar(255), ' + RTRIM(@chrRowHead) + ')'
 9:      ELSE RTRIM(@chrRowHead)
10:      END + ', ' +
11:
12:      CASE
13:      WHEN @intTemp = 3 THEN
14:           CASE
15:           WHEN @inyGrouping IN (1,3) THEN 'datename(' +
16:                CASE @inyGrouping
17:                WHEN 1 THEN 'weekday'
18:                WHEN 3 THEN 'month'
19:                END + ', ' + RTRIM(@chrColHead) + ')'
20:           ELSE CASE @inyGrouping
21:                WHEN 2 THEN '''Week'
22:                WHEN 4 THEN '''Quarter'
23:                WHEN 5 THEN '''Year'
24:                END + '_'' + ' + 'datename(' +
25:
26:                CASE @inyGrouping
27:                WHEN 2 THEN 'week'
28:                WHEN 4 THEN 'quarter'
29:                WHEN 5 THEN 'year'
30:                END + ', ' + RTRIM(@chrColHead) + ')'
31:           END
32:      ELSE CASE @intColType
33:           WHEN 1 THEN 'convert(varchar(255), ' + RTRIM(@chrColHead) + ')'
34:           ELSE RTRIM(@chrColHead)
35:           END
```

continues

13

CROSSTABULATION

Listing 13.17. continued

```
36:      END + ', total = CONVERT(varchar(255),' + RTRIM(@chvType) + '(' +
37:
38:      RTRIM(@chrValue) + ')) from ' + RTRIM(@chrSource) + ' group by ' +
39:      RTRIM(@chrRowHead) + ', ' +
40:
41:      CASE @intTemp
42:      WHEN 3 THEN
43:           CASE
44:              WHEN @inyGrouping IN (1,3) THEN 'datename(' +
45:                   CASE @inyGrouping
46:                   WHEN 1 THEN 'weekday'
47:                   WHEN 3 THEN 'month'
48:                   END + ', ' + RTRIM(@chrColHead) + ')'
49:              ELSE CASE @inyGrouping
50:                   WHEN 2 THEN '''Week'
51:                   WHEN 4 THEN '''Quarter'
52:                   WHEN 5 THEN '''Year'
53:                   END + '_'' + ' + 'datename(' +
54:
55:                   CASE @inyGrouping
56:                   WHEN 2 THEN 'week'
57:                   WHEN 4 THEN 'quarter'
58:                   WHEN 5 THEN 'year'
59:                   END + ', ' + RTRIM(@chrColHead) + ')'
60:           END
61:      ELSE RTRIM(@chrColHead)
62:      END
63: --PRINT @chvExec
64: EXEC(@chvExec)
```

Listing 13.18. A sample of the printed results from Listing 13.16.

```
exec prcrosstab 'stor_id', 'ord_date', 'qty', 'sales', 1, 5

declare colname_cursor3 cursor for
    select stor_id,
           'Year_' + datename(year, ord_date),
           total = CONVERT(varchar(255),SUM(qty))
    from sales
    group by stor_id, 'Year_' + datename(year, ord_date)
```

Take a look at Listing 13.18. Notice that the results create a simple SELECT statement in the cursor with three columns: The row head values, the column names, and the requested aggregate for the value column. Now look at Listing 13.17. The first column (the row head) is defined in lines 7 through 10. An earlier test of the datatype determines whether a conversion to varchar needs to be performed.

The second column (the column head) is a little more complex. It uses a functionality identical to that used to create the column names in the colnames table, so that the correct name is found for the update. Dates are converted to the appropriate grouping (lines 13 through 31).

Other datatypes are converted if they are not of varchar type (lines 32 through 35). The total column is generated on lines 36 and 37. It is a simple conversion of the aggregate value to varchar.

Lines 38 through 62 create the GROUP BY statement again using the same methodology that created the initial column names. Once created, the cursor declaration is executed in line 64. The following results show a sample of the data that you iterate through to perform all the updates to the crosstable. Notice how the second column holds the column names for the crosstable and the last column (in this case) holds the summed values for each pair.

```
stor_id                                         total
------------------------------------------      -----
6380    Year_1994                               8
7066    Year_1993                               50
7066    Year_1994                               75
7067    Year_1992                               80
7067    Year_1994                               10
7131    Year_1993                               85
7131    Year_1994                               45
7896    Year_1993                               60
8042    Year_1993                               55
8042    Year_1994                               25
```

Now that the cursor exists, you are ready to update the crosstable.

Updating the crosstable

By iterating through the cursor just declared, you can update all the values in the crosstable. The next code segment, Listing 13.20, shows the portion of the procedure that performs those updates.

Listing 13.20. Updating the crosstable.

```
 1: /*  Iterate through cursor and update crosstable  */
 2: BEGIN TRAN
 3: OPEN colname_cursor3
 4: FETCH colname_cursor3 INTO @chvRow, @chvCol, @chvVal
 5: WHILE @@fetch_status >= 0
 6: BEGIN
 7:     SELECT @chvColTemp=''
 8:     IF @chvCol LIKE '%[^A-Z0-9]%'
 9:     BEGIN
10:         SELECT @insR = 1
11:         WHILE @insR <= DATALENGTH(RTRIM(@chvCol))
12:         BEGIN
13:             SELECT @chvColTemp = RTRIM(@chvColTemp) +
14:                 CASE
15:                 WHEN SUBSTRING(@chvCol, @insR, 1) LIKE '[A-Z0-9_]'
16:                     THEN SUBSTRING(@chvCol, @insR, 1)
17:                 ELSE ''
18:                 END
19:             SELECT @insR = @insR + 1
20:         END
21:         SELECT @chvCol = @chvColTemp
22:     END
```

continues

13

Listing 13.20. continued

```
23:     SELECT @chvExec = 'update ' + user_name() + '.crosstable set ' +
24:         CASE
25:         WHEN SUBSTRING(@chvCol,1,1) LIKE '[^1234567890]' THEN @chvCol
26:         ELSE '_' + LTRIM(@chvCol)
27:         END + ' = ' +
28:             CASE
29:             WHEN @chvVal IS NULL THEN '0'
30:             ELSE RTRIM(@chvVal)
31:             END + ' where  rowhead = '''
32:     SELECT @chvRow =
33:         CASE
34:         WHEN @chvRow IS NULL THEN 'NULL'
35:         ELSE RTRIM(@chvRow)
36:         END
37:     SELECT @chvRowTemp = ''
38:     IF @chvRow LIKE '%''%'
39:     BEGIN
40:         SELECT @insR = 1
41:         WHILE @insR <= DATALENGTH(RTRIM(@chvRow)) - 1
42:         BEGIN
43:             SELECT @chvRowTemp = RTRIM(@chvRowTemp) +
44:                 CASE
45:                 WHEN SUBSTRING(@chvRow, @insR, 1) LIKE '[^'']' THEN
46:                     SUBSTRING(@chvRow, @insR, 1)
47:                 ELSE ''''''
48:                 END
49:             SELECT @insR = @insR + 1
50:         END
51:         SELECT @chvRow = @chvRowTemp
52:     END
53:     SELECT @chvExec = @chvExec + @chvRow + ''''
54:     --PRINT @chvExec
55:     EXEC(@chvExec)
56:     FETCH colname_cursor3 INTO @chvRow, @chvCol, @chvVal
57: END
```

Listing 13.21. A sample of generated update statements.

```
exec prcrosstab 'stor_id', 'ord_date', 'qty', 'sales', 1, 5

update dbo.crosstable set Year_1994 = 8 where  rowhead = '6380'
update dbo.crosstable set Year_1993 = 50 where  rowhead = '7066'
update dbo.crosstable set Year_1994 = 75 where  rowhead = '7066'
update dbo.crosstable set Year_1992 = 80 where  rowhead = '7067'
update dbo.crosstable set Year_1994 = 10 where  rowhead = '7067'
update dbo.crosstable set Year_1993 = 85 where  rowhead = '7131'
update dbo.crosstable set Year_1994 = 45 where  rowhead = '7131'
update dbo.crosstable set Year_1993 = 60 where  rowhead = '7896'
update dbo.crosstable set Year_1993 = 55 where  rowhead = '8042'
update dbo.crosstable set Year_1994 = 25 where  rowhead = '8042'
```

Listing 13.21 shows the printed results for each update performed. Notice the relationship between the UPDATE statement here and the values shown in Listing 13.20. You use the three values in each row of the cursor to create and dynamically execute each individual UPDATE statement.

Listing 13.20 begins by starting a transaction and opening the cursor. The transaction helps speed the process and is committed only after the procedure is nearly done. Lines 7 through 22 once again take care of invalid column names. Line 23 defines the initial UPDATE statement. Lines 24 through 30 append the Set portion of the update and convert returned null values to 0 to stay consistent with the existing data in the table.

Lines 31 through 53 take care of the WHERE clause portion of the update. The row values are checked for single quotation marks in line 38; if any exist, lines 39 through 52 iterate through the value and add quotation marks, so the final string produces a valid statement. For example, if the WHERE clause were looking for the row with a value of O'Neil, the clause would have to look like this: where rowhead = 'O''Neil'. The two single quotation marks evaluate to a single quotation mark in the string, producing the desired search result.

Finally, line 55 executes the update and the process continues until all updates have been performed. The only thing left to do is to return the results and clean up after yourself.

Finishing Touches

Listing 13.22 shows the last stage of the procedure. First, you close and deallocate the cursor, commit the open transaction, and set the NOCOUNT to off. One last dynamic execution is performed in lines 8 through 11. This returns your data back to the caller of the procedure. Finally, you drop all three tables used by the procedure.

Listing 13.22. The final touches of prCrosstab.

```
 1: CLOSE colname_cursor3
 2: DEALLOCATE colname_cursor3
 3: COMMIT TRAN
 4:
 5: /*  Send back the data from crosstable  */
 6: SET NOCOUNT OFF
 7:
 8: SELECT @chvExec='select * from ' + USER_NAME() + '.crosstable'
 9:
10: --PRINT @chvExec
11: EXEC (@chvExec)
12:
13: /*  Drop the tables  */
14: DROP TABLE #colnames
15: DROP TABLE #rownames
16: DROP TABLE crosstable
```

The code in Listing 13.23 shows all of the PRINT statement results (formatted for readability). This was achieved by removing all of the inline comments(- -) before each PRINT statement from the stored procedure. A simple set of data is chosen to keep the listing short, but larger tables can generate hundreds of lines to be executed. Lines 44 through 51 show the actual results from this crosstabulation. These results are easily retrievable from a Visual Basic application, or even Access.

Listing 13.23. A sample of all dynamic executions and results.

```
 1: exec prcrosstab 'stor_id', 'ord_date', 'qty', 'sales', 1, 5 --The executed
procedure
 2:
 3: --The Print statement results (formatted for readability)
 4:
 5: insert #colnames
 6:     select col1, col2
 7:     from (select distinct col1 = 'Year_' + datename(year, ord_date),
 8:                   col2 = datepart(year, ord_date),
 9:                   col3 = datepart(year, ord_date)
10:            from sales) xyz
11:     order by col3
12:
13: insert #rownames select distinct  stor_id from sales
14:
15: alter table dbo.crosstable add Year_1992 smallint null
16: alter table dbo.crosstable add Year_1993 smallint null
17: alter table dbo.crosstable add Year_1994 smallint null
18:
19: insert dbo.crosstable (rowhead) select
20:     rowname from #rownames
21:
22: declare colname_cursor3 cursor for
23:     select stor_id,
24:            'Year_' + datename(year, ord_date),
25:            total = CONVERT(varchar(255),SUM(qty))
26:     from sales
27:     group by stor_id, 'Year_' + datename(year, ord_date)
28:
29: update dbo.crosstable set Year_1994 = 8 where   rowhead = '6380'
30: update dbo.crosstable set Year_1993 = 50 where  rowhead = '7066'
31: update dbo.crosstable set Year_1994 = 75 where  rowhead = '7066'
32: update dbo.crosstable set Year_1992 = 80 where  rowhead = '7067'
33: update dbo.crosstable set Year_1994 = 10 where  rowhead = '7067'
34: update dbo.crosstable set Year_1993 = 85 where  rowhead = '7131'
35: update dbo.crosstable set Year_1994 = 45 where  rowhead = '7131'
36: update dbo.crosstable set Year_1993 = 60 where  rowhead = '7896'
37: update dbo.crosstable set Year_1993 = 55 where  rowhead = '8042'
38: update dbo.crosstable set Year_1994 = 25 where  rowhead = '8042'
39:
40: select * from dbo.crosstable
41:
42: --The data results
43:
```

```
44: rowhead    Year_1992 Year_1993 Year_1994
45: -------    --------- --------- ---------
46: 6380       0         0         8
47: 7066       0         50        75
48: 7067       80        0         10
49: 7131       0         85        45
50: 7896       0         60        0
51: 8042       0         55        25
```

Summary

If you are asking what else you can do, this book's job is done.

There are many things you could change about this procedure without affecting its final outcome. Experiment with variations, add features—have fun with it. If you find something that would enhance it or have actually coded the addition, please let me know. As stated earlier, an up-to-date version will be kept at www.milori.com.

All the techniques used in this stored procedure are common T-SQL abilities. The combination, however, is quite unique, and demonstrates the full potential of just T-SQL to perform some fantastic feats. As you can see, this procedure would not have been possible without dynamic execution. It is the key. Although the CASE expression made life much easier, all could be replaced using variable and IF statements.

13

CROSSTABULATION

II

PART

SQL Server-Essential Information

Writing Effective Code

IN THIS CHAPTER

CHAPTER

14

In this chapter, I will show you how to leverage your knowledge of Transact-SQL to create stunningly elegant stored procedures. To this end, I'll share some techniques that you can integrate into your everyday coding routine to dramatically improve the effectiveness of your code.

Admittedly, I've presented some fairly loaded and abstract terms in the chapter opening—bizarre and non-technical terms like "elegant" and "effective" code. Purposefully done, I want to get you excited about writing more than just highly efficient, compiler-readable source code. Code that is well planned, structured, and documented for human consumption is not only impressive when encountered, it's an absolute blessing and an asset to its author as well as those who will maintain or reuse it. It may perform precisely the same functions as ill-planned, slipshod code, but it will not induce the headaches, cold sweats, and nausea that the lousy code tends to.

Code elegance is simply code that concurrently communicates process instructions to the human reader as well as the computer. Elegant code, by nature, will meet all the following criteria:

- Performs its objective task
- Is logically easy to follow
- Is visually easy to navigate
- Is self documenting in its context and function
- Is easily maintainable
- Is robust in its application

Taken individually, these criteria each seem simplistic, and they are. The real trick is to adapt a technique that will address each of these issues and to use that technique consistently and methodically. I will give you the technique; it will be up to you to ensure that it is applied conscientiously.

These methods are nothing new, mind you. In fact, you have probably used them yourself, knowingly or otherwise. The difference is that now you will be aware of and perform each distinct step when constructing a stored procedure and will consistently nail all the objectives as a result. Here are the steps:

- Define exactly what your procedure will do.
- Code and test the procedure.
- Optimize and retest the procedure.
- Edit the procedure for readability.

As I define each of these phases in the construction of a stored procedure, you will notice a pattern of iterative design and implementation emerge. Each of the phases addresses the design and construction of the procedure as a whole. By following through each phase, I improve the logic, optimization, robustness, and readability of any procedure I write, while adding minimal overhead to the whole process. In essence, I work smarter, not harder.

Define Exactly What Your Procedure Will Do

A procedure, especially a Transact-SQL procedure should not become a Swiss Army knife of functionality, nor should it deviate from its intended purpose. Whenever you create a new procedure, it's most effective to decide exactly what the procedure will accomplish and stick to that plan throughout construction of the procedure.

Define The Mission

In the text editor you will be using to write your stored procedure, write out, in as few words as possible, what the main objective of the procedure will be. This will serve as your "mission statement" that you can, and should, refer back to it while writing your procedure. When you are satisfied with it, make this the first comment in your procedure.

Make Notes

Next, construct the logic that will meet the objective you just documented. Use high-level English to make notes of what you intend to do within your procedure, separating each logical step on its own line. As you may have guessed, these notes will become comments, so keep that in mind as you are writing these. Also, you may want to indent your notes. Don't get hung up on this, however, since you will perfect your formatting in later steps. Simply indent to the extent that it is helpful to you.

These notes should explain the procedure in logical steps rather than explaining the details of implementation. Here is an example of notes that are just too detailed to translate into useful comments:

```
/* Declare a cursor from the authors table */
/* Open the cursor */
/* Read the fields into variables until the cursor end is reached */
    /* Increment the counter by 1 */
    /* If counter mod 5 then Print the fields */
/* Close the cursor */
```

These notes shroud the intent of what the code is ultimately supposed to accomplish. It simply outlines the implementation of some unknown plan, although if we read every line we can see that it should print every fifth author. Contrast that with the following code:

```
/* Print every fifth author using a cursor */
```

Now that's quite a bit clearer! This example also hints at how the notes will be used in the context of our code. We want our notes to read like headlines so we can focus on creating a plan now and filling in the details later. The latter example makes a great headline for a code paragraph.

Of course, most SQL procedures consist of a single SELECT or other DML statement. In such a case, the essence of functionality lies within one statement that may be quite complex.

To make our notation more valuable in such cases, we can anticipate the entity relationships we will be using and specify these relationships in our notes. For example, our notes for a rather complex SELECT may look like:

```
/* Retrieve a list of publishers who have published titles of @author */
/* by joining @author->titleauthor->titles->publishers */
```

This explanation is so precise that, for a stored procedure with one SELECT statement, it would probably be a sufficient comment for the entire procedure.

But what about a more complex single-statement procedure? I'll give a meatier example now, which I will follow through the construction process to completion. I want to create a query that will return a list of authors who are earning royalties beyond their advances, and I also want to see the book titles. To keep the query from getting out of hand as an example, I will not include store discounts or royalty schedules in the calculations. Here is the completed mission statement and notes for the stored procedure.

```
/* Find authors who are earning royalties beyond their advances per title */
/* by joining authors->titleauthor->titles */
```

Notice I haven't yet begun to contemplate the specifics of the joins. I simply referenced an ER diagram (available in the SQL Server Books Online) and determined the tables that will come into play.

Now that my mission is well defined and my entity relationships are roughed in, I'm ready to code.

Code and Test the Procedure

During coding and testing, the goal is to implement the design to achieve the mission. Most stored procedures are pretty straightforward in their logic. For a procedure that actually takes some thought, it is not imperative that the code is optimized at this phase of construction. The objective of coding and testing is getting it to work—it will be optimized in the next phase. Also be sure to incorporate in this phase the naming and formatting standards that you or your company have decided on. The readability of the code will be refined even further when we edit for readability.

Here is my procedure after completing the coding and testing phase.

Listing 14.1. Rough-coded procedure to select earning authors.

```
/* Find authors who are earning royalties beyond their advances per title */
/* by joining authors->titleauthor->titles */
CREATE PROC prSelEarningAuthors
AS
SELECT t.title_id, au_lname=rtrim(a.au_lname), au_fname=rtrim(a.au_fname),
       advance = t.advance * ta.royaltyper/100,
       royalies = (t.royalty * t.ytd_sales * t.price/100 - t.advance) *
       ➥ ta.royaltyper/100
```

```
FROM authors a, titleauthor ta, titles t
WHERE ta.title_id = t.title_id
AND a.au_id   = ta.au_id
AND (t.royalty * t.ytd_sales * t.price/100 - t.advance) * ta.royaltyper/100 > 0
ORDER BY t.title_id, au_lname, au_fname
GO
```

As with most complex stored procedures, I experimented quite a bit before I got this to work the way I intended. I was not concerned about commenting on what I was doing, nor should have I been. It's a little homely but it works, and that is our goal during the coding and testing phase. I will beautify it when I edit it for readability.

The second portion of coding and testing is, of course, testing. The objectives of testing at this point are:

■ Proof that the procedure meets the objectives in all foreseeable circumstances

■ Validation that the procedure works from the intended client

■ Preparation for the optimization phase

If our overall project is following a formal methodology or framework, we should already have project test plans in place. Depending on how far along the client portion of the system is, construction of a *test harness* may be necessary to accurately exercise the new stored procedure (a test harness is a piece of throw-away code that mimics the actual conditions of the final program for a specific function). Running the test plans, by using the actual program itself or a test harness against the stored procedure, will both prove that the procedure meets the objectives we have set and validate that the procedure works from the intended client.

To prepare for optimization of the stored procedure, it is necessary to gather information about how the rough draft that we have coded can be improved. Showplan is an invaluable tool for spying on the query plan that SQL Server will use when executing the procedure. Effective use of Showplan to optimize queries is covered in depth in Chapter 3, "Optimizing Queries."

Optimize and Retest the Procedure

Although query optimization was covered in depth in Chapter 3, there may be one or more less obvious ways of "preoptimizing" the code at this phase. Before you begin the standard optimization techniques that are covered in Chapter 3, review the stored procedure for the following possibilities:

■ Complexity that could be broken up into separate procedures

■ An improved database design that would obviate the need for the query

■ Enhancement of the query to make it reusable

Using the techniques presented in the following few sections will improve robustness of the query and give you the peace of mind that the query really fits into the larger system.

Reducing Complexity

If possible, reduce complexity by breaking the procedure up into separate stored procedures. A good rule of thumb is to simplify code whenever possible by breaking a large procedure into separate stored procedures and executing them from the parent. This is even more desirable if the spin-off procedures are of a globally reusable nature—strive to make them so if possible. Consider the following complex procedure in Listing 14.2.

Listing 14.2. Complex procedure example.

```
/* Insert or Update an Author */
CREATE PROC prEditAuthor

    @au_id        id,
    @au_lname     varchar(40),
    @au_fname     varchar(20),
    @phone        char(12),
    @address      varchar(40),
    @city         varchar(20),
    @state        char(2),
    @zip          char(5),
    @contract     bit

AS

    /* If the author ID is null then it must be a new author */

    IF (@au_id IS NULL) BEGIN

        INSERT INTO authors
        (
            au_lname,
            au_fname,
            phone,
            address,
            city,
            state,
            zip,
            contract
        )
        VALUES
        (
            @au_lname,
            @au_fname,
            @phone,
            @address,
            @city,
            @state,
            @zip,
            @contract
        )

    END ELSE BEGIN
```

```
      UPDATE authors

      SET au_lname = @au_lname,
          au_fname = @au_fname,
          phone    = @phone,
          address  = @address,
          city     = @city,
          state    = @state,
          zip      = @zip,
          contract = @contract

      WHERE au_id = @au_id

   END

GO
```

The complexity of this procedure could be broken up somewhat by creating separate stored procedures for the INSERT and UPDATE components. The result of this action would look something like Listing 14.3.

Listing 14.3. Reduced complexity example.

```
/*****************************/
/*      Insert an Author     */
/*****************************/
CREATE PROC prInsertAuthor

    @au_lname    varchar(40),
    @au_fname    varchar(20),
    @phone       char(12),
    @address     varchar(40),
    @city        varchar(20),
    @state       char(2),
    @zip         char(5),
    @contract    bit

AS

    INSERT INTO authors
        (
            au_lname,
            au_fname,
            phone,
            address,
            city,
            state,
            zip,
            contract
        )
        VALUES
        (
```

continues

Listing 14.3. continued

```
            @au_lname,
            @au_fname,
            @phone,
            @address,
            @city,
            @state,
            @zip,
            @contract
        )

GO



/******************************/
/*      Update an Author      */
/******************************/
CREATE PROC prUpdateAuthor

    @au_id      id,
    @au_lname   varchar(40),
    @au_fname   varchar(20),
    @phone      char(12),
    @address    varchar(40),
    @city       varchar(20),
    @state      char(2),
    @zip        char(5),
    @contract   bit

AS

    UPDATE authors

    SET au_lname = @au_lname,
        au_fname = @au_fname,
        phone    = @phone,
        address  = @address,
        city     = @city,
        state    = @state,
        zip      = @zip,
        contract = @contract

    WHERE au_id = @au_id
GO



/******************************/
/* Insert or Update an Author */
/******************************/
CREATE PROC prEditAuthor

    @au_id      id,
    @au_lname   varchar(40),
    @au_fname   varchar(20),
    @phone      char(12),
    @address    varchar(40),
```

```
        @city       varchar(20),
        @state      char(2),
        @zip        char(5),
        @contract   bit

AS

    /* If the author ID is null then it must be a new author */
    IF (@au_id IS NULL) BEGIN

        EXEC prInsertAuthor @au_lname,
                            @au_fname,
                            @phone,
                            @address,
                            @city,
                            @state,
                            @zip,
                            @contract

    END ELSE BEGIN

        EXEC prUpdateAuthor @au_id,
                            @au_lname,
                            @au_fname,
                            @phone,
                            @address,
                            @city,
                            @state,
                            @zip,
                            @contract

    END

GO
```

By reducing the complexity in `prEditAuthor`, we gain the reuse of `prEditAuthor` and `prInsertAuthor` across our application. Maybe we will never need these two separate procedures…but then again maybe we will. In any event, the visual complexity of `prEditAuthor` has been broken up. And if experience is any indication, someone down the road will appreciate finding these three handy procedures, ready to use in a situation we could not have anticipated. You'll see another view of this same procedure in the section, "Enhance the Query for Reusability."

Improve the Database Design

In some circumstances, specifically where databases are large, poorly documented or poorly designed, writing code against the tables will uncover a design flaw in the database or an area where improvement is desirable. If a design change is called for, don't let it slide. Small design problems have a way of becoming large implementation problems. Redesigning the database in the early stages is much cheaper than trying to overcome a poor database design later during construction and maintenance. Redesign the database correctly and your client will thank you for it.

Enhance the Query for Reusability

Once again, our stored procedure should not represent a Swiss Army knife of functionality. Notwithstanding, a procedure can be useful in more than one instance without major modification. Having one procedure that performs the same or similar functions in a variety of circumstances is arguably easier to maintain.

Take Listing 14.2, the complex INSERT and UPDATE of the authors table, for instance. I love this example because it seemingly contradicts my Swiss Army Knife abolition. But it does not provide unrelated functionality to various clients, rather, it takes two logically similar but syntactically different Transact-SQL statements, INSERT and UPDATE, and abstracts them into a single, easy-to-use stored procedure. The advantages of this approach become more evident as you begin programming against it from the client. Suddenly INSERTs and UPDATEs from a single client object, a Visual Basic form for example, are simplified because I no longer need to check the value of the author ID or an insert/update flag within my client to determine if the record is to be inserted or updated. Taken one step further, I could now create a client object that can handle maintenance on practically any record—all because I abstracted two syntactically incompatible T-SQL interfaces into a nice, usable (actually multi-use) interface.

Optimizing the Procedure

If the procedure passes these preliminary tests, begin optimization of the procedure. Study the output from Showplan, and restructure the query or create new indexes according to the optimization methods found in Chapter 3. Listing 14.4 is my example procedure with optimizations made.

Listing 14.4. Optimized procedure to select earning authors.

```
/* Find authors who are earning royalties beyond their advances per title */
/* by joining authors->titleauthor->titles */
CREATE PROC prSelEarningAuthors
AS
SELECT t.title_id, a.au_lname, a.au_fname,
       advance = t.advance * ta.royaltyper/100,
       royalies = (t.royalty * t.ytd_sales * t.price/100 - t.advance) *
    ➥ ta.royaltyper/100
FROM authors a, titleauthor ta, titles t
WHERE ta.title_id = t.title_id
AND a.au_id   = ta.au_id
AND (t.royalty * t.ytd_sales * t.price/100 - t.advance) * ta.royaltyper/100 > 0
ORDER BY t.title_id, au_lname, au_fname
GO
```

The first thing I noticed when reviewing my procedure was that I was returning the value of string functions in my SELECT clause which is intrinsically inefficient. I checked to see if I actually needed the calls to RTRIM by performing an sp_help on the authors table. I found that the table had been created with SET ANSI PADDING OFF (evidenced by TrimTrailingBlanks = Yes in the sp_help output) so spaces on varchar columns will be trimmed automatically without a call to RTRIM.

My other major concern is to alleviate the table scans on each table. I've included the output from Showplan for the prSelEarningAuthors sample procedure here for your reference.

```
STEP 1
The type of query is EXECUTE
STEP 1
The type of query is INSERT
The update mode is direct
Worktable created for ORDER BY
FROM TABLE
titles t
Nested iteration
Table Scan
FROM TABLE
titleauthor ta
Nested iteration
Table Scan
FROM TABLE
authors a
Nested iteration
Table Scan
TO TABLE
Worktable 1
STEP 2
The type of query is SELECT
This step involves sorting
FROM TABLE
Worktable 1
Using GETSORTED Table Scan
```

The Showplan output indicates that we need to add some indexes to alleviate all the table scans that are occurring.

There is just one other thought I'd like to leave you with before we depart the topic of optimization. The time/performance tradeoff must be weighed carefully when optimizing code. There are very few non-trivial procedures (in any language) that could not be further optimized in their construction, context, or design. In other words, even if a procedure is optimized, there is probably a more resourceful and clever way to design the system of which it is a part. My point: 'Tis a wise coder who knows when good enough is good enough.

Post-Optimization Testing

Testing after the optimization phase is imperative to re-establish that the procedure is still working properly. Rerun your test cases as you did following the initial coding. If your test cases expose performance flaws, you may need to back up to the coding phase and restructure the procedure.

Edit the Procedure for Readability

The hard part is done—the procedure runs like a Mercedes. But how does it look? Is it "programmer friendly"? If you had to make a major change to it one or two years from now, could you easily grasp its workings and make the change with minimal hassle? How about if someone new to the project needed to understand it? Could that person grasp the purpose and context of the procedure, as well as the logical progression of problem solving that is coded into it?

Of course the answer to all these questions should be yes. But up to this point we have been focusing on feeding the machine high-carb, low-fat code to produce the optimal path to our mission. Sure we have used some standard variable names and we have a handful of useful comments, but the information useful for human consumption is scant at this point. The goal of this phase is to add value to the procedure so that anyone can visually scan the code and not only learn how it works quickly and easily but also modify it painlessly.

In remaining portion of the chapter, I'll focus on the most effective techniques for formatting Transact-SQL code for readability and clarity. This phase is the most valuable phase of construction in that effective formatting of a stored procedure could save untold time and money in maintenance costs later. Plus it will make you look like a coding genius, so what do you have to lose?

Create a Procedure Banner

The first and easiest thing to do is to add a banner to your procedure. A banner provides up-front information about a procedure. It informs someone browsing the code if they are looking at the right procedure or not. It also announces the purpose of the procedure in a standard location. It is simply a comment block containing generally useful information about the procedure. If your organization uses a standard banner, by all means use it in good health. If there is no standard banner available, go ahead and create one. How much information you put into the banner depends mostly on whether or not change-control software, like Visual SourceSafe or PVCS, is being used to track modifications to the source code. If change-control software is used, a banner need not include information such as the DDL file location or modification information like date, author, and notes. Whether or not change-control software is used, a banner should include the following basic information:

- The procedure's name
- The procedure's mission statement
- Special instructions (if applicable)
- Copyright notice

The banner should be easily distinguishable from the rest of the code. The following is a simple example of a procedure banner.

```
/***************************************************************************

Procedure Name: prSelEarningAuthors

Purpose: Find authors who are earning royalties beyond their advances per title.

Special Instructions: This is a test procedure.  Do not use in production.

Copyright © 1998 SAMS Publishing.  All rights reserved.

***************************************************************************/
```

Notice that a single line of no more than 80 characters at the top and bottom of the banner will nicely delimit the banner, distinguishing it from the rest of the procedure. Speaking of 80 characters, it's a good idea to break sentences within the banner to keep lines under 80 characters as well. This will keep the procedure printable on most any machine and will allow full lines to display on most screens. As you continue to format the rest of the procedure, you can visually compare the line widths in the procedure with the delimiting lines in the banner to keep each and every line of the procedure 80 characters or less in width.

Making Your Code More Readable

Beyond the banner, our code awaits. To the computer, our code is an assemblage of foreign words that need to be translated. To us humans, our code is our code. It's a compromised language for both humans and machines to read and understand. Like any human language, written without regard for human interpretation, the syntax can be correct but the meaning becomes less clear. I think of Yoda from the Star Wars movies, how he always talked in object-subject form rather than subject-object as we are accustomed to. I was told by an English professor that grammatically, Yoda's sentences were correct. Yet it sounds strange because we are not accustomed to thinking in object-subject form. So too, Transact-SQL code can be written in a way that takes extra computing time for a human to comprehend it. Conversely, it can also be written so that humans can understand it with considerably less effort if attention is paid to formatting for people-friendly code. I'd like to start my explanation of this by picking nits.

To Capitalize or Not to Capitalize

Rather than start a holy war on capitalization, I will say this. Capitalization of Transact-SQL keywords is used throughout this book so that the occurrence of Transact-SQL keywords will be more apparent. That said, I would not suspect that the use of lower case or initial capitalization (Select, Update, and so on) applied to keywords would adversely effect readability because our vision centers are accustomed to scanning lower case and initial cap words in everyday situations. Bottom line: Consistently use whichever scheme you are most comfortable with.

What's In a Name?

The rule is simple here: use descriptive, useful names for every variable you define in a stored procedure. Transact-SQL doesn't much care what you call a variable, so this is a great opportunity to make your query self-documenting by adhering to prefix-naming standards and creating variables that convey meaning.

> **TIP**
>
> Name parameters in a stored procedure the same as the columns they will be updating, inserting into, or compared with. This will make their purpose apparent even with minimal commenting.

Creating Order from Disorder

The human mind loves to group things. We stereotype, we categorize, we love to find things that have something in common and herd them into a group for easy reference. Almost any human who will look at our code and attempt to decipher it will mentally group lines and commands together to facilitate his or her comprehension. The kindest thing we can do for this person is to preformat our code so that he or she will not have to think so hard—group those things that he or she will mentally group anyway.

Vertical Grouping

Vertical grouping is a method that I'm sure you're quite familiar with. It's simply grouping related lines of code together in blocks and separating these blocks of code with *white space* (one or more blank lines). Vertical grouping provides an excellent visual cue for the eye to find related lines of text quickly and efficiently. The advantages of vertical grouping can be leveraged by placing a comment at the top of a group of related lines that bonds the lines of code together by describing their relation. See Listing 14.9 for an example of vertical grouping.

Horizontal Grouping and Alignment

Horizontal grouping is the grouping of related text in columns that are separated by white space. Alignment is the grouping of columns without respect to white space separation of the columns. If there is a list of languages that could benefit from horizontal grouping and alignment, Transact-SQL tops the list. The appearance of Transact-SQL code is just plain clumsy by default. Generally, a query consists of one or more DML statement that has all sorts of unwieldy clauses with one or more lists of variables, column names, literals, expressions, or any combination of the above mixed together. Horizontal grouping rescues us from visually wading through this jambalaya of gawky ambiguity. Listing 14.5 is a nice example of visual pain.

Listing 14.5. Query example before horizontal grouping.

```
SELECT DATALENGTH(name) FROM syscolumns WHERE id = OBJECT_ID('publishers')
➥AND name = 'pub_id'
```

The agony of having to sequentially scan the line to find what the id is equal to in the WHERE clause is almost unbearable. All right, Listing 14.6 shows what the modern miracle of horizontal grouping can do for this statement.

Listing 14.6. Query example after horizontal grouping.

```
SELECT    DATALENGTH(name)
FROM      syscolumns
WHERE     id    = OBJECT_ID('publishers')
AND       name  = 'pub_id'
```

By placing white space between our clause keywords and the columns and operands that follow them, we've broken the visual mayhem and introduced a new way for a reader to scan for the information he or she is seeking. Notice the ample amount of white space between the columns of information. I recommend 3 or 4 spaces for effective horizontal grouping since fewer spaces do not effectively create visual white space.

Listing 14.7 shows a slightly different example of taming the wild beast with horizontal grouping.

Listing 14.7. Query example with CASE expression before horizontal grouping.

```
SELECT au_lname,
       au_fname,
       contract = CASE contract WHEN 1 THEN 'Yes' ELSE 'No' END
FROM   authors
WHERE  state = 'CA'
```

Actually this beast isn't too wild but could still use some domesticating. We have something approaching horizontal grouping already with the keywords. I would categorize this as alignment rather than grouping, however, because of the small amount of white space between the columns. Also, my eye goes directly into sequential scan mode when I get to the CASE statement. Listing 14.8 is an improvement.

Listing 14.8. Query example with CASE expression after horizontal grouping.

```
SELECT    au_lname,
          au_fname,
          contract =
             CASE contract
                WHEN 0 THEN   'No'
                WHEN 1 THEN   'Yes'
             END
FROM      authors
WHERE     state = 'CA'
```

The columns (groups) are more defined because of the increased white space. The CASE statement has improved because it is using *pure block formatting* which is an indentation of the code to delineate a logical construct. I will cover pure block formatting next in this chapter.

> **NOTE**
>
> Notice too that I dumped the ELSE clause in the CASE statement for an explicit test for 0. The ELSE was unnecessary because a bit can be nothing but 0 or 1 and the explicit test was visually much easier to perceive.

There are a number of ways this example could have been formatted to improve readability—my example is not the only way, nor do I pretend that it is the best. It's simply an improvement based on the use of horizontal grouping.

> **TIP**
>
> Visually, it's most helpful if only related items are aligned or horizontally grouped. It is not necessary to align columns across multiple statements.

Pure Block Formatting

Here's another of those things you have been doing all your programming life but now have a name for. Pure block formatting (technically this formatting in Transact-SQL is known as pure block emulation) is the indentation of a programming construct or a block of code that is delimited by code brackets. Formally, code brackets in Transact-SQL are the CASE...END, IF...ELSE, or BEGIN...END coding constructs. In reality, feel free to use pure block formatting anywhere it makes sense. Pure block formatting can be used successfully with parentheses for example (refer to Listing 14.2).

> **TIP**
>
> Use pure block formatting anywhere that a block of code is logically grouped beneath a higher group or within a programming construct.

I recommend taking advantage of the visual cues that pure block formatting offers by using it in cases where it is not syntactically necessary, if it provides the reader with a clearer depiction of the logical constructs. Look again at Listing 14.2. The BEGIN...END blocks are not necessary because only one SQL statement resides beneath the IF and ELSE statements respectively. The BEGIN...END blocks, however, reinforce to the reader's eye where the END...IF boundaries are. Additionally, if this portion of code is modified, the developer will not have to add the BEGIN...END blocks if another statement is to be added, and there will be no surprise side effects from code that was thought to be inside the construct but wasn't.

Recommenting the Code

By this time the code is probably so self documenting you can read it with your eyes closed. Still, review the procedure one last time. Is every logical step self explanatory or documented in a comment? Is the reason for each line of code apparent? If not, comment it. Are all your previously written comments still accurate and helpful? If a comment is no longer necessary, delete it.

Place comments immediately before their subject code. Align comments with the code they apply to, keeping them visually grouped so as not to confuse the reader about their application.

> **TIP**
>
> Avoid placing comments at the end of a code line whenever possible. End line comments only look nice when they are aligned with each other, which is a pain when you edit the line they are on. Besides, aligning them with each other implies that they are somehow related to each other, which is not necessarily true. And trying to keep a line under 80 characters with them...enough said.

Listing 14.9 is my sample procedure after editing for readability.

Listing 14.9. Optimized procedure to select earning authors.

```
/*****************************************************************************

Procedure Name: prSelEarningAuthors

Purpose: Find authors who are earning royalties beyond their advances per title
         by joining authors->titleauthor->titles

Copyright © 1998 SAMS Publishing.  All rights reserved.

*****************************************************************************/

CREATE PROC prSelEarningAuthors
AS

SELECT     t.title_id,
           a.au_lname,
           a.au_fname,
           advance  =   t.advance * ta.royaltyper/100,

           /* authors share of royalties based on YTD sales less advance */
           royalies =   (t.royalty * t.ytd_sales * t.price/100 - t.advance)
                        * ta.royaltyper/100

FROM       authors      a,
```

continues

14

Listing 14.9. continued

```
           titleauthor   ta,
           titles        t

WHERE      ta.title_id =   t.title_id

AND        a.au_id      =  ta.au_id

           /* authors share of royalties based on YTD sales less advance > 0 */
AND        (t.royalty * t.ytd_sales * t.price/100 - t.advance)
           * ta.royaltyper/100 > 0

ORDER BY   t.title_id,
           au_lname,
           au_fname
GO
```

Excellent! A working stored procedure that is actually commented, is readable, maintainable, *and* looks kind of nice. I wish we could see more of these in real life.

Using Visual Database Tools to Produce Effective Code

I have been content with writing queries and stored procedures in ISQL/w and the SQL Enterprise Manager for years without rebelling against their pitiful authoring features—until now. Finally, Microsoft has given us a proper tool for editing stored procedures as well as managing our database objects—the Microsoft Visual Database Tools. This section will give you some ideas for using Visual Database Tools to create more effective code. Chapter 15, "Taking Advantage of the Tools," gives you many more examples of how to use this tool to speed the development process.

Microsoft Visual Database Tools (MS DataTools) ships with Microsoft Visual InterDev, Visual C++ 5.0 Enterprise Edition, and Visual Basic 5.0 Enterprise Edition. Really, MS DataTools is a built-in feature of Microsoft Developer Studio, the single environment for Visual C++ and Visual InterDev development. If you have installed either of these products, you already have MS DataTools available and ready to run. If you have Visual Basic 5.0 Enterprise, you will need to run the Setup program located in the /Tools/DataTools directory of the Visual Basic 5.0 CD-ROM.

In order to begin working with a SQL Server database in MS DataTools, a Workspace must be created and a Data Connection must be made. The easiest way to do this is to select Files | New and select the Projects tab on the New dialog box. Select Database Project from the list and provide a project name. Clicking the OK button displays the Select Data Source dialog box. Select an existing ODBC data source or create a new one and click OK to connect.

After logging into the SQL Server, click the Data View tab. This view represents the objects in your database. Looks a lot like the SQL Enterprise Manager, doesn't it. Ah, but SQL Enterprise Manager's beauty is only skin deep, comparatively speaking. Open the Tables node and double-click a table. What you get is a wonderful interface for editing the table's data—like a linked table in Access. The database objects you see here are real though, not mere links; delete a table or a view here and it will be gone.

But enough playing around, we are here to write some beautiful stored procedures. There are a few ways to create and run a query in MS DataTools. They are:

- Create a stored procedure.
- Create an ODBC script file.
- Create a query with the Query Designer.

Create a Stored Procedure

In the Data View, we have easy access to stored procedures within our database. Open the Stored Procedures node and right-click a procedure name. You'll see all the options available for manipulating stored procedures in this context menu: Open, Run, New, Copy, Delete, and Rename. Choose the Open command to open the stored procedure, displaying it in the source editor. What a gorgeous breath of fresh air this SQL source editor is! It has all the comforts of your VC++ or VB editor, including keyword and comment color coding. If you have been using ISQL/w for stored procedure creation, you may consider trading up to this beauty.

Create an ODBC Script File

If you are thinking of trading in ISQL/w for the MS DataTools, you might be wondering what replacement DataTools offers for the freestyle querying that is possible in ISQL/w. After all, a stored procedure is usually written only after some trial and error querying has been done. ISQL/w is very handy for jotting off queries, refining, and then compiling the resulting code into a stored procedure. The DataTools substitute is the ODBC script file. An ODBC script file is SQL code that is stored in a file that is associated with your project rather than in the database as a stored procedure. If you have a repository of .sql files that contain all your stored procedures, it may be useful to organize them by creating a Database Project and then associating them with their database. This is done by right-clicking the data connection name in the File View and choosing Add Files from the context menu.

14

WRITING
EFFECTIVE CODE

TIP

Create an ODBC script file strictly for writing experimental code. In File View, select File | New and select ODBC Script File from the Files list. Be sure Add to Project is selected so the script will be available whenever the project is loaded.

Once you have an ODBC script open, type in a simple SELECT statement to run against your SQL Server data connection. To run the query, you must be in Data View and the data connection/database must be selected. Additionally, the focus must be in the source editor window in order for the Run command to be enabled. To run the script, right-click and choose Run, or go to Tools | Run.

Okay, I admit this is a rather shaky replacement for the instant gratification of ISQL/w. Add to this the fact that MS DataTools has no equivalent of highlighting a section of query code and executing the highlighted portion only. The heart of ISQL/w may still be beating for many of us.

Create a Query with the Query Designer

This facility in MS DataTools strongly resembles MS Query and the query building facility in MS Access. Microsoft worked hard to enhance this interface into a frighteningly GUI handholding experience in query construction. To experience this, select File | View and right-click a data connection. Choosing New Query from the context menu will open the Query Designer, which I like to refer to as the Query Tower of Terror, depicted in Figure 14.1.

FIGURE 14.1.

The DataTools Query Designer.

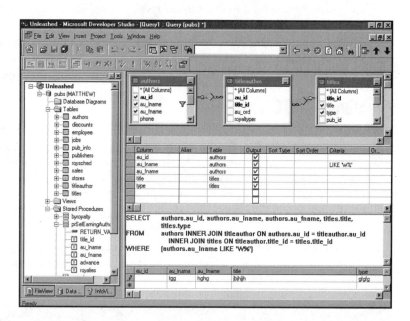

The Tower, er, Query Designer window is divided into four panes, from top to bottom:

- Data Diagram Pane
- Design Grid Pane
- SQL Pane
- Query Results Pane

Kidding aside, it is quite good at constructing and representing many types of queries graphically in the data diagram pane. Try dragging the Authors, TitleAuthors, and Titles tables into the data diagram pane, as shown in Figure 14.1. It immediately graphs the relationships and constructs a template SELECT query in the SQL pane. Check a few output columns in the design grid and click the Run button on the toolbar. Instant gratification ensues in the query results pane. Not bad...not bad at all.

The Verdict

The decision is yours, of course, as to what tool you will use for your daily editing and creation of stored procedures. I recommend giving MS DataTools a fair trial. I find its source editor to be irreplaceable for implementing the advanced formatting techniques I've discussed in this chapter. I still use ISQL/w during my coding phase to develop the specific mechanics of my queries. The stink is that it would be great to have one "Visual Interactive Data Tools Enterprise Manager" rather than three or more clients to cover our needs. The comfort is that we at least have machines that can handle it.

Summary

The steps covered in this chapter will empower you to create consistently effective code that is functionally excellent, maintainable, and lovely to look at. By defining what your procedure will do before you begin (your mission statement), your efforts will be focused and will produce the results intended. Then your mission statement is expanded by creating notes which detail your logic, produce a framework for your code, and provide ready-made comments for that code. Coding, testing, and optimizing place the meat on the bones of the procedure and ensure that the mission statement is met with an efficient solution. Finally, the procedure gets a makeover to make it as presentable as possible for air-breathing folks. Writing good, if not fantastic code is possible, but the key is consistency—make these techniques a part of your routine coding practice and enjoy the rich rewards.

Taking Advantage of the Tools

IN THIS CHAPTER

This chapter focuses on tools that aid in the development of a SQL Server database. Visual Database Tools, which accompanies Microsoft Visual InterDev, allow easy maintenance of some database objects and query development through a visual interface. It also provides a simple mechanism for changing the structure of a database. With the introduction of Visual Basic 5 came the T-SQL Debugger Add-In. This long-awaited tool allows you to debug T-SQL (including stored procedures) from the Visual Basic environment by stepping through the T-SQL, line by line. Finally, some helpful hints on data modeling tools are presented.

Using Visual InterDev's Database Tools

Visual InterDev's Visual Database Tools give developers a graphical interface to generate queries and to modify, drop, and create database objects. It also serves as a mechanism for manipulating table structures without suffering through the creation of pages of SQL scripts. It's a welcome sight for SQL Server developers who have longed for the query tools and the on-the-fly table structure manipulation that Microsoft Access has provided for years.

> **NOTE**
>
> Recently, I entered an international developer's competition where the one- and two-person teams were expected to develop an entire application in 14 hours on one day! There were no stipulations on what tools to use, so my partner, Mark Hunter, and I used a SQL Server database with a Web browser front end. In the past we probably would have chosen to use Microsoft Access, due to the time constraints and its quick drag-and-drop visual features. However, because of the graphical interface of Visual Database Tools, we were able to use the more powerful SQL Server database without losing any time. We designed the tables and their relationships with a few mouse clicks and used Visual Database Tools' local queries to create and verify our SQL. In real life you would never willingly develop an enterprise application within such ridiculous time constraints, but the point is that Visual Database Tools make rapid development with SQL Server a reality. Incidentally, Mark and I placed 3rd in the Internet competition.

Getting Connected

Before we begin, make sure you have the following software requirements covered:

- Visual InterDev, version 1.0 or higher
- SQL Server 6.5 with Service Pack 2 or higher

NOTE

To use the Visual Database Tools with SQL Server, you must first install Service Pack 2 or higher. This service pack can be installed from the Visual InterDev CD-ROM by executing `Server\SQLSrvSp\Setup.exe` on the server machine. This fixes some problems that prevent Visual Database Tools from working well with SQL Server.

Visual InterDev is intended for Web development with a SQL Server back end. However, we will be using it strictly for its Visual Database Tools. Let's start by opening Visual InterDev and creating a new database project called `PubsProject` (see Figure 15.1).

FIGURE 15.1.

Creating the database project `PubsProject`.

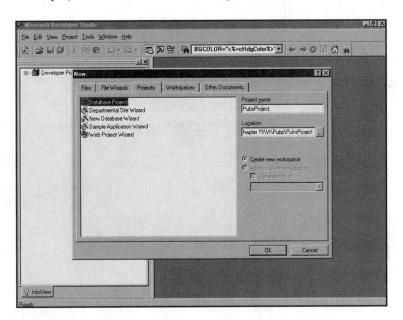

This will create a database project in which you will manipulate the SQL Server `Pubs` database. You will be prompted to supply a data source to use. Select the data source that you have been using for the `Pubs` database. If you have not yet created a data source for the `Pubs` database, you can do so now by clicking the New button on the Select Data Source dialog box or by creating one through the Control panel's ODBC icon.

NOTE

If you click anywhere on the screen outside of the Select Data Source dialog box, it may disappear before you can make your data source selection. To get the dialog box back, right-click PubsProject and select Add Data Connection.

Once you have added the data connection to the Pubs database, you can click on the Data View tab of the Workspace window (or double-click the Pubs database node under the PubsProject) to see the Pubs database and its objects.

Data View Tab

The Data View tab (see Figure 15.2) displays some of the database objects of the connected SQL Server database in a treeview control. Visual Database Tools allow you to view, create, modify, remove, and in some cases execute SQL Server database objects. However, Visual Database Tools currently does not provide access to SQL Server rules, user-defined data types, or defaults. These objects can still be maintained through SQL Server's Enterprise Manager.

FIGURE 15.2.

The Data View tab, displaying some of the Pubs *database's objects.*

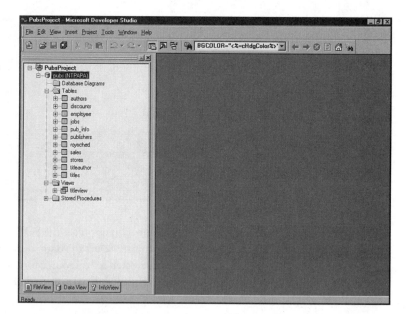

Visual Database Tools Features

So why would you want to use Visual Database Tools instead of using Enterprise Manager or linking to SQL Server via Access? Well, the biggest reason for using Visual Database Tools is the consolidation of Access's query tools and SQL Server's tools, plus the addition of features that neither of the aforementioned tools provide. Let's go through the features of Visual Database Tools at a high level.

> **NOTE**
>
> Don't be alarmed if you notice that a new table was created in your database. In fact, several stored procedures were also created. The first time you use some of the features of the Visual Database Tools, the dtProperties table and several stored procedures are created in your SQL Server database. You can identify these objects by their dt prefix. They are used to manipulate database structural changes that you can apply using the Visual Database Tools' Database Diagrams. The dtProperties table stores information about the Database Diagrams in it. The dt stored procedures are used to manage this information from Visual InterDev. Some of the stored procedures are also used by Visual Database Tools to display the property information in the property dialog boxes in Visual InterDev.

Database Diagrams

Database Diagrams provide a picture of the tables and their relationships in a SQL Server database. Using a Database Diagram, you can

- View all database tables and their relationships.
- Create diagrams to isolate and label individual table relationships.
- Add/edit/remove tables to/from a database.
- Add/edit/remove constraints.
- Add/edit/remove indexes.
- Alter table properties such as nullable columns, identity seeds, and default values.
- Create/edit/remove relationships between tables.

Figure 15.3 shows the entire Pubs database in a diagram. The diagram shows the tables, their columns, the relationships between tables, and the primary keys.

Sometimes a database can have dozens, even hundreds of tables, and just as many relationships between them. A diagram depicting all of these relationships can be very cluttered. That's when it's great to take a subset of those tables and their relationships and see them separated from the rest of the database's relationships. For example, if you only want to see the relationship between authors and the books they write, you can create a new diagram to represent this. Right-click the Database Diagram node in the Data View tab and select New Diagram. Now drag and drop the tables authors, titleauthor, and titles to the new diagram from the Data View tab. Visual InterDev will display the relationships between these tables as you drop them into the diagram window. Finally, save the diagram as Title to Author Relationship (see Figure 15.4). All of the diagrams that you save are displayed under the Database Diagrams node in the Data View tab.

FIGURE 15.3.

The entire Pubs
database in a diagram.

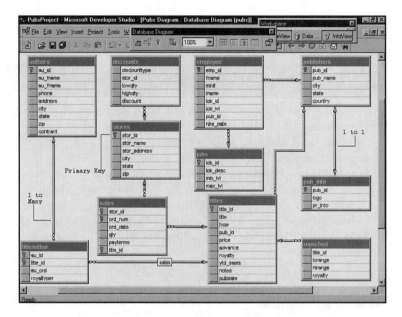

FIGURE 15.4.

*Saving a database
diagram displaying the
relationship between
the* authors,
titleauthor, *and*
titles *tables.*

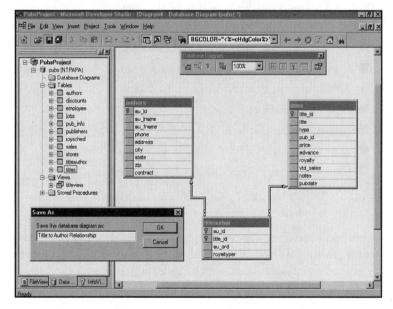

WARNING

When you close a database diagram without saving it, the connected SQL Server database is unaffected. If you save a database diagram, the database may be changed depending on the modifications you made to the diagram. For example, if you delete the relationship between the authors table and the titleauthor table and save the diagram, the foreign key will be deleted from the database. You can preview the changes in the T-SQL script before it modifies the database by clicking on the Save Change Script button on the Database Diagram toolbar. Figure 15.5 shows the T-SQL script that Visual Database Tools generated to drop the foreign key relationship between the authors table and the titleauthor table.

FIGURE 15.5.

Viewing a T-SQL script behind a change in the Database Diagram screen.

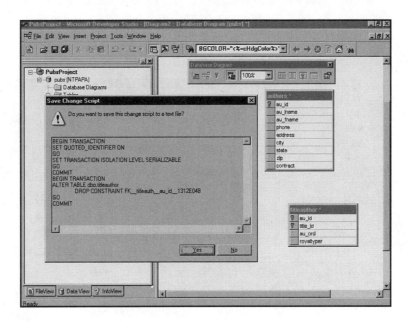

Instead of running the T-SQL in an ISQL window to create, alter, or drop a table, you can use Visual Database Tools to do the same thing without typing any SQL. This is one of the greatest features of Visual Database Tools. I don't know how many times I've gotten stressed out about the hassle of making a change to a table's structure. It even made me reconsider whether the change was really necessary. I had to figure out which foreign keys to drop, bulk copy the data to a text file, drop the table, alter the table's CREATE TABLE script, run the altered script, bulk copy the data back into the table, and re-create the foreign keys. Yuck! What a waste of time. I thought, "Wouldn't it be great if someone made a tool that did all of this for me?" Microsoft has answered this cry with Visual Database Tools.

Let's go through an example that demonstrates how Visual Database Tools can save you countless hours of generating T-SQL scripts and bulk copying files. In this example, we want to change the length of the type field in the table titles to CHAR(24), and change the datatype of pubdate from datetime to smalldatetime. This is a fairly simple task using Visual Database Tools, compared to using SQL scripts as described previously. Open the Title to Author Relationship diagram that you created in the previous example. Select the titles table by clicking in its title bar. Now display the table's properties by either clicking the Show Column Properties button on the Database Diagram toolbar or right-clicking the title bar of the authors table window and selecting Column Properties. All of the columns' properties are displayed, including the datatypes, column lengths, whether they allow nulls, their default values, whether they're identity fields, and if so, their identity seed values and increment values.

Now change the length of the type column to 24. Then change the datatype of the pubdate column to smalldatetime. Notice that when you click on its datatype cell, a combo box displaying all of the datatypes is displayed. Your window should look like Figure 15.6 when you are done.

FIGURE 15.6.

Using the Database Diagram features to alter the titles *table's structure.*

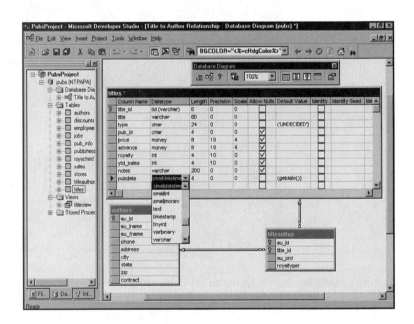

Now click the Save button on the Standard Visual InterDev toolbar. Visual InterDev will confirm the changes with you by displaying what objects will be affected. Notice that along with the titles table the titleauthors, publishers, roysched, and sales tables will also be affected. All of these tables will need to be changed because they have a foreign key that references the titles table.

Before we commit these structural changes, let's find out exactly how Visual Database Tools implement them. Click the No button on the Save dialog box to cancel this table change for now. Let's inspect the T-SQL script that Visual Database Tools use to make this database change. Click the Save Change Script button on the Database Diagram toolbar and look at the T-SQL script. Listing 15.1 shows this script in detail.

Listing 15.1. Visual Database Tools T-SQL script for changing the structure of the `titles` table.

```
 1: BEGIN TRANSACTION
 2: SET QUOTED_IDENTIFIER ON
 3: GO
 4: SET TRANSACTION ISOLATION LEVEL SERIALIZABLE
 5: GO
 6: COMMIT
 7: BEGIN TRANSACTION
 8: ALTER TABLE dbo.titles
 9:     DROP CONSTRAINT FK__titles__pub_id__0E4E2B2E
10: GO
11: COMMIT
12: BEGIN TRANSACTION
13: ALTER TABLE dbo.titles
14:     DROP CONSTRAINT DF__titles__type__0D5A06F5
15: GO
16: ALTER TABLE dbo.titles
17:     DROP CONSTRAINT DF__titles__pubdate__0F424F67
18: GO
19: CREATE TABLE dbo.Tmp_titles_1
20:     (
21:      title_id tid NOT NULL,
22:     title varchar(80) NOT NULL,
23:     type char(24) NOT NULL
     ➥ CONSTRAINT DF__titles__type__0D5A06F5 DEFAULT ('UNDECIDED'),
24:     pub_id char(4) NULL,
25:     price money NULL,
26:     advance money NULL,
27:     royalty int NULL,
28:     ytd_sales int NULL,
29:     notes varchar(200) NULL,
30:     pubdate smalldatetime NOT NULL
     ➥ CONSTRAINT DF__titles__pubdate__0F424F67 DEFAULT (getdate())
31:     ) ON "default"
32: GO
33: IF EXISTS(SELECT * FROM dbo.titles)
34:     EXEC('INSERT INTO dbo.Tmp_titles_1
35:         (title_id, title, type, pub_id, price,
            ➥advance, royalty, ytd_sales, notes, pubdate)
36:             SELECT title_id, title, type, pub_id, price, advance, royalty,
37:                 ytd_sales, notes, CONVERT(smalldatetime, pubdate)
                 ➥ FROM dbo.titles TABLOCKX')
38: GO
39: ALTER TABLE dbo.titleauthor
40:     DROP CONSTRAINT FK__titleauth__title__14070484
41: GO
```

continues

Listing 15.1. continued

```
42: ALTER TABLE dbo.sales
43:     DROP CONSTRAINT FK__sales__title_id__1BA8264C
44: GO
45: ALTER TABLE dbo.roysched
46:     DROP CONSTRAINT FK__roysched__title___1E8492F7
47: GO
48: DROP TABLE dbo.titles
49: GO
50: EXECUTE sp_rename 'dbo.Tmp_titles_1', 'titles'
51: GO
52: CREATE NONCLUSTERED INDEX titleind ON dbo.titles
53:     (
54:     title
55:     ) ON "default"
56: GO
57: ALTER TABLE dbo.titles ADD CONSTRAINT
58:     UPKCL_titleidind PRIMARY KEY CLUSTERED
59:     (
60:     title_id
61:     ) ON "default"
62: GO
63: ALTER TABLE dbo.titles WITH NOCHECK ADD CONSTRAINT
64:     FK__titles__pub_id__0E4E2B2E FOREIGN KEY
65:     (
66:     pub_id
67:     ) REFERENCES dbo.publishers
68:     (
69:     pub_id
70:     )
71: GO
72: GRANT REFERENCES ON dbo.titles TO guest
73: GRANT SELECT ON dbo.titles TO guest
74: GRANT INSERT ON dbo.titles TO guest
75: GRANT DELETE ON dbo.titles TO guest
76: GRANT UPDATE ON dbo.titles TO guest
77: COMMIT
78: BEGIN TRANSACTION
79: ALTER TABLE dbo.roysched WITH NOCHECK ADD CONSTRAINT
80:     FK__roysched__title___1E8492F7 FOREIGN KEY
81:     (
82:     title_id
83:     ) REFERENCES dbo.titles
84:     (
85:     title_id
86:     )
87: GO
88: COMMIT
89: BEGIN TRANSACTION
90: ALTER TABLE dbo.sales WITH NOCHECK ADD CONSTRAINT
91:     FK__sales__title_id__1BA8264C FOREIGN KEY
92:     (
93:     title_id
94:     ) REFERENCES dbo.titles
95:     (
96:     title_id
97:     )
98: GO
```

```
 99: COMMIT
100: BEGIN TRANSACTION
101: ALTER TABLE dbo.titleauthor WITH NOCHECK ADD CONSTRAINT
102:     FK__titleauth__title__14070484 FOREIGN KEY
103:     (
104:     title_id
105:     ) REFERENCES dbo.titles
106:     (
107:     title_id
108:     )
109: GO
110: COMMIT
```

Imagine having to type this script just to change the length of the type column and the datatype of the pubdate column! This is definitely Visual Database Tools' coolest feature. This script may be long, but it is full of extremely basic and short T-SQL statements, which makes it easy to dissect. First, the script turns on the use of quoted identifiers in line 2 of Listing 15.1 so that you can use object names that may be the same as some keywords. Then, on line 4 of Listing 15.1, the script sets the isolation level to SERIALIZABLE so that no other database changes will be noticed while the script is running.

On line 7 of Listing 15.1, the script begins a transaction that will make all of the structural changes necessary to make the two table changes we specified. Then the defaults for these columns are dropped on the titles table. On line 19 of Listing 15.1, the Tmp_titles_1 table is created, incorporating the table changes we specified for the titles table. The data is then copied from the titles table to the new table in lines 33-37 of Listing 15.1. You cannot drop a table without dropping the relationships that reference it, so the T-SQL script drops all of the foreign keys referencing the titles table. Then the script renames the new table to the original table, titles, using the sp_rename stored procedure. The script wraps up by re-creating the primary key of the titles table and the foreign keys that previously referenced the titles table, using the WITH NOCHECK option on the foreign keys. This option tells SQL Server not to verify that the values in the foreign key columns are valid values from the primary keys that they reference. Using this option saves SQL Server from having to check each of these constraints, thus making the script quick. Visual Database Tools is even smart enough to re-create the permissions on this table (see lines 72-76 of Listing 15.1).

The only thing left is to let Visual Database Tools implement these changes. Click the Save button on the Standard Visual InterDev toolbar again. When Visual InterDev confirms the changes by displaying which objects will be affected, click the Yes button on the Save dialog box to commit them.

Tables

In addition to using Database Diagrams to make table changes, you can right-click on an individual table in the Data View treeview and select the Design option from the shortcut menu. If you only need to make changes to a single table, this a more convenient than using a Database Diagram.

There are other aspects of a table that you can modify besides structural changes. You can change a table's name or modify its relationships. Visual Database Tools also let you create, remove, and modify constraints and indexes. For example, you can create a new constraint on the phone column of the authors table that restricts the phone number to a ### ###-#### pattern (see Figure 15.7). Then, if you want to save this new constraint, click the Save button on the Standard toolbar.

FIGURE 15.7.

Creating a new constraint on the phone *column of the* authors *table.*

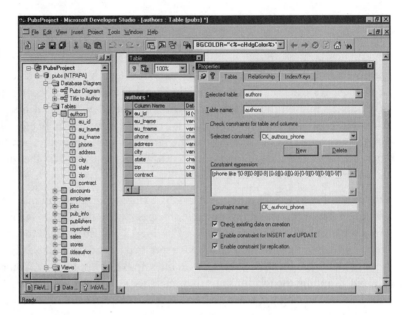

The Index/Keys tab of the Properties dialog box lets you modify indexes, including their fill factor and type of clustering. The Relationship tab provides access to the relationships between tables.

You can create a table by right-clicking the Tables node in the Data View treeview or by selecting Insert|New Database Item|Table. Here you can create columns, specify their datatypes, set their default values, and change several other column-specific attributes.

Figure 15.8 shows how you can create a table and specify which columns allow null values, create default values for columns, and specify a column as an Identity column. This table also uses the Identity Seed and Identity Increment features of SQL Server to customize the customer's number.

As described in previous examples, you can also define constraints, relationships, and indexes on a new table by using the Properties dialog box.

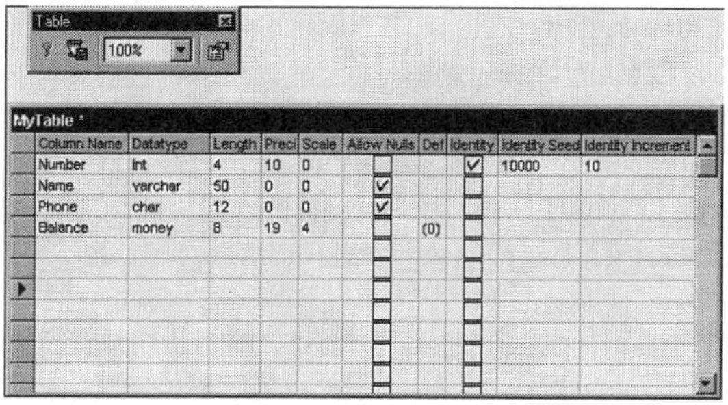

Figure 15.8.

Using Visual Database Tools to create a new table and specify its columns and their attributes.

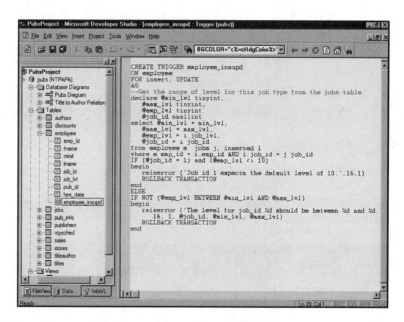

Triggers

You may have noticed that columns are not the only child nodes that are displayed under a Table node in the Data View treeview. Triggers on that table, if any exist, are also displayed under the Table node. Fully expand the employee table node and notice the last child node, employee_insupd. This is a trigger on the employee table that is executed upon INSERT or UP-DATE of the table. If you double-click the trigger, the trigger's code window will appear (see Figure 15.9).

Figure 15.9.

Editing a trigger with Visual Database Tools.

The trigger's code window provides an appealing interface for editing triggers. Using a color-coding system similar to the one Visual Basic uses, Visual Database Tools make coding T-SQL in Enterprise Manager seem about the same as using a simple text editor. T-SQL keywords, comments, and identifiers all appear in different colors, making it easy to differentiate between them.

15

TAKING
ADVANTAGE OF
THE TOOLS

You can create a trigger by right-clicking the table where you want the trigger to be linked and selecting New Trigger, or by selecting Insert|New Database Item|Trigger. A window with the standard trigger syntax will appear, which you can edit as you please. When you are ready to save the trigger, click the Save button on the Standard toolbar (see Figure 15.10). You can also delete a trigger by right-clicking the trigger and selecting Delete. However, make sure that the code window for the trigger you want to delete is closed.

FIGURE 15.10.

Creating a new trigger for insertion in the stores *table, using Visual Database Tools.*

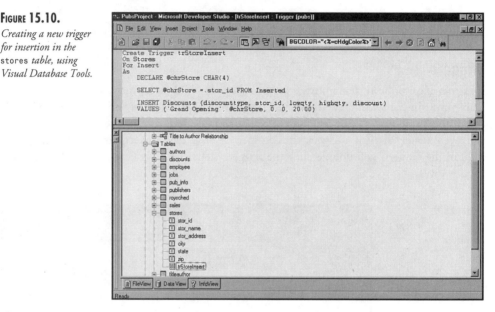

Stored Procedures

Another strength of Visual Database Tools is its robust interface with stored procedures. The Data View treeview displays all stored procedures that are available in the connected database. An expanded stored procedure node displays its return value, all of its parameters, and its results columns.

> **NOTE**
>
> There appears to be a bug in the way Visual Database Tools retrieve the information to display under the stored procedure node of the Data View treeview. A stored procedure that both has parameters and returns results columns does not display the result columns in the Data View treeview. The ByRoyalty stored procedure is a good example of this. However, you can view all of the results columns by opening the code of stored procedure in Visual Database Tools.

Using Visual Database Tools, you can create, modify, and delete stored procedures. You can even execute them and see the results in the Output window. For example, open the `ByRoyalty` stored procedure in the `Pubs` database. (Notice that the stored procedure window is similar to the trigger window in that it color-codes the keywords.)

The `ByRoyalty` stored procedure accepts a percentage and returns all authors who receive that percentage. Execute the stored procedure by right-clicking and selecting Run from the menu or by clicking the Run button on the Database toolbar. When you are prompted for the percentage parameter's value, enter `50`. The results of the stored procedure are displayed in the Output window (see Figure 15.11). The Output window is great for running stored procedures and checking their output during development.

FIGURE 15.11.

Running the ByRoyalty *stored procedure and viewing the results in the Output window.*

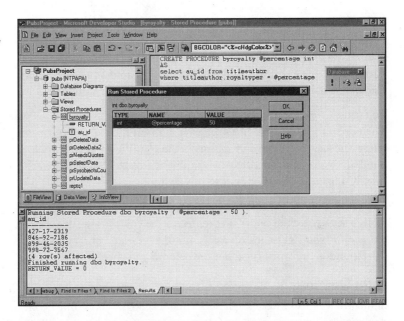

NOTE

You may have noticed that when a stored procedure is executed, Visual Database Tools open the Output window. However, you can explicitly open the Output window by clicking the Output button on the Standard toolbar or by choosing View|Output.

You can create stored procedures by clicking the Insert New Database Item button on the Database toolbar or by choosing Insert|New Database Item|Stored Procedure. In addition to creating stored procedures, you can create triggers, tables, database diagrams, and local queries from this dialog box. Visual Database Tools also let you rename stored procedures and delete them from the database. You can find these features and others by right-clicking a stored procedure and viewing the shortcut menu.

15

TAKING ADVANTAGE OF THE TOOLS

When you run a stored procedure that contains parameters, the Run Stored Procedure dialog box is displayed. Each parameter requires that a value be entered. Visual Database Tools does check datatypes, so make sure that you provide a value that matches the data type of the parameter. If you can't remember the datatype of the parameter, don't worry. The Run Stored Procedure dialog box displays the datatype of the parameter in the first column of its grid.

The flexibility that Visual Database Tools provide for developing and executing stored procedures stops short of a key feature: debugging. This powerful but missing feature is handled by the T-SQL Debugger, which is discussed later in this chapter. However, when you consider all of the features that Visual Database Tools does have, it is quite a consolidated and useful tool.

Views

Unlike triggers and stored procedures, views do not have a special window in which you can manipulate them. Views can only be created or deleted using Visual Database Tools through a query's SQL pane. It is unclear why Microsoft would leave such a basic feature out of Visual Database Tools while providing such an obvious workaround to it.

To create a view, begin by creating a query to return the results you want the view to return. Then open the SQL pane of the query and insert the CREATE VIEW syntax. When you run the query, the view is created and appears in the DataView treeview under the Views parent node. Similarly, you can drop a view by running the DROP VIEW syntax in the SQL pane of a query (the SQL pane is discussed later in this chapter).

You can, however, inspect the columns that a view retrieves in the Data View treeview. Like a table, a view has child nodes that represent the columns (or derived columns) that the object retrieves. If you right-click on a column of a view and choose Properties, you are shown the corresponding information about the column you chose.

Local Queries

Similar to Microsoft Access' queries, Visual Database Tools provide a feature-rich interface for designing and executing queries. Access gives you the choice of seeing either a diagram pane and a grid pane, a results pane, or a SQL pane. Thus, using Access, you can't view all of these windows at once. Visual Database Tools combine all of these features or panes into one window.

The Diagram pane visually displays the joins between the input sources, the columns selected to output, the sort order, and any groupings. The Grid pane supports all column-based options, such as specifying sort orders, columns to output, criteria to select rows by, and column aliases. The SQL pane can be edited to create any type of query, whether that query can be displayed graphically or not. The final pane, the Results pane, shows the results of the most recently executed SELECT statement. All four panes are intended to be used in conjunction with each other, but can function independently.

Because of this feature, you can type in the SQL pane and see the corresponding changes to the Grid and Diagram panes when you click out of the SQL pane. The Grid and Diagram panes are only updated after you leave the SQL pane because Visual Database Tools does not translate the SQL while you type. However, when you make a change in either the Diagram or Grid panes, the other pane and the SQL pane are updated to reflect the change immediately. Visual Database Tools does translate each mouse-click and keyboard movement in these panes as they occur. Thus, the panes can update themselves when appropriate. Figure 15.12 shows a query window with all four panes displayed.

FIGURE 15.12.

A local query showing all four panes and the Query toolbar.

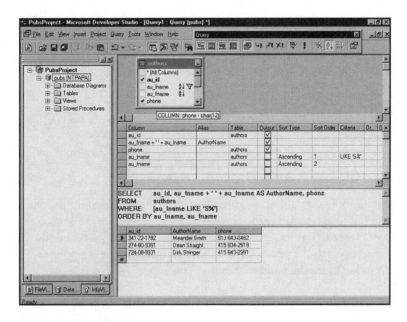

You can create an UPDATE, INSERT, SELECT, or DELETE query using Visual Database Tools' local queries. Also, as discussed previously in this chapter, you can use the SQL pane to execute just about any SQL statement. For example, you can create views, run DBCC statements, and even dump transaction logs.

> **NOTE**
>
> Some T-SQL can't be displayed in the Diagram or Grid panes. In these cases, after typing a DBCC CHECKDB statement in the SQL pane, these other panes are grayed out.

The local query's Properties dialog box can be viewed by right-clicking the mouse anywhere within any of the four panes of the local query window. In this dialog box, you can specify whether the query will only display distinct rows in the results set, or even specify that all columns of all input sources be outputted to the results set. Parameters can also be defined here, as is explained later in the "Grid Pane" section of this chapter.

Diagram Pane

The Diagram pane displays a graphical image of input sources, such as tables and views, and the relationships between them. The Diagram pane can be used to construct most parts of a query by dragging tables and views into the pane and using them as input sources. Dropping input sources into the Diagram pane will automatically update the Grid and SQL panes to reflect the contents of the Diagram pane.

You can create and modify joins between input sources by dragging a column from an input source and dropping it onto another input source's column. A join line will be created, specifying a join between those two input sources on the columns you specified. There are several types of joins that you can specify using the Diagram pane:

- Inner join
- Left outer join
- Right outer join
- Full outer join
- Inner join based on operators (<, >, <=, >=, <>)

Figure 15.13 displays a nonsense query that is intended to display the different types of joins that the Diagram pane can represent. The join between the stores and sales tables is a full outer join and is represented by the solid square icon on the join line. This relationship is also joined using the less than or equal to operators, which is exemplified by those operators being displayed in the diamond within that same square on the join line.

FIGURE 15.13.

A local query showing several different types of joins in the Diagram pane.

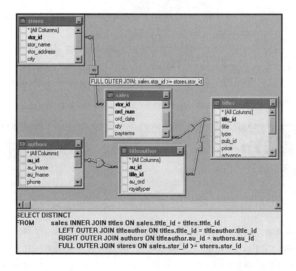

Other than modifying joins in the Diagram pane, the Diagram pane also provides an avenue to specify sort orders and select fields to appear in the query's Results pane. By right-clicking on a column in an input source, you can select an ascending or descending sort order from a shortcut menu. From this same menu, you can specify a column in the select list. These features are expressed visually adjacent to the column they correspond to. Figure 15.12 reiterated some of these features of the Diagram pane.

> **TIP**
>
> ToolTips are not only used to display information about the join they hover over. When placed over a column of an input source, a ToolTip will display the datatype and size of that column.

Grid Pane

If there's something you can't represent about a query in the Diagram pane, you most likely can express it in the Grid pane. The Grid pane represents output columns, sorting columns, grouping columns, derived or calculated columns, target columns for UPDATE statements, and new values for INSERT statements. The columns of input sources are displayed as rows in the Grid pane.

The types of columns on the Grid pane depend upon the types of query that you are designing. See Table 15.1 for details on which columns are present for the different types of queries.

Table 15.1. Types of queries and the columns that correspond to them in the Grid pane.

SELECT	INSERT	UPDATE	DELETE
Column	Column	Column	Column
Alias	Alias	Alias	Alias
Table	Table	Table	Table
Output	Append	New Value	
Sort Type	Sort Type		
Sort Order	Sort Order		
Group By	Group By		
Criteria	Criteria	Criteria	Criteria

> **TIP**
>
> You can easily change the query type by clicking one of the query type buttons on the Query toolbar. All of the panes will be updated automatically to reflect the type of query you choose.

15

TAKING ADVANTAGE OF THE TOOLS

The features of the Grid pane work best if you first provide an input source in the Diagram pane or the SQL pane. For example, let's assume that you are designing a SELECT query. Once you drag one or more tables or views from the Data View treeview to the Diagram pane, you can begin filling in the Grid pane. The column, table, sort type, and sort order columns of the Grid pane all provide drop-down lists of the valid entries for their respective cells. Once an input source is created, you can specify the columns to use in the query by choosing them from a drop-down list. You can then assign an alias to each column and specify whether or not the column should be outputted in the Results pane, any criteria, the sort order, and the sort type of the column, if applicable.

The column can contain a standard column from an input source, a concatenation of columns, a calculated column, or a column within an aggregate function. If you enter an aggregate function in a column cell, upon leaving the cell Visual Database Tools will reformat the Grid pane to express the aggregate function in the Group By column. Note that you can drag fields from an input source on the Diagram pane into the Grid pane. You can also choose the sort order of the query by specifying the sequential order of the columns in the Sort Order column. An ascending or descending sort type is indicated in the Sort Type column of the grid.

As mentioned earlier, the Group By column specifies how to group the columns in the query and whether any aggregate functions are to be displayed in the Results pane. You can choose the Where option in the Group By column to indicate that the corresponding column in the same data row of the grid will be used in a WHERE clause. The Criteria columns display these conditions that limit the query's results set rows. If a GROUP BY clause is specified, Visual Database Tools use the Criteria column for the HAVING clause of the grouping. As you manipulate the Grid pane, the SQL and Diagram panes are updated immediately to reflect the Grid pane's changes. Likewise, the Grid pane is updated when other panes are altered. Figure 15.4 depicts a SELECT query that uses all of these features.

> **TIP**
>
> Just as you can remove a data column by selecting a row and pressing the Delete key, you can clear all contents from a column in the grid by selecting the column and pressing the Delete key. Be careful not to try this on the data field column or it will clear the entire query. If you do, there is always the Undo feature.

Notice in Figure 15.14 that the ord_date column has a condition upon it that its value must be between two values, @FromDate and @ToDate. These two values are parameters that have been designated as such in the Properties dialog box of the query. The Properties dialog box lets you specify any prefix or suffix character to designate parameters. The parameters for this query have been indicated by prefixing their names with a @ character. When this query is executed, Visual Database Tools prompt the user for the values of the parameters before returning a results set.

FIGURE 15.14.

A SELECT query showing off the many visual features of the Grid pane.

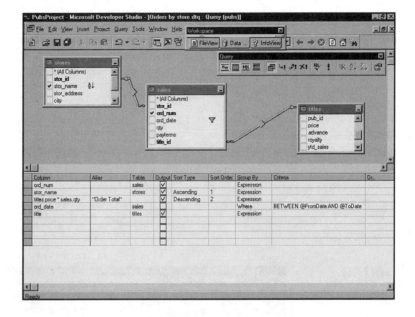

SQL Pane

The SQL pane is the least visually interactive interface, yet it's the most powerful pane in a Query window. You are limited to typing SQL in this pane to create or modify a query, but it does have some strong features. After you type a query in the SQL pane and move the focus outside of the pane, Visual Database Tools format the SQL in the SQL pane by color-coding it and then immediately update the Diagram and Grid panes to reflect the SQL pane's contents. Even better, you can create a query using the visual interfaces of the Diagram and Grid panes and simultaneously watch the SQL pane build the SQL query on-the-fly.

Sometimes you know exactly what the SQL needs to look like for part of a query, but you are not sure how to represent it in the other panes. Similarly, you may be a weak typist (like myself) and prefer to take advantage of the visual interfaces to design a query.

Visual Database Tools will verify the SQL you create and notify you if any part of the query could not be parsed. When you press the Verify SQL button on the Query toolbar, Visual Database Tools parse the query in the SQL pane and determine whether the SQL contains executable SQL. For example, create a new query and enter the following SQL in the SQL pane:

```
SELECT title FROM authors
```

Visual Database Tools will display an error dialog box stating that the `title` column is not a valid column in the `authors` table. The other visible panes will subsequently be dimmed to signify that they no longer represent the SQL displayed in the SQL pane, Also, if the query were valid, Visual Database Tools would confirm its validity with a dialog box.

The most powerful aspect of the SQL pane is its capability to execute SQL Server-specific T-SQL statements. Not only can you create the standard selection queries and action queries, but you can also design T-SQL batches to perform database administration functions. For example, create a new query and enter the following T-SQL in the SQL pane:

```
SELECT getdate(), @@ROWCOUNT, @@IDENTITY, @@ERROR
```

This T-SQL will return the current date and time, the number of rows returned in the most recent query, the most recent Identity value that was created, and the value of the error number after the most recently executed statement. However, when you click the Run button of the Query toolbar, Visual Database Tools tell you that this query cannot be represented in the Diagram and Grid panes. You are then requested to choose whether to continue anyway or to further edit the SQL. When you choose to continue executing the SQL, you will see the values for this SQL Server function and the global SQL Server variables in the Results pane (see Figure 15.15).

FIGURE 15.15.

The SQL pane containing a SQL Server-specific query and the Results pane displaying its results set.

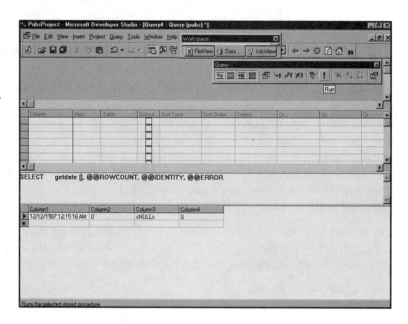

This query happens to return a results set in the Results pane, but that is not always possible or even desired. You could run a database backup or a dump of the transaction log. In those cases, the Results pane serves no purpose because you are not expecting any results back from the database engine.

Results Pane

The Results pane displays the results set of the most recently executed query, if that query returned a results set. If the pane is dimmed, the contents of the Results pane are no longer representative of the query expressed in the other panes. The data in the Results pane can be edited or, in some cases, deleted or appended to. As long as you do not violate any constraints, such as foreign keys, the data in the Results pane can be modified.

Special values, such as nulls and binary data, can be represented in the Results pane. null values are displayed with the symbol <NULL> in the contents of the respective cell. Binary fields are not editable but are visible in the Results pane. Binary data is designated with the symbol <Binary> in the appropriate cell. Dates, times, numbers, and currency values are all displayed in the format specified in the regional settings of the local machine.

When you right-click in the Results pane, the shortcut menu appears (see Figure 15.16). Keep in mind that the Results pane displays a results set that represents the query in the three other panes. Because the results set is a recordset, it can perform the standard recordset navigational methods as well as clear the entire results set or add a new row. As shown in Figure 15.16, the shortcut menu for the Results pane displays the navigational methods available to you.

FIGURE 15.16.

The Results pane's shortcut menu displaying the available methods.

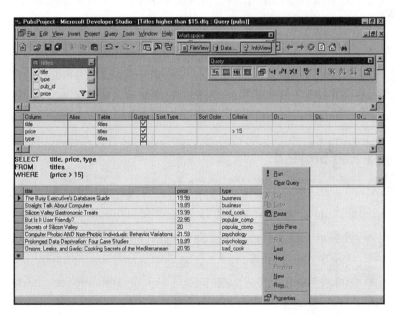

Using the shortcut menu, you can navigate directly to the first, last, next, or previous record of a recordset. You can also go directly to a specific row or even create a new row in a recordset. If data does not fit within the width of a cell, you can widen the column by dragging the column divider until the column is wide enough. Likewise, you can increase the height of a row by dragging its divider down. This will make fields that are too wide appear on multiple lines within their cells. Keep in mind that when you resize one row, all rows are resized as a consequence.

> **WARNING**
>
> If you do not use the Results pane for a period of time, Visual Database Tools will clear its results set. However, you can repopulate the Results pane by rerunning the query.

Visual Database Tools' combination of powerful features and simple interface gives it an edge over all other database tools on the market. Whether you are querying data, editing a relationship, or even running database administration queries, Visual Database Tools is the tool of choice.

Introducing the T-SQL Debugger

The biggest setback from using SQL Server stored procedures has been that they can be extremely difficult to debug. Because you can include complex logic inside of a stored procedure, it is reasonable to assume that you will have to debug the procedure for errors. However, until the advent of the T-SQL Debugger, finding these stored procedure bugs was a hair-tearing experience.

T-SQL Debugger Add-In allows you to debug SQL Server's T-SQL batches and stored procedures from Visual Basic 5. Using the debugger, you can step through the T-SQL line by line to diagnose problems. Another great feature of the T-SQL Debugger is that it allows you to execute a stored procedure using RDO 2.0 and automatically jump into the T-SQL Debugger to debug the stored procedure.

Getting Started

The T-SQL Debugger uses the server's ActiveX dll, SDI.dll, via Remote Automation to debug SQL Server T-SQL. The client configuration is set up automatically when you install Visual Basic 5. In order to use the T-SQL Debugger, you must first satisfy the following requirements:

- Visual Basic, version 5 must be installed on the client machine.
- SQL Server 6.5 with Service Pack 2 or higher must be installed on the server.
- You must log in on a Windows NT account that has administrator's rights.
- Both the client and the server must have either DCOM or Remote Automation installed on them.
- If the client machine is running Windows NT 4.0, run DCOMCNFG and give everyone launch and access permission for the VBSDICLI.exe application.
- The SQL Debugging Interface (SDI) must be installed and registered on the server.

The SQL Server 6.5 Service Pack 2 can be found on the VB 5 CD in the \Tools\TSQL\ SQL65. SP2 folder. Or it can be found on the Visual Studio CD. This service pack includes support files that are required by the T-SQL Debugger for it to debug T-SQL.

If you attempt to use the T-SQL Debugger while being logged onto Windows NT with an account without Administrator's privileges, you will receive the error You must have Privileges to modify the registry. This situation is easily rectified by logging on with an account that has Administrator's privileges.

The SQL Debugging Interface is an ActiveX application that exposes its methods and properties in order to provide access to debug T-SQL. To install SDI, you must run the SDI_NT4.exe program that is included on the Visual Basic 5 CD in the \Tools\T-SQL\SrvSetup folder. You will be prompted by a dialog box requesting the location of the SQL Server installation. It is looking for the folder where the SQL Server was installed, which is usually the \MSSQL folder. The SDI_NT4.exe program will install and automatically register the SDI.dll in this folder.

TIP

If you experience problems using the T-SQL Debugger, make sure the remote procedure call (RPC) and the RPC Locator services are started on the server machine. Also, ensure that SQL Server is not logged on as the SystemAccount. Rather, it should be assigned to log in on an account that has Administrator privileges.

Debugging T-SQL

Now that you have completed the installation required for the T-SQL Debugger to work, add the T-SQL Debugger to the Visual Basic environment through Visual Basic's Add-In Manager. You can then run the T-SQL Debugger from the Add-Ins menu and debug a stored procedure or a T-SQL batch. (Again, for this chapter we will use the Pubs database for our examples.) Then specify the DSN of the Pubs database and a valid User ID and password on the Settings tab of the Visual Basic Batch T-SQL Debugger dialog box (see Figure 15.17). You can also specify the locking type and the type of results set on this tab.

FIGURE 15.17.

Starting a debugging session by opening the T-SQL Debugger and specifying the database connection.

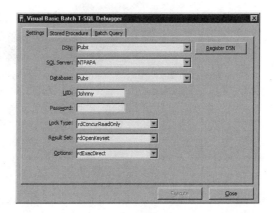

15

TAKING ADVANTAGE OF THE TOOLS

You can debug either a stored procedure or batch T-SQL, depending on which tab you choose on the Visual Basic Batch T-SQL Debugger dialog box. Let's start by entering a simple batch query in the text box on the Batch Query tab. Enter the T-SQL from Listing 15.2 and click the Execute button. This will instantiate the T-SQL Debugger and prepare you for debugging the batch.

Listing 15.2. A T-SQL batch query that updates book prices based on their sales.

```
DECLARE @intQty int

SELECT @intQty = SUM(qty) FROM sales
WHERE title_id = 'PS2091'

IF @intQty > 50
    UPDATE titles SET price = price * 1.10
    WHERE title_id = 'PS2091'
ELSE
    UPDATE titles SET price = price * 0.90
    WHERE title_id = 'PS2091'
```

Before we execute this batch, let's examine the toolbar and menu options of the T-SQL Debugger. From the Edit menu, you can set, remove, or clear all breakpoints just like the debugging interface in Visual Basic. Also similar to the Visual Basic debugging options, you can choose to step into a procedure, step over a procedure, run the batch to the cursor, or run through the entire batch. If you step into the code, the Call Stack menu option is enabled. This option displays the stack of procedure calls that landed you at your current stage.

Now let's debug this batch and identify which branch of the IF statement is traversed. There are several ways to do this: placing breakpoints at both branch levels, placing a breakpoint before the branching point and stepping through code from that point, placing the cursor on the IF statement and running the code to the cursor, or stepping through each line at a time. We'll set a breakpoint at the SELECT statement and keep an eye on the Watch windows to determine which branch will be traversed (see Figure 15.18).

> **NOTE**
>
> In Figure 15.18, notice that the status bar indicates that the AutoRollback mode has been activated. This option specifies that the batch will be rolled back after it is executed. That is why there is no need to place this batch in a transaction while we debug it. This option can be turned on or off from the Options menu or from the Visual Basic Tools|T-SQL Debugger menu.

Now let's run the batch by clicking the Go toolbar button. The code should stop at the breakpoint we set. If you receive the error in Figure 15.19, look in the event viewer's log under the application log for the problem. Refer to the troubleshooting tips described in the "Getting Started" section of this chapter.

FIGURE 15.18.

The T-SQL Debugger stopped while executing a T-SQL batch.

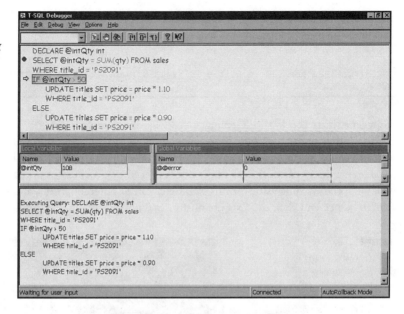

FIGURE 15.19.

The T-SQL Debugger may not function if it is not set up properly.

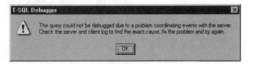

Notice that the @intQty variable is in the Local Variables window in Figure 15.18, along with its current value. We can add our own Watches, as well. Because we did not put any error-handling in this batch, let's add a Watch on the global variable @@error. This will allow us to monitor the error status. To add the Watch, choose Edit | Add Watch, and enter the @@error variable.

Now let's step into (or over) the code to the next line. Notice that the value of the @intQty variable in the Local Variables window has been updated to reflect the SQL statement we just ran. Now that we have been forewarned about which branch will be traversed, we'll just let the rest of the batch execute without breaking. If any errors were encountered, we would have noticed the value of the @@error variable change in the Global Variables window.

Now let's prepare a stored procedure that we can debug (see Listing 15.3). This stored procedure will assign another coauthor to the title PS2091 by inserting a record into the titleauthor table. Create this stored procedure in an ISQL window.

15

TAKING ADVANTAGE OF THE TOOLS

Listing 15.3. The stored procedure `prInsertCoAuthor`.

```
CREATE PROCEDURE prInsertCoAuthor
@chvAuthor VARCHAR(11)
AS
INSERT titleauthor (au_id, title_id) VALUES (@chvAuthor, 'PS2091')
GO
```

Now let's set up the T-SQL Debugger to debug this stored procedure. Go back to the T-SQL Debugger by choosing Debug|Stop Debugging. Go to the Stored Procedure tab of the dialog box and choose the `prInsertCoAuthor` stored procedure from the Procedure Name combo box. Notice that the syntax of the call to the stored procedure provides for the parameter, `@chvAuthor`, that we specified. The value for this parameter can be entered in the Value text box (see Figure 15.20). Once you click the Execute button, we'll begin debugging this example.

FIGURE 15.20.

The T-SQL Debugger's Stored Procedure tab options.

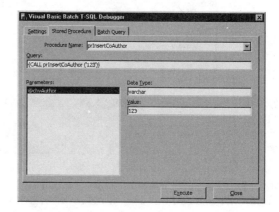

When you run this stored procedure through the debugger, an error is raised. We violated a Foreign Key constraint on the `authors` table because we entered `au_id` `123`. Notice that a dialog box appears indicating the error. Now exit the T-SQL Debugger, reenter the value of the parameter as `172-32-1176`, and rerun the T-SQL Debugger. This time you will not receive any errors.

You know that you can invoke the T-SQL Debugger Visual Basic environment, but did you know that you can invoke T-SQL Debugging while executing Visual Basic code? To utilize runtime debugging, select T-SQL Debugger Options on Visual Basic's Tools menu. The options dialog box allows you to turn on Safe mode, which is synonymous with enabling the AutoRollback mode.

You can also limit the number of rows that appear in the T-SQL Debugger's output window and set the login timeout period that the debugger uses to connect to the database. However, we are interested in turning on Automatic Step into Stored Procedures. This option will activate the T-SQL Debugger whenever you step into an RDO method that runs a stored procedure. For example, if you step into an RDO method that executes the `byRoyalty` stored procedure, the T-SQL Debugger is activated to debug it. After stepping through the `byRoyalty` stored procedure, control is returned to the line after the line of Visual Basic code that executed the stored procedure.

Let's set ourselves up to use this feature of the T-SQL Debugger by creating a new standard Visual Basic project and referencing Microsoft Remote Data Objects 2.0. Make sure the Automatic Step into Stored Procedures option is checked on the T-SQL Debugger Options dialog box. Now place a command button on Form1 and put the code in Listing 15.4 in `Form1`'s code section. The `command1_click` event will execute the stored procedure, which will activate the T-SQL Debugger.

Listing 15.4. The Visual Basic code in Form1.

```
 1: Option Explicit
 2:
 3: Private cnMyCon As New rdoConnection
 4: Private qyMyQuery As rdoQuery
 5: Private rsMyRS As rdoResultset
 6:
 7: Private Sub Command1_Click()
 8:
 9:     Set rsMyRS = qyMyQuery.OpenResultset(Type:=rdOpenForwardOnly,
    ➥ LockType:=rdConcurReadOnly)
10:     Do While Not rsMyRS.EOF
11:         Debug.Print rsMyRS(0)
12:         rsMyRS.MoveNext
13:     Loop
14:     rsMyRS.Close
15: End Sub
16:
17: Private Sub Form_Load()
18:     cnMyCon.CursorDriver = rdUseOdbc
19:     Set cnMyCon = rdoEnvironments(0).OpenConnection(dsname:="Pubs",
    ➥ prompt:=rdDriverNoPrompt, ReadOnly:=True, Connect:="UID=sa")
20:     Set qyMyQuery = cnMyCon.CreateQuery("My SQL", "{call byRoyalty(?) }")
21:     qyMyQuery.rdoParameters(0) = "50"
22: End Sub
23:
24: Private Sub Form_Unload(Cancel As Integer)
25:     Set rsMyRS = Nothing
26:     qyMyQuery.Close
27:     Set qyMyQuery = Nothing
28:     cnMyCon.Close
29:     Set cnMyCon = Nothing
30: End Sub
```

15

TAKING ADVANTAGE OF THE TOOLS

> **WARNING**
>
> If it appears that these steps do not activate the T-SQL Debugger, make sure you are stepping into the line of code that executes the stored procedure. If you run code that executes a stored procedure without stepping into it, the T-SQL Debugger will not be activated.

Place a breakpoint on line 9 of Listing 15.4 so we can step into the T-SQL Debugger. Run the code and click the Command button. When the code breaks on our breakpoint, step into the code by pressing F8. The T-SQL Debugger will activate itself and will be ready for you to walk through and debug the stored procedure. After you debug the stored procedure, the T-SQL Debugger window is closed and Form1's code window gets the focus. Remember, if you are sure your stored procedure works and you do not want the T-SQL Debugger to be activated, simply disable this option.

The long-awaited debugging environment for T-SQL has arrived. It delivers on the functionality, but leaves plenty of room for improvement. For example, it can be a bit moody when you try to install it. Overall, this is a great tool for those of us who have longed for an easier way to debug those multiple-page T-SQL batches.

Modeling Your Data

Data modeling is one of the first steps in creating a relational database. Once you know which entities and attributes exist, you can begin formulating an entity relationship model, either on paper or, more realistically, using a data modeling tool. There are several tools that can aid in your data modeling effort, including Microsoft's Visual Modeler and LogicWorks' ERWin. These tools provide a tremendous amount of flexibility in creating a database model. ERWin, for example, can create a SQL Server database from an ERWin model, including tables, constraints, and triggers. It can also extrapolate an ER model from a SQL Server database, among other databases.

For simple data modeling purposes, though, the Visual Database Tools are up to the task. Visual Database Tools let you create new tables, add columns, define primary and foreign keys, and create triggers for extended relationships. All of the basic functions of data modeling can be performed by Visual Database Tools, making it a sufficient tool to create a database model. If you require more advanced data modeling features, these other tools are better suited for the task. Like Access, Visual Database Tools let you create a database in a very short time through its visual interface.

When you're choosing a data modeling tool, consider whether you prefer to manage your database structure via SQL or through a tool once the database structure is in place. When creating a database, nobody wants to type the SQL to create all of the objects and their relationships. But after you create the database using a data modeling tool, you may want to utilize some of the tool's features to manage the database. If this is the case, ERWin may be your best choice. ERWin is widely used and provides a feature for just about every database management circumstance that you might encounter. In my opinion, ERWin's best feature is its capability to print a legible ER diagram. This is one area where Visual Database Tools and Access fall short.

However, if all you need to do is create a SQL Server database model, Visual Database Tools is the quickest and easiest tool to tackle the job. This contrasts with ERWin and Visual Modeler, whose interfaces can prove to be somewhat cumbersome and even difficult to navigate.

Summary

As you can see from the examples in this chapter, you have a number of positive options to speed development and make troubleshooting your code much easier. Though Microsoft initially intended for Visual InterDev to be used as an aid in creating Web sites, this tool packs a versatility that every SQL Server developer can leverage. Using this tool, you can readily create code behind the scenes by visually manipulating objects on the screen. Then as you look at the code Visual InterDev creates for you, you can more easily follow the logic of the code because of the color-coding scheme.

Every development cycle has its share of bugs, no doubt. So, use T-SQL Debugger to run your queries and spot the problems; it's certainly an easier way to debug your multiple-page T-SQL batches.

Of course, the theorists will tell you that you'll have fewer problems to debug if you start with a more solid plan on the front end with good data modeling. All of the basic functions of data modeling can be performed by Visual Database Tools, making it a sufficient tool to create a database model. If you require more advanced data modeling features, then consider using ERWin and Visual Modeler, but be prepared for a bit steeper learning curve.

Using Multiple Tiers and Client/Server Architecture

IN THIS CHAPTER

Client/server computing has emerged as the development architecture of choice. Client/server technology maintains a high level of performance, a central location for security and control, and balances processing by using client applications.

As you delve deeper into the Internet era, client/server architecture continues to prove that it is the vehicle by which database applications will flourish. Multiple-tiered approaches have evolved due to the influx of Internet technologies to include thin clients, business rules servers, Web servers, database servers, and n-tiered applications.

This chapter discusses how data integrity is maintained by the client/server architecture and why the alternatives are mostly unattractive. Along with SQL Server, RAD (Rapid Application Development) tools can help implement multiple-tiered applications in the client/server arena. Using real-world scenarios, you go through several n-tiered approaches and see how Visual Basic fits into the puzzle. Finally, you can't forget about the technological tidal wave as known as the Internet. You look at how the Internet has provoked us to open the door to thin client implementations of n-tiered applications. First, this chapter begins by defining the current state of client/server architecture and the roles of the client and the server.

Understanding Client/Server Architectures

Client/server architecture most often comprises multiple computers connected via a LAN (Local Area Network), WAN (Wide Area Network), or the Internet. (Do not forget that there is no reason a client/server model can't be implemented on a single computer acting as a database server and a client workstation.) The power behind client/server architecture is the interaction between user workstations and central database servers. The workstations (or clients) run programs that request and update data stored centrally on a database server. These programs are responsible for maintaining the interface to the system users. The central database servers are responsible for accepting data manipulation requests, ensuring data integrity, and returning requested data, all while allowing multiple users to be connected to the database server. Refer to Table 16.1 for more detail on the historical roles of the client and the server.

Table 16.1. The typical roles of the client and the server.

Client	*Server*
Manage user interface	Process database requests
Accept data from user	Maintain integrity checks
Generate database requests	Optimize queries and updates
Transmit requests to server	Format query results
Receive result sets from server	Transmit result sets to clients
Format results from server	Allow for user concurrency
Perform application logic	Recover data, if needed
Manage logical data transactions	

Using Multiple Tiers and Client/Server Architecture

CHAPTER 16

361

16

N-TIER AND
CLIENT/SERVER
ARCHITECTURE

> **NOTE**
>
> Table 16.1 indicates the historical, and possibly the most basic, roles that the client and the server have played. This two-tier approach leaves room for debate regarding the specific responsibilities of the client's and the server's interior functions. For example, on the client: Do you process business-specific logic bundled together with user interface navigation? Where do you separate the logic that formats database instructions from the logic that validates simple data entry? Fortunately, you can break down the roles of the client and the server, so that each tier of the model supports unambiguous and very distinct responsibilities. For now this chapter continues discussing the standard approach in Table 16.1. However, it goes through a detailed outline of the ways to separate your application's functions into multiple tiers in "N-Tier Applications Via RAD Development Tools."

These roles, from Table 16.1, broadly define the responsibilities of a client/server architecture. The client should maintain navigation- and field-level validation while executing all business rules logic. In this scenario, the client must be able to communicate with the database server to retrieve user-requested data, as well as instruct the database server to update data at the request of a user. Clients may also be called upon to instruct the server which data transactions should be executed in logical units. Figure 16.1 outlines the design of the two-tier model, or what has been dubbed the "fat client model." A *fat client* is an application that processes the majority of its logic on the client computer while using the database server merely as a data repository.

FIGURE 16.1.

This two-tier model assigns all business logic, database communication, and validation to the client layer.

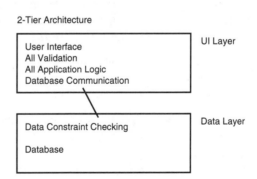

2-Tier Architecture

User Interface
All Validation
All Application Logic
Database Communication

UI Layer

Data Constraint Checking

Database

Data Layer

The server's job is to translate and implement the data manipulation instructions from the client and to return the result set to the client, if any were requested. The server must find the most efficient and quickest route to execute the client's instructions, while ensuring that the data's integrity is not violated.

Ensuring Data Integrity

Maintaining data integrity is the duty of the database in the client/server architecture. Since all database processing is consolidated on a single computer, a high degree of data integrity can be achieved. Since every database request is processed by the server, if database constraints are defined to the server, the server can consistently apply the constraints.

> **TIP**
>
> Utilize the numerous data-integrity checking features of SQL Server where they make sense. Primary keys, foreign keys, defaults, rules, user-defined datatypes, and triggers contribute to solid database design. All of these features, except triggers, are extremely efficient, since they are checked before data is actually changed. A trigger is fired after data is changed. If it determines that data integrity will be violated, the trigger must revert the entire transaction. However, triggers are sometimes the only way to enforce complex business- or data integrity rules. The merits of triggers are discussed at length in Chapter 11, "Specialized Triggers."

If integrity checking is not performed by the server, application programs on the client computers are required to check the constraints. Server-constraint checking is preferred, of course. If the clients are left to check constraints then constraint checking logic must be included in every client application. This is an inefficient and error-prone method of ensuring data integrity. Furthermore, the application programs developers may have different perceptions of the constraints (not to mention the occasional error made when programming the constraints). The developers could program the client application to enforce conflicting constraints, or entirely omit certain constraints due to an ignorance regarding a specific business aspect. Furthermore, if you leave constraint checking to the client applications, all of the constraint checking efforts will be duplicated whenever one is developed.

Do not forget that not all data changes are made through application programs' interfaces. Users can make changes through a query/update language, and data can be imported *en masse*. Seldom are constraints checked for data changes from these sources.

If the server performs constraint checking, constraints need only be defined, verified, and validated once. Further, data changes from all sources are checked for integrity. It won't matter whether a data change is submitted via a client application's interface, an executed SQL statement from a SQL window, or a data import method. Regardless of the data manipulation source, the database ensures the constraints are not violated. This is one of the key elements of client/server architecture.

At face value, the outline in Table 16.1 translates into a two-tier approach. The client (tier one) is processing all user interface functions as well as all business-specific logic and database interfacing. The server (tier two) maintains the data's integrity while performing data retrieval and manipulation. There are, of course, other methodologies of tiered approaches. These are discussed the next section.

N-Tier Applications Via RAD Development Tools

Today's RAD tools, like Visual Basic 5, provide the mechanism to construct client/server applications quickly, easily, and efficiently. By using Visual Basic, you can create robust user interfaces with complex business logic and implement them over multiple tiers. What's the advantage of using a three-tier model in lieu of a two-tier model? It depends on the application you are developing. Two-tier models are adequate for applications that have few or simple business rules, so that the rules can be combined within the user-interface tier.

> **WARNING**
>
> Implementing a two-tier solution can degrade performance or consume heavy memory resources on the client computer. When choosing a tiered approach, consider whether the business rules and database instructions are too heavy a memory burden for client machines to bear.
>
> Also refrain from the two-tier solutions when business rules are apt to change often. For example, if the rules change in a two-tier application, you have to reinstall the software on every client computer. In contrast, if you implement a three-tier solution, you only have to reinstall the business rules software on the server.

The three-tier client/server model, which you can see in Figure 16.2, is ideal for applications that contain complex or dynamic business rules. They reduce the resource burden on the client computer by placing the business rules (or middle tier) on the server, which is usually endowed with more than enough RAM. This means that the client computers can be light on memory, which may prove to be a huge cost savings if you have several client machines.

Another enticement to develop a three-tier client/server architecture is the maintenance factor. Isolating the user interface logic, the business rules logic, and the data layer makes maintenance of these tiers much easier. Now maintenance developers know exactly where to make changes to the application; the best part is that changes to individual tiers won't affect the other tiers.

Visual Basic is an ideal RAD tool for creating a three-tier model. Visual Basic 5, in particular, supports the client/server implementation methods DCOM and remote automation. Both of these methods help client software communicate with server software. N-tiered development has taken huge strides due to the massive number of developers that have embraced Visual Basic as the leading RAD tool. Visual Basic allows developers to design the tiers individually or debug them in an integrated environment. Before you can program your tiers, you have to know where to start. What exactly are these tiers and what are their roles in a client/server architecture? Table 16.2 explains an implementation of the three-tier model.

FIGURE 16.2.

This three-tier model designates all business logic and database communication to the middle tier or the rules layer.

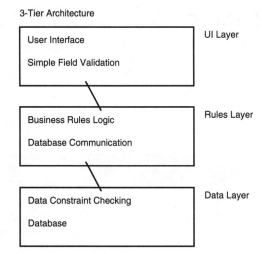

3-Tier Architecture

User Interface Simple Field Validation	UI Layer
Business Rules Logic Database Communication	Rules Layer
Data Constraint Checking Database	Data Layer

Table 16.2. Breakdown of a three-tier implementation of the client/server model.

Tier	Responsibilities
User-interface layer	Accept user inputs
	Process field level validation
	Manage field and screen navigation
	Transmit user inputs to business layer
	Accept results sets from business layer
Business-rules layer	Accept user inputs from the UI layer
	Transmit instructions to the data layer
	Accept result sets from the data layer
	Transmit result sets to the UI layer
	Perform complex data validation
	Execute business logic
Data layer	Accept queries/updates from business layer
	Optimize and perform queries/updates
	Enforce data integrity constraints
	Return result sets to the business layer

The main difference between the two-tier model in Table 16.1 and the three-tier model in Table 16.2 is that all of the business logic has been moved to the middle tier in the three-tier model. By moving this logic to the middle tier, you can either place this layer on the server along with the data layer, or on a separate server. Either way, the business logic is physically located on a single server and not on several client machines. This point is important to note; since the rules reside in a single location, it is a simple task to update the rules without disrupting the client installations.

The three-tier model can be distributed across multiple servers, as well. For rule-intensive applications where speed is of the essence, distributing the business layer and the data layer on separate servers can augment performance. Dedicating a server to support a middle tier of business-rules logic alleviates the database server from having to split its resources amongst the database-intensive processing and complex rules logic.

Instancing and ActiveX Servers

Whether or not you distribute the rules layer and the data layer across separate servers, an important decision needs to be made regarding the type of instancing of the rules layer. Visual Basic allows you to create single-use or multi-use ActiveX servers.

Single-Use ActiveX Servers

A single-use server creates a new occurrence of the ActiveX server in memory for each instantiation by an application. Separate instantiations of these servers allow fast access to rules logic. However, this speed comes at a heavy cost. Each server's instantiation occupies a chunk of memory on the server. For example, if a single-use ActiveX server is referred to by 12 client applications and the ActiveX server allocates 7MB of RAM per instance, then up to 84MB of RAM on the server would be required to run these instantiations. Figure 16.3 is an illustration of this single-use ActiveX server scenario. This is a heavy burden to place on a server, depending on the number of client applications and the amount of RAM required by the Active rules server. However, in a system where there are few users and a business-critical need for speed, single-use servers can prove useful.

> **TIP**
>
> If you haven't already, you are likely to run into applications that require time-critical, complex business rules. A three-tier approach using a single-use rules server is a great way to isolate the business logic. However, the rules server may reserve a few megabytes of RAM and may have several clients. Using the earlier example of 7MB per rules instance with 12 clients, this could certainly tax a server's CPU and memory resources already running SQL Server (not to mention running an IIS as a Web server).
>
> How do you get around this? You can always add more RAM or another CPU to the database server. Another solution is to install the rules layer on a server of its own. This frees the database server from having to reserve some of its memory resources for the rules layer and vice versa. How do you choose? Evaluate the application's requirements. They should help point you to the solution (or combination of solutions) that best fits your situation.

Figure 16.3.

A single-use ActiveX rules server in a three-tier model being accessed by 12 clients.

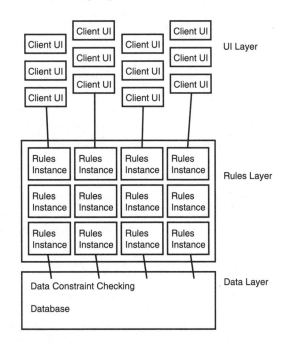

3-Tier Model Using Single-Use ActiveX Rules Server

Multi-Use ActiveX Servers

Conversely, Visual Basic also provides a multi-use server option when creating ActiveX servers. This is more often the choice of developers when choosing an implementation of a rules layer or middle tier. A multi-use ActiveX server allows countless client applications to refer to it using only a single instantiation of the ActiveX server. Notice in Figure 16.4 that 12 client applications can all reference the same rules server. This lowers the memory burden on the computer that houses the ActiveX server, since only one instance of the ActiveX server is created. Each subsequent reference to the server (or rules server, in this case) allots a pointer to the cached version of the rules server. Only when all client applications remove their references to the ActiveX server is the rules server released from memory.

WARNING

You can place all of the business logic within the rules tier in lieu of using triggers, rules, and defaults. The advantages are that your application will always adhere to these rules and that all of the rules all located in one physical code base.

Beware, however, that the database is left unprotected from business-logic violations. For example, a `shirt size` column can only have a value of small, medium, or large.

Normally, you place a SQL Server rule on that column (or a check constraint). However, if you put all of the rules in the rules tier, somebody could update the database to include a size of extra large. You can always put the rules in both places, but you have twice as many places to make the changes if they change. Weigh carefully the consequences of both methods of rules implementation.

FIGURE 16.4.

A multi-use ActiveX rules server in a three-tier model being accessed by 12 clients.

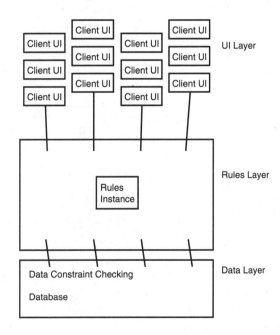

3-Tier Model Using Multi-Use ActiveX Rules Server

Why not always use multi-use servers? Suppose you have several client applications that need simultaneous access to the same chunk of business logic. A multi-use rules server causes these client applications to queue themselves, waiting for each other to traverse the business logic one at a time. This synchronous behavior of multi-use servers may adversely affect the performance of systems that require split second responses. Therefore, these types of systems—order entry, investment trading, and sales applications—should consider using single-use servers.

Each determination regarding the instancing of an ActiveX rules server should be made upon the specific business needs of the application's users. There are, however, other n-tiered models that may better accommodate a business's needs.

Scalability and N-Tiers in the Enterprise

Another implementation of an n-tiered model is to create a data layer separate from the database. Incorporate this concept with the three-tier model in Figure 16.2. Notice that in Figure

16.5 the data layer is separated from the database, resulting in a four-tier architecture. What's the point? The point is that you can isolate all database communication within a single tier. This means that the rules layer can only update or query the database through the data layer.

FIGURE 16.5.

A four-tier model splitting the database interaction from the rules logic.

4-Tier Model Using ActiveX Rules & Database Communication Servers

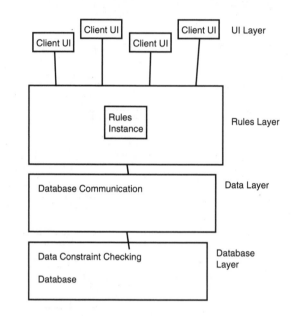

Answering some questions about the data layer will clear some of the confusion: What exactly is a data communication layer? The *data layer* is a translation tool that accepts application-specific rules and converts them into a language (SQL) that the intended database can process. What is the data layer's main goal? The main purpose of a data layer is to create a reusable, generic database communication tool that can be used by any application, regardless of the database or business logic.

The data layer encapsulates all database communication including queries, updates, deletes, inserts, and transactions. It is basically a layer between the application logic and SQL. What does this buy you? If you simplify the interface to the data layer well enough, you create a tier that has few and simple methods that retrieve and update data. Developers on your team all have to access the database in the same manner. This makes application maintenance much easier. Since there is a generic way to access the database, any team member can jump in and debug a problem. If you develop the data layer to handle multiple SQL dialects (Oracle, SQL Server, Access, Excel, and the like), you can switch the back-end database by simply setting a database type flag.

Using Multiple Tiers and Client/Server Architecture

CHAPTER 16

369

16

N-TIER AND
CLIENT/SERVER
ARCHITECTURE

The details of a data layer are up to the development team or department. However, a data communication layer can lay one more brick in the foundation of companywide applications. Once it is developed, there is no end to the number of applications in which it can be used.

User-Interface Managers

You have to put some validation in the user interface (UI). Otherwise, the users have to wait for the validation to occur in the business-rules tier and bubble back up to the client if there is a problem. This can quickly become tiresome to users who have just entered an invalid date or an alphabetic character in a monetary field. On the other hand, you don't want to overburden your client with too much logic, especially if you have numerous or complex screens. It lessens the effect of having an isolated rules tier. What do you do? You could implement a five-tier architecture like the one shown in Figure 16.6.

FIGURE 16.6.

A five-tier model is ideal for applications that have robust user interfaces.

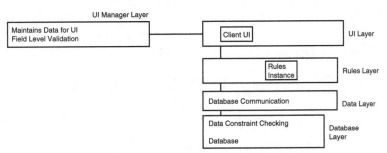

This model demonstrates a UI manager layer that maintains all data required for the UI to function. When data is updated on the UI, the UI Manager records change. When the user wants to save the data, the UI Manager validates the data. Then it either returns a validation error if the data is invalid or returns the valid data to the UI. The UI can act upon the results by either sending the valid data to the rules tier on its way down to the database or can display a message describing the invalid data situation to the user.

The point is that the UI Manager lets the UI stick to maintaining screen and field navigation and general interface usability. The UI Manager maintains all data required for the UI to function, including data values that are not shown on the screens. The UI Manager is also responsible for validating all data before returning it to the UI to be sent to the rules tier. The crucial factor in the UI Manager's power is that it has to bind itself to the fields on the UI's screens. In other words, the fields on the screens need to map directly to the data values stored in the UI Manager. This is how the UI Manager knows which type of field-level validation to perform. The UI Manager can then determine that a date field needs to contain a valid date and so on.

Another major function of the UI Manager is to determine when data has changed on the UI's screen since the last save (or cancel). The UI Manager actually stores two sets of values in its data store: the first for the original data values and the second for the current data values.

The UI Manager can then easily compare these two sets of data values to determine if the data has changed. The original data values are redisplayed on the UI screen when the user presses the UI's Cancel button. You can see that the UI Manager really does all of the dirty work for the UI.

> **TIP**
>
> Essentially, any UI Manager should reveal methods to validate data, bind data to the screen, and populate the screen with the data values.

I have personally used different implementations of the UI Manager on different projects and it has saved me and my colleagues several weeks worth of development efforts. The real savings comes when you have dozens of screens being developed by several developers. Without a UI Manager, everyone would be inventing his or her own way to validate data, populate screens, and refresh from cancels. With a UI Manager, everyone is coding using the same interface, the screens all have a consistent functional behavior, and they get completed faster. To sum it up, a UI Manager makes it easy to implement a robust and user-friendly interface.

Web Browsers, Web Servers, and the Client/Server Model

If you've done any Web development on a sizable system, you're probably thinking that you can't (or don't want to) implement any kind of UI tool on the client computer. Maybe you are developing a Web application on the Internet and you don't want to write a UI Manager using client-side script or a downloadable ActiveX utility. The client-side script has limitations on its power and flexibility while the ActiveX utility could take a long time to download to the client's computer. Maybe the client computer does not allow ActiveX to be downloaded or can't process ActiveX technology. In these cases, you can implement all of the logic, including most types of validation, in the rules layer. You can still use HTML forms to do a minimal level of field validation. However, without ActiveX or client-side script, your options are very limited.

The first question you can ask yourself is whether all of the users will be using an ActiveX-compatible browser. If so, then you do have the option of packaging a UI Manager into a downloadable ActiveX control for the browser to use. This is a very reasonable solution, since the UI Manager ActiveX control will only be downloaded once to the client computer. From that point on, when the client computer accesses your Web application, it can use the UI Manager already on its hard drive. Keep in mind that this method still limits you to users with browsers that support ActiveX.

FIGURE 16.7.

A three-tier thin client model is essential for most applications with browser-based user interfaces.

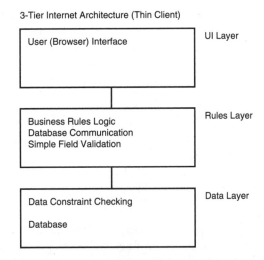

3-Tier Internet Architecture (Thin Client)

| User (Browser) Interface | UI Layer |

| Business Rules Logic / Database Communication / Simple Field Validation | Rules Layer |

| Data Constraint Checking / Database | Data Layer |

TIP

Client-side script is limited in its functionality. It is, however, wonderful for small, client-side interface enhancements such as custom ToolTips.

If you decide against the ActiveX UI Manager approach, you can opt to move the UI Manager down within the rules tier (Figure 16.7 shows this scenario). The browser is completely reliant on the rules tier to validate its data and populate its screens. This situation is referred to as a *thin client*, since the client layer consists solely of the browser. The great thing about thin clients in client/server architecture is that if there is a change to any of the code (rules logic, data communications, validation, and so on), the changes are transparent to the users. This is ideal for systems that have several dozens, or even thousands, of users. As far as the users are concerned, nothing has changed unless the browser interface changes. For more information of the role of the Internet in the client/server world, refer to Chapter 25, "SQL Server on Internet/Intranet Systems."

N-Tier and Stateless Environments

The implementation of a thin client on a Web application cannot maintain state. The very nature of the browser is to connect to a Web server, request information from the Web server, and disconnect itself once it receives the response. The browser reestablishes its connection with the Web server each time the user saves, cancels, or moves to another screen. This is what is called a *stateless environment*. Being stateless also means that you cannot store any data in the lower tiers. Why not? Because the connection to the Web server has been broken.

How does state effect the n-tier client/server models? For scalability, you would be well advised to build stateless environment into your LAN based client/server applications. Imagine your customers tell you they want to include Internet browsers to interface with their system. It would be less difficult to port the application to a Web-based solution if it were already designed to be stateless.

Another reason for moving to stateless environments is for the increased presence of Microsoft Transaction Server (MTS). MTS manages a pool of connections for you. MTS is a complex topic, but in short, it stores previously used (open) connections and assigns them to any requesting application. This reduces the overhead of having connections opened and closed all of the time. Instead, MTS just keeps them open and redistributes them. This point is underscored even more by the inception of the new Microsoft data access tool, RDS. RDS deals with disconnected result sets and basically assumes that no state will be held.

Web development is beginning to redefine n-tiered client/server architecture. With MTS, RDS, ADO, ASP, ActiveX, and many other new and exciting tools, you have many options for implementing a solid client/server application.

Summary

Client/server technology first established itself by distinguishing its data services from its rules and presentation logic. However, more recently client/server is becoming more known for its use of thin clients and n-tiered architectures. With the ever-growing presence of the Internet and intranets, browsers are on almost every desktop. The abundance of browser users warrants a thin client approach to client/server architecture. Without it, the fat client would slowly kill client/server.

The strongest aspect of client/server technology is its resiliency and adaptability. Every time some expert writes an article that "officially" pronounces client/server architecture as dead, client/server manages to survive. It defies the critics because it changes with the need of the market. Client/server architecture has grown into a multi-tiered development model that has the scalability to continue its evolution for years to come.

Replication

Birds do it. Bees do it. Even SQL Server does it. SQL Server's implementation of replication lets data reproduce and distribute itself without writing any code. It puts the power of distributed data into the hands of anyone owning SQL Server version 6.x or above. Still, many business problems require more than the out-of-the-box capabilities that replication has to offer.

In SQL Server's documentation, Microsoft states that replication is designed to allow read-only copies of table-based data to be distributed to other databases. If that was all it did, SQL Server replication would still be a very nice tool. To our benefit, the replication tools included with SQL Server are both flexible and extendable. A bit of design and development creativity, along with SQL Server's standard replication features, can solve some very complex business problems.

There is a dark side to using replication. Aspects of design, development, and administration become more complex. Data modeling entities and attributes develop multiple business roles. Backup and recovery issues give database administrators nightmares, if they can sleep at all. Accidental data modifications, dispersed to many databases, clog network bandwidth and transaction logs and shut down databases. However, these problems can be avoided by having a good understanding of how replication works while you design your solution.

There is another option for replicating data besides the built-in replication tools included with SQL Server. If strict transactional control is required, you can implement a two-phase commit model to replicate your data—but there are no graphical tools included with SQL Server to design and develop this type of model. Except for the administrative setup, all the work to build a two-phase commit solution involves programming.

The first section of the chapter reviews the terminology and mechanisms of SQL Server's built-in replication tools along with the different roles a database can play. This section also looks at two replication models and how they can be used to solve real-world problems. The second section discusses more advanced uses of replication, including SQL-DMO, stored procedures and replication, multiple master replication, and replication over Windows NT Remote Access Services (RAS).

Replication Concepts for Programmers

You go on a quick tour of replication, focusing on what programmers need to know to understand and design a system using it. There are plenty of books that explain how to set up and administer replication. This is not one of them. If you are interested in the setup and administration of servers and databases using replication, check out *SQL Server 6.5 Unleashed, Second Edition* and *Microsoft SQL Server 6.5 DBA Survival Guide*.

This section also includes some information on the two-phase commit model. Unless otherwise noted, when referring to replication in this chapter, the loose consistency model that is provided with the SQL Server product is what is being referred to. This consistency model is described in more detail later in the chapter.

Replication Lingo

Microsoft uses a newspaper publishing analogy to describe their implementation of replication. Here is a list of those terms:

- A publisher is a database with the capability to replicate data.
- A subscriber is a database that can receive published data.
- A distributor is a database that collects published data from one or more publishers and distributes it to one or more subscribers.
- An article is a set of published data from a table.
- A publication is a collection of articles grouped together by a publisher.
- A subscription is the registration by a subscriber to receive a publication from a publisher.

Have that all memorized? If not, you can refer to Figure 17.1 for an illustration of how the replication roles relate to one another.

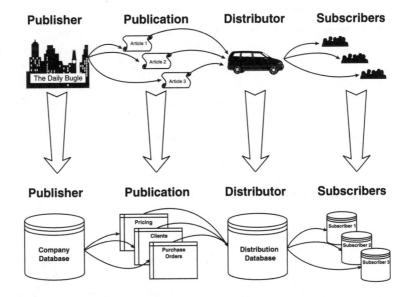

FIGURE 17.1
Each real-world role maps to a role in SQL Server's replication model.

You can install publisher, distributor, and subscriber databases onto a single SQL Server. On the other hand, you can put each database on a separate server on a separate continent. Microsoft has given you plenty of flexibility when it comes to designing a distributed data system. Later in the chapter you look at some of the combinations of publishers, subscribers, and distributors as they apply to specific business scenarios.

Transactions

Transactions are the core of a SQL Server database. They give SQL Server its ability to recover from catastrophes that leave other databases in chaos. A transaction is started implicitly on a single SQL statement or explicitly by programmer definition on all inserts, updates, or deletes to a database. The transaction is committed when the modification is complete. If any part of the transaction fails prior to being committed, the entire transaction rolls back, as if it never happened. This is built into almost all data activity that occurs on a SQL Server database.

SQL Server replication makes use of transactional properties to ensure that data being replicated reaches its destination. If replication fails, SQL Server has notification capabilities that are quite powerful.

Transaction Properties

Before the transaction property of consistency is discussed, make sure you are familiar with the ACID properties of transactions. ACID is an acronym for atomicity, consistency, isolation, and durability. Because each property's full definition is lengthy and redundant, it's been left to the database theorists to explain their exact meanings. Brief definitions of each one follow:

- Atomicity ensures that a transaction either completes perfectly, or not at all. If a SQL statement is updating 20 rows and fails on any row, all rows are returned to their original state and the transaction terminated.

- Consistency extends atomicity to include any applied logical/business rules as part of the success or failure of a transaction. In other words, a consistent transaction fails if any business rule is broken.

- Isolation keeps concurrent uncommitted transactions from interfering with each other. Data-locking strategies ensure correct data modification.

- Durability guarantees that a system failure will not affect committed transactions and will return uncommitted transactions to their last committed state prior to the system failure.

Loose Consistency

SQL Server replication employs what Microsoft calls loose consistency on transactions. *Loose consistency* is described as a replication model that allows a time lag between when the published data is altered and when the subscribing copies are altered. All copies of the data may not be the same at any point in time.

The loose consistency replication model is not ACID-compliant. Although errors are raised by the replication mechanisms if a failure occurs, the entire logical transaction cannot be undone because it is not being dealt with as a single atomic transaction. Sounds bad, doesn't it?

Not really. First of all, SQL Server has a great set of tools to set up and administer replication. This takes a huge workload off database administrators and developers, who don't have to re-invent the replication wheel. Adding a new subscriber is a point-and-click operation.

From the consistency standpoint, looseness is often exactly what you want when replicating data. For example, a traveling sales force with subscribed databases on its laptops cannot be constantly connected to the publishing database (at least not cost-effectively at the time of this writing) to be certain that every salesman always has identical data. Does every branch office of an insurance company need a client's new zip code the minute it is changed at the client's local branch? Probably not.

Another advantage of the loose consistency model is scalability. Adding a new subscriber is simple with the included replication management tools in SQL Server. Many business needs can be met with SQL Server's replication model. Look at an alternative to the loose consistency model.

Two-Phase Commit

Two-phase commit transactions fully comply with the ACID properties. If any part of a transaction fails, the entire transaction fails, even over multiple databases in multiple locations. Replicating data using this data distribution model ensures that all copies are identical at all times.

Financial transactions are the most common example of two-phase commit transactions. When money is transferred between accounts, it is required that both account balances be updated together or not at all. Financial institutions required that it be that way, so they built systems that could handle it. This example of two-phase commit isn't technically replication, since you are updating two different tables, not duplicating information to many places. It does illustrate the tight consistency ACID property that some transactions require. Two phase-commit sounds great in theory, but in reality, it is tough to implement.

There are a few restrictions when using a two-phase commit model. First, it requires that every copy of the data that is part of the transaction be available. If they're not, no changes can be made anywhere, including the original. Imagine making an entire sales force connect to the home office at exactly the same time everyday, so their databases could be updated. If one salesman were missing, no one could make or receive updates. That's no way to make friends with your sales force.

Second, data-locking requirements are rigid. Not only do all the members of the transaction have to be online, but all of the rows affected in every copy have to be available to be updated. Imagine a zip code update failing in a branch office in Toledo because the Boise branch office is printing a customer list and has its customer table locked.

Finally, when using SQL Server, two-phase commit models are code and administration intensive. Everything has to be written from scratch. Adding new databases requires either code changes or designing an administrative system much like the one included with SQL Server replication. This situation is improving with the advent of newer technologies like Microsoft Transaction Server and Microsoft Message Queuing.

17

REPLICATION

> **NOTE**
>
> Remember this: SQL Server replication does not use a two-phase commit model. It would be a huge design error to use the loose consistency model built into SQL Server when your business requirements call for a two-phase commit model. The inverse proposition would be less disastrous, but you would be doing a lot of development work that SQL Server replication handles automatically.

How Replication Works

A Windows NT service included with SQL Server, SQL Executive, manages the execution of replication. SQL Executive is a general task-scheduling engine used by the replication mechanisms to control replication tasks. These tasks are automatically created by SQL Server when databases are marked published, when publications are defined, and when subscribers are added. Look more closely at the function of these tasks in Figure 17.2. The log reader task reads the transaction log to generate SQL statements, which are copied to the distribution database. The distribution task then executes the SQL statements on each subscriber.

FIGURE 17.2.

The log reader and the distribution task in a simple one publisher/ many subscriber replication model.

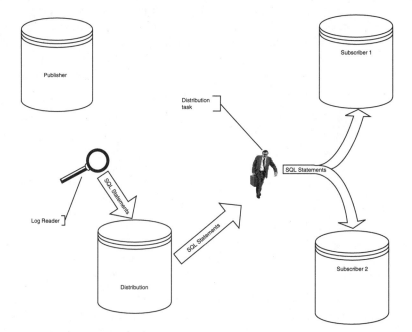

Replication Tasks

The log reader task is created when a database is marked as published. The log reader immediately begins to scan the database's transaction log for committed transactions. When qualifying transactions are found, it creates SQL statements to replicate the changes and puts them in the distribution database. A *qualifying transaction* is one that is committed, published, and subscribed to. This task runs continuously by default.

When a publication is defined, a synchronization task is created for that publication. This task checks the publication every five minutes for article modifications and new subscriptions. If a new subscription is found, the synchronization task creates the files needed for the initial synchronization.

A clean-up task is created when a new subscribing server is registered with the publisher. This task removes completed SQL statements from the distribution database. It runs daily at 1:05 a.m. by default. It is created whether or not any subscribing databases or subscriptions exist.

Finally, a distribution task is created when the subscription is created. This task executes the SQL statements from the distribution database for the subscriber in the order they occurred on the publisher. The SQL statements are grouped into jobs, which are submitted to the subscriber as a single transaction. By default, the distribution task runs continuously on the distribution database.

From a programming standpoint, each of these tasks can be controlled via custom applications developed using the SQL-DMO tools, which are described in more detail in the advanced replication section of this chapter.

Troubleshooting

If you search on the word *troubleshooting* in *SQL Server Books Online*, the first query result takes you to the replication troubleshooting area. It is a must-read if you are responsible for the support of a replication database either in production or in the development and testing phase. Rather than reiterate the contents of *SQL Server Books Online*, this chapter discusses some common issues developers have when working with replicated databases and helps you avoid those issues before they occur.

TIP

If your SQL Servers have access to email, set up an email account for each server and use the account to allow the built-in task-alert capabilities to notify you if your replication tasks fail. Configuring and using mail alerts is covered in Chapter 26, "Integrating SQL Server with Other Microsoft Products."

■ Don't insert test data into subscribed tables. Do all of your data modifications to the publisher's tables and let it replicate. Once publishers and subscribers are out of sync, you lose the data when they are resynchronized. This is the most common cause of replication failure during the development process. An exception to this is if you are testing your replication failure recovery procedures.

■ Make sure your DBA creates transaction logs big enough to handle the largest single transaction you ever expect to have. This is a little tricky. Say you have 10,000 rows in a table that are already published, subscribed to, and synchronized. If a published table is updated with a single SQL statement such as the following, the distribution database receives exactly 1 job with 20,000 SQL commands (yes, 20,000 to 10,000 deletes and 10,000 inserts) that must be distributed to each subscriber as a single transaction.

```
UPDATE MyTable
SET MyColumnData = NULL
```

Each database must have adequate space in its transaction log to handle the size of the transaction as it moves from publisher to distributor to subscribers. If all 20,000 commands are not committed together, the entire transaction rolls back.

■ Get your database backup and recovery plans in place, especially during development. Once you have a fair amount of data being replicated, it is very annoying, time-consuming, and costly to re-create it by hand. This is basic, but often ignored during the development phase of a project.

Replication Limitations

Every product has some limitations. Here are some of the shortcomings of SQL Server replication:

■ Only data is replicated. This makes sense, since SQL Server performs replication by monitoring the publisher's transaction log and sending logged changes to the distributor. Because the system tables are not replicated, neither are changes to database objects—so don't expect a new stored procedure added to a publisher to appear on a subscriber using SQL Server replication. You have to write the code to do that yourself.

■ On subscribed tables, user-defined dataypes (UDDT) are converted to their native dataypes, `timestamps` become `binary(8)`, and identity columns become plain `integer` dataypes. A UDDT is converted because it is defined in the database system table `systypes`, which is not replicated. In addition, non-SQL Server subscribers would not be able to use UDDTs. By definition, a `timestamp` value can only be created and modified by SQL Server. It is guaranteed to be a unique value within a database. If replication were allowed to change a `timestamp` value on a subscriber, non-unique values could be introduced into the subscribing database. For similar reasons, identity columns are converted to their base dataype. If you use these special dataypes, your table designs will differ between publishers and subscribers.

■ It is important to emphasize that SQL Server replication is a high latency, loose consistency replication model. There is no time frame in which the data is guaranteed to be replicated and no guarantee that it will be ever be replicated. It generates an error message eventually, but not when the original data was changed, as in a two-phase commit. You don't want to design a national organ donor availability system or credit card processing system with SQL Server replication. That's not to say that SQL

Server wouldn't be a good choice for those types of applications using a customized replication model; it's just not the right use for SQL Server's built-in replication model.

■ Non-logged operations such as bulk copying and text or image column changes are not automatically replicated. For bulk copying, you must make sure that bulk copying is being logged by having an index on the table importing data or by setting the database SELECT INTO/BULK COPY option to false. Both of these bulk copy settings slow data imports. You have to weigh the benefits and decide what is best for your application. For text and image replication, you must use the Transact-SQL commands WRITETEXT and UPDATETEXT with the WITH LOG option.

Replication Business Models

With the flexibility available from SQL Server there are many ways to combine the three replication roles (publisher, distributor, and subscriber) with one or more servers. This section illustrates two common replication models, along with how they might be used for business solutions. There are many other possible replication models.

> **NOTE**
>
> Easily confused by the many-to-many, *n*-tier, cascading complexity of replication options? Join the crowd. Here are the allowable combinations for replication scenarios. Each publisher can create many publications. Each publication can have many articles. Each subscriber can receive publications from many publishers via each publisher's single distributor. A publisher must have exactly one distributor. A subscriber may subscribe to an entire publication or to any subset of articles within a publication. All of these roles can be performed on a single server or on many servers.

Suppose you have a single database that is being used heavily for data entry and reporting. The problem is that a report that takes 15 minutes to run locks a table that 30 data-entry operators need to update. There they sit, waiting for their screens to refresh. With the model in Figure 17.3, you can replicate the tables needed for reporting to another database, allowing the first database to function as the OLTP (online transaction processing) database for the data-entry operators and the second database to function as the OLAP (online analysis processing) database for people who run reports. This can all be done on a single server or on separate physical servers. If a single server is chosen, replication is very fast and does not create network traffic.

Another common SQL replication scenario is one central subscriber receiving data from many publishers. This scenario can apply to data warehousing applications or point of sale locations reporting back to a centralized database. Sharpen your Transact-SQL skills if you are doing a data warehousing project. Stored procedure replication, which is discussed more fully in the advanced replication section of this chapter, is a useful technique for data scrubbing. Figure 17.4 illustrates an example of this model.

17

REPLICATION

FIGURE 17.3.
*Putting OLTP and
OLAP together without
the locking contention
of a single database.*

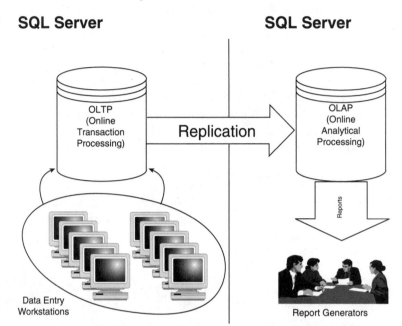

FIGURE 17.3.
*Putting OLTP and
OLAP together without
the locking contention
of a single database.*

FIGURE 17.4.
*A data warehouse
replication model.*

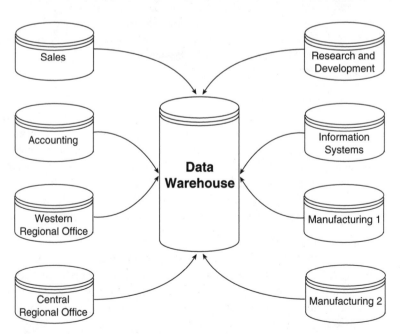

Advanced Replication

The point-and-click replication interface provided by SQL Server has much to offer. With it you can set up complex replication designs. What if that isn't enough? Synthesize your own solutions utilizing the replication mechanisms and tool sets in SQL Server. This chapter's following sections present some ideas to use when programming with replication.

Replication and SQL-DMO

Replication administration is normally managed using SQL Enterprise Manager. SQL-DMO can be used with a development language like Visual Basic or Visual C++ to develop your own replication management applications.

What can you do with SQL-DMO and replication? Say you are publishing from a central database to subscribing databases located on laptops that dial up to receive updates. Each laptop needs to dial up to the main server, start the replication process, and hang up when replication completes. As part of the laptop's database application, you could include a simple module that does the dialing, monitors the replication task, and hangs up when complete. This is possible using SQL-DMO and either a RAS ActiveX component or the RAS API. Take a look at Listing 17.01 for a simple Visual Basic example that runs a replication task using SQL-DMO. Although this example is running a distribution task, you can design an application that will run any task in SQL Executive.

Listing 17.1. A Visual Basic example using SQL-DMO to start and monitor a replication task.

```
'This goes in general declarations
'Windows system function
Private Declare Sub Sleep Lib "kernel32" (ByVal dwMilliseconds As Long)

'The rest goes into your form.  Or in a button.  Or wherever you see fit
Private Sub Form_Load()
    RunSQLExecTask
End Sub

Sub RunSQLExecTask()

    'declare the SQL-DMO objects
    Dim OLESQLObject As SQLOLE.SQLServer
    Dim OLESQLExecutive As SQLOLE.Executive
    Dim OLESQLTask As SQLOLE.Task

    'other misc. declarations
    Dim strTask As String            'name of the replication task to run
    Dim strErrorDesc As String       'minimalist error handler
    Dim dLastRunDate As Date         'when task last ran
    Dim dActiveStartDate As Date     'date upon which task is active
    Dim dActiveEndDate As Date       'date when task becomes inactive
    Dim bTaskEnabled As Boolean      'indicates whether task is enabled
    Dim lStatusNumber As Long        'status of task
    Dim iCheckAgain As Integer       'loop counter
```

continues

Listing 17.1. continued

```
Dim iMaxRetries As Integer      'times to check status of task
Dim iSleepTime As Integer       'frequency of task status checks

On Error GoTo ErrorHandler 'enable error handler

'set number of times to check for completion of SQL task
'each retry waits for iSleepTime milliseconds
iMaxRetries = 100
iSleepTime = 30000

'initialize the server object
Set OLESQLObject = CreateObject("SQLOLE.SQLServer")

' You must use sa as the login name to work with replication tasks
' unless using SQL Server mixed or integrated security.  In that
' case, just pass <servername> to the .Connect method.  If the
' user running the program has sufficient rights to the server,
' the connection will work.
'login to SQL Server <servername> , <login name>, <password>
OLESQLObject.Connect "BUBBA", "sa", ""

'instantiate the SQL Executive object
Set OLESQLExecutive = OLESQLObject.Executive

'name of the task to run - you can get a collection of tasks from
'OLESQLExecutive.Tasks for your UI.  I'm not doing that here.
strTask = "BUBBA_TestPublisher_BUBBA_TestSubs"

'instantiate the SQL Executive task
Set OLESQLTask = OLESQLExecutive(strTask)


'In this section we determine whether to run the task based on
'various attributes
'Check the SQL-DMO enum SQLOLE_COMPLETION_TYPE for the values of
'constants such as SQLOLEComp_Running

'check to see if the task is running
If OLESQLTask.LastRunCompletionLevel <> SQLOLEComp_Running Then

    'get last run information about the task
    dLastRunDate = OLESQLTask.LastRunDate
    'get task's active start date
    dActiveStartDate = OLESQLTask.ActiveStartDate
    'get the task's active end date
    dActiveEndDate = OLESQLTask.ActiveEndDate
    'find out whether the task has been disabled
    bTaskEnabled = OLESQLTask.Enabled

    'check that task is enabled
    If Not bTaskEnabled Then
        strErrorDesc = "Remote task is disabled in SQLExecutive."
        GoTo ErrorHandler
    End If

    'make sure there is a last run date for comparisons
    If Not IsDate(dLastRunDate) Then
```

```
            dLastRunDate = dActiveStartDate
            If Not IsDate(dLastRunDate) Then
                strErrorDesc = "Task is missing remote task start date."
                GoTo ErrorHandler
            End If
        End If

        'check the end date
        If dActiveEndDate <= Now Then
            strErrorDesc = "Task is no longer active."
            GoTo ErrorHandler
        End If

        'start the task
        OLESQLTask.Invoke

        iCheckAgain = 0

        'check the task's completion status every iSleepTime milliseconds
        Do
            iCheckAgain = iCheckAgain + 1
            ' check every iSleepTime milliseconds for completion of tasks
            Sleep (iSleepTime)

            'Update the object
            OLESQLTask.Refresh

            'see if task has finished
            If dLastRunDate < OLESQLTask.LastRunDate Then
                lStatusNumber = OLESQLTask.LastRunCompletionLevel
                iCheckAgain = 0
            End If

        Loop Until (iCheckAgain = 0 Or iCheckAgain = iMaxRetries)

        If iCheckAgain = iMaxRetries Then
            strErrorDesc = "Maximum retries reached, exiting the application."
            GoTo ErrorHandler
        End If

    Else
        'task is already running
        strErrorDesc = "Task status indicates that it is already running"
        GoTo ErrorHandler
    End If

    'clean up and exit
    Set OLESQLTask = Nothing
    Set OLESQLExecutive = Nothing
    Set OLESQLObject = Nothing
    Exit Sub

ErrorHandler:
    'do your error handling stuff
    Set OLESQLTask = Nothing
    Set OLESQLExecutive = Nothing
    Set OLESQLObject = Nothing
    If strErrorDesc = "" Then
```

continues

Listing 17.1. continued

```
        strErrorDesc = "Unknown error"
    End If

    MsgBox strErrorDesc

End Sub
```

The type library, `SQLOLE65.TLB`, is located under the `/mssql/binn` directory where SQL Server is installed. Just add it to your project references in VB or C++ and away you go. Once in your reference list, its description reads `Microsoft SQLOLE Object Library`.

An application was written for one client using SQL-DMO that runs as a `CmdExec` (command-line execution) task under SQL Executive to manage a multiple master RAS replication system. Using SQL Executive's scheduling capabilities, the app dials multiple remote SQL Servers several times a day and invokes the distribution tasks on both the local and the remote severs. Replication tasks 1,500 miles apart run concurrently over 28Kbps dial up lines. When both distribution tasks complete, the application writes a log entry and hangs up the phone.

Another use for the SQL-DMO is writing small applications that allow a user or group of users to control replication task setup and scheduling, without giving them system administrator (sa) or database owner (dbo) authority. If you think the SQL Enterprise Manager interface could be improved, why wait for the next version? The SQL-DMO tool set gives you the power to write your own interface. Through SQL-DMO, Microsoft has put all the power to control SQL Server in your hands.

Stored Procedures

Replication stored procedures are one of the neatest features included with the SQL Server replication tools. They allow you to execute a stored procedure on a remote server based on data changes to a publishing database. In other words, you can use replication to run completely unrelated procedures on a remote server to do anything you want based on data changes on a local server.

Here's a good example: Say there is a remote warehouse running SQL Server with an inventory system. At the home office the accountants are looking for a way to get changes from inventory to the accounting system quickly and on a regular basis. Replication to the rescue! Publish the pertinent table on the inventory system, but instead of storing the data from inventory on the accounting system, update the accounting tables directly using a stored procedure. You can write a little application using SQL-DMO for the accountants that run the distribution task whenever they want the latest warehouse information.

Setting up replication to trigger a stored procedure is easy. Follow the normal process for setting up a publication, but after creating an article using the Edit Publications window in SQL Enterprise Manager, click the article to use for stored procedure processing, then click the Edit button. This opens the Manage Article window. Click the Scripts tab, and you see the screen shown in Figure 17.5.

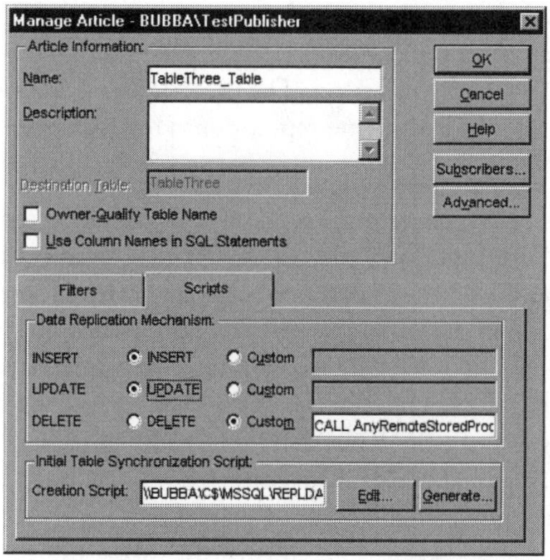

FIGURE 17.5.

*This is where to set up
the stored procedure
replication mechanism.*

Look at the box labeled Data Replication Mechanism. Inside are the options for controlling
how replication handles inserts, updates, and deletes on the subscriber. To change the default
for deletes, click the radio button next to the Delete radio button. The text box to the right
becomes active. To run a stored procedure instead of the default action, type the following:

```
CALL <remote stored procedure name>
```

To disable a default replication mechanism, type the following:

```
NONE
```

It's that simple.

If you call a stored procedure using the replication mechanism, SQL Server does not check to
see if it actually exists on the remote server. A missing stored procedure causes replication failure. The called stored procedure is not invoked until replication actually occurs.

There is nothing special about the replication stored procedures on the remote server. They
can be used like any other stored procedure. However, they need to be written with parameters, such that there is one parameter for each column in the published article and one additional parameter for each column in the primary key of the article's table. These additional
parameters allow the stored procedure to differentiate between the primary key prior to the
data change and the primary key's new values. These additional parameter values can be discarded by the stored procedure if no changes were made to the primary key.

Multiple Master Replication

Multiple master replication is a replication design that allows updates on multiple tables that
are both published and subscribed to each other. It sets up the classic problem in replication:
How do you keep multiple copies of data synchronized when they can be changed in many

places? With SQL Server replication, attempting to implement this design can produce the data equivalent of amplifier feedback, with table 1 sending a change to table 2, which sends the change back to table 1, and so on. The basic implementation of SQL Server replication is not really useful for multiple master replication. However, there are ways to overcome this shortcoming.

In the simplest case, you can use replication's horizontal partitioning feature to allow tables 1 and 2 to be both published and subscribed to each other at the same time. There are some restrictions on this. First, a column in each replicated table must be used to identify the originating publisher of the table. Second, that column must be part of the primary key on the replicated table. Finally, rows can only be modified on the database where they were created. All of this must be handled programmatically. You can see the data from other databases, but not update it. It's sort of a "look but don't touch" design. This design is limited, but it has its uses. For example, regional offices that add their own data but need to see what's going on in other regional offices might find this model useful.

The use of shadow tables is a flexible but complex approach to multiple master replication. Using shadow tables creates a buffer between the multiple copies of tables in a multiple master environment, allowing programmatic resolution to conflicts in the data. It takes up a lot of disk space, but allows high latency connections between servers to keep copies of the data consistent. Figure 17.6 illustrates the shadow table concept.

FIGURE 17.6.

Replication using shadow tables between two databases.

The Shadow Table Knows

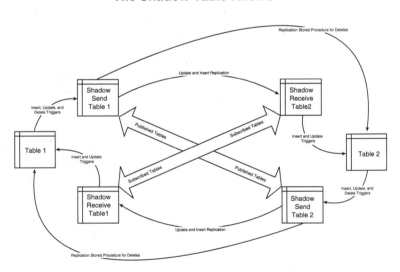

In this example, you have two servers replicating a table to each other. On each table to be replicated, two additional tables with identical schema are created—a shadow send table and a shadow receive table. Each table's schema includes a column to identify which database last affected each row—a database ID column. This column does not need to be a part of the table's primary key.

The original table is not actually published. Instead, the shadow send table is published on each server, using the shadow receive table as the subscribing table. Fortunately, SQL Server replication does not require that a published table and its subscribing table have the same name. Insert and update triggers are then created on the shadow receive table to pass inserts and updates to the subscribing original table. These triggers contain SQL statements with whatever business rules exist for handling exceptions, along with insert or update logic to make changes to the original table. The triggers must also set the database ID value of inserts and updates to the one assigned to the publishing database.

Deletes are handled differently. They use the stored procedure replication mechanism described earlier in this chapter to substitute for the default mechanism used by SQL Server replication when deleting a row. The receiving stored procedure mechanism passes all the columns of the published shadow send table to a stored procedure on the subscribing database. This stored procedure deletes the row in the shadow receive table if it exists, and deletes the row in the subscribing table directly. If you are still awake, you may wonder if handling deletes this way won't cause the DELETE to cascade through the system. It is a little sloppy, but the delete triggers won't be firing anymore once the row is deleted on both servers (since no rows are being affected). Instead of a feedback effect, you get an echo effect.

Hang in there, you're almost finished. The original table on each database needs insert, update, and delete triggers to pass its changes to the shadow send table. Here is where the database ID column plays a big role. The insert and update trigger must be written so that they only fire on rows with the same database ID as the local database. This prevents the replication feedback effect. There is one big implication here: All inserts and updates to rows through normal business processes must set the database ID to the local database to ensure the information is replicated. No one said this would be easy.

The shadow table model can be expanded to multiple servers by designating one of the servers as the primary master. An incredibly complex system can be built by directing all updates to one primary database, then using the shadow table model to distribute and receive the changes. Be sure to have a database administrator who loves challenges.

A final note about multiple master strategies. At the 1997 Microsoft Professional Developer's conference David Marshall, the Microsoft Program Manager for SQL Server development, made it clear that there is no such thing as a completely consistent multiple master strategy. If changes are made in two or more places at the same time, someone wins and everyone else loses. Keep that in mind if you decide to build a multiple master application.

Replicating Over Dial-Up Connections

Microsoft doesn't support replication over RAS connections. RAS replication works, but don't expect much help from Microsoft support if you run into problems. Maybe the next version...

17

REPLICATION

Replication over dial-up lines is basically the same as replication over a LAN or WAN. However, it is slower, and there are sometimes network and security issues involved. There are several programming options to coordinate the dialing and replication tasks. One method is to write it using the SQL-DMO tools and the RAS API.

Another way is to write a batch file that uses the ISQL utility, which comes with SQL Server, to start the SQL replication tasks and the Windows NT RASDIAL.EXE utility to connect to remote subscribers. Put it all in a batch file and automate it using Windows NT's AT scheduling service. There are many options for automating replication.

Here are some issues to be aware of when setting up RAS replication:

- The distribution task needs to be modified after the initial synchronization from an Auto Start task to an On Demand task. Then it can be controlled programmatically, allowing subscribers to dial in and pick up their replicated jobs on demand. Writing applications to do this is where the SQL-DMO tools come in handy.

- For two-way RAS replication, the RAS server has to be on the same server as the distribution database. If the distribution databases cannot directly connect, only one-way replication can be achieved. This makes sense because a RAS client sees the entire remote network. A machine on the network, however, doesn't see the RAS client on the network, which prevents replication from running.

- Unless you like working directly with the Win32 RAS API, get a RAS dialing control. Be sure to get one that allows you to connect synchronously or you'll be writing lots of code to handle your RAS connections.

- One way to avoid security problems is to give the Windows NT login used by SQL Executive the same login ID and password on all SQL Servers involved in replication and on all remote access server's phone books. This is useful when replicating across remote domains.

TIP

If you are going to attempt dial up replication using RAS, you need to know this. RAS connection behavior changed between Windows NT versions 3.51 and 4.0. In version 3.51, dial-up RAS clients stay attached to a RAS server even after a user has logged off the RAS server. In Windows NT 4.0, all RAS connections are disconnected when a user logs off the local machine. Pretty tough on dial-up clients. See Microsoft Knowledge Base article Q158909, *How to Keep RAS Connections Active After Logging Off* for more details. The article says to modify the entry in Windows NT 4.0, but in reality you have to add it yourself. To do it, log on as an administrator and use the Windows NT registry editor to create a new value called KeepRASConnections with a datatype of REG_SZ under HKEY_LOCAL_MACHINE\SOFTWARE\Microsoft\Windows NT\CurrentVersion\WinLogon.

Set the string to a value of 1 (true) to keep RAS connections active.

TIP

Purchase a two-way ring down circuit if you are going to do any extensive RAS replication development. It is basically a phone company in a box the size of a small external modem. When two modems are plugged into it with RJ-11 connectors, the attached computers can emulate real phone lines. You can do performance testing without having to coordinate with a truly remote machine. They are manufactured by Viking Electronics, Inc. of Hudson, Wisconsin, but must be purchased from a local distributor. If you need one of these, you need it badly.

Summary

This chapter only touches on the some of the capabilities of SQL Server replication. Here are the chapter's main points:

- There are three main roles in replication—publishing, distributing, and subscribing.

- SQL Server replication uses loose consistency on replicated data.

- Replication works by reading a published database's committed transaction log entries and converting them into SQL statements, which are replicated on the subscribing database.

- SQL Executive tasks provide the mechanism for replication's operation. Controlling the tasks controls replication.

- Only data is replicated by SQL Server.

- SQL-DMO can be used to programmatically control replication.

- Multiple master replication models are complex and need to be dealt with programmatically.

- Shadow tables are one way to design multiple master replication.

- Although not supported by Microsoft, RAS can be used for replication.

III

PART

Migrating to SQL Server: Data Conversion and Integration

Legacy Databases: Conversion and Integration Issues

IN THIS CHAPTER

There has been a trend for companies to "go client/server" by removing applications from legacy systems on mainframes to a UNIX- or Windows NT-based solution. This chapter focuses on how data can be converted between systems, the tools available with special focus on BCP, and issues about which you should be aware.

Data Conversion Issues

Whether integrating SQL Server into existing legacy systems, or replacing legacy systems entirely with SQL Server, you still need to convert data for replacing the legacy databases or merely transferring data to and from the legacy databases. If the company uses all ASCII-based machines, there should be no problem using SQL Server utilities. However, most mid- to large-sized shops still use IBM, which requires conversion from EBCDIC to ASCII. You have several options for converting EBCDIC to ASCII.

- Converting the data in COBOL
- Using third-party utilities
- Writing a translation program in C or Visual Basic
- Performing the translation within SQL Server

The first method involves using mainframe programmers to extract the data in the desired file format. All of these options require the use of the BCP import/export utility. Refer to the section on using the BCP import/export utility for a detailed explanation on how to use the utility.

Converting the Data in COBOL

COBOL data can be stored as text, binary, or compressed (COMP-3) format. If the data file was completely text, with no number values, you could use the built-in translation process for almost every 3270 terminal emulation program on the market by selecting ASCII translation. In reality, you need number, binary data, or COMP-3 data. The best location to convert data is within the COBOL program being created for providing the data to bring into SQL Server. Use the following guidelines for creating the proper export file.

- For binary data, convert to the numeric equivalent and pass the numeric values to the output file.
- For number data (both numbers and currency), which can include positive or negative values, place a blank if positive or a – if negative in the first position, and fill in the remaining dollar value after the sign or blank space.
- For COMP-3 data, convert to the appropriate number data, and follow the procedures in the previous step.
- Leave all text values intact.
- Add a terminator between each field. This allows the file to have variable length record lengths. If you cannot get a terminator between fields, leave them as fixed length.

Some developers prefer a tilde (~). However, the preference is dependent on the type of data. Tabs are actually a better choice in some cases.

■ At the end of each record, place a carriage return line feed, which should be the equivalent of 0D25.

■ Allow the 3270 emulator to convert the file, which should now be all "text" characters, to ASCII in the download process.

Once you have the file, the only process required of you is to use the BCP copy utility to transfer the file into the table. Refer to the section using the BCP import/export utility for a detailed explanation on how to use the utility.

TIP

Always use an uncommon character, such as a tilde (~) or a tab, to separate fields. The problem with a CSV (comma-separated value) file is that if a field itself contains a comma, it throws the whole import off because BCP—or any import utility, for that matter—assumes it is a field separator. A typical field such as CompanyName could contain commas such as "The Computer Tree, Inc."

Using Third-Party Utilities

There are many utilities, both on the mainframe and the PC, that will perform this conversion from EBCDIC to ASCII. One widely used program is Easytrieve for the mainframe or Easytrieve for the PC. Easytrieve on the mainframe would be able to extract the data from the mainframe file, and output a file in the same format as you would if using COBOL. The advantage to Easytrieve on the mainframe is that you could have a non-programmer write the query and create the output file. The disadvantage is that if a COBOL program is required somewhere in the process besides just for extraction, you may as well code it directly in COBOL.

Easytrieve for the PC assumes you download the EBCDIC file in binary format. You then use this program to define the columns and properties to create the comma-separated value file. The problem with this method is that if you use tildes (~), which you can't produce in the PC version of the package, there is a limit to the number of records that can be processed (at least on version 4.3). The advantage with this option is that you can download small files (under 16,000 records) to the PC and have a non-programmer run the conversion process.

While there may be other third-party utilities, it still makes more sense to maintain the code on the mainframe in COBOL and take the extra ten minutes to program the extraction.

Writing a Translation Program in C or Visual Basic

Again, you can download the EBCDIC file in binary format so no translation takes place. Armed with an EBCDIC to ASCII table, you could easily create an array to perform the character conversion. For the binary data, convert to integer. For COMP-3 data, you need to use bitwise operators to extract the first four bits for one number, and the second four bits for the second number. COMP-3 stores two numbers in one byte. At the last byte, don't forget that the last four bits is the sign, so store this value, and if negative, multiply the result by a −1. The disadvantage with this option is that a fair knowledge of file I/O with C or Visual Basic is required.

Performing the Translation Within SQL Server

Imagine you have no tools to work with except SQL Server. Unfortunately, that scenario is not so far from fiction. SQL Server does allow you to import binary data. You could then use bitwise operators to extract the COMP-3 data, and to decode any signed values. You can also build a table to convert normal text characters. This option can cause problems, especially with characters used in EBCDIC that have special meaning in ASCII that could cause the import to fail.

Using SQL's Bulk Copy Program (BCP)

As you know, the BCP (Bulk Copy Program) provided by SQL Server is run from the command line, not from I/SQL. The file is bcp.exe stored in the MSSQL\BINN subdirectory. The following is the syntax for the bulk copy program.

```
bcp [[[database_name.]owner.]table_name {in | out} datafile
    [-m maxerrors] [-f formatfile] [-e errfile]
    [-F firstrow] [-L lastrow] [-b batchsize]
    [-n] [-c] [-E] [-v] [-a packet_size]
    [-t field_term] [-r row_term]
    [-i inputfile] [-o outputfile]
    [-U login_id] [-P password] [-S servername] [-T]
```

The *database_name* is the name of the database, such as master, pubs, and so on. The *owner* is the owner of the table. The *table_name* parameter is the name of the table to import the data. If you are importing data, use the IN keyword; if you are exporting data, use OUT. The *datafile* is the name of the file to import or export. You can specify the number of maximum errors allowed with *maxerrors*. This is important, because if you import data into a table with an index, and want to discard duplicate data that is contained in the file, the process will stop due to too many errors. Be aware that if an error is encountered, the whole batch as specified with the *batchsize* option will not be committed into the table.

If you use a default import or export format, you can save it with the BCP utility. You would then specify this format with the *formatfile* parameter, saved by default as BCP.FMT. For any imported data that causes errors, specifying the *errfile* will create an output file to store the rows that caused the errors. You can also specify where you want to start within the data file with *firstrow* and where to stop with *lastrow*. If you are copying from SQL Server to SQL Server, use -n for the native database format. For external file import and export, you must use option -c. You can keep the identity values stored in your data file by using the -E switch.

Most important are the terminators. To do this, you would specify the terminator with -t. If you need to specify a row terminator other than carriage return line feed, use -r. For example, to specify a field terminator of tab with a record terminator of carriage return and line feed, the following would be part of your BCP command.

```
-t\t -r\r\n
```

You can redirect input and output to and from the BCP with the *inputfile* and the *outputfile* parameters.

For accessing the table, provide the *login_id*, *password*, and *servername*. Or if you are in the position to make a trusted connection, you can make use of the -T switch.

When importing the data, be sure that the packet size can be handled on the network. The packet size ranges from 512 through 65535. Do not attempt to send 16k files through a 4k token ring network. Any attempt to send a larger packet size that the network can't handle will default to 512 bytes, which makes for a very slow import process. The steps to import a file are as follows:

1. Use sp_dboption to make sure that the value of bulkcopy is set to TRUE. This will allow you to carry out a "fast-BCP" operation.
2. Create a "temporary" table for import. This is not a temporary table in the sense of a SQL Server temporary table, but rather a real table that will only exist for as long as your import operation.
3. Import the data into the temporary table.
4. Verify the accuracy of data.
5. Merge imported data into the appropriate tables.
6. Use sp_dboption to set the bulkcopy value to FALSE.

   The syntax of the sp_dboption is

   ```
   sp_dboption [databasename, option, {TRUE | FALSE}]
   ```

The *databasename* is the name of the database to change the option. The option is any valid option for *sp_dboption*. In this particular case, you are only concerned with the select into/bulkcopy option. Setting the value to TRUE turns the option on and FALSE turns the option off. To allow the pubs database to receive imported data, the format would be

```
sp_dboption pubs, 'select into/bulkcopy' ,TRUE
```

WARNING

Setting this option turns off the capability for transaction log dumps. You need to dump the database once you have turned the option back off in order to continue with log dumps.

The following section steps through an example of this process. You can now create the "temporary" table for import. The code shown in Listing 18.1 is an example of how to create such a temporary work table.

Listing 18.1. Creating the temporary table.

```
IF EXISTS (SELECT * FROM sysobjects
      WHERE id = OBJECT_ID ('bcptest')
      AND sysstat & 0xf = 3)
      DROP TABLE bcptest

GO
CREATE TABLE bcptest(
      TestID     integer NOT NULL PRIMARY KEY ,
      TestName    varchar(30)
)
```

Once the table is created, create a file called `c:\bcpin` with a text editor, word processor, Excel, DOS edit, and so on, to match the contents of Listing 18.2. Just make sure that you save it as a plain text format.

Listing 18.2. Creating the sample import file.

```
1~One
2~Two
3~Three
4~Four
5~Five
6~Six
7~Seven
8~Eight
9~Nine
10~Ten
11~Eleven
12~Twelve
13~Thirteen
14~Fourteen
15~Fifteen
16~Sixteen
17~Seventeen
18~Eighteen
19~Nineteen
20~Twenty
21~Twenty-one
22~Twenty-two
23~Twenty-three
24~Twenty-four
25~Twenty-five
```

Notice the fields have tildes (~) separating one another. To import the data, execute the code in Listing 18.3 from the command prompt.

Listing 18.3. Using BCP to import a data file.

```
bcp mydb..bcptest in c:\bcpin-c -t~ -r\r\n -S SQL -U sa -P dp9966
```

From this code, bcptest is the name of the table to import the data, sa is the user id, dp9966 is the password, and SQL is the name of the SQL Server. Option -c specifies that the data is character data, the field separator is set to a tilde, and the row terminator to carriage return line feed. The name of the server, user, and password will be different for you, so change those accordingly. If you do not specify the password, SQL Server will prompt you for it. If you use this process repeatedly, store the file somewhere on the network server where only you have access, and create a batch file to automate the process.

Just for fun, attempt the process again. Since you set up a primary key on the TestID field, you should receive an error message similar to

```
Violation of PRIMARY KEY constraint 'PK_BCPTEST_TESTID_17E28260':
Attempt to insert duplicate key in object 'bcptest'
```

This is a crude way to remove unwanted duplicate data if the source file contains it. Remember to set your batch size to 1, together with a high maximum of errors allowed.

Once the data has been imported, you need to verify the accuracy of the data. This is a very important step to ensure integrity of the data being added to production tables. You could import data straight into the production table using "slow-BCP" as a logged transaction, but you would have to remove the data if the import failed, and also face potentially filling up your transaction log. Also, triggers are not checked as part of a BCP operation. You can still get bad data into your production table. For these reasons always, but always, import the data into a temporary table and then check the validity of data, such as proper totals, valid range of data, and so on. Failure to do this risks failure of your data integrity. You can verify the data by executing the code in Listing 18.4.

Listing 18.4. Verifying the imported data.

```
select * from bcptest
```

Your output should look like the following:

```
TestID      TestName
----------  ----------------------------
1           One
2           Two
3           Three
4           Four
5           Five
6           Six
...
...
24          Twenty-four
25          Twenty-five

(25 row(s) affected)
```

18

LEGACY DATABASE ISSUES

After you merge the data, you can set the bulk copy option to a value of FALSE to prevent un-authorized imports. To practice exporting data, use the same test table. The command is as follows:

```
bcp mydb..bcptest out c:\bcpout -c -U sa -P dp9966 -S SQL
```

Your newly created file should look like the following:

```
1       One
2       Two
3       Three
4       Four
5       Five
6       Six
7       Seven
8       Eight
9       Nine
10      Ten
11      Eleven
12      Twelve
13      Thirteen
14      Fourteen
15      Fifteen
16      Sixteen
17      Seventeen
18      Eighteen
19      Nineteen
20      Twenty
21      Twenty-one
22      Twenty-two
23      Twenty-three
24      Twenty-four
25      Twenty-five
```

You can even use BCP to gather data out of tables in a fixed block format, which is the standard format for mainframe data transfers. This requires the construction and use of an appropriate format file or the use of a view to collect the data into the right format and then BCP out from the view.

Migrating from Legacy Systems

With the recent demonstration of SQL Server running one billion transactions per second, it does appear that PCs can now rival mainframes. However, careful consideration of the following is necessary before migrating from legacy systems to SQL Server.

- Equipment needs and costs
- Network bandwidth
- Nature of application

Equipment Needs and Costs

Mainframes are notoriously expensive to purchase and maintain, where PCs are significantly cheaper and require less maintenance work. Mainframes do offer a level of performance that PCs are only just getting into the realms of, and you need to run a trial with PC-based hardware to see if the performance can be kept acceptable—which in most cases it can.

Network Bandwidth

There are several outstanding tools that allow for decent networking, such as using Citrix products to run Windows NT Workstation or Windows 95 on any system at acceptable speeds, even on 386 processor-based machines. If you are using SQL Server, and anticipate a lot of users on the network, definitely look at your network architecture, and see where and if you need to increase the bandwidth. You might even have a case where network computers are adequate for most of your data-entry and processing needs.

Nature of the Application

SQL Server can handle most types of applications, from data entry to reporting for decision reporting, very well. As with all systems, you need to examine the volume of transactions that will be occurring and look at how and where best to implement various business functions.

Integrating with Legacy Systems

There are many instances where SQL Server is perfect for interfacing with legacy systems. As pointed out previously, not even UNIX servers, much less PC-based SQL Servers, can handle the upper limits of both the volume and input/output provided by a mainframe. However, since CPU time can be expensive on the mainframe, you can use SQL Server to integrate between legacy systems. The following are some examples:

- Using SQL Server running on a DEC Alpha for handling order transactions over the Internet.

- Offloading financial applications off the mainframe to the PC that are more CPU intensive than volume intensive. Payroll, tracking investments, and purchasing stocks are several transactions easily handled by SQL Server.

- Creating a module in between mainframe systems as a pass-through device. When passing the data from mainframe to SQL Server and then back to the mainframe, use the SQL Server as a Value Added server to perform some required computations, reports, and so on, in case there are not enough resources to handle all requests within the company.

- Using SQL Server as a front-end processor to the mainframe. You can perform security checks, calculations, and so on, before passing the data for processing to the mainframe if required.

Summary

This chapter covers a broad overview of SQL Server and legacy systems. SQL Server can interface with legacy systems; however, you need to translate from EBCDIC to ASCII, and the best method is within the COBOL code required to create the file. Although many clients require interfacing SQL Server with legacy systems, other clients are nearly completely off the mainframe. This chapter should offer you a roadmap for moving from legacy systems to SQL Server.

Outgrowing Access

IN THIS CHAPTER

This chapter includes information for two different but related audiences: the experienced Access developer who is considering whether to move data from Access to SQL Server and has picked up this book to see what SQL Server has to offer, and the SQL Server developer who has been hired to do just that for a client. For this reason, the first part of this chapter provides issues to consider and facts that will help you decide whether you've truly outgrown Access and should, indeed, move on up to SQL Server. The second part of this chapter, beginning with "Moving On: Upsizing from Access 97 to SQL Server 6.5," provides details on the process of the actual move.

Even if you've been using SQL Server for a long time, I urge you to read the first part of this chapter. In case you haven't been hired yet by that prospective Access client, you'll find plenty of information here to help your client make the right choice. When the going gets tough, you'll have plenty of reasons to remind him why he agreed!

> **NOTE**
>
> Throughout this chapter when I refer to Access, I am referring specifically to Access 97, but each point will apply to Access 95 and Access 2.0 as well. Occasionally, a feature or issue might differ somewhat in Access 95 or Access 2.0. This is mentioned when it occurs.

On Moving: Determining the Need to Move from Access to SQL Server

There's no doubt that SQL Server 6.5 is a world-class database. Because of its amazing power and flexibility, you might be tempted to take all your existing Access database solutions and move them posthaste to SQL Server. Before you do, though, you need to ponder a few fundamental questions:

- What's involved in moving from Access to SQL Server?
- What are your options for upsizing?
- Is moving to SQL Server even a good idea?

Chances are that by now you are familiar with many features that make SQL Server a robust client/server solution. It seems as though SQL Server would be the best choice for any database implementation, especially when compared to a desktop product such as Microsoft Access. After all, SQL Server is faster, more reliable, and all around better, isn't it?

Well, not exactly. It is true that SQL Server is capable of processing huge amounts of information with blazing speed and has capabilities that make it a good choice for mission-critical and enterprise installations. However, that doesn't make SQL Server better than Access, only more appropriate for addressing certain kinds of problems.

Before jumping into an upsizing project, you must ask yourself, "Why exactly am I doing this? What am I really trying to accomplish?" When you've begun to define and examine the problem you are trying to solve, the need to upsize will become much clearer.

> **NOTE**
>
> Access refers specifically to the data storage portion of Access and the accompanying Jet engine, not to the forms and VBA modules that might also be stored in the same .mdb file.

SQL Server: The Obvious Choice

Microsoft Access is a powerful desktop database. The Jet database engine effectively incorporates Rushmore Technology, which was originally created for Fox Pro, for surprisingly fast queries on large data sets. The capability to enforce referential integrity rules and user-level security makes it a good choice for many shared databases that otherwise might require a much more expensive client/server solution. All this, and it's relatively easy to use.

There are some things that Access cannot do. It is, in the end, a desktop solution, hampered by the requirement to run on the average user's computer and to provide usable functionality without a high degree of complexity. SQL Server, conversely, typically runs on a more powerful server platform and requires a more advanced level of knowledge to effectively leverage its functionality.

It's not unusual for a single issue or requirement to dictate the need to upsize an Access database. With this in mind, I've listed some situations in which the move to SQL Server from Access would be a no-brainer.

Security

Access has a capable user-level security scheme. Users and groups can be granted various levels of access to tables, queries, and other objects in the database. This user and group information is stored in a separate database file, enabling it to be shared across multiple .mdb files and greatly simplifying administration tasks. Also, because security is implemented by the Jet engine, there is no need to build complex security-handling logic into front-end applications.

Yet, as effective as it is at implementing general security, Access is still at the mercy of the operating system on which it resides. It is commonly accepted that it's not possible to completely secure a desktop database from a motivated individual with the right combination of time, tools, and knowledge. SQL Server, on the other hand, incorporates an even more robust security design that can integrate with Windows NT security for even more protection.

In a nutshell, if your database contains particularly valuable or sensitive information and you've determined security to be of utmost importance, you should definitely move your data from Access to SQL Server.

Capacity

According to Microsoft, an Access 97 database file is capable of growing to nearly 1.2GB. This includes table structures, queries, and data, as well as forms and Visual Basic for Application code modules. SQL Server, however, is capable of holding at least a terabyte of information, a significant difference. Of course, it is possible to create Access databases more than 1.2GB by creating two or more .mdb files and linking the tables to a master database. This adds to the complexity of the database, however, and could have a negative effect on performance. Placing forms and Visual Basic code in a separate file also leaves more room for data storage. Let's face it, there is no way that Access can compare to SQL Server for pure data storage capabilities.

The bottom line is simple: If your data storage needs have grown, or are expected to grow, beyond the storage capacity of a single Access database, moving from Access to SQL Server is certainly justified.

24-Hour Access

Suppose your .mdb file is not quite 1.2GB, but it's getting big nonetheless, say 500–600MB. Chances are that you have some valuable stuff in there, and you (or your boss) would be upset if anything happened to it. Of course, you do the wise thing and back it up nightly, perhaps even more often. But wait, these backups are starting to take a long time and so are those repairs and compacts you need to run every week or so. Then a new shift is added, and you have users who need access to the data 24 hours a day. Now you have a real problem.

Unfortunately, you're not going to solve this easily with Access. Users can't be logged in to an Access database when you back it up, or you run the significant risk of data corruption. Also, there's no such thing as an incremental backup with Access, either. It's the whole .mdb or nothing.

SQL Server provides some flexibility when it comes to backing up. To begin with, you don't have to back up the whole database file every time. Instead, you can back up the main database periodically, maybe weekly or monthly. You can also back it up without logging out the users, by using the DUMP DATABASE command. Then you can back up just the transaction log more frequently. The transaction log maintains a record of every insert, update, or delete applied to the database. It tends to be significantly smaller than the actual data file.

Another advantage to backing up a SQL Server database is that your users don't need to log out when you back up the transaction log. Instead, you can back up the data without interfering with their work.

Multiple Users

An impressive feature of Access and the Jet engine is that the database becomes multi-user simply by placing it in a shared directory and having multiple users connect to it. Access databases, however, are limited to 255 concurrent user connections, though the practical number is much lower. Also, some front-end applications, such as those built with Visual Basic using bound controls, might require several user connections for each user connecting to the database, reducing the number of users even further.

SQL Server, on the other hand, can handle more than 32,000 simultaneous user connections. That's an increased capacity of more than 125 times—and a reasonable justification for moving your data to SQL Server, if you need it.

Insert Locking

Insert locking, or blocking, problems are another good reason for moving from Access to SQL Server. Blocking occurs when multiple users attempt to add rows to a table simultaneously. Access has this problem for two reasons: The first is that all new rows are added to the end of the table, and the second is page locking.

When a user places a new row in an Access table, the Jet engine locks the 2K page on which the new record will reside while it is being written to the table, preventing any other rows from being added. When there are a large number of users entering new data, the potential for blocking increases substantially.

Access will add a new page when an existing page is nearly half full of data, which helps to distribute locking somewhat, but a site with a large number of users—say, more than 15 to 20—doing primarily data entry will still have significant blocking problems.

SQL Server also uses page locking but can alleviate this problem somewhat with a combination of clustered indexes and fill factor. *Clustered indexes* control the physical order of rows in a table. Only one clustered index is allowed on any table, but it can contain multiple columns. The *fill factor* is a definable number that controls how full a page can become before SQL Server will create a new one. By putting a cluster index on columns with a large number of unique values, such as the LastName and FirstName columns in a Customer table, and setting a fill factor to a percentage point somewhat lower than 100, you can greatly reduce the potential for blocking during data entry.

> **NOTE**
>
> Don't place clustered indexes on identity fields in SQL Server because this will force all new rows to be appended to the end of the table, effectively negating the benefit of clustered indexes. Remember, only one clustered index is allowed per table, so choose carefully.

SQL Server 6.5 also has the capability of implementing insert row-level locking. Much ado has been made of this feature, but the truth is, if your database design makes wise use of clustered indexes and a reasonable fill factor, insert row-level locking won't buy you that much. It does help, however, when multiple users are trying to insert data on the same set of data pages ("maybe we're just gonna call the *G*s today") or when rows can be inserted only at the end of the table.

Data Reliability

Here's the scenario: You've written a Visual Basic program that enables a user to maintain a database containing information on all the products your company offers for sale. The database is in an Access .mdb file located on a Windows NT Server box. One feature of this program is that it enables the user to apply price changes to an entire category of products at once. To do so, it uses the following block of VBA code:

```
On Error Goto HandleThis:
    oDB.BeginTrans
    sSQL = "UPDATE Products " & _
            "SET Price = Price * " & iPriceDifferencePercent & _
            " WHERE Category = '" & sCategory & "'"
oDB.Execute sSQL
oDB.CommitTrans
HandleThis:
oDB.Rollback
```

The user enters a percentage by which to change the price and presses the Enter key to start the process. The program is about halfway through the process of writing the updates to the disk when the teenage son of the vice president of Information Technology (the boy is interning for the summer) walks by and trips over the user's workstation cord, shutting off the computer.

No problem—the application was written to use Jet transactions, so the information will be rolled back automatically. No harm done, right? Wrong.

Jet has no way of knowing that a transaction did not complete correctly. If it fails for any reason while writing changes to a database, it leaves the database in an incomplete state, which can lead to a corrupt database, or worse. In this example, there is no way to determine which product records had already been updated when the computer failed. You could restore the last backup of the database and re-execute the program, but what if the database also contains a day's worth of sales data? You probably don't want all that to blow away.

> **NOTE**
>
> The preceding example was contrived to illustrate potential problems with Access databases and Jet transactions. It is true that a good design could easily prevent the problem described, but the point is that Jet transactions don't provide inherent protection against unpredictable hardware failures.

With SQL Server, the preceding scenario would not have been a problem. SQL Server uses the transaction log to apply a more robust commit process. It does this by writing all the insert, update, or delete queries to the transaction log before applying them to the database. When all the changes have been written to the database and confirmed, SQL Server marks them as completed in the transaction log. In the event that SQL Server should shutdown for some reason before both phases of the transaction are completed, when it starts up again, it will know to complete or roll back incomplete transactions in the log, returning the database to a stable condition.

This is probably the most debatable issue so far. A good database design and a little planning can greatly reduce the chance of irrecoverable data loss, and the Jet engine is reliable. You have to ask yourself, though, how critical the data in the database is and how much it would cost to recover in the event of a hardware failure. If the answers to those questions are "extremely" and "too much," respectively, you should probably move your database to the more robust SQL Server platform.

The Not-So-Obvious Choice

By now you might be thinking, "Wow! I should get my Access database ported to SQL Server, pronto!" After all, you've just learned six reasons that would immediately justify upsizing an Access database to SQL Server. In many cases, though, the choice is not clear. There are multiple issues to carefully evaluate before deciding to switch your database platform. The following topics might influence you to upsize but should be considered within the context of a larger picture.

Response Time

This might seem one of the "no-brainer" reasons to upsize that are listed in the previous section, but poor response time with an Access database is more often a design and implementation issue than an actual product limitation.

Multiple problems can affect your response time when working with Access and Jet, but they don't necessitate upsizing to SQL Server, especially in a networked multi-user environment. With this in mind, I've made a list of questions you should ask yourself about performance before deciding to upsize.

- *Would hardware upgrades help?* Nine times out of ten, it *is* the hardware. Often, adding memory or upgrading a processor is more than enough to bring performance up to an acceptable level. Even purchasing an entire new computer is often less expensive than implementing a SQL Server solution.

- *Is there a network problem?* It has been my experience that an application that works well on a standalone computer tends to work well when moved to a network. Data-locking issues aside, in a multi-user environment the network itself is often the culprit when it comes to sudden degradations in response. There are several things you can do to improve your performance over a network:

  - *Segment your users.* This is especially true for Ethernet networks in which a large number of users on a cable segment can cause packet collisions that, in turn, can constrict bandwidth and affect database performance. By dividing your topology so that fewer users are on any one segment, you can reduce collisions and improve response times.

■ *Check for packet spammers.* Poor network performance can also be caused by packet spammers. These are devices or network interface cards that for some reason have malfunctioned and are constantly sending out a large number of packets, slowing down the entire segment. If your database was performing fine on the network and then suddenly slowed to a crawl, a packet spammer would be a prime suspect.

■ *Upgrade your topology.* This isn't as extreme as it might sound, especially if your network uses an older topology technology such as Arc Net. In this case, the cost of upgrading your topology could easily be justified with respect to overall network performance improvement, and not just the improvement of your database application.

■ *Is your database and application optimized for best performance?* I hate to say it, but a lot of database performance problems on any platform are caused by poor or inappropriate design. Upgrading to SQL Server isn't going to improve a fundamentally bad design. There are, however, some optimization methods that are specific to Access database applications. Here are a few quick suggestions to help improve performance.

■ *Split the data from the code.* In applications written using the Access development tools, the Form and VBA code modules are stored with the data in the same .mdb file. Remember, when users access that file, they must suck that whole thing across the network cable. That could take a while. One relatively easy way to improve performance in this case would be to create separate .mdbs for code and data. Then distribute the code .mdb to the users' workstations and place the .mdb containing the data on the network.

■ *Use Query objects whenever possible.* Similar to stored procedures in SQL Server, Query objects are stored, pre-parsed queries that you can use to manipulate data in your database. Unlike stored procedures, queries are run locally on the workstation, but because the Jet engine does not have to parse the query, you'll get an immediate performance gain by using them.

NOTE

Query objects are also a very useful tool for implementing security on an Access database. Because Access security is available only to the table level, you can use a Query object to provide column-level security by giving the user rights to a query, but not the table.

■ *Revisit your database design.* This isn't exactly an Access-specific suggestion, but it's worth considering. Take a second look at your tables. Are they properly indexed, are they overly indexed, do the table structures and relationships make sense, are they normalized? Also, take a look at the queries you are using to manipulate data in your application. Many SQL concepts covered in this book can also be used with the Jet database engine. Apply them.

■ *What is "acceptable performance?"* Maybe you're not getting stellar response with your Access database application, but is it worth the effort and expense to upsize to SQL Server? Are the users satisfied? Ponder the context of your application's environment. Don't allow yourself to fall into the trap of using technology for its own sake.

Business Rules

One of the most frequently touted features of SQL Server is its capability to enforce business rules at the database level. To do this, it provides tools such as stored procedures, triggers, views, default values, and validation rules.

Access, too, shares some of these capabilities—and exceeds them in some cases—but cannot match the sheer power and range of options that SQL Server provides for moving business logic to the database. However, this capability alone isn't a compelling reason for moving your database to SQL Server. With forethought and creative coding, you can emulate much of this functionality in your Jet database applications for potentially less cost than you would incur moving to SQL Server.

One good way to accomplish this is to use a three-tier design with Visual Basic and COM. In a two-tier model, business logic is included as part of each application. In a three-tier model, the business logic is placed in a COM object and reused by each application. Rather than put the logic for accessing data directly in the front-end application, the traditional two-tier model, you can place all the common data access logic for a database in an ActiveX server. This can then be used by your front-end applications. Figure 19.1 illustrates the two-tier and three-tier relationships.

FIGURE 19.1.

The two-tier and three-tier data access models.

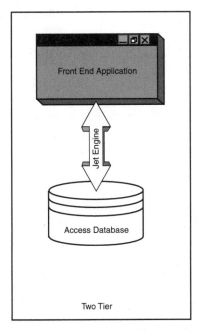
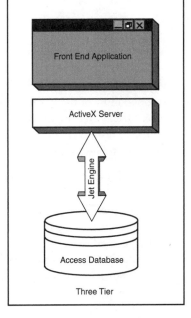

Scalability

Another important feature SQL Server offers is the capability to scale nicely. SQL Server's query engine makes excellent use of the multithreading capabilities in Windows NT. If you add additional processors to your server, SQL Server can instantly make use of them to run multiple process threads simultaneously. This enables it to process requests from multiple users or create additional data pages as needed, without forcing other tasks to wait.

There's no way to achieve this same level of scalability with an Access database, using the Jet engine, but it is possible to design some scalable capacity into your Access database applications. Using a distributed COM object would enable you to encapsulate business logic and leverage the server's processing capability. As an example, take the COM object discussed in the last section and make it a Distributed COM object. Run it on a Windows NT fileserver where the database resides, as shown in Figure 19.2.

FIGURE 19.2.

An example of a three-tier data access model.

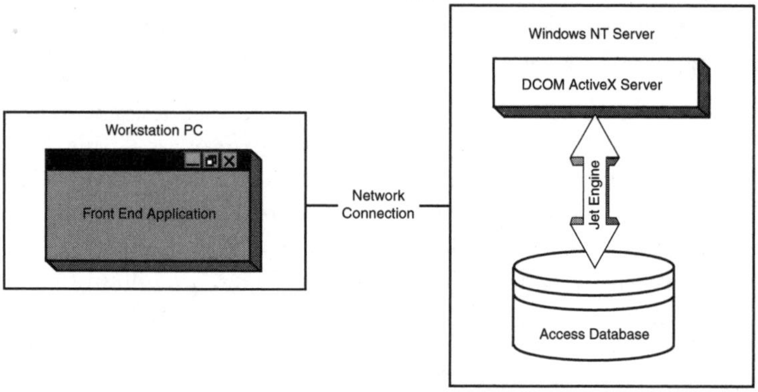

By implementing your data access model in this way, you can improve your data access performance simply by upgrading your server.

Some Other Considerations

Until now, most of the issues to consider before upsizing an Access database to SQL Server have been technical in nature. However, the most convincing arguments for and against upsizing have little or nothing to do with technology. Before you make your final decision, you should consider the following realities:

■ *Knowledge.* SQL Server's many capabilities come at the expense of simplicity. To fully benefit from SQL Server's features requires a fundamental shift in programming techniques. Bound controls and other rapid application development devices are often inappropriate for gaining top performance from a client/server database. Instead, you might need to learn a whole new way of structuring applications and data access methods. You need to ask yourself whether you have the time to invest in acquiring the knowledge necessary to profit from SQL Server, or the budget to hire people who already possess that knowledge.

- *Cost.* When you think about it, nearly every issue boils down to whether the technical advantages offered by SQL Server are worth the investment required to upsize from an Access database. Moving to SQL Server isn't cheap. The price of the product itself, and of the computer on which to run it, is substantially more than the cost of Access. Also, you might need to finance training or even additional employees to get the most out of it.

    You must also consider the cost of revising existing applications that use the Access database. This can involve much more than simply pointing to a different database.

    On the other hand, a SQL Server solution can be more cost-effective to scale. Rather than upgrade several computers to increase overall processing power, with SQL Server you upgrade the server on which it runs.

- *Politics.* Often the need to upsize to SQL Server is based not so much on technical need as on the need to satisfy the wants of the user base. In this case, all the rules for evaluating the decision to upsize fly out the window. Before you blithely acquiesce to the demands of the user, you should still carefully consider all the issues associated with upsizing and help the users evaluate them as well. You might be surprised when you each reach the same conclusions.

In a Nutshell

Throughout this section, criteria is presented for judging the need to upsize an existing Access database to SQL Server. This isn't easy. At various times it seems that one platform or the other is the superior solution. However, neither product is better than the other, only more appropriate for a particular problem and scope.

As you evaluate the prospect of upsizing, ask yourself these questions:

- Are there any mission-critical requirements that can be filled only by the more robust feature set of SQL Server?
- Is there a cost-effective way to achieve the project goals without upsizing?
- Will the overall costs of upsizing the database outweigh the expected benefits?

When you can answer these questions, you will have no difficulty determining whether to upsize your data.

19

OUTGROWING
ACCESS

Moving On: Upsizing from Access 97 to SQL Server 6.5

If you decide that you need to move from an Access database to SQL Server, you find you have a whole new set of issues to consider. In this section, you learn about some of the options you can use to upsize. Then you'll examine the Access 97 Upsize Wizard, how it works, and some of the problems you might encounter.

Upsizing Options

Though the bulk of this section on upsizing methods focuses on the Upsize Wizard, there are a number of options available for upsizing your database. Each has specific advantages that make it more applicable for certain situations, and none can solve every problem you might encounter. In fact, very often the best solution for moving across platforms is to use a combination of techniques.

The most common methods for upsizing from a Microsoft Access database to SQL Server and their strengths and weaknesses are described in the following section.

Export Access Data to SQL Server

Microsoft Access enables you to export data directly to SQL Server, one table at a time. This option correctly creates a table in SQL Server and transfers the data from the Access table you indicate. However, it does not transfer or convert additional schema information such as indexes, AutoNumber fields, table relationships, or cascading deletes and updates. This is a good solution when you are mostly concerned with moving the data and expect to substantially rework the database schema on SQL Server anyway.

Linked Table Queries

If the destination tables already exist on SQL Server, you can link them directly to your Access database and then write queries to move the data. Only data is transferred, but the use of queries gives you much more control over the actual data being exported to SQL Server. This is a good option when the amount of data in the Access database is too great to be transferred all at once, or if the destination SQL Server table structure does not exactly match the Access table's structure.

BCP

BCP (Bulk Copy Program) is a command-line utility used to import data into SQL Server. To use this option, you first export data to a comma- or tab-delimited text file and then use the BCP utility to read the file into SQL Server. As with linked table queries, this option can be used to transfer data only. BCP is a good way to transfer data over WANs, slow connections, or in situations where you need to transfer the data using a floppy disk. You can find more information about BCP in Microsoft's SQL Server Books Online.

Access 97 Upsize Wizard

The Access 97 Upsize Wizard is an Access add-in utility that automates the process of moving an Access database to SQL Server. It transfers table structure and data, as well as schema information such as table relationships, field value defaults, and validation rules, with some caveats. It is an excellent means of moving an existing Access database to SQL Server, but it also makes assumptions and has limitations that you should be aware of before using it. The rest of this chapter focuses on this option.

Effectively Using the Access 97 Upsize Wizard

The Upsize Wizard can greatly reduce the amount of time required to move an Access database to a SQL Server platform. In order to use the wizard effectively, it is important to understand how it implements moving Access database objects and attributes on SQL Server.

In general, the Upsize Wizard re-creates any object in the `.mdb` file that stores data, or is responsible for maintaining the integrity of the data, in addition to the data itself. In many cases it can re-create the objects or attributes directly on SQL Server, but often it will implement similar functionality in SQL Server through the use of other methods. Here is a brief overview of how the wizard implements some of the database schema information.

> **NOTE**
>
> This section describes moving from Access 97 to SQL Server 6.5. Although much of the information is appropriate to older versions of Access and SQL Server, it isn't necessarily so. You can find additional information on upsizing from older versions of Access or to older versions of SQL Server at `http://support.microsoft.com`.

Tables Structures

Tables and fields are implemented much as they are in Access. The Upsize Wizard will reproduce the table structure on SQL Server and convert the field datatypes to the appropriate SQL Server datatype. Table 19.1 lists the datatype conversions performed by the Upsize Wizard.

Table 19.1. Datatype conversions from Access to SQL Server.

Access	SQL Server
Currency	money
Date/Time	datetime
Memo	text
Number (Byte)	smallint
Number (Integer)	smallint
Number (Long Integer)	int
Number (Single)	real
Number (Double)	float
OLE Object	image
Text(n)	varchar(n)*
Yes/No	bit
Hyperlink	none

> **NOTE**
>
> By default, the Upsize Wizard converts the Access Text(n) datatype to the SQL Server varchar(n) datatype. You can change this behavior to always convert Text(n) datatypes to SQL Server char datatypes by changing the UT_USE_CHAR user constant in the Wzcs97.mda database file. For more information, see the section on changing Upsize Wizard user constants later in this chapter.

Indexes

Indexes are created as nonclustered indexes in SQL Server. Unique, required data, and multicolumn indexes are all re-created in SQL Server using similar attributes to maintain functionality. However, SQL Server does not provide for the ascending or descending indexes. The Upsize Wizard names indexes according to the first column on which they are based.

Primary Keys

Like indexes, primary keys are maintained on the SQL Server database and named for the first column on which they are based, but with aaaaa added to the beginning. This ensures that they appear first in a list of indexes.

> **NOTE**
>
> By default, the Upsize Wizard creates SQL Server primary keys as nonclustered, but you can instruct it to create them as clustered by changing the UT_CLUSTERED user constant in the Wzcs97.mda database used by the Upsize Wizard. However, doing so might not always be in the best interest of your table, especially if the Primary Key is on an Identity column. For more information, see the section on changing Upsize Wizard user constants later in this chapter.

AutoNumber Fields

Access AutoNumber fields can generate incremental, random, or replication ID values. The Upsize Wizard handles the different types of AutoNumber fields as follows:

- Incremented AutoNumber fields are implemented as Identity columns, which work nearly identically.

- Random AutoNumber fields are implemented using an insert trigger, which generates a unique number and fills the column whenever a new row is inserted.

- Replication ID AutoNumber fields in Access can generate a 128-bit GUID value. There is no equivalent functionality in SQL Server, so the Upsize Wizard creates a 16-bit varbinary column and transfers the existing data but does not create a method for filling the column.

Defaults

Defaults supply a value to a field if no value is supplied when a row is inserted in a table. Defaults work nearly the same way in Access and SQL Server but are implemented differently. In Access, defaults are considered a part of the table in which the column to which they refer resides. In SQL Server, however, defaults are created independently and can be bound to any number of columns in different tables.

The Upsize Wizard creates defaults on SQL Server and names them according to the table to which they apply. This means that if any two tables have columns with the same default value, SQL Server will create two defaults with different names. The sole exception to this is columns that default to 0, which are all bound to a single default called UW_ZeroDefault.

Table Relationships

The Upsize Wizard implements table relationships in SQL Server by creating either foreign keys or triggers, depending on what you select. The reason for this is that SQL Server does not have any built-in functionality for handling cascade deletes or updates, so the Upsize Wizard supplies it with insert and update triggers. Unfortunately, this is an either/or decision. It would be nice if the wizard were smart enough to automatically use triggers for those tables with cascade delete or cascade update relationships, and foreign keys for standard relationships.

Validation Rules

Even though SQL Server provides a rules object, the Upsize Wizard creates insert and update triggers instead of rules to implement the functionality on SQL Server. This is done because rules don't allow custom error messages.

Required Fields

Like validation rules, SQL Server uses insert and update triggers to provide the functionality because they can return custom error messages. However, in this case you can tell the wizard to use NOT NULL instead, by changing the UT_USE_NULL_CONSTRAINTS user constant in the Wzcs97.mda database. For more information, see the section "Set Wizard Options" later in this chapter.

Hey, What About Queries?

There is good news and bad news about queries. The good news is that the wizard is aware of queries and will go so far as to update the SQL code to reflect differences between SQL Server syntax requirements and Access. Unfortunately, if you are using queries as a method for implementing vertical security (for instance, allowing a user to see only certain fields) or encapsulating business rules, and you plan to move away from the .mdb altogether, you have to implement the functionality yourself in SQL Server. On the bright side, SQL Server provides views, which are much easier to use, so you can continue to implement vertical security. In addition, SQL Server Stored Procedures are head and shoulders above queries for encapsulating business rules.

The Upsize Process

Considering the complexity of the tasks, the process of upsizing an Access database to SQL Server with the Upsize Wizard is straightforward. However, there are some tasks that you will need to complete because the wizard doesn't do them for you. You should also be aware of the implications of certain decisions that the wizard will ask you to make along the way.

> **TIP**
>
> Before you start, it is always a good idea to make sure that SQL Server is up to date with the latest service pack. You can obtain the most recent service pack from Microsoft at http://support.microsoft.com/support/downloads.

Begin with a Backup

Before you begin the process, the first thing you should do is back up the .mdb file. If you are planning to upsize to an existing SQL Server database, you should back it up as well.

Install the Wizard

Obviously, if you have not already done so, you'll need to install the Upsize Wizard. You can find it at http://support.microsoft.com/support. Search for aut97.exe. This file contains the Upsize Wizard and the SQL Server Browser. The SQL Browser is a utility that enables you to browse SQL Server databases from Access. When you obtain the file, run it and follow the directions. The setup will install the needed files and create an entry for the Upsize Wizard on your Tools/Add-Ins menu.

Estimate the Needed SQL Server Database Size

Now is a good time to plan the SQL Server database that will receive the upsized data. In general, you'll need about one and a half to two times the current size of your existing Access .mdb file. Of course, if you expect a lot more data to be added, by all means make more room. As you figure your SQL Server database size, remember that Access .mdb files can contain many objects that aren't upsized, such as forms and code modules.

Create Devices on SQL Server (Optional)

Devices are files in SQL Server that contain the database. Usually, a device will contain one database, and another device will contain the transaction log. The Upsize Wizard can create the devices for you, and this is generally acceptable. However, if you plan to have your database span devices, or you plan to place the database device on one drive and the log device on another, you have to create the devices yourself.

Remember, you can always make devices larger, but not smaller.

Fix Problems Before They Occur

SQL Server has different requirements for table structure than Access. The Upsize Wizard is good at compensating for the differences when it is creating the tables in SQL Server, but you might not be satisfied with the results. It is much easier to resolve these problems in Access before you upsize rather than try to modify the tables in SQL Server. You should check the following items in the Access table structure:

- *Table names contain thirty* chars *or less.* The wizard will truncate any tables with longer names.

- *Table names and field names do not contain spaces.* In SQL Server there cannot be spaces in table or column names. The Upsize Wizard will replace any spaces in the table or field names with underscores (_).

- *Table names and column names consist of only letters, numbers, and* #,$, *and* _ *characters.* These are the only legal characters in a SQL Server table structure. Like spaces, the wizard will replace illegal characters with underscores.

> **NOTE**
>
> When the Upsize Wizard replaces any characters or spaces with underscores, it also creates an aliasing query to redirect data requests to the new data. This is great if your front-end application uses the .mdb file, but useless if your front end will access the data directly from SQL Server.

- *Table and field names begin with a letter or an underscore.* The wizard cannot create a table that begins with anything other than a letter or an underscore. In most cases the wizard will replace the illegal character with an underscore and continue, but in some cases the attempt to upsize the table will fail altogether.

- *Table names don't end with* _local. After a table has been upsized, the wizard will append the local Access table with _local. This tells the wizard not to show the table in the list of tables to select for upsizing. To upsize the table, you'll need to change the name to remove the suffix.

> **TIP**
>
> This is also a good way to re-upsize tables that you changed or did not upsize completely the first time.

- *Tables don't contain fields with hyperlink datatype.* Tables containing hyperlink field types can't be upsized. The wizard won't even try. If you want to upsize a table containing a hyperlink datatype, you'll need to delete the field or move the table data to an Access table that does not contain a hyperlink field and then upsize it. You can also directly create a table on SQL Server, link it to the Access database, and then use linked table queries to move the data.

Create ODBC Data Source Name

The wizard will require an ODBC data source name to link to SQL Server. If you don't have one already, it is better to create one before you start the wizard. In your DSN, set the Database Name parameter to the name of the database to which you intend to upsize. If you intend to create new devices, set the Database Name parameter to master.

If you don't have a SQL Server ODBC driver installed, you'll need to install one. You can find the driver in several places, including the Office 97 CD-ROM. You can always find the most recent driver on the World Wide Web, http://support.microsoft.com/downloads.

Check Your Permissions

When you run the Upsize Wizard, you are going to need sufficient rights to enable it to perform the tasks associated with upsizing the database. The easiest solution is to have SA-level rights by being a member of the Admin group on NT, especially if you plan on creating new devices as part of the upsize process. If this isn't possible, at the very least you'll need CREATE DATABASE rights to create a new database and CREATE TABLE rights to create new tables. For additional information on permissions, check the Administrator's Companion in the Microsoft SQL Server Books Online.

Set Wizard Options

The last task before starting the wizard is to verify that the Upsize Wizard user constants are set the way you need them. The default values are the most appropriate for most upsize projects, but you might want to check them. To do this, open the Wzcs97.mda file in Access. This file is most likely located in the Program Files\Microsoft Office\Office directory.

> **NOTE**
>
> If you've already opened a database in Access, you might receive an error stating that the Wzcs97.mda file can't be opened because it is already opened as a database library. In this case, simply exit Access. Then start it again. This time, select the file by highlighting it in the dialog box that appears when you start Access.

After you've opened the file, click on the Modules tab and locate the UT_modUserConstants module. This module contains user constants that can be set to give some control over how the wizard works. Table 19.2 lists the user settings and their implications.

Table 19.2. Available user constants in the Access 97 Setup Wizard.

Constant	Default	Description Value
UT_CAREFUL	False	If `True`, Access field or table names containing SQL Server reserved words are converted to allow for compliance; otherwise, they are used as the upsized table and column names.
UT_CHECK_FOR_FULL_LOG	True	If `True`, the wizard checks the SQL Server transaction log whenever an ODBC Call Failed error occurs. For a new database, the wizard automatically drops the transaction log, but for an existing database, the wizard asks the user whether he wants to drop the log. Setting this value to `False` can hasten the upsize process, but the process will abort if an ODBC Call Failed occurs.
UT_CLUSTERED	False	If `True`, the wizard creates upsized tables with a clustered primary key; otherwise, primary keys are created as nonclustered.
UT_DELETE_SERVER_XLAT	True	If `True`, the wizard deletes the character translation table created on the server after the upsize process is completed. Setting this value to `False` prevents the wizard from deleting the table. This table can take some time to create, and by not deleting the character translation table, you speed up subsequent upsize sessions to the same database.
UT_EXPORT_GUID	True	If `True`, the wizard exports tables with Replication ID type `AutoNumber` fields; otherwise, the wizard won't export the tables. Note that even if the wizard exports the table, only the field and data is exported. SQL Server has no way of duplicating the `AutoNumber` functionality for this kind of field.

continues

19

Outgrowing Access

Table 19.2. continued

Constant	Default	Description Value
UT_QUIET	False	If True, the wizard won't stop after any errors encountered during the upsize process; otherwise, it displays a message box and waits for user input before continuing.
UT_USE_CHAR	False	If True, the wizard creates columns with the CHAR datatype when upsizing Access Test fields; otherwise, it uses the VARCHAR datatype.
UT_USE_NULL_CONSTRAINTS	False	If True, the wizard sets appropriate NULL or NOT NULL attributes on SQL Server columns created from upsized fields with Primary Key, Unique, or Required properties; otherwise, the wizard duplicates the functionality in SQL Server through the use of triggers. This is done to allow for unique error messages and to enable the nullability of columns to be changed without dropping the table.

Let the Wizard Do the Work for You

Assuming the installation worked correctly, you are now ready to run the Setup Wizard. First, open the .mdb database file that you want to upsize in Access. Then select the Upsize To SQL-Server option on the Tools/Add-Ins menu. The wizard will load and begin its series of dialog boxes. Undoubtedly you've used wizards before, so I'll keep this section brief and to the point.

On the first screen, shown in Figure 19.3, make your first selection: Select Use Existing Database if you have upsized this Access database before or if you want to add new tables and data to an existing database. Otherwise, select Create New Database and click the Next button to continue.

If you select an existing database, the screen in Figure 19.4 presents a list of Data Source Names available on the computer. Select the DSN that you set up earlier. If you are creating a new database, be sure to set the database parameter to master; otherwise, set the database parameter to the existing database to which you are upsizing.

If you selected the Create New Database option on the first screen, the wizard will display a screen like Figure 19.5. You can select an existing device on which to place the new database or create a new device. Be sure that the device you use has enough space to hold the new database.

FIGURE 19.3.

The first screen in the wizard.

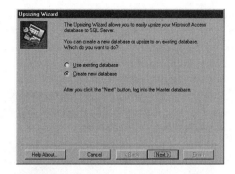

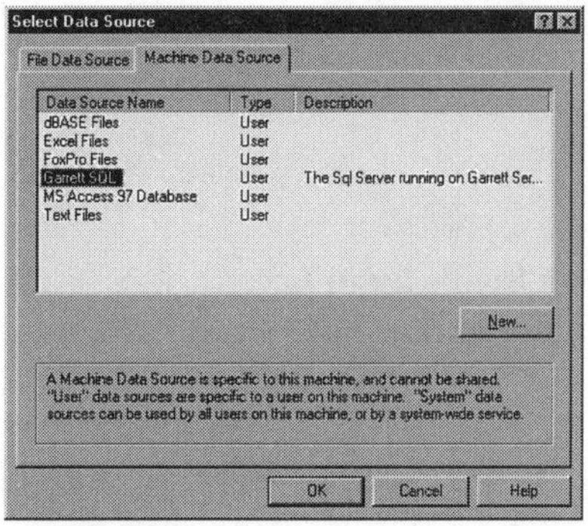

FIGURE 19.4.

Select an ODBC data source.

FIGURE 19.5.

The optional device selection screen.

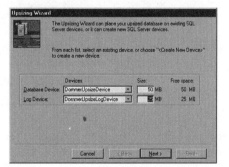

If you want your database device and log device to be on two separate disks, you need to create the devices in SQL Server before running the Upsize Wizard.

TIP

To span devices with a single database or log, create the devices in SQL Server before running the upsizing wizard. Then make them default devices (make sure there are no other default devices). Finally, select what you want for the Default Device when prompted by the upsizing wizard for the database or log. Note that you cannot specify separate sets of default devices for the log and the database.

If you opted to create a new database, the wizard will prompt you to enter a database name and to indicate how large the new database will be on the screen shown in Figure 19.6. Database names can be no longer than 30 characters and can't contain spaces. You should use only letters, numbers, and underscores when naming your database.

FIGURE 19.6.

Create a new database.

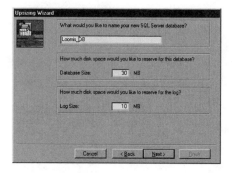

Next, you can select from a list of Access tables, as shown in Figure 19.7, that you can upsize to SQL Server. Tables with a `_local` suffix don't show in the Available Tables list.

FIGURE 19.7.

Use this screen to select tables to upsize.

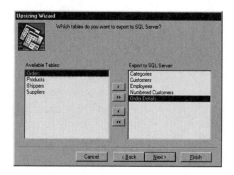

At this point, and on all the screens from here on, you can click Finish and continue straight to upsizing without moving to the next screen.

Selecting Table Attributes

The screen in Figure 19.8 enables you to select table attributes to export, choose data options, and decide how the Access database is modified.

FIGURE 19.8.
Selecting table attributes.

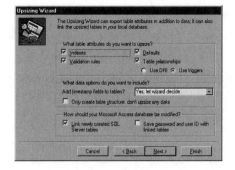

The Upsize Wizard enables you to select the following table attributes to move to SQL Server:

- *Indexes.* Moving indexes, especially on large tables, can significantly slow down the upsize process. In some cases, you might be better off not upsizing the indexes but, instead, creating them after the fact on SQL Server. Another option would be to upsize the database in two passes. On the first pass, upsize the smaller tables with their indexes, and on the second, upsize the larger tables without their indexes.

- *Validation Rules.* The Upsize Wizard uses Access validation rules, rather than SQL Server rules, with triggers. If you want validation rules on your SQL Server database to be implemented with other rules, you should deselect this option and create the rules yourself in SQL Server.

- *Defaults.* The Upsize Wizard will create a new SQL Server default for every field with a default value attribute. If you would rather reuse SQL Server defaults, deselect this option. After the upsize is completed, you can create the defaults in SQL Server and bind them to the appropriate columns.

- *Table Relationships.* This option requires more forethought than the others. You have two choices for enforcing table relationships: Declarative Referential Integrity (DRI) and triggers. If you choose Use DRI, the wizard will implement table relationships using SQL Server DRI, namely foreign keys, but the database will not support cascade deletes or cascade updates. Choosing Use Triggers, on the other hand, instructs the wizard to enforce table relationships using triggers, which has the advantage of supporting cascade deletes and cascade updates but the disadvantage of generally slowing the database. Unfortunately, the wizard doesn't automatically use the best option for the type of table relationship. This is another situation where two passes through the process would be a good idea. On one pass you could upsize tables with standard relationships (for instance, no cascade deletes or cascade updates), and on another you could upsize tables with extended relationships. A third option is to ignore table relationships altogether and create them yourself after the process is complete.

19

OUTGROWING ACCESS

Selecting Data Options

The Upsize Wizard enables you to set the following data options:

- *Timestamp Columns.* A `timestamp` column is a special SQL Server column that receives a unique value every time a row is inserted or updated. The reason for timestamps is to enable an application to compare the `timestamp` in a row it is holding in local memory with the timestamp for the same row in the database. If the values have changed, the application can be prevented from saving changes that could overwrite changes another user already saved to the table. The downside to `timestamps` is that they add overhead to every update or insert statement for the table in which they reside, thus slowing the database performance.

  By default, the wizard creates `timestamp` columns in any Access table containing single floating point, double floating point, memo, or OLE fields. You can specify whether this is acceptable or whether the wizard should create a `timestamp` for every table, or ignore `timestamps` altogether.

  How you set this option depends largely on how you expect your tables to be used. If a table's rows are generally inserted once and then not updated, a `timestamp` column isn't really called for. If, however, you expect the table's rows to be updated frequently by several users, and the rows are too large to effectively select for comparison, a `timestamp` would be a good idea. Unfortunately, you can't indicate to the Upsize Wizard which tables should receive `timestamp` columns.

- *Create Table Structure Only.* This is a very useful option if the amount of data in the Access tables is so great that the system can't move it all at once. This feature enables the wizard to go ahead and create the table structures and other schema information. Then you can perform linked table queries to move subsets of the data to the new SQL Server tables.

TIP

If you do decide to attempt to move a large dataset anyway, you can prevent problems by increasing the value of the ODBC `QueryTimeout` registry key. To do so, use the registry editor to change the value in the registry at

`\HKEY_LOCAL_MACHINE\Software\Microsoft\Jet\3.5\Engines\ODBC`

You can increase the value or set it to `0`. Setting it to `0` effectively disables the `QueryTimeout` value. Use it with caution.

Modifying Access Database Options

These options control how the Upsize Wizard will modify the `.mdb` file from which you are upsizing.

■ *Attach Newly Created SQL Server Tables.* Selecting this option causes the new SQL Server tables created by the upsize process to be linked to the Access database and the local tables to be renamed with _local suffixes. This option is absolutely essential if you plan to connect to the SQL Server data through the .mdb file or to use linked table queries to pass data from the Access database to SQL Server. Otherwise, deselecting it can speed up the upsize process somewhat, especially if there are a large number of tables to upsize.

■ *Save Password and User ID with Linked Tables.* This option is provided as a convenience to users so that they don't have to log in to SQL Server every time they open an Access database with linked tables. However, it can also create a gaping hole in your SQL Server security if there is no security on the Access database. If you don't plan to use the Access database file to connect to SQL Server, this option is academic; otherwise, I would advise using it with caution and only on SQL Server databases where security isn't a priority.

Creating an Upsizing Report

You can also create an upsizing report from the final screen in the wizard. The upsizing report contains a list of all the upsized tables, both their original name and the name used in SQL Server. The report also shows Transact SQL code used to create triggers and default to enforce referential integrity. That's not all. The report also lists any aliasing queries that were created, as well as any errors that occurred during the process. Generating an upsizing report is highly recommended.

> **NOTE**
>
> During the upsize process, the wizard creates a table for translating extended ASCII characters on the SQL Server database. If the upsize process terminates prematurely, you might want to delete this table from SQL Server.

Completing the Upsize Process

Now that the wizard has successfully run, you still need to perform a number of tasks to prepare the new database for human contact and to enable your front-end applications to get the most out of the new platform.

The first thing you'll want to do, of course, is to back up your new SQL Server database and the Access .mdb file. After that, you'll need to prepare the SQL Server database so that the users can use it and then look over the client applications for possible problems.

Setup SQL Server Security

Unfortunately, the Upsize Wizard does not export security information along with the database schema, so one of the first things you need to do is to ensure that the intended users have the appropriate access to the new SQL Server database. To do this, you perform several tasks.

19

OUTGROWING
ACCESS

> **NOTE**
>
> Access has no control over the security on linked tables. This means that even if you plan to access the SQL Server database using the current Access database, you'll still need to set up user security on SQL Server.

- *Add users and groups.* Initially, the new database is accessible only to the database owner and the system administrators. You'll need to add users and groups to the database.
- *Create views.* If necessary, you'll create views to allow users to view only certain information, rather than grant them rights to a particular table.
- *Set up object permissions.* After you add users and groups, you need to grant rights to newly created tables, views, and stored procedures.
- *Plug Access security holes.* If you select the option to allow usernames and passwords to be saved with the original Access database, this is also a good time to ensure that the security on the Access database is sufficient to prevent unauthorized access to the SQL Server database.

It's possible that you'll change your mind about allowing users to store their usernames and passwords with the Access database. If this happens, you can perform the following steps to remove the option from the user.

- Locate or create a table called `MsysConf` in the SQL Server database in which the linked tables reside. The table structure should match the structure shown in Table 19.3. Be sure to create the table and column names exactly as shown.

- Grant `SELECT` permissions to all users for this table; only the system administrator should have `INSERT`, `UPDATE`, and `DELETE` permissions.

- `INSERT` a row in the table and set the `nValue` column value to 0 and the `Config` column to 101. You can ignore the other two columns. If a row already exists with a `Config` value of 101, simply `UPDATE` the row to set the `nValue` column to 0.

That's it. The changes take effect the next time the Access database attempts to connect to SQL Server. Note that this change applies to any Access database that attempts to connect to this SQL Server database.

Column name	Datatype	Allows Null?
Config	smallint	No
chValue	VARCHAR(255)	Yes
nValue	int	Yes
Comments	VARCHAR(255)	Yes

Inspect Your Client Applications

By design, the Upsize Wizard assumes that the original Access database will be used to connect to SQL Server. This enables the fastest possible upsize path, but it does so at the expense of functionality and performance. You need to decide whether you want to continue using the existing Access database to access the data or whether you want to access data directly from SQL Server.

Regardless of which path you choose, you'll still need to take a close look at your applications and change them to accommodate differences in accessing SQL Server. The following are some common tasks that you might perform to ensure compatibility or to leverage the SQL Server platform.

- *Convert SQL statements.* The wizard changes all the SQL syntax used to create queries in the Access database. Unfortunately, it does not do so in Access macros or modules, nor can it change code in other languages, such as Visual Basic, that use the Access database as a back end. Instead you'll need to go through your applications and update any SQL statements that are built into the application to conform to SQL Server, instead of Access, syntax. This would also be a good time to investigate moving some of these queries to SQL Server stored procedures.

- *Optimize design.* Optimizing application design for client/server solutions is a book unto itself. Therefore, I mention it only briefly. Make sure that you are accessing data intelligently. Rather than pull across an entire table, use SQL queries to limit the amount of data coming across the network. Obviously, this will be neither easy nor cheap with existing applications, but if you don't do it, you will gain little, if anything, from upsizing your database.

- *Remove obsolete code.* If your application is using DAO to access your data, you need to remove references to objects and methods that don't apply to ODBC databases. You might think about moving to another data access technology, such as RDO. Again, this could be potentially messy and expensive, but the gains will far outweigh the cost.

Summary

Although moving to SQL Server from Access seems like an obvious move, you need to weigh the costs of upsizing against the expected increase in functionality and performance. There are some reasons for upsizing that are in themselves a justification, but other reasons need to be considered in a larger context.

If you do decide to upsize from Access to SQL Server, you should first consider your options and then choose the tool that is most appropriate to your needs. The Access 97 Upsize Wizard is an excellent method for upsizing, but you need to be aware of how it works and some of the assumptions that it makes. After you upsize, you must still implement security on your new SQL Server database and potentially rework client applications in order to fully benefit from the power and flexibility of SQL Server.

The Oracle Transition

IN THIS CHAPTER

Although Oracle and Microsoft utilize a standard SQL form, there are many differences between T-SQL and PL/SQL. This chapter serves as a blueprint for making the switch from using Oracle to using Microsoft SQL Server. You find numerous examples of syntax, real-world examples, and a table of information on the variations. You can use these now to learn the differences and to refer to as you troubleshoot any existing conversions. The process of converting is never easy—especially the first time through—but the information in this chapter should help make that move smoother both for you, the developer, and eventually for your end-user. The chapter concludes with a few tips and hints to add to your checklist as your begin (or repeat) this process.

Datatypes

When making the transition, you need to know the available datatypes before you can create the database. Table 20.1 summarizes the datatypes available to PL/SQL, the equivalent to T-SQL and the range of values, and any additional nuances. Keep in mind that Oracle provides almost every character set in existence, whereas SQL Server only uses ASCII. This has major implications when integrating the database across different platforms.

Table 20.1. Datatype equivalents from PL/SQL to T-SQL.

PL/SQL Datatype	T-SQL Datatype	Description/Variances
NUMBER or DECIMAL	DECIMAL or NUMERIC	Can create any type of number (for example, float, integer, real) by accepting parameters of precision and scale. Both allow a maximum precision of 38, but SQL Server defaults to 28 for backward compatibility with front ends like Visual Basic.
FLOAT	FLOAT	Derivative of NUMBER; specify the number of decimal places.
REAL	REAL	Derivative of number.
NUMBER	MONEY, SMALLMONEY	SQL Server adds a datatype that has two decimal places. Can create this as a user-defined datatype in Oracle. Money values are represented as double-precision integers. Storage size is eight bytes.
LONG	DECIMAL or NUMERIC	Can create user-defined datatype in SQL Server to account for LONG values using NUMBER or DECIMAL.

PL/SQL Datatype	T-SQL Datatype	Description/Variances
INTEGER, BINARY_ INTEGER, PLS_ INTEGER	INTEGER	Value range -2,147,483,648 through 2,147,483,647.
SMALLINT	SMALLINT	Value range -32768 through 32767.
NUMBER or DECIMAL	TINYINT	Value range 0 through 255. Need to create user-defined datatype in Oracle to duplicate this datatype.
DOUBLE PRECISION	DOUBLE PRECISION	Same value range as FLOAT.
NATURAL	DECIMAL or NUMERIC	Value range 0 through 2,147,483,647. Need to create user-defined datatype in SQL Server.
NATURALN	DECIMAL or NUMERIC	Value range 0 through 2,147,483,647 with no NULL values. Need to create user-defined datatype in SQL Server.
POSITIVE	DECIMAL or NUMERIC	Value range 1 through 2,147,483,647. Need to create user-defined datatype in SQL Server.
POSITIVEN	DECIMAL or NUMERIC	Value range 1 through 2,147,483,647 with no NULL values. Need to create user-defined datatype in SQL Server.
CHAR, CHARACTER	CHAR, CHARACTER	Same value range of one or more characters specified; however, Oracle has the ability to code in different formats such as EBCDIC or ASCII. No such option in SQL Server. In addition, SQL Server stores a maximum of 255 values; Oracle can hold standard 32768 or over 2GB if LONG.
VARCHAR, STRING	VARCHAR	Same function in both packages; holds characters of variable length; trailing blanks are removed.

continues

Table 20.1. continued

PL/SQL Datatype	T-SQL Datatype	Description/Variances
VARCHAR2	VARCHAR	No real SQL Server equivalent. Holds character values for multi-byte characters. SQL Server does not allow for multi-byte characters.
RAW, LONG RAW	TEXT, IMAGE	Both store large binary or text objects.
DATE	DATETIME, SMALLDATETIME	Both values store date and time; SQL Server uses SMALLDATETIME to go to minute values. Oracle retains complete control to thousands of a second, which can be retrieved through DATE.
BOOLEAN	BIT	SQL Server does allow you to get down to the bit level to store a single bit. Uses less storage and great for a yes/no indicator. Oracle does have BOOLEAN to store TRUE or FALSE to perform similar functions.
ROWID	TIMESTAMP	A binary or variable binary value stored in a table column; updated every time a row is inserted or updated. Oracle has the same feature called ROWID, and does not have to have a column specified as TIMESTAMP, since this automatically occurs.

NOTE

Keep in mind that SQL Server also allows an abbreviation. The reader may encounter INT, which is INTEGER.

User-Defined Datatypes

In almost every case, SQL Server has an equivalent to Oracle for a matching datatype. Since both databases allow for user-defined datatypes, you could make both databases with identical variable datatypes.

SQL Server uses the system stored procedure `sp_addtype` to create a user-defined datatype. You can then make the datatype available to all databases. The following is an example of creating a user-defined datatype in SQL Server:

```
sp_addtype ssn, 'varchar(11)', 'NOT NULL'
```

In Oracle, you can specify your user-defined datatypes, referred to as *subtypes*, in the `DECLARE` section. An Oracle example follows:

```
SUBTYPE ssn IS varchar2(11);
```

Both achieve the same concept using different coding methods.

Implicit and Explicit Datatype Conversions

Both Oracle and SQL Server have methods for handling implicit datatype conversions when assigning a variable of one datatype to a value of another datatype. However, to make sure that the PL/SQL and T-SQL code always converts in the desired manner, it is better to use explicit datatype conversions. In SQL Server, the `CONVERT` function can convert from one datatype to another. In Oracle, this is accomplished using `TO_CHAR`, `TO_DATE`, and `TO_NUMBER`.

The format for the `CONVERT` function is as follows:

```
CONVERT(datatype[(length)],input_data[,style])
```

The `datatype` parameter specifies the new datatype desired. The `length` parameter, which is optional, specifies the length of the new datatype. The default value is `30`. The `input_data` parameter is the source data to be converted. Optionally, the `style` input parameter is used when formatting date conversions to string datatypes.

Use the following code to convert a character string `'123'` to a number value `123`:

```
CONVERT (INTEGER , '123')
```

In Oracle, the same conversion is as follows:

```
TO_NUMBER('123')
```

The following sample illustrates the differences in using a `CONVERT` statement in Oracle or in SQL Server:

Original statement:
```
SELECT (fn CONVERT (SSN, SQL_INTEGER)} FROM STUDENT
```
Converted Oracle statement:
```
SELECT TO_NUMBER(SSN) FROM STUDENT
```
Converted SQL Server statement:
```
SELECT CONVERT(INT,SSN) FROM STUDENT
```

In SQL Server, by specifying the datatype, you eliminate the need for the several functions that are provided in Oracle (TO_DATE, TO_NUMBER, and TO_CHAR).

Variables

In SQL Server, local variables are preceded with the @ symbol, and global variables are preceded by two @ symbols (@@). Oracle local variables do not require the @ symbol at the first position, and Oracle uses the % symbol for global system variables. Both databases have a limit of 30 characters for a variable name. Remember, though, that in SQL it is a maximum of 29 characters (if you include the @ symbol).

Assigning a value to a variable is also completely different between the two databases. In Oracle, you use the common method of the assignment operator "=" to assign the lvalue with the expression or value of the rvalue. An example follows:

```
SSN := '123-45-6789' ;
```

It is important to know the differences between permanent and temporary objects. The following minitable describes the differences and similarities of the permanent and temporary objects.

Oracle	SQL Server
1–30 characters in length. (Oracle database names can be a maximum of 8 characters, database link names can be a maximum of 128 characters.)	1–30 characters in length. (Temporary objects names should not exceed 13 characters in length.)
Identifier names must begin with an alphabetic character and contain alphanumeric characters, or the _, $, or # characters.	Identifier names must begin with an alphabetic character or one of three symbols (_, @, #) and contain either alphanumeric characters, or the _, $, and # characters. Additionally, an object beginning with @ is defined as a local variable; an object beginning with a single # defines a local temporary object, and an object beginning with two ## defines a global temporary object.

In SQL Server, you must always use the SELECT statement to assign a value. This is a different method than using Oracle's SELECT ... INTO method of assigning a value to a variable. The syntax for SQL Server is as follows:

```
SELECT @variable = {expression ¦ select_statement}
      [, @variable = {expression ¦ select_statement}...]
[FROM table_list]
[WHERE search_conditions]
[GROUP BY clause]
[HAVING clause]
[ORDER BY clause]
```

The @variable parameter is the lvalue variable. You can assign a constant value, an expression, or even another SELECT statement. Optionally, you can specify a table, including any search conditions and group methods. You use the following to assign the same value to SSN:

```
SELECT @SSN = '123-45-6789'
```

There are a few additional datatypes in Oracle not found in SQL Server. The first is %rowtype, which assigns an entire row to a variable. In SQL Server, you have to assign a concatenated string to a CHAR or VARCHAR variable, making sure to use the CONVERT function. The other method is to create all the variables and assign the values to each individual variable.

The %TYPE attribute is the second variable assignment method not found in SQL Server. Instead of declaring a variable, later modifying the database, and having to update all instances of the variable to match the definition on the table, %TYPE automatically assigns the variable the same datatype assigned to the column in a database. Again, since this important feature does not exist in SQL Server, good documentation is more important than ever.

The CONSTANT variable declaration is not available in Microsoft SQL Server. You have to create a variable and then assign a constant value with the SELECT statement.

Operators

Almost all of the operators and order of operations are identical between the two database packages. Table 20.2 lists the operators and their equivalents from both database packages in the order of operations, except for the comparison operators. The comparison operators are broken down in Table 20.3. See Chapter 8, "Advanced String Manipulation and Bitwise Operators," for more detailed explanation of these operators.

Table 20.2. Operator equivalents from PL/SQL to T-SQL.

PL/SQL Operator	T-SQL Operator	Description/Variances
()	()	Items in parentheses are evaluated first.

continues

Table 20.2. continued

PL/SQL Operator	T-SQL Operator	Description/Variances
**	EXP (function)	Exponentiation operator in Oracle has only equivalent function in SQL Server.
NOT	NOT	In SQL Server takes precedence over AND and OR operators. Same purpose for both operators, but different order of operations.
+, -	N/A	Identity, negation.
N/A	Bitwise ~	Bitwise ~ in SQL Server allows access to bit level operations.
*, /, MOD	*, /, %	Multiplication, Division, and MOD operator. In SQL Server, the % symbol is used for calculating the remainder. In Oracle, the function MOD is used. The % symbol in Oracle is reserved for datatypes.
+, -, ||	+, -, +	Addition, subtraction, and concatenation. The concatenation operator differs between the two database packages.
N/A	Bitwise ^	Bitwise exclusive OR. No comparable operator in Oracle.
N/A	Bitwise &	Bitwise AND. No comparable operator in Oracle.
N/A	Bitwise [vb]	Bitwise OR. No comparable operator in Oracle.
AND	AND	Compare two values, conjunction.
OR	OR	Compare two values, inclusion.

Table 20.3 The comparison operators for Oracle and SQL Server.

Operator	Oracle	SQL Server
Equal to	=	=
Greater than	>	>
Less than	<	<

Operator	Oracle	SQL Server
Greater than or equal to	>=	>=
Less than or equal to	<=	<=
Not equal to	!=, ^=, < >	!=, <>
Not greater than	N/A	!>
Not less than	N/A	!<
In any member in set	IN	IN
Not in any member in set	NOT IN	NOT IN
Any value in set	ANY, SOME	ANY, SOME
All values in set	ALL	ALL
Like pattern	LIKE	LIKE
Not like pattern	NOT LIKE	NOT LIKE
Value between	BETWEEN	BETWEEN
Value not between	NOT BETWEEN	NOT BETWEEN
Value exists	EXISTS	EXISTS
Value does not exist	NOT EXISTS	NOT EXISTS
Value {is | is not} NULL	IS NULL, IS NOT NULL	IS NULL, IS NOT NULL

The only difference in the order of operations is that the keyword NOT has a higher order in Oracle than in SQL Server. In SQL Server, NOT precedes the comparison operators AND and OR. If you are copying and pasting code from one database package to the other, make sure that the computations work properly. When in doubt, always use parentheses. In addition, SQL Server offers bitwise manipulation with several operators not found in Oracle. Refer to Chapter 8 for a more detailed explanation. Since SQL Server does not support other character sets, use of bitwise operators for conversion is extremely important. Oracle also provides identity and negation operators not available in SQL Server. The last major difference is that the concatenation operator is now + instead of ||. This takes some getting used to when coding SQL Server.

Tables and Indexes

There are quite a few differences when setting up tables in Oracle and when setting up tables in SQL Server. You observe the differences when creating a table, joining tables, and managing indexes. While most of the changes are syntactical, this section saves you time by pointing out these slight variances, thereby saving a lot of frustration.

20

THE ORACLE TRANSITION

Differences in Creating a Table

There are many differences you need to account for between the two database packages when creating tables. One major difference is that Oracle stores a value ROWID automatically for each row in the table. While this takes up space, the ROWID could be put to good use. In SQL Server, this process is not automatic; however, with DASD so inexpensive, you should create a timestamp on one column in SQL Server, which acts similarly to ROWID in SQL Server. The syntax for creating a table in SQL Server and Oracle is identical:

```
CREATE TABLE [database.[owner].]table_name
(
    {col_name column_properties [constraint [constraint [...constraint]]]
    ¦ [[,] constraint]}
        [[,] {next_col_name ¦ next_constraint}...]
)
```

> **NOTE**
>
> In SQL Server, table and column names can be case sensitive, depending on the character sort order installed. When SQL Server is first set up, the default sort order is dictionary order, not case sensitive.

While the syntax for creating the table is the same, the implementation varies slightly. Listing 20.1 works verbatim in both database packages.

Listing 20.1. A CREATE TABLE statement that looks alike for both, but works differently.

```
CREATE TABLE salesmw (
    StoreID    integer NOT NULL
        REFERENCES store(StoreID),
    CDID    integer  NOT NULL
        REFERENCES CD(CDID),
            CONSTRAINT smw PRIMARY KEY(CDID,StoreID,SalesDate),
    QtySold    integer,
    SalesDate    datetime)
```

However, Listings 20.2 and 20.3 begin to show some differences in syntax.

Listing 20.2. The Oracle format to create the Classification table.

```
CREATE TABLE classification (
    ClassifID    integer  CONSTRAINT pk_classif NOT NULL PRIMARY KEY,
    Classification    varchar(25),
        CONSTRAINT class UNIQUE (Classification))
```

Listing 20.3. The SQL Server version of the `Classification` table.

```
CREATE TABLE Classification (
    ClassifID    integer  NOT NULL PRIMARY KEY,
    Classification    varchar(25)
        CONSTRAINT class UNIQUE (Classification))
```

When only one field is involved, the primary key in SQL Server does not require the keyword `CONSTRAINT`.

Another syntax difference is seen when creating the `Store` table. Listing 20.4 shows the Oracle table's creation and Listing 20.5 creates the table in SQL Server:

Listing 20.4. Creating the `Store` table for Oracle.

```
CREATE TABLE Store   (
    StoreID    integer CONSTRAINT pk_st NOT NULL PRIMARY KEY,
    StoreName    varchar(30) ,
        CONSTRAINT stname UNIQUE (StoreName,Address,City,State),
    Address    varchar(40),
    City    varchar(20),
    State    varchar(2),
    ZipCode    varchar(10),
    ManFName    varchar(25),
    MI    varchar(1) NULL,
    ManLName    varchar(30),
    RegionCode    char(2) NOT NULL   )
```

Listing 20.5. Creating the `Store` table in SQL server:.

```
CREATE TABLE Store(
    StoreID    integer NOT NULL PRIMARY KEY,
    StoreName    varchar(30) NOT NULL
        CONSTRAINT stname UNIQUE (StoreName,Address,City,State),
    Address    varchar(40),
    City    varchar(20),
    State    varchar(2),
    ZipCode    varchar(10),
    ManFName    varchar(25),
    MI    varchar(1) NULL,
    ManLName    varchar(30),
    RegionCode    char(2) NOT NULL )
```

When creating a unique index that requires more than one field, the Oracle database requires a comma between the field name and the constraint, whereas SQL Server does not.

As you can see, the minor subtleties in the syntax of the CREATE TABLE statement produce difficult-to-find errors in SQL Server. PRIMARY KEY, FOREIGN KEY, UNIQUE CONSTRAINT, DEFAULT CONSTRAINT, and CHECK CONSTRAINT follow the same implementation in both database packages. The DROP and ALTER TABLE commands are identical between the two database packages. In addition, the INSERT, UPDATE, DELETE, COMMIT, and ROLLBACK statements work identically in both packages.

Differences in Joining Tables

The standard method for joining tables with the WHERE clause works identically. However, SQL Server provides an additional way to join tables, which complies with the new ANSI method. The ANSI method joins are demonstrated in Chapter 1, "Beyond the Basics of Data Manipulation Language."

Differences in Creating and Managing Indexes

There are many major differences in the handling of indexes between the two database packages. Observe the differences in the syntax for each database. The syntax for SQL Server is as follows:

```
CREATE [UNIQUE] [CLUSTERED ¦ NONCLUSTERED] INDEX index_name
      ON [[database.]owner.]table_name (column_name [, column_name]...)
[WITH
      [FILLFACTOR = x]
      [[,] IGNORE_DUP_KEY]
      [[,] {SORTED_DATA ¦ SORTED_DATA_REORG}]
      [[,] {IGNORE_DUP_ROW ¦ ALLOW_DUP_ROW}]]
[ON segment_name]
```

The syntax for Oracle is as follows:

```
CREATE [UNIQUE] INDEX index_name
     ON [CLUSTER] [[database.]owner.]table_name (column_name ASC, DESC
           [, column_name ASC DESC]...)
[INITRANS integer
MAXTRANS integer
TABLESPACE tablespace
STORAGE storage_clause
PCTFREE integer
NOSORT {RECOVERABLE ¦UNRECOVERABLE }
PARALLEL parallel_clause]
```

Both packages offer the UNIQUE keyword to make sure all values in the index are unique, with no duplicates. Both systems also allow you to have up to 16 columns contained in one index. Oracle provides ASC and DESC keywords to maintain compatibility with DB2; however, all indexes are stored in ascending order. SQL Server does allow for the use of non-clustered indexes as Oracle, but you must specify the index as NONCLUSTERED.

A non-clustered index is an index sorted in ascending order, but the physical rows remain in the same order. A pointer in the index points to the physical location of a row in the table. This allows you to sort a table in the most frequently queried format, yet create additional indexes for fast retrieval on other sorts. In conjunction with this feature, Oracle uses NOSORT to specify that rows are not to be sorted, whereas SQL Server performs this action by default. The optional FILLFACTOR in SQL Server works in the same manner as STORAGE in Oracle; however, you do have more control in Oracle as to the percentage of free space to maintain.

IGNORE_DUP_ROW, which allows duplicate values to be entered, is an additional SQL Server feature. Use this with caution—the use of this feature is not recommended. Finally, both Oracle and SQL Server provide the capability to prevent logging the transactions as indexes are created by specifying UNRECOVERABLE. Preventing transactions from logging speeds the process of creating indexes on large tables.

In summary, SQL Server does provide most of the flexibility Oracle does, but Oracle allows more control over storage requirements. In SQL Server, you must specify CLUSTERED or NONCLUSTERED, whereas Oracle requires the keyword CLUSTER, but defaults to NONCLUSTERED. If using NONCLUSTERED indexes, SQL Server by default does not sort the rows, whereas you need to specify the NOSORT option in Oracle to prevent this from occurring. One last dangerous option in SQL Server is the capability to override the checks for duplicate records and allow for the insertion of duplicate records.

The following is an example of a NONCLUSTERED index in Oracle:

```
CREATE INDEX empid ON employee (employeeid)
    NOSORT
```

The same index in SQL Server is as follows:

```
CREATE NONCLUSTERED INDEX emplid ON employee (employeeid)
```

While there are several differences in the order, keywords, and syntax for creating indexes, there is equal variation on managing the indexes of both databases. In Oracle, the system tracks and keeps statistics on all indexes for faster retrieval. You can remove the statistics, but it is not necessary and leads to longer access time by queries. In SQL Server, you must maintain the indexes with the UPDATE STATISTICS statement. This statement is covered in detail in Chapter 12, "Updating Table Indexes and Statistics," where you learn how to create a utility to update each index statistics in a database for faster retrieval of data in a query.

Cursor Variances

Most of the differences are, again, syntactical and keywords usage. In order to better discuss the variances, first look at Table 20.4, which shows the differences in syntax. For example, MS SQL Server does not need the semicolon (;) after each DECLARE statement or step of the cursor. Listing 20.6 shows a cursor created in SQL Server, and Listing 20.7 shows the goal accomplished from Oracle.

Table 20.4. Syntax examples for the differences in MS SQL Server and Oracle.

Operation	PL/SQL	Transact-SQL

Declaring a cursor	`CURSOR cursor_name`
	`[(cursor_parameter(s))]`
	`IS select_statement;`
		`DECLARE cursor_name`
		`[INSENSITIVE] [SCROLL]`
		`CURSOR FOR select_statement`
		`[FOR {READ ONLY ¦ UPDATE`
		`[OF column_list]}]`

Opening a cursor	`OPEN cursor_name` `[(cursor_parameter(s))];`	`OPEN cursor_name`

Fetching from cursor	`FETCH cursor_name INTO`
	`variable(s)`
		`FETCH [[NEXT ¦ PRIOR ¦`
		`FIRST ¦ LAST ¦ ABSOLUTE`
		`{n ¦ @nvar} ¦ RELATIVE`
		`{n ¦ @nvar}] FROM]`
		`cursor_name`
		`[INTO @variable(s)]`

Listing 20.6. A cursor created in SQL server.

```
DECLARE
     @empname VARCHAR(40),
     @salary MONEY,
     @empid integer
DECLARE getemp_curs CURSOR
     FOR
          SELECT empid, empname, rate
          FROM employees
          WHERE employeetype = "C"
OPEN getemp_curs
FETCH NEXT FROM getemp_curs into @empid, @empname, @salary
WHILE @@FETCH_STATUS = 0 BEGIN
     UPDATE employees
          SET rate = @salary
               WHERE empid = @empid
FETCH NEXT FROM getemp_curs into @empid, @empname, @salary
END
CLOSE getemp_curs
DEALLOCATE getemp_curs
```

Listing 20.7 The goal accomplished from Oracle.

```
DECLARE
     v_empname VARCHAR2(40);
     v_empid    INTEGER;
     v_rate   NUMBER (9,2);
CURSOR c_getemp IS
SELECT empid, empname, rate
```

```
       FROM employees
         WHERE employeetype = "C";
BEGIN
OPEN c_getemp;
LOOP
    FETCH c_getemp INTO v_empid, v_empname, v_rate;
    UPDATE employees
       SET rate = @salary
            WHERE empid = @empid;
    EXIT WHEN c_getemp%NOTFOUND;
END LOOP;
CLOSE c_getemp;
END;
```

Starting with the DECLARE section, all variables defined in Oracle end with the semicolon punctuation (;). In SQL Server, you need to separate all variables declared with a comma (,); otherwise, you have to type DECLARE for each variable. When you DECLARE a cursor in Oracle, the keyword IS follows the cursor; SQL Server uses the keyword FOR. In addition, the location of the keyword CURSOR is switched from Oracle to SQL Server. Another punctuation variance is that Oracle repeatedly needs a semicolon at the end of each ending SQL statement as a delimiter, whereas SQL Server does not require any punctuation as a delimiter. This can be seen in the WHERE clause.

The next variance occurs when testing to see if any more rows can be fetched. Oracle uses %NOTFOUND whereas SQL Server relies on the global variable @@fetch_status for a value of zero if more rows can be fetched. By using this method, the loop required to access all records returned from the cursor is different. With Oracle, a simple LOOP until %NOTFOUND is TRUE suffices. SQL Server uses the WHILE loop to test the value of @@fetch_status = 0. The final variance occurs when a cursor is closed. In Oracle, the CLOSE statement closes the cursor and frees the utilized resources. SQL Server requires the CLOSE statement, and then the DEALLOCATE statement to free the resources used.

While you can update records in both packages, only Oracle allows you to INSERT records into a table from a cursor. You need to create a different method in SQL Server to accomplish this task, such as creating the table desired with the records desired, and using UPDATE to add the values, such as a calculation to the new table.

One last important feature available only in SQL Server: the ability to scroll within a cursor. The commands used to scroll within a cursor are summarized in Table 20.5.

Table 20.5. Statements used to scroll within cursors.

PL/SQL Cursor Statement	Description
NEXT	Retrieves next row.
PRIOR	Retrieves prior row.

continues

20

THE ORACLE TRANSITION

Table 20.5. continued

PL/SQL Cursor Statement	Description
FIRST	Retrieves first row.
LAST	Retrieves last row.
ABSOLUTE	Can access the *n*th record from the first record by specifying the number. For example, an ABSOLUTE 5 would retrieve the fifth record.
RELATIVE	Can access the *n*th record from the current cursor location by specifying the number. For example, a RELATIVE 5 would retrieve the fifth record from the current location of the cursor.

The capability to scroll through cursors provides you unlimited opportunities to test data, arrange data, update data, and so on. You now have full control over the cursor results. As a bonus, you can update the cursor values with the UPDATE statement.

> **TIP**
>
> One advantage of moving through cursors deals with rounding issues. Suppose you had a case where you multiplied a single number by multiple percentages out to 12 decimal places and the total should come back to the single number. If you use the ROUND function, carrying out computations usually results in the number being off several dollars or cents. One great feature with cursors is that you can scroll back to the number with the highest value and add or subtract the difference between the expected number and the current result.

Conditional Branching Variances

The main branching statements used in both packages are the IF statement, its derivatives, and the CASE statement.

The IF Statement

One interesting aspect of SQL Server when testing BOOLEAN conditions such as AND is that if the first expression is FALSE, the second expression is still tested. In most other databases, including Oracle, if the first condition is FALSE, the remaining conditions are not evaluated. The simple IF statement itself has differences. In Oracle, the syntax is as follows:

```
IF <true_condition> THEN
<perform_statements>
END IF;
```

The same syntax in SQL Server is as follows:

```
IF <true_condition>
<perform statements>
```

First, Oracle uses the keyword THEN, whereas SQL Server does not. When listing more than one statement to perform if the condition is TRUE, Oracle can only list the statements, whereas SQL Server requires the keywords BEGIN and END surrounding all statements to perform if the condition is TRUE. Finally, Oracle requires the END IF statement, and a semicolon after each statement. By checking to see if an ID is over 499, the next example demonstrates these differences. The example looks like the following in Oracle:

```
IF v_ID >= 500 THEN
    rate := rate * 1.05;
END IF;
```

The example looks like the following in SQL Server:

```
IF @ID >= 500
    SELECT rate = rate * 1.05
```

The other variances are derivatives of the IF statement. Adding the ELSE keyword in both databases performs the same function if the expression is evaluated FALSE. When nesting IF statements, Oracle requires the keyword ELSIF. With SQL Server you use the ELSE keyword with the IF statement. In Oracle, an example of ELSIF is as follows:

```
IF v_Score >= 90 THEN
    v_LetterGrade := 'A';
ELSIF v_Score >= 80 THEN
    v_LetterGrade := 'B';
ELSIF v_Score >= 70 THEN
    v_LetterGrade := 'C';
ELSIF v_Score >= 60 THEN
    v_LetterGrade := 'D';
ELSE
    v_LetterGrade := 'E';
END IF;
```

In SQL Server, your code would look like the following:

```
IF @Score >= 90
    SELECT @LetterGrade = 'A'
ELSE IF @Score >= 80
    SELECT @LetterGrade = 'B'
ELSE IF @Score >= 70
    SELECT @LetterGrade = 'C'
ELSE IF @Score >= 60
    SELECT @LetterGrade = 'D'
ELSE
    SELECT @LetterGrade = 'E'
```

Again, notice that SQL Server does not require THEN, does not requires punctuation of semicolons, does not require END IF, and uses ELSE IF, not ELSEIF.

20

THE ORACLE
TRANSITION

The CASE Statement

Your applications that used the CASE statement require being changed to IF statements. SQL Server treats CASE as an operator, not a statement, so SQL Server uses CASE primarily when printing options in a SELECT clause. To get a better understanding of the CASE operator, refer to Chapter 13, "Crosstabulation."

> **TIP**
>
> When converting Oracle CASE to SQL Server IF statements, make sure to code BEGIN..END blocks for the series of statements and don't forget to use the RETURN statement to stop SQL Server from evaluating each of the IF statements.

Looping Differences

Oracle provides the statements LOOP, FOR, WHILE, and REPEAT..UNTIL to repeat a series of iterations until the exit condition occurs. In SQL Server you only need to worry about coding the WHILE loop. The syntax for the WHILE loop in Oracle is as follows:

```
WHILE <true> LOOP
     <perform_statements>
END LOOP;
```

The syntax for the WHILE loop in SQL Server is as follows:

```
WHILE <true> BEGIN
     <perform_statements>
END
```

While Oracle provides where the block of statements begins and ends with END IF, END LOOP, and so on, SQL Server uses BEGIN...END to denote the statements to execute within the block. The WHILE loop is flexible enough to handle all your needs in SQL Server. The following examples in Oracle are translated to SQL Server:

The following shows the FOR loop in Oracle incremented by a value of 2:

```
FOR v_loopcounter IN 1..6 LOOP
    IF MOD(v_loopcounter,2)=0 then
         v_test :=  vtest * v_loopcounter;
    END IF;
END LOOP;
```

In SQL Server

```
SELECT @counter = 2
WHILE @counter != 8 BEGIN
        SELECT @test = @test * @counter
        SELECT @counter = @counter + 2
END
```

The WHILE loop in Oracle

```
v_testvalue := 0;
WHILE v_testvalue < 10 LOOP
    v_salary := v_salary * 1.05;
    v_testvalue := v_testvalue + 1;
END LOOP;
```

The same loop in SQL Server

```
SELECT @testvalue = 0;
WHILE @testvalue < 10 BEGIN
    SELECT @salary = @salary * 1.05
    SELECT @testvaue = @testvalue + 1
END
```

As you can see, SQL Server can handle any looping construct needed by the application. BREAK and CONTINUE work the same way in both database packages.

Functions and Aggregates

One noticeable difference between Oracle and SQL Server is that you can't create functions in SQL Server! The good news is that SQL Server has more flexible coding in stored procedures, which can accomplish the same tasks as your function. The bad news is that if you are converting from Oracle to SQL Server, you have to re-code the functions as stored procedures. Another major difference is the handling of date values. SQL Server uses the CONVERT function for displaying date values. Tables 20.6 through 20.11 summarize the Oracle and SQL Server functions and any variances between the two functions.

Table 20.6. Character function equivalents from PL/SQL to T-SQL.

PL/SQL Function	T-SQL Function	Description/Variances
ASCII	ASCII	Returns decimal equivalent.
CHR	CHAR	Returns corresponding character of decimal value.
CONCAT, ¦¦	+ (operator)	Combines string data.
N/A	DIFFERENCE	Shows how close a match is made by comparing SOUNDEX to character string. Anything with a value of 3 or more is most likely the match desired.
INITCAP	N/A	Creates sentence case for entire sentence.
INSTR	PATINDEX	Finds the occurrence of a string within a string.

continues

20

THE ORACLE
TRANSITION

Table 20.6. continued

PL/SQL Function	T-SQL Function	Description/Variances
INSTRB	N/A	Finds the occurrence of a string within a string.
LENGTH	DATALENGTH	Returns length of a string, including any padded spaces if a CHAR value.
LENGTHB	DATALENGTH	Returns length of a string, including any padded spaces if a CHAR value.
LOWER	LOWER	Converts all values to lowercase.
LPAD	N/A	Pads a string of characters on the left side of a string value.
LTRIM	LTRIM	Removes leading blanks.
NLS_INITCAP	N/A	Same as INITCAP according to NLS parameter.
NLS_LOWER	N/A	Same as LOWER according to NLS parameter.
NLS_UPPER	N/A	Same as UPPER according to NLS parameter.
NLSSORT	Can use system stored procedure sp_configure to change sort order.	Changes sort methodology.
REPLACE	N/A	Can replace occurrences of a string with specified string value.
N/A	REPLICATE	Repeats character string *x* number of times.
N/A	REVERSE	Reverses the order of characters in a string.
SUBSTR	RIGHT	Extracts *x* amount of characters from the right of the string.
RPAD	N/A	Pads a string of characters on the right side of a string value.
RTRIM	RTRIM	Removes trailing spaces.
SOUNDEX	SOUNDEX	Returns phonetic representation of character string.
N/A	SPACE	Returns string of spaces specified.
TO_CHAR	STR	Returns character data from numeric data.
SUBSTR	SUBSTRING	Extracts all or part of a string.

PL/SQL Function	T-SQL Function	Description/Variances
SUBSTRB	SUBSTRING	Extracts all or part of a string.
TRANSLATE	STUFF	Similar to search and replace, with replacing part of a string with values in the replace string.
UPPER	UPPER	Changes all values to uppercase.

Most of the functions that do not exist in SQL Server can easily be created by using stored procedures combined with functions. See both Chapters 5, "Effective Use of Built-in Functions," and 8 on implementing some of these missing functions in SQL Server. The math functions are listed in Table 20.7.

Table 20.7. Mathematical function equivalents from PL/SQL to T-SQL.

PL/SQL Function	T-SQL Function	Description/Variances
ABS	ABS	Returns the absolute value of a number.
ACOS	ACOS	Returns the arc cosine in radians.
ASIN	ASIN	Returns the arc sine in radians.
ATAN	ATAN	Returns the arc tangent in radians.
ATAN2	ATN2	Returns the arc tangent of two numbers (y/x).
CEIL	CEILING	Returns the value representing the smallest integer that is greater-than or equal to the input parameter.
COS	COS	Returns the cosine.
COSH	N/A	Returns the hyperbolic cosine.
N/A	COT	Returns the cotangent of an angle in radians.
N/A	DEGREES	Degrees converted from radians of the numeric expression.
EXP	EXP	Returns e raised to the *n*th power.
FLOOR	FLOOR	Returns the value representing the largest integer that is less than or equal to the input parameter.

continues

Table 20.7. continued

PL/SQL Function	T-SQL Function	Description/Variances
LN	LOG	Returns the natural logarithm.
LOG	LOG10	For SQL Server, returns the base-10 logarithm. Oracle accepts an additional parameter, which allows you to compute the logarithm for any base.
MOD	% (operator)	Returns the remainder of one integer divided by another integer.
N/A	PI	Constant value of 3.141592653589793.
POWER	POWER	Returns input value x raised to y power.
N/A	RADIANS	Radians converted from degrees of the numeric expression.
N/A	RAND	Generates a random number.
ROUND	ROUND	Rounds number to x places. If the places to round is specified as a negative, it rounds to the left of the decimal.
SIGN	SIGN	Used to check the sign of a number. Returns 1 if positive, 0 if zero, and -1 if negative.
SIN	SIN	Returns the sine of a number.
SINH	N/A	Returns the hyperbolic sine.
SQRT	SQRT	Returns the square root of a positive value.
TAN	TAN	Returns the tangent of a number.
TANH	N/A	Returns the hyperbolic tangent.
TRUNC	N/A	Truncates to the exact place without rounding. If the value is negative, rounds to the left of the decimal. Refer to Chapter 5 to create a similar function.

With regards to mathematical functions: Even if both packages do not possess the same functions, they can easily be created. Some of the functions that are great in SQL Server include the ability to generate a random number, and the ability to translate from radians to degrees and vice versa. Date functions are next reviewed in Table 20.8.

Table 20.8. Date/Time function equivalents from PL/SQL to T-SQL.

PL/SQL Function	T-SQL Function	Description/Variances
ADD_MONTHS, NEXT_DAY	DATEADD	DATEADD is more flexible than ADD_MONTHS, because you can specify which part of the date to add to, such as year, month, day, hours, and so on.
MONTHS_BETWEEN	DATEDIFF	DATEDIFF can perform the functions of MONTH_BETWEEN, but can also tell you how many days between, years between, and so on, by specifying the datepart.
TO_CHAR	DATENAME	Returns the name of the datepart, such as Monday, January, and so on. TO_DATE offers a full range of flexibility for date output.
N/A	DATEPART	Returns integer to represent part of the date.
SYSDATE	GETDATE	Retrieves system date and time.
LAST_DAY	N/A	Returns last day in a given month.
NEW_TIME	N/A	Displays time in another time zone.
ROUND	N/A	Can round to nearest hour, minute, second, and so on.
TRUNC	N/A	Truncates the date and time.

Oracle clearly has an advantage with date functions; however, all of these functions can be created in PL/SQL within SQL Server. The DATEADD function in SQL Server does offer a major advantage, since it can add any datepart desired, such as day, week, and month. However, this too could be created as a function within Oracle. Other functions with differences are text and image functions, which are listed in Table 20.9.

20

THE ORACLE TRANSITION

Table 20.9. Text/Image function equivalents from PL/SQL to T-SQL.

PL/SQL Function	T-SQL Function	Description/Variances
BFILENAME	N/A	Returns pointer to physical location of binary file
EMPTY_BLOB	N/A	Initializes a BLOB
EMPTY_CLOB	N/A	Initializes a CLOB
N/A	TEXTPTR	Returns pointer to first page of text
N/A	TEXTVALID	Determines if given text pointer is valid
N/A	SET TEXTSIZE	Can limit the maximum size of an image or text object

There are few correlating functions. Oracle handles text and image objects differently than SQL Server. Next, Table 20.10 reflects conversion techniques.

Table 20.10. Conversion function equivalents from PL/SQL to T-SQL.

PL/SQL Function	T-SQL Function	Description/Variances
CHARTOROWID	N/A	Converts CHAR or VARCHAR2 from Oracle external format to its internal binary format.
CONVERT	N/A	Converts from one character set to another.
HEXTORAW	N/A	Converts hex string values.
RAWTOHEX	N/A	Converts internal RAW to hex.
ROWIDTOCHAR	N/A	Converts ROWID to external 18-character string format.
TO_CHAR	CONVERT	Can convert dates, numbers, labels to characters. SQL Server only needs CONVERT.
TO_DATE	CONVERT	Can convert numbers, characters to date. SQL Server uses CONVERT.
TO_LABEL	N/A	Converts CHAR or VARCHAR2 to MLSLABEL.
TO_MULTI_BYTE	N/A	Converts single-byte to multi-byte characters. SQL Server does not offer other character sets.

PL/SQL Function	T-SQL Function	Description/Variances
TO_NUMBER	CONVERT	Can convert characters to numbers. SQL Server uses CONVERT.
TO_SINGLE_BYTE	N/A	Converts multi-byte to single byte. SQL Server does not offer other character sets.

Since SQL Server does not support multiple character sets, most functions in Oracle are not available for SQL Server. This does pose a problem for converting data between legacy IBM systems and SQL Server. The last functions available to SQL*PLUS are the aggregate functions, which are summarized in Table 20.11.

Table 20.11. Aggregate function equivalents from PL/SQL to T-SQL.

PL/SQL Function	T-SQL Function	Description/Variances
AVG	AVG	Calculates the average value of a column
COUNT	COUNT	Counts the number of rows selected in a column
COUNT(*)	COUNT(*)	Counts all rows, even NULL values
GLB	N/A	Greatest Lower Bound
LUB	N/A	Least Upper Bound
MAX	MAX	Finds largest value in a column
MIN	MIN	Finds smallest value in a column
STDDEV	N/A	Finds the standard deviation in a column
SUM	SUM	Adds the values in a column
VARIANCE	N/A	Calculates the variance in a column of all values selected

The manner works identically (except for punctuation of a semicolon at the end of each complete statement in Oracle), except SQL Server provides two additional operators; they provide additional summary results. These two operators are the CUBE and the ROLLUP operators. Both of these operators allow for additional summary information. If you were to GROUP BY on a field in Oracle or SQL Server, you would not receive grand totals (unless you created a variable to track and print the overall grand totals). The CUBE operator performs summary statistics on all items listed in the GROUP BY clause. An example follows.

20

THE ORACLE
TRANSITION

```
SELECT classification.Classification,
    Count(CD.CDID) "Total Offerings"
FROM CD,classification
    WHERE CD.ClassifID = classification.ClassifID
        GROUP BY classification.Classification with CUBE
```

Your output should look like the following:

```
Classification           Total Offerings
-----------------------  ---------------
Alternative              3
Country & Western        2
Heavy Metal              7
Pop Rock                 19
(null)                   31

(5 row(s) affected)
```

As you can see, the last row specified by NULL has an overall summary. For more information on the CUBE and ROLLUP operators, refer to Chapter 2, "Using Advanced Data Manipulation Language."

Stored Procedures

Stored procedures allow for the most flexibility in any SQL environment. Again, there are many differences, mostly syntactical, between the two database packages. As far as added features go, SQL Server is definitely better than Oracle. In addition, SQL Server already has several built-in system stored procedures to access every system element with ease. The syntax for creating a procedure in SQL Server is as follows:

```
CREATE PROC[edure] [owner.]procedure_name
  [parameter1,parameter255]
{FOR REPLICATION} ¦ {WITH RECOMPILE}
      [{[WITH] ¦ [,]} ENCRYPTION]]
AS sql_statements
```

The syntax for creating a stored procedure in Oracle is as follows:

```
CREATE {OR REPLACE} PROCEDURE procedure_name
    [(parameters {IN¦OUT¦INOUT}]type,)]
    {IS ¦ AS} sql_statements
```

One item missing from SQL Server is the capability to overwrite a stored procedure. You can no longer use the optional OR REPLACE. You must DROP the procedure before you can create the procedure, if it exists. Syntactically, PROCEDURE can be shortened to PROC, IS, or AS, which are treated the same in Oracle; they must be specified in SQL Server using AS, and the parameter specifications for input and output are different. With Oracle, you have IN, OUT, and INOUT parameters, with the default parameter IN if nothing is specified. With SQL Server you list all input parameters, but must specify OUTPUT for any output parameters. One additional feature offered within SQL Server is the capability to encrypt the stored procedure with the ENCRYPTION keyword. Listing 20.8 shows an example using Oracle for replacing a stored procedure, and Listing 20.9 shows the same process using DROP in SQL Server.

Listing 20.8. Replacing a stored procedure in Oracle.

```
CREATE or REPLACE PROCEDURE pr_copyuser (
     p_UID varchar2(30) )
AS
BEGIN
INSERT INTO oldusers
     SELECT *
          FROM myusers
          WHERE UserID = p_UID;
DELETE myusers -- Remove user from myusers table
     WHERE UserID = p_UID;
END;
```

Listing 20.9. Using DROP to overwrite the procedure in SQL Server.

```
DROP PROC pr_copyuser
     GO
CREATE PROC pr_copyuser (@UID varchar(30) )
AS
INSERT INTO oldusers -- Database archiving the data
     SELECT *
          FROM myusers
          WHERE UserID = @UID
DELETE myusers -- Remove user from myusers table
     WHERE UserID = @UID
```

In addition to the syntactical differences, Oracle requires that the statements be surrounded by the keywords BEGIN..END.

To execute the stored procedure within a stored procedure, SQL Server requires the EXEC[UTE] statement; in Oracle this is optional. In addition, when executing stored procedures in Oracle, you need parentheses around the parameters. Do not use parentheses in SQL Server; instead, separate each parameter with a space delimiter. One of the nicest features SQL Server has over Oracle is several built-in system stored procedures. For more information on stored procedures, consult Chapter 6, "Effective Use of Stored Procedures as an Administrative Tool" and Appendix C, "System Stored and Extended Stored Procedures Quick Reference."

20

THE ORACLE TRANSITION

Converting an Oracle Database into a SQL Server Database

Besides total development in Oracle, you may need to convert a database from Oracle to SQL Server. Some guidelines are listed here:

- Export all tables in Oracle in a comma-separated value (CSV) format. Make sure no LOBs are used; they are incompatible with SQL Server.

- Create the tables in SQL Server, making sure all datatypes agree with the data in the CSV file. Your best bet is to copy and paste the CREATE TABLES statements from Oracle into SQL Server and make any necessary changes.

- Use the BCP program to import the data into the tables.

- No matter which word processor you are using, create macros to convert the differences with functions, operators, and syntax differences using search and replace methods. Save these files, and then copy and paste into SQL Server and save.

- Attempt to run the SQL blocks, making any necessary corrections.

- Back up your work when completed!

Summary

This chapter demonstrates several differences between SQL Server and Oracle in an attempt to make the transition easier. As with migrating from any similar package, most of the differences were in naming conventions, punctuation, or placement of parameters. You see differences in datatypes, variables, operators, creating tables and indexes, cursors, conditional branching, looping, functions and aggregates, stored procedures, and some basic steps to convert an Oracle database to SQL Server. While SQL Server does offer some benefits, one flaw holding this database package back from being a true leader is the capability to work with different character sets, especially when trying to integrate into a mixed computing environment.

Making the Switch
from Sybase SQL
Server

CHAPTER 21

Why Sybase SQL Server and MS SQL Server Are So Similar

Long ago, before they started competing against each other in the relational database world, Sybase and Microsoft were partners.

In the second half of the 1980s, Sybase teamed with Microsoft to develop and promote SQL Server for the Intel processor, initially for OS/2 and Novell. Microsoft eventually ported SQL Server to Windows NT as well. Around version 4.2 of both Sybase's and Microsoft's SQL Servers, they agreed to disagree, and both sides took the SQL Server code base and went their separate ways. Sybase released System 10, System 11, and Sybase Adaptive Server version 11.5. Microsoft released v6.0, v6.5, and plans to release v7.0 sometime in 1998. As the two companies have traveled different paths, their SQL Server products have become more dissimilar. This trend will continue as newer versions are released.

Sybase has taken a more architectural and administrative focus with their product, targeting larger companies with larger databases. They've added features like named caches, which allows tables and databases to be bound to their own memory space, and table partitioning, which allows a table to maintain separate page chains to distribute inserts and support parallel query operations. Sybase has worked to improve performance of maintenance activities like DBCC. These are useful features for database administrators who want to solve particular performance problems, but most users couldn't care less.

Microsoft, since v6.0, has focused on workgroup-sized databases. This isn't to say that MS SQL Server can't handle very large databases—it can. Still, most of the enhancements to MS SQL Server make it easier to use for end users, programmers, and especially those who are administering SQL Server for the first time.

In particular, MS SQL Server provides a suite of Windows-based management tools for administering their database. The Enterprise Manager hides a great deal of the complexity of managing a complex RDBMS, and provides a familiar, Microsoft-style GUI interface for the administrator's daily chores. It also includes a scheduler for SQL backups, SQL, or any other task.

These tools were lacking in Sybase's early offerings. The company is working to provide them (a product called Sybase Central is in development), but Microsoft has had them in place since 6.0.

Administration of Sybase versus Microsoft

Because the two servers started from a common source, they retain a common history that carries over into their everyday administration tasks. Each database ships with a set of common system stored procedures that assist in the management of the database. Some of the underlying code of these procedures has changed, but their functions remain the same. This is to retain compatibility with older versions and ease the learning curve of people stepping up to newer versions. Most importantly for the conversion effort, the procedures' names and parameters have remained the same.

If you have a database creation script that creates some tables, adds some rules and defaults and binds them to the tables, inserts some static data, and builds indexes, the Sybase script will run without any modifications on MS SQL Server.

For administration procedures, a Sybase SQL script that updates the statistics of all of your indexes and runs some DBCC check commands every Sunday night will port effortlessly.

In most cases, it's really easy to make the transition from Sybase to Microsoft. There are some exceptions, though. To take advantage of some of the better performance features of Microsoft, you will want to tweak some of your code. There are a few differences between the two database systems that are not compatible. These include changes to Transact SQL (T-SQL) and modifications to the programming libraries.

SYSTEM STORED PROCEDURE STORAGE LOCATION

One important difference between Sybase and MS SQL Servers is the location of system stored procedures. As of System 10, Sybase maintains these procedures in a separate database, sybsystemprocs. Microsoft keeps them in the master database. If you have a lot of these, you will need to increase the size of master to accommodate them.

The best way to transfer them to Microsoft is to create them, with a database creation script, in the master database. They will continue to be available in all database contexts, just as they were in Sybase.

Converting Sybase T-SQL to MS T-SQL

Ever since the split, Microsoft has added and implemented more neat stuff to their version of SQL. They've implemented parts of the ANSI SQL-92 standard that Sybase hasn't. The good news is that almost every query that runs on Sybase will run *with no changes* on MS SQL Server.

Both Sybase and Microsoft use a dialect of SQL called T-SQL. T-SQL builds on the ANSI SQL syntax, implementing standard commands like SELECT, INSERT, and DELETE, and adding things not specified in ANSI SQL, like CREATE INDEX and EXECUTE (for stored procedures, an extension in themselves). T-SQL also adds some enhancements to the standard commands, like optimizer hints on SELECT (see the tip following this paragraph) and allowing joins in UPDATE and DELETE statements. The good news is that these extensions to SQL are the same on both Sybase and Microsoft. Database objects, including views, defaults, constraints, rules, user-defined datatypes, triggers, and even stored procedures will compile and run on Microsoft without any changes to the SQL code.

OPTIMIZER HINTS

Both Sybase and Microsoft employ a pessimistic query optimizer that decides the most efficient way to access requested data each time you issue a query. Sometimes the optimizer makes a bad choice, usually because it doesn't know something (such as the number of rows in a table, if statistics are out of data, or if the size of variable length rows tends to be much smaller or larger than it expects).

An optimizer hint is a way to ask the server to access data in a specific way, without optimizing the query. The formats are slightly different between the two databases. Sybase requires the words INDEX <Indexname>. Microsoft requires an equal sign:

```
select *
from HugeTable (index=CLHugeTable)
where id between 5 and 14023
```

While it would be a major undertaking to present all the T-SQL differences between Sybase and MS SQL Server, here are some of them:

- Chained Mode
- Slightly different cursor syntax
- Different PRINT syntax
- Different raiserror syntax
- No flushmessage connection option in Microsoft
- No rollback trigger command in Microsoft
- Additional reserved keywords in Microsoft
- No administration roles in Microsoft
- Temp tables max name length is 20 characters in Microsoft (Sybase's is 30)
- Differences in identity columns
- Optimizer hints are different

Things Microsoft Does Better

You will see performance differences between the two servers. In most cases, you will be pleasantly surprised by Microsoft's better performance. This is a partial list:

- Microsoft can walk an index backwards to support a query using ORDER BY DESC, while Sybase cannot. Sybase, in versions 11.0.x and earlier, uses temporary work tables to re-sort the data in the requested order, which introduces more overhead. Version 11.5 can perform reverse index scans.

■ Microsoft has enhanced cursor functionality. I recommend against using cursors whenever possible, but there are times when cursors are either unavoidable or make a complex process less so. This added functionality comes at a price—scrollable cursors will perform generally worse than their nonscrollable, Sybase counterparts. Look for performance differences in your code between Sybase and MS. The jury is still out on whose cursors perform better under the same circumstances. Keep in mind that cursors still offer generally worse performance than set-based SQL statements on either Sybase or MS SQL Server.

■ The CASE expression, part of the ANSI SQL-92 standard, was implemented by Microsoft, but not by Sybase until their 11.5 release. CASE won't give you immediate performance improvements; you must use it in your SQL code. It does allow some problems to be solved more efficiently. CASE makes crosstab reports very easy, and allows you to generate crosstabs with a single table scan.

Just as there are performance gains, you will find performance reductions. Once the conversion is done and you have had a chance to catch your breath, you should keep an eye out for poorly performing queries. Users are great at bringing these to your attention—if their report runtime goes from five seconds to five minutes, you'll hear about it.

Things Sybase Does Better

One thing that Sybase does better has to do with the allocation of new pages in an extent. Sybase uses OAM (object allocation map) pages to keep track of which pages are used and which are free. When the database is relatively small (under a gigabyte) this isn't such a big deal. As the page chains grow very large, though, the delay can be noticeable. You'll see this most often during large insert operations. A large, daily bcp in is an example of this. BCPs require the rapid allocation of new pages as they blast in large volumes of new data.

The Query Optimizer

The query optimizer is the part of the server that developers at both companies have spent the majority of their time improving. This has caused performance differences to pop up in places that are difficult to predict. Due to differences in the query optimizers and how some queries are recognized and processed, and also due to some of the architectural differences between the two systems (Sybase uses a prefetch cache, Microsoft uses a similar, but technically different read ahead cache, named caches in Sybase, LRU/MRU strategies, and so on), you may be unpleasantly surprised to find that a procedure that used to run in half a minute now takes half an hour. It could just as easily come out the other way around.

Some basic performance and tuning steps can smooth out these little bumps. Some more good news is that all the tricks and tips you learned for Sybase apply to Microsoft SQL Server. SET SHOWPLAN ON is still a wonderful way to get a glimpse of the optimizer choices, and for the DBAs who know what I'm talking about, DBCC TRACEON(3604, 302, 310) remains the query troubleshooter's best friend.

Chained Mode

In chained mode, the `begin transaction` command is implicitly issued whenever an `INSERT`, `UPDATE`, `DELETE`, `FETCH`, or `SELECT` statement is executed, but commits must be issued explicitly. Listing 21.1 is an example of chained mode SQL.

Listing 21.1. Sample chained mode SQL.

```
SET CHAINED ON
GO
INSERT Names(7, "John", "W", "Smith")
INSERT Invoices(7, getdate(), $750)
COMMIT TRAN
```

The first line turns on chained mode behavior. In this example, two inserts are performed before I issue a `COMMIT`. There is no matching `BEGIN TRANSACTION` command. Chained mode begins transactions automatically when an `INSERT`, `UPDATE`, `DELETE`, `FETCH`, or `SELECT` statement is executed.

If you use chained mode in your SQL queries, or your stored procedures use it, you have two options. The most painless is to use the Microsoft `SET IMPLICIT_TRANSACTIONS ON` statement. New to 6.5, this corresponds to the Sybase chained mode. Your other option is to convert your old queries. This is a pretty painless process: simply insert `begin tran` wherever chained mode would have begun an implicit transaction for you.

Cursor Syntax

Cursors in Microsoft have enhanced features. Sybase cursors can travel in only one direction: forward. Microsoft cursors can be defined as either forward-only cursors or scrollable cursors. Using scrollable cursors may enhance a Sybase process that requires multiple cursors, or requires opening and closing a single cursor many times.

> **TIP**
>
> Cursors introduce overhead into a process. This is especially true for very small queries, because cursors require their own memory allocations and memory spaces on the server to prepare them to run. Try to use set-based SQL whenever possible. Scrollable cursors introduce even more overhead. Resist the temptation to solve a problem with cursors, and the database engine will reward you.

The differences in cursor syntax between Sybase and Microsoft are trivial enough that you needn't lose sleep over them, but important enough that you will need to recode any queries or procedures that use them before they will work. There are four cursor differences you need to know when moving from Sybase to Microsoft:

■ Inside the cursor loop, a global variable is checked to determine the status of the last cursor fetch. The name of this variable is `@@sqlstatus` in Sybase, and `@@fetchstatus` in Microsoft.

■ Return codes for the fetch status are positive in Sybase, and negative in Microsoft.

■ To deallocate a cursor in Sybase, you say `deallocate cursor <cursorname>`. In Microsoft, you say `deallocate <cursorname>`.

■ Unless the cursor is in a stored procedure, Sybase requires you to declare the cursor in its own batch before it can be opened. Microsoft allows the cursor to be used in the same batch in which it is declared.

Listing 21.2 is a simple cursor example in Sybase, and Listing 21.3 is the same example in Microsoft. The cursor reads rows from the titles table. If the title is a business book, the price is inflated by 25 percent. If there is no defined price for the book, a special "No Pricing" message is printed. Also notice that I use the `print` statement to return data, instead of `SELECT`, and a `raiserror` command to show differences between the two database systems:

Listing 21.2. A simple Sybase cursor.

```
SET NOCOUNT ON
GO
declare title_curs cursor
for
select    title, type, price
from      titles
order by type, title
for read only
go

open title_curs
declare @type char(12), @price money, @title char(22),
print "Title                     Price"
print "---------------------    ---------"
fetch title_curs into @title, @type, @price
while @@sqlstatus = 0 begin
   if @type = 'business'
       select @price = @price * 1.25
   if @price is null
       print "%1! --No pricing--", @title else
       print "%1! %2!", @title, @price
fetch titles_curs into @title, @type, @price
end

if @@sqlstatus = 1
       raiserror 50000, "An error occurred during the cursor fetch."
close title_curs
deallocate cursor title_curs
```

Listing 21.3 is the Microsoft cursor. Note the preponderance of minor differences between the two:

Listing 21.3. A simple Microsoft cursor.

```
set nocount on

declare title_curs cursor
for
select    title, type, price
from      titles
order by type, title
for read only
go

open title_curs
declare @type char(12), @price money, @title varchar(80),
        @tempstr varchar(40)
print "Title                    Price"
print "---------------------  ---------"
fetch next from title_curs into @title, @type, @price
while @@fetch_status = 0 begin
   if @type = 'business'
       select @price = @price * 1.25
   if @price is null
       select @tempstr = convert(char(22), @title) + "  --No pricing--"
   else
       select @tempstr = convert(char(22), @title) + convert(char(7), @price)
   print @tempstr
   fetch next from title_curs into @title, @type, @price
end

if @@fetch_status = -2
       raiserror ("An error occurred during the cursor fetch.", 16, -1) with log

close title_curs
deallocate title_curs
```

There are five coding differences between the two examples above.

First, Sybase requires the cursor declaration to occur in its own batch. I've indicated that with the directive GO, for use in ISQL. It doesn't hurt to have them in separate batches in Microsoft so the transition won't be affected by multiple batches.

The name of the global variable is `@@sqlstatus` in Sybase, and `@@fetch_status` in Microsoft. These changes will be easy to make, and any that you miss will be easy to find: you'll simply get a 137 error, `Must declare variable @@sqlstatus`.

The `raiserror` command in Sybase allows a user-defined error number to be passed. Microsoft always returns error number `50000` from a `raiserror` with a static string. To pass a different error, it should be defined with `sp_addmessage`. `sp_addmessage` is available in both Sybase and Microsoft, and is used to add custom error messages to the server.

The following are some important points worth noting about errors and how Microsoft SQL Server implementation differs from Sybase:

- User-defined error numbers: Both Sybase and Microsoft allow user-defined error messages to be added. Sybase allows these values to be higher than `20000`. Microsoft requires they be at least `50000`. If you have user-defined errors under `50000`, you will need to redo them.

- Alternate syntax for `raiserror`: Microsoft also allows an alternate syntax for `raiserror` (for backward-compatibility) that does not use commas. This allows you to raise an error number of your choice, with a custom error string. For example:

```
RAISERROR 56000 "This is a sample error."
```

- Tracking errors: Sybase tracks custom error messages by database. Each database has a system table, `sysusermessages`, containing all user-defined messages. Microsoft tracks these in a single table in the `master` database. Both user-defined and system messages reside in `sysmessages` in Microsoft. If you have databases that use the same error numbers but different messages, you will have to find a way to agree on who gets to use the error number.

Furthermore, the return codes differ. The return codes for cursor fetches are `0`, `1`, or `2` for Sybase, and `0`, `-1`, or `-2` for Microsoft. Table 21.1 summarizes the return values. Note that the other company's return values cannot be had simply by multiplying by –1; an error is indicated by 1 in Sybase, but –2 in Microsoft.

Table 21.1. Cursor return values in Sybase and Microsoft.

Sybase Value	MS Value	Description
0	0	Successful fetch
1	-2	Error during fetch
2	-1	No more rows available in the cursor keyset

flushmessage

Often used in debugging Sybase procedures, the `flushmessage` option is a connection-level setting that tells the server to send back results whenever a `print` or `raiserror` is encountered. Usually, the server waits until a network packet is completely full or the batch is complete.

Microsoft does not have an equivalent to the `flushmessage` option. Fortunately, there are other ways to debug T-SQL, some of them much more user-friendly. Refer to Chapter 15, "Taking Advantage of the Tools," where the T-SQL debugger is covered.

rollback trigger

Sybase implemented a `rollback trigger` command in System 10 to undo the work done inside a trigger, and the statement that fired the trigger, without rolling back the entire transaction that the statement happened to be inside. Microsoft does not have a `rollback trigger` command. Fixing this will require some work.

Listing 21.4 is a piece of Sybase code that demonstrates `rollback trigger`.

Listing 21.4. rollback trigger example.

```
create trigger trSalesTrig on Sales for update
as

if datepart(dd, getdate()) not in (1, 15)
  rollback trigger with raiserror 50000
  "Sales must be updated on the 1st or 15th of the month."

return
go

begin tran
insert Sales values(20665, $350, "1/12/1998")
update Sales set Amount = $650 where SalesID = 12477
insert Sales values(20667, $25, "1/12/1998")
commit tran
```

The trigger code assumes that an update can fail without invalidating the inserts. If this piece of code were run on the third of the month, the update would be rolled back. However, the two inserts would still be made, and the transaction could still commit successfully.

To convert this example to Microsoft, you have two choices. First, the `rollback trigger` could be replaced with a `rollback transaction`, and each statement in the calling batch could be placed in its own transaction. This is the easiest way, but does not maintain exactly the same functionality as the Sybase code. Listing 21.5 shows this new trigger.

Listing 21.5. Updated trigger and calling batch in Microsoft.

```
create trigger trSalesTrig on Sales for update
as

if datepart(dd, getdate()) not in (1, 15)
begin
    rollback
    raiserror 50000 "Sales must be updated on the 1st or 15th of the month."
end
return
go

-- begin tran REMOVED... each statement in its own transaction
insert Sales values(20665, $350, "1/12/1998")
update Sales set Amount = $650 where SalesID = 12477
insert Sales values(20667, $25, "1/12/1998")
```

This allows the two inserts to succeed and the update to fail, which is exactly what would have happened in Sybase. However, if the third insert failed (due to deadlock, for example), you would not be able to roll back the first insert and the update together.

A more painful option is to recode all of your triggers to simulate the behavior of rollback trigger. Listing 21.6 demonstrates the trigger enhancements.

Listing 21.6. Simulating `rollback trigger` in MS SQL Server.

```
create trigger trSalesTrig on Sales for update
as

/* set a savepoint to rollback only the trigger actions */
save tran tr1

/* Check date */
if datepart(dd, getdate()) not in (1, 15) begin
    rollback tran tr1
    raiserror 50000 "Sales must be updated on the 1st or 15th of the month."
end
return
go

/* Calling batch looks substantially more complex! */
begin tran
insert Sales values(20665, $350, "1/12/1998")

/* set a savepoint for this insert statement */
save tran save1
update Sales set Amount = $650 where SalesID = 12477
if @@error = 50000 --Trigger found a problem and raised an error
    rollback tran save1

insert Sales values(20667, $25, "1/12/1998")

commit tran
```

In this code, we're only worried about what happens to the update statement: if you had insert triggers, you would need to surround each statement in the original transaction with save tran <label> and check for a raised trigger error.

If you have used rollback trigger extensively, consider whether modification statements that fire triggers should be included inside a transaction. If they are, do the conditions that indicate failure inside the trigger invalidate just the results of a single modification, or the results of everything inside the transaction?

Other Transaction Processing Differences Inside Triggers

In addition to rollback trigger, transaction processing with rollback transaction in triggers is different between Sybase and MS SQL Server. In MS, a rollback transaction in a trigger rolls back to the outermost begin transaction, but batch processing continues—no abort or error message. In Sybase, the batch is aborted. This could lead to a significant difference in how transactions are processed when migrating from Sybase to MS SQL Server, and will require recoding of the applications to avoid transactional integrity problems.

Consider the code for Sybase in Listing 21.7.

Listing 21.7. Transactions in a trigger.

```
create table t1 (a int, b int)
go
create trigger tr1 on t1 for insert
as
if exists (select * from inserted where a = 100)
begin
  rollback tran
raiserror 50000 "Danger Will Robinson"
end
return
go

begin tran
insert t1 values (10, 10)
insert t1 values (10, 20)
insert t1 values (100, 30)
insert t1 values (10, 40)
go
select * from t1
```

When run in Sybase, the batch is aborted when the `rollback tran` is caused by the third `insert` statement. The fourth statement is skipped. The end result: no rows are inserted into table t1.

This same code, when executed in MS SQL Server, will continue processing after the `rollback tran` is encountered. The end result: one row, the fourth, gets inserted into the table. To avoid the fourth `insert` being executed (and transactional integrity being lost), you need to add error-checking after each `insert` statement that would have aborted the batch in the event of an error. This error-checking would already be there in a perfectly designed SQL app, but we all tend to take shortcuts when we know how the DBMS behaves. Listing 21.8 shows how to preserve transactional integrity in MS SQL Server.

Listing 21.8. Maintaining transaction integrity in a Microsoft trigger.

```
create table t1 (a int, b int)
go
create trigger tr1 on t1 for insert
as
if exists (select * from inserted where a = 100)
begin
  rollback tran
  raiserror 50000 "Danger Will Robinson"
end
```

```
return
go

begin tran
insert t1 values (10, 10)
if @@trancount = 0 /* if @@trancount is 0, then the transaction has been aborted */
   goto abortbatch
insert t1 values (10, 20)
if @@trancount = 0 goto abortbatch
insert t1 values (100, 30)
if @@trancount = 0 goto abortbatch
insert t1 values (10, 40)

abortbatch:
/*
  The abortbatch label is necessary here, because MS does not allow the RETURN
  statement to run outside stored procedures. We'd use RETURN instead of GOTO
  if this were in a stored proc.
*/

go
select * from t1
```

NOTE

Although @@error could be used to test the error level, I've found that @@trancount is safer to use when checking after a trigger. Depending on how the trigger is written, if any other commands are executed in the trigger after the raiserror statement, the error number will be lost.

Optimizer Hints Are Different

Optimizer hints are dangerous tools, a lot like circular saws. A circular saw is a great thing to have around when you're undertaking a major project. A master craftsman or even a reasonably skilled handyman can get more done with it in a shorter time than if he had to ask the lumberyard to cut everything for him. The neophyte, on the other hand, may get good results from his new toy, but is just as likely to lop off some fingers.

If you've used optimizer hints in Sybase, my first recommendation is to remove them entirely when you move to Microsoft. See if the MS query optimizer makes the same mistakes that you needed to fix in Sybase. Because the two optimizers started from the same seed, the MS optimizer is just as likely to guess wrong in similar circumstances as it is to surprise you and pick the most efficient query plan. If it does guess wrong, familiarize yourself with the new MS optimizer hints.

The optimizer hints relating to the Sybase MRU/LRU cache and prefetch strategies are not available in Microsoft. The index hints remain the same except for a slight syntax difference, however, as shown in Listing 21.9.

Listing 21.9. Index hints in Sybase and MS.

```
/* Sybase hint */
select  salesmanID, sum(sales)
from    HugeTable (index CLHugeTable)
group by salesmanID

/* MS hint */
select  salesmanID, sum(sales)
from    HugeTable (index=CLHugeTable)
group by salesmanID
```

Converting CT-Library Applications

CT-Library is a Sybase-specific API. There is no easy way to port your existing CT-Lib applications to Microsoft. It's not the end of the world, though. Sybase provides a guide for porting DB-Library applications to CT-Library. This guide was intended for one-way travel, but can be used to go backwards as well. Major applications will have a tough time doing this, but smaller apps should port with relative ease back to DB-Library.

Most of the commands in CT-Library have DB-Library equivalents. Whereas ct_open() is called to open a connection, DB-Library uses dbopen(). If you undertake a conversion effort for a CT-Library application, be prepared to completely rewrite sections of your code. The strategies used in a CT-Lib program may not be appropriate for a DB-Lib program.

CONNECTING TO MS SQL SERVER WITH EXISTING CT-LIB APPS

Sybase's objective with CT-Library was to develop a less product-specific API for their database system. Their vision was that developers all over the world would use CT-Lib apps to connect to any number of different databases. Sound familiar? It should: Microsoft had the same vision for ODBC.

I have received unconfirmed reports from colleagues that existing CT-Lib apps can connect to and run against MS SQL Server. I haven't been able to make that work, but you're welcome to give it a try. The CT-Lib layer should convert calls to the TDS layer, which may or may not be the same between Sybase and MS versions. The TDS layer is a proprietary protocol that may change as time goes on. Because the companies have never released a TDS spec, they're free to change the protocol without warning.

Your best bet for continued reliability in CT-Lib apps is to convert them to a supported MS API.

Converting ODBC Applications

ODBC applications should port effortlessly. ODBC was intended to make the database back end transparent. A developer can write a software product that makes calls to the ODBC layer, and then depend on the strength of the ODBC driver to translate between the application and the database.

Are ODBC Apps Slower Than DB-Lib Apps?

The quick answer is, "In Sybase, yes. In Microsoft, no."

In Sybase, ODBC applications perform worse than the same applications that write directly to the DB-Lib or CT-Lib layer. This is because Sybase's ODBC driver translates all ODBC calls to one of those libraries. For System 10 and later ODBC drivers, the ODBC calls are translated to CT-Library. Previous driver versions translated the calls to DB-Library. Figure 21.1 shows the path a call must take to get to Sybase SQL Server.

FIGURE 21.1.

ODBC calls must pass through the DB-Lib or CT-Lib layer in Sybase apps.

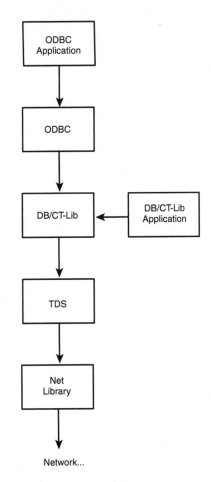

In Sybase, ODBC is nothing more than an intermediate layer. Applications that make direct CT-Lib calls will always be more efficient, because they're taking one less step. They will be quicker and will have a smaller footprint.

In both Sybase and Microsoft, the DB-Lib (and CT-Lib) API translates the database call into the Tabular Data Stream, or TDS. The TDS is a proprietary protocol ensuring that all interaction with SQL Server, from whatever type of hardware and whatever API, looks the same once it gets to the server. To get to the server over various network types (TCP/IP, NETBEUI, Appletalk, and so on), these TDS packets must be wrapped in the transport layer's packets. This is where the network library comes in.

Now that you understand all the layers involved, you can see why ODBC is no slower on Microsoft. The MS ODBC driver for SQL Server does not translate database calls into DB-Lib; it writes directly to the TDS layer. An ODBC call is as efficient as a DB-Lib call, because calls are traveling through the same number of layers no matter which API you use.

FIGURE 21.2.

ODBC calls in MS SQL Server take the same number of steps as DB-Lib calls.

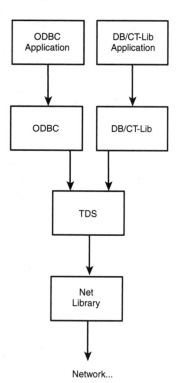

Switching ODBC Drivers

You do not need to make any changes to an ODBC project to connect to MS SQL Server. However, you must replace the current Sybase SQL Server ODBC driver on each client machine with an MS SQL Server ODBC driver. This change is made using the Control Panel on each client machine. For 32-bit apps, use the ODBC32 icon. For 16-bit apps, use the ODBC icon.

The next time your program runs, use the new ODBC data source to connect to MS SQL Server.

ODBC DRIVER DIFFERENCES

The ODBC specification has undergone a number of changes since its inception. Driver manufacturers are required to write their drivers to specifically defined compliance levels. When those compliance levels are different between drivers (usually due to age, as later compliance levels might not have existed when the driver was released), you may encounter some minor differences.

This may manifest in specific ODBC calls that contained previously optional arguments, which a later compliance level defined as required. The newer driver then insists on a parameter being passed, and since the app doesn't, an error occurs.

These changes should be relatively easy to overcome, but will require code changes and recompilations.

Converting DB-Library Applications

A few years ago, it was possible to write a DB-Lib application that could connect to either type of server. All you needed to do was make the right DB-Lib DLL available and you were in business. No recompilation was necessary.

This isn't possible any longer. Part of the reason is that each company has made changes to DB-Lib. It is still open to debate whether these changes were for technical reasons or marketing reasons. Microsoft renamed the DB-Lib DLL from W3DBLIB.DLL to MSDBLIB3.DLL. The old DLL is still available as a stub, which simply passes any calls it receives directly to the new library. In the few cases where function parameters have changed, this stub makes the proper substitution.

Sybase translates DB-Lib calls to CT-Library before passing the call on to SQL Server. It uses a similar stub strategy, but the Sybase W3DBLIB.DLL actually translates each call to CT-Lib before passing it on.

To convert a DB-Lib application today, you will need to recompile the application.

Migrating 16-Bit to 32-Bit

The 32-bit DB-Library has a number of differences from the 16-bit DB-Library. The most important of these is its asynchronous communications model. A 16-bit program operated as a single thread. If your program called `dbsqlexec()`, Windows appeared to hang until the function returned.

To avoid this, developers used asynchronous communication in their DB-Lib programs. A query was sent to the server (using `dbsend()`), and the connection was checked from time to time (with `dbdataready()`) for results. In 32-bit DB-Lib programs, it is common to implement routines where each call to `dbsqlexec()` spawns a new thread. This allows the thread to wait patiently for `sqlexec`, a synchronous function, to return results without hanging either the application or the operating system.

If you are converting from 16-bit to 32-bit, consider removing asynchronous communications from your app. This will result in more efficient processing. To do this, you must spawn a thread (or maintain a pool of threads) for each call to `dbsqlexec()`.

Converting a C Application

The DB-Lib API itself has changed very little between Sybase and Microsoft. This code works exactly the same on either Sybase or MS SQL Server.

An important change that must be made when converting from Sybase to MS involves the header files. Sybase calls its header files `SYBFRONT.H` and `SYBDB.H`. Microsoft header files are `SQLFRONT.H` and `SQLDB.H`. The header files perform the same functions: defining macros, datatypes, and structures.

Converting a VB Application

Sybase VB programs usually implement DB-Library by using a VB control, such as Embarcadero's SQL-Sombrero product or Sybase's older VBSQL control.

To convert these projects, you must provide a new reference to Microsoft's VBSQL object library. The VBSQL object library is available in the Microsoft SQL Server Developer's Kit. In VB, go to Tools|References and check the VBSQL object library.

Once the library is referenced, the DB-Library function calls must be changed to conform to the new object library. Going from Sybase VBSQL to Microsoft VBSQL is pretty straightforward. Functions are named the same in both libraries—`SqlSend()` is still `SqlSend()`, and `SqlOpen()` is still `SqlOpen()`.

If you are migrating from a third-party vendor, their tools' functions will have different names. You will need to change the names, although the parameters will be nearly identical. This is because third-party tools for VB are just thin layers that map a VB function to a C function. DB-Library is really a C call level API, a collection of C functions that implements communication with SQL Server.

Summary

Moving from Sybase to MS SQL Server is a lot easier than this chapter makes it seem. In most situations, you can convert to MS SQL Server in a few days, and with a minimum amount of downtime.

There's a saying in our industry about conversion efforts: you spend 90% of your time on 10% of the conversion. I've tried to give you the 10% you're most likely to battle.

IV

PART

Programming Internal and External Connections

Using the
DBLibrary

CHAPTER

22

IN THIS CHAPTER

This chapter demonstrates the use of DBLibrary in two development environments, Visual Basic and C/C++. Using Visual Basic, you will create a simple query application with DBLibrary. Specifically, you use the Visual Basic VBSQL control. Many of the concepts presented are applicable to C/C++ programming as well; the only difference is the syntax used for each DBLibrary function call, and a few functions that aren't supported in Visual Basic.

This is followed up with some C/C++ code samples. These applications demonstrate some of the features that are not supported in Visual Basic, specifically, advanced Bulk Copy functions.

DBLibrary Architecture

If you have been a developer in the computer industry for any length of time, you realize that computer science seems to be able to solve any problem by adding another level of abstraction. Data access methods such as DAO, RDO, ODBC, and ADO are just that, abstractions of lower-level protocols, or programming APIs.

DBLibrary is, arguably, the native client API to SQL Server. If you wanted to be technical, you could say that TDS over IPC is the native method in which to talk to SQL Server. Unless you are the type of developer who enjoys assembly-language programming, delving any deeper than DBLibrary isn't suggested.

Learning DBLibrary before jumping into ODBC or RDO is akin to writing a Windows application with the Win32 SDK before writing an application in Visual Basic. It never hurts to know the underlying plumbing of the environment in which you are working.

> **NOTE**
>
> For those that are really curious about what is being sent back and forth between the client and the server, it is known as *Tabular Data Stream (TDS)*. The TDS uses tokens that describe column names, datatypes, events, and return statuses. Only the DBLibrary and ODBC interfaces write directly to the TDS. These APIs wrap the TDS complexities, relieving application developers of the need to understand the details behind TDS.

DBLibrary enables tight integration between an application and SQL Server. Transact-SQL statements can be placed, programmatically, right in your application. In addition, values from the database can be bound to program variables for manipulation by the application.

One advantage DBLibrary has over other Data Access APIs (like ODBC or RDO) is its support for various operating systems. DBLibrary runs on top of Net-Library, which is implemented as a terminate-stay-resident (TSR) driver in the MS-DOS operating system. With 16-bit Windows, Windows 95, Windows NT, and OS/2, the Net-Libraries are implemented as dynamic-link libraries (DLLs). The Net-Library needs to load the appropriate driver based on the IPC method, which can include Named Pipes, SPX, TCP/IP sockets, VINES, or DECnet.

Windows does have the advantage of being able to load multiple Net-Libraries, whereas MS-DOS can have only one active at a time.

SQL Server also includes AppleTalk, DECnet, and TCP/IP network protocols; with the correct DBLibrary, clients such as Apple Macintosh, VMS, and UNIX can access SQL Server as well. A block diagram of the Net Library architecture is shown in Figure 22.1.

FIGURE 22.1.
Net-Library architecture.

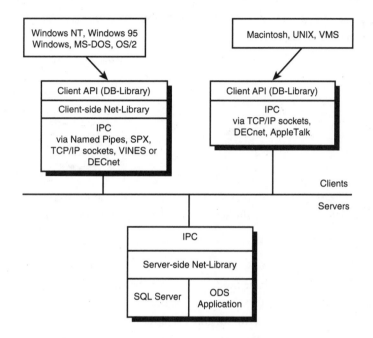

When a call is made to open a connection to SQL Server (dbopen), DBLibrary determines which client-side Net-Library should be loaded to communicate with SQL Server.

DBLibrary handles all the connections to SQL Server, and negotiates which network protocol to use. When you write an application using DBLibrary, you call SQL Server's native API functions. This approach offers a rich set of functions to the developer, yet introduces complexities that are hidden in some of the other interfaces you will discuss in later chapters.

You can do all of the following with DBLibrary:

- Browse available servers
- Open connections
- Format queries
- Send query batches to the server and retrieve the resulting data, including multiple result sets returned from a single query
- Bulk-copy data from files or program variables to and from the server
- Bind columns to your own variables
- Control two-phase commit operations between several participating SQL Servers
- Execute stored procedures on remote servers

FIGURE 22.2.

The DBLibrary interface automatically loads the appropriate Net-Library. Different operating systems require a different DLL to be loaded.

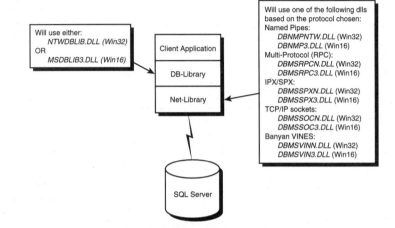

The libraries' functions provide developers with fine-grained control of data flow back and forth between the client and the server. DBLibrary supports C/C++ compilers and Visual Basic.

When developing with a C/C++ compiler, you may choose from one of several environments:

- A multithreaded dynamic link library (DLL) for the Windows NT operating system
- Medium and large model static link libraries for MS-DOS for both Microsoft and Borland compilers
- A DLL for the Windows operating system
- A DLL for the OS/2 operating system

WARNING

Although programming DBLibrary with Win32 enables the creation of threads, you need to be aware that DBLibrary functions that access the same DBPROCESS are not reentrant.

Visual Basic and DBLibrary

With Microsoft Visual Basic, you can create applications with similar functionality to those built with C/C++ compilers. The Visual Basic Library for SQL Server (VBSQL) is a version of the DBLibrary API specifically tuned for use with Visual Basic that provides virtually all the functions available in DBLibrary.

The VBSQL Library is provided as a custom control. To use VBSQL, you need to include either VBSQL.VBX (Win16), or VBSQL.OCX (Win32) in your Visual Basic application. There are a few points to note when using VBSQL:

- You cannot create multithreaded applications in Visual Basic, yet C compilers can.
- You cannot bind column names to variables.
- The VBSQL control must convert Visual Basic Pascal calling convention to the C calling convention (CDECL).
- The VBSQL control converts data coming back from SQL server to a Visual Basic string.

Pros and Cons of Using the DBLibrary API

Whether you're programming in Visual Basic or C/C++, DBLibrary gives application developers a powerful set of functions to interact with SQL Server. But, this wide range of functionality does have a tradeoff: added complexity. Please refer to the following comparisons when determining the feasibility of DBLibrary programming for your particular situation.

Advantages include the following:

- Access to virtually all SQL Server functions.
- A native interface to SQL Server.
- Specific API calls to address each SQL Server feature.
- API for Bulk Copy (BCP) functions.
- Interrupt driven error and message handling.
- Server side cursor support on SQL 6.0 and later.
- Application interfaces for several operating systems: MSDOS, Win16, Win32, OS/2. Code written for DBLibrary can be ported to various operating systems with little or no alterations.

Disadvantages include the following:

- Provides access only to Microsoft SQL Server (and some versions of Sybase); not portable to another DBMS.
- Larger learning curve than other higher level API's.
- Direct interaction with the Win32 API and with DBLibrary increases the risk of Access Violations (the error formerly known as GPF).
- All data binding to user interface controls must be programmed manually.
- Queries to be sent to SQL Server must be formatted in its native language: Transact-SQL.

DBLibrary Development Environment

To try the examples listed in this chapter, you need a C/C++ compiler, access to the DBLibrary C/C++ header files and link libraries, Visual Basic 4.0 or later, the DBLibrary control VBSQL.OCX, and a connection to SQL Server with the pubs database installed. In addition, the code can be downloaded from the Web site, as described at the end of the book.

The pubs sample database is typically created when SQL Server is installed. If for some reason you need to install it, you can install it from the SQL Server CD by running the following on the command line (replace options with your user name, password, server name, and CD-ROM drive letter):

```
isql /Usa /Ppassword /Sserver -i\sql\install\instpubs.sql
```

> **NOTE**
>
> Test your connection to SQL Server before trying the sample code. Use one of the client utilities that ship with SQL Server, and verify that you have a working connection and the Net-Library components are working.

DBLibrary Documentation and Resources

The SQL Server Books Online contain the most up-to-date information on DBLibrary programming. In addition, you may want to subscribe to the Microsoft Developers Library, which provides in-depth coverage of every Windows API and SDK available, including DBLibrary. In addition, the BackOffice SDK gives you access to online references related to all the BackOffice components.

Comparing VBSQL to DBLibrary Programming in C

Most of the Visual Basic DBLibrary functions directly map to a similar C DBLibrary function. The only difference is the prefix for the functions. The VBSQL functions all start with SQL whereas the C functions start with db. For example, the VBSQL function SQLLogin maps to dblogin in C. Therefore, the concepts you learn in this chapter can be easily applied to C programming.

The DBLibrary in C provides a few functions not available in Visual Basic. dbaltbind, dbbind, dbconvert, and dbwillconvert are available only as C functions. These functions enable your program variables to be bound to a result column. Every time a new row is fetched, your program variables will be updated with the data in the bound column. In addition to the data binding functions, the two-phase commit functions aren't available in VBSQL.

Portability of Your DBLibrary Code

Both VBSQL and C applications can be ported easily between 16-bit and 32-bit if a few guidelines are followed.

In Visual Basic, the 16-bit DBLibrary functions might use type-declaration characters in their declarations. The majority of the functions either return a string or an integer. For example,

SQLOpenConnection% returns an integer (thus the % type-declaration character). In 32-bit VBSQL, all the parameters and return values that were previously integers are now of type *Long*—a long integer is a variable stored as a signed 32-bit (4-byte) number. If you're starting out with 16-bit VBSQL, you may want to avoid using type-declaration characters throughout your code. When it comes time to port between 16-bit and 32-bit you'll be able change your code in one location, the function declaration section. The sample code for this chapter includes the module VBSQL.BAS. This module defines the calls made available in VBSQL.OCX, and is intended for the 32-bit platform.

> **TIP**
>
> Visual Basic 4.0 and later allows for conditional compilation. You can wrap your 16-bit and 32-bit declarations in an #If...Then...#Else statement as follows:
>
> ```
> #If Win32 Then
> Declare Function SqlOpenConnection Lib "VBSQL.OCX" (Server As String,
> ➥LoginID As String, Pwd As String, WorkStation As String,
> ➥Application As String) As Long
> #Else
> Declare Function SqlOpenConnection Lib "VBSQL.VBX" (Server As String,
> ➥LoginID As String, Pwd As String, WorkStation As String,
> ➥Application As String) As Integer
> #End If
> ```
>
> Before creating the executable file, choose Tools | Options, click the Advanced tab in the Options dialog box, and enter an argument such as Win32=-1 in the Conditional Compilation Arguments field. This action causes the Win32 directive to return True.

Two C DBLibrary functions, dbprhead and dbprrow, aren't supported in 16-bit Windows because they send output to STDIO, but are supported in the Win32 API and can be used when developing applications for the console subsystem. These functions provide a convenient way to send results to the default output device. If these functions aren't used, you should be able to link in either the 16-bit or 32-bit library.

Visual Basic Sample Application

With VBSQL, you can build a simple yet powerful query utility. This sample application will provide functionality similar to that of the ISQL/w utility that ships with SQL Server. All VBSQL applications that send queries and retrieve results perform a common sequence of functions:

1. Initialize VBSQL with SqlInit.
2. Allocate a login structure with SqlLogin.
3. Connect to SQL Server with the login structure, using SqlOpen.
4. Send a query, using SqlCmd.
5. Execute the query, using SqlExec or a combination of SqlSend and SQLOk.

6. Process the results with `SqlResults`, and retrieve the rows for each result with `SqlNextRow`.

7. Close the connection with `SqlClose` or close all SQL Server connections with `SqlExit`, and then release the memory referenced by VBSQL with `SqlWinExit`.

With your VBSQL Test application, the following sections examine each of these functions, discussing the enhancements and error handlers that have been implemented.

NOTE

The Visual Basic sample code will work in both Visual Basic 4.0 and 5.0. The sample code uses the grid control, which no longer ships in Visual Basic 5.0. There is a directory on the Visual Basic 5.0 CD that contains all the ActiveX Controls that shipped with Visual Basic 4.0 Professional and Enterprise Editions. You will need your Visual Basic 5.0 installation CD. Here you need to look in the directory `VB5.0\Tools\Controls`. Follow the instructions to register the old controls in your Visual Basic 5.0 environment.

The sample code can be found on this publication's related Web site.

Initializing VBSQL and the Error Handlers

A call to `SqlInit` is used to prepare Visual Basic to use DBLibrary. It also initializes the error handlers that you've provided in your code. The VBSQL control has only two events—`Error` and `Message`. These events enable you to capture errors from DBLibrary and messages returned from SQL Server. These may include informational messages that shouldn't be treated as severe errors, or syntax error messages returned from SQL Server.

There are two informational messages that you always ignore in your sample application: 5701 and 5703. Message 5701 simply informs you that the query caused the database context to change, as in `USE pubs`. SQL Server supports multiple languages; Message 5703 indicates that the language setting has changed, and isn't a severe error.

In addition to SQL Server-generated messages, you can generate your own informative messages to be returned to the user. For example, if in a query you use the `print` command, it will generate a message that's captured in the VBSQL message handler.

Listing 22.1 shows the VBSQL initialization code and the error handlers.

Listing 22.1. The VBSQL initialization code and error handlers.

```
Sub Main()
    'Initialize VBSQL.
    Dim strReturn As String

    strReturn = SqlInit()
    If strReturn = "" Then
```

```
        MsgBox "VBSQL could not been initialized."
        End
    End If


    frmLogin.Show
End Sub

Private Sub Vbsql1_Error(ByVal SqlConn As Long, ByVal Severity As Long,
➡        ByVal ErrorNum As Long,ByVal ErrorStr As String,
➡        ByVal OSErrorNum As Long, ByVal OSErrorStr As String,
➡        RetCode As Long)

    MsgBox ("DBLibrary Error: " + Str$(ErrorNum) + " " + OSErrorStr)
End Sub

Private Sub VBSQL1_Message(ByVal SqlConn As Long, ByVal Message As Long,
➡        ByVal State As Long, ByVal Severity As Long, ByVal MsgStr As String,
➡        ByVal ServerNameStr As String, ByVal ProcNameStr As String,
➡        ByVal Line As Long)
' It is common practice to ignore the following messages
    ' Message 5701, Changed database context to '%.*s'.
    ' Message 5703, Changed language setting to '%.*s'.
    ' They are informative, and should not be dealt with as fatal errors

    If Message <> 5701 And Message <> 5703 Then
        MsgBox ("SQL Server Message: " + IIF(Message = 0, "",
➡        Str$(Message)) + " " + MsgStr)
    End If
End Sub
```

Opening a Connection to SQL Server

When a connection is established with SQL Server, you need to pass a login structure, along with the name of the server to which you're connecting. To create a login structure, you use the SqlLogin function. This will return a pointer to a structure that can be passed to several other functions, which can supply values to the structure. These functions include all the following:

- SqlSetLUser—Supplies the login (user) ID.

- SqlSetLPwd—Supplies the user's password. The password is required only if the user has a password on SQL Server.

- SqlSetLHost—Supplies the workstation name. The workstation name is useful when viewing a server's current activity. The activity monitor (in Enterprise Manager) shows the user name, computer name, and application name.

- SqlSetLApp—Supplies the application name. Like SqlSetLHost, this information is useful when monitoring current server activity. It also may be useful when tracing events logged by SQL Server.

- SqlSetLNatLang—Supplies the national language preferred.

- ■ SqlSetLPacket—Supplies the TDS packet size. For large data transfers, such as bulk copy, increasing the packet size may improve network efficiency because fewer reads and writes need to be performed. If you want to increase the packet size, stick with a range between 4092 and 8192.
- ■ SqlSetLSecure—Requests a secure connection.
- ■ SqlSetLVersion—Sets DBLibrary 6 behavior. If this function isn't called, DBLibrary will default to Version 4.2 behavior.
- ■ SqlBCPSetL—Enables bulk copy operations. By default, SQL Server connections aren't enabled for bulk copy operations.

After the login structure has been allocated with SqlLogin, it's passed to SqlOpen with the name of the server to which you're attempting to connect. The sample application adds an enhancement to this process by enumerating the available servers and presenting them in a combo box. The function SqlServerEnum enumerates the available servers on the network, or those configured locally. This function returns a string that contains all the servers found, and separates them with NULL. A special Visual Basic function needed to be written to parse out the server names, and you'll see this done in FindNullInString.

After the connection is established, the value returned from SqlOpen is stored in the global variable SqlConn. This connection value is passed to all subsequent DBLibrary functions. Listing 22.2 shows this login and connection sequence in Visual Basic.

Listing 22.2. Logging in to SQL Server and creating a connection.

```
Option Explicit

Function FindNullInString(nStart As Integer, sString As String) As Integer

    ' return 0 if pointing to a Null character
    If Mid(sString, nStart, 1) = Chr$(0) Then
        FindNullInString = 0
        Exit Function
    End If

    Do While nStart < Len(sString)
        If Mid(sString, nStart, 1) = Chr$(0) Then
            FindNullInString = nStart
            Exit Function
        Else
            nStart = nStart + 1
        End If
    Loop

End Function

Private Sub cmdExit_Click()
    'Close connection and exit program.
    SqlExit ' Close and free all SQL Server connections.
    SqlWinExit ' Release memory referenced by VBSQL
    End
```

```
End Sub

Private Sub cmdLogin_Click()
    'Get a Login record and set login attributes.
    Dim Login As Long
    Dim strLoginID As String, strPwd As String, strServer As String

    Login = SqlLogin()
    strLoginID = txtLoginID.Text
    strPwd = txtPassword.Text

    Result = SqlSetLUser(Login, strLoginID)
    Result = SqlSetLPwd(Login, strPwd)
    Result = SqlSetLApp(Login, "VBSL Sample")

    'Get a connection for communicating with SQL Server.
    strServer = cbServerName.Text
    SqlConn = SqlOpen(Login, strServer)
    If (SqlConn <> 0) Then
     Unload Me
     frmQuery.Show
    End If
End Sub

Private Sub Form_Load()

    Dim sServers As String, sName As String
    Dim nNumEntries As Long
    Dim nPos As Integer, nLastPos As Integer

    CenterForm Me
    sServers = Space(128)
    Call SqlServerEnum(LOCSEARCH + NETSEARCH, sServers, nNumEntries)

    ' Fill the combo box with the servers we found
nLastPos = 1
    nPos = FindNullInString(1, sServers)    'Look for nulls
    Do While nPos <> 0
        sName = Mid$(sServers, nLastPos, nPos - nLastPos)
        cbServerName.AddItem sName
        nLastPos = nPos + 1
        nPos = FindNullInString(nPos + 1, sServers)    'Look for nulls
    Loop
    If nNumEntries > 0 Then 'only if we found something
        cbServerName.Text = cbServerName.List(0)
    End If
End Sub
```

Sending a Query

The command `SqlCmd` fills the command buffer with the query that needs to be sent to SQL Server. When the buffer holds the query text, one of two methods can be used to execute the query: synchronous or asynchronous.

The synchronous method is the easiest to code, as it uses only the one command SqlExec. The downside to this method is that control isn't returned to your application until SQL Server has completed the query. The function SqlSetTime is used to set the number of seconds DBLibrary will wait for SQL Server responses.

> **WARNING**
>
> By default, SqlSetTime is set to an infinite timeout. If the timeout value isn't changed, SqlExec has the potential of hanging forever. It might be wise to reduce the timeout period with SqlSetTime, or use the asynchronous method.

The asynchronous method pairs up the functions SqlSend and SqlOk. SqlSend starts the query, and immediately returns control to your application. You then need to call SqlDataReady to determine that SQL Server has finished processing your request. At this time, you need to call SqlOk, which checks the correctness of the batch and allows further processing of the results. Listing 22.3 shows how to use the SqlDataReady function in a loop, which gives the user feedback as the query executes, and enables him to cancel the query at any time. If the query is canceled, a call to SqlCancel must be made to free the connection and stop the current batch. If this isn't done, you receive the DBLibrary 10038 Results Pending error whenever you attempt to call another DBLibrary function.

Listing 22.3 shows the portion of the code executed when the user sends a query. Notice that the code is using the asynchronous method, and is periodically checking for data readiness. The asynchronous method shown here uses a global variable bStop (Boolean) that is set to TRUE when the user selects the Stop button.

Listing 22.3. Code executed when the user sends a query.

```
'Put the command into the command buffer.
   sSql = txtSQL.Text
   Result = SqlCmd(SqlConn, sSql)

   'Send the command to SQL Server and start execution.
#If 0 Then ' this waits until SQL Server returns results
   Result = SqlExec(SqlConn)
#Else     ' this will allow user input as it waits for SQL Server results
   nWait = 0
   txtWait = ""
   Result = SqlSend(SqlConn)
   While SqlDataReady(SqlConn) = 0
       DoEvents    ' Allow user to stop query
       If bStop Then
```

```
        SqlCancel (SqlConn)
        GoTo Exit_Query
      End If
    txtWait = "Waiting ." + String(nWait, ".")
    nWait = nWait + 1
    If nWait > 5 Then nWait = 0
  Wend
  Result = SqlOk(SqlConn)
  If Result <> SUCCEED Then GoTo Exit_Query
#End If
```

You'll have to run a query that takes a measurable amount of time to execute in order to see the asynchronous method in action. For example, if you have a large database called `catalog`, and a complex stored procedure called `SalesReport`, you would type the following into the query window:

```
USE catalog
execute salesreport
```

As the stored procedure runs, the animated `Waiting` text gives you feedback that the query is executing. At any time, clicking the Stop button cancels the query.

Retrieving the Results

After the query executes, DBLibrary has pending results to return to your application. You must either retrieve all results, or call `SqlCancel`. This procedure for retrieving results, and the rows of each result, is common to most DBLibrary applications. The flow chart in Figure 22.3 shows how the sample application processes results returned to DBLibrary. This order of operations can be applied to other DBLibrary applications as well.

When looking at the flowchart in Figure 22.3, you see that the outer loop is making calls to `SqlResults` until it returns `NOMORERESULTS`. This is necessary because a query batch may return several sets of results. The various result sets shouldn't be confused with the multiple rows you receive from each result set. The following is an example of a query that may return several results:

```
select * from jobs
select * from authors
```

This may look like two queries that could have been sent separately, but keep in mind that SQL Server allows query batches. Several requests can be put into a single batch. In addition, stored procedures may return several result sets.

Feel free to follow along in code Listing 22.4.

FIGURE 22.3.

*This flowchart shows
how results are
retrieved in most
DBLibrary applica-
tions.*

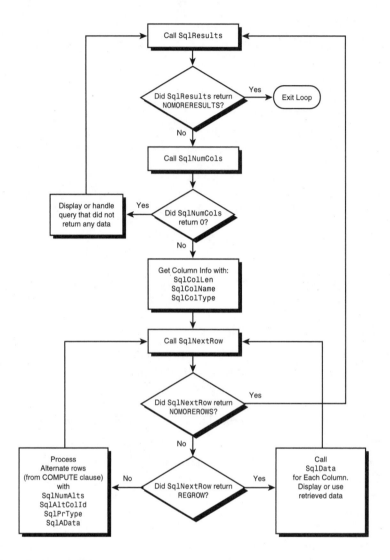

Listing 22.4. Looping through returned data.

```
Private Sub cmdExecute_Click()

    If optUseGrid Then
        UseGrid
        Exit Sub
    End If

    Dim nCols As Long
    Dim nRows As Long
    Dim nWait As Long
    Dim nStartTime As Long
    Dim OutString As String
```

```
        Dim x As Long
        Dim nPad As Integer
        Dim sStr As String, sData As String, sSql As String
        Dim Columns() As ColumnInfo
        Dim hdr1 As String, hdr2 As String
        Dim ResultProcess As Long, ResultRows As Long

        cmdExecute.Enabled = False

        nStartTime = GetTickCount()

        txtResults = ""   ' Clear text boxes
        txtTime = ""
        txtFetchTime = ""
        txtRows = ""
        bStop = False

        'Put the command into the command buffer.
        sSql = txtSQL.Text
        Result = SqlCmd(SqlConn, sSql)

        'Send the command to SQL Server and start execution.
#If 0 Then ' this waits until SQL Server returns results
        Result = SqlExec(SqlConn)
#Else    ' this will allow user input as it waits for SQL Server results
        nWait = 0
        txtWait = ""
        Result = SqlSend(SqlConn)
        While SqlDataReady(SqlConn) = 0
            DoEvents    ' Allow user to stop query
            If bStop Then
                SqlCancel (SqlConn)
                GoTo Exit_Query
             End If
            txtWait = "Waiting ." + String(nWait, ".")
            nWait = nWait + 1
            If nWait > 5 Then nWait = 0
        Wend
        Result = SqlOk(SqlConn)
        If Result <> SUCCEED Then GoTo Exit_Query
#End If

        txtTime = CStr((GetTickCount() - nStartTime) / 1000)

' We need to check SqlResults repeatedly in case
' the query return several batches
Do Until ResultProcess = NOMORERESULTS
        ResultProcess = SqlResults(SqlConn)
        If ResultProcess = NOMORERESULTS Or ResultProcess = FAIL Then Exit Do

          'Retrieve and print the result rows.
          nCols = SqlNumCols(SqlConn)
          If nCols = 0 Then
            txtResults.SelStart = Len(txtResults) + 1
            txtResults.SelText = "The query did not return any data." + CRLF
          Else
            ReDim Columns(1 To nCols)
            hdr1 = ""
```

continues

Listing 22.4. continued

```
     hdr2 = ""
     For x = 1 To nCols
         Columns(x).colLen = SqlColLen(SqlConn, x)
         Columns(x).colName = SqlColName(SqlConn, x)
         Columns(x).colType = SqlColType(SqlConn, x)
         ' Print header for columns
         nPad = Columns(x).colLen - Len(Columns(x).colName)
         If nPad < 0 Then
          nPad = 0
         End If
         sStr = Columns(x).colName + Space(nPad)
         hdr1 = hdr1 + sStr + " "
         If Columns(x).colLen < Len(Columns(x).colName) Then
          nPad = Len(Columns(x).colName)
         Else
          nPad = Columns(x).colLen
         End If
         hdr2 = hdr2 + String(nPad, "-") + " "
     Next x

     txtResults.SelStart = Len(txtResults) + 1
     txtResults.SelText = hdr1 + CRLF + hdr2 + CRLF
   End If

   nRows = 1
   ResultRows = SUCCEED
   Do Until ResultRows = NOMOREROWS
     ResultRows = SqlNextRow(SqlConn)
     If ResultRows = NOMOREROWS Then Exit Do
     If ResultRows <> REGROW Then
         ProcessAltRows ResultRows, OutString, nRows, Columns
         txtResults.SelStart = Len(txtResults) + 1
         txtResults.SelText = OutString
     Else

       sStr = ""
       For x = 1 To nCols
           sData = SqlData(SqlConn, x)
           nPad = Columns(x).colLen - Len(sData)
           If Columns(x).colLen < Len(Columns(x).colName) Then
            nPad = Len(Columns(x).colName) - Len(sData)
           End If
           sStr = sStr + sData + Space(nPad) + " "
       Next x
       sStr = sStr + CRLF

       ' Do error checking, in case we run over 64K limit of text box
       On Error Resume Next

       txtResults.SelStart = Len(txtResults) + 1
       txtResults.SelText = sStr

       If (Err) Then
         MsgBox "The maximum lines for display in the text
                     ➥box has been reached."
         SqlCancel (SqlConn)
```

```
        Exit Do
      End If

      On Error GoTo 0     ' turn of resume next handler

      If (nRows Mod 10 = 0) Then
        ' call DoEvents every 10 rows
        DoEvents   ' Allow user to hit stop
      End If

      If bStop Then
        SqlCancel (SqlConn)
        Exit Do
      End If
      nRows = nRows + 1
      End If
      txtRows = nRows
    Loop ' Row loop
Loop ' Results loop

Exit_Query:

    txtRows = nRows
    cmdExecute.Enabled = True
    txtFetchTime = CStr((GetTickCount() - nStartTime) / 1000)
    txtFetchTime = txtFetchTime + " sec."

    ' See if this query caused database name to change
    CheckDatabaseName

    cmdExecute.SetFocus

End Sub
```

After SqlResults determines that results are available, SqlNumCols can be used to begin retrieving column information. The sample application checks this against 0 to see whether the query returned any data. If valid column information exists, the application calls the functions SqlColLen, SqlColName, and SqlColType to retrieve column information, to format the width of text columns that are subsequently displayed in the query results window.

The innermost loop calls SqlNextRow continually until it returns NOMOREROWS. When no more rows are available, the outer loop again uses SqlResults to determine whether the results from the entire batch have been retrieved.

For each column from which you want to retrieve data, you need to pass the column number to SqlData. The return value from SqlData is a string containing the data in a result column. For the SQL Server datatypes binary, varbinary, and image, SqlData returns a string of binary data with one character in the string per byte of data in the result column. For all other datatypes, SqlData returns a string of readable characters. When there's no such column or when the data is NULL, an empty string is returned. To make sure that the data really is NULL, always check for a return of 0 by using SqlDatLen.

> **TIP**
>
> This distinction between an empty string and NULL is important. An empty string still has a length of 1 byte—the NULL *character*—in other words, a string that contains the character CHR$(0). A truly NULL value has a length of zero, as indicated by SqlDatLen returning 0.

Retrieving Alternate Columns from compute Clauses

There are special cases when the row returned doesn't have data that maps directly to all the columns. SqlNextRow returns the constant REGROW (-1), 0 for failure, NOMOREROWS (-2) when it has reached the end of the result set, or the identification number of the compute clause. These alternate rows are a result of a query that contains compute clauses, as in the following query:

```
SELECT title, type, price, advance
FROM titles
WHERE ytd_sales IS NOT NULL
AND type IN ('trad_cook', 'psychology')
ORDER BY type DESC
COMPUTE AVG(price), SUM(advance) BY type
COMPUTE SUM(price), SUM(advance)
```

To handle these compute clauses, you call your own procedure, ProcessAltRows. This procedure in turn uses the DBLibrary functions SqlNumAlts, SqlAltColId, SqlPrType, SqlAltOp, and SqlAData. The function SqlAltColId tells us to which column the compute clause (resulting from MIN, MAX, AVG, SUM, or COUNT) applies. In the example, AVG(price) will return a column ID of 3 because price is the third column in the select clause. SqlAltOp is then used to determine the type of aggregate function in a compute column. This type can be converted to a readable string, using SqlPrType.

The following is the portion of the ProcessAltRows procedure that checks each alternate column, and extracts the type and data:

```
numalts = SqlNumAlts(SqlConn, Result)
    For x = 1 To numalts
        AltCol = SqlAltColId(SqlConn, Result, x)
        AltType = SqlPrType(SqlAltOp(SqlConn, Result, x))
        AltValue = SqlAData(SqlConn, Result, x)

        nLen = 0
        For y = 1 To AltCol - 1
            nLen = nLen + colpositions(y).colLen + 1
        Next y
        nLen = nLen + 1
        Mid$(AltStr1, nLen, Len(AltType)) = AltType
        Mid$(AltStr2, nLen, Len(AltType)) = String(Len(AltType), "-")
        Mid$(AltStr3, nLen, Len(AltValue)) = AltValue

    Next x
```

Selecting, Changing, and Retrieving the Current Database

For this to be a truly useful query tool, it should present to the user a list of databases available for the current SQL Server connection. This functionality is part of the sample application, and demonstrates the use of the DBLibrary functions SqlName and SqlUse.

In the Form_Load event for frmQuery, you perform a query on the master database's sysdatabases table. This table holds the names of all databases available in SQL Server. This list is then presented to the user in a drop-down combo box. When the user makes a selection from the combo box, a call to SqlUse actually performs the database context change.

The sample application uses a helper subroutine named CheckDatabaseName to determine whether the database context has changed, and if so, it updates the current combo box selection to reflect this change. Note that the CheckDatabaseName subroutine is called after any query has been executed, in case the query itself changed the database context, as in the query USE pubs.

Listing 22.5 shows the code for the Form_Load event and the CheckDatabaseName subroutine.

Listing 22.5. The Form_Load event and the CheckDatabaseName subroutine demonstrate database context-change capabilities of DBLibrary.

```
Sub Form_Load()

    Dim sSql As String, sDatabase As String

    CenterForm Me

    ' Get the names of all the databases on the SQL Server.
    sSql = "Select name from master..sysdatabases"
    Result = SqlCmd(SqlConn, sSql)
    'Send the command to SQL Server and start execution.
    Result = SqlExec(SqlConn)
    Result = SqlResults(SqlConn)

    'Process the command.
    If Result = FAIL Then
        MsgBox "Error, Could not retrieve database names."
        Exit Sub
    Else
        While SqlNextRow(SqlConn) <> NOMOREROWS
            cbDatabases.AddItem SqlData(SqlConn, 1)
        Wend
    End If

    ' Place current database name in combo box
    CheckDatabaseName

    ' Select text in query edit box
    txtSQL.SelStart = 0
    txtSQL.SelLength = Len(txtSQL)
End Sub
```

continues

Listing 22.5. Continued

```
Sub CheckDatabaseName()
    Dim sDatabase As String
    ' Place the current database name in combobox text
    sDatabase = SqlName(SqlConn)
    cbDatabases.Text = sDatabase
End Sub
```

Timing, Benchmarking, and Limitations

The Windows API call `GetTickCount` is used to determine the time it took to execute the query, as well as how long it took to retrieve the results. Due to the nature of the Visual Basic edit box, the retrieval of the results is somewhat sluggish. Every time a new row is received, it must be appended to the end of the edit box text. The call to `DoEvents` also introduces some overhead.

The Visual Basic edit box has a 64KB limit under Windows 95, and under Windows NT it's limited by available memory. If you retrieve a large number of results under Windows 95, the text box displays only the first 64KB worth of text.

The time it takes to execute the query isn't affected by the method you chose to retrieve the results, and is a good way to benchmark how efficiently you've written a query or a stored procedure. In the sample application, the value after `Execution Time (sec):` indicates how long it took for the query to execute.

In the sample application, the amount of time it took to actually retrieve the rows is listed after the `Rows Retrieved` label.

There are some methods with which you may want to experiment, which increase the speed at which this sample query application retrieves the rows. You may want to call `DoEvents` less often. Right now it's called every 10 rows, although the frequency with which you check for events directly correlates with how responsive the Stop button is.

Another improvement is to use a control other than the edit box to display the query results. The sample application has an option called Use Grid. If you select this check box, the Visual Basic grid control is used to display query results (although the grid control isn't well-suited for queries that return multiple results or include `compute` clauses). When you use the sample application with the grid control enabled, you see only the first set of results in a query with multiple batches. The remaining results are discarded with `SqlCancel`. For large result sets, retrieving rows into the grid can be twice as fast as the edit box method.

Developing with C/C++

When working in C/C++ you have the option of creating DBLibrary applications in one of several operating systems. There are some specifics to note when working in each environment.

The header files that you need to include remain the same for all target platforms. They are sqlfront.h and sqldb.h. When using these header files, you will want to set up the correct preprocessor definitions first. In addition, you will want to link with the appropriate library file.

- In MS-DOS you define DBMSDOS, and link with rmdblib.lib or rldblib.lib (pick the correct library based on memory model).
- In Windows 3.x you define DBMSWIN, and link with msdblib3.lib.
- In 32-bit Windows you define DBNTWIN32, and link with ntwdblib.lib.

The header files and libraries needed to compile the C/C++ examples can be found on the Platform SDK. The Platform SDK is available on MSDN. You will also find the necessary files in the PTK directory of SQL Server Developer Edition found in the Visual Studio Enterprise version, or on the SQL Server Workstation CD. Be sure to add the location of these include files and library files to your development environment. One way to do this is shown in Figure 22.4. This is specific to Visual C++ 5.0, and is only one of many ways to set this up.

FIGURE 22.4.

This Microsoft Visual C++ 5.0 Options screen is found under the Tools | Options menu. It can be used to configure additional include and library directories.

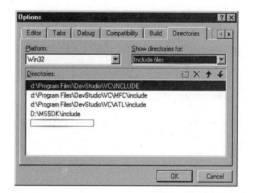

Common DBLibrary Calls in C/C++

With C/C++, you will find that initializing DBLibrary and connecting to a server is done in a similar fashion to Visual Basic. One key difference is that Visual Basic used events to handle DBLibrary messages and errors. In C/C++ you pass dbmsghandle and dberrhandle a reference to your own function handlers. Setting up the logon structure and calling dbopen are all that is needed to get connected. Most of your DBLibrary C/C++ applications will have a similar skeleton to the one found in Listing 22.6. This shows a complete DBLibrary application that initializes, connects to a server, creates and drops a database, and finally disconnects.

Listing 22.6. Basic functions typically found in a DBLibrary application written in C/C++.

```c
/* example1.c */

#if defined(DBNTWIN32)
#include <windows.h>
#endif

#include <stdio.h>
#include <conio.h>

/* DBLibrary specific includes */
#include <sqlfront.h>
#include <sqldb.h>

/* Forward declarations of the error handler and message handler functions. */

int err_handler(DBPROCESS*, int, int, int, char*, char*);
int msg_handler(DBPROCESS*, DBINT, int, int, char*);

main(int argc, char *argv)
{

LOGINREC      *login;
DBPROCESS     *dbproc;

dbinit();     /* initialize dblib */

/* Install user-supplied error and message handling */
dbmsghandle((DBMSGHANDLE_PROC)msg_handler);
dberrhandle((DBERRHANDLE_PROC)err_handler);

/*    Allocate and initialize the LOGINREC structure to be used
      to open a connection to SQL Server. */
login = dblogin();
DBSETLUSER(login, "sa");
DBSETLPWD(login, "");
DBSETLAPP(login, "example1");
DBSETLVERSION(login, DBVER60);

/* change following line to match your server name */
dbproc = dbopen(login, "reznor");
printf("Calling create database.\n");
    dbcmd(dbproc,"create database example");
dbsqlexec(dbproc);
dbresults(dbproc);

// drop the database we just created
printf("Calling drop database.\n");
dbuse(dbproc,"master");
dbcmd(dbproc,"drop database example");
dbsqlexec(dbproc);
dbresults(dbproc);
printf("Press a key to continue.\n");
getch();

/* close down DBLibrary */
dbexit();
return(STDEXIT);
}
```

```
int err_handler(DBPROCESS *dbproc,
int severity,      int dberr,
int oserr, char *dberrstr,
char *oserrstr)
{

printf("DBLIBRARY error:\n\t%s\n", dberrstr);

if (oserr != DBNOERR)
printf("Operating-system error:\n\t%s\n", oserrstr);
if ((dbproc == NULL) || (DBDEAD(dbproc)))
return(INT_EXIT);

return(INT_CANCEL);
}

int msg_handler(DBPROCESS *dbproc, DBINT msgno,
➡       int msgstate, int severity, char *msgtext)
{
/*    There are many messages that are informational only, and do not
need to be treated as severe.  One example is message 5701, severity 0.
This message is returned any time the database context is switched. */

printf ("SQL Server message %ld, state %d, severity %d:\n\t%s\n",
msgno, msgstate, severity, msgtext);
return(0);
}
```

Bulk Copy Operations in C/C++

The code in Listing 22.5 is a good starting point, but there is more DBLibrary functionality left to uncover in C/C++. It is worth exploring the functionality available in C/C++ that cannot be directly accessed in Visual Basic. Specifically, you will look at some of the advanced Bulk Copy operations.

The bulk copy functions in C/C++ enable the reading and writing of bulk copy format files, and give you the capability to bind program variables to bulk copy columns. By binding program variables to bulk copy columns, you can do bulk inserts without the need for a data file. This might be useful for doing bulk inserts of real-time data.

There are some things you need to note when inserting data into a table with bulk copy functions. When copying data in, bulk copy is fastest if your database table has no indexes.

To do a non-logged insert with bulk copy, you may want to use the sp_dboption system procedure to set the Select Into/Bulk Copy option for that database to true. If the option isn't set, SQL Server generates a warning message and will log the bulk inserts.

```
sp_dboption 'pubs', 'select into/bulkcopy', 'true'
go
use pubs
go
checkpoint
```

For a table that has indexes, you don't need to set the Select Into/Bulk Copy option, because bulk inserts into tables with indexes are always logged. Be aware though, there is a performance penalty for copying data into a table that has indexes in place. If you are copying a large number of rows, you have a few options to speed up the process.

The first option is to drop all the indexes beforehand with DROP INDEX, enable Select Into/BulkCopy, copy the data into the table, dump the database, and then re-create the indexes. If the incoming bulk data is sorted prior to the copy, rebuild the clustered index with the option WITH SORTED DATA.

Another common approach with bulk copy is to use an intermediate work table. Instead of copying data directly into your production table, copy it into a similar work table. This work table can even exist in a separate database. This will give you the added advantage of enabling looser datatype conversions on your incoming bulk copy. You can offload the conversion process onto a stored procedure that converts the columns from the work table to the appropriate datatype in the production table. The stored procedure that moves the working copy into the production table could be set up to perform several tasks: run on a schedule, only insert new fields, only update fields that have changed (reducing log file size), and delete fields if not present in new data.

The bulk copy operations in DBLibrary can also be used to create datafiles from your database tables. Listing 22.7 is the portion of the code that differs from the template you created earlier in Listing 22.6.

Listing 22.7. Bulk copy data from a table to a local text file.

```
    /* be sure to define the following somewhere above
    RETCODE      rc;
    DBINT        dbiRows;
    */
login = dblogin();
    DBSETLUSER(login, "sa");
    DBSETLPWD(login, "");
    DBSETLAPP(login, "example2");
    DBSETLVERSION(login, DBVER60);
    BCP_SETL(login, TRUE);          // enable Bulk Copy for this login

    /* change following line to match your server name */
    dbproc = dbopen(login, "reznor");

    rc = bcp_init ( dbproc, "pubs..authors", "authors_out.txt",
                   ➡"authors_err.txt", DB_OUT );
    if (rc == FAIL) exit (ERREXIT);

    bcp_columns(dbproc, 9);
    bcp_colfmt(dbproc, 1, SQLCHAR, 0, -1, "\t", 1, 1);
    bcp_colfmt(dbproc, 2, SQLCHAR, 0, -1, "\t", 1, 2);
    bcp_colfmt(dbproc, 3, SQLCHAR, 0, -1, "\t", 1, 3);
    bcp_colfmt(dbproc, 4, SQLCHAR, 0, -1, "\t", 1, 4);
    bcp_colfmt(dbproc, 5, SQLCHAR, 0, -1, "\t", 1, 5);
    bcp_colfmt(dbproc, 6, SQLCHAR, 0, -1, "\t", 1, 6);
```

```
bcp_colfmt(dbproc, 7, SQLCHAR, 0, -1, "\t", 1, 7);
bcp_colfmt(dbproc, 8, SQLCHAR, 0, -1, "\t", 1, 8);
bcp_colfmt(dbproc, 9, SQLCHAR, 0, -1, "\r\n", 2, 9);

bcp_writefmt(dbproc, "my_fmtfile.txt");
rc = bcp_exec(dbproc, &dbiRows);
if (rc == FAIL) printf ("Bulk copy failed, only copied %ld row%s.\n",
                dbiRows, (dbiRows == 1) ? "": "s");
```

When you compile this sample, be sure to change the server name in the dbopen call to match yours.

When you run this application, it should create three text files: authors_out.txt, authors_err.txt, and my_fmtfile.txt.

The first file, authors_out.txt, is the content of the authors table as found in the pubs database. The second file, authors_err.txt, will most likely be empty, and would contain any error information if generated. The final file, my_fmtfile.txt, contains the format file that could subsequently be used to reload the table with the authors_out.txt data.

The DBLibrary functions of interest are BCP_SETL, bcp_init, bcp_columns, bcp_colfmt, and bcp_writefmt.

WARNING

Be sure to include a call to bcp_colfmt for every column in your target table. The number of columns should also match the value passed into the last parameter of bcp_columns. If not, you will see an unhanded exception error.

The function BCP_SETL sets a field in the LOGINREC structure that tells SQL Server that the DBPROCESS connection can be used for bulk copy operations. This should be called before dbopen.

The bcp_init function initializes the bulk copy operation. In this example, it sets the database to pubs, and the table to authors. It then sets the file name to authors_out.txt. This is the file that will be created with the bulk copy data. The next parameter is the file for the error log. If you don't want to use an error log file, you may set it to NULL. Finally, the DB_OUT constant is used to signify that the data is to be moved from the table to the file.

If you want to bulk copy into a table, the final parameter would be set to DB_IN. You can essentially replace the DB_OUT with DB_IN and recompile this sample. In this case, you will have an application that loads a table. If you try this, remember that the authors table is already populated and has foreign key constraints on it. You may want to create a test table, and change the parameters in `bcp_init`. To do this, use SQL Server Enterprise Manager, and switch to the pubs database. Run the following script:

```
USE pubs
GO
CREATE TABLE dbo.authors2 (
    au_id id NOT NULL ,
    au_lname varchar (40) NOT NULL ,
    au_fname varchar (20) NOT NULL ,
    phone char (12) NOT NULL ,
    address varchar (40) NULL ,
    city varchar (20) NULL ,
    state char (2) NULL ,
    zip char (5) NULL ,
    contract bit NOT NULL
)
GO
```

This script created a table called `authors2`. Change `bcp_init` to match this table name, and set the direction to `DB_IN`:

```
rc = bcp_init ( dbproc, "pubs..authors2", "authors_out.txt",
                ➡"authors_err.txt", DB_IN );
```

With these changes, you can see how data can be bulk copied into a table.

When programming DBLibrary with C/C++, you also have the option of binding program variables to columns in a table. The process involves first calling `bcp_bind` for each of the columns in the table. As the program variables are updated for each row, a call to `bcp_sendrow` is made. To demonstrate this procedure, create a new table in the pubs database called `timer`. Use the following script:

```
USE pubs
GO
CREATE TABLE dbo.timer (
    id int NOT NULL ,
    time varchar (40) NOT NULL
)
GO
```

The code in Listing 22.8 shows two variables bound to the two columns of your new timer database. The example simply binds an integer to the `ID` column, and a string to the `time` column. Then the current time is captured from the operating system, and copied into your program variable. For each row, a call is made to `bcp_sendrow`.

Listing 22.8. DBLibrary functions used to bind program variables to columns during a bulk copy.

```
/*    example3.c */

#if defined(DBNTWIN32)
#include <windows.h>
#endif

#include <stdio.h>
#include <conio.h>
#include <time.h>
#include <sys/timeb.h>
```

```
/* DBLibrary specific includes */
#include <sqlfront.h>
#include <sqldb.h>

/* Forward declarations of the error handler and message handler functions. */

int err_handler(DBPROCESS*, int, int, int, char*, char*);
int msg_handler(DBPROCESS*, DBINT, int, int, char*);


main(int argc, char *argv)
{

    LOGINREC     *login;
    DBPROCESS    *dbproc;
    RETCODE       rc;
    DBINT         dbiRows;
    char          co_time[MAXNAME];
    DBINT         co_id;
    DBINT         nRow;
    struct _timeb tstruct;
    char          tmpbuf1[32];
    char          tmpbuf2[32];


    dbinit();          /* initialize dblib */

    /* Install user-supplied error and message handling */
    dbmsghandle((DBMSGHANDLE_PROC)msg_handler);
    dberrhandle((DBERRHANDLE_PROC)err_handler);

    /*    Allocate and initialize the LOGINREC structure to be used
        to open a connection to SQL Server. */
    login = dblogin();
    DBSETLUSER(login, "sa");
    DBSETLPWD(login, "");
    DBSETLAPP(login, "example3");
    DBSETLVERSION(login, DBVER60);
    BCP_SETL(login, TRUE);          // enable Bulk Copy for this login

    /* change following line to match your server name */
    dbproc = dbopen(login, "reznor");

    /* Initialize bcp. */
    rc = bcp_init(dbproc, "pubs..timer", (BYTE *)NULL,    (BYTE *)NULL, DB_IN);
    if (rc == FAIL)
        exit(ERREXIT);

    /* Bind program variables to table columns. */
    if (bcp_bind(dbproc, (BYTE *)&co_id, 0, (DBINT)-1, (BYTE *)NULL,
            ➥0, 0,    1)    == FAIL)
    {
        fprintf(stderr, "bcp_bind, column 1, failed.\n");
        exit(ERREXIT);
    }
```

continues

Listing 22.8. continued

```
    if (bcp_bind
        (dbproc, co_time, 0, (DBINT)-1, "", 1, 0,     2)     == FAIL)
    {
        fprintf(stderr, "bcp_bind, column 2, failed.\n");
        exit(ERREXIT);
    }

    for (nRow = 0; nRow < 100; nRow++)
    {
        /* Create test data data. */
        co_id = nRow;
        /* create time with milliseconds */
        _strdate( tmpbuf1 );
        _strtime( tmpbuf2 );
        _ftime( &tstruct );
        sprintf( co_time, "%s %s:%u", tmpbuf1, tmpbuf2, tstruct.millitm );

        /*  Send the data. */
        if (bcp_sendrow(dbproc) == FAIL)
            exit(ERREXIT);
    }

    /* Terminate the bulk copy operation. */
    if ((dbiRows = bcp_done(dbproc)) == -1)
        printf("Bulk-copy unsuccessful.\n");
    else
        printf ("Bulk-copy successfully sent %ld row%s.\n",
                            dbiRows, (dbiRows == 1) ? "": "s");

    printf("Press a key to continue.\n");
    getch();

    /* close down DBLibrary */
    dbexit();
    return(STDEXIT);
}
```

This code uses most of the skeleton code again. In addition, you added the calls to bcp_bind and bcp_sendrow, and did not pass any filenames into bcp_init.

The loop that generates the sample data simply updates the program variables with a counter and the current date/time. This would be where your own custom data updates would take place.

The most confusing function in this example is probably bcp_bind. It uses the following syntax:

```
RETCODE bcp_bind (
    PDBPROCESS dbproc,
    LPCBYTE varaddr,
    INT prefixlen,
    DBINT varlen,
    LPCBYTE terminator,
```

```
INT termlen,
INT type,
INT table_column );
```

The following lists the detail of the syntax:

- ◼ dbproc—The DBPROCESS structure created for this connection.

- ◼ varaddr—The address of the program variable from which the data is copied. If *type* is SQLTEXT or SQLIMAGE, varaddr can be NULL. A NULL varaddr indicates that text and image values are sent to SQL Server in chunks by bcp_moretext, rather than all at once by bcp_sendrow.

- ◼ Prefixlen—The length, in bytes, of any length prefix this column can have; valid length prefixes are 0, 1, 2, or 4 bytes. Strings in some non-C programming have a 1-byte length prefix, followed by the string data itself. If the data doesn't have a length prefix, set prefixlen to 0.

- ◼ varlen—The length of the data in the program variable, not including the length of any length prefix or terminator. Setting varlen to 0 signifies that the data is NULL. Setting varlen to -1 indicates that the system should ignore this parameter.

  For fixed-length datatypes such as integers, the datatype itself indicates to the system the length of the data. Therefore, for fixed-length datatypes, varlen must always be -1 except when the data is NULL, in which case varlen must be 0. In Listing 22.7, the variable co_id is bound to the first column of the table. Because the first column of the table is an integer, the varlen is set to -1, which suggests that it is to use the default system length of an integer.

- ◼ terminator—A pointer to the byte pattern, if any, that marks the end (terminator) of this program variable. In Microsoft's Compilers, C strings usually have a 1-byte terminator whose value is 0. If there is no terminator for the variable, set terminator to NULL. If you want to designate the C null terminator as the program variable terminator, use an empty string ("") as terminator and set termlen to 1, because the null terminator constitutes a single byte. For instance, to use a C null terminator:

  ```
  bcp_bind (dbproc, co_lname, 0, -1, "", 1, 0, 2)
  ```

  If there is no terminator:

  ```
  bcp_bind (dbproc, co_lname, 0, -1, NULL, 0, 0, 2)
  ```

- ◼ termlen—The length of this program variable's terminator, if any. If there is no terminator for the variable, set termlen to 0.

- ◼ type—The datatype of your program variable. The data in the program variable is automatically converted to the type of the database column. If this parameter is 0, no conversion is performed. The datatypes definitions are the same used in dbconvert.

- ◼ table_column—The column number in the database. Column numbers start at 1.

If you map your C variable datatypes as closely as possible to the datatypes in the target table, you will be able to get by without needing to define a type. When working with strings, be sure to use a double quote (" ") as a terminator, and set the termlen to 1.

Summary

In this chapter, you created a query tool and a bulk copy application that demonstrates the core functionality required of most DBLibrary applications.

The VBSQL concepts presented in this chapter can be applied to any C/C++ DBLibrary development that you undertake. In addition, all the sample code can be converted to the 16-bit Visual Basic equivalent by replacing the 32-bit definitions with the 16-bit definitions, and using the VBSQL.VBX control in place of the 32-bit OCX control.

The DBLibrary calls commonly needed for C/C++ development were presented, and expanded upon. These samples are complete enough that they can easily be modified to fit your specific needs.

Using ODBC and Visual C++ with SQL Server

IN THIS CHAPTER

Microsoft's *Open Database Connectivity Interface (ODBC)* is a library of functions that enable access to a variety of DBMSs using SQL. The ODBC interface offers vendor-independent manipulation of a wide variety of DBMS types through this standard set of 57 function calls. ODBC maximizes the interoperability of the various DBMSs. Your application can access multiple DBMSs and can be built without knowledge of the DBMS's specifications.

Software written using ODBC to access one DBMS can be moved to SQL Server as the database grows. Centralizing the data is SQL Server's strong point. It is now common for a developer to build with a desktop database such as Access but deploy with SQL Server to handle the larger volume of data. Microsoft has released upsizing wizards that allow you to quickly move data into SQL Server but continue to use your desktop applications by reassigning where ODBC looks for the data. Stored queries in SQL Server are more efficient than desktop database queries. By writing your application to take advantage of this, you can manipulate larger datasets just as quickly. In this chapter we will look at building Visual C++ applications that manipulate data in SQL Server using ODBC.

In ODBC the SQL statement is a string, usually constructed at runtime. It is flexible enough that the same object is used against different DBMSs. The application can ignore the communication with the DBMS and know that data is being returned to it in the application's own formats.

The idea is very much the same as printer drivers in Windows NT. You can format text and send it out to the Device Context for the printer without knowing which printer is attached. ODBC embodies a similar set of database drivers, each a DLL. ODBC is a division of labor. The application, the ODBC driver manager, and the ODBC driver DLLs all have separate chores. Figure 23.1 shows these relationships.

ODBC has three components: your application, the driver manager, and the DBMS's ODBC driver. Each has specific tasks, but the power of ODBC is that you only have to provide the tasks for the application. Two-thirds of the work is done for you.

The application requests the connection to the DBMS and defines the data storage formats. Once connected, the application sends SQL statements. The SQL statements are the requests for results from the DBMS and the method the application uses to process errors. The application also reports the query results to the user. In transaction processing, the application requests the commit and rollbacks. Lastly, it is the application's job to terminate the connection to the DBMS.

Before your application can use ODBC to connect to a database, you have to link the database with the appropriate driver manager. This is done through ODBCAD32.EXE, the ODBC Administrator, shown in Figure 23.2. This manages entries in the NT Registry's ODBC key values.

FIGURE 23.1.

The relationship of the application to the driver manager, the drivers, and the DBMS data.

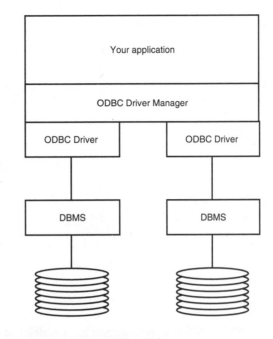

FIGURE 23.2.

Control Panel's ODBC Administrator applet.

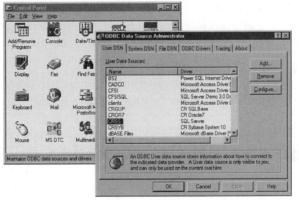

The ODBC Device Manager actually loads the appropriate driver when it receives the function calls of either `SQLBrowseConnect`, `SQLConnect`, or `SQLDriverConnect`. It uses the Registry key values to get the mappings from DBMS to the appropriate driver. The Device Manager then processes the ODBC initialization and provides ODBC entry point addresses for the available function calls. The Device Manager also has the job of validating the parameters passed by the ODBC function calls.

ODBCAD32.EXE provides a list of the drivers available, as seen in Figure 23.3. You may have many databases, all of which use the same driver. When a DBMS system is installed, if it provides ODBC support, it will install a new driver in this list.

FIGURE 23.3.

Installed ODBC drivers.

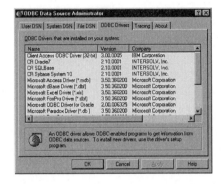

The ODBC driver's jobs include establishing the connection to the database. The requests from the application are submitted to the DBMS in the format it recognizes. The driver translates data into the format the DBMS requires as well and returns results in the format the application requires. Different DBMSs use different error code values, and these are translated into those standard to ODBC. The driver manages the position of the cursors you have set, pointing to the row of data you're manipulating. Lastly, the driver manager handles transaction processing, storing changes until your application calls for them to be committed to the database.

What this all means to you, the programmer, is that two-thirds of the work is being done for you by the Driver Manager and the ODBC driver. You are responsible for the final third: the application.

ODBC and SQL Programming

From the developer's standpoint, it would be ideal if all DBMSs supported the same set of ODBC function calls and SQL statements. This is not the case. Each DBMS has its own set of features, strengths, and weaknesses. To address this, ODBC has conformance levels for its drivers that address two areas: the ODBC API and the SQL grammar. To claim that it supports a conformance level, the driver must support all of the functionality at that level. It may provide more, but it cannot provide less. Three calls can be used to determine what conformance level is supported: SQLGetInfo, SQLGetFunctions, and SQLGetTypeInfo. But this is getting a little ahead of ourselves in the discussion. For now, it is enough to know SQL Server 6.5 is compliant with API Level 2 and SQL Level 1.

ODBC Setup

When you installed NT 4.0 or any one of the Microsoft Office products, the ODBC DLLs were installed in your WINNT\SYSTEM32 or in Windows 95's windows\system directory, and the ODBC 32-bit administrator was installed as an applet in the Control Panel. When you install a DBMS, it will install its own ODBC drivers. When you define a database using the DBMS, you need to go into the ODBC Administrator applet (ODBCAD32.EXE) and link the appropriate driver to your database, giving the data source a name: the DSN.

With Windows NT and ODBC, the information is written into the registry in an ODBCINST.INI key. With versions of ODBC prior to 2.1, driver information was written to a ODBCINST.INI file and database connections were listed in the ODBC.INI file. These files were in the windows directory for Windows 3.11 and NT 3.0 and 3.5. ODBCINST.INI is simply a listing of installed drivers, followed by each driver's path to its particular DLL, and lastly the conformance level the driver can provide.

The same information as the registry listing for a SQL Server database would have been written to the ODBCINST.INI file on an earlier version of ODBC.

The setting options for both the Registry and the older ODBCINST.INI file are as follows. APILevel can be 1, 2, or 0. The value CreateDSN is just the data source name. The ConnectFuntions values are either Y or N for SQLConnect, SQLDriverConnect, and SQLBrowseConnect. DriverODBCVer is the major version number, which can be 1.00, 2.00, or 3.00. The value FileUsage can be 0, 1, or 2, where 0 is not single-tier (usually a client/server DBMS where a client passes SQL statements to server software that it processes), 1 is single-tier with data files as tables (as in Xbase), and 2 is where the driver treats files in data files as qualifiers (like Microsoft's Access, where one file contains many tables). The FileExtensions value is simply that—a file extension, like *.mdb for Access or *.dbf for Xbase. Lastly, SQLLevel is the level of grammar supported, where a 0 is minimal grammar, 1 is core grammar, and 2 is extended grammar.

The translators key of the Registry is what ODBC uses in processing the SQL statements between your application and the driver when different character formats are used.

Once the driver for a DBMS is set up under NT, you can use the ODBC Administrator from the Control Panel to register your application's data source. This information is written to the ODBC.INI file in the windows directory for ODBC 2.0 or to the ODBC.INI key of the registry for more current versions. The system is very important because it enables the application to change data sources without being recompiled. It is common to build a Visual C++ application using a data source file called MYSOURCE, typically a Microsoft Access database that is used in development and testing. When the application is finished and is to be deployed in the work environment, you define an SQL Server database with the same tables and columns. The SQL Server database is named MYSOURCE. Go into the ODBC Administrator and change MYSOURCE to point to the SQL Server database instead of the Access database. This last capability is what makes ODBC a powerful tool for writing applications.

In the ODBC.INI key, the parameter trace is set to 1 when tracing is enabled. In Windows 3.1 tracing was always enabled for all ODBC applications, but in NT it is enabled by each individual application, beginning when an application calls SQLAllocEnv. TraceFile is the output file name.

TraceAutoStop is like Trace. In NT the individual application disables tracing when you call SQLFreeEnv.

Developing an Application

An ODBC application follows the flow of Table 23.1. You initialize the connection, process a set of SQL statements, and then terminate the connection. Whether you develop a console application or use the Visual C++ Database Wizard, you will find the process always follows these same steps.

Table 23.1. Always the same steps!

Process	*Steps in Each Process*
Connect	Allocate environment handle with SQLAllocEnv
	Allocate connection handle with SQLAllocConnect
	Connect to server with SQLConnect
	Allocate statement handle with SQLAllocStmt
SQL Processing	Submit statements
	Retrieve results
	Process results
Disconnect	Free statement handle with SQLFreeStmt
	Disconnect from server with SQLDisconnect
	Free connection handle with SQLFreeConnect
	Free environment handle with SQLFreeEnv

The following is a very simple application run from the command line that illustrates these steps and their order. It assumes that you have used the ODBC Administer applet to set up a DSN, CFSI, pointed to an existing database.

```
#include <windows.h>
#include <string.h>
#include <sql.h>
#include <sqlext.h>
#define MAX_DATA 100

int WINAPI WinMain(HANDLE hInstance, HANDLE hPrevInstance,
➡ LPSTR lpszCmdLine, int nCmdShow)
{
RETCODE rc;
HENV henv;
HDBC hdbc;
```

```
HSTMT hstmt;
char szData[MAX_DATA];
SDWORD cbData;

SQLAllocEnv(&henv);
SQLAllocConnect(henv, &hdbc);
SQLConnect(hdbc, (UCHAR *)"CFSI", SQL_NTS,NULL,0,NULL,0);
SQLAllocStmt(hdbc, &hstmt);


rc = SQLFetch(hstmt);
SQLGetData(hstmt, 2, SQL_C_CHAR, szData, sizeof(szData), &cbData);

MessageBox(NULL, szData, "Chapter xx", MB_OK);

SQLFreeStmt(hstmt, SQL_DROP);
SQLDisconnect(hdbc);
SQLFreeConnect(hdbc);
SQLFreeEnv(henv);
return(TRUE);

}
```

The environment handle is of type HENV, the connection handle of type HDBC, and the statement handle of type HSTMT. Each of these is a memory storage location holding the specifics of the DBMS to which you are connecting. An environment handle can contain multiple connection handles, but each connection handle is associated with only one environment handle. Likewise, each connection handle can have many statement handles, but each statement handle is associated with only one connection handle.

Your application passes data to the driver as the address and length of an input buffer. Afterwards you receive data back as an address, length, and possibly the additional address of the maximum amount of data available in the output buffer. The application needs to allocate memory for these buffers. When the driver returns data that may be in its own SQL format, it is responsible for converting it into the format that ODBC SQL requires. This usually applies to providing NULL-terminated strings.

Whenever you call an ODBC function, the driver returns a predefined code. I defined it above as RETCODE rc. The following are the return codes:

SQL_SUCCESS	SQL_INVALID_HANDLE
SQL_SUCCESS_WITH_INFO	SQL_STILL_EXECUTING
SQL_NO_DATA_FOUND	SQL_NEED_DATA
SQL_ERROR	

Both SQL_ERROR and SQL_SUCCESS_WITH_INFO return additional information that is accessed through a call to SQLError. One of the important functions of the driver is to return a predefined set of error codes.

The syntax for SQLError is

```
RETCODE SQLError(henv, hdbc, hstmt, szSQLState,
➥ pfNativeError, szErrorMsg, cbErrorMsgMax, pcbErrorMsg)
```

23

USING ODBC AND VISUAL C++ WITH SQL SERVER

szSQLState is a pointer to the NULL-terminated 5-byte string, the output of the call. Every error has an associated SQLSTATE return code. These state strings are checked by the application in structure error handling. The SQLSTATE code is a two-character class value followed by a three-character subclass value. The class values of 01 indicate warnings and are accompanied by SQL_SUCCESS_WITH_INFO. Class IM values indicate an ODBC implementation warning or error. SQL_SUCCESS has an SQLSTATE return value of 00000. These values were standardized in the ANSI SQL-92 document:

pfNativeError is the database's native error code; output.

szErrorMsg is a pointer to the error message string; output.

cbErrorMsgMax is the maximum length of the szErrorMsg.

pcbErrorMsg is a pointer to the maximum number of bytes in szErrorMsg.

These error codes tell you if the error came from the database or from one of the components of the ODBC connection, such as the driver. The format changes to indicate the source of the error.

A component error would have the following text form:

```
[vendor][component identifier]error text
```

Here is an example of the error message string:

```
[Microsoft][ODBC dBase Driver]Unable to allocate sufficient memory.
```

An error from the database itself would also identify the data source as

```
[vendor][component identifier][data source]error text
```

The following is an example of the error message string:

```
[Microsoft][ODBC dBase Driver][dBase]
➡ Invalid file name: file TEST.DBF not found.
```

In MFC database programming, we will deal with record sets defined in the class CRecordset. MFC provides structure exception handling through class CDBException. Error handling is usually omitted for readability throughout the rest of the examples in this chapter, but you should use it. The following is an example of using an error string in try/catch error handling:

```
try{
  m_pSet->ReQuery();
  }
catch (CDBException* e) {
  AfxMessageBox(e->m_strError);
  }
```

or

```
try{
  m_pSet->ReQuery();
```

```
   }
catch (CDBException* e) {
   AfxMessageBox(e->m_strStateNativeOrigin);
   }
```

The second form gives you the complete error string, including the native error code, which is useful if you are familiar with the DBMS and its error codes. The results of `m_strStateNativeOrigin` follow:

```
State:S0022,Native:207,Origin:[Microsoft][ODBC SQL Server Driver][SQL Server]
```

`m_strError` would just be `Invalid column name, MyColumn`.

Summing Up the Introduction

The first portion of this chapter examined the history of SQL and ODBC. It defined the basic components of ODBC, the driver, and the driver manager. It listed the basic process of writing an ODBC application: first getting the environment handle, the connection handle, and the statement handle, and then processing multiple SQL statements and reversing the process, freeing the handles. Lastly, an outline of the error handling process was provided. Microsoft has wrapped the database API into several classes, which will be examined before SQL statements and ODBC are discussed again.

MFC Database Class Programming

Back in MFC 3.2, Microsoft introduced four new classes to wrap the most frequent ODBC functions. In subsequent versions of MFC, new methods of database access were introduced, such as DAO for the Jet Engine, OLE-DB for Web applications, and Active Server Pages. The MFC classes really haven't changed since it was introduced. Using the Application Wizard in Visual C++, it became trivial to build a simple ODBC application.

All the connection and data exchange was handled for one table in the initial frame through a `CRecordView`. Visual C++ even provided a set of VCR-type controls to step through the database. It used `CDatabase` and `CRecord set` to open a connection, retrieve a table's data, and close the connection. This chapter assumes that you are familiar with this process and have looked at the sample ODBC tutorial included with Visual C++ 5.0. There you had to get a connection to a database before you could use a `CRecord set` object. You constructed a `CDatabase` object and called its `Open` member function. When you constructed the `CRecord set` object, you passed a pointer to the `CDatabase` object. You finished by calling the `CDatabase Close` member and destroying the `CDatabase` object. This is the basic design of the MFC Database classes. You may not however know you did all of this because the AppWizard handled all of the work!

Class CDatabase

`CDatabase` provides member functions to open a database, close a database, begin/end/reverse transactions, and query the database via SQL statements. `CDatabase` is derived from `CObject` and has one data member, m_hdbc, the connection handle of type HDBC. You construct the object and then call Open to initialize or establish a connection to the database.

The following example shows a typical code snippet to declare an instance of a CDatabase and open that database:

```
class CMyDocument : public Cdocument
{
public:
  CDatabase m_myDB;

}CDatabase* CMyDocument::GetDatabase()
{
  if(!m_myDB.IsOpen() && !m_myDB.Open(NULL))
    return NULL;
  return &m_myDB;
}
```

Creating the class doesn't open the data source—you must call CDatabase's member function Open to make the connection.

```
CDataBase::Open
virtual BOOL Open(Ltual BOOL Open(Ltual BOOL Open(Ltual BOOL
        ➡Open(Ltual BOOL Open(Ltual BOOL Open(LtPCSTR lpszDSN = NULL,
        ➡BOOL bExclusive = FALSE, bReadOnly = FALSE, LPCSTR lpszConnect = "ODBC;",
        ➡BOOLbUseCursorLib = TRUE)
```

The parameters for the code are as follows:

lpszDSN is a string of the data source name. If you pass NULL, the Data Source dialog box asks the user to which data source it should connect. If you specify the lpszConnect string as shown, it will just be ignored, but in future versions of ODBC this may change. Normally you can just set this value to NULL. BExclusive is always FALSE in current versions of MFC because a data source must be shared (non-exclusive). BReadOnly is usually FALSE because you want to be able to read and write to the database. You would set this to TRUE for a data source that you read but don't want the user to change. LpszConnect is a connect string. It always begins with the characters ODBC;, but future versions of CDatabase may support other types of connections. The data source name, the user ID, the user password (if required), and the other information required by your particular database follows. If you don't supply the required information, the Data Source dialog is presented to the user. BUserCursorLib is TRUE when you use the ODBC Cursor library DLL. Set it to FALSE if you wish to use

```
    connect +=uid;
    connect +="; PWD=";
    connect +=password;

pD0c->m_myDB.Open(NULL,FALSE,FALSE,connect,FALSE);
}
```

The following shows another example of Open, where the application hard-codes the database name and connection information:

```
CDatabase m_myDB();
m_myDB.Open("MYDATABASE",FALSE,FALSE,"ODBC;");
```

You also can query the user for connection information by using just the `Open(NULL)`:

```
m_myDB.Open(NULL);
```

It is important to note that opening the database can take several seconds. Most applications open the database once globally and then use that connection throughout the application. `Open` is usually stored in either the `CDocument` class or the main application's `InitInstance`. In the following example, we open the database in the application's call to `InitInstance`.

In the application's header file:

```
CDatabase myDB;
```

In the application's `InitInstance`:

```
try
{
  myDB.Open("MYDATABASE",FALSE,FALSE,"ODBC;");
}
catch (CDBException *e)
{
  AfxMessageBox(CString("Didn't open database.\n") + e->m_strError);
  throw;
}
```

Wherever you need to open a `CRecord set` to get a pointer to the application, open the record set as

```
CMyApp *app=(CMyApp *)AfxGetApp();
CMyRecord set myset(&(app->myDB));
myset.Open(CRecord set::dynaset);
...
```

If you open the database in the document, you need a pointer to the database. The pointer is gotten from the document, as the following example shows:

```
CDatabase *pDoc = GetDocument()->m_pDatabase;
CDatabase::Close();
virtual void Close();
```

The only thing to remember about `CDatabase::Close` is that you need to close the record sets before you close the database connection. If you don't, the record set is left in an undefined state and transaction processing rolls back. This does not destroy the `CDatabase` object—you may need it to connect to a different data source.

The preceding example uses the attribute `IsOpen`, which returns nonzero if the `CDatabase` object is connected. Also available are `GetConnect()`, the ODBC connect string; `GetDatabaseName()`, a string of the database in use; `CanUpdate()`, which returns nonzero if you didn't make the connection read-only; `CanTransact()`, which returns nonzero if the database supports transaction processing; `InWaitForDataSouce()`, which returns nonzero when the `CDatabase` object is waiting for a server response; `SetLoginTimeout()` and `SetQueryTimeout()`, which enable you to specify how many seconds to wait; and SetSynchronousMode(), which enables synchronous processing for record sets and SQL statements. Asynchronous processing is the default. CDatabase::Cancel is used to cancel an asynchronous operation in progress.

CDatabase supports transaction processing, which is a set of reversible SQL calls—AddNew(), Edit(), Delete() and Update() member functions of CRecord set. If the data source supports transaction processing, all of the statements are held in a state where they can each be reversed. To begin, the statement BeginTrans() is called, followed by a set of statements. When the user specifies that all is okay, CommitTrans() is called and the set of statements is executed. In addition to the preceding, CDatabase has the operation RollBack() to reverse changes since BeginTrans().

One of the most-used database operations is CDatabase::ExecuteSQL. The member function takes a pointer to the SQL statement. The next chapter, "Connecting to SQL Server from Visual Basic," looks at two ODBC functions, SQLExecDirect and SQLExecute, which enable you to pass every SQL statement to our DBMS driver and get back record sets of data. However, CDatabase::ExecuteSQL is not used to retrieve datasets—it's used in row operations such as UPDATE and DELETE. In MFC programming, you should try to limit direct SQL calls via ::ExecuteSQL so that functionality is not supported by the MFC class. This function doesn't return an MFC dataset:

```
Void ExecuteSQL(LPCSTR lpszSQL);
```

An example code snipped using ExecuteSQL to execute an SQL statement:

```
CString myName = "Update CLIENTS Set LASTNAME = "Hamilton"
➥    WHERE CLIENTNO eq 1345";
IF(!m_myDB.ExecuteSQL(myName);
{
//handle error
}
```

CRecord set

The CRecord set class encapsulates a collection of database records called a record set. Record sets support scrolling through records, adding, editing, and deleting records, specifying filters to the records, sorting, and parameterization of the record set. You need a separate CRecord set class for every database table and every join you use. The Class Wizard creates this for you and sets up member variables to handle the data exchange between the class and the dialog or the view where you manage the data. Don't modify the code generated by Class Wizard in this class. If you redefine the database table, Class Wizard regenerates over your changes. The class-specific code to manipulate the data can be in either the Dialog class or a separate class you inherit from your CRecord set class.

The CRecord set class should be created and deleted as needed. Each instance takes up RAM, but creating and deleting is fast and efficient. Don't open the classes globally, as you did with the database connection. Open record sets as you need them, then close them after you use them. You can also let them go out of scope by opening them in your dialog class functions. In the following OnOK() function for a dialog box, you see that the record set object will be deleted after the OnOK() function is complete because the function's local variables go out of scope and die:

```
void CMyDialog::OnOK()
{
  UpdateData(TRUE);
  try
  {

    CMyApp *app=(CMyApp *)AfxGetApp();
    CMyRecord set myset(&(app->myDB));
    myset.Open(CRecord set::dynaset);
    myset.AddNew();
    myset.m_name = m_NameID;
    myset.Update();
  }
catch(CDBException *e)
{
  AfxMessageBox(e->m_strError);
  e->Delete();
  return;
}
Cdialog::OnOK();
} //after this function exits the above Crecord set
// goes out of scope and is deleted
```

Deleting the record set frees up the RAM.

CRecord set is a large class. Record sets come in two types: dynasets and snapshots. A dynaset stays synchronized with updates that the user makes, while a snapshot is a set of data from the database at the time you created the CRecord set. There is also an open type, Forward Only, which sets up a read-only forward-scrolling record set. This enables the MFC classes to work with older drivers that only support this type of scrolling.

The functions of CRecord set enable you to scroll through, update, sort, and further filter the data, and to parameterize the record set. Parameterizing enables you to change the filter without parsing the entire SQL phrase again. The Open member function has already been discussed. There is also a Close member function.

The data members of CRecord set are simple:

>   *m_hstmt* is the statement handle.

>   *m_pDatabase* is a pointer to the database's CDatabase class.

>   *m_nFields* is a UINT to the number of data fields in the record set.

>   *m_nParams* is the number of parameter data members.

>   *m_strFilter* is a CString with the SQL WHERE clause.

>   *m_sort* is a CString with the SQL ORDER BY clause.

23

USING ODBC
AND VISUAL C++
WITH SQL SERVER

CRecord set operations edit the record set and move through the record set.

AddNew prepares the record set for a new row (Update actually adds it).

Delete deletes the current record from the record set.

Edit prepares the record set for changes (Update actually changes it).

Update completes the AddNew and Edit member functions.

Move positions the record set at one record.

MoveFirst positions to the first record in the record set.

MoveLast positions to the last record in the record set.

MoveNext and MovePrev position the record in the record set.

DoFieldExchange implements RFX between field member data of the record set and database.

GetDefaultConnect gets the default connect string.

GetDefaultSQL gets the default SQL string.

OnSetOptions sets options for the ODBC statement.

OnWaitForDataSource is called to yield processing time to other applications during asynchronous operations.

When you're moving through the record set, you need to check if you are at the end or beginning of the record set with the following:

```
if (!myRecset.IsBOF() && !myRecset.IsEOF())
    myRecset.MoveNext();
```

CRecord set has a large set of attributes (see Table 23.2) to give you information on the record set and changes to the field. All attributes that are "checks if " return nonzero if TRUE.

Table 23.2. CRecord set attributes.

Attribute	Purpose
CanAppend	Checks if new records can be added.
CanRestart	Checks if requery can be called.
CanScroll	Checks if you can scroll through the records.
CanTransact	Checks if transactions are supported.
CanUpdate	Checks if the record set can be updated.
GetRecordCount	Gets the number of records in the record set.
GetStatus	Gets the status of the record set: the index of the current record and whether a final count of the records has been obtained.
GetTableName	Gets the name of the table of the record set.
GetSQL	Gets the SQL string used to select the record set.

Attribute	Purpose
IsOpen	Checks if Open has been called previously.
IsBOF	Checks if the record set has been positioned before the first record. There is no current record.
IsEOF	Checks if the record set has been positioned after the last record. There is no current record.
IsDeleted	Checks if the record set is positioned on a deleted record.

CRecordView

CRecordView enables your application to display fields in a dialog box. Dialog Data Exchange (DDX) and Record Field Exchange (RFX) enable you to automatically exchange data between your view and the dialog box. CRecordView supports movement between records, updating records, and automatically closing the record set when the view closes.

In MFC programming, the standard approach to developing a database application is via document/view. You open a file and have multiple views of the data in that file. If this still confuses you, think about Microsoft Word. When you type a .DOC file, you can change how you view the text in four ways: Normal, Outline, Page Layout, and Master Document. When you create a document you use Normal to view spacing. When you review a document you probably switch to Master, a more convenient reading mode.

The concept of multiple views becomes nebulous with databases. The document is actually a collection of files or tables. You often want to look at a union of several tables. Multiple views are even harder to define in client/server applications when you are passing messages to another application. In database applications the record set is the document. It is often easier to embed the record set in the frame window, but this precludes having multiple views on the data. CRecordView is a class developed as a view directly connected to a record set.

CRecordView is a view created from a dialog template that displays the fields in a CRecord set. This class uses both DDX and RFX to automate the movement of data between controls and fields in the record set. When you did your first ODBC tutorial, you saw the power of CRecordView when the AppWizard created a view and record set. AppWizard even created a toolbar to navigate through the record set. However, in most cases you will use CRecord set and a CView, but not CRecordView. CRecord set has many more features for manipulating data from your database dialog box.

CFieldExchange (RFX) and Special Handling of CLongBinary

CFieldExchange is a helper class for the RFX mechanism. It exchanges data between the record set class and the actual database. CFieldExchange supports a number of operations, including binding parameters, binding data members, and setting flags on the current record. It has two class members: IsFieldType returns the number of the field if the operation is appropriate for the type, and SetFieldType specifies the type of the record set data member. The ClassWizard generates a field map and handles the typing for you, as the following example shows:

```
//enroll tutorial
void CSectionSet::DoFieldExchange(CFieldExchange* pFX)
{
//{{AFX_FIELD_MAP(CSectionSet)
pFX->SetFieldType(CFieldExchange::outputColumn);
RFX_Text(pFX, _T("[CourseID]"), m_CourseID);
RFX_Text(pFX, _T("[SectionNo]"), m_SectionNo);
RFX_Text(pFX, _T("[InstructorID]"), m_InstructorID);
RFX_Text(pFX, _T("[RoomNo]"), m_RoomNo);
RFX_Text(pFX, _T("[Schedule]"), m_Schedule);
RFX_Int(pFX, _T("[Capacity]"), m_Capacity);
//}}AFX_FIELD_MAP
pFX->SetFieldType(CFieldExchange::param);
RFX_Text(pFX,"CourseIDParam",m_strCourseIDParam);
}
```

The pFX is the context for doing the data exchange and is similar to CArchive::Serialize. It gets and sets data to an external data source, in this case a CDatabase class member variable. RFX supports the operations shown in Table 23.3.

Table 23.3. Operations supported by RFX.

Name	Operation
BindParam	Indicates where ODBC should retrieve parameter data.
BindFieldToColumn	Indicates where ODBC must retrieve/deposit outputColumn data.
Fixup	Sets CString/CByteArray lengths, sets NULL status bit.
MarkForAddNew	Marks dirty (changed) if value has changed since AddNew call.
MarkForUpdate	Marks dirty if value has changed since Edit call.
Name	Appends field names for fields marked dirty.
NameValue	Appends <column name>=? for fields marked dirty.
Value	Appends ? followed by separator, like , or .
SetFieldDirty	Sets status bit dirty for field.
SetFieldNull	Sets status bit indicating NULL value for field.
IsFieldDirty	Returns value of dirty status bit.
IsFieldNull	Returns value of NULL status bit.
IsFieldNullable	Returns TRUE if field can hold NULL values.
StoreField	Archives field value.
LoadField	Reloads archived field value.
GetFieldInfoValue	Returns general information on a field.
GetFieldInfoOrdinal	Returns general information on a field.

If your binary data is long, you will need to retrieve it into a CLongBinary, which can be as large as the available memory. One additional step is needed to do the field exchange, which is calling SetFieldDirty to ensure that the field is included in UPDATE operations.

Class CLongBinary simplifies working with *BLOBs (binary large objects)* in a database. A BLOB is an object in the database, such as a bitmap, but it may be larger than available memory. In this case you would need to process in a piecemeal fashion using ODBC's function SQLGetData. When you create a CRecord set, the CLongBinary object is an embedded member of that class. RFX handles loading the data and storing it back in the database. CLongBinary has two class members: m_hData, an HGLOBAL handle to the actual data, and m_dwDataLength, the object's size in bytes. If the BLOB is too large, you get an AFX_SQL_ERROR_SQL_NO_TOTAL or a standard memory exception. You can check this by calling ::GlobalSize on the m_hData member. The next chapter discusses the ODBC function SQLGetData.

CDBException

The class CDBException provides exception handling for runtime errors during ODBC processing. It provides member functions that enable your application to access both the error return codes and the strings associated with them. Its format is as follows:

```
try
  {
    CMyApp *app=(CMyApp *)AfxGetApp();
    CMyRecord set myset(&(app->myDB));
    myset.Open(CRecord set::dynaset);
    myset.AddNew();
    myset.m_name = m_NameID;
    myset.Update();
  }
catch(CDBException *e)
{
  AfxMessageBox(e->m_strError);
  e->Delete();
  return;
}
```

The next chapter deals extensively with SQL and ODBC errors and their SQLSTATE return codes.

Some Examples

One of the most common questions asked about developing database applications is, "How do I create a join?" In Example 1, I will do just that. Example 2 makes a modified CRecord set base class with added functionality that can be reused, saving you some typing time.

Example 1

A join is a common database activity. To make a join using MFC, you add the second table to the GetDefaultSQL() in your first record class:

```
CString CMyRSet::GetDefualtSQL()
{
  return _T("Employees", "Payroll");
}
```

This example joins tables `Employees` and `Payroll`. You then assign the new member variables as normal. If you have columns with the same name, you need to remember that column names in `DoFieldExchange` must be unique. So you would set table name to column name as

```
void CMyRSet::DoFieldExchange(CFieldExchange* pFX_
{
//{{AFX_FIELD_MAP(CMyRSet)
pFX->SetFieldType(...)
RFX_TEXT(pFX,"Employees.EmpLastName," m_Lastname);
...
//}}AFX_FIELD_MAP
}
```

Also you need to add the table name to the field name in the sort and filter strings. This tells the compiler which `EmpLastName` tables you are referring to. Demarcate the fields with the table name as

```
m_pSet->m_strFilter = "Employees.EmpLastName = Payroll.EmpLastName";
```

Example 2

Load `ComboBox` in the `CRecordset` derived class. For every table or view you create, you build a `CRecord` set. The ClassWizard generates the code for you, but when you change the database schema and regenerate, your custom code changes within the `CRecord` set can be lost. One technique is to create a class derived from your `CRecord` set and define class functions in it. This example fills a combo box. The `CRecord` set used here is `CRSEmployee`, and its derived class will be `CRSDEmplyee`:

```
//RSDemployee.h
#include "rsdemployee.h"
class CRSDEmployee : public CRSEmployee
{
public
  CRSDEmployee(CDatabase* pDatabase = NULL);
  void LoadCombo(class CComboBox &cb);
  DECLARE_DYNAMIC(CRSDEmployee)
};

//rsdemployee.cpp
#include "stdafx.h"
#include "myCDatabase.h"
#ifdef _DEBUG
#undef THIS_FILE
static char BASED_CODE THIS_FILE[] = _FILE_;
#endif
IMPLEMENT_DYNAMIC(CRDEmployee, CRSEmployee)
CRSDEmployee::CRSDEmployee(CDatabase* pdb)
  :CRSEmployee(pdb)
{
}
```

```
void CRSDEmployee::LoadCombo(CMyApp *)afxGetApp();
int index;
m_strSort = "Lname ASC, Fname ASC";
m_strFilter = "";
try
{
  Requery();
  cb.ResetContext();
  while (!IsEOF())
  {
    index = cb.AddString(m_Lname + ", " + "m_Fname);
    cb.SetItemData(index, m_EmpID);
    MoveNext()
 }
catch(CDBException* e)
{
  AfxMessageBox(e->m_strError);
  e->Delete();
}
#ifdef _DEBUG
... rest of class code
#endif //_DEBUG
```

You would use this class and call this function from your application's `OnInitDialog` as

```
BOOL CMyDialog::OnInitDialog()
{
  CMyApp *app = (CMyApp*)AfxGetApp();
  CRSDEmployee emp(&(app->db));
  emp.Open(CRecord set::dynaset);
  Cdialog::OnInitDialog();
  emp.LoadCombo(m_pSet);  //this is function call
}
```

The Call Level Interface (CLI)

The preceding sections demonstrated ODBC programming by using the MFC Database classes, which wrap the ODBC function calls into easier-to-use classes. This is similar to how MFC wraps the Win32 API functions into classes. This section focuses on the specifics of how you implement an ODBC-enabled application using those function calls.

In an early Pascal programming class, I remember being given a totally unknown file from which I needed to extract some demographic data. I had to devise a plan to open the file and search for patterns in the data. At the time, it seemed like such an obscure problem. Now this type of problem happens every day, however, when your company sells software to a new client and you need to convert the existing data to your format. In most cases, you know the file types and data definitions. However, with the new concept of the "global village," more and more often you won't know the data format.

For the sake of example, say you need to write a report that includes sales of widgets by month. You know the sales data is located in the accounting domain's computers. You know that accounting has an SQL Server, and you have the correct privileges. In the past you would have called accounting and asked for the data over the "sneakernet." But today you can connect with your spreadsheet or report writer, have the data structure presented to you as a series of list boxes, query the data, and get results in the format your report needs. This section discusses writing the report-writing software behind the report.

In the standard CLI (call level interface), there are 57 functions to support database access. At first they seem threatening, but once you know one of the family, they are all similar. They all take input parameters as a pair made up of string address or NULL, and length or ignore. They all pass back output parameters as string address, length of data you want, and, optionally, the address of the amount of data available to you. This last output parameter can be confusing unless you think of it as having a very long column description available, (like My_Still_Working_Employees), although you only need a short report heading (Employees). This chapter uses Hungarian notation as sz (a NULL-terminated string), cb (count of bytes), and pcb (pointer to a count of bytes). pcb is usually the total number of bytes available. If pcb is pointing to a string, it is without the NULL terminator. Throughout this chapter NULL-terminated strings are cast as (UCHAR *) because .cpp (C++) files and type checking are generated more tightly than .c (C). Most outside examples you see don't include this cast on the NULL-terminated strings and are thus standard C files.

The CLI specified functions can be broken down into 11 groups, making the task of learning all 57 functions somewhat easier:

- Allocating and deallocating handles (eight calls)
- Getting and setting attributes (ten calls)
- Opening and closing database connection (two calls)
- Accessing descriptors (six calls)
- Executing SQL statements (nine calls)
- Retrieving results (eight calls)
- Accessing schema metadata (four calls)
- Performing introspection (four calls)
- Controlling transactions (two calls)
- Accessing diagnostic information (three calls)
- Canceling functions (one call)

If you're new to ODBC, one of the best resources is called ODBCTEST (the file is actually ODBCTE32.EXE), included with the ODBC 3.0 SDK. The ODBC SDK is available on Level II or Level III MSDN. Each of the SQL functions throughout this section is listed. ODBCTE32.EXE enables you to execute each statement, one by one, and test your syntax. It's a good idea to add it to your VC++ 5.0 tools menu so that it's available for debugging your ODBC application. If you have an older version of ODBC, ODBC 3.0 is available on CompuServe's WINEXT forum or through ftp.microsoft.com in the /developer/ODBC/public/ subdirectory.

Whether you are writing for a single PC or for a company's worldwide application, it is best to envision the client/server model. The application sends messages that the server interprets. The server retrieves data from a DMBS that is sent back to the client with another stream of messages. In ODBC, the middleware is the driver.

ODBC defines three types of drivers. Although each type functions differently, the application doesn't have to know about it. In ODBC programming, the application doesn't care if the data is on your local hard drive, across the network, or on a different continent. In ODBC, a *one-tier* driver accesses an ISAM or flat file. Usually the database is on your local PC. In this case, the driver is the SQL engine and it does all the SQL statement processing.

Figure 23.4 is a one-tier driver typical of what you will use in developing a PC-based database application.

FIGURE 23.4.

ODBC one-tier type driver.

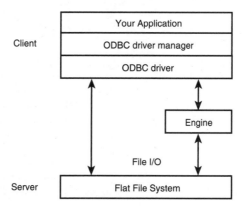

A two-tier driver is the more typical NT office setup. The application is usually placed on an NT workstation and the DBMS on an NT server. This is what is usually referred to as *client/ server*. ODBC calls the two-tier driver maps to the DBMS's native SQL. SQL Server uses a two-tier ODBC driver. Figure 23.5 shows that the server end of the system is intelligent, parsing and optimizing SQL statements as well as scheduling their execution. The client handles the connection to the DBMS and the processing of results.

In a three-tier driver, the client connects to a server that acts as a gateway to the network, as shown in Figure 23.6. The DBMS may be on a large mainframe computer. The gateway is responsible for routing and translating requests. In a sense, the application on the client has a one-tier driver to the gateway machine. The gateway machine has either a one- or two-tier driver to the DBMS. The gain is that by off-loading work requirements to a gateway machine, more clients can access the DBMS.

FIGURE 23.5.

SQL Server's two-tier type driver.

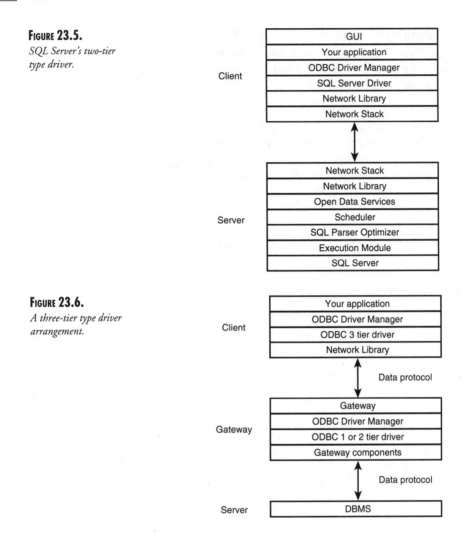

FIGURE 23.6.

A three-tier type driver arrangement.

Connecting to a Data Source

When you're connecting to a database, you must evaluate two scenarios—the first is where you have a target database in mind and know its schema, and the second is where your application must behave like Excel or Crystal Reports and connect to any ODBC data source. In the second case, you need to use the ODBC catalog functions to determine which capabilities are available.

SQLAllocEnv

Before you can call any ODBC function, you must initialize ODBC and establish the environment. ODBC uses this environment to keep track of which data sources are in use. Remember that you have one environment per application but can have many connections. The first call is always to SQLAllocEnv, which returns a pointer to the memory location of the environmental handle. The environmental handle privately tracks the number of connections, the connections' states (connected vs. disconnected), and the passing of environment errors to SQLError. Within the henv handle are also the enumerates of the data sources and the drivers available, as well as the ability to control the transaction processing on all connections.

This handle is of type HENV. Handles in ODBC are like those you have seen in programming for Windows NT. They are an index into a table entry, identifying program data that is private. Windows has all types of handles, memory handles, device contexts, instance handles, and ODBC handles. Privacy is important in that each driver developer can do what they need to do to get the job done inside a block of code that is used by the application in a consistent way. This is called the *interface*. Handles have constant interfaces. ODBC drivers provide uniform error handling, tying the error to the function that generated the error condition. In a multithreaded environment like Windows NT, if one process starts a thread to do something, another can control or terminate that thread. There are actually a pair of handles generated. The application generates a handle passed to the driver manager, and the driver manager generates a handle to share with the DBMS's actual ODBC driver.

The return value from SQLAllocEnv is SQL_SUCCESS or SQL_ERROR. Generally, SQL_ERROR means a memory error and handle would be set to SQL_NULL_HENV. The following is a general outline of the process:

```
#include <windows.h>
#include <sql.h>
HENV henv;
HDBC hdbc;
SQLAllocEnv(&henv);
SQLAllocConnect(&hdbc)
SQLConnect(hdbc, MYDATABASE",SQL_NTS,"MYUSERID",SQL_NTS,"MYPASSWORD",SQL_NTS);

//preform application ODBC functions

SQLDisconnect(hdbc);
SQLFreeConnect(hdbc);
SQLFreeEnv(henv);
```

SQLAllocConnect

Just as you got the previous environment handle, you need a handle to the actual connection or connections. For every data source your application uses, you need one connection handle. SQLAllocConnect returns a pointer to a memory location, the connection handle, of type hdbc. SQLAllocConnect can return the same codes as above with the SQLSTATE codes of 01000, S1000, S1001 (memory allocation error) and S1009 (invalid argument value). SQLAllocConnect is a call into the Driver Manager DLL. Inside the private structures of hdbc is all the information about one single connection, including the server/directory/file information, for the driver to be used. The greatest feature of an hdbc is that all the function calls provided by the driver have pointers stored in an array to provide function call routing. hdbc passes connection errors to SQLError. Transaction isolation is done within this handle, as well as time-out information:

```
HDBC hdbc;
SQLAllocConnect(henv, &hdbc);
```

You also need to allocate a handle to the statements you will use. Again, every connection can have many statements, but each statement applies to only one connection. All SQL statements and catalog functions get the hdbc handle from the hstmt handle to know which driver has the actual function code. hstmt also maintains state information so that the application can call the functions in the correct order. hstmt locks results sets together and holds the cursor name and network information. But all of its member variables are private, available only to Windows and ODBC to access via an interface. The syntax is

```
rc = SQLAllocStmt(hdbc, phstmt);
```

phstmt is a far pointer to the storage area of the statement handle.

SQLState return codes are 01000, 08003 (connection not open), IM001, S1000, S1001 (memory allocation failure), and S1009 (invalid argument).

SQLConnect

At this point you have two handles. The ODBC connection is said to be initialized, but you have not yet specified which data source you want or made the actual connection. SQLConnect is the only ODBC function available at the Core API Level to make the connection. In the ODBC installation section, I introduced various methods of passing the DSN (data source name) and database specifics, like user ID (UID) and password (PWD), via SQLConnect. The SQLConnect parameters are

```
SQLConnect(hdbc, szDSN, cbDSN, szUID, cbUID, szPWD, cbPWD)
```

Throughout this chapter, the type definitions are always

```
HDBC hdbc;
char szDSN[SOME_LENGTH];
SDWORD bcDSN;
```

This is a good place to point out a similarity between the parameter values used for all ODBC function calls. First comes a handle, then a parameter, then that parameter's size, then another parameter, then that parameter's size. This is always the pattern—remember it when you get stuck. This pattern makes internalizing the function calls easier to remember. If the strings are NULL-terminated, you can pass SQL_NTS for the length of the DSN. In most single-tiered databases, you only need to supply the connection handle and the DSN.

SQLConnect returns general SQLSTATE return codes: 01000, 08001 (unable to connect), 08002 (connection in use), 08004 (data source rejected connection), 08S01 (communication link failure), and 28000 (invalid authorization). It also returns driver codes: IM001 (function not supported), IM002 (no default driver), IM003 (driver not loaded), IM004 (SQLAllocEnv failed), IM005 (SQLAllocConnect failed), and IM006 (SQLSetConnectOption failed). It also returns IM009 and SQL codes: S1000, S1001, S1090 (invalid string length), and S1T00 (timeout). SQL_INVALID_HANDLE sets the hdbc to SQL_NULL_HDBC.

```
RETCODE rc;
rc = SQLConnect(hdbc, "MYDATABASE",SQL_NTS,"MYUSERID",
➥ SQL_NTS,"MYPASSWORD",SQL_NTS);
```

In a normal application, you might have a dialog box in which the user provides a username and password. In this case you would build a string, the connection string, which could be passed to SQLConnect or its friends SQLDriverConnect and SQLBrowseConnect. SQLDriverConnect is an extension Level 1 function that takes a connection string rather than a set of parameters and uses standard user interface elements. Therefore, if you are writing to Windows, Macintosh OS, or OS/2, this is applicable. If you are writing to MS-DOS, it doesn't help you because you don't have graphical dialog boxes available. You saw SQLDriverConnect wrapped in CDatabase, with its ability to ask the user for the string information with dialog boxes. In that case, the call had no supplied parameters:

```
rc = SQLDriverConnect(hdbc, hwnd, NULL, 0, NULL, 0, 0, SQL_DRIVER_COMPLETE);
```

You need to supply the hwnd, a handle to the window in which you want questions asked. The function builds the message boxes and displays them:

```
#define MAXBUF 512
{
HDBC hdbc;
HWND hwnd;
char szConStrIn[MAXBUF+1];  //input string
SWORD cbConStrIn; //length of string
char szConStrOut[MAXBUF+1]; //connection string for later use
SWORD cbConStrOutMax;
SWORD pcbConStrOut; // pointer to total number bytes in csConStrOut
UWORD fDriverCompletion;
rc = SQLDriverConnect(hdbc, hwnd, szConStrIn, MAXBUF, szConStrOut,
   ➥MAXBUF, &pcbConStrOut, fDriverCompletion);
```

Using ODBCTEST, you can simulate what your user will see. First choose SQLAllocEnv, SQLAllocConnect, and then SQLDriverConnect, and you are presented with your default dialog boxes, as shown in Figure 23.7, and the dialog box to input the username and password, as shown in Figure 23.8.

FIGURE 23.7.

SQLDriverConnect *to the data source.*

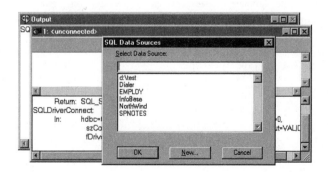

FIGURE 23.8.

SQLDriverConnect
retrieves connection
information.

The magic that brings up these dialog boxes is done in the last parameter, which can be either SQL_DRIVER_PROMPT (put up the SQL Data Sources dialog with all DSNs for the user to pick one), SQL_DRIVER_COMPLETE (checks the szConStrIn for DSN and connects when enough information is available), SQL_DRIVER_COMPLETE_REQUIRED (same as above, but must have full connection string to proceed), or SQL_DRIVER_NOPROMPT (don't ask).

In Windows NT, you may be tempted to develop a DLL that encapsulates the application's ODBC functions, sharing them between several applications. ODBC handles are unique to their tasks and cannot be shared because their memory allocation does not use the DDE_SHARE option on the GlobalAlloc() call. A better approach than developing a separate DLL is to develop a DDE server application. By doing so, you are not trying to share handles and the server application will still have all the ODBC calls and will send messages to your other applications.

The return codes for SQLDriverConnect has the same SQLSTATEs as SQLConnect.

SQLBrowseConnect is the third method of connecting to a data source. It enables you to control the user interface. Your application goes step by step, first asking the driver what information is needed, then prompting the user for that information. You repeat the process with the next bit of information until the entire connection string is completed. If you repeatedly called SQLBrowseConnect, the driver gives you the next piece of the connection string and returns SQL_NEED_DATA. Why? You would use SQLBrowseConnect when attempting to connect to a foreign data source, perhaps a source on a mainframe computer where even the format of the data may need to be translated. The database might have many personal attributes, such as HOSTNAME, ALIASs, multiple levels of passwords, and so on. An example follows:

```
HSTMT hstmt
RETCODE rc;
UCHAR szConStrIn[100] = "MYDSN";
UCHAR szConStrOut[100];
SWORD cbConStrOut;
do
{
rc = SQLBrowseConnect(hstmt, szConStrIn, SQL_NTS, szConStrOut,
 ➥sizeof(szConStrOut),&bcConStrOut);
}
while
{
(rc == SQL_NEED_DATA)
}
```

The input and output strings are always in the following form:

`KEYWORD=VALUE;`

`SQLBrowseConnect` has extensions that enable you to query the user in the form of

`KEYWORD:PROMPT=?;`

`PROMPT` is your string to the user. Another extension uses the form

`KEYWORD:PROMPT={CHOICE1,CHOICE2,CHOICE3}`

This gives the user three choices. The attributes like `UID` (username) and `PWD` (password) must be in all capital letters. The prompt can be mixed case. If you precede an attribute with an asterisk (*), it is optional.

Now the question is, which connection function is best? Here are a simple set of rules:

- If the application works with a fixed set of drivers, use `SQLConnect` or `SQLDriverConnect` and hard-coded connection strings.

- If your data source requires more than the three parameters for `SQLConnect`, you need to use `SQLDriverConnect`.

- If you use dialog boxes to prompt users for information to log in, use `SQLDriverConnect` or `SQLBrowseConnect`.

- If the driver supports only core-level functions, use `SQLConnnect`. If it supports Level 1, use either `SQLConnect` or `SQLDriverConnect`.

- If the application doesn't know which drivers are available, use `SQLDriverConnect`.

- If your application will have multiple users and passwords, it is usually best to prompt the users for data with a dialog box in the application, so call `SQLConnect` or `SQLDriverConnect`.

- If users can decide on a data source, call `SQLDriverConnect` or `SQLBrowseConnect`.

- If the application has no idea what the connection string might look like, call `SQLBrowseConnect`.

You may want to build a quick, simple Visual C++ application to make sure all this really works as described. The following is a fairly basic application that I also listed earlier. Open a data source and get a piece of data from a table. In Visual C++ you open a new workspace, choose a name, and choose Application. Add a new file to the project and type it in. This procedure does nothing more than display a list box with the data element you went looking for. All the usual error checking has been removed for simplicity. Your application should function like this, but don't follow this form because without error handling, ODBC applications become very difficult to debug. You may not even know if the database is open, let alone why you are getting strange characters for the results.

```
//text1.cpp
#include <windows.h>
```

```
#include <sql.h>
#include <sqlext.h>
#define MAX_DATA 100

int WINAPI WinMain(HANDLE hInstance, HANDLE hPrevInstance,
➥ LPSTR lpszCmdLine, int nCmdShow)
{

HENV henv;
HDBC hdbc;
HSTMT hstmt;
char szData[MAX_DATA];
SDWORD cbData;

SQLAllocEnv(&henv);
SQLAllocConnect(henv, &hdbc);
SQLConnect(hdbc, (UCHAR *)"SPNOTES", SQL_NTS,NULL,0,NULL,0);
SQLAllocStmt(hdbc, &hstmt);

SQLFetch(hstmt);
SQLGetData(hstmt, 2, SQL_C_CHAR, szData, sizeof(szData), &cbData);

MessageBox(NULL, szData, "Chapter SQL Server", MB_OK);

SQLFreeStmt(hstmt, SQL_DROP);
SQLDisconnect(hdbc);
SQLFreeConnect(hdbc);
SQLFreeEnv(henv);
return(TRUE);
}
```

To explain what is happening behind the scenes, let's back up a bit. When you build your application, Visual C++ links in ODBC32.LIB. When your user runs the application, ODBC.DLL is loaded into memory. The driver manager contains the function entry points for every one of its functions. Windows NT may not load ODBC.DLL if it is already running (the instance count is nonzero). When your application allocates the preceding handles, two sets are actually allocated: one for the application/driver manager connection, and one for the driver manager/driver connection. When you call SQLConnect to the DSN, the driver manager calls LoadLibrary and loads the driver DLL.

At this point the driver manager polls the driver DLL, using the Windows function GetProcAddress to build an array of function entry points and associate that array with your HDBC handle. From this point on, the driver DLL is just another data file to Windows NT. The driver manager then uses the second set of HENV and HDBC to make the calls into the driver DLL. It is this two-step process that makes connecting to an ODBC data source time-consuming to the user. After all these steps, the driver sends the user ID and password to the DBMS. Throughout this process, your application's call to SQLConnect has been waiting for its return.

Using the Data Source

The data source in ODBC is the combination of the driver and the DBMS. You have already seen the definition of the DBMS in the registry ODBCINST.INI folder, but how did it get there?

The obvious way was that the user loaded a new data source with the ODBC applet from the Control Panel. However, most applications install data sources as part of the program installation. This would certainly lower the number of support calls you receive about how to install the data source. You could also manually edit the registry. Telling a user to do so, of course, is guaranteed to get you all the support calls you can handle. The prescribed method is `SQLConfigDataSource`. The prototype is

```
BOOL SQLConfigDataSource(hwnd, UINT fRequest,
➡ LPCSTR lpszDriver, LPCSTR lpszAttributes);
```

The following is an example for an Excel spreadsheet you want to access via ODBC:

```
#include <odbcinst.h>
SQLConfigDataSource(NULL,ODBC_ADD_DSN, "Excel Files (*.xls)",
    ➡ "DSN=MyFancySpreadsheet\0", "Description=Save the Company Spreadsheet\0",
    ➡ "FileType=Excel\0","DataDirectory=C:\\ROOT\0", "MaxScanRows=20\0");
```

The data source in the case of an Excel spreadsheet is the directory of the spreadsheet itself. ODBC 2.5 introduced the functions `ConfigDriver`, `SQLConfigDriver`, `SQLInstallTranslator`, `SQLRemoveDriver`, `SQLRemoveDriverManager`, and `SQLRemoveTranslator`. These all alter the entries in the NT registry under SOFTWARE | ODBC | ODBCINST.INI.

The following is an example of an Access database:

```
char  szDriverName[] = "Microsoft Access Driver (*.mdb)";
char  szAttributes[] = "DSN=sample\0
➡ DefaultDir=\\\0 DriverId=25\0DBQ=sample.mdb\0";
char  szAttributesCreateMDB[] = "CREATE_DB=\\sample.mdb General\0";

SQLConfigDataSource(NULL, ODBC_ADD_DSN, szDriverName,szAttributesCreateMDB);
SQLConfigDataSource(NULL, ODBC_ADD_DSN, szDriverName,szAttributes);
```

The syntax of the new installer functions is

```
BOOL ConfigDriver(hwnd, fRequest lpszDriver, lpszArgs,
➡ lpszMsg cbMsgMax and pcbMsgOut);
BOOL SQLConfigDriver(hwnd, lpszDriver, lpszArgs,
➡ lpszMsg cbMsgMax and pcbMsgOut);
```

The difference is that `SQLConfigDriver` calls the driver's `ConfigDriver` routine without knowing the name of the setup DLL. Your setup program would have installed the DLL prior to the call.

The parameters are: `hwnd`, the parent window handle; `fRequest`, either `ODBC_INSTALL_DRIVER` or `ODBC_REMOVE_DRIVER`; `lpszDriver`, the name of the driver to install; `lpszArgs`, a `NULL`-terminated string of arguments; `lpszMsg`, `NULL`-terminated string output message; `cbMsgMax`; and `pcbMsgOut`. The function returns `TRUE` or `FALSE`.

```
BOOL SQLRemoveDriver(lpszDriver, FRemoveDSN, lpdwUsageCount)
BOOL SQLRemoveDriverManager(lpdwUsageCount)
```

Both of these return `TRUE` or `FALSE`.

23

USING ODBC AND VISUAL C++ WITH SQL SERVER

The parameters are: lpszDriver, the name of the driver; fRemoveDSN, either TRUE or FALSE; and lpdwUsageCount, the usage count of the drive after this function has been called. The last parameter is an output parameter that is decremented with each call until the UsageCount goes to 0, at which point the registry entry is removed.

SQLInstallTranslator adds information about a translator to the ODBCINST.INI section of the registry and increments the translator's UsageCount by one.

```
BOOL SQLInstallTranslator (lpszInfFile, lpszTranslator, lpszPathIn, lpszPathOut,
    cbPathOutMax, pcbPathOut, fRequest, lpdwUsageCount)
BOOL SQLRemoveTranslator(lpszTranslator, lpdwUsageCount);
```

Both functions return TRUE if successful.

The parameters are: lpszInfFile, the full path of the ODBC.INF file; lpszTranslator, the key in ODBC.INF that describes the translator; lpszPathIn, where to install it; lpszPathOut, the path of prior installation; cbPathOutMax, the length; pcbPathOut, the pointer to the number of bytes available; fRequest, either ODBC_INSTALL_INQUERY or ODBC_INSTALL_COMPLETE; and lpdwUsageCount, the usage count after the translator is installed.

In addition to the preceding functions, ODBC 2.5 introduced eight additional installer functions to support Uninstall software:

- SQLConfigDataSouce
- SQLCreateDataSource
- SQLGetPrivateProfileString
- SQLInstallDriver
- SQLInstallDriverManager
- SQLInstallODBC
- SQLManageDataSources
- SQLWritePrivateProfileString

The ODBC SDK includes software for installing drivers into the Windows NT registry on your client's machine. While shipping an application, you probably need to check that ODBC itself is installed. The ODBC SDK has samples for writing setup routines to check and install ODBC, your driver, and your application's DSN into the customer machine. You also can use the sample software to install a driver you are missing in your registry. Copy the driver DLLs to the directory where you have the ODBC SDK's SETUP32. Make sure you have the ODBC.INF file, which identifies which DLLs are needed. Once all of these are in the directory, run DRVSTP32.EXE.

Tables, Columns, Indexes, and Stored Procedures

The function of the driver is to let the world know the capabilities of the data source. It does this with a well-defined interface. In SQL-92, DBMSs provided their structure with schema information tables, which are views in the database. These views list the information about tables, columns, sizes, and so on. But these schema tables were not implemented in many DBMSs. Before you access data in an unknown data source, you need to know its schema. And to get that, you need to query the database.

Querying the database for a list of its tables, columns, indexes, or stored procedures is part of the ODBC catalog functions. All of them take a similar set of parameter values and include the standard wildcard characters: * for all chars, _ for any one char, and % for any combination of zero or more chars. For example, %dave% brings up all fields with *dave* in any position.

The following catalog functions are defined in SQL-92:

- Core Level—None
- Level 1—`SQLTables`, `SQLColumns`, `SQLStatistics`, `SQLSpecialColumns`
- Level 2—`SQLTablePrivileges`, `SQLColunmPrivileges`, `SQLPrimaryKeys`, `SQLForeignKeys`, `SQLProcedures`, `SQLProcedureColumns`

This chapter looks at each of the Level 1 functions. Every call has the first seven parameters in common and returns the same first three attributes about their target.

SQLTables

`SQLTables` returns a list of tables in the data source. The syntax is

```
rc = SQLTables(hstmt, szTableQualifier, cbTableQualifier,
➥ szTableOwner, cbTableOwner, szTableName,
➥ cbTableName, szTableType, cbTableType)
```

In a relational database, each table has a qualifier (usually the database), a table owner, and a name. You can implicitly call any table as this example. The table type value is either NULL or one or more of the following values: TABLE, VIEW, SYSTEM TABLE, GLOBAL TEMPORARY, LOCAL TEMPORARY, ALIAS, SYNONYM. The two temporary table types are base tables that hold intermediate results of queries and are flushed at the end of a transaction or session. An example would be `Accounting."Dave".AccountsRec`, which is the accounts receivable table from the accounting database owned by Dave. Using wildcards can make this easier:

```
rc = SQLTables(hstmt, "%", SQL_NTS, "%", SQL_NTS,
➥ "%", SQL_NTS, "'TABLE','VIEW','SYSTEM TABLE'", SQL_NTS)
```

The preceding example shows all the tables, views, and system tables. The following example shows all tables:

```
rc = SQLTables(hstmt, "",0,"%",SQL_NTS,"",0,"",0)
```

The following example shows all VIEWs from MYDATABASE owned by Dave:

```
rc = SQLTables(hstmt, "MYDATABASE", SQL_NTS, "DAVE",
➥ SLQ_NTS,"%", SQL_NTS, "'VIEW'", SQL_NTS)
```

The result set has five items for each table:

TABLE_QUALIFIER	Varchar(128)	qualifier name
TABLE_OWNER	Varchar(128)	owner of table
TABLE_NAME	Varchar(128)	name of table
TABLE_TYPE	Varchar(128)	type of table
REMARKS	Varchar(254)	remarks

SQLTables returns SQLSTATEs 01000, 08S01, 24000 (invalid cursor state), IM001, S1000, S1001, S1008 (operation canceled), S1010, S1090, S1C00 (driver not capable), and S1T00.

However, it may be that you have a mixed bag of tables when you don't initially know the data source. In that case, extra error checking is required:

```
TRY
{
// set any options, like timeouts, scrolling options
OnSetOptions(m_hstmt);

// call the ODBC catalog function with data member params

AFX_SQL_ASYNC(this, (::SQLTables)(m_hstmt,
➥ (m_strQualifierParam.IsEmpty()? (UCHAR FAR *)NULL:
➥  (UCHAR FAR *)(const char*)m_strQualifierParam), SQL_NTS,
    (m_strOwnerParam.IsEmpty()? (UCHAR FAR *)NULL:
➥ (UCHAR FAR *)(const char*)m_strOwnerParam), SQL_NTS,
➥ (m_strNameParam.IsEmpty()? (UCHAR FAR *)NULL:
➥ (UCHAR FAR *)(const char*)m_strNameParam), SQL_NTS,
    (m_strTypeParam.IsEmpty()? (UCHAR FAR *)NULL:
➥ (UCHAR FAR *)(const char*)m_strTypeParam), SQL_NTS));

if (!Check(nRetCode))
  {
   AfxThrowDBException(nRetCode, m_pDatabase, m_hstmt);
  }
     // load first record
     MoveFirst();
}
CATCH_ALL(e)
{
  Close();
  THROW_LAST();
}
END_CATCH_ALL
  return TRUE;
}
```

SQLColumns

SQLColumns is just like SQLTables, except that it returns column information. The first seven parameters are the same, and the last two parameters are changed to szColumnName (usually a search string) and cbColumnName. A large database may have hundreds of columns, so you may need to use wildcards to return only a subset with the search string (for example, PAT* for all the patient-related columns).

The return set from SQLColumns has 12 items for each column, as shown in Table 23.4.

Table 23.4. SQLColumns return set values.

Name	Type	Comments
TABLE_QUALIFIER	Varchar(128)	
TABLE_OWNER	Varchar(128)	
TABLE_NAME	Varchar(128)	
COLUMN_NAME	Varchar(128)	
DATA_TYPE	SMALLINT	ODBC SQL datatype
TYPE_NAME	Varchar(128)	DBMS data type
PRECISION	int	Maximum digit
LENGTH	int	Length you want
SCALE	SMALLINT	Maximum digits after decimal
RADIX	SMALLINT	*
NULLABLE	SMALLINT	Columns accept NULL as value
REMARKS	Varchar(254)	Remarks

*RADIX is always either 10 or 2. If it is 10, use PRECISION and SCALE to get the number of decimal points in the column. If it is 2, PRECISION and SCALE define the number of bits in the column.

23

USING ODBC
AND VISUAL C++
WITH SQL SERVER

Disconnecting from Data Source

The preceding example showed how the process of connecting to the data source was reversed. You will always call SQLDisconnect, SQLFreeConnect, and SQLFreeEnv, in that order.

SQLDisconnect

SQLDisconnect, discussed earlier, frees allocated statement handles. When your application calls SQLDisconnect, the driver manager calls both SQLFreeConnect and SQLFreeEnv within the driver, then calls FreeLibrary to unload the ODBC driver DLL and free up memory. If any SQL statements are still executing (you would be in asynchronous mode), the disconnect fails with SQLSTATE S1010 (function sequence error). Connecting to a data source can take several seconds and slow your application down. In general, you connect to the data source once when your application starts. However, your DBMS might override this decision. An example would be a DBMS like MicroRim's Rbase, where you purchase connection licenses in groups of five. You might only be able to use five connections at a time and need to disconnect users to enable others' access.

The `SQLDisconnect` form is

```
SQLDisconnect(hdbc);
```

It returns `SQLSTATE`s `01000`, `01002` (disconnect error), `08003` (connection not open), `25000` (invalid transaction state), `IM001`, `S1000`, `S1001`, and `S1010`. You can reuse the `hdbc` to connect to another data source after the `SQLDisconnect` without reallocating the handle.

SQLFreeConnect

`SQLFreeConnect` releases the resources you allocated for the connection. You cannot reuse the `hdbc` handle after this call, because it no longer exists—its memory has been freed. The form is simply

```
SQLFreeConnect(hdbc);
```

The `SQLSTATE` codes returned are `01000`, `08S01`, `S1000`, and `S1010`.

SQLFreeEnv

Just before closing the application, you need to free up this memory space with `SQLFreeEnv` in the same manner. `SQLFreeEnv` can return `SQL_SUCCESS`, `SQL_SUCCESS_WITH_INFO`, `SQL_ERROR`, or `SQL_INVALID_HANDLE`. These `SQLSTATE` return codes are `01000` (general warning), `S1000` (general `SQL_ERROR`), or `S1010` (function sequence error). The most common reason for `SQL_ERROR` is that you haven't freed a connection handle. You would get the `S1010` `SQLSTATE` return code to indicate that. Always call `SQLDisconnect` and `SQLFreeConnect` prior to calling `SQLFreeEnv`.

SQLExecute

Most SQL statements take a statement handle as their first parameter and return a standard set of `SQLSTATE` codes and data in a result set of columns and rows. Previously you saw SQL functions that returned information with the output parameters of the function call. From this point on, the functions return result sets, which can contain hundreds of rows and columns of data. This becomes somewhat more complicated in that you will always have a two-step process: generate the result set, then retrieve the results. The next two sections examine both steps. Figure 23.9 is a general outline of the process. This flowchart details your choices after you have initialized the connection and gotten a statement handle. You first ask yourself if the statement will be executed multiple times and if you need to know information about the result set prior to execution. If you can answer no to both of these questions, you proceed using `SQLExecDirect`. Otherwise, you need to use the `SQLPrepare`, `SQLExecute` combination. This is the first process examined in this section.

FIGURE 23.9.

General flow of ODBC function processing.

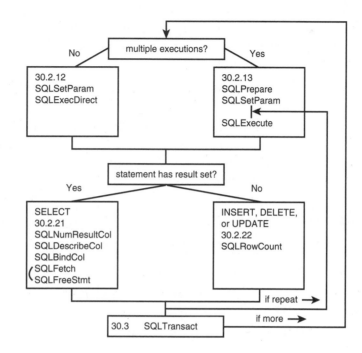

Generating Result Sets

Prior to executing a valid SQL Statement, you need to allocate memory for the statement handle. This is done as

```
HSTMT hstmt;
RETCODE rc;
rc = SQLAllocate(hdbc, &hstmt);
```

The SQLSTATE return codes are 01000, 08003, IM001, S1000, S1001, and S1009.

Different DBMSs can support different numbers of open SQL statements. If you are using an unknown data source, this number is obtained with SQLGetInfo's SQL_ACTIVE_STATEMENTS parameter. A value of 0 means that there is no limit. Some DBMSs restrict the number of active statements but enable multiple connections in exchange. This is a poor exchange because, as you have seen, connecting takes time and resources. It is best to allocate a statement handle, use it, free it with SQLFreeStmt, and then reuse it. This minimizes the resources your application needs.

SQLFreeStmt

SQLFreeStmt takes two parameters: the hstmt and an option. The options are: SQL_CLOSE (close cursor and discard results, but keep hstmt around and keep bound parameters and results bound), SQL_DROP (close cursor, disregard results, and free hstmt), SQL_UNBIND (release buffers that you bound with SQLBindCol), or SQL_RESET_PARAMS (release all parameter buffers). Binding is the process of associating a dataset with the application's variables. You have already seen SQLBinCols. The next section looks at SQLBindParameter, but the basic concept is that you need to store the results somewhere or they'll get discarded.

SQLFreeStmt has the SQLSTATE return codes of 01000, IM001, S1000, S1001, S1010, and S1092 (option type out of range).

ODBC provides several functions to execute SQL statements. Functions are executed either by *direct* or *prepared* execution. Direct execution is fast and is the easiest way to execute an SQL Statement. It is used when the SQL statement is to be executed only once and when no information is needed about the result set prior to execution. Prepared execution is more flexible.

SQLExecDirect

SQLExecDirect executes the SQL statement exactly once. Its syntax is

```
rc = SQLExecDirect(hstmt, szSqlStr, cbSqlStr);
```

The szSqlStr is any valid SQL statement, such as SELECT * FROM ACCOUNTREC. The resulting function example is

```
rc = SQLExecDirect(hstmt, "SELECT * FROM ACCOUNTREC", SQL_NTS);
```

Use SQLExecDirect when you want a result set that will not change throughout your application—filling a list box with available products you offer. You generally know the format of the data and the table and type of data being returned.

SQLExecuteDirect has the SQLSTATE return code:

```
01000, 01004, 01006, 01S03, 01S04, 07001, 08S01, 21S01, 21S02, 22003,
➡ 33005, 22008, 22012, 23000, 24000, 34000, 37000, 40001, 42000,
➡ IM001, S0001, S0002, S0011, S0012, S0021, S0022, S1000, S1001,
➡ S1008, S1009, S1010, S1090, S1109, S1C00, S1T00
```

There are six basic steps in executing any SQL statement. Using SQLExecDirect, all six steps are executed:

1. The SQL statement is formed by the application or user.
2. The SQL statement is sent to DBMS.
3. The SQL statement is parsed.
4. The parsed SQL statement is optimized to develop the execution plan. The optimizer of each database has rules for using indexes and the ordering of statements to get the result set the quickest way.
5. The execution plan is executed.
6. The client and the server interact to send status information and data to the client.

In using SQLPrepare, the first four steps are done first and stored. The last two steps are then performed later by SQLExecute. In a stored procedure, these first four steps are stored back into

DBMS to be used over and over. By preprocessing the first four steps, you can gain more flexibility and speed. The parsing step of a complex SQL statement can be quite time-consuming!

SQLPrepare

Prepared execution is more flexible in that you can break the execution into two steps. The first step is to find out information about the result set, and the second is to execute the statement and get the result set. One example is to find out the number of rows returned to format a printed report. A second example is where the user forms the SQL SELECT statement at runtime and you need to check its grammar. A final example is to ensure that only one row meets your criteria prior to performing a DELETE.

The two step process is

```
rc = SQLPrepare(hstmt, szSqlStr, cbSqlStr);
rc = SQLExecute(hstmt);
```

SQLPrepare returns SQLSTATE codes: 01000, 08S01, 21S01, 21S02, 22005, 24000, 34000, 37000, 42000, IM001, S0001, S0003, S0012, S0021, S0022, S1000, S1001, S1008, S1009, S1010, S1090, and S1T00. ODBC 2.5 added S1C00 (driver not capable).

SQLExecute returns SQLSTATE codes: 01000, 01004, 01006, 01S03, 01S04, 07001, 08S01, 22003, 22005, 22008, 22012, 23000, 24000, 40001, 42000, and IM001.

Always test SQLExecute, SQLExecDirect, and SQLPrepare for the return of SQL_SUCCESS or SQL_SUCCESS_WITH_INFO. If you didn't get one of these returned, the statement was not executed. If you don't test, you won't know if you made database changes or not.

SQLPrepare's statement is parsed into its data access path, which makes information about the source available, as you saw with the catalog functions. If you have multiple calls to SQLExecute, the preparsed data access path can speed things up considerably as well. This is the same thing you see with parameterized statements.

Let's look again behind the scenes at what is actually happening in a call to SQLExecute. When you called SQLAllocStmt, the driver manager again made a similar call to the driver and allocated a second statement handle for the communication between the driver manager and the driver. It is important to remember that when you are done using a HSTMT handle, reuse it! SQLExecDirect actually sends whatever string you give it to the server, which parses the string and determines if it can act on the information you provided. It does not return results until you specifically ask for them—it just returns the success or failure of your statement.

Parameterization

Parameterized statements are formed by specifying a ? as a placeholder in an SQL statement. This placeholder gets changed each time the statement is executed, but the entire SQL statement doesn't need to be parsed again—the substitution needs to be made. When you bind a parameter, you tie it to a particular storage location of memory, to be retrieved at execution time.

It was mentioned earlier that you need to save the parameters of SQL statements or they'll get discarded. Binding the results means setting up a pointer to a memory buffer that holds the results. If you had a parameterized statement such as INSERT INTO CLINIC(city, state, zipcode) VALUES (?,?,?), you would need three bindings to retain the three parameter values.

SQLBindParameter binds a buffer to a single parameter. If you want to save multiple parameters, you must call SQLBindParameter multiple times. The syntax is as follows and its explanation appears in Table 23.5.

```
rc = SQLBindParameter(hstmt, ipar, fparType, fCType, fSqlType,
➥ cbColDef, ibScale, rbgValue, cbValueMax, pcbValue);
```

Table 23.5. The SQLBindParameter parameters.

Parameter	Description
ipar	Integer for which parameter to save
fparType	Either SQL_PARAM_INPUT, SQL_PARAM_OUTPUT, or SQL_PARAM_INPUT_OUTPUT
fCType	C Data type
FSqlType	SQL Data type
cbColDef	Precision of column
ibScale	Scale of column
rgbValue	Pointer to buffer for parameter's data
cbValueMax	Maximum length of buffer
pcbValue	Pointer to buffer for parameter length

NOTE

A variation on calling the function SQLBindParameter passes the parameter value at execution time. To evoke this form, set pcbValue to SQL_DATA_AT_EXEC and the rgbValue is set to a 32-bit token passed by SQLParamData and SQLPutData. This is useful when the parameter is a large amount of data, such as a binary object.

SQLSTATE return codes for SQLBindParameter are: 01000, 07006, IM991M, S1000, S1001, S1003 (C type not valid), S1004 (SQL Type not valid), S1009, S1010, S1090, S1093 (invalid parameter number), S1094 (invalid scale number), S1104 (invalid precision number), S1105 (invalid parameter type), and S1C00.

The following is an example using SQLBindParameter:

```
HSTMT hstmt;
UCHAR szName[NAME_LEN];
SDWORD cbName = SQL_NTS;
```

```
//allocate a statement and prepare it
rc = SQLAllocStmt(hdbc, &hstmt);
if (RETCODE_IS_SUCCESSFUL(rc))
   {
     rc = SQLPrepare(hstmt, "INSERT INTO CLINIC (name) VALUES (?)", SQL_NTS);
   }
//bind the parameter
if (RETCODE_IS_SUCCESSFUL(rc))
  {
     rc = SQLBindParameter(hstmt, 1, SQL_PARAM_INPUT,
➥    SQL_C_CHAR, SQL_CHAR, NAME_LEN, 0, szName, 0, &cbName);
  }
//input the parameter data
strcopy(szName, "Dave's Clinic");
//execute
if (RETCODE_IS_SUCCESSFUL(rc))
  {
     rc = SQLExecute(hstmt);
  }
```

The preceding example is somewhat contrived. In reality, the whole concept of parameters assumes you will reuse the SQL statement over and over, and the benefit is that you don't need to reparse the entire statement. A collection of parameters is passed with SQLParamOptions as

```
HSTMT hstmt;
UCHAR szNames[][NAME_LEN] = {"Dave's clinic","Bill's clinic","Sam's clinic"};
SDWORD cbName[] = {SQL_NTS, SQL_NTS, SQL_NTS};
UWORD irow;
//allocate a statement and prepare it
rc = SQLAllocStmt(hdbc, &hstmt);
if (RETCODE_IS_SUCCESSFUL(rc))
  {
     rc = SQLPrepare(hstmt, "INSERT INTO CLINIC (name) VALUES (?)", SQL_NTS);
  }
// tell we have 3 parameters, we are going to insert 3 rows,
// irow is number of current row
if (RETCODE_IS_SUCCESSFUL(rc))
  {
     SQLParamOptions(hstmt, 3, &irow);
  }
//bind the parameter
if (RETCODE_IS_SUCCESSFUL(rc))
  {
     rc = SQLBindParameter(hstmt, 1, SQL_PARAM_INPUT,
➥ SQL_C_CHR, SQL_CHAR, NAME_LEN, 0, szNames, 0, cbName);
  }
//execute
if (RETCODE_IS_SUCCESSFUL(rc))
  {
     rc = SQLExecute(hstmt);
  }
```

The syntax for SQLParamOptions follows:

```
rc = SQLParamOptions (hstmt, crow, pirow);
```

The parameter crow is the number of parameters, and pirow is a pointer to the current row number. If pirow is a NULL pointer, no row number is returned.

The SQLSTATE return codes are: 01000, IM001, S1000, S1001, S1010, and S1107 (row value out of range).

Getting Results from Result Sets

All the preceding functions address each function's return code, which tells us about success or failure. Where are the actual results, though? SQL SELECT and the catalog functions each return result sets, rows, and columns of data. SQL DELETE, SQL UPDATE, and SQL INSERT all return a row count, which is the number of rows affected by the statement.

Once you execute SQLDirect or SQLExecDirect, the results still reside on the server as a subset of the database. Even if you are using a local database, think of it as a server. You still need to fetch the rows from the result set. Why? What if you tried something like SQLExecDirect(hstmt, "SELECT * FROM NY_PHONEBOOK"), where NY_PHONEBOOK was immense? Where would the results go? They are still on the server, with a *cursor* pointing to the first row of results. You move the cursor and fetch its contents with SQLFetch and SQLExtendedFetch. Before you gather this information, you still need to know about the result set. You might know a lot about the data (if you designed the database rows and columns), or you might not even know which data is coming back. The ODBC catalog functions were introduced first because they help you find out what you are going to get back.

Getting to Know the Result Set

Figure 23.11 is an expansion on the lower half of Figure 23.9. The left box shows the process of retrieving results from the result set. You loop through the rows with SQLFetch.

SQLRowCount

If you followed the right half of Figure 23.10, your statement was either INSERT, DELETE, or UPDATE. You could also have used SQLSetPos with SQL_UPDATE, SQL_ADD, or SQL_DELETE. The results are the number of rows you inserted, deleted, or updated. The syntax is

```
rc = SQLRowCount(hstmt, pcrow);
```

pcrow is the output, which is the number of rows affected by the statement or -1 if that number is not available.

The SQLSTATE return codes are 01000, IM001, S1000, S1001, and S1010.

SQLNumResultCols

If your call gives you a result set, on the other hand, the first thing you need to know is the number of columns in that result set. You need this for both allocating memory and displaying the information on your monitor. The simplest way to get this information is with SQLNumResultCols, which has the following syntax:

```
rc = SqlNumResultCols(hstmt, pccol);
```

FIGURE 23.10.

ODBC result processing flow chart.

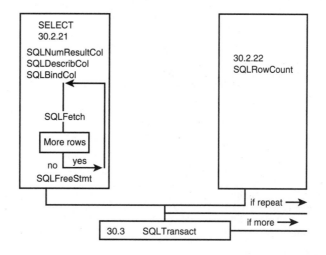

hstmt is the handle to the statement you just executed, and pccol is the returned number of columns. If pccol is 0, your executed SQL statement was of the type that returns rows, not a result set such as INSERT, DELETE, or UPDATE. These statements use SQLRowCount to return the number of rows affected by the call.

The SQLSTATE return codes are 01000, IM001, S1000, S1008, S1010 (common error code when your function calls out of sequence), and S1T00.

It has been several pages since you actually typed something into Visual C++ to ensure that all this is working. Take the simple console application from earlier in this chapter and modify it as follows. Remember, SPNOTES is the sample data source name and VDATA just one of its tables. Change these to your test data source:

```
#include <windows.h>
#include <sql.h>
#include <sqlext.h>
#define MAX_DATA 100
#define MAX_COLNAME 100
int WINAPI WinMain(HANDLE hInstance, HANDLE hPrevInstance,
➥ LPSTR lpszCmdLine, int nCmdShow)
{
// setup vars
HENV henv;
HDBC hdbc;
HSTMT hstmt;
char szData[MAX_DATA];
SDWORD cbData;
// vars for descriptions
SWORD cCols;
SWORD iCol;
char szColName[MAX_COLNAME +1];
char szTypeName[MAX_COLNAME +1];
SWORD cbColName;
SWORD fSQLType;
UDWORD cbPrec;
SWORD cbTypeName;
```

23

USING ODBC
AND VISUAL C++
WITH SQL SERVER

```
SWORD cbScale;
SWORD fNullable;


SQLAllocEnv(&henv);
SQLAllocConnect(henv, &hdbc);
SQLConnect(hdbc, (UCHAR *)"SPNOTES", SQL_NTS,NULL,0,NULL,0);
SQLAllocStmt(hdbc, &hstmt);

//example of just getting some data
SQLExecDirect(hstmt, (UCHAR *)"SELECT * from VDATA", SQL_NTS);
SQLFetch(hstmt);
SQLGetData(hstmt, 2, SQL_C_CHAR, szData, sizeof(szData), &cbData);
MessageBox(NULL, szData, "Column Data", MB_OK);

//example of getting number of columns
SQLNumResultCols(hstmt, &cCols);
wsprintf(szData, "%d columns returned\n", cCols);
MessageBox(NULL, szData, "Column's received", MB_OK);

//example of column description
for (iCol = 1; iCol <=cCols; iCol++)
{
  SQLDescribeCol(hstmt, iCol, (UCHAR *)szColName, MAX_COLNAME,
➥ &cbColName, &fSQLType,&cbPrec, &cbScale, &fNullable);
  SQLColAttributes(hstmt,iCol, SQL_COLUMN_TYPE_NAME, szTypeName,sizeof(szTypeName),
&cbTypeName,0);
  wsprintf(szData, "Column %d name = '%s'\n type is %02d (%s)\n max length =
%3ld\n",
➥  iCol, szColName, fSQLType, szTypeName, cbPrec);
  MessageBox(NULL, szData, "Column description", MB_OK);
}


SQLFreeStmt(hstmt, SQL_DROP);
SQLDisconnect(hdbc);
SQLFreeConnect(hdbc);
SQLFreeEnv(henv);
return(TRUE);
}
```

SQLDescribCol

The next thing you probably want to know is the names of the columns and the type of data they hold. The preceding example shows just how simple it is to get the basic description of a column's data. SQLDescribeCol returns the name, type, precision, scale, and nullability of your result set. The syntax is

```
rc = SQLDescribeCol(hstmt, icol, szColName, cbColName,
➥ pcbColName, pfSqltype, pcbColDef, pibScale, pfNullable);
```

You would call SQLDescribeCol after a call to SQLPrepare and either before or after SQLExecute. You could also call SQLDescribeCol after SQLExecDirect. This function call returns information about one column only, the one you specify in the integer, icol. To get information on all the columns, you need to call SQLDescribeCol once for each result column from 1 to the number you got with SQLNumResultCols. Here's the parameter list: SzColName is the column name;

`cbColName` is the maximum length of the name you want returned; `pcbColName` is the total maximum length of the column name; `pfSqlType` is the SQL data type; `pcbColDef` is the precision or how large a buffer you need to hold the result set; `pibScale` is the number of digits to the right of the decimal point; and `pfNullable` is either `SQL_NO_NULLS`, `SQL_NULLABLE`, or `SQL_NULLABLE_UNKNOWN`.

SQLSTATE return codes are `01000`, `01004` (data truncated), `24000`, `IM001`, `S1000`, `S1001`, `S1002` `S1008`, `S1010`, `S1090`, and `S1T00`.

SQLColAttributes

`SQLColAttributes` returns even more detailed information about the columns in the result set. In the sample console application we just built, `SQLDescribeCol` returned the `SQLType` in the parameter `fSqlType`. If you don't know that type 5 in your data source is a `SHORT`, this doesn't help much. You need to be able to get more detailed information, like in the example, to get the text string representing the various SQL types. The function `SQLColAttributes` is somewhat unusual in that you can get either text returned, as in the preceding example, or a 32-bit signed value. The returned information is in the output parameter `pfDesc` (if `pfDesc` is a signed value, the drive ignores `rbgDesc`, `cbDescMax`, and `pcbDesc`). The syntax is

```
rc = SQLColAttributes(hstmt, icol, fDescType,
➥ rgbDesc, cbDescMax, pcbDesc, pfDesc);
```

Returned `SQLColAttribute` information is shown in Table 23.6.

Table 23.6. Returned `SQLColAttribute` information.

fDescType	*Output Param*	*Results*
SQL_COLUMN_AUTO_INCREMENT	pfDesc	TRUE or FALSE
SQL_COLUMN_CASE_SENSITIVE	pfDesc	TRUE or FALSE
SQL_COLUMN_COUNT	pfDesc	Number of columns in set
SQL_COLUMN_DISPLAY_SIZE	pfDesc	Number of chars to display column
SQL_COLUMN_LABEL	rgbDesc	Label or title
SQL_COLUMN_LENGTH	pfDesc	Bytes transferred each SQLFetch
SQL_COLUMN_MONEY	pfDesc	TRUE or FALSE
SQL_COLUMN_NAME	rgbDesc	Column name
SQL_COLUMN_NULLABLE	pfDesc	SQL_NO_NULLS or SQL_NULLABLE or SQL_NULLABLE_UNKNOWN
SQL_COLUMN_OWNER_NAME	rgbDesc	Owner of table

continues

Table 23.6. continued

fDescType	*Output Param*	*Results*
SQL_COLUMN_PRECISION	pfDesc	Precision
SQL_COLUMN_QUALIFIER_NAME	rbfDesc	Qualifier of table
SQL_COLUMN_SCALE	pfDesc	Scale
SQL_COLUMN_COLUMN_SEARCHABLE	pfDesc	SQL_UNSEARCHABLE or SQL_LIKE_ONLY or SQL_ALL_EXCEPT_LIKE or SQL_SEARCHABLE
SQL_COLUMN_COLUMN_TABLE_NAME	rgbDesc	Name of table
SQL_COLUMN_COLUMN_TYPE	pfDesc	SQL data type
SQL_COLUMN_TYPE_NAME	rgbDesc	Data source data type
SQL_COLUMN_UNSIGNED	pfDesc	TRUE or FALSE
SQL_COLUMN_UPDATABLE	pfDesc	SQL_ATTR_READONLY or SQL_ATTR_WRITE or SQL_ATTR_READWRITE_UNKNOWN or SQL_COLUMN_UPDATABLE

The SQLSTATE return codes are: 01000, 01004, 24000, IM001, S1000, S1001, S1002, S1008, S1010, S1090, S1091 (descriptor out of range), S1C00, and S1T00.

The information you choose to retrieve depends on how you use it. If you're going to display to the monitor, you need SQL_COLUMN_DISPLAY_SIZE, and if you're going to do a large UPDATE, you should know beforehand if the column is SQL_COLUMN_UPDATABLE.

Both SQLColAttributes and SQLDescribeCol assume that you don't know about the column. In many of your applications you will be the person that designed the data source, and you'll execute the SQL statement, bind the columns, and then use the results. A simple example follows:

```
UCHAR szName[30], szAddress[30], szCity[10], szState[3], szZipcode[6];
SDWORD cbName, cbAddress, cbCity, cbState, cbZipcode;
rc = SQLExecDirect(hstmt, "SELECT Name, Address, City, State, Zipcode
➥ FROM CUSTOMERS",SQL_NTS);
if (retcode = SQL_SUCCESS)
  {
    SQLBindCol(hstmt, 1, SQL_C_CHAR, szName, 30,&cbName);
    SQLBindCol(hstmt, 2, SQL_C_CHAR, szAddress, 30, &cbAddress);
    SQLBindCol(hstmt, 3, SQL_C_CHAR, szCity, 10, &cbCity);
    SQLBindCol(hstmt, 4, SQL_C_CHAR, szState, 3, &cbState);
    SQLBindCol(hstmt, 1, SQL_C_CHAR, szZipcode, 6, &cbZipcode);
    while (TRUE)
    {
```

```
      retcode = SQLFetch(hstmt);
      if (retcode == SQL_SUCCESS ¦¦ retcode == SQL_SUCCESS_WITH_INFO)
      {
//print strings 1 less than length for \0
   fprintf(out, "%*s %*s %*s %*s %*s"
➥,29,szName,29,szAddress,9,szCity,2,szState,5,szZipcode);
      }
      else
      {
      break;
      }
   }
 }
```

ODBC uses either `SQLBindCol` or `SQLGetData` to assign a storage location after `SQLFetch` or `SQLExtendedFetch`. Use `SQLGetData` to bind large data objects, which may have to be retrieved in parts due to their size. You can actually mix the two calls as long as you call `SQLGetData` after you have bound the columns with `SQlBindCol`. Although you used `SQLGetData` above, it is discussed in greater detail as it relates to BLOBs in our discussion of binary data near the end of this chapter.

SQLBindCol

As we have demonstrated, `SQLBindCol` is used to pass a pointer to the storage buffer for the column of data. It also specifies how the data is converted from SQL data types to C data types. These default conversions are shown in Table 23.7.

Table 23.7. ODBC 3.0 default data types.

SQL DATA TYPE	C DATA TYPE
SQL_CHAR	SQL_C_CHAR
SQL_VARCHAR	SQL_C_CHAR
SQL_LONGVARCHAR	SQL_C_CHAR
SQL_DECIMAL	SQL_C_CHAR
SQL_NUMERIC	SQL_C_CHAR
SQL_BIT	SQL_C_BIT
SQL_TINYINT	SQL_C_STINYINT or SQL_C_UTINYINT
SQL_SMALLINT	SQL_C_SSHORT or SQL_C_USHORT
SQL_INTEGER	SQL_CV_LONG or SQL_C_ULONG
SQL_BIGINT	SQL_C_CHAR
SQL_REAL	SQL_C_FLOAT
SQL_FLOAT	SQL_C_DOUBLE
SQL_DOUBLE	SQL_C_DOUBLE

continues

Table 23.7. continued

SQL DATA TYPE	*C DATA TYPE*
SQL_BINARY	SQL_C_BINARY
SQL_VARBINARY	SQL_C_BINARY
SQL_LONGBINARY	SQL_C_BINARY
SQL_DATE	SQL_C_DATE
SQL_TIME	SQL_C_TIME
SQL_TIMESTAMP	SQL_C_TIMESTAMP

The syntax for SQLBindCol is

```
rc = SQLBindCol(hstmt, icol, fcType, rgbValue, cbValueMax, pcbValue);
```

The columns in the result set are numbered from left to right, with the first column being number 1. fcType is the C data type to which you want the column converted. All SQL types can be converted to SQL_C_CHAR. RgbValue is the pointer to the storage space.

The SQLSTATE return codes are 01000, IM001, S1000, S1001, S1002, S1003, S1009, S1010, S1090 and S1C00.

Once a column is bound, it remains bound until you call SQLFreeStmt with either the SQL_UNBIND or SQL_DROP option. You can also unbind any one column by calling SQLBindCol again with that column's number, but setting rgbValue to a NULL pointer.

Column-wise, binding is the default. You can also bind row-wise by using the statement SQLSetStmtOption (hstmt, SQL_BIND_TYPE, sizeof(MytableStruc). In this case, MytableStruc is a typical C structure, defined as follows:

```
typedef struct {
  UCHAR szLname[30];
  SDWORD cbLname;
  UCHAR szAddress[30];
  SDWORD cbAddress;
} MytableStruc;
```

MytableStruc is declared as

```
MytableStruct rrows[100];
```

and bound as

```
SQLBindCol(hstmt, 1, SQL_C_CHAR. rrow[0].szLname,
➥ sizeof(szLname),&rrow[0].cbLname);
```

SQLFetch

As you saw previously, `SQLFetch` simply fetches one row of your result set. You need to call it over once per row to get the entire result set. Its syntax couldn't be simpler:

```
rc = SQLFetch(hstmt);
```

The `SQLSTATE` return codes are: `01000`, `01004`, `07006` (could not convert data type), `08S01`, `22003` (number out of range), `22012` (division by zero), `24000`, `40001` (serialization failed), `IM001`, `S1000`, `S1001`, `S1002`, `S1008`, `S1008`, `S1010`, `S1C00`, and `S1T00`. ODBC 2.5 added `22005` (error in assignment) and `22008` (datetime overflow).

Every call to `SQLFetch` advances the cursor one row until the cursor is positioned after the last row, at which point it returns `SQL_NO_DATA_FOUND`.

`ODBCTEST` (`ODBCTE32.EXE`) has been mentioned before, and it is probably the best way to learn the ODBC functions. The next few paragraphs discuss extended ODBC functions. If you find that a section of your application won't work, stepping through the ODBC function calls with `ODBCTEST.EXE` can ensure that your parameters are correct and also show you what results are being returned. This application is part of the ODBC SDK. Nearly every ODBC function is available and in the order you would call the function. Using the `SQLError` function returns string and `SQLSTATE` information on each call. Several calls are bundled, such as `GetDataAll` and `FullConnect`. You also have the option of building groups of SQL statements into autotest suites. In this manner, you can test your application when unusual data is returned. A sample autotest is provided with the ODBC SDK, as shown in Figure 23.11.

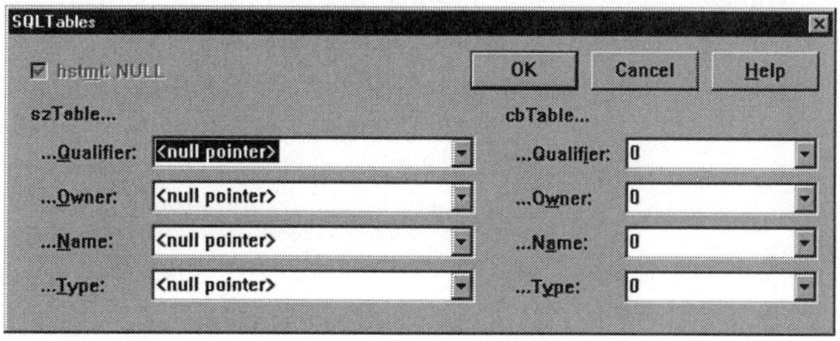

FIGURE 23.11.
Microsoft `ODBCTE32.EXE` *input of parameters for SQL drivers.*

SQLExtendedFetch

ODBC SDK 3.0 provides an extended set of functions that enable you to perform more advanced operations on a result set, such as blocking cursors, making scrollable cursors, modifying the result set, and retrieving multiple result sets. The function returns the result set in the form of an array. `SQLExtendedFetch` has `fFetchType` options of `SQL_FETCH_NEXT`, `SQL_FETCH_PRIOR`, `SQL_FETCH_RELATIVE` (use value in `irow` to move that many rows), `SQL_FETCH_FIRST`, `SQL_FETCH_LAST`, `SQL_FETCH_ABSOLUTE` (use value in `irow` as starting point), and `SQL_FETCH_BOOKMARK`. Other options are available by setting parameters in `SQLSetStmtOption`.

A bookmark is a 32-bit value that uniquely identifies the row. Like the bookmark you're familiar with, it enables you to quickly return to your place (the row) in the result set. The syntax is

```
rc = SQLExtendedFetch(hstmt, fFetchType, irow, pcrow, rgFRowStatus);
```

The `irow` parameter is the number of rows to return, `pcrow` is the number of rows actually fetched, and `rgfRowStatus` is an array of status values.

The `SQLSTATE` return codes are the same as `SQLFetch`, with the addition of `01S01` (error in row), `S1106` (fetch type out of range), `S1107` (row out of range), and `S1111` (invalid bookmark value).

To use block cursors, you first call `SQLSetStmtOptions` with the `fOption` `SQL_ROWSET_SIZE` and the `vParam` of the number of rows you want in the block. This can decrease network traffic because you are sending the server fewer calls. If your block size was 20, one call to `SQLExtendedFetch` returns 20 rows, the same as 20 separate calls to `SQLFetch`.

Scrollable cursors enable you to move about the result set. You first call `SQLSetStmtOption` with the `fOption` parameter of `SQL_CURSOR_TYPE` and your choice of the following: `SQL_CURSOR_STATIC` (your result set won't change throughout the calls, the same as MFC snapshot); `SQL_CURSOR_DYNAMIC` (your result set will change and the cursor should process data as it changes); or `SQL_CURSOR_KEYSET_DRIVEN` (similar to dynamic with changes and deletions, but ignores newly inserted rows).

Just as a cursor marks your position in a word processing document, an ODBC cursor marks your current position in a result set. The simplest type of cursor is forward-only, where the cursor points to a row in the result set. Each subsequent fetch call moves it forward one row. The forward-only cursor is the most common, but cursors with the ability to scroll backward, page up, and page down, as well as cursors that point to a group of rows, are more flexible in your applications. When a cursor can move back and forth in the result set, it is said to be *scrollable*. This might seem overly simplistic, but scrollable cursors in result sets are fairly new and may not be supported by your ODBC driver. A cursor that enables you to update the data to which it is pointing is said to be a scrollable, updatable cursor.

In SQL you would say

```
DECLARE MyCursor Cursor for SELECT * FROM client where Lastname like "HAMELTON"
UPDATE client SET Lastname = "Hamilton" WHERE CURRENT of MyCursor
```

This is simple until you examine the effect of more than one user accessing the data at one time. Should user 1 or user 2 get to update the result set, and who sees what after the update? This is called *sensitivity*, or the visibility of data after changes are made by a cursor owner. An *insensitive* set of data would be like a *snapshot*, which is a copy of the result set at the point in time when the cursor was set. A *static* cursor is said to give a snapshot view of the data. To change the result set, you need to close the cursor and reopen it (a second snapshot). The opposite of this is a *dynamic* cursor, where all changes are immediately visible. In-between these two cursor types is a *keyset* cursor, which has a unique *keyvalue* for each row in the result set. The keyvalue maintains order, with inserts being put at the end of the result set.

Intertwined in these cursor types is the concept of *row locking*. Once a user gets a result set to work on, should the entire result set be locked for total access by other users by using exclusive locking (X-LOCK), or should it be shown to them in read-only mode with a shared lock (S-LOCK)? Should you just lock the row that is being updated (U-LOCK), or should you lock a page of memory? You might use *optimistic* locking—if no one else is looking at your data when you get it, your application assumes that no other transaction will update our data until you are finished. Suddenly the whole concept of cursors has become quite a bit more complex.

Like so many things in the computer world, row locking has its trade-offs (see Table 23.8).

Table 23.8. Cursor models and trade-offs.

Cursor Type	Accuracy	Consistency	Concurrency	Performance
STATIC	Poor	Excellent	Good	Varies
KEYSET_DRIVE	Good	Good	Good	Good
DYNAMIC	Excellent	Poor	Excellent	Varies
MIXED	Varies	Fair	Good	Good

Concurrency is set by SQLSetStmtOption or SQLSetScrollOptions or determined with the partner function SQLGetStmtOptions. The choices follow:

SQL_CONCUR_READ_ONLY	No updates will be attempted.
SQL_CONCUR_LOCK	Data is locked as fetched. Some DBMSs use an update lock (U-LOCK).
SQL_CONCUR_ROWVER	Versioning type optimistic locking.
SQL_CONCUR_VALUE	Optimistic locking uses value checking to detect changes.

SQLSetScrollOptions is used as

```
rc = SQLSetScrollOptions(hstmt, fConcurrency, crowKeyset, crowRowset);
```

The fConcurrency values are SQL_CONCUR_READ_ONLY, SQL_CONCUR_LOCK, SQL_CONCUR_ROWVER, or SQL_CONCUR_VALUES. crowKeyset is the number of rows to buffer or the scroll method by SQL_SCROLL_FORWARD_ONLY, SQL_SCROLL_STATIC, SQL_SCROLL_KEYSET_DRIVEN, or SQL_SCROLL_DYNAMIC. CrowRowset is the number of rows in the rowset.

The SQLSTATE return codes are 01000, IM001, S1000, S1001, S1010, S1107, S1108 (concurrency option out of range), and S1C00.

Static (snapshot) cursors have the members, order, and values of the result set fixed at the time the cursor is opened. The result set is usually a copy of the data, and it is easiest to think of this result set as a copy. When data is updated in the static cursor result set, it can't be seen by other users because the update was made to the copy. You also cannot see updates made by other cursors because you're working with a local copy of the data. This copy is usually in memory, but it can be spooled to a file if the data is excessive. In Table 23.12, this data has excellent consistency because you are always looking at the same set of data. The data has poor accuracy, however, because another user may have changed all of it while you were looking at the copy. The database may implement this with a temporary table for the data on the server instead of actually making a copy of the data on the client. Most DBMSs lock all the rows and make the other users wait.

Dynamic cursors show you the changes the cursor owner makes to the data as they are being made, as well as changes other cursors make. Updates affect the members, order, and values of the result set. The result set is said to be dynamic and have excellent accuracy because it always mirrors the current state of the data. DBMSs usually implement this by assigning an index to the result set. This index is also dynamic, initially set by the order you specify in your ORDER BY or GROUP BY clause. As rows are deleted or updated, this index value changes to enable you to move through the result set without holes.

A keyset cursor has a constant set of members and a constant order, but its values can be updated. If another cursor were to delete a row, you would still see that row in your cursor's result set. Inserts by other cursors are not seen, but inserts by your cursor are put at the end of the result set. To develop a keyset cursor, you need a unique index column in your result set. The keyset is built from these unique values. When you update a value in a row, using this unique value requeries only the row, not the entire result set. The keyset may also include more rows than just the cursor row. This is to buffer the data, assuming you will be moving through the data by repositioning the cursor, which leads to greater performance. On your network, this larger result set can decrease traffic.

A *mixed* cursor is like the keyset cursor in that it is always larger than the rows specified by the cursor, but never larger than the result set itself. It moves through this set like a keyset cursor, but can move to rows outside the set and behave like a dynamic cursor. As it moves to the row past the defined keyset, a new keyset is built.

You can set and get the current cursor name with a pair of ODBC functions. Cursor names are used in positioned updates and deletes, like UPDATE variable ...WHERE CURRENT of szCursor.

```
rc = SQLGetCursorName(hstmt, szCursor, cbCursorMax, pcbCursor);
rc = SQLSetCursorName(hstmt, szCursor, cbCursorMax);
```

The szCursor name is a pointer to the cursor name, cbCursorMax is the length of szCursor, and pcbCursor is the total bytes available to return in szCursor.

The SQLSTATE return codes are 01000, 01004, Im001, S1000, S1001, S1010, S1015 (no cursor name), and S1090.

```
#include <windows.h>
#include <sql.h>
#include <sqlext.h>
#define MAX_DATA 100
```

```
#define MAX_COLNAME 100

int WINAPI WinMain(HANDLE hInstance, HANDLE hPrevInstance,
➥ LPSTR lpszCmdLine, int nCmdShow)
{
// setup vars

HENV henv;
HDBC hdbc;
HSTMT hstmt1;
HSTMT hstmt2;
RETCODE rc;

// change lastname of patient via cursors

SQLAllocEnv(&henv);
SQLAllocConnect(henv, &hdbc);
SQLConnect(hdbc, (UCHAR *) "SPNOTES",SQL_NTS,NULL,0,NULL,0);
SQLAllocStmt(hdbc, &hstmt1);
SQLAllocStmt(hdbc, &hstmt2);

UCHAR szLastName[MAX_DATA];
UCHAR szAccount[MAX_DATA];
SDWORD cbLastname;

SQLSetCursorName(hstmt1, (UCHAR *)"MyCursor", SQL_NTS);
SQLExecDirect(hstmt1, (UCHAR *)"SELECT PLastName, PAccount
➥ FROM PAT FOR UPDATE of PLastName", SQL_NTS);
SQLBindCol(hstmt1, 1, SQL_C_CHAR, szLastName, MAX_DATA, &cbLastname);
do
SQLFetch(hstmt1);
while ((rc == SQL_SUCCESS || rc == SQL_SUCCESS_WITH_INFO)
➥ && (strcmp((CHAR *)szLastName, "Boyer")));
if (rc == SQL_SUCCESS || rc == SQL_SUCCESS_WITH_INFO)
{
SQLExecDirect(hstmt2,(UCHAR *)"UPDATE PAT SET PLastName = \"Hamilton\"
➥ WHERE CURRENT OF MyCursor", SQL_NTS);
}
SQLFreeStmt(hstmt1, SQL_DROP);
SQLFreeStmt(hstmt2, SQL_DROP);
SQLDisconnect(hdbc);
SQLFreeConnect(hdbc);
SQLFreeEnv(henv);
return(TRUE);
```

As stated previously, there are trade-offs in setting concurrency and setting isolation levels. There is also some common sense. If you set the isolation level to SERIALIZABLE, you are saying that no other transactions can affect your result set and you can't affect theirs. Therefore, you need not set further locks. The more you take control over the locking and isolation, the more checking your application needs to do to ensure the data in the result set is correct.

Block cursors and scrollable cursors can be combined to give both traffic savings and flexibility.

Unfortunately, SQLExtendedFetch is a Level 2 call and not available to all DBMSs.

The working example can be changed to use SQLExtendedFetch:

```
#define ROWS 100
UCHAR szName[ROWS][30], szAddress[ROWS][30], szCity[ROWS][10];
UCHAR szState[ROWS][3], szZipcode[ROWS][6];
SDWORD cbName, cbAddress, cbCity, cbState, cbZipcode;
UDWORD crow, irow;
UWORD rgfRowStatus[ROWS];
RETCODE rc;
SQLSetStmtOption(hstmt, SQL_CONCURRENCY, SQL_CONCUR_READ_ONLY);
SQLSetStmtOption(hstmt, SQL_CURSOR_TYPE, SQL_CURSOR_KEYSET_DRIVEN);
SQLSetStmtOption(hstmt, SQL_ROWSET_SIZE,ROWS);

rc = SQLExecDirect(hstmt,
 ➥ "SELECT Name, Address, City, State, Zipcode FROM        CUSTOMERS",SQL_NTS);

if (rc = SQL_SUCCESS)
   {
      SQLBindCol(hstmt, 1, SQL_C_CHAR, szName, 30,&cbName);
      SQLBindCol(hstmt, 2, SQL_C_CHAR, szAddress, 30, &cbAddress);
      SQLBindCol(hstmt, 3, SQL_C_CHAR, szCity, 10, &cbCity);
      SQLBindCol(hstmt, 4, SQL_C_CHAR, szState, 3, &cbState);
      SQLBindCol(hstmt, 1, SQL_C_CHAR, szZipcode, 6, &cbZipcode);

      while (TRUE)
      {
        rc = SQLExtendedFetch(hstmt, SQL_FETCH_NEXT, 1 &crow, rgfRowStatus);
        if (rc == SQL_SUCCESS || retcode == SQL_SUCCESS_WITH_INFO)
        {
//print strings 1 less than length for \0
        for(irow = 0, irow < crow ,irow++)
          {
          if(rgfRowStatus[irow] != SQL_ROW_deleted &&
 ➥ rgfRowStatus[irow] != SQL_ROW_ERROR)
          fprintf(out, "%*s %*s %*s %*s %*s",29
 ➥,szName[irow],29,szAddress[irow],9,szCity[irow],2,szState[irow],5,szZipcode[irow]);
          }
        }
        else
        {
        break;
        }
      }
   }
```

A good time to remember SQLExtendedFetch is when your application needs to print a long report. You know the page length and the length of the header and footer, so set the block size to the rows of data to print per page. Each page would require only one fetch call to the server.

SQLSetPos

After that long discussion of cursors, most of you want to know how a cursor is actually set. SQLSetPos sets the cursor position in a row set and enables you to refresh, update, delete, or add data to the rowset. The syntax is

```
rc = SQLSetPos(hsmt, irow, fOption, fLock);
```

The parameters are: irow, the number of the row to which the operation is to be performed (if irow is zero, the operation is on the whole rowset); fOption is either SQL_POSITON, SQL_REFRESH, SQL_UPDATE, SQL_DELETE or SQL_ADD; and fLock is either SQL_LOCK_NO_CHANGE, SQL_LOCK_EXCLUSIVE (row lock), or SQL_LOCK_UNLOCK. Also note that while SQL_ADD can have an irow value of any number, it is logical that the remaining fOption values have irow values less than or equal to the number in the rowset.

The SQLSTATE return codes are 01000, 01004, 01S01, 01S03 (no rows updated or deleted), 21S02, 22003, 22005, 22008, 23000, 24000, 42000, IM001, S0023, S1000, S1001, S1008, S1009, S1010, S1090, S1107 (row out of range), S1109 (invalid cursor position), S1C00, or S1T00.

Positioned Updates

Another Level 2 function is to modify data that is part of the result set. These are called *positioned updates* or *positioned deletes*. The SELECT statement uses the phrase FOR UPDATE, which may lock the entire result set on most DBMSs. An example is SELECT * FROM Customers WHERE zipcode eq "68510" FOR UPDATE of zipcode. Although this is a very clean way of updating data in the result set, there are not many DBMSs that support positioned updates. To determine this, you call SQLGetInfo with the fInfoType of SQL_PS_POSITIONED_UPDATE or SQL_PS_SELECT_FOR_UPDATE.

The steps are to first get the name of the cursor for the SELECT FOR UPDATE, then position the cursor with SQLFetch, then SQLExecute the SELECT using the cursor name. An example is the easiest way to show this:

```
RETCODE rc;
UDWORD fPos;
SWORD cbValue;
UCHAR szUpdateSQL{512];
UCHAR szCursor{SQL_MAX_IDENTIFIER+LEN + 1];
HSTMT hstmt;
SWORD cbCursor;
rc = SQLGetInfo(hdbc, SQL_POSITIONED_STATEMENTS, &fPos, sizeof(fPos), &cbValue);
if (RETCODE_IS_SUCCESSFUL(rc)
{
  rc = SQLGetCursorName(hstmt1, szCursor, sizeof(szCursor), &cbCursor);
}
if (RETCODE_IS_SUCCESSFUL(rc)
{
  rc = SQLAllocStmt(hdbc, &hstmt2);
}
if (RETCODE_IS_SUCCESSFUL(rc)
{
 sprintf(szUpdateSQL, "SELECT * FROM Customers WHERE zipcode eq "68510"
➥ FOR UPDATE of zipcode WHERE CURRENT of %s", szCursor);

rc = SQLExecDirect(hstmt2, szUpdateSQL, SQL_NTS);
SQLFreeStmt(hstmt1, SQL_DROP);
}
return rc;
}
```

`SQLGetCursorName` has the following syntax:

```
rc = SQLGetCursorName(hstmt, szCursor, cbCursorMax, pcbCursor);
```

The output parameters are `szCursor` and `pcbCursor`.

The `SQLSTATE` return codes are: `01000`, `01004`, `IM001`, `S1000`, `S1001`, `S1010`, `S1015` (no cursor name), and `S1090`.

Multiple SQL Statements

Some DBMSs enable you to submit more than one SQL statement at once. This would be true in the case of a stored procedure. In this case, you need to be able to retrieve one result set, then move to the next result set. `SQLMoreResults` simply does that. It moves to the next result set associated with a single `hstmt`. The syntax is

```
rc = SQLMoreResults(hstmt);
```

The `SQLSTATE` return codes are `01000`, `IM001`, `S1000`, `S1001`, `S1008`, `S1010`, and `S1T00`. The following is a simple example:

```
rc = SQLExecDirect(hstmt, "SELECT * FROM Customers"; "SELECT * FROM Friends");
while(rc != SQL_NO_DATA_FOUND)
{
rc = SQLFetch(hstmt);
//nonsense function mail
mail(Christmas cards);
}

SQLMoreResults(hstmt);

while(rc != SQL_NO_DATA_FOUND)
{
rc = SQLFetch(hstmt);
//worked above, use it again
mail(Christmas cards);
}
```

Date and Time Literals

DBMSs support many different types of date and time formats. The ISO standard is represented as yyyy-mm-dd. Your application can use a special *escape clause* to pass the ODBC format and the driver interprets it. This is done as {d '1996-02-20'}. To Microsoft SQL Server, this comes across as "02-20-1996". There are similar escape clauses for time and timestamps.

Outer Joins

Just as you saw with data escape clauses, ODBC has defined a syntax for an outer join syntax:

```
outer_join ::=table_name[correlation_name]
LEFT OUTER JOIN {table_name[correlation_name] ¦ outer_join}
 ON search_condition
```

Scalar Functions

ODBC supports 60 scalar functions for strings, numerics, system, time/date, and data type conversions. Numeric functions are like SELECT {fn log10(fMyNumber)} FROM Mytable or SELECT {fn rand(iMyint)} FROM Mytable. These take a single parameter and act upon it. String functions extract substrings, determine string length, and concatenate strings as in SELECT {fn concat(LastName, FirstName)} FROM PAT. Date functions do time-based calculations on a column and work like SELECT {fn dayofweek(idate)} FROM CALENDAR or SELECT * FROM MySchedule WHERE MyTIMESTAMP = {fn now()}. System functions return the name of the database, the user, and if a value is NULL in the form SELECT * FROM PATIENTS WHERE PAT = {fn user()}. The data type conversion functions work like SELECT EMPLOYEENO FROM EMPLOYEES where {fn convert(EMPLOYEENO, SQL_CHAR) LIKE '1%'.

The LIKE predicate is the percent character (%), which matches zero or more of any character. Using underscore (_) matches any one character. Using these characters in an SQL statement usually requires an escape clause, or the compiler might mix up the number of parameters you are passing. You see this as SELECT LASTNAME, FIRSTNAME FROM EMPLOYEE WHERE LASTNAME LIKE '\%HAM%' {escape '\'}. This might be messy, but if you have been using C or C++ for a while, you see the problem that it solves. This assumes the escape character is (\). Your DBMS may vary, and you may need to call SQLGetInfo with the SQL_LIKE_ESCAPE_CLAUSE to determine it.

Stored Procedures

In the 1980s, stored procedures were introduced by Sybase as a way to enforce general business rules on its DBMS. An example was that if an order dropped inventory below a certain level, a reorder for a given number of inventory units was automatically created. A stored procedure is a group of SQL statements (get new inventory level, check against rule minimum level if low order level is specified) that's given a procedure name and executed as a unit by calling that name. This procedure would be used by many applications assessing the inventory data. It looks like a function call with a name, parameters, and return values.

DBMSs differ widely in the format of a stored procedure. To overcome this, ODBC has another escape clause:

```
{[?] call procedure)name[(arg1m arg2, ...)]}
```

The calling format is

```
{?= CALL monthend (?)}
```

This format calls the monthend procedure. The ?= specifies an output parameter (your results), the second ? the input parameter. Before you call the procedure, you use SQLBindParameter with the fParamType of SQL_PARAM_INPUT_OUTPUT (assuming you have both input and output parameters). The results are returned in a result set in the same fashion as the other SQL statements. To find out if your DBMS supports stored procedures, you can call SQLGetInfo with fInfoType of SQL_PROCEDURES. The return is either Y or N.

Transaction Processing

Imagine the amount of code you would need to write to track every possible database change and reverse it if necessary. You would need to store the original data so that you could reverse any updates or deletions. You would need to store changes and deletions so that you could reverse them. You would need to store the sequence of the changes. And so on. This would be a huge application just to provide the ability to undo. Most true DBMSs provide built-in transaction processing.

A *transaction* is a group of one or more SQL statements that are to be executed as a unit. Either all or none are executed. *Commit* means executing the unit, *rollback* means returning the database to its state prior to the execution of the unit. Transactions are used to maintain data integrity. In accounting, you learned to debit one account and credit another. The two steps are one transaction, and both must be performed in order for your accounts to stay in balance. If one cannot be performed, neither should be, and the transaction is rolled back so that your books are as they were before. Those are the basics of transaction processing. If both can be executed, you commit the unit. If not, you reverse the action of the partial steps in a rollback.

The DBMS has to be capable of detecting deadlocks between multiple executing transactions. When a deadlock occurs, the transaction that is initiated must be rolled back and the application informed. The application then restarts the transaction. This is an area were standardization of error codes is essential, as the following example shows:

```
if(!strcmp(SQLSTATE,"40001"))
//restart transaction
```

The first thing your application needs to do is determine if the data source supports transaction processing. You saw this step in SQLGetInfo with the parameter SQL_TXN_CAPABLE. SQLGetInfo returns SQL_TC_NONE if it's not supported, while SLQ_TC_DML indicates that data definition language (DDL) statements cannot be used in transactions (like CREATE TABLE or DROP TABLE (to delete a table)). SQL_TC_DDL_COMMIT indicates that any DDL statement fires off a commit, and SQL_TC_DDL_IGNORE indicates that any DDL statement in the transaction is ignored. And lastly, SQL_TC_ALL means transaction processing of both DDL and DML statements is supported. You also need to know if multiple transactions can be active at one time on any one connection. SQLGetInfo provides this in the SQL_MULTIPLE_ACTIVE_TXN by returning either Y or N.

Transaction processing involves three steps:

1. Set up transaction processing in SQLSetConnectOptions to manual commit.

2. Execute multiple SQlPrepare, SQLExecute or SQLExecDriect statements as a unit.

3. Commit or roll back the statements using SQLTransact.

SQLSetConnectOptions

You have two choices in the setup of SQLSetConnectOptions: auto commit and manual commit. Auto commit is the default state, where each SQL statement is committed as it executes.

Because auto commit is the default, you must set up manual commit to do the transaction processing yourself.

NOTE

```
SQLSetConnectOptions(hdbc, SQL_AUTOCOMMIT, SQL_AUTOCCOMMIT_OFF)
```

can return SQLSTATE of S1C00 (driver not capable) if the mode is already set to manual. If you hadn't called SQLGetInfo's SQL_TXN_CAPABLE before this call, you wouldn't know why you got this error.

After you set the manual commit mode, every SQL statement is part of a transaction unit. You usually commit if the whole unit succeeds or roll back if any one statement fails. A good example is DELETE, where you assume that you are only deleting one row. You can save yourself by ensuring that SQLRowCount is 1 prior to the commit.

In manual commit mode, the driver begins a transaction when an application submits an SQL statement and no transactions are open. It commits or rolls back upon the call to SQLTransact. In autocommit mode, each SQL is a single, complete transaction. The driver commits once per statement. All statement handles belonging to a single connection handle are in the same transaction space. SQLTransact commits or rolls back all statements in the same transaction space. If you have two statements, you need to be aware that this happens. Each statement is associated with a cursor. If a cursor is open when SQLTransact is called, one of three things can happen:

- The cursor may be closed and deleted, and any prepared statements will be lost.
- The cursor may be closed but not deleted. The application needs to reexecute any prepared statements.
- The cursor is preserved and the application can continue to use the cursor after the call to SQLTransact.

Your design needs to be aware of possibilities when using multiple statement handles in a transaction mode.

The following is a simple transaction example:

```
RETCODE rc;
SDWORD cRow;
rc = SQLConnectOption(hdbc, SQL_AUTOCOMMIT, SQL_AUTOCOMMIT_OFF);
if (RETCODE_IS_SUCCESSFULL(rc))
  {
    rc = SQLExecute(hstmt);
  }
if (RETCODE_IS_SUCCESSFULL(rc))
  {
    rc = SQLRowCount(hstmt, &cRow);
  }
```

```
if (RETCODE_IS_SUCCESSFULL(rc) && cRow <=1L)
  {
    SQLTransact(henv, hdbc, SQL_COMMIT);
  }
else
  {
    SQLTransact(henv, hdbc, SQL_ROLLBACK);
  }
```

SQLTransact

As shown in the preceding example, SQLTransact takes three parameters: the environment handle, the database handle, and either SQL_COMMIT or SQL_ROLLBACK.

The SQLSTATE return codes are: 01000, 08003, 08007 (connect failed during transaction), IM001, S1000, S1001, S1010 S1012 (invalid transaction code), and S1C00.

SQLTransact requests a commit or rollback on all active operations of the statement handles associated with a connection. This immediately raises questions of multi-user environments and the concept of *transaction isolation levels*. Think of two users: the first edits some data but hasn't committed the changes, and the second user polls the same data. Should they see the edited data or the original? What if they make different changes to the data? What if user 1 is adding a bunch of new data? User 2 polls the same data, and then user 1 decides to roll back so that data is never in the actual database. Three terms are used to describe the state of the data. A *dirty read* is when user 1 changes data that is read by user 2, then user 1 rolls back. A *nonrepeatable read* is when both user 1 and user 2 poll the same data, user 2 deletes some data and commits, and user 1 rereads the same data, which has changed. And a *phantom read* is when user 1 reads data, user 2 inserts new data, and user 1 requeries and gets the new data.

ODBC provides five sets of locking instructions to prevent these situations or combinations of themes, as some may be desirable in your situation. The syntax is

```
rc = SQLSetConnectOption(hdbc, SQL_TXN_ISOLATION, SQL_TXN_READ_UNCOMMITTED)
```

There is a trade-off between reading the most current data and reading consistent data. There are also trade-offs when you lock users out of data. This is called *concurrency* locking. The more consistency the more rows need to be locked, so there is less concurrency. To provide a high level of consistency, like SQL_TXN_SERIALIZABLE, you may need to lock entire tables. Because each DBMS has its own record locking scheme, the best you can do is call SQLGetInfo with fInfoType SQL_TXN_ISOLATION_OPTION and see what levels are available—very few DBMSs support all 5 levels. Often you do the opposite and set up an acceptable level to make the application more robust. This function returns the levels shown in Table 23.9.

Table 23.9. ODBC transaction isolation levels.

Isolation level	Dirty reads	Non-repeatable reads	Phantom reads
SQL_TXN_READ_UNCOMMITTED	Yes	Yes	Yes
SQL_TXN_READ_COMMITTED	No	Yes	Yes
SQL_TXN_REPEATABLE_READ	No	No	Yes
SQL_TXN_SERIALIZABLE	No	No	No
SQL_TXN_VERSIONING	No	No	No

Read Uncommitted places no restrictions on reads. Data that is inserted, edited, or deleted is immediately available to the next query; therefore, you have a high level of concurrency. Because you have no locks, however, you will see all three types of read problems and thus you have very low consistency.

Read Committed restricts only dirty reads so that transactions do not read uncommitted data. It has slightly better consistency in the data but the dataset is slightly less concurrent.

Repeatable reads is a usual level for multiple user systems. Because reading many rows locks those rows, you should try to have small result sets to give as many users concurrent access as possible.

Serializable transactions means if that if two transactions are executed immediately in order (serial), you will always get the same result set. However, because this may require an entire table to be locked, your multiuser performance will suffer.

Versioning is when a high-performance DBMS keeps separate pages of data for each transaction. Multiple users each have their own page of data and fewer records need to be locked per transaction. This is a good trade-off of concurrency versus consistency, but this approach can fail if the server goes down while many transactions are pending.

Also note that if you fail to issue SQLTransact after a group of statements, the transaction is still open and further statements are added to that unit. Some DBMSs have limits on the number of transactions in a unit.

Explicit Locking

In most cases you won't have complete control over the preceding transaction options. Instead, the DBMS will have set a default isolation level. Sometimes, though, you cannot let the DBMS manage the locking scheme—the application must control the locks. At this point you need to dig out the API manuals for the DBMS you choose. Some have specific record locking functions, most do not. You need to know about the data source. A `SELECT FOR UPDATE` on some systems does row locking on the rows. You also can use `SQLSetPos` locking functions, discussed earlier. If you're using MFC record sets, you can also use `CRecord set::SetLockingMode` for optimistic or pessimistic locking.

Summary

This chapter has touched on approximately one-half of the ODBC functions available to you using Visual C++ and SQL Server. SQL Server provides a rich, stable data store, while Visual C++ lets you build full-featured Windows applications using that data. Although most of the examples by necessity have been short console applications, they can be easily cut and pasted into your Windows application's class functions.

Connecting to SQL Server from Visual Basic

CHAPTER 24

This chapter looks at all the various methods of connecting to SQL Server from Visual Basic. First you explore the methods of extracting data by developing the same simple application using each object model—the simplest data control application to direct ODBC API calls are all covered here. There is a section on using VBA to format and present data with a sample Excel application. Finally, you use SQL-DMO to manage the SQL Server itself, demonstrating the full power of the Visual Basic connection.

Which Connection Is Right for You?

There are many ways in which you can connect to SQL Server from Visual Basic, but which is the best? Not one solution can be used in all circumstances. Some connections have limitations, and others are extremely complex and difficult to work with but extremely powerful. In this chapter you follow the code to make the same application using each of the techniques. This gives you an idea of what is involved in using each connection and helps you pick which one to use in future projects. As a summary before you try each of the connections, Table 24.1 shows some comparison information about each connection.

> **TIP**
>
> Whenever you are working on an application with a connection to SQL Server, use the Current Activity dialog box in SQL Enterprise Manager to ensure that you are not leaving a trail of dead connections behind you.
>
> If you simply double-click the connection that you want to cancel, check that it is the one you want to remove and click the Kill Process button. This cancels the process. This is particularly important if the process is holding any locks on the server.

In Table 24.1, the difficulty in writing is rated from 1 (easy) to 10 (difficult). Code Required refers to the approximate number of lines necessary to produce the same output using each code type.

Table 24.1. Comparing connection models from Visual Basic.

	Data Control	DAO	OLE DB/ADO	RDO Library	DB-API	ODBC
Difficulty in Writing	1	3	4	5	7	10
Execution Speed	Good	Good	V Good	V Good	V Good	V Good
Code Required (lines)	50	75	65	70	80	105

	Data Control	*DAO*	*OLE DB/ADO*	*RDO Library*	*DB-API*	*ODBC*
SQL Functions Exposed	Some	Some	Some	Most	All	Most
Connection Management	Automatic	Simple	Simple	Average	Simple	Complex
Data Management	Simple	Average	Average	Average	Complex	Complex
Other DB Connections Supported	Yes	Yes	Yes	Yes	No	Yes

Some programmers believe that by connecting with the ODBC API directly they are achieving a significantly faster application. Although this might have been true in earlier versions of Visual Basic, the newer connection models of ODBCDirect and the RDO provide simple fast interfaces with ODBC databases. Many of the earlier concerns about speed come from using the original JET connections, which were slow. Now much of the overhead of JET can be avoided by using the ODBCDirect connection type within the DAO model. You can then write simple code, calling a small library of C++ functions rather than lines of Visual Basic code that call the ODBC API directly. Another problem with using the more direct techniques such as DBLibrary or the ODBC API is that without careful connection management, dead connections can be left open and memory won't be reclaimed.

Setting Up an ODBC Data Source Name (DSN)

Most of the connections that you will set up require a data source name (DSN) as the basis for the connection. It is possible to create a data source name at runtime with the more advanced connection types. However, to avoid complication you use the same basic connection that is established here for all ODBC type connections in this chapter.

1. Open the ODBC manager in the Control Panel. In the ODBC Data Source Administrator dialog box, click the User DSN tab. Click Add to create a new data source, and select a driver. In this case the SQL Server driver is needed, as shown in Figure 24.1.

FIGURE 24.1.

Selecting on ODBC driver for the connection.

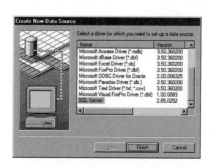

24

SQL SERVER AND VB

2. Now press Finish, and the ODBC SQL Server Setup dialog box will appear. Leave most entries at their default values and give the connection a name. The server entry is the name of your server without the preceding forward slashes (for example, NTSQL not //NTSQL). The completed dialog box is shown in Figure 24.2.

FIGURE 24.2.

The completed ODBC SQL Server Setup dialog box.

Connecting Using the Different Methods

Throughout this section you use the same basic application and achieve the same objectives, but by using each of the connection methods in turn. This way you can see how they compare and contrast in opening, retrieving data, managing connections, and disconnecting. The view of the test application in Figure 24.3 shows how the final application will look using any of the connection methods. Although the application looks the same on the surface, some of the methods are very different underneath.

FIGURE 24.3.

The test application at runtime.

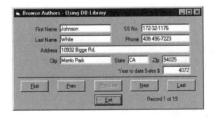

You write the application in the same way each time to make direct comparisons. The connection is opened in the Form_Load event procedure of frmData. After the form has loaded press the Populate button on the form. This opens the data from the database and fills the text boxes with the first record. You then can use any of the four navigation keys to step through the records individually or to move directly to the first or last record. Finally, the connection is dropped when you press the Exit button, and any resources are reclaimed.

For clarity, most error trapping has not been included except where it is necessary for function or to help you understand how to manage the connection.

Setting Up the Base Form for the Project

Open a standard EXE new project in Visual Basic. Paste in the controls that you see in Figure 24.4.

FIGURE 24.4.

The application form at design time.

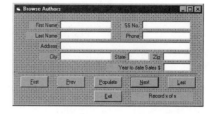

Set the controls' properties to the values shown in Listing 24.1, which shows the common header for each of the applications.

Listing 24.1. The form header of `frmData`.

```
 1: VERSION 5.00
 2: Begin VB.Form frmData
 3:    Caption         =    "Browse Authors"
 4:    ClientHeight    =    3105
 5:    ClientLeft      =    2595
 6:    ClientTop       =    2265
 7:    ClientWidth     =    6585
 8:    LinkTopic       =    "Form1"
 9:    ScaleHeight     =    3105
10:    ScaleWidth      =    6585
11:    Begin VB.TextBox txtYTD
12:       Alignment    =    1   'Right Justify
13:       Height       =    285
14:       Left         =    5220
15:       TabIndex     =    23
16:       Top          =    1680
17:       Width        =    975
18:    End
19:    Begin VB.CommandButton cmdPopulate
20:       Cancel       =    -1  'True
21:       Caption      =    "&Populate"
22:       Height       =    375
23:       Left         =    2820
24:       TabIndex     =    22
25:       Top          =    2160
26:       Width        =    975
27:    End
28:    Begin VB.CommandButton cmdExit
29:       Caption      =    "&Exit"
30:       Height       =    375
```

continues

24

SQL SERVER AND VB

Listing 24.1. continued

```
31:        Left            =    2820
32:        TabIndex        =    20
33:        Top             =    2640
34:        Width           =    975
35:    End
36:    Begin VB.TextBox txtID
37:        Height          =    285
38:        Left            =    4485
39:        TabIndex        =    3
40:        Top             =    240
41:        Width           =    1695
42:    End
43:    Begin VB.TextBox txtLastName
44:        Height          =    285
45:        Left            =    1605
46:        TabIndex        =    5
47:        Top             =    600
48:        Width           =    1815
49:    End
50:    Begin VB.TextBox txtAddress
51:        Height          =    285
52:        Left            =    1605
53:        TabIndex        =    9
54:        Top             =    960
55:        Width           =    4575
56:    End
57:    Begin VB.TextBox txtCity
58:        Height          =    285
59:        Left            =    1605
60:        TabIndex        =    11
61:        Top             =    1320
62:        Width           =    1815
63:    End
64:    Begin VB.TextBox txtState
65:        Height          =    285
66:        Left            =    4005
67:        TabIndex        =    13
68:        Top             =    1320
69:        Width           =    735
70:    End
71:    Begin VB.TextBox txtZip
72:        Height          =    285
73:        Left            =    5205
74:        TabIndex        =    15
75:        Top             =    1320
76:        Width           =    975
77:    End
78:    Begin VB.TextBox txtPhone
79:        Height          =    285
80:        Left            =    4485
81:        TabIndex        =    7
82:        Top             =    600
83:        Width           =    1695
84:    End
85:    Begin VB.TextBox txtFirstName
86:        Height          =    285
87:        Left            =    1605
```

```
88:        TabIndex       =    1
89:        Top            =    240
90:        Width          =    1815
91:     End
92:     Begin VB.CommandButton cmdPrev
93:        Caption        =    "&Prev"
94:        Height         =    375
95:        Left           =    1515
96:        TabIndex       =    17
97:        Top            =    2160
98:        Width          =    975
99:     End
100:    Begin VB.CommandButton cmdNext
101:       Caption        =    "&Next"
102:       Default        =    -1    'True
103:       Height         =    375
104:       Left           =    4095
105:       TabIndex       =    18
106:       Top            =    2160
107:       Width          =    975
108:    End
109:    Begin VB.CommandButton cmdLast
110:       Caption        =    "&Last"
111:       Height         =    375
112:       Left           =    5385
113:       TabIndex       =    19
114:       Top            =    2160
115:       Width          =    975
116:    End
117:    Begin VB.CommandButton cmdFirst
118:       Caption        =    "&First"
119:       Height         =    375
120:       Left           =    225
121:       TabIndex       =    16
122:       Top            =    2160
123:       Width          =    975
124:    End
125:    Begin VB.Label lblYtd
126:       Alignment      =    1    'Right Justify
127:       Caption        =    "Year to date Sales $"
128:       Height         =    195
129:       Left           =    3240
130:       TabIndex       =    24
131:       Top            =    1740
132:       Width          =    1875
133:    End
134:    Begin VB.Label lblRecordcount
135:       Alignment      =    2    'Center
136:       Caption        =    "Record x of x"
137:       Height         =    255
138:       Left           =    4140
139:       TabIndex       =    21
140:       Top            =    2700
141:       Width          =    2115
142:    End
143:    Begin VB.Line Line1
```

24

SQL SERVER AND VB

continues

Listing 24.1. continued

```
144:        X1              =    120
145:        X2              =    6420
146:        Y1              =    2040
147:        Y2              =    2040
148:     End
149:     Begin VB.Label lblCity
150:        Alignment       =    1   'Right Justify
151:        Caption         =    "City"
152:        Height          =    195
153:        Left            =    885
154:        TabIndex        =    10
155:        Top             =    1380
156:        Width           =    615
157:     End
158:     Begin VB.Label lblZip
159:        Alignment       =    1   'Right Justify
160:        Caption         =    "Zip"
161:        Height          =    195
162:        Left            =    4485
163:        TabIndex        =    14
164:        Top             =    1380
165:        Width           =    615
166:     End
167:     Begin VB.Label lblFirstname
168:        Alignment       =    1   'Right Justify
169:        Caption         =    "First Name"
170:        Height          =    195
171:        Left            =    525
172:        TabIndex        =    0
173:        Top             =    300
174:        Width           =    975
175:     End
176:     Begin VB.Label lblLastname
177:        Alignment       =    1   'Right Justify
178:        Caption         =    "Last Name"
179:        Height          =    195
180:        Left            =    405
181:        TabIndex        =    4
182:        Top             =    660
183:        Width           =    1095
184:     End
185:     Begin VB.Label lblPhone
186:        Alignment       =    1   'Right Justify
187:        Caption         =    "Phone"
188:        Height          =    195
189:        Left            =    3765
190:        TabIndex        =    6
191:        Top             =    660
192:        Width           =    615
193:     End
194:     Begin VB.Label lblAddress
195:        Alignment       =    1   'Right Justify
196:        Caption         =    "Address"
197:        Height          =    195
198:        Left            =    885
199:        TabIndex        =    8
```

```
200:        Top              =    1020
201:        Width            =    615
202:    End
203:    Begin VB.Label lblState
204:        Alignment        =    1   'Right Justify
205:        Caption          =    "State"
206:        Height           =    195
207:        Left             =    3285
208:        TabIndex         =    12
209:        Top              =    1380
210:        Width            =    615
211:    End
212:    Begin VB.Label lblID
213:        Alignment        =    1   'Right Justify
214:        Caption          =    "SS No."
215:        Height           =    255
216:        Left             =    3765
217:        TabIndex         =    2
218:        Top              =    300
219:        Width            =    615
220:    End
221: End
```

Data Controls

The first connection type to consider is the quickest to program and simplest of all: the data control-based connection. This connection is often ignored as a trivial connection, but for developing a prototype or a quick test program it can be very useful.

The type of data control that the example uses is the simple Microsoft data control. It works almost identically to the remote data control.

Registering the Components

Compared to the other connections, you don't need to do much here. You simply must select the data control in the Visual Basic toolbox and draw it on the form. Set the name property of the data control to DatDataCtrl.

Go to the Project menu and select References, and in the dialog box place a check in the box next to the Microsoft DAO 3.5 Object Library. You use several constants that are defined in this file.

Global Variables

No global variables are required when you use the data control.

Getting Connected Using the Data Control

Set the DataSource property of each of the text boxes to DatDataCtrl before you start. It is not possible to set the DataSource property at runtime; it must be done at design time.

24

SQL SERVER AND VB

Listing 24.2 shows the code for creating the connection with the data control. At the beginning of the `Form_Load` event procedure the data control is set to point to the `pubs` DSN that was created earlier in this chapter. The `DefaultType` is set to use ODBCDirect rather than the slower JET-based connection. The `RecordsetType` property is set to use a snapshot-type record set, and the `ReadOnly` property is set to `True` because the data will only be looked at rather than modified. After the data control is set up, the navigation buttons enabled are set to `false` to prevent the code from being activated until there are records to move around in.

Listing 24.2. Connecting using the data control.

```
Private Sub Form_Load()
    With DatDataCtrl
        .Visible = False
        .Enabled = True
        .DefaultType = dbUseODBC
        .RecordsetType = vbRSTypeSnapShot
        .Connect = "odbc;uid=;pwd=;DSN=pubs"
        .ReadOnly = True
    End With
    ' Disable the navigation buttons until there is data!! *
    cmdFirst.Enabled = False
    cmdPrev.Enabled = False
    cmdNext.Enabled = False
    cmdLast.Enabled = False
End Sub
```

Retrieving the Records Using the Data Control

Now that a connection has been established, the required data must be pinpointed. The next step is to set a string equal to the SQL statement that will be used to select the data. The `RecordSource` property is set to this string, and then the record set is refreshed. The next group of code sets each `datafield` of the text box on the form to point to a field in the results of the query. As each `datafield` is set you will see the value appear in the form. When all the text boxes are set, the record pointer label (`lblRecordCount`) on the form is updated using the `AbsolutePosition` and `Recordcount` properties of the underlying record set to the data control. Listing 24.3 shows how the records are returned using the data control.

Listing 24.3. Retrieving the records using the data control.

```
Private Sub cmdPopulate_Click()
    Dim strDC As String, intEnum As Integer
    ' Build SQL statement
    strDC = "SELECT ta.au_id, a.au_fname, a.au_lname, a.phone, a.address, "
    strDC = strDC & "a.city, a.state, a.zip, Sum(t.ytd_sales) Ytd_sales "
    strDC = strDC & "FROM pubs..authors a, pubs..titles t, "
    strDC = strDC & "pubs..titleauthor ta "
    strDC = strDC & "WHERE ta.au_id = a.au_id AND ta.title_id = t.title_id "
    strDC = strDC & "GROUP BY ta.au_id, a.au_fname, a.au_lname, a.phone, "
    strDC = strDC & "a.address, a.city, a.state, a.zip "
    With DatDataCtrl
```

```
            .RecordSource = strDC
            .Refresh
    End With
    ' Set the txtboxes to connect to the fields in the query
    txtFirstName.DataField = "au_fname"
    txtLastName.DataField = "au_lname"
    txtID.DataField = "au_id"
    txtPhone.DataField = "phone"
    txtAddress.DataField = "address"
    txtCity.DataField = "City"
    txtState.DataField = "State"
    txtZip.DataField = "zip"
    txtYTD.DataField = "ytd_sales"
    ' Refresh all controls attached to the datacontrol
    DatDataCtrl.UpdateControls
    lblRecordcount = "Record " & (DatDataCtrl.Recordset.AbsolutePosition + 1) _
    & " of " & DatDataCtrl.Recordset.RecordCount
    cmdPopulate.Enabled = False
    cmdFirst.Enabled = True
    cmdPrev.Enabled = True
    cmdNext.Enabled = True
    cmdLast.Enabled = True
End Sub
```

Navigating Using the Data Control

You move to the first and last records by using the movefirst and movelast methods on the record set associated with the data control. Listing 24.4 shows the full code for the two procedures. The second line in each procedure updates the form record pointer.

Listing 24.4. Moving to the first and last records.

```
Private Sub cmdFirst_Click()
    DatDataCtrl.Recordset.MoveFirst
    lblRecordcount = "Record " & DatDataCtrl.Recordset.AbsolutePosition + 1 _
                            & " of " & DatDataCtrl.Recordset.RecordCount
End Sub

Private Sub cmdLast_Click()
    DatDataCtrl.Recordset.MoveLast
    lblRecordcount = "Record " & DatDataCtrl.Recordset.AbsolutePosition + 1 _
                            & " of " & DatDataCtrl.Recordset.RecordCount
End Sub
```

24

SQL SERVER AND VB

Moving to the next and previous record is nearly as simple, except that a check must be made to prevent the pointer from moving past the end of the record set or before the first record. The movements in each case are performed using MoveNext and MovePrevious methods on the record set. After the MoveNext method the record set is checked using the EOF property to see whether the pointer is at the end of the file. If the pointer is at the end of the file, the MoveLast method is used to reposition the pointer at the last record, a beep is sounded to remind the user that he is at the end of the records, and then the procedure is exited. If the move was successful the pointer information on the form is updated.

Similar code (see Listing 24.5) is used for the previous record navigation, but `BOF` and `MoveFirst` are used.

Listing 24.5. Moving to the next and previous records.

```
Private Sub cmdNext_Click()
    DatDataCtrl.Recordset.MoveNext
    If DatDataCtrl.Recordset.EOF Then
        DatDataCtrl.Recordset.MoveLast
        Beep
        Exit Sub
    End If
    lblRecordcount = "Record " & DatDataCtrl.Recordset.AbsolutePosition + 1 _
                            & " of " & DatDataCtrl.Recordset.RecordCount
End Sub

Private Sub cmdPrev_Click()
    DatDataCtrl.Recordset.MovePrevious
    If DatDataCtrl.Recordset.BOF Then
        DatDataCtrl.Recordset.MoveFirst
        Beep
        Exit Sub
    End If
    lblRecordcount = "Record " & DatDataCtrl.Recordset.AbsolutePosition + 1 _
                            & " of " & DatDataCtrl.Recordset.RecordCount
End Sub
```

Closing the Connection Using the Data Control

Again using the data control, the management of the connection is something you do not have to worry much about. To close the connection object and recover resources all you must do is close the form and the control, and the dirty work is done for you. The code for exiting the data control application is shown in Listing 24.6.

Listing 24.6. Exiting the application.

```
Private Sub cmdExit_Click()
    Unload frmData
End Sub
```

Using the Data Access Object (DAO) with a JET-Based Connection

The previous section used DAO and the data control. This section deals with a connection using only the DAO in a standalone mode. The main reason why you would choose this type of connection would be if you were trying to join two data sources of different types, which JET allows you to do quite painlessly.

Registering the Components

The only addition to the default Visual Basic standard EXE project is to load the Microsoft DAO 3.5 Object Library. You do this by selecting References from the Project menu and checking the box next to Microsoft DAO 3.5 Object Library.

Global Variables

Several objects are used throughout the project. The statements in Listing 24.7 need to be added to the `General Declarations` section of the form.

Listing 24.7. Global variable definitions.

```
Private WSJet As Workspace
Private DBPubs As Database
Private rsDAO As Recordset
```

Getting Connected Using DAO/Jet

To manually open a connection, you must first establish a workspace by using the `CreateWorkspace` method to create a workspace object. The method requires a workspace name, a valid username, and password for a user in the `Users` collection of the Jet workspace object. The final parameter for `CreateWorkspace` specifies that you want a JET connection rather than an ODBCDirect connection.

After you have successfully opened a workspace, you can open a database within that workspace using the `OpenDatabase` method. The parameters for the `OpenDatabase` method are the name of the DSN used to connect, `False` for open in non-exclusive mode, `True` for open as read only, and the connect string.

After the connection has been established the navigation buttons are disabled and the procedure exits in Listing 24.8.

Listing 24.8. Connecting to the database.

```
Private Sub Form_Load()
    Dim strCon As String
    ' Create Jet workspace object
    Set WSJet = CreateWorkspace("NewJetWorkspace", "admin", "", dbUseJet)
    ' Define connect string and open the database
    strCon = "ODBC;UID=;PWD=;"
    Set DBPubs = WSJet.OpenDatabase("Pubs", False, True, strCon)
    cmdFirst.Enabled = False
    cmdPrev.Enabled = False
    cmdNext.Enabled = False
    cmdLast.Enabled = False
End Sub
```

24

SQL SERVER AND VB

WARNING

Keep this in mind when you use workspaces with a secure database: If you add the workspace to the workspaces collection, any other application can browse through the workspace and use your connection and security to access any data through your workspace.

Retrieving the Records Using DAO/Jet

Listing 24.9 shows the code used to open the record set. As with all the connections, first a string that contains the query is constructed. Next, a snapshot-type (non-updateable) record set is opened using the `OpenRecordset` object on the database object, created in the `Form_Load` event procedure.

The record set object now exists, but it must be filled with data by moving to the last item and back to the first item using the `MoveLast` and `MoveFirst` methods.

Listing 24.9. Retrieving the records.

```
Private Sub cmdPopulate_Click()
Dim strSQLdao As String
    strSQLdao = "SELECT ta.au_id, a.au_fname, a.au_lname, a.phone, a.address, "
    strSQLdao = strSQLdao & "a.city, a.state, a.zip, Sum(t.ytd_sales) " & _
                                                        "as Ytd_sales "
    strSQLdao = strSQLdao & "FROM authors a, titles t, titleauthor ta "
    strSQLdao = strSQLdao & "WHERE ta.au_id = a.au_id AND ta.title_id = " & _
                                                        "t.title_id"
    strSQLdao = strSQLdao & " GROUP BY ta.au_id, a.au_fname, a.au_lname, "
    strSQLdao = strSQLdao & "a.phone , a.address, a.city, a.state, a.zip "
    ' Open snapshot type recordset
    Set rsDAO = DBPubs.OpenRecordset(strSQLdao, dbOpenSnapshot)
    ' To size recordset move to last and then position at first record
    rsDAO.MoveLast
    rsDAO.MoveFirst
    ' Update Display
    Call TextBoxUpdate_DAO
    cmdPopulate.Enabled = False
    cmdFirst.Enabled = True
    cmdPrev.Enabled = True
    cmdNext.Enabled = True
    cmdLast.Enabled = True
End Sub
```

After the record set has been populated, the `TextBoxUpdate_DAO()` procedure is called to update the form. Listing 24.10 shows the code in the `TextBoxUpdate_DAO()` procedure. Each text box is updated by assigning its text property to the value of each of the fields in the fields collection of the record set. Notice how you can use the database field names directly by enclosing them in brackets rather than referring to the field by its numeric position in the fields collection.

Listing 24.10. Updating the form.

```
Private Sub TextBoxUpdate_DAO()
    ' Update Display
    txtFirstName = rsDAO.Fields![au_fname]
    txtLastName = rsDAO.Fields![au_lname]
    txtZip = rsDAO.Fields![zip]
```

```
    txtAddress = rsDAO.Fields![address]
    txtCity = rsDAO.Fields![city]
    txtState = rsDAO.Fields![State]
    txtPhone = rsDAO.Fields![phone]
    txtID = rsDAO.Fields![au_id]
    txtYTD = rsDAO.Fields![Ytd_sales]
    lblRecordcount = "Record " & (rsDAO.AbsolutePosition + 1) & _
                                 " of " & rsDAO.RecordCount
End Sub
```

At the end of the procedure the `AbsolutePosition` and the `RecordCount` property are used to provide the position information for the `lblRecordCount` label.

> **NOTE**
>
> The `AbsolutePosition` property must have 1 added to it, because it is zero based. The maximum value to which you can set the `AbsolutePosition` property is the value of the `RecordCount` property, 1.

Navigation Using DAO/Jet

Navigation is almost identical to the data control, except that the `TextBoxUpdate_DAO()` procedure is required to update the text boxes on the form. Listing 24.11 shows how to code the procedures for the `First` and `Last` command button `click` events.

Listing 24.11. Moving to the first and last records.

```
Private Sub cmdFirst_Click()
    rsDAO.MoveFirst
    ' Update Display
    Call TextBoxUpdate_DAO
End Sub

Private Sub cmdLast_Click()
    rsDAO.MoveLast
    ' Update Display
    Call TextBoxUpdate_DAO
End Sub
```

Listing 24.12 shows how similar the strategy for moving forward and backward one record is to the data control `Next` and `Prev` command button click events. In each case the pointer is moved one record, then checked to see whether it falls outside the records. If the pointer falls outside, a move is made to the extreme of the records, and the procedure is exited after warning the user with a beep. If the move is successful the form is updated.

Listing 24.12. Moving to the next and previous records.

```
Private Sub cmdNext_Click()
    rsDAO.MoveNext
    If rsDAO.EOF Then
        Beep
        rsDAO.MoveLast
    Else
        ' Update Display
        Call TextBoxUpdate_DAO
    End If
End Sub

Private Sub cmdPrev_Click()
    rsDAO.MovePrevious
    If rsDAO.BOF Then
        Beep
        rsDAO.MoveFirst
    Else
        ' Update Display
        Call TextBoxUpdate_DAO
    End If
End Sub
```

Closing the Connection When Using DAO/Jet

Listing 24.13 shows how to close the connection with the database. Each of the objects must be closed using the `Close` method. This closes its connection to the database, but to reclaim any resources each of the object variables must be set to `Nothing`.

Listing 24.13. Closing the connection.

```
Private Sub cmdExit_Click()
    ' Close each of the objects used and set to nothing
    rsDAO.Close
    Set rsDAO = Nothing
    DBPubs.Close
    Set DBPubs = Nothing
    WSJet.Close
    Set WSJet = Nothing
    Unload frmData
End Sub
```

Using DAO With ODBC Direct

Once again this connection will use DAO as in the last section, but this time it uses the faster ODBCDirect connection rather than a Jet-based connection. Changing the connection type means that different objects are used to get connected, but after the connection is made, things will be very similar to the DAO/Jet connection until the connection is closed.

Registering the Components

The only addition to the default Visual Basic standard EXE project is to load the Microsoft DAO 3.5 Object Library. To do this, select References from the Visual Basic Project menu, and check the box next to Microsoft DAO 3.5 Object Library.

Global Variables

Listing 24.14 shows the global variables that are used throughout the application and must be placed in the Declarations section of the form.

Listing 24.14. Global variable declarations.

```
Private WSodbc As Workspace
Private conpubs As Connection
Private rsODBCd As Recordset
```

Getting Connected with DAO/ODBCDirect

As with the DAO/Jet application, a workspace is created, but this time the dbUseODBC option is used so that the workspace will initialize in the ODBCDirect connection mode. Instead of opening a database object, a connection object is created in the workspace. The connect string is similar to the DAO/Jet, but this time a slightly different syntax is used. The DSN in Listing 24.15 is specified in the connect string, and the OpenConnection method's first parameter is used to set a name for the connection. The original syntax used in Listing 24.8 to open the database uses the DSN name as the first parameter. Both are valid uses; this second method allows increased flexibility if you must name the connection something other than the DSN name.

After the connection has been established, the command buttons are disabled until some data has been fetched from the database.

Listing 24.15. Creating a database connection.

```
Private Sub Form_Load()
Dim szConOdbc As String
    ' Create ODBCDirect Workspace object.
    Set WSodbc = CreateWorkspace("NewODBCWorkspace", "admin", "", dbUseODBC)
    ' Define connect string and connect to the database
    szConOdbc = "ODBC;UID=;PWD=;DSN=Pubs"
    Set conpubs = WSodbc.OpenConnection("ODBCDirect", _
                            dbDriverCompleteRequired, True, szConOdbc)
    ' Update button status
    cmdFirst.Enabled = False
    cmdPrev.Enabled = False
    cmdNext.Enabled = False
    cmdLast.Enabled = False
End Sub
```

24

SQL SERVER AND VB

> **NOTE**
>
> In the `OpenConnection` method in Listing 24.15 the options parameter is set to `dbDriverCompleteRequired`. This means that if insufficient or incorrect information is supplied in the connect string then the ODBC driver will present a dialog box asking for the additional information required to connect. To test this try changing the connect string in Listing 24.15 to an invalid `UID`. When the application is run, a SQL Server login dialog box will appear asking for a valid username and password.

Retrieving Records with DAO/ODBCDirect

A record set object must be defined and populated under the connection object that was created in the `From_Load` event procedure. Listing 24.16 shows the required code to create and populate the record set.

The first lines of Listing 24.16 create the SQL statement that is used to create the record set. A snapshot-type, read-only record set is created using the `OpenRecordset` method on the connection object. Because the query does not have any parameters, the `dbExecDirect` parameter is passed to make the query execution quicker.

In the DAO/Jet connection a move was made to the last record in the record set to populate it. This step is not required in the ODBCDirect connection, and the `TextBoxUpdate_ODBCDirect()` procedure is called to update the controls on the form.

Listing 24.16. Creating and populating the record set object.

```
Private Sub cmdPopulate_Click()
    Dim strSQLodbc As String
    strSQLodbc = "SELECT ta.au_id, a.au_fname, a.au_lname, a.phone, a.address,"
    strSQLodbc = strSQLodbc & " a.city, a.state, a.zip, Sum(t.ytd_sales) " & _
                                                            "as Ytd_sales "
    strSQLodbc = strSQLodbc & "FROM authors a, titles t, titleauthor ta "
    strSQLodbc = strSQLodbc & "WHERE ta.au_id = a.au_id AND ta.title_id = " & _
                                                            "t.title_id "
    strSQLodbc = strSQLodbc & "GROUP BY ta.au_id, a.au_fname, a.au_lname, "
    strSQLodbc = strSQLodbc & "a.phone, a.address, a.city, a.state, a.zip "
    Set rsODBCd = conpubs.OpenRecordset(strSQLodbc, dbOpenSnapshot, _
                                        dbExecDirect, dbReadOnly)
    ' Update Display
    Call TextBoxUpdate_ODBCDirect
    cmdPopulate.Enabled = False
    cmdFirst.Enabled = True
    cmdPrev.Enabled = True
    cmdNext.Enabled = True
    cmdLast.Enabled = True
End Sub
```

Listing 24.17 shows the common code that is used throughout the application to update the controls on the form. As with the DAO/Jet application, it identifies the field in the fields collection of the rsODBCd record set by using the field names. At the end of the procedure the lblRecordCount is updated using the AbsolutePosition and RecordCount properties of the record set.

Listing 24.17. Updating the form.

```
Private Sub TextBoxUpdate_ODBCDirect()
    ' Update Display
    txtFirstName = rsODBCd.Fields![au_fname]
    txtLastName = rsODBCd.Fields![au_lname]
    txtZip = rsODBCd.Fields![zip]
    txtAddress = rsODBCd.Fields![address]
    txtCity = rsODBCd.Fields![city]
    txtState = rsODBCd.Fields![state]
    txtPhone = rsODBCd.Fields![phone]
    txtID = rsODBCd.Fields![au_id]
    txtYTD = rsODBCd.Fields![Ytd_sales]
    lblRecordcount = "Record " & (rsODBCd.AbsolutePosition + 1) & _
                                  " of " & rsODBCd.RecordCount
End Sub
```

Navigation Using DAO/ODBCDirect

Using the record set object as in the DAO/Jet example, the MoveFirst and MoveLast methods move the pointer in the record set to the first and last records, respectively. After the pointer is moved the form controls are updated using the TextBoxUpdate_ODBCDirect() procedure in Listing 24.17. The code for navigating to the first and last records is shown in Listing 24.18.

Listing 24.18. Moving to the first and last records.

```
Private Sub cmdFirst_Click()
    rsODBCd.MoveFirst
    ' Update text boxes
    Call TextBoxUpdate_ODBCDirect
End Sub

Private Sub cmdLast_Click()
    rsODBCd.MoveLast
    ' Update Display
    Call TextBoxUpdate_ODBCDirect
End Sub
```

Listing 24.19 shows the code required for moving forward and backward a single record. These lines are almost identical to those used in the DAO/Jet connection; by using the BOF and EOF properties of the record set, you can ensure that the pointer does not advance beyond the limits of the record set. When the move is complete, the form controls are updated using the TextBoxUpdate_ODBCDirect() procedure.

24

SQL SERVER AND VB

Listing 24.19. Moving forward and backward by single records.

```
Private Sub cmdPrev_Click()
    rsODBCd.MovePrevious
    If rsODBCd.BOF Then
        Beep
        rsODBCd.MoveFirst
    Else
        ' Update Display
        Call TextBoxUpdate_ODBCDirect
    End If
End Sub

Private Sub cmdNext_Click()
    rsODBCd.MoveNext
    If rsODBCd.EOF Then
        Beep
        rsODBCd.MoveLast
    Else
        ' Update Display
        Call TextBoxUpdate_ODBCDirect
    End If
End Sub
```

Closing the Connection When Using DAO/ODBCDirect

To close any active connections and reclaim any resources, each object used in the application is closed and then set to nothing. After each of the objects is unloaded the form closes, exiting the application. Listing 24.20 shows the complete code to close each object and close the form.

Listing 24.20. Closing the connection.

```
Private Sub cmdExit_Click()
    ' Close each of the objects used and set to nothing
    rsODBCd.Close
    Set rsODBCd = Nothing
    conpubs.Close
    Set conpubs = Nothing
    WSodbc.Close
    Set WSodbc = Nothing
    ' Unload the form
    Unload frmData
End Sub
```

Remote Data Objects (RDO)

The remote data object (RDO) provides a very powerful database connection model. It has a good execution speed with relatively easy connection management, and it exposes most functions of the connected database.

Registering the Components for Using RDO

To use any RDO objects within your application you must add the RDO object library to your project. To do this, select References from the Visual Basic Project menu. In the References dialog box place a check next to the Microsoft Remote Data Object 2.0 reference and click OK.

RDO Global Variables

Listing 24.21 shows the three global variables that are used in the application to manage the RDO connection.

Listing 24.21. Global variable definition.

```
Private RDOcon As New rdoConnection
Private qyRDO As New rdoQuery
Private rstRDO As rdoResultset
```

Getting Connected Using RDO

To open the RDO connection, set the `connect` property of the RDO connection object to the connect string, then use the `EstablishConnection` method to open the connection. The `rdDriverCompleteRequired` constant means that the connection will be established from the information in the connect string. If there is not enough information, the SQL Server Login dialog box will be shown to allow the user to manually complete the connection. The `True` at the end of the establish connection sets the connection as a read-only connection.

After the connection is established, the command buttons are disabled until there is data in the form to manipulate. Listing 24.22 shows the necessary code to open the RDO connection.

Listing 24.22. Opening a connection.

```
Private Sub Form_Load()
    ' Define connect string and open connection to the database
    RDOcon.Connect = "uid=;pwd=;DSN=pubs;APP=VBRDO"
    RDOcon.EstablishConnection rdDriverCompleteRequired, True
    ' Update command buttons
    cmdFirst.Enabled = False
    cmdPrev.Enabled = False
    cmdNext.Enabled = False
    cmdLast.Enabled = False
End Sub
```

Retrieving Records Using RDO

Listing 24.23 shows the code for connecting to the database and getting an RDO result set. The code should be pasted into the `cmdPopulate_click` event procedure.

To create a query using RDO use the `rdoQuery` object that is created in the global declarations section of the form. The `SQL` property of the `rdoQuery` object is set to the SQL statement to be executed. The `ActiveConnection` property of the `rdoQuery` object is set to the `RDOcon` connection object that was created in the `Form_Load` event procedure.

To retrieve the records from the `rdoQuery` object, use the `OpenResultset` method on the `rdoQuery` object. When the result set is opened, specify that it is to use a static cursor with the `rdOpenStatic` constant and set it as read-only using the `rdConcurReadOnly` constant.

24

SQL SERVER AND VB

Now the result set is opened, the code fills the text boxes with the data by calling the TextBoxUpdate_RDO() procedure.

Listing 24.23. Retrieving the records.

```
Private Sub cmdPopulate_Click()
    Dim strSQLrdo As String
    strSQLrdo = "SELECT ta.au_id, a.au_fname, a.au_lname, a.phone, a.address, "
    strSQLrdo = strSQLrdo & "a.city, a.state, a.zip, Sum(t.ytd_sales) " & _
                                                             "Ytd_sales "
    strSQLrdo = strSQLrdo & "FROM authors a, titles t, titleauthor ta "
    strSQLrdo = strSQLrdo & "WHERE ta.au_id = a.au_id AND ta.title_id = " & _
                                                             "t.title_id "
    strSQLrdo = strSQLrdo & "GROUP BY ta.au_id, a.au_fname, a.au_lname, "
    strSQLrdo = strSQLrdo & "a.phone, a.address, a.city, a.state, a.zip "
    ' Setup query
    qyRDO.SQL = strSQLrdo
    Set qyRDO.ActiveConnection = RDOcon
    ' Open resultset
    Set rstRDO = qyRDO.OpenResultset(rdOpenStatic, rdConcurReadOnly)
    ' Update text boxes
    Call TextBoxUpdate_RDO
    cmdPopulate.Enabled = False
    cmdFirst.Enabled = True
    cmdPrev.Enabled = True
    cmdNext.Enabled = True
    cmdLast.Enabled = True
End Sub
```

Listing 24.24 shows the code for the TextBoxUpdate_RDO() procedure. The text property of the text boxes is set to the value in the columns collection of the result set object. The column in the result set is specified by using the column name rather than by using the numeric position of the column in the collection.

Listing 24.24. Updating the form controls.

```
Private Sub TextBoxUpdate_RDO()
    ' Update text boxes
    txtFirstName = rstRDO.rdoColumns![au_fname]
    txtLastName = rstRDO.rdoColumns![au_lname]
    txtZip = rstRDO.rdoColumns![zip]
    txtAddress = rstRDO.rdoColumns![address]
    txtCity = rstRDO.rdoColumns![city]
    txtState = rstRDO.rdoColumns![state]
    txtPhone = rstRDO.rdoColumns![phone]
    txtID = rstRDO.rdoColumns![au_id]
    txtYTD = rstRDO.rdoColumns![ytd_sales]
    lblRecordcount = "Record " & rstRDO.AbsolutePosition & " of " & _
                                                  rstRDO.RowCount
End Sub
```

The last line in the TextBoxUpdate_RDO() procedure updates the lblRecordcount label. It does so by using the AbsolutePosition property to find the pointer's position in the result set and by using the RowCount property to find the size of the result set.

Navigation Using RDO

Navigation in the RDO result set is similar to the navigation methods in a DAO record set—the same `MoveFirst`, `MoveLast`, `MoveNext`, and `MovePrevious` methods can be used. The `EOF` and `BOF` properties are also supported by the result sets.

Listing 24.25 shows the code required to move to the first and last records in the result set. To move to the first record use the `MoveFirst` method on the result set `rstRDO`. Use the `MoveLast` method to move to the last record. After the move the `TextBoxUpdate_RDO()` is called to update the form controls.

Listing 24.25. Moving to the first and last records.

```
Private Sub cmdFirst_Click()
    rstRDO.MoveFirst
    ' Update Display
    Call TextBoxUpdate_RDO
End Sub

Private Sub cmdLast_Click()
    rstRDO.MoveLast
    ' Update Display
    Call TextBoxUpdate_RDO
End Sub
```

Listing 24.26 shows how the movement by a single record is handled. As in the DAO examples, the move is made to the next record using the `MoveNext` or `MovePrevious` methods, and then the `BOF` and `EOF` properties are used to make sure that the pointer is still within the bounds of the result set.

Listing 24.26. Moving forward and backward by a single record.

```
Private Sub cmdNext_Click()
    rstRDO.MoveNext
    If rstRDO.EOF Then
        Beep
        rstRDO.MoveLast
    Else
        ' Update Display
        Call TextBoxUpdate_RDO
    End If
End Sub

Private Sub cmdPrev_Click()
    rstRDO.MovePrevious
    If rstRDO.BOF Then
        Beep
        rstRDO.MoveFirst
    Else
        ' Update Display
        Call TextBoxUpdate_RDO
    End If
End Sub
```

Closing an RDO Connection

The code required to close the database connections is shown in Listing 24.27. The objects must be closed in the correct order: first the result set is closed, and then the rdoQuery, and then the connection. After each object is closed, the variable it is using is set to nothing to reclaim any resources that it is using.

Listing 24.27. Closing the connection.

```
Private Sub cmdExit_Click()
    ' Close resultset
    rstRDO.Close
    Set rstRDO = Nothing
    ' Close query
    qyRDO.Close
    Set qyRDO = Nothing
    ' Close connection
    RDOcon.Close
    Set RDOcon = Nothing
    ' Unload form
    Unload frmData
End Sub
```

OLE DB/ADO (ActiveX Data Objects)

The OLE DB-based connection is very much the new kid on the block, but it is simple to use and has high speed and a small overhead. Unlike RDO or DAO, the object hierarchy is less important; you can independently create objects without navigating a tree of objects. This makes the OLE DB model easier to use because it's easier to track a smaller number of objects through your applications.

Over the next few years, OLE DB will become the most widely used data access model, replacing the DAO and RDO models.

Registering the Components for Using OLE DB/ADO

The OLE DB support files will be on your system only if you have a full installation of Microsoft Internet Information Server, or you have the OLEDB SDK installed on your system. You can download the OLEDB SDK from www.microsoft.com/data/oledb/.

To use ActiveX data objects within your application, you must add the OLE DB object libraries to your project. To do this select References from the Visual Basic Project menu. In the References dialog box place a check next to the Microsoft OLE DB ActiveX Data Objects 1.0 Library and the Microsoft OLE DB Error Library reference, and then click OK.

OLE DB Global Variables

Listing 24.28 shows the two global variables that are used in the application to manage the OLE DB application.

Listing 24.28. Global variable definition.

```
Dim rsOLEDB As Object
Dim intpointer As Integer
```

Getting Connected Using OLE DB/ADO

Because OLE DB supports connectionless objects, you do not have to open a connection in order to use a record set in the application. Listing 24.29 shows code to set up the command buttons for the application. OLE DB does have a connection object that can be reused—it is used in much the same way as the RDO connection object. In this simple application, the connection is established in the same command that opens the record set.

Listing 24.29. Opening a connection.

```
Private Sub Form_Load()
    'disable the navigation buttons
    cmdFirst.Enabled = False
    cmdPrev.Enabled = False
    cmdNext.Enabled = False
    cmdLast.Enabled = False
End Sub
```

Retrieving Records Using OLE DB/ADO

Listing 24.30 shows the code required to open and populate the record set. First the rsOLEDB is created in line 4. Lines 5 through 12 set up the SQL query string. In line 14, the rsOLEDB record set is opened passing the query string, the connection string, and cursor and locking options. After the connection has been opened, the rest of the procedure enables the navigation buttons and updates the form with the first row of data.

Listing 24.30. Retrieving the records.

```
 1: Private Sub cmdPopulate_Click()
 2:     Dim strOLEDB As String
 3:     ' Create ADO OLEDB workspace object
 4:     Set rsOLEDB = CreateObject("ADODB.Recordset")
 5:     strOLEDB = "SELECT ta.au_id, a.au_fname, a.au_lname, a.phone, a.address, "
 6:     strOLEDB = strOLEDB & "a.city, a.state, a.zip, Sum(t.ytd_sales) " & _
 7:                                                     "as Ytd_sales "
 8:     strOLEDB = strOLEDB & "FROM authors a, titles t, titleauthor ta "
 9:     strOLEDB = strOLEDB & "WHERE ta.au_id = a.au_id AND ta.title_id = " & _
10:                                                     "t.title_id"
11:     strOLEDB = strOLEDB & " GROUP BY ta.au_id, a.au_fname, a.au_lname, "
12:     strOLEDB = strOLEDB & "a.phone , a.address, a.city, a.state, a.zip "
13:     ' Single command to open, recordset and set options
14:     rsOLEDB.Open strOLEDB, "ODBC;UID=Sa;PWD=;DSN=pubs", adOpenStatic, _
15:                                                     adLockReadOnly
16:     intpointer = 1
17:     ' Update Display
```

continues

24

SQL SERVER AND VB

Listing 24.30. continued

```
18:      Call TextBoxUpdate_OLEDB
19:      cmdPopulate.Enabled = False
20:      cmdFirst.Enabled = True
21:      cmdPrev.Enabled = True
22:      cmdNext.Enabled = True
23:      cmdLast.Enabled = True
24:  End Sub
```

Listing 24.31 shows the code for the TextBoxUpdate_OLEDB() procedure. The text property of the text boxes is set to the value in the columns collection of the record set object. The field in the record set is specified by using the field name rather than the numeric position of the field in the collection.

Listing 24.31. Updating the form controls.

```
Private Sub TextBoxUpdate_OLEDB()
    ' Update Display
    txtFirstName = rsOLEDB.Fields![au_fname]
    txtLastName = rsOLEDB.Fields![au_lname]
    txtZip = rsOLEDB.Fields![zip]
    txtAddress = rsOLEDB.Fields![address]
    txtCity = rsOLEDB.Fields![city]
    txtState = rsOLEDB.Fields![State]
    txtPhone = rsOLEDB.Fields![phone]
    txtID = rsOLEDB.Fields![au_id]
    txtYTD = rsOLEDB.Fields![Ytd_sales]
    lblRecordcount = "Record " & intpointer & _
                                " of " & rsOLEDB.RecordCount
End Sub
```

The last line in the TextBoxUpdate_OLEDB() procedure updates the lblRecordcount label by using the intpointer global variable to find the position in the record set and the RecordCount property to find the size of the record set.

Navigation Using OLE DB/ADO

Navigation in the OLE DB record set is similar to the navigation methods in the RDO and DAO record sets. You can use the same MoveFirst, MoveLast, MoveNext, and MovePrevious methods. The EOF and BOF properties are also supported by all these record set objects.

Listing 24.32 shows the code required to move to the first and last records in the record set. To move to the first record use the MoveFirst method on the record set rsOLEDB, or use the MoveLast method to move to the last record. After the move the pointer variable intpointer is updated and TextBoxUpdate_rsOLEDB() is called to update the form controls.

Listing 24.32. Moving to the first and last records.

```
Private Sub cmdFirst_Click()
    rsOLEDB.MoveFirst
    intpointer = 1
    ' Update Display
    Call TextBoxUpdate_OLEDB
End Sub

Private Sub cmdLast_Click()
    rsOLEDB.MoveLast
    intpointer = rsOLEDB.RecordCount
    ' Update Display
    Call TextBoxUpdate_OLEDB
End Sub
```

In Listing 24.33 the code shows how to handle movement by a single record. As in the DAO and RDO examples, the move is made to the next record using MoveNext or MovePrevious methods, and then the BOF and EOF properties are used to make sure that the pointer is still within the bounds of the record set. Depending on the position after the move the intpointer is either incremented, decremented, or set to either extent of the record set.

Listing 24.33. Moving forward and backward by a single record.

```
Private Sub cmdNext_Click()
    rsOLEDB.MoveNext
    If rsOLEDB.EOF Then
        Beep
        rsOLEDB.MoveLast
        intpointer = rsOLEDB.RecordCount
    Else
        intpointer = intpointer + 1
        ' Update Display
        Call TextBoxUpdate_OLEDB
    End If
End Sub

Private Sub cmdPrev_Click()
    rsOLEDB.MovePrevious
    If rsOLEDB.BOF Then
        Beep
        rsOLEDB.MoveFirst
        intpointer = 1
    Else
        intpointer = intpointer - 1
        ' Update Display
        Call TextBoxUpdate_OLEDB
    End If
End Sub
```

24

SQL SERVER AND VB

Closing an OLE DB/ADO Connection

The code required to close the database connections is shown in Listing 24.34. The only object that is open, rsOLEDB, is closed and then is set to nothing to reclaim any resources it is using. After the object has been closed, the form is unloaded.

Listing 24.34. Closing the connection.

```
Private Sub cmdExit_Click()
    ' Close the object used and set it to nothing
    rsOLEDB.Close
    Set rsOLEDB = Nothing
    Unload frmData
End Sub
```

Using DBLibrary

Whenever you are using the DBLibrary always remember that the routines are written in C++, and you will have to take that into account when calling the library functions and passing variables.

Registering the Components for DBLibrary

If you do not already have the DBLibrary installed you must follow the installation instructions in Chapter 22, "Using the DBLibrary."

With the base form loaded in Visual Basic, use the Add File option from the Project menu. Find the vbsql.bas file included with the DBLibrary installation and add it to your project. This file contains the declarations for the routines and constants in the DBLibrary.

DBLibrary Global Variables

The global definitions in the DBLibrary shown in Listing 24.35 are not objects as in the RDO and DAO examples. Several long variables are used to communicate with the C++ routines in the library and to keep track of the output from the library.

Listing 24.35. Global variable definition.

```
Private lngDBlibCon As Long
Private lngCursorID As Long
Private lngCursorRow As Long
Private lngRows As Long
Private lngCols As Long
```

Getting Connected Using DBLibrary

You establish a connection with the DBLibrary by calling a single function, the SqlOpenConnection() function. Listing 24.36 shows the completed code required to open the connection using DBLibrary. Because the DBLibrary does not use the ODBC driver, a DSN is not used to describe the connection to the server. The information for the connection is passed directly to the function in its calling arguments. The syntax of the function call is

```
SqlOpenConnection(Server, LoginID, Password, Workstation, Application)
```

The `Workstation` is the network name of the computer that is opening the connection, and the `Application` is the application name. These help the system administrator monitor the connections to the database, and provide useful troubleshooting information.

After the connection function is called, a check is made to make sure that the connection was successful. If the connection did not succeed then a message box is shown to the user. After that is acknowledged the application exits. If the connection was successful, the navigation command buttons are disabled.

NOTE

When using the DBLibrary the ODBC DSN is not used because the connection is not using the ODBC drivers that all the other connections used here are. The connection will not succeed with the incorrect login information in the `SqlOpenConnection()` function call in Listing 24.36. Replace the server name, username, and password in the listing with your own when you enter the code.

Listing 24.36. Opening a connection.

```
Private Sub Form_Load()
lngDBlibCon = SqlOpenConnection("NTSQL", "Sa", "", "WS_NTSQL", "VBDBLIB")
    If lngDBlibCon = 0 Then
        MsgBox "DBLibrary connection did not succeed!" & Chr(10) _
            & "Check SqlOpenConnection statement", vbCritical + vbOKOnly, _
            "DB Library Connection Error"
        End
    End If
    ' Update command buttons
    cmdFirst.Enabled = False
    cmdPrev.Enabled = False
    cmdNext.Enabled = False
    cmdLast.Enabled = False
End Sub
```

Retrieving the Records Using DBLibrary

Listing 24.37 shows the completed code for getting the records. Lines 2 through 12 define the SQL statement used to select the data from the database. At line 15 a local variable is declared to hold the maximum number of rows that the query can return. This is normally set to a slightly higher value than is expected to ensure that all the data is returned.

Next a function is called to open a cursor based on the query that is defined in the SQL statement. Included in the call is the variable lngDBlibCon, which contains the connection identifier, and constants declaring the type of cursor and setting the cursor to read-only.

To populate the cursor a move is made to the last record by calling the SqlCursorFetch() function using the FETCHLAST constant. After moving to the last record, the listing moves to the first record by using the same function, but specifying the FETCHFIRST constant. Because the cursor is pointed to record 1, the local pointer variable lngCursorRow is set to 1 on line 23.

On line 24 the size of the cursor set is established and passed into two local variables, lngCols for the number of columns and lngRows for the number of rows. Lines 26 through 32 check that the query returned data. If it did not, an error is displayed, cmdExit_click() is called to close the connection, and the application exits. If the query was successful and data was returned the TxtBoxUpdate_DBLib() procedure is called, updating the controls on the form. The command buttons are also enabled allowing navigation through the records.

Listing 24.37. Retrieving the records.

```
 1: Private Sub cmdPopulate_Click()
 2: Dim strSQLdblib As String, lngSQLres As Long
 3:     strSQLdblib = "SELECT ta.au_id, a.au_fname, a.au_lname, a.phone, "
 4:     strSQLdblib = strSQLdblib & "a.address, a.city, a.state, a.zip, "
 5:     strSQLdblib = strSQLdblib & "Sum(t.ytd_sales) Ytd_sales "
 6:     strSQLdblib = strSQLdblib & "FROM pubs..authors a, " & _
 7:                                 "pubs..titles t, pubs..titleauthor ta "
 8:     strSQLdblib = strSQLdblib & "WHERE ta.au_id = a.au_id AND " & _
 9:                                 "ta.title_id = t.title_id "
10:     strSQLdblib = strSQLdblib & "GROUP BY ta.au_id, a.au_fname, " & _
11:                                 "a.au_lname, a.phone, a.address," & _
12:                                 " a.city, a.state, a.zip "
13:     Dim intRowMax As Integer
14:     ' Define the maximum rows expected from the query
15:     intRowMax = 50
16:     ' Open cursor
17:     lngCursorID = SqlCursorOpen(lngDBlibCon, strSQLdblib, CURKEYSET, _
18:                                 CURREADONLY, intRowMax)
19:     ' Position to last row, and then to first to populate cursor
20:     lngSQLres = SqlCursorFetch(lngCursorID, FETCHLAST, 0)
21:     lngSQLres = SqlCursorFetch(lngCursorID, FETCHFIRST, 0)
22:     ' Set pointer to 1, cursor is pointed at first record
23:     lngCursorRow = 1
24:     ' Get size of results
25:     lngSQLres = SqlCursorInfo(lngCursorID, lngCols, lngRows)
26:     If lngCols <= 0 Or lngRows <= 0 Then
27:         MsgBox "DBLibrary based query did not return " & Chr(10) _
28:                 & "any rows, check Query!", vbCritical + vbOKOnly, _
29:                     "DB Library Query Error"
30:         cmdExit_Click
31:         End
32:     End If
33:     ' Update the text boxes
34:     Call TextBoxUpdate_DBLib
35:     ' Update the command buttons
36:     cmdPopulate.Enabled = False
37:     cmdFirst.Enabled = True
38:     cmdPrev.Enabled = True
```

```
39:    cmdNext.Enabled = True
40:    cmdLast.Enabled = True
41: End Sub
```

To update the text boxes on the form the `SqlCursorData()` function is called. This returns a value from the data based on a cursor row number held in the variable `lngCursorRow` and a column number. Listing 24.38 shows the `SqlCursorData()` function being called for each text box on the form.

To update the record counter the global variables are used to return the current record and the number of records in the cursor.

Listing 24.38. Updating the form controls.

```
Private Sub TextBoxUpdate_DBLib()
    ' Update the text boxes
    txtID = SqlCursorData(lngCursorID, lngCursorRow, 1)
    txtFirstName = SqlCursorData(lngCursorID, lngCursorRow, 2)
    txtLastName = SqlCursorData(lngCursorID, lngCursorRow, 3)
    txtPhone = SqlCursorData(lngCursorID, lngCursorRow, 4)
    txtAddress = SqlCursorData(lngCursorID, lngCursorRow, 5)
    txtCity = SqlCursorData(lngCursorID, lngCursorRow, 6)
    txtState = SqlCursorData(lngCursorID, lngCursorRow, 7)
    txtZip = SqlCursorData(lngCursorID, lngCursorRow, 8)
    txtYTD = SqlCursorData(lngCursorID, lngCursorRow, 9)
    lblRecordcount = "Record " & lngCursorRow & " of " & lngRows
End Sub
```

Navigation Using DBLibrary

To navigate using the DBLibrary, there are no `movefirst` or `movelast` methods to call, but the same code is possible using the local pointer `lngCursorRow`. To move to the first record, the pointer is set to 1, and then `TextBoxUpdate_DBLib()` is called.

To move to the last record the pointer is set to the number of records in the cursor, and then the `TextBoxUpdate_DBLib()` is called to update the controls on the form.

The code for the Last and First command buttons is shown in Listing 24.39.

Listing 24.39. Moving to the first and last records.

```
Private Sub cmdFirst_Click()
    lngCursorRow = 1
    ' Update the text boxes
    Call TextBoxUpdate_DBLib
End Sub

Private Sub cmdLast_Click()
    lngCursorRow = lngRows
    ' Update the text boxes
    Call TextBoxUpdate_DBLib
End Sub
```

24

SQL SERVER AND VB

To move record by record through the cursor, the local pointer is used to return the relevant records. Listing 24.40 shows the code required to move through the records individually.

To move forward through the cursor, a check is made to see whether the value of the pointer variable lngCursorRow is not equal to the number of rows in the cursor. If it is, a beep sounds to warn the user and the procedure exits. If the pointer variable is not equal to the number of rows, its value is incremented by 1 and the TextBoxUpdate_DBLib() procedure is called.

Moving back through the cursor follows the same method, but the pointer value is checked to see that is not less than or equal to 1 (the first row). If the pointer value is greater than 1, the value is decremented and the TextBoxUpdate_DBLib() procedure is called to update the controls on the form as shown in Listing 24.40.

Listing 24.40. Moving forward and backward by single records.

```
Private Sub cmdNext_Click()
    If lngCursorRow >= lngRows Then
        Beep
    Else
        lngCursorRow = lngCursorRow + 1
        Call TextBoxUpdate_DBLib
    End If
End Sub

Private Sub cmdPrev_Click()
    If lngCursorRow <= 1 Then
        Beep
    Else
        lngCursorRow = lngCursorRow - 1
        Call TextBoxUpdate_DBLib
    End If
End Sub
```

Closing a DBLibrary Connection

The DBLibrary gives a simple way to close the connection by using the SqlClose() function. To close a connection pass the connection identifier to the function and the DBLibrary routine takes care of closing the connection. The SqlExit() and SqlWinExit functions release any other memory and handles used in the connections.

Listing 24.41. Closing the connection.

```
Private Sub cmdExit_Click()
    ' Close connection
    SqlClose (lngDBlibCon)
    SqlExit
    SqlWinExit
    Unload frmData
End Sub
```

Using the ODBC API

The ODBC API is the most difficult connection to establish, and maintaining the connection and manipulating the data requires significant code. Unless you have a specific reason for using the ODBC API, it is best avoided. It exposes most functions of the SQL Server, but not all. Execution speed is good, but any gain from calling the C++ ODBC functions directly is offset by the amount of Visual Basic code required to support the calls.

Registering the Components for ODBC API

Copy the `ODBC32.TXT` file from the `/ODBC` directory on the CD to the `/ODBC` directory under your Visual Basic installation. With the base form loaded in Visual Basic, use the Add File option from the Project menu. Find the `ODBC32.TXT` file you have just copied and add it to the project. This file contains the declarations for the routines and constants in the ODBC API.

ODBC API Global Variables

Listing 24.42 shows the variable declarations required for the application using the ODBC API. These definitions must be placed in the `Declarations` section of the form. As with the DBLibrary no objects are declared, just variables for holding connection information and manipulating the data.

Listing 24.42. Global variable definitions.

```
Private intODBCret As Integer
Private intRowStatus(50) As Integer
Private lnghenv As Long
Private lnghconn As Long
Private lngFetchRows As Long
Private lngRowPtr As Long
Private lngRows As Long
Private lngstmt As Long
```

Getting Connected Using the ODBC API

Of all the connection sections, using the ODBC API is the most complex. There is no layer between you and the ODBC API doing any behind the scenes work that you have been shielded from until now. Listing 24.43 shows the code required to connect via the ODBC API.

Before opening a connection you must use `SQLAllocEnv()` to get an environment handle—this call is shown on line 4. After the handle is allocated the return value is checked in lines 5 through 9. If the allocation failed a message box is generated and the application exits.

The allocated environment handle is used to get a connection handle using the `SQLAllocConnect()` procedure on line 10. The return value is checked for success at lines 11 through 15, returning an error message and exiting if the allocation was not successful.

Line 16 defines the connect string and line 17 initiates the connection using the SQLDriverConnect() function. The SQLDriverConnect() function has a complicated parameter list, it requires the connection handle, the handle of the calling window, the connect string, and the length of the connect string. The last three parameters are the returned finished connect string, the length of the supplied string (Microsoft advises that this string be at least 255 characters long), and the actual returned length of the final connect string. The last argument in the function call is the SQL_DRIVER_COMPLETE_REQUIRED parameter, which will force the ODBC connect dialog box to collect any further information required to complete the connection.

If the connection was successful, the procedure finishes by disabling the command buttons.

Listing 24.43. Opening a connection.

```
 1: Private Sub Form_Load()
 2:     Dim intOut As Integer, strConnect As String * 100
 3:     Dim strconnected As String * 255
 4:     intODBCret = SQLAllocEnv(lnghenv)
 5:     If intODBCret <> SQL_SUCCESS Then
 6:         MsgBox "Environment Handle Allocation Failure", vbCritical + _
 7:                                 vbOKOnly, "ODBC Connection Failure"
 8:         End
 9:     End If
10:     intODBCret = SQLAllocConnect(lnghenv, lnghconn)
11:     If intODBCret <> SQL_SUCCESS Then
12:         MsgBox "Connection Handle Allocation Failure", vbCritical + _
13:                                 vbOKOnly, "ODBC Connection Failure"
14:         End
15:     End If
16:     strConnect = "uid=Sa;pwd=;DSN=pubs;DATABASE=pubs;APP=VBODBCapi"
17:     intODBCret = SQLDriverConnect(lnghconn, frmData.hWnd, strConnect, _
18:                                 Len(strConnect), strconnected, _
19:                                 Len(strconnected), intOut, _
20:                                 SQL_DRIVER_COMPLETE_REQUIRED)
21:     If intODBCret <> SQL_SUCCESS_WITH_INFO Then
22:         MsgBox "Connection Failed", vbCritical + _
23:                                 vbOKOnly, "ODBC Connection Failure"
24:         End
25:     End If
26:     cmdFirst.Enabled = False
27:     cmdPrev.Enabled = False
28:     cmdNext.Enabled = False
29:     cmdLast.Enabled = False
30: End Sub
```

Retrieving the Records Using the ODBC API

Listing 24.44 shows the code used to retrieve the data from the database. Lines 2 through 13 define the SQL statement that will select the data from the database. Line 15 uses the SQLAllocStmt() procedure to allocate a statement handle based on the connection handle. Line 17 sets the cursor type to a keyset-driven cursor by calling the SQLSetStmtOption() procedure.

The SQL statement is executed in line 20 by passing the SQL statement to the SQLExecDirect() function. The cursor is populated by calling the SQLExtendedFetch() function in line 22, with the SQL_FETCH_LAST constant to position it at the last record.

The SQLGetStmtOption in line 25 returns the current row when used with the SQL_ROW_NUMBER constant, which is the number of rows in the cursor; the current row is the last row. After getting the row count, the cursor is moved back to the first row using SQLExtendedFetch() with the SQL_FETCH_FIRST constant. With the cursor set to the first row, the local row pointer lngRowPtr is set to 1.

Now the records are retrieved, the TextBoxUpdate_ODBCapi() procedure is called to update the form, and the navigation command buttons are enabled.

Listing 24.44. Retrieving the records.

```
 1: Private Sub cmdPopulate_Click()
 2:     Dim strODBCsql As String
 3:     ' Define SQL statement
 4:     strODBCsql = "SELECT ta.au_id, a.au_fname, a.au_lname, a.phone, "
 5:     strODBCsql = strODBCsql & "a.address, a.city, a.state, a.zip, " & _
 6:                                      "Sum(t.ytd_sales) Ytd_sales "
 7:     strODBCsql = strODBCsql & "FROM pubs..authors a, pubs..titles t," & _
 8:                                      "pubs..titleauthor ta "
 9:     strODBCsql = strODBCsql & "WHERE ta.au_id = a.au_id AND " & _
10:                                      "ta.title_id = t.title_id "
11:     strODBCsql = strODBCsql & "GROUP BY ta.au_id, a.au_fname, a.au_lname"
12:     strODBCsql = strODBCsql & ", a.phone, a.address, a.city, " & _
13:                                      "a.state, a.zip"
14:     ' Allocate a statement handle
15:     intODBCret = SQLAllocStmt(lnghconn, lngstmt)
16:     ' Setup statement option
17:     intODBCret = SQLSetStmtOption(lngstmt, SQL_CURSOR_TYPE, _
18:                                   SQL_CURSOR_KEYSET_DRIVEN)
19:     ' Execute the SQL statement
20:     intODBCret = SQLExecDirect(lngstmt, strODBCsql, Len(strODBCsql))
21:     ' Populate cursor
22:     intODBCret = SQLExtendedFetch(lngstmt, SQL_FETCH_LAST, _
23:                                   0, lngFetchRows, intRowStatus(0))
24:     ' Get number of rows returned
25:     intODBCret = SQLGetStmtOption(lngstmt, SQL_ROW_NUMBER, lngRows)
26:     ' Reposition at first row and set local pointer to 1
27:     intODBCret = SQLExtendedFetch(lngstmt, SQL_FETCH_FIRST, _
28:                                   0, lngFetchRows, intRowStatus(0))
29:     lngRowPtr = 1
30:     ' Update the text boxes
31:     Call TextBoxUpdate_ODBCapi
32:     cmdPopulate.Enabled = False
33:     cmdFirst.Enabled = True
34:     cmdPrev.Enabled = True
35:     cmdNext.Enabled = True
36:     cmdLast.Enabled = True
37: End Sub
```

24

SQL SERVER AND VB

The code in Listing 24.45 shows a procedure and a function it calls to update the controls on the form with the current record information. In the procedure `TextBoxUpdate_ODBCapi()` each text box is assigned the returned value from the `Get_Data()` function.

The `Get_Data()` function is passed the column number to be returned. It uses the `SQLGetData()` ODBC API function to get the column value in the current row from the database. `SQLGetData()` is passed the statement handle, the column number, the C variable type of the column, a string in which to return the value, the maximum length of the returned value, and the actual length that is returned. The part of the C string that contains data is assigned to the return value of the function.

The `TextBoxUpdate_ODBCapi()` procedure finishes by updating the `lblrecordcount` label with the current position in the database. It uses the global pointer `lngRowPtr` to return the current row, and the global variable `lngRows`, which contains the number of rows in the cursor.

Listing 24.45. Updating the form controls.

```
Private Sub TextBoxUpdate_ODBCapi()
    txtID = Get_Data(1)
    txtFirstName = Get_Data(2)
    txtLastName = Get_Data(3)
    txtPhone = Get_Data(4)
    txtAddress = Get_Data(5)
    txtCity = Get_Data(6)
    txtState = Get_Data(7)
    txtZip = Get_Data(8)
    txtYTD = Get_Data(9)
    lblRecordcount = "Record " & lngRowPtr & " of " & lngRows
End Sub

Private Function Get_Data(intColNum) As String
    Dim strretn As String * 40, lngRetlen As Long
    intODBCret = SQLGetData(lngstmt, intColNum, SQL_C_CHAR, strretn, _
                                        Len(strretn), lngRetlen)
    Get_Data = Left(strretn, lngRetlen): strretn = ""
End Function
```

Navigation Using the ODBC API

The procedures to move to the first and last records are shown in Listing 24.46. The `SQLExtendedFetch()` function is called with either the `SQL_FETCH_FIRST` or `SQL_FETCH_LAST` constant. With the cursor set to the correct position, the local pointer `lngRowPtr` is updated and then the form controls are updated by calling the `TextBoxUpdate_ODBCapi()` procedure.

Listing 24.46. Moving to the first and last records.

```
Private Sub cmdFirst_Click()
    intODBCret = SQLExtendedFetch(lngstmt, SQL_FETCH_FIRST, _
                        0, lngFetchRows, intRowStatus(0))
    lngRowPtr = 1
    Call TextBoxUpdate_ODBCapi
```

```
End Sub

Private Sub cmdLast_Click()
    intODBCret = SQLExtendedFetch(lngstmt, SQL_FETCH_LAST, _
                        0, lngFetchRows, intRowStatus(0))
    lngRowPtr = lngRows
    Call TextBoxUpdate_ODBCapi
End Sub
```

To move row by row through the cursor `SQLExtendedFetch()` is used again, but this time with the `SQL_FETCH_ABSOLUTE` constant, as shown in Listing 24.47.

Before the function is called a check is made to ensure that the cursor is not at the first or last record. If the cursor is already at the limit of the data in the cursor, then a beep is made to warn the user and the procedure is exited. If the move can be made, the local pointer variable `lngRowPtr` is updated, then the `SQLExtendedFetch()` function is called. When using the `SQL_FETCH_ABSOLUTE` constant the local pointer is used to position the cursor at the desired row.

With the cursor correctly positioned the `TextBoxUpdate_ODBCapi()` procedure is called, updating the form.

Listing 24.47. Moving forward and backward by single records.

```
Private Sub cmdNext_Click()
    If lngRowPtr >= lngRows Then
        Beep
        Exit Sub
    Else
        lngRowPtr = lngRowPtr + 1
        intODBCret = SQLExtendedFetch(lngstmt, SQL_FETCH_ABSOLUTE, _
                        lngRowPtr, lngFetchRows, intRowStatus(0))
        Call TextBoxUpdate_ODBCapi
    End If
End Sub

Private Sub cmdPrev_Click()
    If lngRowPtr <= 1 Then
        Beep
        Exit Sub
    Else
        lngRowPtr = lngRowPtr - 1
        intODBCret = SQLExtendedFetch(lngstmt, SQL_FETCH_ABSOLUTE, _
                        lngRowPtr, lngFetchRows, intRowStatus(0))
        Call TextBoxUpdate_ODBCapi
    End If
End Sub
```

24

SQL SERVER AND VB

Closing an ODBC API Connection

To close the connection, each of the handles must be freed using several ODBC API functions. Listing 24.48 shows the collection of functions that must be called to close the connection. The functions must be called in the correct order to ensure that a clean disconnect is achieved.

Listing 24.48. Closing the connection.

```
Private Sub cmdExit_Click()
    'free the statement handle
    intODBCret = SQLFreeStmt(lngstmt, SQL_CLOSE)
    'disconnect from the database
    intODBCret = SQLDisconnect(lnghconn)
    'free the connection handle
    intODBCret = SQLFreeConnect(lnghconn)
    'free the environment handle
    intODBCret = SQLFreeEnv(lnghenv)
    Unload frmData
End Sub
```

How to Connect with VBA

Any of the code and connection methods that were used in the earlier sections of this chapter can be used within a VBA application without modification. To illustrate this, the next section uses DAO to connect to a SQL Server, and then transfers the results into a spreadsheet and produces a graph from the results. The output from the application is shown in Figure 24.5.

FIGURE 24.5.

Output of the sample VBA application.

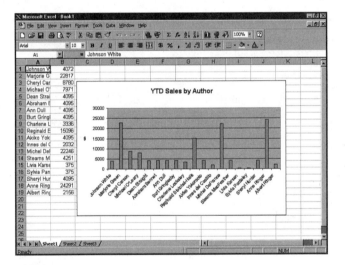

Setting Up the Application

To reproduce this application, follow these steps:

1. Open Microsoft Excel.

2. Start the Visual Basic editor. It is located under the Macro option of the Tools menu.

3. Select References from the Tools menu. In the dialog box add the Microsoft DAO 3.5 Object Library to the project references.

4. Insert a new UserForm into the project.

5. Create a CommandButton named cmdProcessQuery, a CommandButton named cmdExit, and a TextBox named txtQuery.

6. Place the code in Listing 24.49, later in this chapter, in the Declarations section of the UserForm.

Connecting to the SQL Server

The DAO/ODBCDirect connection is made in the cmdProcessQuery_Click() event procedure at lines 19 through 24 in Listing 24.49. Next a snapshot record set is opened based on the SQL query loaded into the txtQuery text box in the UserForm_Load() event procedure.

After the record set is opened a procedure FillSheet() is called. The code for this procedure is shown in lines 54 through 62. In this procedure a For..Next loop is used to iterate through the rsDAO record set object and place the results into cells on the Sheet1 worksheet. The au_fname and au_lname fields are concatenated and placed in the A column, and the Ytd_sales are placed in the B column of the sheet.

After the results are placed in the sheet, the CreateChart() procedure is called. The code for the CreateChart() procedure appears at lines 42 through 52. This procedure creates a chart object on Sheet1 and then uses the Excel ChartWizard method to form the chart from the data in the sheet that was fetched from the database.

After the chart has been created the cmdExit_click() event procedure is called to close the database connection and reset the object variables that were used. If you now look at Sheet1 in Excel, the data and graph will have been created, similar to that shown in Figure 24.5.

Listing 24.49. The Excel VBA application.

```
 1: Option Explicit
 2: Private WSJet As Workspace
 3: Private DBPubs As Database
 4: Private rsDAO As Recordset
 5: Private oChart As ChartObject
 6:
 7: Private Sub cmdExit_Click()
 8:     ' Close each of the objects used and set to nothing
 9:     rsDAO.Close
10:     Set rsDAO = Nothing
11:     DBPubs.Close
12:     Set DBPubs = Nothing
13:     WSJet.Close
14:     Set WSJet = Nothing
15:     Unload UserForm1
16: End Sub
17:
18: Private Sub cmdProcessQuery_Click()
19:     Dim strCon As String
20:     ' Create Jet workspace object
```

continues

Listing 24.49. continued

```
21:    Set WSJet = CreateWorkspace("NewJetWorkspace", "admin", "", dbUseODBC)
22:    ' Define connect string and open the database
23:    strCon = "ODBC;UID=sa;PWD=;"
24:    Set DBPubs = WSJet.OpenDatabase("Pubs", False, True, strCon)
25:    ' Open snapshot type recordset
26:    Set rsDAO = DBPubs.OpenRecordset(txtQuery, dbOpenSnapshot)
27:    Call FillSheet
28:    Call CreateChart
29:    Call cmdExit_Click
30: End Sub
31:
32: Private Sub UserForm_Initialize()
33:    TxtQuery.MultiLine = True
34:    txtQuery = "SELECT ta.au_id, a.au_fname, a.au_lname, " & _
35:                              " Sum(t.ytd_sales) as Ytd_sales "
36:    txtQuery = txtQuery & "FROM authors a, titles t, titleauthor ta "
37:    txtQuery = txtQuery & "WHERE ta.au_id = a.au_id And ta.title_id = " & _
38:                              "t.title_id "
39:    txtQuery = txtQuery & "GROUP BY ta.au_id, a.au_fname, a.au_lname"
40: End Sub
41:
42: Private Sub CreateChart()
43:    Set oChart = Worksheets("sheet1").ChartObjects.Add(100, 30, 400, 250)
44:    oChart.Chart.ChartWizard Source:=Worksheets("sheet1").Range("a1:b19"), _
45:       gallery:=xlColumn, Title:="YTD Sales by Author", CategoryLabels:=1 _
46:       , HasLegend:=False, ValueTitle:="$"
47:    oChart.Chart.Axes(xlValue).TickLabels.Font.Size = 8
48:    oChart.Chart.Axes(xlValue).AxisTitle.Font.Size = 8
49:    oChart.Chart.Axes(xlValue).AxisTitle.Orientation = xlHorizontal
50:    oChart.Chart.Axes(xlCategory).TickLabels.Font.Size = 8
51:    oChart.Chart.ChartTitle.Font.Size = 12
52: End Sub
53:
54: Private Sub FillSheet()
55:    Dim intloopvar As Integer
56:    For intloopvar = 0 To rsDAO.RecordCount - 1
57:        Sheet1.Range("a" & intloopvar + 1) = rsDAO.Fields![au_fname] & _
58:                              " " & rsDAO.Fields![au_lname]
59:        Sheet1.Range("b" & intloopvar + 1) = rsDAO.Fields![Ytd_sales]
60:        rsDAO.MoveNext
61:    Next
62: End Sub
```

Connecting with SQL-Distributed Management Objects

Before you can create any SQL-DMO based objects, an object library must be added to the references in your project. Use the References option from the Project menu in Visual Basic to add the Microsoft SQLOLE object library to your project. If the library does not show up in your list, use the Browse button to find the library. The library is contained in the SQLOLE65.tlb file, located in the BINN directory under your SQL Server installation.

> **NOTE**
>
> Remember that this application is only an example of how to use SQL-DMO and only touches on the available objects. Other SQL-DMO objects are all harnessed in a similar way to the ones shown in the example. For example, refer to Chapter 17, "Replication," for another way that you can use SQL-DMO to create an interface that streamlines that task.

The connection is made with the SQL Server in the `cmdConnect_click()` event procedure shown in Listing 24.50. A new `SQLOLE.SQLServer` object is created to hold the connection. The `LoginTimeout` property of the connection object is set to 10 seconds.

> **TIP**
>
> Always set the connection timeout property to a reasonable value. If the timeout is set too long and the connection cannot be made, the application will freeze until the connection timeout returns control to the application.

Listing 24.50. Connecting with SQL-DMO.

```
Private Sub cmdConnect_Click()
    'Create new SQLOLE.SQLServer object
    Set oSQLServer = New SQLOLE.SQLServer
    'Set login timeout to 10 seconds
    oSQLServer.LoginTimeout = 10
    'Ensure the connection is disconnected
    oSQLServer.DisConnect
    'Connect with the user information in the form text boxes
    oSQLServer.Connect txtServer.Text, txtLogin.Text, txtPassword.Text
    'Fill the TreeView with data
    FillTreeView
End Sub
```

Managing Tables with SQL-Distributed Management Objects

The main SQL-DMO part of the application supplies the `TreeView` control with information about the `pubs` database on the connected server object. It iterates through each of the collections adding the name of each member to the correct branch of the `TreeView`. For example, in line 10 the `oSQLItem` object variable is set to the `pubs` database object. In line 17 the `For Each` construct is used to iterate through the `tables` collection. Each item in the `tables` collection is added to the TreeView control `tvwSQL` in line 23. To decide which table tree the table should be placed, the `SystemObject` property of the table is checked in line 18.

24

SQL SERVER AND VB

Similar code is used in the remainder of the procedure to fill the other branches of the tree. This code is shown in Listing 24.51.

Listing 24.51. Filling the TreeView control with data.

```
 1: Private Sub FillTreeView()
 2:     Dim oSQLItem As Object, oSQLItem2 As Object, oSQLItem3 As Object
 3:     Dim strTableType As String, nodX As node
 4:     ' Add server branch
 5:     Set nodX = tvwSQL.Nodes.Add(, , "server", "SQL Server - " & _
 6:                                              txtServer, 2, 1)
 7:     ' Add Database branch
 8:     Set nodX = tvwSQL.Nodes.Add("server", tvwChild, "databases", _
 9:                                              "Databases", 2, 1)
10:     Set oSQLItem = oSQLServer.Databases("Pubs")
11:     Set nodX = tvwSQL.Nodes.Add("databases", tvwChild, oSQLItem.Name & _
12:                              "database", oSQLItem.Name, 2, 1)
13:     Set nodX = tvwSQL.Nodes.Add(oSQLItem.Name & "database", tvwChild, _
14:             "tables" & oSQLItem.Name & "database", "Tables", 2, 1)
15:     Set nodX = tvwSQL.Nodes.Add(oSQLItem.Name & "database", tvwChild, _
16:         "systables" & oSQLItem.Name & "database", "System Tables", 2, 1)
17:     For Each oSQLItem2 In oSQLServer.Databases(oSQLItem.Name).Tables
18:         If oSQLItem2.SystemObject Then
19:             strTableType = "systables"
20:         Else
21:             strTableType = "tables"
22:         End If
23:         Set nodX = tvwSQL.Nodes.Add(strTableType & oSQLItem.Name & _
24:             "database", tvwChild, strTableType & oSQLItem.Name & _
25:                         oSQLItem2.Name, oSQLItem2.Name, 2, 1)
26:         Set nodX = tvwSQL.Nodes.Add(strTableType & oSQLItem.Name & _
27:         oSQLItem2.Name, tvwChild, oSQLItem.Name & oSQLItem2.Name & _
28:                             "columns", "Columns", 2, 1)
29:         Set nodX = tvwSQL.Nodes.Add(strTableType & oSQLItem.Name & _
30:         oSQLItem2.Name, tvwChild, oSQLItem.Name & oSQLItem2.Name & _
31:                             "indexes", "Indexes", 2, 1)
32:         Set nodX = tvwSQL.Nodes.Add(strTableType & oSQLItem.Name & _
33:         oSQLItem2.Name, tvwChild, oSQLItem.Name & oSQLItem2.Name & _
34:                             "keys", "Keys", 2, 1)
35:         Set nodX = tvwSQL.Nodes.Add(strTableType & oSQLItem.Name & _
36:         oSQLItem2.Name, tvwChild, oSQLItem.Name & oSQLItem2.Name & _
37:                             "triggers", "Triggers", 2, 1)
38:         For Each oSQLItem3 In _
39:          oSQLServer.Databases(oSQLItem.Name).Tables(oSQLItem2.Name).Columns
40:             Set nodX = tvwSQL.Nodes.Add(oSQLItem.Name & oSQLItem2.Name _
41:                         & "columns", tvwChild, oSQLItem.Name & _
42:                     oSQLItem2.Name & oSQLItem3.Name & "column", _
43:                                 oSQLItem3.Name, 3)
44:         Next
45:         For Each oSQLItem3 In _
46:          oSQLServer.Databases(oSQLItem.Name).Tables(oSQLItem2.Name).Indexes
47:             Set nodX = tvwSQL.Nodes.Add(oSQLItem.Name & oSQLItem2.Name & _
48:                 "indexes", tvwChild, oSQLItem.Name & oSQLItem2.Name & _
49:                         oSQLItem3.Name & "index", oSQLItem3.Name, 3)
50:         Next
51:         For Each oSQLItem3 In _
52:             oSQLServer.Databases(oSQLItem.Name).Tables(oSQLItem2.Name).Keys
```

```
53:                   Set nodX = tvwSQL.Nodes.Add(oSQLItem.Name & oSQLItem2.Name & _
54:                       "keys", tvwChild, oSQLItem.Name & oSQLItem2.Name & _
55:                               oSQLItem3.Name & "keys", oSQLItem3.Name, 3)
56:               Next
57:               For Each oSQLItem3 In _
58:               oSQLServer.Databases(oSQLItem.Name).Tables(oSQLItem2.Name).Triggers
59:                   Set nodX = tvwSQL.Nodes.Add(oSQLItem.Name & oSQLItem2.Name & _
60:                       "triggers", tvwChild, oSQLItem.Name & oSQLItem2.Name & _
61:                       oSQLItem3.Name & "triggers", oSQLItem3.Name, 3)
62:               Next
63:           Next
64:           ' Add views
65:           Set nodX = tvwSQL.Nodes.Add(oSQLItem.Name & "database", tvwChild, _
66:                       "views" & oSQLItem.Name & "database", "Views", 2, 1)
67:           For Each oSQLItem2 In oSQLServer.Databases(oSQLItem.Name).Views
68:               Set nodX = tvwSQL.Nodes.Add("views" & oSQLItem.Name & "database", _
69:                       tvwChild, oSQLItem2.Name & "views", oSQLItem2.Name, 3)
70:           Next
71:           ' Add Stored Procedures
72:           Set nodX = tvwSQL.Nodes.Add(oSQLItem.Name & "database", tvwChild, _
73:               "sProcs" & oSQLItem.Name & "database", "Stored Procedures", 2, 1)
74:           For Each oSQLItem2 In _
75:               oSQLServer.Databases(oSQLItem.Name).StoredProcedures
76:               Set nodX = tvwSQL.Nodes.Add("sProcs" & oSQLItem.Name & _
77:                   "database", tvwChild, oSQLItem2.Name & "SProcs", _
78:                                           oSQLItem2.Name, 3)
79:       Next
80: End Sub
```

To fill the properties text box for the current selected branch, the NodeClick() event procedure of the TreeView is used. The code for updating the properties text box is shown in Listing 24.52. The text box is initially set to an empty string. To find the current object, the object variable obj1 is set the output from a recursive function RecurseDMO(), which returns the current selected object. If the returned object variable is set to nothing, then the procedure exits with an empty text box.

If the object variable has a value, then the For..Each construct is used to loop through the properties collection for that object. As the collection is iterated, the property name and its value are added to the text box.

Listing 24.52. Updating the properties text box.

```
Private Sub tvwSQL_NodeClick(ByVal node As ComctlLib.node)
    Dim prop As Property, obj1 As Object, obj2 As Object
    On Error Resume Next
    txtProp = ""
    Set obj1 = RecurseDMO(node)
    If obj1 Is Nothing Then
        Exit Sub
    End If
    For Each prop In obj1.Properties
        txtProp = txtProp & prop.Name & ":  " & prop.Value & vbCrLf
    Next
End Sub
```

24

SQL SERVER AND
VB

The recursive function `RecurseDMO()` that is called in the `NodeClick()` event procedure of the TreeView control is shown in Listing 24.53. The first step is to check whether the current node is the root; if it is, then the return object is set to the `oSQLServer` object.

The `select case` statement in lines 7 through 12 keeps recursing the function, passing the `node.parent.parent` to the function until the parent is not one of the specified cases. The specified cases are the nodes that are object types, not an object in a collection. When the parent of the current node is anything other than an object type, then the function exits to its last call. If the parent of the original node is an object type, the second `select` statement in lines 14 through 33 will return the correct object type to the calling procedure. If the parent of the original node is not an object type, the function returns an object variable set to `nothing`.

Listing 24.53. Recursive function to return a selected object in TreeView.

```
 1: Private Function RecurseDMO(node As ComctlLib.node) As Variant
 2:     Dim objLocal As Object
 3:     If node.Root = node.Text Then
 4:         Set RecurseDMO = oSQLServer
 5:         Exit Function
 6:     End If
 7:     Select Case LCase$(node.Parent.Text)
 8:         Case "columns", "indexes", "keys", "triggers", "indexes", _
 9:             "views", "stored procedures", "tables", "databases"
10:             Set objLocal = RecurseDMO(node.Parent.Parent)
11:         Case Else
12:             Set RecurseDMO = Nothing
13:     End Select
14:     Select Case LCase$(node.Parent.Text)
15:         Case "columns"
16:             Set RecurseDMO = objLocal.Columns(node.Text)
17:         Case "indexes"
18:             Set RecurseDMO = objLocal.Indexes(node.Text)
19:         Case "keys"
20:             Set RecurseDMO = objLocal.Keys(node.Text)
21:         Case "triggers"
22:             Set RecurseDMO = objLocal.Triggers(node.Text)
23:         Case "indexes"
24:             Set RecurseDMO = objLocal.Indexes(node.Text)
25:         Case "views"
26:             Set RecurseDMO = objLocal.Views(node.Text)
27:         Case "stored procedures"
28:             Set RecurseDMO = objLocal.StoredProcedures(node.Text)
29:         Case "tables", "system tables"
30:             Set RecurseDMO = objLocal.Tables(node.Text)
31:         Case "databases"
32:             Set RecurseDMO = objLocal.Databases(node.Text)
33:     End Select
34: End Function
```

Closing the SQL-DMO Connection

To close the SQL-DMO connection, the cmdExit_Click() event procedure is called when the user presses the Exit button on the form. This in turn calls the Form_Unload() event procedure. The two procedures are shown in Listing 24.54.

In the Form_Unload() procedure the disconnect method is called to close the connection. The SQLServer object is closed using the close method, and the oSQLServer object variable is set to Nothing, releasing any resources that it was using.

Listing 24.54. Disconnecting the SQL-DMO connection.

```
Private Sub cmdExit_Click()
    ' Unload the form
    Unload Me
End Sub

Private Sub Form_Unload(Cancel As Integer)
    ' Disconnect from the server
    oSQLServer.DisConnect
    ' close the object
    oSQLServer.Close
    ' set the object variable to nothing
    Set oSQLServer = Nothing
End Sub
```

Summary

Visual Basic provides many models for connecting to SQL Server, and each has its strengths and weaknesses. It is important to look at the needs of your application before picking the connection to use. The future for data access seems to be heavily based on the OLE DB model, so watch for additional capabilities being added as this newcomer grows up.

CHAPTER 25

SQL Server on Internet/Intranet Systems

The Web creates a real twist in client/server development. Just a few months were spent from static HTML to dynamic HTML. During that time, the intranet concept interested a lot of people.

The RDBMS very quickly emerged as the right storage area for data pushed to the Web and pulled from the Web users. SQL Server has not waited long to be a bright tool for creating Web dynamic applications.

This chapter makes a quick and complete tour of all the needed technologies for developing bright Internet and intranet applications. From simple Internet Database Connector to Remote Data Services and ActiveX Data Objects.

> **WARNING**
>
> You need to have knowledge in HTML to read this chapter, because HTML subtleties are not discussed here. Instead, this chapter focuses on data exchange between a Web browser and SQL Server using IIS.

The Essentials of Web Database Development

It can be said that the Web did not change a lot of things as far as client/server is concerned. If you take a look at Figure 25.1, you see the common three-tier model.

FIGURE 25.1.

Three-tier model.

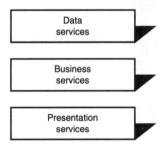

In traditional two-tier model with SQL Server, the business logic is, for one part on the server—with stored procedure—and for one part on the client. The Web server is in charge of the presentation services with Internet and intranet technologies. It receives HTTP requests from the client Web browser and sends HTTP-format answers.

As far as business logic is concerned, it is generally performed by the Web server. In Figure 25.2, you see a classical Web database connected application.

The Web server is in charge of getting connected—not necessarily on the same machine—to the database server and for sending request and presenting result sets sent by the DBMS.

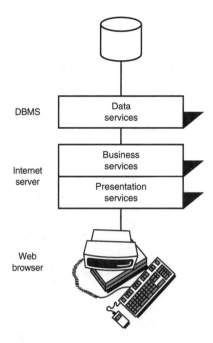

These tasks were generally done with CGI scripts, until Microsoft Internet Information Server (IIS). IIS is shipped with its own API interface, ISAPI, which enables communication between IIS and the "outer word."

For two years, Microsoft shipped three major releases of IIS. From version 2 to version 4, the communication interfaces from IIS to databases evolved. The number of possibilities is getting more and more important each day.

You can keep focusing on six available technologies:

1. CGI scripts
2. ISAPI and OLEISAPI
3. Internet Database Connector
4. Active Server Pages and ActiveX Data Objects (ADO)
5. Remote Data Service (formerly called Active Data Connector)
6. The SQL Server Web assistant

NOTE

Microsoft dbWeb is not mentioned here on purpose, since this technology has totally been abandoned by Microsoft.

This chapter focuses on the most interesting leverage technologies.

SQL Server Web assistant

The SQL Server Web assistant is probably the simplest of the group's technologies. In fact, it's not a technology. It's a wizard. The wizard allows you to easily create Web pages based on SQL Server Data. These Web pages can be updated on a scheduled basis or with triggers. Figure 25.3 gives you the overall scheme.

Figure 25.3.

The Web assistant is pushing data to the Web server.

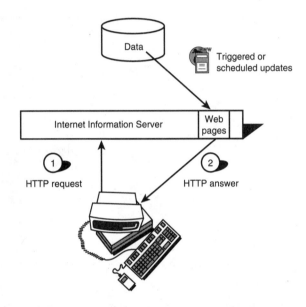

When you get connected to the Web server, you ask for .htm files and receive them without any active scripting or program launching. In fact, these Web pages are what can be called "pseudo-dynamic." The contained data are static, but can be updated by the Web-stored procedures and scheduled tasks.

Nevertheless, you can neither update data with the Web assistant nor send a specific query.

The big interest of the Web assistant is the reduction of overhead on the database server. In fact, none of the Web browsers ever get connected to the database. This is so a great tool to offer Web browsers simple information, like a list of employees or products.

IDC

Internet Database Connector was introduced in Internet Information Server 1.0. It is based on Web page models, which are needed to present query feedback. Figure 25.4 gives you the overall scheme.

The query is hard coded, with the connection information, in the IDC file. During the initial request for this file, the client has the ability to send parameters (including logon information). The query is then sent to the database server.

FIGURE 25.4.

Internet Database Connector flow of data.

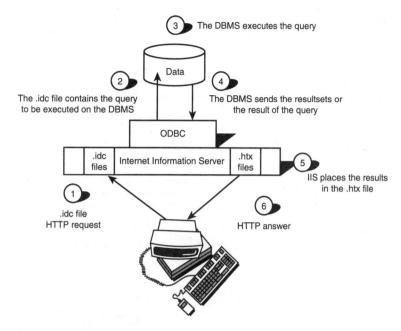

Any ODBC database can be used. All DML and DDL queries can be sent to the server, so it is definitely possible to update tables or insert records based on the information typed by the user.

Once executed, the result (if any) is placed into an HTX file. This file, despite its name, is an HTML file. It has special tags to insert data and is sent back to the client Web browser.

Although this is a simple way to query a database, IDC avoids the need for programming. Furthermore, FrontPage 97 and 98 wizards help create the IDC and HTX files.

ASP/ADO/RDS

Here comes the most accomplished, and complicated, technology, from the one you have just seen. Appearing with Internet Information Server 3.0, Active Server Pages goes beyond the data connection, and offers the needed environment for active scripting, in VBScript or JScript (Microsoft JavaScript version). Figure 25.5 gives you the overall scheme of data connection and retrieval.

Figure 25.05 is simpler than the complete model. Active Server Pages is not limited to data connection, but is shipped with active components (ad rotator, browser capabilities, and so on) and supports ActiveX objects.

Referencing all needed objects and code in the same file, or in included files, is the main idea in Active Server Pages. That means an active server page file (ASP) can contain HTML, server-side scripting, client-side scripting, or an ActiveX object reference.

FIGURE 25.5.

Active Server Pages, ADO, and RDS.

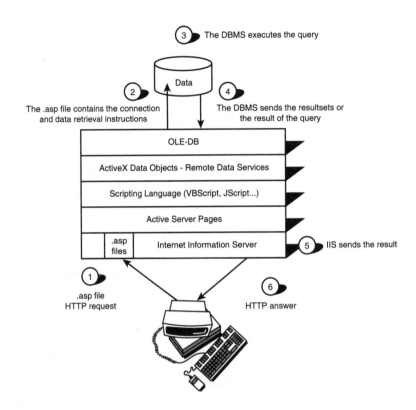

The possibilities of using Active Server Pages and ADO with databases include those of RDO—and in some case go beyond RDOs.

> **NOTE**
>
> Remote Data Services 1.5 was formerly called Active Data Connector 1.0. Designed for making it easier to create and deploy Web-based (or LAN-based) applications, they have now been integrated into ActiveX Data Objects.

The Push/Pull Models

As you could read in the previous sections, the Web server either receives data (Web assistant), or asks for data (IDC and ASP/ADO/RDS). This situation creates two different models from an RDBMS point of view: Either the RDBMS pushes data to the Web server, or the Web server pulls data from the DBMS. A simplified data retrieval schematic is shown in Figure 25.6.

FIGURE 25.6.
The push/pull models.

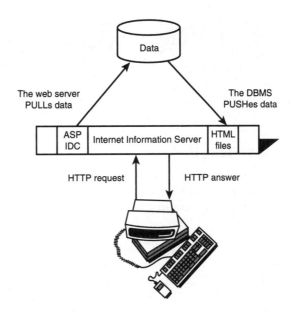

The model choice depends on your need. Generally, the first reaction is this: Forget the Web assistant and IDC, and head for ASP. That is so quick a decision! Here are some hints when using such technology:

- Web assistant   Reducing DBMS overhead; publishing read-only data; high transfer rate between Web browser and Web server.

- IDC   You want to avoid coding (HTML excepted); all the processing can be done server-side with queries or stored procedures.

- ASP/ADO/RDS   You need to use a disconnected record set to process calculation or update the client side; you want to use ASP components.

Nevertheless, ASP/ADO/RDS offers the most interesting features, but has the most significant overhead for Web and database servers. Remember, that it is possible to mix all of these technologies on the same Web site.

Internet Information Server

The client-side is quite obvious (for the client, not necessarily for the developer. All you need to do is reference an URL. As far as the server goes, you had better prepare the environment.

If you want your URL to send back files, you need a Web server and an alias on a directory. Microsoft Internet Information Server 4.0 offers the possibility of transforming your Windows NT Server machine into a Web server, creating virtual directories that can be referenced through an URL and HTTP protocol.

NOTE

Internet Information Server is shipped with Web, FTP, and Gopher servers. The Web server is focused on in this chapter. If you want other information on Internet Information Server features, see `http://www.microsoft.com/iis`.

Creating a Virtual Directory

Whatever technology you choose, you need to create a new Web site, or at least the virtual directory containing your Web files (HTM, ASP, IDC, or HTX). Figure 25.7 gives you an overview of the Virtual Directory properties dialog box.

This operation is probably as simple as using the Internet. Once you have created your directory, start Microsoft Management Console (or Internet Service Manager, if you are using IIS 3.0). Make sure the Web service is started. Right-click your default Web site, and then choose New, Virtual Directory. Follow the Web site wizard's instructions: Give your virtual directory an alias, browse to choose the directory containing your Web file, make sure to allow script access if you want to run IDC or ASP files, and click Finish. Then right-click your new virtual directory and choose Properties; open your Virtual Directory property sheet.

FIGURE 25.7.

Virtual Directory properties dialog box.

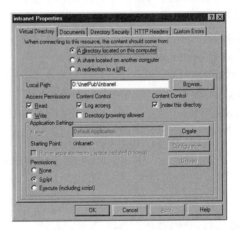

Ensure that all the settings are correct as far as scripting is concerned (Application Settings frame). You can define a default page if your home page is not default.ASP or default.HTM, as is shown in Figure 25.8.

From here, you can close the properties dialog box.

FIGURE 25.8.

Setting the default page.

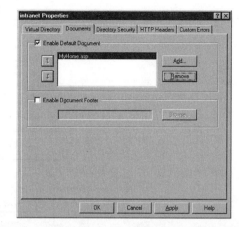

> **WARNING**
>
> If your virtual directory contains executable files and you select only the Read check box, the scripts won't be executed; instead, they'll be sent as plain text to the client Web browser.

You are now ready to create your data access Web files.

Internet Database Connector (IDC)

IDC is probably the simplest technology to enter the world of dynamic data access over the Web. IDC is shipped with IIS, and is present on the disk through the DLL `httpodbc.dll`.

> **WARNING**
>
> You cannot use a DSN-less connection with IDC, so you should create an ODBC Data Source Name before creating IDC files.

An Overview of IDC

An IDC connection is based on three files:

- A normal HTML file referencing the IDC file
- A text file (IDC) containing all the necessary information to get connected to the database and to send a query
- An HTML file (HTX) that acts as a template for the results sent by the DBMS and sent back to the client Web browser

Figure 25.9 gives you the overall architecture and flow of IDC data.

FIGURE 25.9.

Getting connected and retrieving data with IDC.

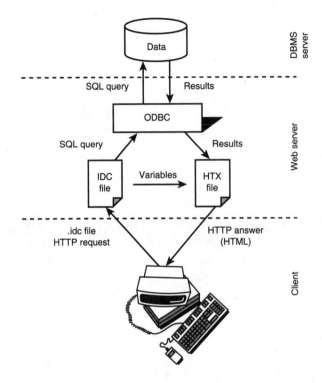

Now take a look at IDC and HTX files.

Getting Connected

The first thing to do is to create the IDC file and reference it into an HTML file. It's quite simple, as you see here.

The IDC File

Listing 25.1 gives you the basic syntax of an IDC file.

Listing 25.1. Basic syntax of an *IDC* file.

```
Datasource: <An ODBC Data source name>
Username: <User account to open a connection>
Password: <Associated password>
Template: <URL of a HTX template file>
SQLStatement: <line of SQL Statement>
+ <next line of SQL Statement>
```

The Datasource line indicates the name of the ODBC DSN that points to the database from which to retrieve data.

> **WARNING**
>
> Knowing how to create an ODBC System Data Source Name is important for use with IDC and ASP. If you create a user DSN, it is saved in the user profile and cannot be used by a Windows NT service.

The other lines are self explanatory enough to understand, and are shown in Listing 25.2.

Listing 25.2. Basic syntax of an *IDC* file.

```
Datasource: Pubs
Username: marc
Password: mypwd007
Template: authors.htx
SQLStatement: SELECT * FROM authors
+ WHERE au_lname='%txtau_lname%'
```

This IDC file gets connected to the Pubs DSN, with the account marc (password mypwd007), sends the query SELECT * FROM authors, and sends the result back in the HTX file called authors.htx, which is situated in the same virtual directory as the IDC file. Quite simple!

> **NOTE**
>
> You can use a variety of options with the SELECT statement (or another statement, like UPDATE), including aliasing column names, joining tables, and so on. The only restrictions are SQL Server's.

Referencing the IDC File

The IDC file can easily been referenced through the <FORM> or the <A> tag in an HTML file, as in Listing 25.3.

Listing 25.3. Referencing an *IDC* file with a *<FORM>* tag.

```
<html>
<head>
<title>Querying Authors</title>
<meta http-equiv="Content-Type" content="text/html; charset=iso-8859-1">
<meta name="GENERATOR" content="Microsoft FrontPage 3.0">
</head>
<body>
```

continues

25

SQL SERVER ON
INTERNET/
INTRANET SYSTEMS

Listing 25.3. continued

```
<form action="authors.idc" , method="post">
  <p>Enter the author name :
  <input type="text" name="txtau_lname" size="20">
  <input type="submit" value="Get author" name="cmdGetAuthor"></p>
</form>
</body>
</html>
```

Clicking the `cmdGetAuthor` button calls the `IDC` file, connects, and sends the query with the asked author name.

> **TIP**
>
> A POST method is used, to avoid displaying the parameters in the URL, but the GET method could have been used. With a GET, the parameters are clearly displayed. For example: `http://EMA/Pubs/authors.idc?txtau_lname=Ringer&cmdGetAuthor=Get+author`. Another limitation is that URL strings are limited to 256 characters.

Referencing the `IDC` file with the `<A>` tag is almost the same, parameters excepted. With that kind of link, it is impossible to submit the value of the parameters to the `IDC` file. You should either know beforehand the values of the parameters or recreate the URL before sending it, as you can see in Listing 25.4.

Listing 25.4. Referencing an *IDC* file with a *<A>* tag.

```
<A HREF="authors.idc?txtau_lname=Bourne">
...
</A>
```

In the previous example, the `IDC` file receives the parameter and sends the query to the database server.

Displaying Results

Once the DBMS has executed the query sent by the `IDC` file, it returns the results to the `HTX` file. The results can be displayed using the `<%variable_name%>` placeholder. The variables used in the `IDC` file can be displayed using the `<%idc.variable_name%>` placeholder.

If you want to display the first name, the last name, and the phone number of the author, you can use the code shown in Listing 25.5 in the `HTX` file.

Listing 25.5. Displaying results in the *HTX* file.

```
<p>Last name: <%idc.txtau_lname%></p>
<p>First name : <%au_fname%><p>
<p>Phone : <%phone%><p>
```

These few lines are fine if your results contain only one line, otherwise, only the first line of the result set is displayed. You create a loop enabling the display of all the lines with the <%BeginDetail%><%EndDetail%> tags, as shown in Listing 25.6.

Listing 25.6. Displaying multi-line results.

```
<p>Last name: <%idc.txtau_lname%></p>
<%BeginDetail%>
    <p>First name : <%au_fname%>    Phone : <%phone%><p>
<%EndDetail%>
```

Of course, you can create an HTML table to display the results, as shown in Listing 25.7.

Listing 25.7. Displaying multi-line results in a table.

```
<p>Last name: <%idc.txtau_lname%></p>

<table border="1" width="100%">
  <tr>
    <td width="50%">First Name</td>
    <td width="50%">Phone number</td>
  </tr>
  <%begindetail%>
  <tr>
    <td width="50%"><%au_fname%></td>
    <td width="50%"><%phone%></td>
  </tr>
  <%enddetail%>
</table>
```

User Variables

You have seen in the previous examples, you could retrieve parameters value from the client and send them to the database server, with the %*control_name*% syntax in the IDC file. It is similar in the HTX file, with <%*variable_name*%> or <%idc.*variable_name*%>.

First of all, you should know this method can be used for any lines in the IDC file. Look at Listing 25.8, which gives you a sample IDC file.

Listing 25.8. Coding the user's name and password.

```
Datasource: Pubs
Username: <%txtUsername%>
Password: <%txtPassword%>
```

continues

Listing 25.8. continued

```
Template: authors.htx
SQLStatement: SELECT * FROM authors
+ WHERE au_lname='%txtau_lname%'
```

You can ask the remote user to identify him or herself before running the query. You could even ask for the data source, the template file, or the SQL statement (or options).

> **TIP**
>
> You should use integrated security with Web or intranet sites. In fact, once Windows NT identifies the user, SQL Server trusts Windows NT and retrieves the username. You have a more secure connection and Web site, and can simplify the IDC files, since the lines Username and Password are no longer needed.

IDC and HTTP Environment Variables

IDC offers the developer built-in variables, IIS, and the HTTP environment variables, which are usable in the HTX file. Table 25.1 shows the IDC variables.

Table 25.1. IDC built-in variables.

Variables	*Description*
CurrentRecord	Indicates the record number at which you are pointing
MaxRecords	Indicates the total number of records in the result set

All the IIS HTTP environment variables are usable. Table 25.2 gives you the most useful of these variables.

Table 25.2. Most useful HTTP environment variables.

Variables	*Description*
LOGON_USER	The Windows NT user account used
QUERY_STRING	The string following the question mark character in the HTTP request
REMOTE_ADDR	Client's IP address
REMOTE_HOST	Client's name or IP address
SCRIPT_NAME	Script file's virtual path

As column names or IDC user variables, the HTTP environment variables should be enclosed between <%...%>. For instance: <%REMOTE_ADDR%>.

The variables you probably use the most are CurrentRecord and MaxRecords. You can test their values to determine if the result set contains at least one record, as well as how many records it contains.

> **NOTE**
>
> Always test CurrentRecord and MaxRecords after the <%BeginDetail%><%EndDetail%> section; otherwise their values are undefined (generally 0).

Conditions

Since IDC offers variables, it also offers possibilities to test them, like in Listing 25.9.

Listing 25.9. Testing the number of records.

```
<p>Last name: <%idc.txtau_lname%></p>
<%BeginDetail%>
    <p>First name : <%au_fname%>    Phone : <%phone%><p>
<%EndDetail%>
<%if currentrecord EQ 0%>
    Sorry, we don't know this author...
<%endif%>
```

If the result set is empty, the Web server sends it the information; otherwise, the Web page would be empty. You need the following tags to test values:

    <%if...%>

    <%else%>

    <%endif%>

You have to test an equality (EQ stands for "equal to"). Table 25.3 gives you the possible comparison operators.

Table 25.3. Comparison operators.

Operator	Description
EQ	Equal to.
LT	Less than
GT	Greater than.
CONTAINS	The left side string contains the right side string.

You test built-in variables here, but it is possible to test IDC parameters or values returned by the database server.

Hyperlinks

You can, of course, reference other IDC files in the HTX file and create logical links that way. Listing 25.10 creates a link on each first name that jumps to the complete record of the selected author.

Listing 25.10. Creating hyperlinks on authors' last names.

```
<p>Last name: <%idc.txtau_lname%></p>

<table border="1" width="100%">
  <tr>
    <td width="50%">First Name</td>
    <td width="50%">Phone number</td>
  </tr>
  <%begindetail%>
  <tr>
    <td width="50%"><a HREF="AuthorRecord.idc?au_id='<%au_id%>'">
    <%au_fname%> </a></td>
    <td width="50%"><%phone%></td>
  </tr>
<%enddetail%>
</table>
```

An <A> tag shows you can use that tag with variables coming from the database. You can use this technique to create detailed and summary information.

Updating Records

Until now, you have selected data. What about updating them? Everything is possible with IDC: INSERT, UPDATE, and DELETE (if you have the rights in the database).

There are no particular things to say about updating data. Listing 25.11 is a simple example of an IDC file.

Listing 25.11. Inserting a new record.

```
Datasource: Pubs
Username: sa
Password:
Template: insertauthor.htx
SQLStatement: INSERT authors
+ VALUES('%txtau_id%', '%txtau_lname%', 'txtau_fname', 'txtphone',
+ 'txtaddress', 'txtcity', 'txtstate', 'txtzip', 'chkcontract')
```

The only thing you need to have is the right controls in your HTML file and the `insertauthor.htx` file to give the user feedback.

Advanced Techniques

You probably find all these things quite simple (even basic). You were warned: There is nothing fabulous with IDC, just plain, simple techniques. Nevertheless, you can leverage your application (with almost no programming) with these advanced techniques.

Required Parameters and Default Values

The `RequiredParameters` line of the `IDC` file indicates the parameter(s) absolutely needed, like that in the Listing 25.12.

Listing 25.12. Required parameters.

```
Datasource: Pubs
Username: marc
Password: mypwd007
RequiredParameters: txtau_lname
Template: authors.htx
SQLStatement: SELECT * FROM authors
+ WHERE au_lname='%txtau_lname%'
```

If the user fails to enter one of these parameters, IDC automatically generates an error page.

> **WARNING**
>
> It is impossible to specify required parameters with the IDC wizard shipped with Microsoft FrontPage.

In the same area, if a parameter is not required, it can have a default value, defined with a `DefaultParameters` line in the script file, shown in Listing 25.13.

Listing 25.13. Default value.

```
Datasource: Pubs
Username: marc
Password: mypwd007
DefaultParameters: txtau_lname=%
Template: authors.htx
SQLStatement: SELECT * FROM authors
+ WHERE au_lname like '%%%txtau_lname%%%'
```

Multiple SQL Statements

It is possible to send multiple queries in the same IDC file, as shown in Listing 25.14.

Listing 25.14. Default value in an IDC script.

```
Datasource: Pubs
Username: marc
Password: mypwd007
Template: authors.htx
SQLStatement: SELECT * FROM authors
+ WHERE au_lname = 'txtau_lname'
SQLStatement: SELECT * FROM titles
```

To display the two result sets, use two <%BeginDetail%><%EndDetail%>.

Stored Procedures

You can speed your queries with the stored procedures. You run a stored procedure as if it were an *ad hoc* query. The procedure is shown in Listing 25.15.

Listing 25.15. A stored procedure with one parameter.

```
CREATE PROCEDURE SelPhone @chvau_lname varchar(40) AS
SELECT * FROM authors WHERE au_lname=@chvau_lname
```

It is possible to call it the following way:

```
SQLStatement: SelPhone 'txtau_lname'
```

> **NOTE**
>
> If your stored procedure returns more than one result set, you can display each of them with a separated <%BeginDetail%><%EndDetail%> section, as if you had multiple SQLStatement lines.

IDC Options

You can select several options for your IDC script file, most of them concerning ODBC and the result set. The most interesting options concern the ODBC trace file and the transaction isolation level. If you want explanations on all the others, read the Help file shipped with the IDC Wizard.

Active Server Pages

Active Server Pages is the definitive Microsoft Web dynamic technology. Active Server Pages is quite a monster and the product deserves a full book. ASP is introduced to help you understand ActiveX Data Objects and Remote Data Service.

An Overview of Active Server Pages

Active Server Pages is a complete part of Internet Information Server. In fact, it is the main difference between IIS 2.0 and IIS 3.0. Figure 25.10 shows you the overall functioning from a database point of view; as you later see, there are other components that can be used.

FIGURE 25.10.

The functioning of Active Server Pages.

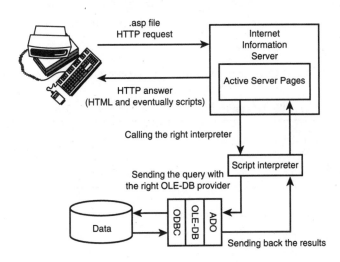

The client sends an HTTP request to the Web server. The server understands this is an active server page, calls the right interpreter (VBScript, JScript, or something similar) and sends the query to the database. It finishes the page with the results obtained and sends it back to the client.

The page can contain client-side scripting to be executed on the client, added to HTML code. By default, ASP accepts VBScript and JScript as scripting language, but you can use any other compatible scripting language, like PerlScript.

To reference an active server page, use these classical techniques: <A HREF>, <FORM ACTION>, or the <FRAME SRC> tag. This is shown in Listing 25.16.

Listing 25.16. Referencing an active server page.

```
<A HREF="/asp/login.asp?name='Tony'">, Click to login <A>

<FORM ACTION="/asp/login.asp" METHOD="Post">

<FRAME SRC="/asp/login.asp" NORESIZE>
```

When you know what you must do, you have to decide how to code your page.

Client-Scripting and Server-Scripting

Three types of scripts exist in active server pages:

- Scripts executed on the server as the page is created
- Scripts that can be executed on the server as functions or subroutines
- Scripts executed on the client as the page is interpreted

Server-Side Scripts

You enclose scripts executed during page creation between <% and%>. Look at Listing 25.17.

Listing 25.17. VBScript executed on the server during page creation.

```
<% if txtspeedlimit > 55 then%>
You should be on a highway
<% else %>
Ok, your speed is correct
<% end if%>
```

Lines 1, 3, and 5 are VBScripts and lines 2 and 4 are information for display on the HTML page. The result send to the client is only either line 2 or 4, depending on the value of the txtspeedlimit variable.

If you want to create functions or subroutines executed on the server if necessary, enclose them in <SCRIPT></SCRIPT> tags, like those shown in Listing 25.18.

Listing 25.18. VBScript executed on the server, if necessary.

```
<SCRIPT LANGUAGE=VBScript RUNAT=Server>
Function PriceWithTax(curPrice as real) as real
   PriceWithTax = curPrice * 1.008
End Function
</SCRIPT>
```

> **WARNING**
>
> In fact, you cannot write code between <SCRIPT></SCRIPT> tags if it is not a function or a subroutine, or if it has to be executed server-side.

Client-Side Scripts

Client-side scripts are always enclosed between <SCRIPT></SCRIPT> tags, but there's a slight difference between these and the server-side scripts. Take a look at Listing 25.19.

Listing 25.19. VBScript executed on the client.

```
<SCRIPT LANGUAGE=VBScript>
MsgBox "Welcome to the BigCorp Intranet"
Sub btnLogon(name, password)
   ...
End Sub
</SCRIPT>
```

The difference is that you can place code outside functions or subroutines, executed as the page is interpreted by the client. Note the other important difference: No RUNAT statement is necessary in the <SCRIPT> tag, as the client is the default for ASP.

Application and `global.asa` File

As a developer, you have already created an application. From that point of view, an application is an EXE (or COM) file, and eventually a set of DLLs.

From an Internet (or intranet) point of view, an *application* is the set of files contained in the virtual directory and the associated subdirectories. For example, if you create a virtual directory called MyApp, all the files under that directory are part of a single application.

As a matter of fact, you have no single EXE file, so the notion of a global variable might seem difficult. You can create a file called `global.asa` that contains three type of declarations for your application:

- Application or session OnStart event
- Application or session OnEnd event
- Object tags

The `global.asa` file is read each time a new session starts (each time a user opens a file of the application). Listing 25.20 gives you an example of a `global.asa` file for a connection to a SQL Server. The file keeps a visitor counter in a text file and defines a connection string to a database.

Listing 25.20. A *global.asa* file.

```
<SCRIPT LANGUAGE=VBScript RUNAT=Server>
SUB Application_OnStart
    Set FileObject = Server.CreateObject("Scripting.FileSystemObject")
    CounterFilename = Server.MapPath ("/MyApp") + "\counter.txt"
    Set objFile = FileObject.OpenTextFile (CounterFilename, 1, FALSE, FALSE)
    Application("visitors") = objFile.ReadLine
    Application("CounterFilename ") = CounterFilename
END SUB

SUB Application_OnEnd
    Set FileObject = Server.CreateObject("Scripting.FileSystemObject")
```

continues

25

SQL SERVER ON
INTERNET/
INTRANET SYSTEMS

Listing 25.20. continued

```
    Set objFile= FileObject.CreateTextFile
    ➥ (Application("CounterFilename"), TRUE, FALSE)
    objFile.WriteLine(application("visitors"))
END SUB

SUB Session_OnStart
    Application.lock
    Application("visitors")= Application("visitors") + 1
    intVisitors = Application("visitors")
    Application.unlock
    Session("VisitorID") = intVisitors

    'Saving file for security purposes, every 100 visitors
    If t_visitors MOD 100 = 0 Then
        SET FileObject = Server.CreateObject("Scripting.FileSystemObject")
        Set objFile = FileObject.CreateTextFile
    ➥ (Application("CounterFilename"), TRUE, FALSE)
        Application.lock
        objFile.WriteLine(intVisitors)
        Application.unlock
    End If

    ' If the store manager has been here before,
    ➥ there is a cookie called "stor_id"
    ' that is the primary key to the Stores table in the database
    CustomerID = Request.Cookies("store_id")
    If CustomerID = "" Then ' New store
        CustomerID = 0
    Else ' They've been here before - get manager name from the cookie
        Session("StoreManagerName") = Request.Cookies("StoreManagerName ").Item
    End If
    Session("store_id") = store_id   ' Put on session for later use

    ' set ADO Connection string
    ' we use integrated security - we don't need to give username and password
    ' and will open a new connection on each page.
    Session("ConnectionString") = "dsn=Pubs"

END SUB
</SCRIPT>
```

You can use this file as a template for your future application, but note that while the global.asa file is optional, but strongly recommended.

As you can see, you use different objects, like Server or Application. These are objects of the Active Server Pages' object model.

Active Server Pages Object Model

To create and maintain easily active pages, ASP offers a simple and efficient object model, which is shown in Figure 25.11.

FIGURE 25.11.

Active Server Pages object model.

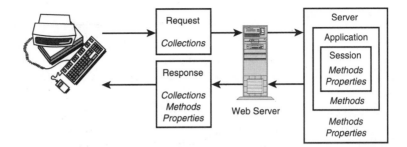

> **NOTE**
>
> The Session object is included in the Application and in the Server object, but this is just for the following explanations. In fact, there is no programmatic hierarchy between these objects, but a logical one.

If you worked, for example, with DAO or RDO, you are used to object models. This model can be used as a particularity: You do not need to create the objects. They are built in. You can use them right away.

You take a quick tour of this object model, because you need it when you want to get connected to a database.

Server

The Server object concerns the properties and methods of the server. It has four methods and one property, shown Table 25.4.

Table 25.4. *Server* object property and methods.

Property/Method	Syntax	Description
ScriptTimeout	Server.ScriptTimeout = *numseconds*	Number of seconds a script can run before being canceled by the server. (If this value is less than the registry setting HKEY_LOCAL_MACHIN\SYSTEM\ CurrentControlSet\ Services\W3SVC\ASP\ Parameters\ScriptTimeout, the value defined in the registry setting is used.)

continues

Table 25.4. continued

Property/Method	Syntax	Description
CreateObject	Server.CreateObject ([vendor.]componentname [.version]	Creates an object of the specified class.
HTMLEncode	Server.HTMLEncode(string)	Applies HTML encoding to the string.
MapPath	Server.MapPath (virtualpath)	Maps a virtual or relative path to a physical path on the Webserver.
URLEncode	Server.URLEncode(string)	Applies URL encoding to the string.

As far as databases is concerned, you use the Server object to create the ADO connection to the database server, as shown in Listing 25.21.

Listing 25.21. Creating an ADO connection.

```
<% Set conPubs = Server.CreateObject("ADODB.Connection") %>
```

> **WARNING**
>
> The CreateObject method creates an object with page scope, by default. If you want to keep your connection open until the end of the user's session, for example, you need to define a session scope object explicitly:
>
> ```
> <% Set Session("conPubs") = Server.CreateObject("ADODB.Connection") %>
> ```

Application

The Application object is generally used to share information among all the users of the same application. Remember that an application, from an ASP point of view, consists of all the files in the virtual directory and in the subdirectories.

The Application object has two methods and two events, shown in Table 25.5.

Table 25.5. *Application* object methods and events.

Method/Event	Syntax	Description
Lock	Application.Lock	Prevents other users to modify application variables

Method/Event	Syntax	Description
Unlock	Application.Unlock	Allow the other users to modify application variables
OnStart	Sub Application_OnStart	Defines the statements to run at the beginning of the application (the first time a page of the application is referenced)
OnEnd	Sub Application_OnEnd	Defines the statements to run at the end of the application (after the last Session_OnEnd event)

You find examples of Lock and Unlock methods in Listing 25.20 of the global.asa file. Because an Internet application is multiuser, you need to prevent two users modifying the same variable at the same time and serialize modifications with Lock and Unlock methods.

You generally use the Application object to store global variables, like a connection string, a connection timeout, or an ADO Connection object, as in Listing 25.22.

Listing 25.22. Creating an ADO connection with an application scope.

```
<% Set Application("conPubs") = Server.CreateObject("ADODB.Connection") %>
```

Session

The Session object "belongs" to one user. That is, each time a user references a page of the application for the first time, the Session object keeps the values of the variables stored in the Session object until the session is abandoned with the Abandon method, or until the session expires (after the delay defined with the Timeout property).

The Session object has two properties, one method, and two events, which are shown in Table 25.6.

Table 25.6. *Session* object properties, method, and events.

Property/ Method/Event	Syntax	Description
SessionID	Session.SessionID	Returns a unique identifier for the user session.
Timeout	Session.Timeout = number_of_minutes	Specifies the delay before the server abandons the session, after the last hit of the session user. The default value is 20 minutes.

continues

Table 25.6. continued

Property/ Method/Event	Syntax	Description
Abandon	Session.Abandon	Kills the Session object after the last script of the page has been executed. Once you abandon the session, its variables are usable until the user jumps to another page. If the user jumps to a page within the same application, the server opens a new Session object for that user.
OnStart	Sub Session_OnStart	Defines the statements to run at the beginning of a session (that is the first time a user references a page of the application).
OnEvent	Sub Session_OnEnd	Defines the statements to run at the end of a session (when the session is abandoned or when it is timed out).

The Session object is useful for keeping track of what's happening for a specific user. Listing 25.20 of the global.asa file shows where the OnStart event is used to count the number of application visitors, gets the cookie information, and defines the connection string.

You can also use this event to define session scope variables, as in Listing 25.23.

Listing 25.23. Creating variables and an ADO connection with a session scope.

```
<%
Session("MaxBooks")=20
Set Session("conPubs") = Server.CreateObject("ADODB.Connection")
%>
```

The two remaining objects are probably the most useful, because they define the interaction between the client and the server.

Request

As its name implies, this object retrieves the values of the HTTP request sent by the client to the server.

The Request object has five collections, shown in Table 25.7.

Table 25.7. *Request* object collections.

Collection	Syntax	Description
ClientCertificate	Request. ClientCertificate (*key[subkey]*)	Returns the certification information of the client if the secure HTTP protocol (https:, instead of http:) is used; returns EMPTY otherwise.
Cookies	Request.Cookies (*cookie*)[(*key*) ¦.*attribute*]	Retrieves the values of the cookie sent by the HTTP request.
Form	Request.Form(*parameter*) [(*index*)¦.*Count*]	Retrieves the element posted by a form with a POST method.
QueryString	Request.QueryString (*variable*)[(*index*) ¦.*Count*]	Retrieves the values encoded after the question mark of an HTTP request.
ServerVariables	Request.ServerVariables (*variable*)	Retrieves the value of the Web server environment variables.

NOTE

As for each collection, you can omit the default collection name. In fact, there is no default collection, but a search order: QueryString, Form, Cookies, ClientCertificate, and ServerVariables. If you reference a variable with Request("Myvar"), ASP searches this object among all the collections, in the order given here. If the same object exists in two collections, the first one found is used.

For performance reasons, it is preferable to indicate the right collection.

The main advantage with collections is the ability to scan them for a For each statement, as in Listing 25.24. It's assumed in Listing 25.24 that all the parameters are char or varchar.

Listing 25.24. Scanning the *QueryString* parameters to use in a stored procedure.

```
http://authors.asp?para="Smith"&para="John"

<%
For each MyPar in Request.QueryString("para")
    TxtStoredProc = txtStoredProc & "'" & Mypar & "',"
Next
TxtStoredProc = Left(TxtStoredProc, Len(TxtStoredProc)-1)
%>
```

NOTE

You find all the necessary parameters, variable names, and so on in the ADO documentation. You can freely download this documentation from `http://www.microsoft.com/data`.

Response

The `Response` object is the most used, since it contains the information sent back to the client. It is the most complex object, since it has one collection, five properties, and eight methods. They are shown in Table 25.8.

Table 25.8. *Response* object collection, properties, and methods.

Collection/ Property/Method	Syntax	Description
Cookies	Response Cookies (*cookie*)[(*key*) ¦.*attribute*]=*value*	Sets the values of the cookie sent back to the client. If the cookie does not exist, it is created.
Buffer	Response.Buffer=*flag*	Indicates if the page should be buffered on the server before sending it complete, or until a Flush or End method. This line should be the first one of the page.
ContentType	Response.ContentType= *ContentType*	Indicates the HTTP content type for the response. The common values are "text/HTML", "text/plain", "image/GIF", or "image/JPEG".

Collection/ Property/Method	Syntax	Description
Expires	Response.Expires= *number*	Indicates the delay (in minutes) before the page cached on the client expires.
ExpireAbsolute	Response. ExpireAbsolute=[*date*] [*time*]	Indicates the date and expiration time of a page cached on the client.
Status	Response.Status=*string*	Indicates the three-digit status code of the server, as defined in HTTP specification.
Addheader	Response.Addheader *name, value*	Adds an HTML header with the specified name and value. It cannot be removed, nor can it replace another header of the same name.
AppendToLog	Response.AppendToLog *string*	Appends a new string to the Web server log.
BinaryWrite	Response.Binarywrite *data*	Writes the data to the HTTP output, without character conversion.
Clear	Response.Clear	Erases the output buffer body, not the header.
End	Response.End	Stops processing and sends back the results to the client.
Flush	Response.Flush	Sends immediately the output buffer to the client, if the Response.Buffer property has been set to true.
Redirect	Response.Redirect URL	Connects the client to the URL specified.
Write	Response.Write *string*	Writes the specified string to the HTTP output.

As you can see, this object is quite complete. You see examples of the use of this method and properties in the ADO and RDS sections.

25

Server-Side Includes

If you are a C programmer, you are familiar with library files, whose purpose is sharing code between different application. It is possible to do almost the same thing with ASP and the server-side includes (SSIs).

SSIs are mechanisms used to insert information into your page before being processed. ASP implements only the #INCLUDE directive to insert the content of a file into your page, shown in Listing 25.25.

Listing 25.25. Including the *ADO* constant file for VBScript.

```
<!-- #INCLUDE FILE="Includes/adovbs.inc" -->
```

This file can contain HTML code, scripts, functions, subroutines, variable declarations, constant definitions, or object definitions. For example, you can use SSI to define style and default footer for all the pages of your site (with the style sheet, this method tends to be obsolete, but still works fine), or to define constants and functions used in all the sites. Listing 25.26 gives you a partial output of the file adovbs.inc used to declare the global constants. The file is shipped with the ADOs, which contain the global constants.

Listing 25.26. Partial output of the *adovbs.inc* include file.

```
<%
'-----------------------------------------------------------------
' Microsoft ADO
' (c) 1996 Microsoft Corporation.  All Rights Reserved.
' ADO constants include file for VBScript
'-----------------------------------------------------------------

'---- CursorTypeEnum Values ----
Const adOpenForwardOnly = 0
Const adOpenKeyset = 1
Const adOpenDynamic = 2
Const adOpenStatic = 3

'---- CursorOptionEnum Values ----
Const adHoldRecords = &H00000100
Const adMovePrevious = &H00000200
...
'---- SchemaEnum Values ----
...
Const adSchemaProcedureParameters = 26
Const adSchemaForeignKeys = 27
Const adSchemaPrimaryKeys = 28
Const adSchemaProcedureColumns = 29
%>
```

That should remind to the VB programmers the constant.txt file used in Visual Basic 3 and previous versions. Just remind include files are plain HTML or script files, so writing them should be no problem.

Server Components and Script Objects

The last, but not least, concerns the server components and the performance enhancements you can obtain with the <OBJECT> tag.

Server Components

ASP is shipped with five pre-built server components, or ActiveX server objects:

- **Ad Rotator** To automate the rotation of advertisement on Web pages.
- **Browser Capabilities** To provide the description of the capabilities of the client Web browser.
- **Data Access Objects** To access OLE-DB– or ODBC-structured data.
- **Content Linking** To manage a list of URLs.
- **File Access** To retrieve and update data in server files.

These components are not alone. Because they are based on ActiveX technology, any developer or vendor can create its own server components. Because these components are ActiveX objects, an instance has to either be created with the Server.CreateObject method or with the <OBJECT> tag.

You focus on ADO in the next section, but first look at the <OBJECT> tag.

Script Objects

You have seen, with the Server object, how to create server objects with applications, session scopes, or page scopes, like an ADO connection. Nevertheless, an instance of the object is created immediately with this method, even it won't be used in the future.

To save resources for application and session scope, you can declare objects in the global.asa file with the <OBJECT> tag, as in Listing 25.27. The result is almost identical to the CreateObject method, but the instance of the object is created during the first reference to this object in a script.

Listing 25.27. Defining an ADO connection with an *<OBJECT>* tag in the *global.asa* file.

```
<% OBJECT RUNAT=Server SCOPE=Session ID=ConPubs PROGID="ADODB.Connection">
</OBJECT>
```

This object can be used in any scripts within the same application, as in Listing 25.28.

Listing 25.28. Using the ADO connection in an *ASP* file.

```
<% ConPubs.ConnectionString="DSN=Pubs">
```

All the objects need to be closed, or set to Nothing, at the end of an application or a session. If you forget to do it, Active Server Pages does it for you. You see these statements in the following section.

OLE DB and ActiveX Data Objects (ADO)

OLE DB is the keystone of Microsoft Universal Data Access. In fact, that strategy is the Microsoft response to the Oracle Universal Data Server. The main purpose of these two strategies is to simplify access to data, whatever their formats.

OLE DB is the Microsoft system-level programming interface to different data sources, and ADO is the application programming interface to OLE DB.

The Universal Data Access is based on the three levels of the multi-tier paradigm:

- **Data providers** Expose data using a rowset abstraction, such as ISAM files, ODBC databases, spreadsheets, and the like.
- **Services** Use (consumes) and produce OLE DB data, like a query processor.
- **Consumers** Consume OLE DB data, like the Active Data Objects.

The overall architecture, from an SQL Server access point of view, is described in Figure 25.12.

FIGURE 25.12.

Universal Data Access example from SQL Server point of view.

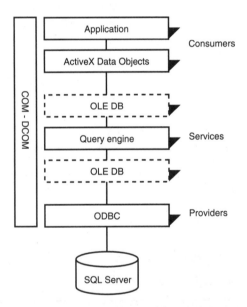

TIP

If you are interested in OLE DB and want to know more about the internal architecture of services and providers, consult the OLE DB site at http://www.microsoft.com/oledb and read the file that's found at http://www.microsoft.com/data/ado/sigmod98.htm.

OLE DB has been designed to leverage the existing ODBC drivers and allow various ODBC driver vendors to smoothly transform their drivers into OLE DB providers, in an effort to enhance performance.

For the moment, ODBC is used, and the most interesting part for the application developer is the ActiveX Data Objects.

An Overview of ADO

ADO is to OLE-DB what RDO is to ODBC. If you know RDO (or DAO), attempting ADO won't be a problem. Like DAO and RDO (and ASP), ADO exposes an object model, which is shown in Figure 25.13.

FIGURE 25.13.

ADO object model.

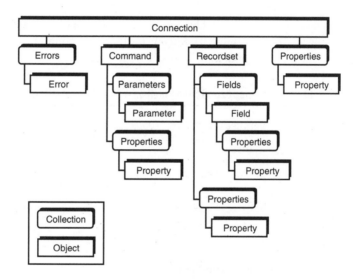

You find in the following sections the different necessary operations to get connected to SQL Server, retrieve and update data, execute stored procedures, and handling errors.

> **NOTE**
>
> In all the following examples, you see constants such as adXactIsolated. To use these constants, you must include the adovbs.inc or adojavas.inc files, depending on the scripting language used.

Getting Connected

First, you need to get connected to an ODBC data source. Once you have created an ODBC data source name, you get connected to that data source, as in Listing 25.29.

Listing 25.29. Getting connected to a DSN.

```
<%
Set conPubs = Server.Createobject("ADODB.Connection")
conPubs.Open "Pubs"
%>
```

> **WARNING**
>
> ASP uses system DSN, as it is a process that gets connected to the data source. Be careful to define system DSN, not to define a user DSN.

The previous example is probably the simplest way to open a connection on SQL Server. You probably want to define more parameters for the active connection. For that, you can use the ConnectionString method, as in Listing 25.30.

Listing 25.30. Using *ConnectionString* method with a classical ODBC connection string.

```
<%
Set conPubs = Server.Createobject("ADODB.Connection")
conPubs.ConnectionString ="DSN=Pubs;UID=sa;PWD=password"
conpubs.ConnectionTimeout=20
conpubs.CommandTimeout=60
conPubs.IsolationLevel = adXactIsolated
conPubs.Open
%>
```

The previous example opens a connection on the Pubs database, waits for 20 seconds (maximum) to open the connection, waits (at most) 60 seconds for the query result, and uses the serializable transaction isolation level.

> **NOTE**
>
> See Chapter 3, "Optimizing Queries," to know more about isolation transaction level.

As you can see, the connection string is the same as the one used with DAO and RDO. The ConnectionString method has its own parameters, as shown in the script in Listing 25.31.

Listing 25.31. Using *ConnectionString* method with a classical ODBC connection string.

```
<%
Set conPubs = Server.Createobject("ADODB.Connection")
conPubs.ConnectionString ="Data source=Pubs;User ID=sa;Password=password"
conpubs.ConnectionTimeout=20
conpubs.CommandTimeout=60
```

```
conPubs.IsolationLevel = adXactIsolated
conPubs.Open
%>
```

The two previous examples needed a system DSN to get connected. It is possible to use a DSN-less connection, as in Listing 25.32.

Listing 25.32. Using *ConnectionString* method with a classical ODBC connection string.

```
<%
Set conPubs = Server.Createobject("ADODB.Connection")
conPubs.ConnectionString ="DRIVER={SQL
Server};SERVER=SaoPaulo;UID=sa;PWD=password;DATABASE=pubs"
conpubs.ConnectionTimeout=20
conpubs.CommandTimeout=60
conPubs.IsolationLevel = adXactIsolated
conPubs.Open
%>
```

> **TIP**
>
> When you are designing applications, always keep in mind that the user is unpredictable. You should always check the state of the connection. Its State property helps you. If its value is adStateClosed (&H00000000), the connection has been closed. If it is adStateOpen (&H00000001), then the connection is still open. From page to page, checking the connection state before sending any request is a safe attitude.

You can, of course, define your connection with the <OBJECT> tag in the global.asa file and give it the necessary scope. Once your connection is open, however, the most important is to come: executing queries.

Executing a Query

You can do two things on your database: read data and update data. The first operation sends back a record set (same name in DAO, equivalent to result set in RDO). The second one sends nothing, except for either a stored procedure's output parameters or a return value.

You send the query depending on whether you have a SELECT query.

Running an Action Query

An action query is an INSERT, UPDATE, DELETE, or EXECUTE statement (for the EXEC, the stored procedure does not contain any interesting SELECT to send back to the client). Running such a statement is easy, as shown in Listing 25.33.

Listing 25.33. Running an *UPDATE* query depending on the page parameters.

```
<%
strAu_id = Request.QueryString("txtau_id")
strAu_lname = RequestQueryString("txtau_lname")

strSQL = "UPDATE authors SET au_lname='" & strAu_lname
strSQL = strSQL & "' WHERE au_id='" & strAu_id & "'"
conPubs.Execute strSQL
%>
```

You can apply the same strategy for the UPDATE, DELETE, and EXECUTE statements. You see, in this chapter's "Record Set" section, you can use record set methods to achieve the same operation with cursors.

Listing 25.34 shows how you can achieve the same operation with the Command object.

Listing 25.34. Running an *UPDATE* query with a *Command* object.

```
<%
set comUpd = Server.CreateObject("ADODB.Command")
comUpd.ActiveConnection=conPubs

strAu_id = Request.QueryString("txtau_id")
strAu_lname = RequestQueryString("txtau_lname")

strSQL = "UPDATE authors SET au_lname='" & strAu_lname
strSQL = strSQL & "' WHERE au_id='" & strAu_id & "'"
comUpd.CommandText=strSQL
comUpd.Execute
%>
```

The differences between these two examples are not extraordinary, since the results are identical. Nevertheless, the Command object allows more flexibility.

If you need to execute a query more than once, it can be useful to create a stored procedure, or let ODBC create it with the Prepared option set to true. The first time you run that command, the execution is slowed by the creation of the stored procedure, but the consecutive executions are faster.

SQL String and Stored Procedure

With SQL Server, you can execute either an *ad hoc* or a stored procedure. As always, if you don't say anything, the ADO tries to know what kind of query you are asking for. It is better to clearly specify the type of query you are going to run, like in Listings 25.35 and 25.36. A stored procedure named update_authors is used in those listing.

Listing 25.35. Specifying the type of query with the *Connection* object.

```
<%
...
strSQL = "UPDATE authors SET au_lname='" & strAu_lname
strSQL = strSQL & "' WHERE au_id='" & strAu_id & "'"
conPubs.Execute strSQL,, adCmdText
...
conPubs.Execute "update_authors '" & strAu_lname & "',
➥ '" & strAu_id & "'",, adCmdStoredProc
%>
```

Listing 25.36. Specifying the type of query with the *Command* object.

```
<%
...
strSQL = "UPDATE authors SET au_lname='" & strAu_lname
strSQL = strSQL & "' WHERE au_id='" & strAu_id & "'"
comPud.CommandTypeEnum=adCmdText
comUpd.CommandText=strSQL
comUpd.Execute
...
comPud.CommandType=adCmdStoredProc
comUpd.CommandText="update_authors '" & strAu_lname & "', '" & strAu_id & "'"
%>
```

If you don't specify the type of query, the type is adCmdUnknown. With this type, the system must do intensive testing on the string to evaluate the best type, slowing the process.

Parameters

In the previous queries, appending the textbox values to the string created the queries' parameters. With the Command object, you can take profit of the Parameters collection to define more precisely the procedure or the query parameters.

Listing 25.37 defines the UPDATE query's two parameters.

Listing 25.37. Defining the query parameters.

```
<%
set comUpd = Server.CreateObject("ADODB.Command")
comUpd.ActiveConnection=conPubs
...
comPud.CommandTypeEnum=adCmdStoredProc
comUpd.CommandText="update_authors"
Set parAu_id = comUpd.CreateParameter("au_id", adVarchar, adParamInput, 11)
Set parAu_lname = comUpd.CreateParameter("au_lname, adVarchar, adParamInput, 40)
comUpd.Parameters.Append parAu_id
comUpd.Parameters.Append parAu_lname
parAu_id.value= Request.QueryString("txtau_id")
parAu_lname.Value= RequestQueryString("txtau_lname")
comUpd.Execute
%>
```

You might think this a lot of work for just two parameters—but if you have return value or output parameters for your query, it is the only way to go.

> **WARNING**
>
> Always give the size of the parameter before appending it. Otherwise, you provoke a runtime error. You can give it in the `CreateParameter` method (fourth parameter) or with the `Size` method of the parameter object.

You can see the name of the stored procedure in the `CommandText` property, which afterward defines the parameters. For a simple query, the problem is a little different, as you can see in Listing 25.38.

Listing 25.38. Specifying the type of query with the *Command* object.

```
<%
...
strSQL = "UPDATE authors SET au_lname=? WHERE au_id=?"
comPud.CommandTypeEnum=adCmdText
comUpd.CommandText=strSQL

Set parAu_id = comUpd.CreateParameter()
parAu_id.Type=adVarchar
parAu_id.Direction=adParamInput
parAu_id.size=11
parAu_id.value= Request.QueryString("txtau_id")

Set parAu_lname = comUpd.CreateParameter()
parAu_lname.Type=adVarchar
parAu_lname.Direction=adParamInput
parAu_lname.Size=40
parAu_lname.Value= RequestQueryString("txtau_lname")

comUpd.Parameters.Append parAu_id
comUpd.Parameters.Append parAu_lname
comUpd.Execute
...
comPud.CommandType=adCmdStoredProc
comUpd.CommandText="update_authors '" & strAu_lname & "', '" & strAu_id & "'"
%>
```

In this example, the parameterized values are replaced by a question mark, and properties of the `Parameter` object are used to define the characteristics of both parameters. You usually need to read these values and parameters before updating data. The `Recordset` object is there to help you.

Working with Record Sets

If you have worked with DAO and Jet, you are familiar with the `Recordset` object. OLE DB uses a rowset abstraction to present data to the consumers, and ADO uses this possibility to offer applications record set. You are going to see a lot of similarities between RDO/DAO and ADO.

Creating a Record Set

There are many ways to create a record set, whether you use a `Command` object or not. Listing 25.39 shows you how to create a record set with an `Execute` method.

Listing 25.39. Creating a record set with an *Execute* method of a *Connection* object.

```
<%
Set conPubs = Server.Createobject("ADODB.Connection")
conPubs.ConnectionString ="DSN=Pubs;UID=sa;PWD=password"
conPubs.Open
...
strSQL = "SELECT * FROM authors"
set rsAuthors=conPubs.Execute(strSQL)
...
%>
```

You can directly open a new record set with the `Open` method, as shown in Listing 25.40.

Listing 25.40. Creating a record set with an *Open* method.

```
<%
Set conPubs = Server.Createobject("ADODB.Connection")
conPubs.ConnectionString ="DSN=Pubs;UID=sa;PWD=password"
conPubs.Open
...
strSQL = "SELECT * FROM authors"
set rsAuthors=Server.CreateObject("ADODB.Recordset")
rsAuthors.open strSQL, conPubs, adOpenKeyset, adLockBatchOptimistic, adCmdText
...
%>
```

It is possible to specify the cursor type and the lock type with this version of record set creation. It would have been possible to define other properties prior to the opening. As in the case of the action query, you need the `Command` object to use the parameterized query, as shown in Listing 25.41.

Listing 25.41. Defining the query parameters for the record set.

```
<%
set comUpd = Server.CreateObject("ADODB.Command")
comUpd.ActiveConnection=conPubs
...
```

25

SQL SERVER ON INTERNET/INTRANET SYSTEMS

continues

Listing 25.41. continued

```
comUpd.CommandType=adCmdStoredProc
comUpd.CommandText="SELECT * FROM authors WHERE au_lname=?"
Set parAu_lname = comUpd.CreateParameter("au_lname, adVarchar, adParamInput, 40)
comUpd.Parameters.Append parAu_lname
parAu_lname.Value= RequestQueryString("txtau_lname")
set rsAuthor=comUpd.Execute
%>
```

If you compare the `comUpd.Execute` line in Listings 25.41 and 25.37, you see that if the query is an action one, no result is returned; if the query is a SELECT, a record set is returned.

Table, Queries, and Stored Procedures

Until now, you have seen SQL queries and stored procedure calls. If you have worked with DAO and Jet, you are familiar with the `db_open_table` option of the `OpenRecordset` method. This possibility was lost when working with DAO or RDO on a remote table, but you can do it with ADO, simplifying standard work. This is shown in Listing 25.42.

Listing 25.42. Opening a table directly without the *Command* object.

```
<%
...
rsAuthor.open "authors", conPubs, , , adCmdTable
...
%>
```

Listing 25.43. Opening a table directly with the *Command* object.

```
<%
...
comPud.CommandType=adCmdTable
comUpd.CommandText="authors"
set rsAuthor=comUpd.Execute
...
%>
```

In these two cases, with the `adCmdTable` option, the executed query is a SELECT * FROM tablename. This option is here just to quickly open a table, without having to write an SQL query.

Choosing a Cursor and a Lock Type

No matter what method you choose to open your cursor, you can choose the cursor type and location, and the lock type used. The `Recordset` object has three properties dedicated to these choices: `CursorType`, `CursorLocation`, and `LockType`.

The choice can have a significant impact on performance. The main rule is the same as in typical client/server architecture: Always use the cursor and lock you need, do not consume too many resources.

By default, the defined cursor and lock are forward only and read only, to minimize the overhead on the DBMS. If you need an updatable or scrollable cursor, define more precise options. Table 25.9 shows the different types of cursors.

Table 25.9. Types of cursors for *CursorType* property.

Cursor	Description
adOpenForwardOnly	Default. Static, forward-only cursor.
adOpenDynamic	All types of movement and modifications are allowed, and all others modifications are seen.
adOpenKeyset	Dynamic cursor without the ability to see others add.
AdOpenStatic	Static copy of data, fully scrollable.

These cursor types are equivalent to those proposed in RDO.

You can choose your cursor's location with the CursorLocation property, either client-side with the adUseClient constant (or adUseClientBatch in ADO 1.1), or server-side (default) with adUseServer. Table 25.10 shows the different types of locks.

Table 25.10. Types of locks for *LockType* property, from a SQL Server point of view.

Cursor	Description
adLockReadOnly	Default. Only shared locks on pages.
adLockPessimistic	Locks pages from edit to update.
adLockOptimistic	Locks pages only during the execution of the Update method.
adLockBatchOptimistic	Required for batch updates.

As you are going to see, ADO offers two types of updates: immediate or batch. In the section, "Batch Updates" later in this chapter, you'll see how this type of update can be very useful with Remote Data Services.

Moving Through a Record Set

Moving in an ADO record set is not much different than moving in an RDO result set or a DAO record set.

The classical Move methods still exist: MoveFirst, MoveLast, MovePrevious, MoveNext, and Move, with the EOF and BOF properties to test the limits of the record set, as shown in Listing 25.44.

Listing 25.44. Moving through a record set.

```
<table>
<%
Set rsAuthor=Server.CreateObject("ADODB.Recordset")
rsAuthor.open "authors", conPubs, , , adCmdTable
Do While not rsAuthor.EOF %>
    <tr><td><% =rsAuthor("au_lname") %></td></tr>
    <% rsAuthor.Movenext
Loop
rsAuthor.close
%>
</table>
```

The previous example scans the authors table and display each author name in an HTML table.

Two of the most interesting properties of the Recordset for Web application are PageSize and PageCount, along with the AbsolutePage method. The PageSize property allows you to define a "page" of n records to display to the user, avoiding the creation of too long a page. The PageCount property gives the number of pages in the record set, and the AbsolutePage property allows the user to jump to the nth page, as shown in Listing 25.45.

Listing 25.45. Moving through a different page each time the user clicks *Next*.

```
<SCRIPT>
Sub cmdNext_OnClick()
Session("intNumPage")= Session("intNumPage") + 1
RsAuthor.AbsolutePage= Session("intNumPage")
Response.Write ("<table>")
For intRecord=1 to RsAuthor.Pagesize
    Response.Write ("<tr><td>")
    Response.Write =rsAuthor("au_lname")
    Response.Write ("</tr></td>")
    rsAuthor.Movenext
Next
End Sub
</SCRIPT>
```

As in DAO and RDO, the Bookmark property allows you to save a bookmark on a record and go back at anytime to that bookmark.

Updating a Record Set

ADO offers updates through record sets. There are two kinds of updates: direct and batch. If you are used to direct updates with DAO and RDO, you probably did not work with batch updates (unless you worked with RDO 2.0).

Batch updates are great as far as Internet applications go, since you can work with a server-side cursor, make all your updates locally, and send them back to the server as a batch.

Direct Updates

To update a record through a record set, you just have to modify the value of its fields, and call the Update method, as in Listing 25.46.

Listing 25.46. Updating a record through a record set.

```
<SCRIPT>
Sub cmdUpdate_OnClick()
    rsAuthor("au_lname")=Request.QueryString("txtau_lname")
    rsAuthor.Update
End Sub
</SCRIPT>
```

> **WARNING**
>
> You must be in Edit mode to update records in DAO and RDO. There is no equivalent with ADO. If your record set is updatable, you update fields directly. Be careful—if you forget the Update method, the system automatically updates your data with the next Move method.

You can choose your locking method when you update records directly. Updatable record sets supports two methods: optimistic (adLockOptimistic) or pessimistic (adLockPessimistic). You define the method with the LockType property before opening the record set.

The choice of locking can have a dramatic impact on your application. You know SQL Server locks pages. If you intend to modify a record with the pessimistic strategy (the most secure), the exclusive lock page is held until the end of the Update method, blocking all pending transactions needing access to that page. Try to write as updates that are short as possible. Never let the user commit an update after having began editing. If the user decides to take a coffee break, he can block a lot of other users.

> **TIP**
>
> Because it is more secure to use adLockPessimistic, it is a good idea to keep the update as short as possible. If you need to use long updates, add a timestamp column and use it to compare the selected record to what it is the moment the record is to be updated.

Adding a new record is almost as simple (take a look at Listing 25.47), except you use the Addnew method to create a blank record before inserting new values in the fields.

Listing 25.47. Inserting a new record through a record set.

```
<%
If not IsEmpty(Request.Form)
...rsAuthor.Addnew
    rsAuthor("au_id")= Request.Form("txtau_id")
    rsAuthor("au_lname")=Request.Form("txtau_lname")
...
    rsAuthor.Update
End If
%>
```

The Form object and the Submit button are used to add the new record, avoiding the creation of a specific subroutine. The same locking rules apply to the Insert.

To delete a record, use the Delete method. The Delete is immediately done, does not need to be validated and cannot be canceled.

You can cancel a single update/insert with the CancelUpdate method, prior to a move. Remember that the update is validated once you have moved.

Batch Updates

If the user has to make a large number of updates/inserts/deletes, it is better to group and send them as a batch. SQL Server responds more quickly with 10 updates in the same batch than it does with the same 10 updates in individual batches. This feature is really helpful over the Internet; the connection does not have to be left open during multiple, but separate transactions when the user is modifying data.

To use batch updates, you need to use batch-locking mode with the adLockBatchOptimistic lock mode. This mode sends an automatic update after each Move statement (as it would be with direct update locking). Listing 25.48 shows you how to use batch updates.

Listing 25.48. Batch update.

```
<%
    rsAuthor.LockType=adLockBatchOptimistic

        'Make all necessary update/delete/insert

    rsAuthor.UpdateBatch
%>
```

If you created a sessionwide record set, you can jump from page to page in the same application and update at the end. The updates are on specific pages and the Commit button is on every page, so that the user can commit the changes at any moment.

> **TIP**
>
> If you want to improve your updates' performance for a Web application, you can use the *marshaling* technique. This technique sends only the updated rows to the server, not to all the record sets, preserving bandwidth. To do that, define the `MarshalOptions` property of the record set with the `adMarshalModifiedOnly` value.

Transactions

Even if a batch updates more than one record at a time, SQL Server does not consider it a transaction. If one update fails, the others are completed. If you want to enforce transaction, you need to declare it with the `Connection` object's `BeginTrans` method.

Every update included between `BeginTrans` and `CommitTrans` (or `RollbackTrans`) is part of the transaction—and that mean that locks are held until the end of the transaction. Keep your transactions short! This is particularly true over the Web.

A nice ADO feature is the capability to know the nesting level of the transaction, as shown in Listing 25.49.

Listing 25.49. Identifying the nesting level of a transaction.

```
<%
...
    intNestLevel=conPubs.BeginTrans()
...
%>
```

If the `intNestLevel` value equals 1, the transaction is top level. If it equals 2 or more, this transaction is nested.

> **NOTE**
>
> You might prefer starting transactions with the Transact-SQL `BEGIN TRAN` statement inside a stored procedure. That way, you know what exactly SQL Server is doing, and nothing is hidden by ODBC. If you don't need to port your front-end application on other databases, use a stored procedure and manage transactions from within the stored procedure.

Remote Data Service (RDS)

Formerly called Active Data Connector (ADC), Remote Data Services (version 1.5 as of December 1997) leverages the power of ActiveX Data Objects into Web pages for Internet and intranet applications.

With RDS, you can use data-aware controls on your Web page, avoiding long programming, but you can cache data on the client-side very easily. Client data caching is a nice feature that helps you avoid data round trip on the network, especially on Internet applications.

Remote Data Services is compatible with three-tier applications, Microsoft Transaction Server, OLE-DB, and SSL. You can quickly create powerful, secure transaction applications.

RDS is automatically installed with Internet Information Server 4.0, or can be downloaded from the Web at `http://www.microsoft.com/adc` (`msadc15.exe` for Windows NT on Intel).

WARNING

Remote Data Services is part of Internet Explorer 4.0. If your browser is a former version of IE, you need to install the Remote Data Service Client Components on your computer, downloadable at the previously given address. These components have not been tested on Netscape browsers.

RDS works client-side with the Active Data Control object (`RDS.Datacontrol`, a kind of invisible RDC for RDO, or DAC for DAO), and works server-side with the `RDSServer.Datafactory` object, by default.

Linking the Web Page to the Data

To create an RDS application, the first step is to create an instance of the data object, as in Listing 25.50.

Listing 25.50. Creating an instance of the Active Data Control object.

```
<OBJECT CLASSID="clsid:BD96C556-65A3-11D0-983A-00C04FC29E33"
ID="MyADC">
</OBJECT>
```

You then need to describe the connection elements, like the DSN, the Web server name, and the SQL string to be executed, as in Listing 25.51.

Listing 25.51. Getting connected with the Active Data Control object.

```
<%
MyADC.Server="http://" & Request.ServerVariables("SERVER_NAME")
MyADC.Connect="DSN=Pubs"
MyADC.SQL="SELECT * FROM authors"
%>
```

The parameters could have been defined between the `<OBJECT></OBJECT>` tags, using `<PARAM>` tags.

Displaying Data

To easily display data, you can use the Sheridan Data bound grid control shipped with RDS 1.5, as shown in Listing 25.52.

Listing 25.52. Displaying data in a data bound grid.

```
<OBJECT CLASSID="clsid:AC05DC80-7DF1-11d0-839E-00A024A94B3A"
CODEBASE="http://<%=Request.ServerVariables("SERVER_NAME")%>/RDS/ssdatb32.cab"
ID=grdResult DATASRC=#MyADC HEIGHT=125 WIDTH=495>
    <PARAM NAME="BackColor" VALUE="-2147483643">
    <PARAM NAME="BackColorOdd" VALUE="-2147483643">
    <PARAM NAME="ForeColorEven" VALUE="0">
    <PARAM NAME="AllowAddNew" VALUE="TRUE">
    <PARAM NAME="AllowDelete" VALUE="FALSE">
    <PARAM NAME="AllowUpdate" VALUE="TRUE">
</OBJECT>
```

Among the parameters, the most significant is DATASRC, which binds the grid to the Active Data Connector.

If you have ever worked with the Data Access Control (with DAO), you are used to referencing the underlying Recordset object. This is the equivalent. For example, you can create a typical button to move to the last record by using the code shown in Listing 25.53.

Listing 25.53. Creating a Movelast button.

```
<INPUT TYPE=BUTTON NAME="cmdLast" VALUE=">>">
...
<SCRIPT LANGUAGE=VBScript>
...
Sub cmdLast_OnClick
    grdResult.Recordset.MoveLast
End Sub
...
</SCRIPT>
```

It is also possible to use Recordset properties and methods (MoveNext, MovePrevious, MoveLast, MoveFirst, EOF, BOF, and so on). However, in order to allow a quicker interface, the record sets are populated asynchronously—even if you can ask for synchronous population using the ExecuteOptions and the FetchOptions of the ADC.

Records can be updated through the data bound controls. Nevertheless, all modification is done on the client, since you are working with disconnected record sets. If you want to update the data source with the modification done on the client, call the SubmitChanges method on the ADC object. If you want to discard them, use CancelUpdate. Note that CancelUpdate refreshes the bound control with the original values.

> **TIP**
>
> Asynchronous data fetching can always run. If you intend to update records through RDS, you must always check that the ADC's ReadyState property does not equal adcReadyStateInteractive.

Internet Explorer 4.0 extends the <OBJECT> tag and allows almost any control to be data aware, with the new DATASRC (ADC source of data), DATAFLD (the field to display), and DATAFORMATAS (the field's format). This new feature makes creation of Web pages even easier.

There are a lot of things to say about RDS, because you can develop your own business object to replace the RDSServer.Datafactory default object on the middle tier. If you are interested by this new fantastic technology, download the RDS documentation from http://www.microsoft.com/adc.

Web Assistant

The two previous technology (IDC and ASP) where pull technologies. The client gets connected to the server and retrieves (or updates) data from the database server.

SQL Server offers a simple and powerful tool for creating Web pages automatically from data stored on the server: the Web Assistant. This wizard is based on the SQL Server stored procedure sp_makewebtask.

> **NOTE**
>
> The Web Assistant is much more convenient than the stored procedure and has the same functionality. If you are not convinced, look for the procedure in Books Online and see for yourself.

Creating a Simple Page

The creation of a simple Web page is a very simple task. Run the SQL Server Web Assistant and perform the following steps:

1. Get connected to your server with an account that has SELECT rights on the data you are going to read, and INSERT rights in the msdb database (since a new task is going to be created).

2. Choose to create a query from a database hierarchy, to enter a query as free text, or to use a stored procedure.

3. Decide when you are going to create and refresh the page. If you choose Now, a task is created with an On Demand schedule. If you choose When Data Changes, the system asks you to specify the tables in which you want to add (or modify) triggers for running the created task. All the other options are classical schedule tasks.

4. Give the Web page a name, a title, and eventually an URL.

5. Choose formatting options for the results display.

You have finished, the page is created—or will be created—if you ask to delay the creation.

Updating the Page

The underlying data will probably change, and the page needs to be refreshed. You have two possibilities for updating the Web page:

- Scheduled task
- Triggered task

As far as scheduled tasks are concerned, a new task is created to be managed by SQL Executive, as shown Figure 25.14.

FIGURE 25.14.

The task created to update the Web page on a schedule basis.

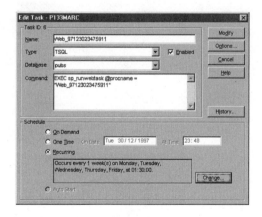

The wizard runs the `sp_makewebtask` to create a stored procedure (`WITH ENCRYPTION`) in the database. The scheduled `sp_runwebtask` executes this stored procedure.

This is a convenient way to update the page during off hours. Of course, a Web user connected on Tuesday does not see the updates until Wednesday at 1 a.m.. If you need tighter updates, you should trigger the page update. Listing 25.54 shows you the Insert trigger created by the Web assistant.

Listing 25.54. The *Insert* trigger created to update the page.

```
CREATE TRIGGER Web_16003088_1 ON dbo.authors FOR INSERT AS
begin
   exec sp_makewebtask
               @outputfile='C:\WEB2.HTML',
               @query='select a.* from pubs.dbo.authors a',
               @fixedfont=1,
               @bold=0,
               @italic=0,
               @colheaders=1,
               @lastupdated=1,
               @HTMLheader=2,
               @username='dbo',
               @dbname='pubs',
               @webpagetitle='SQL Server Web Assistant',
               @resultstitle='Query Results',
               @maketask=0,
               @rowcnt=0
end
GO
```

Equivalent triggers are created for Update and Delete.

> **NOTE**
>
> Note the numerous parameters of sp_makewebtask! An almost complete chapter would be required in order to fully explain them.

Using a Template

The page you obtain with such a method is not the prettiest Web page on Earth (though it is not the ugliest, either). Instead of creating a Web page, you can use a template. In fact, a template is a plain HTML (or ASP or HTX) page with a special <%Insert_data_here%> tag.

Be careful—if you ask to insert an updated timestamp within a template file, this information is not included!

How to Write Client/Server Internet Applications

This title is ambitious—a complete book could be written on this topic. If you want to write client/server Web-based application, you have to make a lot of difficult choices.

This section gives you a few hints about what to do, possible directions, and the best choices, for what you intend to do. You start server side.

Server Side

The server-side problem is quite simple: Windows NT and IIS. The only question? Do you use the same machine for SQL Server? In fact, everything depends on the activity on your Web server and on your database.

One thing is sure: the quality/price ratio is better on two machines (IIS on one side and SQL Server on the other) connected through a 100Mbps network, than on a more powerful system trying to cope with different applications. Dedicated servers are easier to tune.

Of course, the other question remains: Are ASP and IIS performing well? The following sections explain how fast they are.

Server-Side Scripting

IIS is probably one of the fastest and most simple Web administration server on the market. Furthermore, if you pay close attention to the hardware, you probably have the best basis for creating a great Web site.

As far as server-side scripting goes, it is plainly interpreted code. Because of that, it runs as fast as possible. Don't expect VBScript or JavaScript to be as efficient as a C DLL (this is discussed in a moment), but you have to pay a slight price for the simplicity.

Nevertheless, don't try to create scripts that are too complex. Put the load on the database server. You know SQL Server stored procedures are fast, pre-compiled, and sharable code—so use it like you would on a typical client/server configuration.

Furthermore, there is no browser limitation with server-side scripting. If you use only typical HTML code and objects, any type of client browser can connect to your database.

If you want to improve server-side scripting, rely on Server components. They are fast, reliable, and simple.

Server Components

The server component is ActiveX DLL, which runs on the server. It is sharable, optimized code, generally written in C++ (you can write the code in Visual Basic or in Java, but the performance will be better in C).

IIS 4.0 is shipped with lots of components, like the ad rotator or the database access (ADO) used to access your SQL Server. Of course, you find new server components next month. If you develop in VB or VC++, you are familiar with OCX objects and don't make a fuss about it; it's the same with server components. If you use them, both your life and the lives of your clients will be easier.

Database Side

You must pay close attention to the database side of your application. Remember that your application's client is not the Web browser, but the Internet server.

Remember that the network and another server stand between your client and the database. Think of it while you develop; otherwise, you take the risk of being disappointed by the performance. Develop code to be run on the server (server-side scripting) and use stored procedures extensively.

Stored procedures are, nonetheless, a very good performance optimization, but it is a gateway to your security. Allowing access to your data exclusively through a stored procedure simplifies the code on your Web server, increases the independence of your application from the design of the database, and increases the security of your database application.

Security

Security is the major concern in regards to Web sites. There are security concerns on an intranet system, but they are not as pressing as those on the Internet; anybody can get connected to your site on the Internet. If you allow anonymous access to your Web server, anybody can write a quick and dirty Web page to access your database, knowing an ODBC data source on the server.

Giving a password to the SA is the first thing to do. (In one case, 90 percent of the SQL Server sites did not go give the SA the password; 50 percent of the 90 percent give SA access to everybody—it was hard coded in the application). Imagine an administrator Windows NT account without a password: Come in, the door is wide open.

Anonymous Access

Anonymous access via the Web is obvious. You cannot do without it if you want anyone to sign in. Just make sure to give the rights to the IUSR_server account on your Windows NT Server; use Integrated security on SQL Server, mapping this account to a SQL Server account with SELECT, INSERT, UPDATE, or DELETE rights on the right tables. (It is even better to only do this with EXEC rights on stored procedures.) Figure 25.15 shows you the different authentication methods.

FIGURE 25.15.

*Authentication
Methods dialog box.*

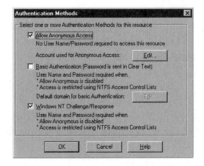

Logging the WWW Activity

Log the WWW activity if you want to check, for a while, that unauthorized people are not trying to enter backside. In Microsoft Management Console, right-click your Web server, and choose Properties. Check the Enable Logging check box. You can log on to a file (using a different format), or log on to an ODBC database.

If you choose to log on to a file (see Figure 25.16 for text files' logging properties), choose the New Log Time Period (a new file is created for each period), and choose the information to log in the Extended Properties pane.

FIGURE 25.16.

Logging properties for text files.

If you choose to log your WWW activity on SQL Server, create the logging table in a database, and create an ODBC DSN to point to that table. The script for creating the table is shown in Listing 25.55.

Listing 25.55. The *InternetLog* SQL Server table.

```
CREATE TABLE InternetLog(
   ClientHost varchar(255),
   UserName varchar(255),
   LogTime datetime,
   Service varchar(255),
   Machine varchar(255),
   ServerIP varchar(50),
   ProcessingTime int,
   BytesRecvd int,
   BytesSent int,
   ServiceStatus int,
   Win32Status int,
   Operation varchar(255),
   Target varchar(255),
   Parameters varchar(255))
```

Logging on SQL Server offers the possibility of querying the table easily and finding specific connections, while discarding classical operations to identify possible hackers.

Client Side

The client side could be a big problem. In fact, if you are developing for an intranet, you probably have the ability to deploy the Web browser of your choice, in addition to the hardware and software platforms of your company.

You don't know the client on the Internet. If you want a really universal application, use the browser-capable server components, to test the possibility of your client browser before sending code or objects. Of course, you have to code different types of pages to answer the different issues, but that's the price you pay to be universal.

Client-Side Scripting

The war is hard as far as client-side scripting goes. Microsoft and Netscape try to be compatible, but also try to impose their own standards. Choosing between JavaScript and VBScript is no matter of taste. Java is probably the best scripting choice for the Internet. However, going to VBScript is painless if you have a good knowledge of Visual Basic, but probably better for an intranet.

ActiveX or Not ActiveX?

It is the same for ActiveX components. Few browsers support ActiveX objects. A Java applet or a Perl script is sometimes better, but a lot of things can be done with simple HTML objects if you have to develop simple and functional Web database applications.

An object like the Active Data Connector (or Remote Data Services) is fine and simple to use. Whether you want to be fully compatible is your choice.

Adapting Applications for a Corporate Intranet

Designing a Web application for an intranet is slightly different than designing one for the Internet. In fact, the major difference relies on what information you want to publish for anonymous connections, and for an intranet-logged user. You need to secure the site in both cases.

Securing the Site

Probably the best thing to do is create a border between intranet and Internet pages; store files for the Internet site in a specific directory, and the files for the intranet site in another directory.

You can use NTFS file and directory permissions with IIS, as well as apply different authentication methods on each virtual directory. Furthermore, if you use ASP, you can use the `Request.ServerVariables` property to get the `LOGON_USER` or `REMOTE_ADDR` variables to test your client.

Security

If you want to protect your intranet site, enable an authentication method—take advantage of Windows NT security and Integrated security on your Web server.

Windows NT File Security

With Windows NT file and directory security, you can allow or forbid users to access directories and files. Windows NT security is simple and reliable. Use it.

Opening a Session

Enable an authentication method, either basic authentication or Windows NT challenge/response mode, if you need to ask your users to open a session before accessing the intranet site. The advantages of the second method is that the communication between the Web browser and the server is encrypted, but this strategy only works with Microsoft Internet Explorer. The advantage of the first one is that the password is sent as clear text on the network, and works with most of the Web browsers.

Coding the Application

Coding an Internet or an intranet application are equivalent, if your security of well designed. Furthermore, if you are used to Remote Data Objects or Data Access Objects, you can leverage your knowledge with ActiveX data objects.

If you try, you are on the edge of discovering a new way to code applications. Be ready to discover things you have to forget in two or three months. Everything goes fast with Internet technologies, so jump in. You won't regret it.

Summary

If you were familiar with classical client/server applications, you probably discovered a new world of opportunities. If you are familiar with Web technologies, you probably discovered the same, from another point of view.

You have seen the different possibilities for getting connected to SQL Server through the Web. You made the difference between push and pull models, and are aware of security issues.

You ran through Internet Database Connector and saw how easy it was to create dynamic HTML pages, knowing only HTML. You discovered the limits of IDC and jumped to Active Server Pages and ActiveX Data Objects.

Once in ADO, you discovered several things: scanning a table, updating records, and so on. With Remote Date Services, you discovered even more! Disconnected record sets are a reality. They are simple to program and powerful to use.

The Web Assistant released all the limits of the pull model, allowing automatic static Web pages updating.

At last, you compared Internet and intranet applications, and learned how to leverage IIS, Windows NT, and SQL Server to create great Web applications.

V

PART

Programming Real-World Implementations

Integrating SQL with Other Microsoft Products

CHAPTER

26

Somewhere deep within the walls of Microsoft, I am convinced there hangs a largish bronze plaque that reads "No Product Is An Island." True to this creed, SQL Server is designed to integrate with other Microsoft products to create highly customizable, hybrid solutions. One product that can give SQL Server data a GUI interface in no time flat is Microsoft Access.

Using Access as a Front End

Let's face it, ISQL/w is powerful and tons of fun at parties, but pretty it is not. When I am creating hardcore stored procedures in SQL Server, I couldn't be happier with my ISQL/w. But when the job calls for poking data into 35 lookup tables before lunch, I reach for Microsoft Access.

The GUI Advantage

Although Access does have its limitations, it also brings some outstanding strengths to the table… strengths that are quite endearing to the developer who is up to his or her ears in "Rapid Application Development." To a professional SQL Server developer, Access is the ticket to quick-and-dirty database maintenance solutions.

The quickest method to a GUI interface for SQL Server data is to link SQL tables into an Access database via ODBC. This is accomplished by creating a new database in Access (examples in this chapter will use Access 97). In Access, choosing File | Get External Data | Link Tables will bring up the Link dialog box shown in Figure 26.1.

FIGURE 26.1.

The Link dialog box.

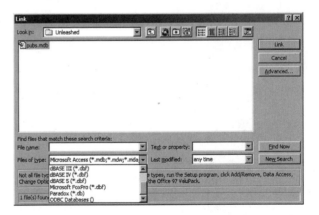

In the Files of Type drop-down list, selecting ODBC Databases from the bottom of the list immediately displays a Select Data Source dialog box. Selecting a SQL Server ODBC Data Source Name (DSN) from this dialog box will bring up a SQL Server Login dialog box.

> **TIP**
>
> If you are running ODBC 3.0 or later, the login prompt can be easily bypassed by creating a File DSN with a predefined user ID and password.

After logging in, Access will display the Link Tables dialog box. The example shown in Figure 26.2 shows the list of tables from the Pubs sample database. Notice that even though the dialog box is called Link Tables, views are included in the list as well.

FIGURE 26.2.

The Link Tables dialog box.

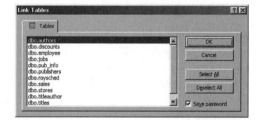

The list in the Link Tables dialog box is a simple multiselect. No need to use the Ctrl key when clicking here. The Select All button is handy for linking every available data object (tables or views) into the Access database at once. And the Save Password option will save the login/password so you will not be prompted when reopening this database. Access will begin linking the selected data objects when the OK button is clicked.

> **WARNING**
>
> Checking the Save Password option in the Link Tables dialog box will allow anyone who can open the Access database to view and modify the SQL Server data linked to it without entering a login and password. If you select this option when linking, you may wish to set a password on the Access database in Tools | Security to prevent unauthorized access.

During the linking process, if Access encounters a view or a table that was created without a primary key constraint, it will display the Select Unique Record Identifier dialog box, shown in Figure 26.3.

For our purposes, creating a unique identifier, or pseudo-index, is only necessary when linking to SQL views. Specifying a pseudo-index that includes all the unique columns within the view enables Access to create an updateable dynaset from the view. If a pseudo-index is not defined, Access can only create a snapshot of the view that will not allow record editing.

FIGURE 26.3.

The Select Unique Record Identifier dialog box.

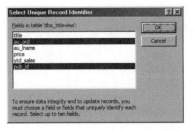

You can demonstrate this with the titleview view in the pubs database. Follow the steps we have covered to link the titleview view into an Access database. When the Select Unique Record Identifier dialog box appears, click the Cancel button. Double-click the link to the view in Table View and try to edit one of the records. Of course, you can't edit a record because what you are viewing is a read-only Snapshot recordset. Link the table again, but this time select the au_ord and pub_id fields in the Select Unique Record Identifier dialog box. Editing is now enabled and will update the tables on which the view is based.

> **NOTE**
>
> Linking a SQL Server table into Access does not expose the database structure to editing, but only the data within the tables. You cannot edit or delete (DROP) a table object through the Access interface. Deleting a linked table via the Edit | Delete menu only serves to remove the link to the table from the Access database—the table on SQL Server will remain intact.

Data Editing Made Easy

Once the SQL Server tables are linked into the Access database, the data in the table may be viewed, queried, and modified much like native Access table data. Probably the most readily useful characteristic of a linked table or view is the availability of the data in the default table view. This is the consummate quick-and-dirty method for editing SQL Server lookup tables. In the Database window, select the Tables tab to see the list of tables. Selecting a table and clicking the Open button will display the table's data in a datasheet. Typing data into the last row of the datasheet will cause an INSERT of the new data to be executed at the server once the focus leaves that row. Likewise, editing data on any row causes an UPDATE to be executed. Selecting a row by clicking the row's select button, located to its immediate left, and pressing the Delete key causes a DELETE of the row at the server.

Fast, Full-Featured Forms

For more sophisticated, permanent solutions, such as back-end data administration and maintenance, it may be necessary to organize the interface a bit more and provide some visual relationships of the data being maintained. Fortunately it's quite easy to design a simple interface suitable for data maintenance by using Access Forms. As an example, I've created the Employee Maintenance form shown in Figure 26.4.

FIGURE 26.4.

The Employee Maintenance form.

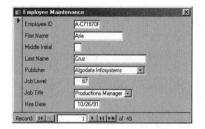

This example was created in about three minutes using the Form Wizard. It's a fully functional maintenance screen that saves changes automatically when a record loses the focus. Record navigation is provided automatically via the navigation buttons at the bottom of the form, as is record insertion. Deletion is made possible using the Record selector bar on the left margin of the form.

To get a feel for the process of creating a maintenance form like the Employee Maintenance form, go to the Forms view and click the New button. Select the Form Wizard from the list and the `dbo_employee` table from the drop-down list. Click OK and the Form Wizard is displayed. Click the Select All (>>) button to move all the fields from the `employee` table into the Selected Fields list. Click the Next button, which brings you to a choice of form layouts; I chose Columnar for the example. Click Next again and you'll be presented with a choice of fancy backgrounds. I went with the standard background so as not to offend any tender users. Click Finish to conclude your consultation with the Wizard. After the Wizard leaves, you will find yourself viewing the form that you've created.

At this point, the form is actively displaying records from the `employee` table. It doesn't look quite like the form I've created yet because I also added two drop-down lists to my example, one for the Publisher and one for the Job Title. To add these, switch to the Design View (View | Design View) and delete the `job_id` and `pub_id` fields from the form. Add two combo boxes to display rows from the `jobs` and `publishers` tables. The Combo Box Wizard will walk you through the simple process of associating the primary key IDs from the two tables with their respective members in the `employee` table.

The astounding speed with which a data maintenance solution can be concocted using a simple form like the Employee Maintenance form is great leverage when a project is under a time crunch. No time to create that Web site and a sophisticated data maintenance suite? Put your time and energy into creating a robust Web site and whip up the maintenance module in a day using Access as a front end.

Reporting

Another excellent feature of Access is its fine report engine. Linked views and tables can be transformed into reports rapidly, with Wizards guiding your every step if desired. Complex reports can be created, without resorting to the creation of server table `views`, by basing the reports on Access queries.

The main limitation of Access reports running against linked tables is restricted scalability. For this reason, Access reports are generally useful for limited administrative reporting and other special situations where the user base is characteristically small and manageable.

Programming SQL Mail

Do you ever wish SQL Server could just send you a page or an email to let you know what's going on? Okay, maybe it's not everyone's dream, but it is a reality. The SQL Mail features of SQL Server enable the sending and receiving of mail messages via the Windows NT mail application programming interface (MAPI). Additionally, a message received by SQL Mail can be processed as a query and return a result set to the sender. But before we can write our first query to SQL Mail, we have more than a little configuring to do.

Installing and Configuring SQL Mail

All the basic components that allow SQL Mail to function are present when Windows NT 4.0 Server (with the Windows Messaging components) and SQL Server 6.5 are installed. In addition to these installations, I strongly recommend installing the latest Service Packs for Windows NT, SQL Server, and the latest Exchange client (or Outlook 97, which phantom-installs Windows Messaging 5.0). Installing these updates should avert many of the known SQL Mail configuration problems.

WARNING

The Microsoft SQL Server 6.5 online documentation gives outdated instructions on how to configure SQL Server. These instructions apply to SQL Server 6.0 and NT 3.51 configurations of SQL Mail but are not reliable for configuring SQL Server 6.5 on NT 4.0.

SQL Server and the Windows Messaging client require careful configuration before SQL Mail will function properly. The major configuration steps are

- Configuring the MSSQLServer service
- Configuring an Exchange Client Profile for MSSQLServer
- Configuring SQL Mail to use the new profile

Integrating SQL with Other Microsoft Products

CHAPTER 26

681

26

INTEGRATING SQL
WITH MICROSOFT
PRODUCTS

Configure the MSSQLServer Service

In order for SQL Mail to function properly, the MSSQLServer service must be run under a user account. Create a new user who is a member of the Administrators and Users groups— SQLUser, for example. Then, in Control Panel | Services, configure the MSSQLServer service to start up as SQLUser. Be sure to stop and restart the service to effect the change.

Configure an Exchange Client Profile for MSSQLServer

This step assumes that a mail server, such as Exchange Server, Microsoft Mail, or an SMTP/ POP3 mail server, can be reached from the SQL Server computer. If no mail server is available, you can create a Microsoft Mail post office on the SQL Server computer.

> **NOTE**
>
> It is imperative that you follow the subsequent instructions while you're logged in as the user that MSSQLServer logs in as.

While logged in as the MSSQLServer user (SQLUser), add an Exchange client profile in Control Panel | Mail and Fax. The Microsoft Exchange Setup Wizard will assist in the creation of a new profile when the Add button is clicked.

> **TIP**
>
> When the Mail and Fax profile list is empty, the Exchange Setup Wizard steps you through the creation of a new profile without presenting the option of naming the profile. For the first profile created, the name may be "MS Exchange Settings" or "Windows Messaging Settings" depending on the version of the Exchange client you are running. You cannot rename this initial profile without editing the registry, but you can click the Copy button to make an instant copy and then rename the copy. I recommend giving the copied profile the same name as the login name (SQLUser, in our example).

After creating the profile that SQL Mail will use, make it the default for Windows Messaging by selecting it in the drop-down list, as shown in Figure 26.5. This allows additional options to be set in the inbox.

To set additional mail client options, start Windows Messaging, also known as Microsoft Exchange or the inbox. First, we want to remove the default setting that causes the saving of all sent messages. This can be done under Tools | Options | Send. Uncheck the option to save copies to the Sent Items folder.

We should also set the delivery intervals to be small so that messages to and from SQL Mail get processed as quickly as possible. The tricky thing is that Microsoft has scattered these settings hither and yon.

FIGURE 26.5.

The Windows Messaging Mail and Fax settings.

If you are using Microsoft Mail for SQL Mail delivery, go to the Tools | Options | Services tab. Bring up the properties for Microsoft Mail click the Delivery tab and change the mail check interval to 1 minute.

If an Internet mail transport is installed, the setting for the delivery interval is found on the Tools | Options | Internet E-mail tab.

Once the mail client profile is configured, test the new profile by sending yourself mail using the inbox program.

Configure SQL Mail to Use the New Profile

Now that the mail profile exists, SQL Server must be instructed to use it to access its mail. At the same time, we will configure SQL Mail to start when the SQL Executive starts. To perform these two tasks, run the SQL Setup program from the Microsoft SQL Server 6.5 program group. Continue through the dialog boxes until you reach the Microsoft SQL Server 6.5 - Options dialog box. Click the Set Server Options radio button and click Continue. Ensure that the Auto Start Mail Client checkbox is checked and click the Mail Login button. The Exchange Login Configuration dialog box appears, as shown in Figure 26.6. Enter the name of the mail profile that was created in the previous step. By the way, this dialog box offers a refreshingly accurate explanation of precisely what should be entered here.

FIGURE 26.6.

The Exchange Login Configuration dialog box.

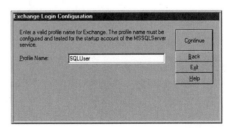

Once SQL Mail has been configured to use the correct mail profile, click the Change Options button on the Select Server Options dialog box to accept the changes. SQL Mail should now be properly configured and ready to run.

Up to this point, we have not configured SQL Mail to actually process incoming messages. Because I really want to help you get the most you can out of SQL Mail, I'll explain the workings of SQL Mail and allow you to craft your own solutions based on your newfound knowledge of it. Then I'll examine configuration possibilities for mail message processing.

The SQL Mail Engine

SQL Mail is powered by six extended stored procedures nestled in the small (67KB) SQLMAP60.DLL file. These extended stored procedures are listed in Table 26.1.

Table 26.1. SQL Mail extended stored procedures.

Procedure	Description
xp_startmail	Starts a SQL Mail session
xp_stopmail	Stops a SQL Mail session
xp_findnextmsg	Finds the next mail message
xp_readmail	Reads a mail message
xp_sendmail	Sends a mail message to a recipient list
xp_deletemail	Deletes a mail message by ID

In addition, there is a single system stored procedure, sp_processmail, that encapsulates the functionality of the SQL Mail extended stored procedures. Let's take a look at each procedure and extract all the value we can from each one.

xp_startmail

SQL Mail, which is a MAPI client, requires us to initialize a mail client session before inbox operations can be performed. If there is a session already running, xp_startmail will not start a new one. xp_startmail performs the same job as right-clicking the SQL Mail node in SQL Enterprise Manager and choosing Start from the context menu.

Previously, we configured SQL Server to auto-start the mail client when the MSSQLServer service starts, which, in effect, automatically performs the execution of this procedure.

The syntax for xp_startmail is as follows:

```
xp_startmail user, password
```

user

This parameter optionally specifies a mail client profile name to use. The profile must be in the list of profiles created for the user account under which the MSSQLServer service runs. If no user is specified, the mail session will be created using the profile that was specified in the Exchange Login Configuration dialog box (see Figure 26.6).

password

The `password` parameter specifies the password for the profile. If the `user` is specified and no password is specified, SQL Mail will attempt to log in with the password saved in the profile settings.

The following are all valid examples of calls to `xp_startmail`:

```
xp_startmail 'SQLUser', 'password'

xp_startmail 'SQLUser'

xp_startmail
```

xp_stopmail

`xp_stopmail`'s sole purpose in life is to stop the current MAPI client session. This procedure has no parameters.

xp_findnextmsg

True to his name, this fellow finds the next message in the inbox and, optionally, returns its message ID, a unique string that uniquely identifies the message. The syntax is

```
xp_findnextmsg msg_id [output], type, unread_only
```

msg_id

The `msg_id` parameter is an input parameter and an output parameter. On input `msg_id` specifies the current `msg_id`, and on output it specifies the next message ID. If `msg_id` is null on input (the default), the first message ID is returned. If `output` is not specified, the message ID is returned in a single-column, single-row record set with the column name `Message ID`.

type

Interpersonal Messages (IPM) and Interprocess Communications (IPC) are the two message classes that are supported under Microsoft Mail for PC Networks. However, IPC messages do not appear in the mail client inbox and can only be read by setting the `type` parameter to `IPC`. By default, this parameter is `IPM`.

unread_only

This `varchar` parameter specifies whether or not messages that have been read should be filtered from the list of returned messages. Valid values are `true` and `false`. The default value is `false` (finds read and unread messages).

`xp_findnextmessage` returns a `0` on success or `1` on failure.

The following example passes in a value for `msg_id` and requests the next message ID in the list of read and unread messages.

```
EXEC @status = xp_findnextrecord @msg_id = @msg_id OUTPUT,
                                 @unread_only = 'false'
```

Integrating SQL with Other Microsoft Products

CHAPTER 26

685

26

INTEGRATING SQL
WITH MICROSOFT
PRODUCTS

xp_readmail

This procedure uses the `msg_id` gained from `xp_findnextmsg` to retrieve information contained within the message. The syntax is

```
xp_readmail msg_id,
            type            [output],
            peek,
            suppress_attach,
            originator      [output],
            subject         [output],
            message         [output],
            recipients      [output],
            cc_list         [output],
            bcc_list        [output],
            date_received   [output],
            unread          [output],
            attachments     [output],
            skip_bytes      [output],
            msg_length      [output]
```

msg_id

Specifies the message ID to read. If a null `msg_id` is specified or no `msg_id` is specified, `xp_readmail` returns a record set containing the information from all messages.

> **NOTE**
>
> By design, running `xp_readmail` with a null `msg_id` will create temporary files for attachments. Specify `suppress_attach = 'true'` to keep SQL Mail from creating temporary files.

Also, by specifying a null `msg_id` and a `type`, you can retrieve specific messages, including those not found in the inbox.

For instance,

```
xp_readmail @type = 'IPC'
```

returns a record set containing pending interprocess communication messages with type names beginning with IPC.

type

This is an input/output parameter. On output, it returns the message class as described in the type parameter of `xp_findnextmsg`. On input, this must match the type of the message to be read. Specifying a `type` when `msg_id` is null returns a record set of messages of `type`.

This parameter is ignored if the input value is null (the default value).

peek

The `peek` parameter specifies if the message is to be read without changing the mail status to read. Valid values are `true` and `false`. The default value is `false` (mark the mail as read).

> **TIP**
>
> Although calling `xp_readmail` with no parameters is extremely handy for checking SQL Server's mail message queue, it will mark all the messages in SQL Server's inbox as read. The `sp_processmail` procedure does not process messages marked as read, so checking messages without specifying `@peek = 'true'` will essentially invalidate all the messages in the inbox. If you know you will use `xp_readmail` often, create a wrapper procedure for `xp_readmail` where `@peek = 'true'` by default to sidestep this behavior.

suppress_attach

When this parameter is `false`, `xp_readmail` creates temporary files to contain the message's attachments and returns the paths to these `attachments` in the attachments output parameter. Valid values are `true` and `false`, with the default value being `true` (do not create files for attachments).

originator

This is an output-only parameter that returns the mail address of the message sender. Use a variable defined as `varchar(255)` for this parameter.

subject

An output-only parameter that returns the subject line of the message. Use a variable defined as `varchar(255)` for this parameter.

message

An output-only parameter that returns the message body of the mail message. In the context of SQL Mail, this text is expected to be a `query` command. Use a variable defined as `varchar(255)` for this parameter. To read messages longer than 255 characters, use the `skip_bytes` and `msg_length` parameters (see Listing 26.1).

recipients

An output-only parameter that returns the complete list of recipients with individual addresses separated by a semicolon (;). Use a variable defined as `varchar(255)` for this parameter.

cc_list

An output-only parameter that returns the complete list of copied (cc:) recipients with individual addresses separated by a semicolon (;). Use a variable defined as `varchar(255)` for this parameter.

bcc_list

An output-only parameter that returns the complete list of blind copied (bcc:) recipients with individual addresses separated by a semicolon (;). Use a variable defined as `varchar(255)` for this parameter.

Integrating SQL with Other Microsoft Products

CHAPTER 26

687

26

INTEGRATING SQL
WITH MICROSOFT
PRODUCTS

date_received

This output-only parameter is actually the date and time that the mail message was sent (not the date received, as the name implies). Use a variable defined as varchar(255) for this parameter. This parameter is optional.

> **WARNING**
>
> Server-side code that performs a comparison between a message's date_received information and the local date and time will not work properly. The date_received is a remote timestamp created on a computer that is probably not synchronous with the server.

unread

This output-only parameter specifies that the message has not been previously read. Output values are true and false. Use a variable defined as varchar(5) for this parameter.

attachments

This output-only parameter returns a list of temporary paths to file attachments. The individual paths are separated by a semicolon (;). Use a variable defined as varchar(255) for this parameter.

skip_bytes

This is a numeric input/output parameter. On input, it specifies the number of bytes to skip before returning a value to the message parameter. After skipping the designated number of bytes, the lesser of 255 bytes or the remainder of the message is returned in the message parameter. This makes the retrieval of messages larger than 255 possible, as demonstrated in Listing 26.1.

On output, skip_bytes will return with the byte location of the next starting point within the message. Use a variable defined as INT for this parameter.

msg_length

This output-only parameter returns the total length of the message body. Used in conjunction with skip_bytes, it is possible to retrieve messages longer than 255 bytes. An example of how to do this is shown in Listing 26.1. Use a variable defined as INT for this parameter.

Listing 26.1. Read messages greater than 255 bytes.

```
DECLARE @msg_id      VARCHAR(255)
DECLARE @message     VARCHAR(255)
DECLARE @skip_bytes  SMALLINT
DECLARE @msg_length  SMALLINT
DECLARE @status      INT

SET NOCOUNT ON
```

continues

Listing 26.1. continued

```
/* loop through all messages */
SELECT @status = 0
WHILE (@status = 0) BEGIN

    /* get next message id */
    EXECUTE @status = master..xp_findnextmsg
                @msg_id       = @msg_id  OUTPUT,
                @unread_only  = 'false'

    IF (@msg_id IS null) BREAK

    /* retrieve complete message body in 255 byte chunks */
    SELECT @skip_bytes = 0
    WHILE (1 = 1) BEGIN

        EXECUTE @status = master..xp_readmail
                    @msg_id      = @msg_id,
                    @message     = @message    OUTPUT,
                    @skip_bytes  = @skip_bytes OUTPUT,
                    @msg_length  = @msg_length OUTPUT

        IF (@status != 0) BREAK


        SELECT 'msg_id'   = @msg_id,
               'msg_part' = @message


        IF @skip_bytes = @msg_length BREAK

    END

END
```

xp_sendmail

The xp_sendmail procedure performs much of the magic of SQL Mail. That is, it not only sends mail, but it communicates with SQL Server to run a query and obtain the results to be forwarded to the mail recipient. The syntax of xp_sendmail is

```
xp_sendmail recipients,
            message,
            query,
            attachments,
            copy_recipients,
            blind_copy_recipients,
            subject,
            type,
            attach_results,
            no_output,
            no_header,
            width,
            separator,
            echo_error,
```

Integrating SQL with Other Microsoft Products

CHAPTER **26**

689

26

INTEGRATING SQL
WITH MICROSOFT
PRODUCTS

```
set_user,
dbuse
```

recipients

A list of email addresses, separated by semicolons (;), that will receive this mail message.

message

Contains the body (text) of the message to be sent.

query

A SQL Server query to be processed and the results sent with this mailing. The query results will be appended to the message text or attached as a file depending on the value of the attach_results parameter.

attachments

A list of paths to files to send as with this mail message. The individual paths are separated by a semicolon (;). Use a variable defined as varchar(255) for this parameter.

copy_recipients

A list of email addresses, separated by semicolons (;), that will receive a copy (cc:) of this mail message.

blind_copy_recipients

A list of email addresses, separated by semicolons (;), that will receive a blind copy (bcc:) of this mail message.

subject

Specifies a subject line for the mail message. If no subject is supplied, "SQL Server Message" is used as the default.

type

Specifies the message class type for the message. Interpersonal Messages (IPM) and Interprocess Communications (IPC) are the two message classes that are supported under Microsoft Mail for PC Networks. However, IPC messages do not appear in mail client inbox and can only be read by setting the type parameter to IPC. By default, this parameter is IPM.Note.

attach_results

Specifies that results from the query should be returned as an attachment. Valid values are true and false. The default is false (results are returned appended to the message body). If attach_results is true and attachments is not null, the first filename in attachments is used for the results file name. If attach_results is true and attachments is null, a file name of the format SQLnn.TXT is generated.

no_output

Specifies that no output message is to be sent to the client when executing this procedure. Valid values are true and false. The default value is false (output messages will be sent to the client).

no_header

Specifies that no header should be returned on the result set from the `query`. Valid values are `true` and `false`. The default value is `false` (headers are returned).

Use this when returning results sets that will be processed by another program (such as a spreadsheet).

width

Sets the character line width of the query results. The default line width is 80 characters. The value must be 10 or greater.

You can set this parameter to a large width for queries that return long output rows. For example:

```
xp_sendmail @recipients     = 'johndoe',
            @query          = 'select * from pubs.dbo.authors',
            @attach_results = 'true',
            @attachments    = 'results.txt',
            @width          = 512
```

This returns a nicely formatted attachment named `results.txt` with rows that do not wrap lines.

separator

Specifies the character used to separate columns in the query result set. If no `separator` is specified, columns are of fixed widths and are padded with spaces. Use this parameter to create output that can be imported into spreadsheets or other databases.

echo_error

Specifies that the count of rows and any server messages or DBLibrary errors that occur while executing the `query` be appended to the mail message body rather than writing them to the error log.

> **NOTE**
>
> If echo_error is true, xp_sendmail will always return a status of 0 if the mail message was delivered, even if errors occurred during query processing.

set_user

Specifies the security context to run the `query` under. This parameter is `guest` by default.

dbuse

Specifies the database context for running the `query`. When not specified, this is set to the user's default database.

xp_deletemail

Deletes a mail message by its message ID. Its syntax is

```
xp_deletemail msg_id
```

msg_id

Specifies the ID of an inbox message to be deleted.

Putting It All Together—sp_processmail

Now that you are familiar with the SQL Mail engine, I would like to show you one way of putting them all together into a useful package—the sp_processmail system stored procedure. I say "one way" because sp_processmail is, by all accounts, a no-frills direct flight to getting the job done. There are no provisions for fancy security and plenty of trip mines to detonate if you're not aware of them. I'll help you start designing some of the missing features and touch off the trip mines without losing your foot.

sp_processmail Query Syntax

First, allow me to present the procedure syntax:

```
sp_processmail subject,
               filetype,
               separator,
               set_user,
                  dbuse
```

subject

Specifies a subject line `filter` for processing mail queries. If a `subject` is specified, only mail messages received with this subject will be processed as queries. By default, all messages are processed as queries.

filetype

Specifies a file extension for the query results file attachment. If no `filetype` is specified, TXT is used by default. Contrary to the parameter name, the output format is unaffected by this parameter.

separator

Specifies the character used to separate columns in the query result set. If no `separator` is specified, columns are tab-delimited. Use this parameter to create output that can be imported into spreadsheets or other databases. For example,

```
sp_processmail @filetype = 'CSV', @separator = ','
```

processes pending messages in SQL Server's inbox, returning query results in an attached, comma-delimited file suitable for import into Microsoft Excel or Access.

set_user

Specifies the security context to run the query under. This parameter is `guest` by default.

dbuse

Specifies the database context for running the query. When not specified, this is set to the user's default database.

SQL Server Mail Processing Scheduling

Because sp_processmail will process queries we send to it, it would be easy enough to use an email program to send a query command and have it executed. SQL Mail will process the query as the guest user and return the results to the account that originated the message, copying anyone whom we include on the cc: line of the original message. Of course, sp_processmail needs to be scheduled to run before any of this can take place.

If you do not want sp_processmail to look for incoming mail and process it, this step is optional. However, if you would like to take advantage of SQL Mail's ability to run queries that are mailed to it, scheduling the processing of incoming mail is necessary.

I've laid out the inner workings of the SQL Mail engine for you to consider. You may have already been pondering some of the possibilities that SQL Mail opens up. I'll guide you through one last official configuration step of SQL Mail—mail process scheduling—before we begin to gently nudge the envelope.

To use SQL Enterprise Manager to schedule sp_processmail, navigate to Server|Scheduled Tasks or right-click on the SQL Executive node beneath the appropriate server and choose Manage Scheduled Tasks. Click the New Task button, which is the leftmost button on the toolbar. Give the task an appropriate name, designate the command to be executed as sp_processmail, and click the Add button. The Task Schedule dialog box will appear.

For the quickest response when sending email commands to SQL Mail, you will probably want to schedule mail processing to occur once every minute. Figure 26.7 is an example of the Task Schedule dialog box configured for the task to run at the top of each minute.

FIGURE 26.7.

*The Task Schedule
dialog box.*

> **NOTE**
>
> Round-trip processing of an email query command sent from a remote machine will almost certainly take more than one minute to complete. The processing of pending messages by SQL Server will take place once each minute. However, query processing time, Microsoft Exchange client scheduling of delivery, and transport time all add up. The average round trip may take two minutes or more... an important fact to remember when you're designing a program that interacts with SQL Mail.

Once the task is scheduled, you can check the history of task executions by right-clicking on the item in the task list and choosing History from the context menu.

SQL Mail Security

The simplest way to secure SQL Mail against unauthorized access to data is to require a password for query execution to take place. A password can be included in the `subject` parameter of `sp_processmail` and, using the `set_user` parameter, can restrict access to as much or as little data as necessary. When a `subject` is specified, the query of an incoming mail message will only be processed if its subject matches the `subject` parameter of `sp_processmail`. For example, scheduling the commands in Listing 26.2 to execute every minute would enable the processing of mail messages with different access rights depending on their subject line passwords.

Listing 26.2. Subject line password processing with `sp_processmail`.

```
EXEC sp_processmail @subject = 'novera',  @set_user = 'norm',  @dbuse = 'pubs'
EXEC sp_processmail @subject = 'gopostal', @set_user = 'cliff', @dbuse = 'pubs'
```

Messages using this method of security should also utilize a form of message encryption suitable to the situation to prevent interception of the subject line.

Note that the `dbuse` parameter is used to set the database context of the query. It does not prevent the query from accessing other databases if the user's rights allow them to do so.

Cleaning Up Unprocessed Mail

If you use subject-line validation of queries exclusively, messages with invalid subject lines will pile up in SQL Server's inbox. There is no built-in mechanism for dealing with the stack of unprocessed mail that will accumulate in SQL Server's mailbox. You may toy with the idea of using the `date_received` output parameter to return a mail message after a certain expiration period. But the `date_received` is actually a date stamp created on the sending machine, which is probably not in sync with our server and might not even be in the same time zone.

One viable solution is to create a table that records all the mail message IDs currently in the inbox before processing. When processing is finished, delete all the messages that have IDs in our temp table. This is a simple solution that does not require tweaking code in sp_processmail. In fact, Listing 26.3 contains the complete code to build the system stored procedures and accompanying table.

Listing 26.3. The SQL Mail purging procedures.

```
/* Create a table in master to hold message ids */
USE master
GO

CREATE TABLE spt_inboxids (msg_id VARCHAR(64))
GO

CREATE UNIQUE CLUSTERED INDEX spt_inboxids
    ON spt_inboxids(msg_id)
GO


/* record all the message id's in the inbox */
CREATE PROC sp_recordinbox
AS

DECLARE @msg_id  VARCHAR(64)
DECLARE @status  INT

/* read all the message id's from the inbox into our table */
WHILE (1 = 1) BEGIN

    EXEC @status = master..xp_findnextmsg @msg_id = @msg_id OUTPUT

    IF (@status != 0) OR (@msg_id IS NULL) BREAK

    INSERT spt_inboxids VALUES (@msg_id)

END

GO


/* remove all recorded messages that remain after processing */

CREATE PROC sp_purgeinbox
AS

DECLARE @msg_id     VARCHAR(64)
DECLARE @originator VARCHAR(255)
DECLARE @message    VARCHAR(255)
DECLARE @msgtext    VARCHAR(255)
DECLARE @status     INT

/* Read all the message id's from the inbox and perform
   a look up in our table.  If it exists then it was
   unprocessable.  Return a message to the sender
   and delete the message.
*/
```

```
SELECT @status = 0
WHILE (@status = 0) BEGIN

    EXEC @status = master..xp_findnextmsg @msg_id = @msg_id OUTPUT


    /* Loop exit */
    IF (@status != 0) OR (@msg_id IS NULL) BREAK


    IF EXISTS(SELECT @msg_id
              FROM    master..spt_inboxids
              WHERE   msg_id = @msg_id)
    BEGIN
        /* get the originator's address from the message */
        EXEC @status = master..xp_readmail
              @msg_id     = @msg_id,
              @originator = @originator OUTPUT,
              @message    = @message    OUTPUT

        IF (@status != 0) OR (@msg_id IS NULL) BREAK


        /* delete the message from the inbox */
        EXEC @status = master..xp_deletemail @msg_id

        IF (@status != 0) OR (@msg_id IS NULL) BREAK


        /* Alert the originator that the query was not processed. */
        SELECT @msgtext = 'Your query was refused at the server.' +
                      CHAR(13) + CHAR(10) + @message

        EXEC @status = master..xp_sendmail
              @recipients = @originator,
              @message    = @msgtext
    END


END


/* Wipe the table if success */
IF (@status = 0) BEGIN
    TRUNCATE TABLE master..spt_inboxids
    RETURN 0
END ELSE
    RETURN 1


GO
```

Now it's a simple matter of scheduling the following commands to execute once each minute. The following is an example of mail processing commands that could be entered into SQL Enterprise Manager's task scheduler:

Listing 26.4. Sample SQL Mail purging commands for the scheduler.

```
EXEC sp_recordinbox
EXEC sp_processmail @subject = 'novera',   @set_user = 'norm',  @dbuse = 'pubs'
EXEC sp_processmail @subject = 'gopostal', @set_user = 'cliff', @dbuse = 'pubs'
EXEC sp_purgeinbox
```

The net result is any mail messages with subjects "novera" or "gopostal" will get their queries processed, and any other messages will return an email to their originator explaining that their query was refused. Additionally, all mail will be deleted after processing.

Alert—You've Got Mail

Now that you have SQL Mail configured and trading messages with you, there is another mode of server communication that is available to you—email and pager notification of alert messages. Admittedly, there is not a big need for customization of these facilities via programming, so I won't bog you down with the proper syntax of sp_addalert and the like. However, it's a short step to take advantage of this powerful facility once you have SQL Mail properly configured. Alert notification parameters can be suitably administrated from the SQL Enterprise Manager (SQL-EM). And the first order of business when configuring SQL Server to notify someone when trouble is afoot is to define "trouble."

Alerts Defined

What exactly is an alert anyway? Actually, that's for you to define. Alerts are configured to occur when an SQL Server exception that you define takes place. And you define alerts in SQL-EM's Manage Alerts and Operators dialog box, which is available by navigating to Server | Alerts. A sample of this dialog box is shown in Figure 26.8.

FIGURE 26.8.

The Manage Alerts and Operators dialog box.

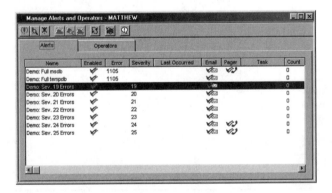

Of interest to us here is the column denoting email and pager notifications. Alerts with the email or pager column checked are covered by one or more operators and will dispatch a message if the alert occurs.

Integrating SQL with Other Microsoft Products

CHAPTER 26

697

26

INTEGRATING SQL
WITH MICROSOFT
PRODUCTS

Alert Messaging

The recipient of an alert message is the trusty operator. In the SQL-EM, the list of operators is managed under Server|Alerts/Operators in the Manage Alerts and Operators dialog box. Selecting the Operators tab in this dialog box displays a rather plain list of configured operators and their email contact information. Clicking the New Operator button displays a more interesting dialog box, Edit Operator. This dialog box, shown in Figure 26.9, is where the routing of alert messages is defined.

FIGURE 26.9.

The Edit Operator dialog box.

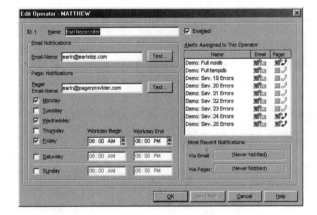

Despite its busy appearance, it is self-explanatory. Give the operator a name, define his email address, define a pager address and pager duty hours (if applicable), and check off the alert messages that he should receive while defining their delivery method. The Help button is sheer overkill here.

Once all the operators have been defined, click on the Alert Engine Options button to bring up the Alert Engine Options dialog box. Here you can designate a fail-safe operator that will receive notification of an alert if SQL Mail is unable to deliver the alert message. This situation could arise due to an invalid or unreachable pager or email address or a gap in pager coverage at the time the alert occurred. A message sent to the fail-safe operator will contain text indicating that it was sent as a fail-safe message.

On the Pager tab of the Alert Engine dialog box, any special formatting required by a page service can be entered.

> **NOTE**
>
> Notice that the pager address is simply an email address. Many paging service providers now have Internet page addresses. If you are using a provider with an Internet pager address, you will need to configure the Exchange client for Internet mail access from SQL Mail.

Using SQL Server with Internet Explorer

Remember the olden days (6 months or so ago, which is a long time in Microsoft years), when creating a multiuser application meant deciding between a two-tier or n-tier architecture? Well, welcome to today, my friend, because a new architecture is heading straight into the mainstream… intranet architecture.

Today's choices for deploying your latest enterprisewide intranet application using Microsoft technologies are something along these lines:

- Server-side data access via Active Server Pages/ADO
- Client-side data access via Active Script/ADO
- Client-side data access via ActiveX Documents
- Any combination of the above

Server-Side Data Access

You've already reviewed the possibilities of Active Server Pages and ADO in Chapter 25, "SQL Server on Internet/Intranet Systems." The strengths of this architecture revolve around the highly controllable environment created by centrally locating the code base. Here we have virtually no custom deployment issues to worry about, and we can make changes in functionality immediately available to everyone. And because we can place our Internet Information Server next to our SQL Server, data access is controllably fast.

The main tradeoff here is the one-way, two-dimensional interface. HTML is no Visual Basic, no matter how much Active Script you use. The limited interaction between client and server restricts any application we create to a send-a-page/receive-a-page paradigm. Internet Explorer 4.0 has made some strides in this area through Dynamic HTML and Client Pull technologies, however, the interface still does not offer all the simple control that developers have come to know and love—and expect.

Client-Side Data Access Via Active Script/ADO

To break out of the send-a-page/receive-a-page routine, we could develop our application with the data access code on the client machine. Accessing our data from the client allows our application to leverage client-side Active Script to provide a more interactive interface. This approach maintains our centrally maintained code base and the immediate deployment benefits.

Access to SQL Server data, or any other data server for that matter, is accomplished using ADO, precisely the same methods as those used for server-side data access. We'll need to install ODBC 3.0 on our client machines in order to use the DSNless connections that allow us to keep our code centrally located. Also, security may now become an issue because login/password information, as well as the query calls to the server, must now originate from the client rather than being hidden safely on the server.

In most environments, the security concern rising from client-side access of data will be negligible. Where it is an issue, data access can be encapsulated into an ActiveX DLL where measures can be taken to hide the sensitive or proprietary information.

However, we are still left with a severely limited interface. Happily, the savvy Visual Basic programmer and the ambitious Visual C++ programmer have yet another alternative... ActiveX Documents.

Client-Side Data Access Via ActiveX Documents

ActiveX documents are somewhat like ActiveX controls in that they are embedded within Internet Explorer. However, they allow the programmer to develop an interface using multiple forms in a single language that is much more familiar than coding piecemeal in HTML, Active Script (VBScript or JavaScript), and Visual Basic or Visual C++ for ActiveX controls. ActiveX documents allow the developer to create a robust interface while preserving all the benefits of the centralized code base. Deployment is just as painless as any of the other architectures.

The Combination Intranet

In the real world, different problems call for different solutions. None of the architectures mentioned here is "the best." In fact, the best approach is to pick and choose among them all, using suitable technologies to produce suitable solutions. The important thing is that each of these architectures can peacefully and synergistically coexist with the others.

Summary

In the course of this chapter, I've shown you how to take advantage of the interoperability of a few Microsoft products to extend the usefulness of SQL Server.

Microsoft Access offers a quick and robust interface to SQL Server data through its default table view and customizable forms. It also provides a simple reporting tool that can be useful for ad hoc reporting. SQL Mail, a feature of SQL Server, allows us to send and receive mail messages with SQL Server. Once it is properly configured, it can be used in a variety of situations, such as to obtain remote server reporting and server alert messaging.

Microsoft Internet Explorer offers a new paradigm for building and deploying client/server applications. By placing the data server next to the intranet server (such as Microsoft Internet Information Server on an isolated network segment with SQL Server), an application client can expect increased data performance. Using Internet Explorer in conjunction with ActiveX technology gives us the ability to create applications with the full-featured interfaces that users have come to expect from enterprise applications.

Programming a Line-of-Business Solution

IN THIS CHAPTER

SQL Server offers an excellent solution for handling the needs of a specific line of business. In most cases, standard or even custom packages require modification to run in any business environment. For example, while banking may be considered standardized, there are many facets of banking that can be handled differently by each company, and from personal experience, usually are. This chapter will walk you through the steps needed to produce a successful business solution.

Designing a Programming Solution

Currently, there are several methodologies employed to program a solution to a specific line of business needs, such as the Andersen or IBM methodologies. The following steps seem to provide for an optimized solution for programming SQL Server to accomplish the tasks at hand.

- Define the primary business objective.
- Understand the business.
- Define the requirements.
- Normalize the data.
- Determine the tools required.
- Create a prototype.
- Allow users to test the prototype.
- Complete the application.
- Document the system.
- Train the employees.
- Monitor the application.

This chapter will walk through the steps, using the example of an actual business utilizing SQL Server.

Define the Business Objective

While the company usually provides this, you may need to help in defining the true business objective. Some general objectives include:

- Gain market share through product differentiation
- Utilize technology to achieve growth
- Improve workflow with technology
- Gain market share through acquisitions

While these general objectives may seem mundane or too vague, I have provided examples of SQL Server solutions.

An example of the first objective in the list is where SQL Server was used as a data warehouse, to sort through data providing the market segmentation so businesses knew how to differentiate their products. Several companies have used technology to reduce work. Imagine if no computers were available, and you had to use people to handle the credit card transactions at Christmas!

The third objective was met by using SQL Server as an imaging solution for legal documents. The legal documents had specific data filled in the forms. There is plenty of OCR software that also recognizes handwriting. The certificates were scanned, the form data was saved as ASCII fields in SQL Server, and the path to the graphical image was saved in a field for access using any GIF viewer or Web browser. Implementation of IIS 4.0 would have been ideal to access the data from SQL Server using Internet Explorer, Netscape Navigator, or any other browser, but the company had no plans for such an investment.

The example you concentrate on in this chapter is a solution for an insurance company. Their goal was the last objective, to increase market share through acquisitions of similar commercial insurance businesses. This integration requires two parts: merging direct insurance premium and claims, and integrating reinsurance. Direct insurance consists of the typical policies that a commercial business or a typical person would purchase such as personal and commercial property protection, auto insurance, workman's compensations, and so on. Most insurance companies have decent systems in place to handle the direct portion of the business.

Reinsurance, however, is a different matter. Reinsurance is basically insurance for insurance companies. Imagine insuring the space shuttle for four billion dollars. When the Challenger exploded in 1986, if only one company had insured the space shuttle, the company would now be out of business. Reinsurance allows the spread of risk, by giving each participant a share of the premium dollars, and if losses occur, a share of the losses.

What is amazing is that almost none of the major insurance companies have a truly integrated reinsurance system in place, particularly when you consider that effectively using reinsurance improves the bottom line of a company. These companies may use separate databases, spreadsheets, and yes, even ledger sheets! Why is reinsurance so difficult to add to a direct premium and loss database? Reinsurance can require several complicated calculations. However, there should be no excuse for integrating insurance with reinsurance. Since the business objective requires growth through acquisitions, reinsurance plays more of an important role to reduce the risks. SQL Server can be applied very effectively to this role, to provide an interface between the direct premium and loss systems to the accounts payable and accounts receivable portion of the reinsurance system, by acting as a calculation engine. Now that the business objective and scope have been defined, you can start to understand the industry.

Understand the Business

Once the business objectives have been defined, the next logical step is to learn the business. Unfortunately, this step—one of the most important—is often ignored. Understanding the business means not only understanding how the industry works, but also how the company applies the industry standards to its business. You should become familiar with the terminology both internal to the company and external to the industry. In addition, you should try to meet with as many people as possible who understand the nature of the business, from sales, to accounting, to technical. Not truly learning the business will most likely result in:

■ Creating a product that follows the requirements provided, but is not an optimal solution

■ Problems with workflow and integration

■ Rewriting the database because functionality is not complete

Several examples deal with an insurance company that was growing through acquisitions. While the industry terminology was used, this company's interpretation of the terminology, and the application of the terminology, was different from several other insurance companies. Originally, the company required the production of a statistics file for reinsurance. This file was provided but, based on an understanding of the industry, it was appropriate to question how it was going to process reinsurance once the merger was finalized.

It turns out that the company was going to process reinsurance manually, similar to other acquisitions. However, the book of business was so large that it would have to hire almost an entire wing of people just to handle the additional work manually. In addition, anytime you process something manually, the likelihood of mistakes increases dramatically. There is a product using SQL Server that can accommodate the company's needs by mechanizing the entire process without adding to the current staff's workload.

From this example, you can see that the original solution was not optimal, and the final solution required extensive rework. The rework was required because the new process had little in common with the statistical file originally requested. Also, the original process would have hampered workflow because the department's workload would have increased dramatically. By applying business knowledge and industry standard practices, you can make yourself invaluable to any company. While it may take extra hours to learn and define requirements, it will result in shorter development time, an increase in productivity, and customer satisfaction.

Define the Requirements

Once you have a solid grasp of the industry and the business objective, it is much easier to define the requirements. Since end users often do not fully understand technology, you can apply your business and technical knowledge to help them meet their business objective. This phase should be the longest, and it can be the most challenging. You may encounter either of the following scenarios.

■ Management will have asked their internal people for requirements and present those to you.

■ You interface to management and the actual end user.

The second scenario is the best scenario, because these are the people who have full knowledge of the business and will use the system. Unfortunately, the first scenario is more common, which often will result in a system redesign before the project is successfully complete. When you review the requirements, you should ensure the following questions are answered.

- What inputs are necessary to obtain the required outputs?
- What systems may need to be integrated or interfaced to extract the necessary inputs?
- What internal processing is required to change the inputs to the desired outputs?
- What calculations need to be performed on the data?
- Which systems are required to extract additional data?
- What are the expected outputs?
- What systems may need to be interfaced to the expected outputs?
- What format is the output data required in, and, if necessary, how can the input data be converted to the output format required?

> **TIP**
>
> Before you begin the requirements phase, it is extremely important to see the "big picture." This means to see how people perform their job in today's environment. You should also see the systems with which you will interact, understand the flow of data from one system to the next, and understand how this flow will be integrated into your project.

In the example of the insurance companies' reinsurance system, moving to the integrated and automated system instead of the manual one had a big impact on the project. The change in requirements midway into the project meant significant work had to be redone, putting the project behind schedule. This example shows the importance of spending time investigating the requirements of the project up front, rather than rushing ahead with the implementation.

Normalize the Data

Once you have all of the project requirements and know the data flow—including calculations, conversions, and so on—you can start to normalize the data. Normalizing the data is a way to store the data to reduce redundancy of stored data and to make for faster retrieval and storage of information. For instance, in an order entry system, you would not want to enter the complete customer information for every line item in the order. But you'd rather use a customer number for the entire order that references back to the customer's information.

Determine the Tools Required

Once you have the complete flow of data, the tables normalized, and understand the user requirements, you can select the tools to create the finished product. First, take an inventory of available tools. You may have everything you need in-house. Most typical components required are:

- The database package
- A front-end package for clients to access the database on the server
- A method to convert character sets from EBCDIC to ASCII
- Sufficient network bandwidth
- Tools to move data from one network or system to another network or system

The Database Package

Most mid-size to large companies will already have some database package in-house. The common packages include IMS, DB/2, Oracle, Sybase, SQL Server, or Access. Many businesses will already have the Microsoft BackOffice suite, which contains SQL Server. Using SQL Server over a mainframe is becoming more popular to remove applications that are storage intensive, but do not require the horsepower of the mainframe. These applications are typically payroll, applications to solve a business problem, internal phone book/employee list, and so on. Small businesses can take advantage of SQL Server as a total solution, including using SQL Server as their main accounting database. Several third-party solutions offer accounting packages written especially for SQL Server.

In the reinsurance example, the company had DB/2, Oracle, SQL Server, Dataease, and Access. Oracle was being used for a specific third-party package. IMS was primarily mainframe, with too few storage resources or programmers to solve the business problem at hand. SQL Server was a great solution in this environment because the business was moving toward SQL Server as its enterprise database to integrate with the various mainframe databases.

Front-End Package for Clients to Access the Database on the Server

In most cases, you will need employees to access the database. While they could all use I/SQL, this is not always the best solution. Your choices will typically include Visual Basic, Delphi, PowerBuilder, Java with Web Browser, or Visual C++. By building a front-end screen, your design concepts should include the following:

- Minimizing the amount of data entry
- Minimizing data-entry mistakes
- Decreasing query times
- Allowing for flexible query capabilities

Always attempt to minimize data entry whenever possible. Allowing users to select from list or combo boxes, rather than using text boxes, is a good way to ensure data uniformity. By limiting the amount of data entry required, you improve on efficiency and decrease the chance for error.

Imagine the possibilities when reporting someone with a poor payment history to a credit bureau. If a separate data-entry system was used, and the social security number was off just by one digit, you would be destroying someone else's credit. Unfortunately, experience with major credit bureaus shows that this is more fact than fiction.

Another major design component is to decrease query times. It would be terrible if a customer service representative queries a customer's account and it takes over 30 seconds to display on the screen. This scenario has been seen in a customer service application shared by major banks. Due to slow network bandwidth and poor design, it took twenty minutes to transmit the screens to access the Sybase database, and then sometimes up to five minutes to access a customer's account. Instead of downloading the screens to the customer service PCs, the company should have localized the data entry and search screens, passing updates to the screen when needed.

Finally, you should add flexible query capabilities to allow for searching on many fields. One major problem often encountered with an online banking system is the lack of search abilities. The system was made almost unworkable when the users were unable to use searching to trace transactions. A few extra search options in their interface would have made the difference between a satisfied customer and an unhappy one.

27

PROGRAMMING A
LINE-OF-BUSINESS
SOLUTION

> **WARNING**
>
> When adding flexible queries to your application, be sure to stay away from the freeform SQL dialog box that would allow people to write potentially damaging queries. Using a dialog box that allows select queries to be "built" by selecting fields from list boxes is much safer.

Often Visual Basic is a good choice, because of its enhanced 32-bit, multitasking capabilities and ease of use. Being a Microsoft product, it integrates seamlessly with SQL server. However, you can accomplish your tasks with any of the front-end options previously listed. Since you should use front-ends mostly for screen data entry and queries, you will not need the horsepower of Visual C++. Java is still in its infancy, but as faster real-time compilers are developed, it, too, might become a viable option. The reinsurance business solution does not need a front-end system because all data will always be fixed in the tables, and new data is selected and imported from the mainframe.

Method to Convert Character Sets from EBCDIC to ASCII

If you are integrating mainframe-based data to SQL server, you will need some method to convert from the EBCDIC character set to the ASCII character set. Chapter 18, "Legacy Databases: Conversion and Integration Issues," covers multiple methods for the conversion process in depth.

The best method would be to convert all binary and packed fields on the mainframe to character equivalents, and to place the sign to the left of the number on the mainframe. Almost all emulators will translate between the two-character sets, provided all data is character data. The reinsurance solution uses the mainframe emulator Rumba for character translation, and uses the mainframe to convert back and forth between binary and packed fields.

Sufficient Network Bandwidth

No matter how efficient the server and queries are, if there is insufficient network bandwidth the application will crawl. Make sure the network infrastructure is in place to support the application. Use LAN- and WAN-based packet analyzers and other tools to monitor network performance.

Tools to Move Data from One Network or System to Another

If you are using other data sources besides SQL Server or ODBC-compliant databases, you will need some method to transport files from network-to-network or system-to-system. Many public domain tools support FTP over TCP/IP. Other tools provided by Netware have support for moving files over IPX. While there are many choices, make sure you can obtain, or have in-house, the means to pass files. In the reinsurance example, a COBOL job creates the file, and then uses FTP to end the file through a firewall to the waiting server. The FTP program on the server waits for the transmission. Once the transmission occurs, it launches a batch file which then imports the data using BCP into SQL Server. The internal T-SQL code manipulates the data, and then uses BCP to export the data. The file is then sent back to the mainframe using FTP.

In summary, for the mechanization of the reinsurance program, the following tools were used.

- SQL Server
- FTP capabilities for mainframe to PC
- TCP/IP capabilities on the mainframe and PC
- Rumba for character translation

Create a Prototype

Once you have completed the analysis phase, you are ready to start the development cycle. In the prototype stage, you will need to do the following:

- Create the tables.
- Create the SQL and T-SQL code.
- Create the front-end screens.
- Run every possible variation of test data through the system and review for desired results. If possible, use actual data.
- Run a stress test with a lot of data to make sure you do not need a complete redesign to handle large data loads. If possible, stress test on the production network with several users accessing the application.
- Correct problems as they occur and fix the problems.

Once the initial prototype is ready, you can demonstrate the product to the end users.

Allow Users to Test the Prototype

There are many reasons for allowing the end user to test a prototype of the application. These include the following:

- Provide suggestions for improvement.
- Review output for errors.
- Make sure application performs all functions desired.
- Provide suggestions to reduce data-entry.

> **NOTE**
>
> When allowing users to test the prototype, make sure they stay focused on the application. What consistently seems to happen are gripes on the appearance of the front-end screens rather than the functionality and ease of use of the application. Simply providing a method that the end user can use to customize his or her own colors will save a lot of time. Believe it or not, these petty arguments do come up often!

Complete the Application

After the users have tested the prototype, make any changes necessary and repeat the process until you have a functional product that meets the business requirements. You can then go back and make the front-end screens more presentable.

> **TIP**
>
> At this point in the development cycle, it is easy to get into a continuous cycle of adding features, having user tests; the users want more features and the cycle begins again! Set deadlines for new feature requests and be realistic about what adds value to the product.
>
> Always consult more than one user; what one user loves, another will hate. The final product must be a balance that pleases everybody most of the time, not one person all of the time!

Document the System

Once the system is finalized, you will need to document it. This requires two sets of documentation, one for the end users and one for the technical users. The end-user documentation should take the user step-by-step through the application. All input and output should be reflected in the documentation. The technical documentation should include all SQL and T-SQL code, all tables, entity relationship diagrams, data flow diagrams, front-end screen code, and an overview of the process. Whenever any changes are made, make sure the documentation is always updated to reflect them.

Train the Employees

You will need to train the employees, using the documentation, and then train the technical users to handle the maintenance of the system. Time spent here with the users can make the difference between success and failure. If you teach them well, and the application is well designed, they will be able to work more effectively.

Monitor the Application

Once complete, ensure that the application continues to meet its objectives. Even after a successful test, often you may find that an interaction of unusual conditions will cause a bug to rear its ugly head! If this does happen, fix the code and update the relevant documentation. To give the application a longer life cycle, you can issue a new version with added features that were missed from the original version or take into account changes in the industry or its business rules.

Summary

When starting out on a new programming solution, always take time to thoroughly investigate the business—the requirements of the application. In doing this, you ensure that your final product meets its customers' expectations and will provide many years of useful service. Also, after spending many hours producing your solution, always take the extra time to document your work and to train users and support personnel.

Data Warehousing and Online Transaction Processing (OLTP)

Designing a database is certainly a difficult—and often poorly done—part of a global information system project. But it's more difficult to create a universal database that accepts long-running complex queries and quick small transactions. My purpose isn't to show you how to perform such a miracle, but just to give you the right directions to create a decision support system (DSS) database, based on a data warehouse, or an online transaction processing (OLTP) database.

The purpose of these databases is quite different, but the former is sometimes based on the latter: an OLTP application is used to take orders online (assume more than 10 inserts per second), whereas the last months records are used to draw charts and find trends.

This chapter has three major goals: to show you how to create a data warehouse and DSS database; to discuss the main issues concerning transaction systems and their creation with SQL Server; and to give you hints about creating these two types of applications on the same server or even the same database. Of course, it is important for you to be familiar with SQL Server, indexing and locking issues, and creating stored procedures and remote stored procedures. If these subjects are not yet clear to you, review the first part of this book. For those who are fine with these subjects, let's continue.

SQL Server as a Data Warehouse

As I was writing the outline of this chapter, I faced a major "chicken and egg"-like dilemma. I didn't know how to start, I changed my mind probably ten times just finding good reasons to start with so and so, but finding other good reasons five minutes later. So, I made a decision: let's do things like in real world.

This chapter will follow the same pattern as a real-world data warehouse. First I give you a broad definition and the main issues of a data warehouse. Then, you discover how to create a good warehouse, considering necessary software and hardware configuration. The main problems begin at this time: how will you fill you warehouse? We'll discover how to use a good fill-up strategy, mixing stored procedure, data importation, and replication. At last, you study the classical queries used on a data warehouse, and what you need to consider as far as indexes and locks are concerned. To finish with that section, you are reminded of some standard maintenance tasks you should do to maintain a good level of speed.

Essentials of a Data Warehouse

As its name implies, a *data warehouse* is a huge set of data stored in one place. Though the name appeared a few years ago, the concept is older. The main purpose of a data warehouse is to hold almost all the data of a company. From that point, the warehouse is a starting point to decision support systems (DSS).

Assume you have a data warehouse holding all the sales records for the past three years, along with the order amount, product name, the store's name and address, age of the customer, and city. With these simple data, it is possible to find trends and make decisions on the evolution of the sales. The tricky part is writing the right queries that obtain the answer as fast as possible.

The problem is to have a fast answer; the database should be well designed. And that is the main point of a data warehouse: being huge and fast. SQL Server has all the necessary features to create really nice warehouses no bigger than 1 Tb, but that should be sufficient to begin with. So let's create the warehouse.

Implementing a Data Warehouse

First of all, it is important to design your warehouse well. With an efficient database architecture, you can achieve really good performance. Some points seen in this section are not SQL Server specific, especially the ones about the normal forms, but I thought they would be worthwhile just to remind you of the virtue of denormalization. For those who are really familiar with these concepts of normal forms and denormalization, feel free to skip this small section.

Creating the Database

Among the differences between a DSS and an OLTP database is often size. A DSS database can really be huge (many Gigabytes), and cannot fit in memory even with the 3 affordable Gigabytes of SQL Server Enterprise Edition.

Nevertheless, a user querying that database should not wait hours to have the results. Otherwise, he will soon forget this invaluable tool, and all you efforts will be lost. It is important to offer your users good performance in term of throughput and speed. You should use good hardware. Take a look at the physical design issues.

Physical Design

When you think of creating your database, you have to first create the database devices. If you have only one disk, forget all the I/O improvement solutions: they involve at least two disks.

Of course, the transaction log isn't discussed here. It shouldn't be a major subject of concern in a data warehouse (except for the loading of data), but is discussed later in this chapter. In a standard warehouse, all the data is read-only; so there is no need to use the transaction log. The focus is on reading data from disk to cache.

SQL Server and Windows NT offer three I/O improvement solutions:

- RAID 0—Disk Stripe set
- RAID 5—Disk Stripe set with parity
- Segments

And SQL Server offers one automatic read I/O improvement: read ahead.

28

DW AND OLTP

The segments can be used to share I/O among different disks. The main problems with this are:

- You are not sure how to equally share the I/O.
- The segments probably won't be supported in the next SQL Server version.

If you consider the split scheme of Figure 28.1, it is possible to put the big tables in the User1 segment, or split indexes and tables in two different segments (for example, tables in the User1 segment and indexes in the Default segment).

FIGURE 28.1.

Splitting the database in different segments.

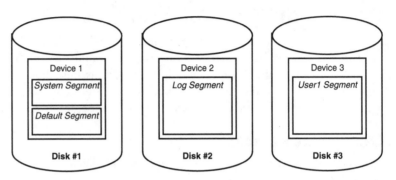

Here are the different steps, with the Transact-SQL syntax, needed to create and fill user segments:

1. Create the necessary devices and the database.

2. Create the new segment:

   ```
   sp_addsegment 'segment_name', 'device_name'
   ```

3. Drop the default and system segments (and the log segment, if your log has not been separated from the data) on the same device:

   ```
   sp_dropsegment 'default', 'device_name'
   sp_dropsegment 'system', 'device_name'
   ```

4. Create the tables/indexes on this new device, with the ON clause in the CREATE TABLE and CREATE INDEX statement.

WARNING

If you don't delete the system and default segment on your device, they compete for device space with your new segment, and you lose the benefit of using the segments.

Even if you think hard about your database segmentation, it will always be less efficient than a RAID solution. The only exception to that postulate occurs if you need to store archive data or binary large objects (BLOB) that are used infrequently.

Imagine that you have a 10,000-products table, and you have a picture of almost all your products. If you store these pictures along with your data, the table will be quite big, and you run the risk of fragmenting data or mixing binary information (pictures) and character/numeric information. It is more effective to split the table in two, with a one-to-one relationship enforced by a Foreign Key constraint, and then store the picture table on a separate disk, as shown in Figure 28.2.

FIGURE 28.2.

Splitting a table in two segments may increase the overall throughput.

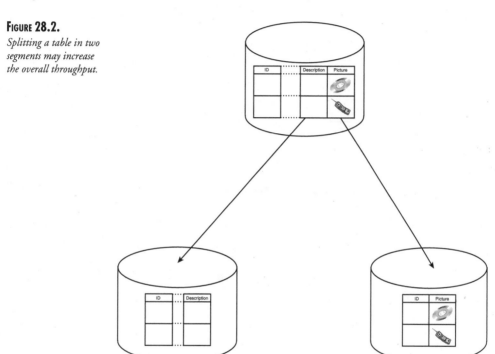

Concerning the disk organization in RAID, a hardware solution is always better than a software solution. But if you don't have a RAID disk controller, you can easily profit from the software RAID solutions of Windows NT.

With a RAID 0 or 5 array, like the one shown in Figure 28.3, the throughput is increased.

Furthermore, SQL Server uses read ahead. This means that when a query is issued, more threads are used to move the data from disk to memory, as shown in Figure 28.4.

FIGURE 28.3.
*A RAID array increases
the data output.*

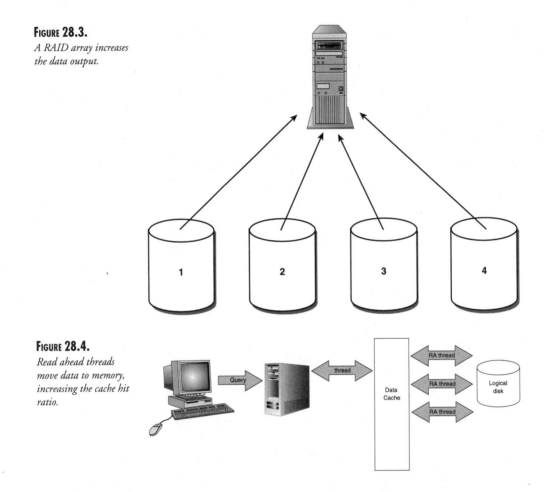

FIGURE 28.4.
*Read ahead threads
move data to memory,
increasing the cache hit
ratio.*

From a global perspective, the read ahead is a good thing, because as the main thread is calculating the result set, read ahead threads scrub data. Nevertheless, this particular feature can be enhanced with a good disk array and a good disk controller. Disk transfers are generally slower than memory transfers. But if you have a good I/O subsystem and an SMP machine, try to increase the RA Worker thread option.

This configuration parameter describes the number of read ahead threads. As a rule of thumb, multiply the number of processors by a number between three and five (see the ratio given Table 28.1), depending of the quality of your I/O subsystems. But remember to always monitor your modifications.

Table 28.1. Number of processors and number of RA worker threads.

# of processors	# of RA worker threads
1	3 to 5
2	6 to 10
3	9 to 15
4	12 to 20

> **NOTE**
>
> Read ahead offers other parameters, but your purpose isn't to describe all the insight of SQL Server read ahead. If you'd like to learn more about the subtleties of read ahead, pick up *SQL Server 6.5 Unleashed*, Sams Publishing, 1997.

It is important for you to consider the physical design of your database. The design can have a dramatic impact on the performance and transform a failure into success. As a quick summary, in order of importance, consider the following points before implementing your warehouse:

- Use a disk array, with a RAID 5 controller.
- Use a disk array, with software RAID 5.
- Use a disk array, with a RAID 0 controller.
- Use a disk array, with software RAID 0.
- Use segments.

> **TIP**
>
> As you are using Windows NT Server, the software solution is free (except for the disks). Consider using it before thinking of a segment solution.

After you have chosen a possible and affordable solution, go back to the conceptual design.

Normal Forms and Warehousing

I won't go into the normal forms discussion here; I assume you already know how to design your database in third normal form.

Instead I will focus on the benefit of denormalization. Data warehouses must be prepared for long-running complex queries. Normally, the more joins, the slower the query (this isn't always true, but I'll explain indexing the warehouse in the next section). So, be prepared to

28

DW AND OLTP

denormalize your data. This operation is particularly important if you intend to create datacubes (see "How to Scrub (Prepare) Data for Warehouses" later in this chapter).

For the moment, look at an example: You have been asked to create a data warehouse for a bank. You need information on customers and their accounts. Create the logical design shown in Figure 28.5.

FIGURE 28.5.

Logical design in third normal form.

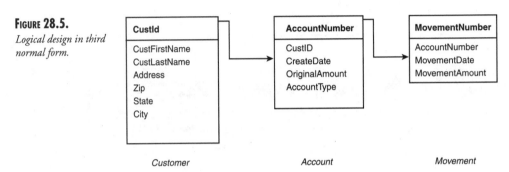

This bank has 100,000 customers, and each customer has an average of 2.5 accounts (so, 250,000 accounts) and an average of 1 movement a day per account (365×250,000 = 91,250,000 movements a year). With this figure, each join is a pain for input/output. Now, one of the main queries done on that system is calculating each account balance at the end of the year. The query to do that is shown in Listing 28.1.

Listing 28.1. Calculating the account balance with three tables.

```
SELECT C,CustID, C.CustLastName, A.AccountNumber,
       Balance = Sum(MovementAmount)
FROM Customer AS C JOIN
     (Account AS A ON C.CustID=A.CustID) JOIN
     (Movement AS M ON A.AccountNumber=M.AccountNumber)
GROUP BY C.CustID, A.AccountNumber
```

That query can really be long running, even if it is simple (in fact, it's made simpler here, because I don't take into account the initial amount of each account). If you are in a hurry, you'd better change your design. In fact, because the optimizer is using nested iteration, even if you have good indexes SQL Server will scan the account table 100,000 times—once for each customer—and scan the movement table (remember the number of lines…) 250,000 times—once for each account.

This query is a simple one! Some can be much more complex and long running. What about a really complex query, with ORDER BY, more tables, and more calculation? Now that you're thinking of it, maybe you should denormalize your database (see Figure 28.6).

FIGURE 28.6.
Denormalized logical design.

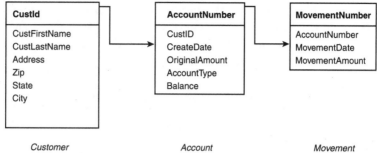

	Customer		Account		Movement

The new query is shown in Listing 28.2.

Listing 28.2. Calculating the account balance with two tables.

```
SELECT C,CustID, C.CustLastName, A.AccountNumber, Balance
FROM Customer AS C JOIN
     (Account AS A ON C.CustID=A.CustID)
ORDER BY C.CustID, A.AccountNumber
```

You don't have to calculate the balance for each account, because it has already been calculated and maintained up to date, either by a trigger or by weekly batches. (Maintaining a denormalized model is discussed further in "How to Scrub (Prepare) Data for Warehouses," later in this chapter.)

With such an approach, the amount of I/O is reduced and the query runs faster. You have what you wanted. The join is the feature to kill when you write a DSS query. Keep that rule in mind: lowering the number of joins can be painful, but almost always a win. Sometimes good indexes make an efficient work.

Row Width and I/O speed

Another area of concern is the number of records per page. Remember that SQL Server uses 2KB pages to store table data. One page can store 1 to 256 records. While you are working with a data warehouse, you should keep in mind that space management could be your enemy, or your ally.

Look at your balance account example. At the end of the year, you have 91,250,000 movements. If the movement table were created the way Listing 28.3 was, the row length is 24 bytes (4+4+8+8). A page can store 2,016 bytes, or 80 records (the offset table takes 1 byte per record at the end of the page). The movement table needs 1,140,625 pages (1.09GB).

Listing 28.3. Creating an optimistic movement table.

```
CREATE TABLE Movement
    (MovementNumber    Int NOT NULL IDENTITY(1,1),
     AccountNUmber     Int NOT NULL,
     MovementDate      Datetime NOT NULL,
     MovementAmount    Money NOT NULL)
```

If you create that table the way Listing 28.4 was created, the row length is 16 bytes (4+4+4+4). 118 records can be stored on a page, so the movement table needs 773,306 pages (756MB). You can see that changing two datatypes on a narrow table can have a dramatic impact on the physical storage (you spare more than 250MB).

Listing 28.4. Creating a pessimistic but compact movement table.

```
CREATE TABLE Movement
     (MovementNumber    Int NOT NULL IDENTITY(1,1),
      AccountNUmber     Int NOT NULL,
      MovementDate      SmallDatetime NOT NULL,
      MovementAmount    SmallMoney NOT NULL)
```

Of course, you can tell that physical disk is cheap. Buying a new 2GB disk is generally not a problem. But what about transferring 250MB from disk to RAM? Even if you have very quick disks, it can take few seconds. Spare it—the more space you spare, the quicker your queries, due to the reduction of I/O.

> **NOTE**
>
> Decreasing the row width increases the number of rows on a page and increases the number of duplicates on the same page, decreasing the I/O for a given value.

In calculating the number of pages, I did not take into account the index pages. If your query use indexes, remember that index pages need to be transferred into RAM to be used. So the economy should be greater.

Indexing the Database

Indexes play a major role in warehouses. Because your database is read-only, indexes don't disturb the record updates. So over-indexing the database isn't a problem.

But before creating a large number of indexes, you need to really understand their different types (if you don't feel comfortable with indexes, review Chapter 3, "Optimizing Queries"). I will give you a few hints on what columns need to be indexed in a data warehouse, and how to check the used indexes.

Clustered Indexes

The purpose of a warehouse is to store a huge amount of data. (If you think I've already said that, you're right, but I think this is something you should keep in mind at every instant.) Clustered indexes are your diamond: you can only have one on each table, so choose wisely.

Here are clustered index choices you should think twice about:

- Primary key
- Unique column searched frequently on a single value

On a DSS system, you'll probably have more than one index on each table. It's a good idea to choose other cases than the two listed previously for the clustered index.

The difference between a clustered and a nonclustered index on highly selective columns (few to no duplicates) is so tiny (generally 1 page), you should always choose a nonclustered index. The only exception to that rule is an ORDER BY or a GROUP BY clause.

If you need to sort your query on that column(s), a clustered index will be helpful (if it is chosen by the optimizer, instead of another strategy), because the data are already sorted. But you can use that on only one group of columns.

> **TIP**
>
> Remember covering indexes. They are what I call nonclustered clustered indexes: a query using only the columns defined in a nonclustered index (no other columns for the table) "cover" the index. The optimizer doesn't need to read the data pages; all the necessary data is on the index leaf level.

Now you've been told you about the bad choices, you get to hear about good ones:

- Column(s) used in range queries (BETWEEN...AND, >, <, >=, <=)
- Column(s) sorted or grouped
- Foreign key

For the first two, I don't think you have any problems understanding the reasons. For the third one, the reason is also obvious, if you have a one-to-many relationship. Remember your balance example? If you create a clustered index on the Movement.AccountNumber column, we are sure all the movement for a specific account will be on the same page, or on contiguous pages. That decreases the number of I/O (always the man to kill).

Nonclustered Indexes

From what you just learned concerning clustered indexes, you could imagine that choosing the nonclustered indexes is an easy task. Don't fool yourself. Deciding is always difficult.

Nevertheless, deciding for a nonclustered index is always easier than for a clustered index. But be careful, an index isn't always interesting. Assume you run a stored procedure, named find_cust_city, on your warehouse:

```
SELECT * FROM customer WHERE city = @strCityName
```

28

DW AND OLTP

If the variable `@strCityName` equals `"Shoshone"`, and if only 3 out of 100,000 customers live in Shoshone, CA, a nonclustered index on City can be useful because of the selectivity of the value. But if the variable equals `"Los Angeles"`, and 30% (30,000) of your customers live in Los Angeles, a table scan will be used instead of the index.

Everything depends on the selectivity of the data in the column. Nonclustered indexes are useful with a selectivity of less than 15% (that means the query can eliminate more than 85% of records). But with a parameter in a stored procedure, the selectivity isn't calculated, but read in the distribution page. In your "Shoshone versus Los Angeles" case, the selectivity of the table would have been too high to select the index, even in the case of `"Shoshone"`.

So when choosing a nonclustered index, monitor your creation. Use a range of different values and `DBCC SHOW_STATISTICS` to see whether your index is used or not.

Over-Indexing the Databases

As I said at the beginning of this section, you have a chance in a warehouse; you are not bothered by the updates.

> **WARNING**
>
> Don't read the preceding sentence too quickly and create indexes all over the table. First, you need to update your database from time to time—the more indexes, the longer it takes. Second, indexes consume physical storage—the more indexes, the more disks it uses.

Don't think, for the moment, of updating data—that time will come. Over-indexing a table can be a good thing, because the optimizer can choose among different indexes, and with more choices can take a better decision.

Remember that SQL Server uses only one index per table (except with certain OR queries). Having a lot of different indexes increases your chance of using an index.

It isn't uncommon to have more than ten indexes on a single table in a data warehouse. Nevertheless, always make sure your indexes are used.

> **NOTE**
>
> A lot of people are using tools like Business Objects or Microsoft Access to query data. The problem with this kind of tool is that you don't know the queries the users are going to write. Over-indexing the tables increases their chances to use indexes. But, it is better to know in advance what kind of query they write (sometimes, they run the same WHERE clause, or query the same cubes).

To finish, remember that column order is important in an index. Assume you created the following index:

```
CREATE INDEX ncLastFirst ON Customer(CustLastName, CustFirstName)
```

If you query the table with

```
SELECT * FROM Customer WHERE CustFirstName='John' AND CustLastName='Doe'
```

the `ncLastFirst` index will probably be used. Of course if you run the query

```
SELECT * FROM Customer WHERE CustFirstName='John'
```

the `ncLastFirst` index probably won't be used. Now if you had created this other index

```
CREATE INDEX ncFirstLast ON Customer(CustFirstName, CustLastName)
```

the second `SELECT` query could have used it. But the same for the first. It all depends on the selectivity. If you have 2% of 'John' and 10% of 'Doe,' when you are looking for John Doe, the `ncFirstLast` index is more selective than the `ncLastFirst` index.

This is another example of the selectivity of the index. So over-indexing the tables can have surprising consequences. But, when you are implementing your warehouse, always keep in mind that increasing the number of indexes increases the number of choices of the optimizer, and increase the chances you have to decrease the number of I/O.

How to Scrub (Prepare) Data for Warehouses

Creating the physical structure should be done prior to loading. SQL Server offers many ways to load data and constitute the huge warehouse you are expecting.

You can load data with one of these five methods:

- Bulk Copy Program
- `INSERT` and `INSERT...SELECT`
- Replication
- `CUBE` and `ROLLUP`
- Online Triggers and Batches

Each solution has its virtues, as detailed in the following sections.

Loading Data with bcp

Bcp is probably the first tool you use to load data from a heterogeneous source, either alone or in conjunction with SQL Transfer Manager. The only advantage to this solution is its speed.

> **TIP**
>
> If you intend to load data regularly with bcp, drop all the indexes first (don't forget primary key and unique constraints), load the data, and then re-create all the indexes (beginning with the clustered index). Just to give you an idea of the speed gain: loading 1 million records in a table with three indexes (on a height-processor parallel sequent computer) took me 26 hours. Doing the same thing in a script, dropping the indexes, loading the data, and then re-creating indexes took 2 hours!

I won't go into bcp details; the Books Online have all the necessary information for you to run bcp, and learn all its case-sensitive parameters. Let's go to more modern solutions.

Loading Data with Stored Procedure

It is possible to create stored procedures containing INSERT or SELECT...INTO statements to fill the table, either in a trigger or in a batch procedure. But the results and constraints are different if you are on the same server or on different servers.

Loading a Warehouse Situated on the OLTP Server

If you want to fill a table named Customer in the Warehouse database from the table Customer in the Sales database, you can use the procedure fill_warehouse_customer, shown in Listing 28.5.

Listing 28.5. Creating a procedure filling one table from another table.

```
CREATE PROC fill_warehouse_customer
AS
INSERT INTO Warehouse..Customer
   SELECT * FROM Sales..Customer
   WHERE cust_insert_date = convert(char(8),GETDATE(),101)
```

This procedure is convenient and easy to set up. But you can do better with SQL Server 6.5.

The 6.5 version introduced the INSERT...EXECUTE statement. With this new statement, it is possible to load a table from the result of a stored procedure. You now create the procedure in the Sales database, as shown in Listing 28.6.

Listing 28.6. Creating a procedure by selecting data.

```
CREATE PROC select_today_customer
AS
SELECT * FROM Sales..Customer
WHERE cust_insert_date = convert(char(8),GETDATE(),101)
```

Now you are able to use this procedure from the warehouse database, as shown in Listing 28.7.

Listing 28.7. Calling a procedure to insert its result in another table.

```
INSERT Warehouse..Customer
  EXECUTE Sales..select_today_customer
```

Of course, it is possible to launch this statement off-hours, or use optimizer hints to avoid blocking problems (blocking issues between OLTP and DSS databases are discussed later in this chapter). But one of the main advantages of loading this way is you can use this statement from another server, with the remote stored procedure.

Loading a Warehouse Situated on Another Server

The remote stored procedure offers the possibility of running a procedure on another server, as shown in Figure 28.7. It is also possible to insert the result of a stored procedure in a local server.

FIGURE 28.7.

Inserting locally remote results.

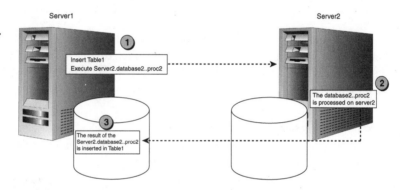

The only thing to do is to configure the remote servers, with the Remote Servers command in the Server Menu. To configure Server1 and Server2, follow these steps:

On Server1:

1. Declare Server2 the remote server, either with SQL Enterprise Manager or with `sp_addserver 'server2'`.

2. Declare Server1 the local server, either with SQL Enterprise Manager or with `sp_addserver 'server1', local`.

On Server2:

1. Declare Server1 the remote server, either with SQL Enterprise Manager or with `sp_addserver 'server1'`.

2. Declare Server2 the local server, either with SQL Enterprise Manager or with `sp_addserver 'server2', local`.

3. Map the necessary Server1 logins on Server2 logins.

You can now run stored procedure (if you have the rights) on Server2, from Server1.

> **CAUTION**
>
> Watch the case! If you installed your server with a case-sensitive sort order (like binary, for instance), you must declare the server names with the right case.

After you've performed these operations, it's possible to run an INSERT...EXECUTE statement. If your Sales database is on the SalesManagement server (the select_today_customer, shown in Listing 28.6, is in this database), and your Warehouse database is on the DSS server, you can load your customer table with the query shown in Listing 28.8.

Listing 28.8. Calling a remote stored procedure to insert its result in another table.

```
INSERT Warehouse..Customer
    EXECUTE SalesManagement.Sales..select_today_customer
```

You can schedule this statement to be executed on a daily or weekly basis with SQL Executive. Nevertheless, this method has its own drawback. For example, how can you update your data? Unfortunately, there is no way to UPDATE...EXECUTE or DELETE...EXECUTE. One of the answers lies in replication.

Loading Data with Replication

Replication is probably the simplest way to regularly maintain a perfect copy of your OLTP server. Of course, a data warehouse will not fully synchronize with your OLTP databases, but the majority of cases this isn't a big problem. The warehouse is generally here to help you find trends on a long-term point of view, not to react to a sudden modification of data.

Replication is a perfect tool to duplicate data quickly and efficiently. The SQL Server replication is based on a Publisher-Subscriber metaphor.

In your case, a warehouse is the subscriber of one or many publishers, like in Figure 28.8.

You schedule the replication tasks when you need them. This is the first step. I won't go into details on setting up a replication model here; you'll find the necessary information in Chapter 17, "Replication." But I'll focus on the important role the developer can have.

Normally, you replicate the same modification. If an insert occurs on the publisher, the same insert will occur on the subscriber. But sometimes, more often than not in fact, the data models between the OLTP database and the warehouse are not the same. The replication is then forgotten. What a pity! What are the stored procedures for?

It is possible to modify the original INSERT, UPDATE, and DELETE statements into stored procedures. Let's look at a quick and easy example of what you can do.

When you insert a new customer in your Sales..customer table, you want to feed, with replication, three tables on your warehouse. Figure 28.9 shows the Sales..customer table.

FIGURE 28.8.
One subscriber (data warehouse) and many publishers.

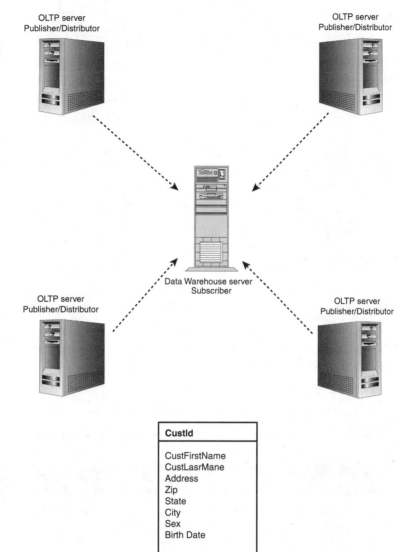

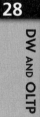

28

DW AND OLTP

FIGURE 28.9.
The
`Sales..Customer`
table.

CustId
CustFirstName
CustLasrMane
Address
Zip
State
City
Sex
Birth Date

You need to calculate statistics dynamically on your customer's gender, age, and city of residence. It's possible to calculate that information when you need it (see "Hypercubes," later in this chapter) or take profit of stored procedure to do the operation dynamically on the subscriber.

On the subscriber side, you have the tables shown in Figure 28.10.

Figure 28.10.

The three aggregate tables.

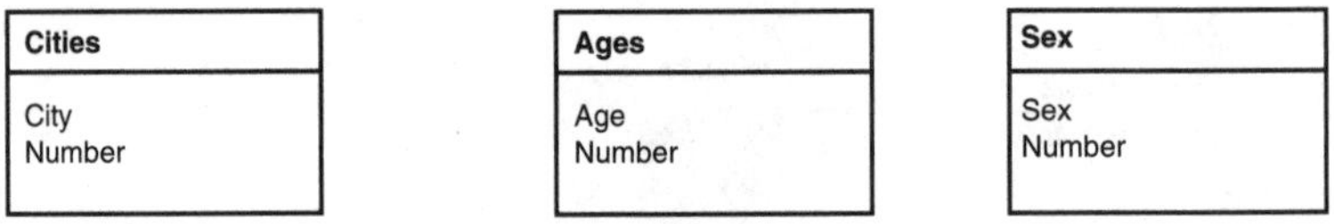

Cities
City
Number

Ages
Age
Number

Sex
Sex
Number

If you want to replicate to these three tables, you can write the following stored procedure to update these three tables from the `Sales..customer` table, as shown in Listing 28.9.

Listing 28.9. Replication stored procedure.

```
CREATE PROCEDURE update_aggregate_tables
     @chvfname varchar(40),
     @chvlname varchar(40),
     @chvadd varchar(50),
     @chrzip char(5),
     @chrstate char(2),
     @chrcity varchar(20),
     @bitsex char(1),
     @datbirth smalldatime,
     @intcustid int
AS
BEGIN TRAN
     UPDATE cities
        SET number = number +1
        WHERE city = @chrcity
     UPDATE sex
        SET number = number +1
        WHERE sex = @bitsex
     UPDATE ages
        SET number = number +1
        WHERE ages = DATEDIFF(year, @datbirth, getdate())
COMMIT TRAN
```

> **TIP**
>
> I used the CONVERT function with the 101 parameter (century on 4 digits). Remember that in a few months you change century. Calculating dates on 2 digits should be prohibited in all your programs; otherwise, you'll have slight date calculation problems.

This procedure has to be created in the subscriber database, because it is executed on the subscriber machine. Let the subscriber do the job.

After you've done that, in the article definition, instruct SQL-Server to replicate the INSERT statement with your stored procedure, in the article management window.

Of course, you can apply this strategy to delete and update as well, if necessary. And of course you can make more complicated calculation. You are going to see how to perform really complicated calculations the simplest possible way with the CUBE and ROLLUP statements.

Hypercubes

For those of you who are unfamiliar with the term *hypercube*, I should tell you it has nothing to do with hyperspace or any Star Trek or Star Wars stuff. Nevertheless, those who have worked with relational databases for awhile, know that creating an *n* dimension data cube with only one query is a little bit Science Fiction.

The preceding example was a simple one because you knew how many men or women were in your database, and how many customers lived in Los Angeles. But if you want to know the sales for 26-year old women living in Los Angeles, the task is impossible with the simple warehouse you have. Let's create a cube.

Creating the Cube

You can have many types of information in a GROUP BY query, as shown in Listings 28.10.

Listing 28.10. Classical GROUP BY query.

```
SELECT city, BirthYear = RIGHT(CONVERT(char(10), BirthDate, 101),4),
➥ sex, Sum_sales=SUM(sales)
FROM Customer C JOIN Sales S ON C.Cust_ID = S.Cust_ID
GROUP BY city, RIGHT(CONVERT(char(10), BirthDate, 101),4), sex

city                 BirthYear sex Sum_sales
------------------   --------  --  -------------------------
Ann Arbor            1938      0   389,78
Berkeley             1949      1   410,05
Berkeley             1965      0   413,04
Covelo               1978      1   457,90
Lawrence             1971      1   386,12
Los Angeles          1939      0   360,21
Los Angeles          1940      0   481,80
Los Angeles          1949      0   535,63
Los Angeles          1956      1   414,69
Los Angeles          1971      0   433,97
Menlo Park           1972      1   352,24
Nashville            1956      0   406,05
Oakland              1936      1   362,19
```

Fine, but what about the sales for a particular city (without birth year and sex)? This is handled similarly (see Listing 28.11).

Listing 28.11. CUBE GROUP BY query.

```
SELECT city, BirthYear = RIGHT(CONVERT(char(10), BirthDate, 101),4),
➥sex, Sum_sales=SUM(sales)
FROM Customer C JOIN Sales S ON C.Cust_ID = S.Cust_ID
GROUP BY city, RIGHT(CONVERT(char(10), BirthDate, 101),4), sex
WITH CUBE

city                 BirthYear sex Sum_sales
------------------   --------  --  -------------------------
```

28

DW AND OLTP

continues

Listing 28.11. continued

```
Ann Arbor          1938       0     389,78
Ann Arbor          1938       (nul389,78
Ann Arbor          (null)     (nul389,78
Berkeley           (null)     1     410,05
Berkeley           (null)     (nul410,05
Berkeley           1965       0     413,04
Berkeley           1965       (nul413,04
Berkeley           (null)     (nul823,08
Covelo             1978       1     457,90
Covelo             1978       (nul457,90
Covelo             (null)     (nul457,90
Lawrence           1971       1     386,12
Lawrence           1971       (nul386,12
Lawrence           (null)     (nul386,12
Los Angeles        1939       0     360,21
Los Angeles        1939       (nul360,21
Los Angeles        1940       0     481,80
Los Angeles        1940       (nul481,80
...
Los Angeles        (null)     1     414,69
Menlo Park         (null)     1     352,24
Oakland            (null)     1     801,81
Salt Lake City     (null)     1     408,06
San Jose           (null)     1     337,29
Shoshone           (null)     1     463,55
Walnut Creek       (null)     1     894,83
(null)             (null)     1   4 926,54
```

Okay, the result is rather confusing, because of the NULL values. You learned how to handle NULL values in Chapter 1, "Beyond the Basics of Data Manipulation Language." But here you can have two types of NULL values. Let's look at an example. If you read the third line of Listing 28.11, the two NULL values represent an aggregate. That line is the result of the total sales for all sales for the city of Ann Arbor. But look at the second and fifth lines for Berkeley. It seems these lines are identical. In fact, the first one represents a sale for a customer whose birth date has not been inserted, so this birth date is NULL (the BirthDate column accepts NULL values).

This can be rather confusing when you read the results. So you can slightly modify the query with the GROUPING function, as shown in Listing 28.12.

Listing 28.12. GROUPING CUBE query.

```
SELECT city,
       BirthYear = RIGHT(CONVERT(char(10), BirthDate, 101),4),
       RealNull=GROUPING(RIGHT(CONVERT(char(10), BirthDate, 101),4)),
       sex, Sum_sales=SUM(sales)
FROM Customer C JOIN Sales S ON C.Cust_ID = S.Cust_ID
GROUP BY city, RIGHT(CONVERT(char(10), BirthDate, 101),4), sex
WITH CUBE

city                 BirthYear RealNull sex Sum_sales
-------------------- --------- -------- -- -------------------------
Ann Arbor            1938      0         0   389,78
```

Ann Arbor	1938	0	(nul389,78
Ann Arbor	(null)	1	(nul389,78
Berkeley	(null)	0	1 410,05
Berkeley	(null)	0	(nul410,05
Berkeley	1965	0	0 413,04
Berkeley	1965	0	(nul413,04
Berkeley	(null)	1	(nul823,08
Covelo	1978	0	1 457,90
Covelo	1978	0	(nul457,90
Covelo	(null)	1	(nul457,90
Lawrence	1971	0	1 386,12
Lawrence	1971	0	(nul386,12
Lawrence	(null)	1	(nul386,12
Los Angeles	1939	0	0 360,21
Los Angeles	1939	0	(nul360,21
Los Angeles	1940	0	0 481,80
Los Angeles	1940	0	(nul481,80
...			
Los Angeles	(null)	1	1 414,69
Menlo Park	(null)	1	1 352,24
Oakland	(null)	1	1 801,81
Salt Lake City	(null)	1	1 408,06
San Jose	(null)	1	1 337,29
Shoshone	(null)	1	1 463,55
Walnut Creek	(null)	1	1 894,83
(null)	(null)	1	1 4 926,54

The result of the GROUPING function is 1 if the NULL value represents an aggregate, and 0 if it is a real NULL value in the data. You now know how to make the difference between real NULL values and aggregate NULL values. A major problem remains: you are doing this job to create a warehouse. But who will use that warehouse? Probably simple users, with little to no knowledge about NULL values.

So you have to use other functions to create a readable cube. Let's have a look at the one shown in Listing 28.13.

Listing 28.13. A readable datacube.

```
SELECT
City=CASE WHEN (GROUPING(city)=1) THEN 'All'
    ELSE ISNULL(city, 'Unknown')
    END,
BirthYear = CASE WHEN (GROUPING(BirthDate)=1) THEN 'All'
    ELSE ISNULL(RIGHT(CONVERT(char(10), BirthDate, 101),4),'Unknown')
    END ,
Sex = CASE WHEN (GROUPING(sex)=1) THEN 'All'
    ELSE ISNULL(sex, 'Unknown')
    END,
Sum_Sales=SUM(sales)
FROM Customer C JOIN Sales S ON C.Cust_ID = S.Cust_ID
GROUP BY city, BirthDate, sex
WITH CUBE
```

28

DW AND OLTP

Partial results of the readable datacube would look like this:

```
City                  BirthYear Sex Sum_Sales
--------------------  -------- --  --------------------------
Ann Arbor             1938      0    389,78
Ann Arbor             1938      All  389,78
Ann Arbor             All       All  389,78
Berkeley              Unknown   1    410,05
Berkeley              Unknown   All  410,05
Berkeley              1965      0    413,04
Berkeley              1965      All  413,04
Berkeley              All       All  823,08
Covelo                1978      1    457,90
Covelo                1978      All  457,90
Covelo                All       All  457,90
Lawrence              1971      1    386,12
Lawrence              1971      All  386,12
Lawrence              All       All  386,12
Los Angeles           1939      0    360,21
Los Angeles           1939      All  360,21
Los Angeles           1940      0    481,80
Los Angeles           1940      All  481,80
...
Los Angeles           All       1    414,69
Menlo Park            All       1    352,24
Oakland               All       1    801,81
Salt Lake City        All       1    408,06
San Jose              All       1    337,29
Shoshone              All       1    463,55
Walnut Creek          All       1    894,83
All                   All       1    4,926,54
```

As you can see, there is now a clear difference between grouping and standard NULL values.

Of course, it is possible to create a stored cube with a SELECT INTO instead of a normal SELECT statement. With your new table—let's call it sales_cube—you can find all the sales for 26-year old women living in Los Angeles, with the query shown in Listing 28.14.

Listing 28.14. Querying the cube.

```
SELECT * FROM sales_cube
WHERE sex='0'
AND Birthyear=convert(char(4),DATEPART(yy, GETDATE())-26)
AND city='Los Angeles'
```

The output would look like this:

```
City                  BirthYear Sex Sum_Sales
--------------------  -------- --  --------------------------
Los Angeles           1971      0    433,97
```

Creating the cube is no problem. The problem is now to keep the cube up-to-date.

Maintaining the Cube

Your previous cube is a static one. If you want to have it up-to-date, you need to execute the same query again, or you can maintain it. In fact, it should be updated if you update the sales table. For example, if you insert a new sale, run the procedure shown in Listing 28.15, on the insert replicated statement.

Listing 28.15. Updating the cube if a new sale is inserted.

```
CREATE PROCEDURE Update_Sales_Cube @intcustid int, @mnysales money
AS
UPDATE sales_Cube
SET sum_sales = sum_sales + @mnysales
WHERE
 (city=ISNULL((SELECT city FROM customer WHERE cust_id=@intcustid), 'Unknown')
 OR city='All') AND
 (sex=ISNULL((SELECT sex FROM customer WHERE cust_id=@intcustid), 'Unknown')
 OR sex='All') AND
 (BirthYear=ISNULL((SELECT RIGHT(CONVERT(char(10), BirthDate, 101),7)
 FROM customer WHERE cust_id=@intcustid), 'Unknown')
 OR BirthYear='All')
```

This stored procedure must be created in the subscription database and used instead of the classical replicated INSERT statement. Of course, you can do the same thing for the DELELE and UPDATE statement.

Batch Processing

The last possibility of creating the data warehouse is by using batch jobs to insert, delete, or update data. Using bcp or standard scripts isn't really difficult when you know how to use SQL Executive and the task manager.

The major problem of data warehouses is the time spent running queries. You are now going to focus on that subject and see how you can transform your queries into "rocket-style" queries.

Large Queries and Performance Optimization

After you create your warehouse and set up all the necessary update procedures, it becomes clear how people are going to use it. Here comes probably the toughest part of all.

A lot of companies don't create a special querying application but use instead a standard tool like Business Objet or Microsoft Access. The problem comes from the fact that you don't know what data is going to be queried. It becomes important to create access paths with views or stored procedures. But you should be aware of what's happening when you create and use them.

28

DW AND OLTP

Querying Data

You saw in the previous section how to create the warehouse, and the datacubes. Now when a user queries these data, he can avoid waiting hours and hours for the result. Here are a few tips discussed in detail in Part I, but here focused on large result sets.

Analyzing the Query

The query analyzer will give you precious information to decide on the indexes to use. Chapter 3 gives you a good overview of what can be done with this optimizer. When you come to data warehouse, it becomes important that you know its limits and optimize your query manually.

I won't talk about index choices here (go back a few pages, to the indexing section), but about table order. The optimizer is optimizing join order with four-table groups. That means if you have the following query:

```
SELECT C1, C2, C3, C4
FROM T1, T2, T3, T4, T5
WHERE ...
```

the system will optimize the join between tables T1, T2, T3, and T4. Then, it will optimize the results of the previous join with T5. As far as large volume sets are concerned, that can be a catastrophe.

Let's take a precise example of what to do. In your warehouse, you have five tables: customers, sales, sales_details, products, and suppliers. One of your users needs to query these five tables to find a possible correlation between the product suppliers and the customer's city of residence.

The WHERE clause is the following: city='Los Angeles' and product_name='New P1'. In the FROM clause, the user declared the tables with the order Customers, suppliers, sales, sales_details, products. The optimizer will join the first four tables, and then join the results with the products table.

But the products table is referenced in the WHERE clause. With that order, the system will extract the customers, suppliers, and sales information for the city of Los Angeles (that can do a lot of information), and then join that result with the product table.

If you write the FROM clause this way: Customers, products, suppliers, sales, sales_details, the optimizer will reduce the number of rows for the first four-table join, due to the WHERE clause. The query will be quicker, and the user more satisfied.

So when analyzing a query with SET SHOWPLAN ON or with the trace flag 310, have a look at table order and try to change it if there are more than four tables. If there are fewer than four tables, don't bother.

You can also enable the SET FORCEPLAN option, to force the table order. I don't think it is a good thing. Nobody knows better the data distribution than SQL Server (if the statistics are up-to-date, of course). So it is better to disable that option and create a four-table group function of the WHERE clause.

Another thing to think of is the use of optimizer hints.

Optimizer Hints

Optimizer hints are modifications in the behavior of the optimizer, such as index choice, lock choice, and obtaining the first row quickly. As far as lock is concerned, you should not be concerned with update activity, so there is no use asking for update lock, for example.

> **TIP**
>
> If you want to speed your SELECT query, you'd better use no locks. You have three ways to do that: use the NOLOCK option, or TRANSACTION ISOLATION LEVEL READ UNCOMMITTED, or set the database to read only. But pay attention to the fact that this tip applies only to a read only data warehouse.

In a warehouse, you are mainly concerned with crucial index choices and obtaining the first row as fast as possible.

INDEX

The INDEX hint is used to force the optimizer to use a specific index or a table scan. Normally, the optimizer knows its job. But in special cases, it can be useful, because, the optimizer can make mistakes. Nevertheless, always check that your choice is really useful with STATISTISC IO and STATISTISC TIME.

FASTFIRSTROW

The optimizer always tries to reduce the number of read pages. If you are programming your front-end and the query you are writing is a long running and sorted one, your user is blocked until the result set is fully populated.

Let's take the query shown in Listing 28.16 on the datacube.

Listing 28.16. Querying a large datacube.

```
SELECT *
FROM Sales_Cube
WHERE city = 'Shoshone'
ORDER BY Sum_sales
```

You created a nonclustered index on the Sum_sales column and a clustered index on the City column. Normally, the optimizer will choose the clustered index to minimize the number of I/Os. Problems arise when it takes a long time to find and sort the right rows, and the user is blocked till the end of the sort.

28

DW AND OLTP

With the FASTFIRSTROW hint and the possibility of running an asynchronous query from your front-end, the nonclustered index will be used to quickly find the first row. On a long-running DSS query, the FASTFIRSTROW can be a major advantage, because the user thinks everything is fast, but only the first row comes fast.

Views

It is impossible to ask your user to know all the subtleties of T-SQL. But you can program them into views. You or your users can use views like tables, and take advantages of optimizer hints on complex queries.

Views are particularly useful with more than four-table queries, or with a cube (see Listing 28.17).

Listing 28.17. View of a datacube.

```
CREATE VIEW Sales_cube
AS
SELECT
Customer_city = CASE WHEN (GROUPING(city)=1) THEN 'All'
     ELSE ISNULL(city, 'Unknown')
     END,
BirthYear = CASE WHEN (GROUPING(BirthDate)=1) THEN 'All'
     ELSE ISNULL(RIGHT(CONVERT(char(10), BirthDate, 101),4),'Unknown')
     END ,
Gender = CASE WHEN (GROUPING(sex)=1) THEN 'All'
     ELSE ISNULL(sex, 'Unknown')
     END,
Sum_Sales=SUM(sales)
FROM Customer C JOIN Sales S ON C.CustID = S.CustID
GROUP BY city, BirthDate, sex
WITH CUBE
```

This view is equivalent to the previous cube. You could use optimizer hints to fasten the selection of data.

Stored Procedures

For querying warehouses, stored procedures can be used to create complicated SELECT queries, with or without cursors. The main point is to obtain fast results, and sometimes a quick recompilation should be necessary.

Parameters and Recompilation

The recompilation of a stored procedure is a subject for discussion. In my humble opinion, it should be considered with a lot of concern for the warehouse, due to the huge amount of data. Imagine my Customer table has 10 million rows and a nonclustered index on the column Cust_id. You create the procedure included in Listing 28.18.

Listing 28.18. A procedure that needs to be recompiled.

```
CREATE PROCEDURE List_Customers @intcustid int
AS
SELECT * FROM Customer
WHERE Cust_id > @intcustid
```

If the first user runs the procedure with `@intcustid = 9,999,999`, the execution plan in the procedure cache uses the nonclustered index, and the answer is fast. If the second user runs the procedure with `@intcustid = 100`, that user will use the plan created for the first user. But in this case, a table scan would have been smarter, and would have been calculated if the procedure had been recompiled.

Remember that recompilation concerns only the optimization and the creation of the execution plan. On a data warehouse, as the number of manipulated rows is generally important, you should test your procedure with different values of parameters and with SHOWPLAN ON, to see if different execution plans can be generated. If this is the case, create your procedure WITH RECOMPILE.

Warehouse Maintenance Tasks

A data warehouse is, first of all, a database. So you need to program maintenance tasks in order to have a fully secure and optimized systems. I recommend to program the following tasks:

1. DBCC DBREINDEX all tables SORTED_DATA_REORG every week.
2. UPDATE STATISTICS every day.
3. sp_recompile all the tables every day, after UPDATE STATISTICS.
4. DUMP TRAN every day (if you update the database dynamically with replication, or remote stored procedure).
5. DBCC CHECKDB, NEWALLOC, and CHECKCATALOG every day.
6. DUMP DATABASE every week.

All these tasks have already been described in detail in other chapters. Nevertheless, the first two are particularly important on a huge set of data, because if your indexes are not up-to-date, you shouldn't expect good performances.

That completes the data warehouse discussion; you are now going to look at a more "dynamic" section: transaction systems.

SQL Server and OLTP Systems

An OLTP (Online Transaction Processing) system is characterized by a large amount of transactions per second. The Transaction Processing Council (www.tpc.org) offers benchmarks for transaction systems. SQL Server is now one of the fastest and cheapest transaction system, if you give credit to TPC benchmarks.

OLTP Issues

The main characteristics of an OLTP system are the following:

■ Small and fast transactions.

■ A large number of transactions per second.

■ Very selective queries.

■ Fastest possible response time and best possible throughput.

Of course, what a developer should have in mind while developing such a system is creating as fast as possible queries. Remember to write down the expected response times and throughput. Developers should have a comparison scale. Saying as fast as possible isn't an answer. But writing less than half a second is measurable!

Creating the Database

An OLTP database is generally quite different from a DSS database. In fact, generally, that kind of database is in third normal form, because you try to update, insert, or delete data—not read a huge amount of data.

So you are going to take examples of normalized versus denormalized transactional databases, and study the impact of the row width on I/O and updating speed.

Normal Forms and OLTP

I think you'll agree to put your database in third normal form. You don't have any redundancy of data, so updating data only has to be done in one place.

If you take the database example of Figure 28.5, if you have to insert a new movement you don't need to make other updates—the insert operation has chances to be fast. But if you denormalize the database for DSS purposes on each insert operation (refer to Figure 28.6), you need to calculate the balance for each account to receive consistent data. So the insert operation will be slowed down by the update of the Account table, even if the table is updated by a trigger.

Of course, this update can be done during an off-hour batch operation. In that case, the denormalization isn't painful for transaction operations, but users should be aware that some data are updated off-hours, so temporary inconsistency can be encountered sometimes.

For example, the balance for account #101 is $1,000.00. You credit $1,000.00 on this account. If the balance is updated off-hours, the balance will still be $1,000.00, and not $2,000.00 as it should have been if it was updated immediately.

The first rule of an OLTP system is to minimize the length of transactions. If this rule is followed, the impact of locks will be minimized at the same time.

Row Width and Page Splitting

If the row is small, the insert should be quicker than if it is larger. However, this isn't always true, because it depends on the type of update/insert operation.

In fact, the row width has a slight impact on the speed of the transaction, because, just a few lines had to be extracted from the database. You are not on a DSS system. But the impact is on the page splitting.

If you have a clustered index, and all the inserts are done at the end of the database, you are not for the moment concerned by page splitting. But what happens if you have inserts or updates all over the table? The answer, of course, is pages split.

If there isn't enough space in the page for this record when inserting a new record, the page splits. Half of the records stay in place, and the other half go to the new page. Figure 28.11 shows the page before the insert operation, and Figure 28.12 shows the page after the insert operation.

FIGURE 28.11.

A page before the insert operation.

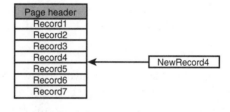

FIGURE 28.12.

The pages after the insert operation.

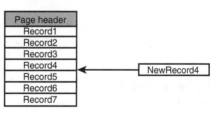

The page allocation can be a long operation, especially if the page has to be allocated on a new extent. So it is a good idea to try to avoid it. To do so, create a clustered index with a fillfactor. If you had created the table with a clustered index and a fillfactor value of 50, there would have been space in the page to insert the new row without splitting the page.

So the second rule of the OLTP database is to leave space in the pages with the fillfactor during index creation, and reindex the table to avoid page splitting.

Indexing the Database

Indexing an OLTP database is a very important part of the creation of the application. Too many indexes slow down the update/insert/delete operation, but too few of them slow down the selections. You have to find a compromise.

Clustered Indexes

Remember what you learned about data warehouses: You can have only one clustered index per page, so choose it purposefully. Your worst enemy in an OLTP application is the clustered index, but it doesn't have to be. Consider it your best friend if you can.

The clustered index is sorting data physically. If your data are equally spread along the table, and equally inserted along the table, you'll probably encounter page splitting. But if your inserts are only at the end of the table, everything runs smoothly. All the inserts don't necessarily have to be done at the end of the table, but it's a good choice. (Because you have insert row locking in version 6.5, it can really be an excellent choice.)

But the clustered index should be reserved for foreign keys and/or columns used in range queries. You can avoid page splitting with fillfactor—and one megabyte of hard disk is cheaper than ever. Furthermore, you can apply the fillfactor to non-leaf levels with the PAD_INDEX option; you can avoid page splitting even in non-leaf index pages. Why bother reserving your clustered index to insert rows at the end of the table?

Of course, if you are always inserting at the end of the table, without any update at all (such as accounting application, SAP/R3, or BAAN), create your clustered index with a fillfactor of 100.

Nonclustered Indexes

Updating a nonclustered index is more expensive than a clustered index, due to the number of levels. It is interesting to use STATISTICS IO ON during your test to see the number of pages accessed and updated by your statement. In fact, the more indexes you have, the more updates have to be done.

Reserve your nonclustered indexes for exact queries on unique (or almost unique) values and for primary keys. If you can avoid nonclustered indexes, you'll speed the updates operations.

Right-Indexing the Databases

Right-indexing an OLTP database, as I have already said, is a difficult task. But you should make a precise *CRUD (Create, Retrieve, Update, Delete) analysis* to determine the really useful indexing. In fact, for each stored procedure you are going to write, you should follow these steps to test the usefulness of indexes (as you will soon learn, always use stored procedures in OLTP applications):

1. Write down the results of logical reads for your procedure.
2. Study the search arguments and the join arguments of your query and create indexes on each of them. Over-index if you feel it is necessary (even create different indexes on the same columns).
3. Run your procedure, and write down the number of logical reads and the indexes used.
4. Drop all the unused indexes.

5. Run your procedure again, and check that the number of logical reads is fewer than the number obtained in the first step.

6. Check the effect of the new indexes on all the other stored procedures. If they dramatically slowed down the other procedures, decide whether to drop them.

These steps are long and painful ones, but they must be taken if you want to know if your indexes are really used and useful. An OLTP application is a compromise. But the first goal to reach is excellent response time and throughput.

So, the third rule for OLTP applications is to create only useful indexes, and drop all the others.

Transactions

Transactions are the sinews of war! If your transactions are well written on a well-designed database, your project will be a complete success.

I won't go into the details of writing transactions (see Chapter 3, "Optimizing Queries," to learn about it). Instead, I focus on special transaction traps you can encounter while developing an OLTP application. So let's see how to write efficient transactions.

Writing Efficient Transactions

First of all, always remember the fourth rule of OLTP application: keep transactions short. The shorter, the better. What do I mean by short? The amount of time between a BEGIN TRAN and the associated COMMIT or ROLLBACK, not necessarily the number of lines. For instance, a single update on 10 million rows is longer than ten updates on one row (the locking and isolation level can have a dramatic impact on transactions, which I will discuss about it in a moment).

As a rule of thumb, keeping your transaction as short as possible is the first step to writing efficient transactions.

Nested Transactions

SQL Server offers the possibility to nest transactions. You can create up to 16 levels of transactions.

> **CAUTION**
>
> Remember that triggers can count in the number of nested transactions. You should precisely know what triggers you have, and if they increase the numbers of nested transactions.

Nested transactions can be very useful, because you can develop small, fast transactions, and nest them to create larger transactions. For example, imagine the stored procedure shown in Listing 28.19.

Listing 28.19. Classical update stored procedure.

```
CREATE PROCEDURE update_customer
@intcustid integer, @chvcity varchar(25)
AS
DECLARE @chvoldcity varchar(25)
BEGIN TRAN
    SELECT @chvoldcity=city FROM customer WHERE cust_id=@intcustid
    UPDATE customer SET city=@chvcity WHERE cust_id=@intcustid
    UPDATE cities SET number=number-1 WHERE city=@chvoldcity
    UPDATE cities SET number=number+1 WHERE city=@chvcity
COMMIT TRAN
```

You can then run the script included in the Listing 28.20.

Listing 28.20. Nesting procedure in a transaction.

```
BEGIN TRAN
    EXEC update_customer 12234, 'Walnut Creek'
    INSERT sales DEFAULT VALUES
COMMIT TRAN
```

Here is a convenient way to do update/insert/delete operation. But what seemed like a short transaction (Listing 28.20) is in fact longer, due to the nested transaction in the stored procedure. That can cause the whole system to slow down. If that happens, the following section shows you how to track problems.

Correcting Slow Transactions

What I call a slow transaction is a transaction that doesn't fit in the time asked for. If your user asks for less than half a second for a transaction, and that transaction is running in more then two seconds, it is a slow transaction.

The first step to correct that slowness is to identify whether locks are concerned or not. To find out, set the `single user` option on, and then run the transaction. You'll see whether it is faster. If it isn't faster, this isn't a locking or concurrency problem. If it is fast as lighting, it is probably a (b)locking problem, so jump to the next section.

For the moment, it is important to know what's happening. Unfortunately, SQL Server doesn't offer a procedure call tree, so you have to track the different procedure calls with the PRINT statement.

> **TIP**
>
> The following stored procedure can be used to calculate the number of minutes, seconds, and milliseconds between two datetime variables (this function isn't totally accurate to the millisecond, but will give you a broad idea of execution time):

```
CREATE PROCEDURE MinSecMil
     @start datetime,
     @end datetime,
     @chvresults varchar(9) OUTPUT

AS
DECLARE @intmin int, @intsec int, @intmil int, @intint int
SELECT @intint=DATEDIFF(ms, @start, @end)
SELECT @intmil= @intint % 1000
SELECT @intsec= ((@intint-@intmil)/1000) % 60
SELECT @intmin= (@intint-@intmil-(@intsec*1000))/60000
SELECT @chvresults=CONVERT(varchar(2), @intmin) + ":" +
➥     CONVERT(varchar(2), @intsec) + ":" +
➥     CONVERT(varchar(3), @intmil)
```

The statements shown in Listing 28.21 can be inserted in all the procedures and triggers while debugging.

Listing 28.21. Debugging statements.

```
DECLARE @dtmstart datetime, @chvduration varchar(9), @dtmend datetime
PRINT "Entering procedure¦trigger procname"
PRINT "Transaction count: "
SELECT convert(varchar(2), @@TRANCOUNT)
SELECT @dtmstart=GETDATE()
...
SELECT @dtmend=GETDATE()
EXEC MinSecMil @dtmstart, @dtmend, @chvduration OUTPUT
PRINT @chvduration
PRINT "Exiting procedure¦trigger procname"
```

After you know precisely all the procedure and trigger calls for a single procedure, you can test each procedure¦trigger individually with STATISTICS IO and STATISTICS TIME to find the weakest.

In all the cases I've encountered and audited, the problem was not the number of nested transactions but one slow transaction, due to lack of indexing. Adding or modifying an existing index has always been the solution. But in some cases, you need to consider the design of the database.

Distributed Transactions

Distributed computing is an important and complex subject. When you talk about distributed transactions, you generally refer to the two-phase commit.

Chapter 4, "Advanced Transact-SQL Statements," introduced the distributed transactions and the Distributed Transaction Coordinator (DTC). One crucial thing about distributed transaction with SQL Server 6.5 is its great facility. All you need to know is how to call a remote stored procedure and to use BEGIN DISTRIBUTED TRAN instead of BEGIN TRAN.

DTC is such an interesting concept that it has been the base of Microsoft Transaction Server. An entire book could be written on Microsoft Transaction Server, but the thing you need to know about that product is the incredible simplicity of creating distributed transactions. In fact, if you know how to create an ActiveX DLL, you almost know how to write a Transaction Server package.

Microsoft Transaction Server is the cornerstone for three-tier multidatabase provider applications. If this product interests you, I suggest you go and surf the www.microsoft.com\transactions Web site.

Locking

Locks are a major concern on OLTP applications, because many transactions mean many locks, leading to potential blocking problems. You should precisely know all the types of locks (see Chapter 3 for more information on locks), the potential blocking problems, and the way to correct them if they occur. Of course, you should be aware of when to use insert-row locking.

Identifying and Correcting the Blocking Problems

First of all, blocking doesn't mean deadlock, as you'll see if you run the queries shown in Listing 28.22, which shows two different connections (you can try this with ISQL/w, for example).

Listing 28.22. Locking query.

```
Query 1
BEGIN TRAN
    UPDATE customer SET city = 'Walnut Creek' WHERE cust_id=12234

Query 2
BEGIN TRAN
    UPDATE customer SET city = 'Shoshone' WHERE cust_id=12235
COMMIT TRAN
```

If you run Query 1 first and then Query 2, Query 2 will wait indefinitely for lock. The problem here is Query 1 has not committed or rollbacked its transaction, so an exclusive lock remains on the page. If the rows for customers 12234 and 12235 are on the same page, Query 2 waits for the exclusive lock to be released. There is no timeout on lock, so Query 2 will wait until the administrator kills the connection or the users abort the transaction.

This blocking problem is frequent on OLTP systems, either due to the missing of a COMMIT or ROLLBACK statement, or to a bad programming strategy.

> **TIP**
>
> If you want to check if you have all the associated COMMIT and ROLLBACK statements, use the @@TRANCOUNT global variable. After the last COMMIT or ROLLBACK, the value of this variable should be 0. If it is 1 (or more), you forgot one (or more) COMMIT or ROLLBACK.

A common mistake is to separate the BEGIN TRAN and the COMMIT statement, associating them with different buttons on the user's screen. But what happens if that user takes a coffee break? The system hangs until she presses the commit button. If you decide to use this dangerous strategy, always add a timer. If the user isn't doing anything after few minutes, rollback the transaction, releasing the locks. I don't think this is the best strategy to use on OLTP systems.

If you have a blocking problem, you can track them with SQL Enterprise Manager or with the stored procedure sp_lock2 and sp_who, as shown in Listing 28.23.

> **TIP**
>
> sp_lock2 gives you the table and database name instead of their ID as in sp_lock. But I experienced some problems with it under heavy load: sp_lock ran fine, and sp_lock2 was blocked.

Listing 28.23. sp_who and partial results.

```
sp_who
spid   status    loginame   hostname     blk   dbname     cmd
-----  --------  ---------  -----------  ----  --------   -----------------
1      sleeping  sa                      0     master     MIRROR HANDLER
2      sleeping  sa                      0     master     LAZY WRITER
3      sleeping  sa                      0     master     CHECKPOINT SLEEP
4      sleeping  sa                      0     master     RA MANAGER
10     sleeping  sa         P133MARC     0     master     AWAITING COMMAND
...
14     sleeping  sa         P133MARC     0     Receiver   AWAITING COMMAND
15     sleeping  sa         P133MARC     14    Receiver   UPDATE
16     runnable  sa         P133MARC     0     Receiver   SELECT
```

The preceding results indicate (thanks to the blk columns) that process #15 is blocked by process #14. It is then possible, with the sp_lock2, to know what kind of lock is blocking. For example, you'll see the table and database name. If you use the DBCC INPUTBUFFER(*spid*) statement, you'll see what statement has been issued by the blocking process (or you can use SQL Trace, if the trace has been activated).

> **WARNING**
>
> If the statement has been handled by the SQL Server RPC manager, it won't appear with the DBCC INPUTBUFFER statement. This is particularly true when using dbrpcexec() with DB-Library, and SQLPrepare(), SQLBindParameter(), and SQLExecDirect() with ODBC.

Of course, the answer to such blocking problems is row locking. The next version of SQL Server will probably implement row locking for each kind of statement. But for the moment, it is a good habit to keep the transactions as short as possible.

Insert-Row Locking

Concerning insert operations, it is now possible to ask for row locks. Row locking can minimize contention if many inserts occur at the same time, which happens frequently in OLTP applications. If all the inserts go into the same page (probably at the end of the table), the page locking will block simultaneous inserts, and the system will be sequential.

If you have this type of application, you can activate insert row locking as shown in Listing 28.24.

Listing 28.24. Activating insert-row locking on sales table.

```
sp_tableoption 'sales', 'insert row lock', true
```

> **TIP**
>
> If you need to activate insert row locking on all tables, you can use tokens in sp_tableoption. For example, you activate insert-row locking for all tables by executing sp_tableoption '%', 'insert row lock', true.

Remember that row locking is more expensive than page locking. Activate that kind of locking only if you really need it.

Deadlocks

Deadlock is an infinite blocking problem. SQL Server automatically handles deadlocks, but don't think you don't have to worry about them—they can kill your application performance. It is important for you to make a clear distinction between blocking and deadlocking, so let's have a look first at the types of deadlocks, and then the ways to handle or avoid them.

The Two Types of Deadlocks

You can encounter two types of deadlocks in SQL Server:

- *Cycle deadlock.* Occurs when a transaction owns an exclusive lock and wants to acquire another exclusive locks held by a transaction trying to obtain the first held lock.

- *Conversion deadlock.* Occurs when a transaction owns a shared lock and need to acquire an exclusive lock.

These two types of deadlocks can occur with page, table, or even row locks. Let's take a detailed look at these.

Cycle Deadlock

Cycle deadlock is the classic and most known type of deadlock. If you try the two queries shown in Listing 28.25 in two different connections, one of the two queries will be killed, receiving the 1205 error.

Listing 28.25. Provoking a cycle deadlock.

Query 1

```
WHILE 1=1
BEGIN
BEGIN TRAN
    UPDATE customer SET city='Walnut Creek' WHERE cust_id=12234
    WAITFOR DELAY '00:00:02'
    UPDATE sales SET amount='100' WHERE sales_id='6789'
COMMIT TRAN
END
```

Query 2

```
WHILE 1=1
BEGIN
BEGIN TRAN
    UPDATE sales SET amount='100' WHERE sales_id='6789'
    WAITFOR DELAY '00:00:02'
    UPDATE customer SET city='Walnut Creek' WHERE cust_id=12234
COMMIT TRAN
END
```

28

DW AND OLTP

NOTE

The WAITFOR statement is here only to speed up the moment of the deadlock. The deadlock will occur with or without the WAITFOR statement.

The 1205 error would look like this:

```
(Msg 1205, Level 13, State 1)
Your server command (process id #5) was deadlocked with another process and
has been chosen as deadlock victim. Re-run your command.
```

The other query finishes normally. So when a deadlock is detected, SQL Server kills the query that closed the circle; that is, the query that asked for the lock that provoked the deadlock.

> **NOTE**
>
> In SQL Server 4.x and 6.0, SQL Server killed the query owned by the process that consumed less CPU time. That algorithm has been abandoned in SQL Server 6.5.

The two transactions use the tables in different orders, possibly acquiring locks alternately.

Conversion Deadlock

The other type of deadlock is probably more subtle. Run the query shown in Listing 28.26 simultaneously in two different connections.

Listing 28.26. Provoking a conversion deadlock.

```
SET TRANSACTION ISOLATION LEVEL SERIALIZABLE
WHILE 1=1
BEGIN
BEGIN TRAN
    SELECT * FROM customer WHERE cust_id=12234
    WAITFOR DELAY '00:00:02'
    UPDATE customer SET city='Walnut Creek' WHERE cust_id=12234
COMMIT TRAN
END
```

One of the two transactions will be killed receiving the 1205 message. This time the deadlock is due to the transformation of the shared lock acquired by the SELECT statement. The two transactions hold a shared lock on the same page, and cannot transform it into exclusive locks for the UPDATE statement.

Avoiding Deadlocks

Experiencing deadlock is never pleasant, so you should always try to avoid it. The following sections show you some possible solutions.

Many people think that row locking is the solution to deadlocking. But deadlocks occur with row locking. Imagine having row locking on update operation. If a transaction needs to update two records on the same page, it needs to acquire two row locks. But in the meantime, another transaction needs to acquire the same locks in reverse order. The deadlocks that occur could have been avoided with page lock, so row locking isn't the solution to all deadlocks.

Cycle Deadlock

Cycle deadlock occurs when two transactions access at least two tables in reverse order. The main solution to this kind of deadlock is to always access tables in the same order in all the transactions.

So it is crucial to define at the beginning of the project the access order of tables. If all the procedures access the tables in the same order, you can almost eliminate cycle deadlocks.

You can still encounter deadlocks on indexes or on locks that protect internal resources, but you lower the risk to almost zero.

Conversion Deadlock

Conversion deadlock occurs with Serializable or Repeatable read isolation level. In fact, with these levels, the shared locks are held until the end of the transactions. You have two possibilities to avoid that kind of deadlock. The first is to use another isolation level if possible. The second is to ask for an update lock, as shown in Listing 28.27.

Listing 28.27. Avoiding conversion deadlock.

```
SET TRANSACTION ISOLATION LEVEL SERIALIZABLE
WHILE 1=1
BEGIN
BEGIN TRAN
    SELECT * FROM customer (UPDLOCK) WHERE cust_id=12234
    WAITFOR DELAY '00:00:02'
    UPDATE customer SET city='Walnut Creek' WHERE cust_id=12234
COMMIT TRAN
END
```

The update lock is incompatible with another update lock, so if the two transactions are run at the same time, the first that acquires the update lock blocks the others (but no deadlock occurs) until the commit; then the other one runs normally.

> **WARNING**
>
> Always place the lock hint between brackets, otherwise SQL Server will think it is a table alias.

Handling Deadlocks

You cannot completely avoid deadlocks, so you should always prepare your code to receive the 1205 error.

> **WARNING**
>
> You cannot test the 1205 error in Transact-SQL because, following a deadlock, the process is killed by the system. You need to test it client-side.

Listing 28.28 shows you a possible Visual Basic error handler in case of deadlock.

28

DW AND OLTP

Listing 28.28. Deadlock error handler.

```
Error_Handler:
    If rdoErrors(0).Number=1205 Then
        intNbErr = intNbErr + 1
        If intNbErr<10 then
            Resume 'Restart the stored procedure call
        Else
            Msgbox "The update fails, please reexecute it later !"
            Exit sub
        End If
    End If
```

In this example, I insert a retry counter and decide to stop reexecuting the procedure if the system receives the 1205 error 10 times. You can modify this error handler to handle more cases, but remember to always include a 1205 error handler in your OLTP applications.

Optimizing SQL Server as an OLTP System

After you decide to create an OLTP database, you should configure your system the following way, monitor it, and of course follow the transaction check list to see whether you forgot something.

Transaction Check List

The following checklist has to be checked on all transactions and tables of your system:

1. *Keep your transaction short.* Place variable declaration, loops, and so on outside of the transaction and keep it as short as possible. If it can be shortened, shorten it.

2. *Use fillfactor.* Use fillfactor to leave space for inserts and updates in pages, avoiding page splits.

3. *Create only the useful indexes; drop all the others.* Indexes are useful for finding and selecting data, but they slow down updates; so keep only the ones that speed up the queries. All the others should be dropped.

4. *Always use the correct isolation level.* If you don't need Repeatable Read or Serializable, don't use them; otherwise you'll overuse your shared locks. If you need this isolation level, think of update locks.

5. *Define table access order.* Always accessing tables in the same order dramatically lowers the possibilities of cycle deadlocks.

6. *Always test deadlocks.* Testing and handling deadlocks enables you to reexecute a killed transaction without any message to the end user.

Of course, if you follow all these rules, you are not sure to have a fast and reliable application. You need to modify certain configuration options.

Configuration Options

Some configuration options can be checked and modified to obtain the best response time and throughput.

Fillfactor

Modifying the fillfactor value provides you with some insurance—if you always create your indexes with the right fillfactor value. Nevertheless, I prefer asking for a particular fillfactor with CREATE INDEX or DBCC REINDEX statements, rather than setting the same fillfactor for all indexes.

LE Threshold

The lock escalation threshold must be changed. The default values are not adapted to OLTP database, because the escalation occurs too soon, locking the table instead of the pages. To my mind, setting a high value for LE Threshold maximum and a reasonable one for LE Threshold percent is preferable—for example, 10,000, and 30% respectively. But the maximum value depends on the size of your tables.

Log Write Sleep

The default value (0) for this option is generally good, because it delays the transaction log write if other transactions are pending, lowering the number of physical I/O. Nevertheless, that value has a slight impact on performance if your I/O subsystem is a performing one, and if your transaction log is on its own disk.

Max Async IO

My advice is to always use brilliant I/O subsystems (controller and disks). With Mylex or Compaq controllers, you can set higher values, improving the I/O throughput. Values greater than 20 are typical with such controllers.

Procedure Cache

Generally, OLTP databases have a lot of stored procedures. You should monitor the number and size of your stored procedure to define a correct value for that option.

Recovery Interval

This option indicates the frequency of the cache flushing to disk. If that operation is too frequent, the overall performance will lower, because of the amount of physical I/O. The default is 5 minutes. In fact, the 5 minutes are evaluated from the number of transaction log records. The system estimates each record requires 10 ms to be redone. So a recovery interval of 5 minutes equals 30,000 (5 * 60 *1000/10) transaction log records.

On an OLTP system, with an average of 200 transactions per second, the physical checkpoint occurs every 2.5 minutes. If you have 100MB of memory dedicated to SQL Server, and a maximum physical throughput of 10Mbits/s (classical practical throughput for SCSI systems), the cache flushing will require 80 seconds. So every two and a half minutes, the I/O subsystem hangs for more than a minute.

You need to think of giving a higher value to recovery intervals on heavy transaction systems. Values greater than 60 are generally good ones, if you have a good backup strategy and a UPS on your server.

Physical Data Repartition

If you need to increase the capacity of your I/O subsystems, I recommend to you the following hardware:

- *Raid 5 for data.* Excellent reading performance, and protection against one media failure.
- *Raid 1 for transaction log.* Excellent writing performance, and protection against one media failure. If possible, use disk duplexing instead of simple mirroring.

If you set a correct value for recovery interval, you won't have a lot of writing on your data—all the updates are done in data cache. But the transaction log writing is almost continuous (really continuous on heavy transactions systems). If the log is alone on its own disk, the disk heads are not moving away between two log writes, so the I/O subsystem is fully optimized.

At least physically separate data and log, and put the log alone on its own disk.

Monitoring Performances

Every modification you do on your system should be monitored. You have different tools to monitor your system performance, from DBCC to Windows NT Performance Monitor.

Here are some hints about what to monitor and what to do.

Cache Hit Ratio

The cache hit ratio indicates the percentage of chance to find data in memory instead of reading it from disk.

The cache hit ratio should always be greater than 80. You can monitor it with the Windows NT Performance monitor (Object: SQL Server, counter: Cache hit ratio), or DBCC SQLPERF(LRUSTATS). If you have an average cache hit ratio of less than 70, try to increase the memory allocated to SQL Server or check that the procedure cache isn't overallocated.

Procedure Cache

You can monitor the size of the procedure cache used either with Windows NT Performance monitor (Object: SQL Server—Procedure cache, counter: Procedure cache used %), or with DBCC PROCCACHE. If your are near 100% increase its size. If you are far from 100%, reduce the size. At the maximum capacity, you should be around 80%.

Input/Output

You should always keep in mind to lower the use of the disk to the profit of the memory. You monitor the effectiveness of the memory with the cache hit ratio. But make sure that you don't overuse the disk.

First of all, you should know the physical limits of your I/O subsystem. As a rule of thumb, I use the 10Mbits/sec value as an average throughput for SCSI systems. Then you can measure the effective throughput.

You should try to lower the number of batch writes (Object: SQL Server, counter I/O—batch writes/s. or DBCC SQLPERF(IOSTATS)). That value should always be zero except during cache flushing—increasing recovery interval decreases the frequency of cache flushing. During cache flushing, you probably want to increase the overall throughput. Increasing the max async IO (with a good I/O subsystem) can have a positive impact on the throughput.

Transactions

You'll probably want to know how many transactions per second your system is able to manage. You can monitor this value with Windows NT Performance Monitor (Object: SQL Server, counter: I/O—Transaction/s.) or DBCC SQLPERF(IOSTATS). Of course, the higher the better; there is no perfect value. But remember, this isn't really the number of transactions per second, but the number of batches per second.

You can monitor a lot of other counters, but the ones I discussed are really the most important concerning OLTP databases.

Creating DSS and OLTP Applications

DSS and OLTP applications don't get on happily together. So, creating a DSS and an OLTP application on the same server, even with the same database, is a very difficult task. But nothing's impossible.

I will give you a few hints to create good, if not brilliant, different applications on the same server and on the same database. I hope you will avoid classical traps.

Creating Applications on the Same Server

All the things I discussed in this chapter can apply to one server, except probably some of the configuration options I talked about in the OLTP section. Here are a few hints on loading the DSS database and configuring the SQL Server.

Loading the Database

No remote stored procedure here, you are on the same server. Standard procedure is probably the simplest way to load your warehouse. You can use SQL Transfer Manager, or even replication. I try to avoid replication, because of the overhead of the log reader process. I think batch jobs are well suited for these kinds of applications.

Anyway, if your OLTP database isn't too heavily updated, think about triggers to update the DSS database on-the-fly.

Configuration Options

All the options seen in the OLTP sections apply except Lock Escalation, which needs to be thought of more precisely. In fact, in the two databases, you need to lower the number of locks. Try to favor OLTP, and use READ UNCOMMITTED isolation level in the DSS database.

Of course, if both databases are used simultaneously, you'd better think about adding more memory to your system. A good tool to monitor memory use is DBCC MEMUSAGE. You'll have a nice idea of which database uses the most memory.

Handling Dual Applications on the Same Database

This is the toughest part of all—dealing with the impossible extraordinary application, made of both and OLTP *and* a DSS on the same database. If you can avoid this situation, please do it. If you inherit that kind of database, try to do your best, knowing it is almost a lost match.

Here are the main problems you are going to encounter:

- You need a lot of indexes for the DSS application, compared to just a few of them for the OLTP application.
- The shared locks issued by the SELECT statement of the DSS application block the update operations of the OLTP application.
- You manipulate a large amount of data in memory, and probably need a lot of memory to store all the data.

If you're asked to create this type of application, you've got your work cut out for you. You can't totally satisfy both applications. If you want to increase speed of the DSS application, you must over-index the database or denormalize it, lowering the speed of the OLTP application.

On the other hand, if you want to increase the speed of the OLTP application, you need to have a third normal form design, and few indexes, but that increase the number of needed computation for DSS queries. Everything is compromise, but a much harder compromise than using a single application, and having to handle only the stored procedure.

If you can avoid that situation, I recommend splitting the two databases, even on the same server. Hard drives are cheap nowadays. Otherwise, tell everybody you cannot do miracles, even with faster machines.

Summary

Saying that you now know everything you should know about data warehouses and OLTP systems with SQL Server would be a lie, although you know enough to create great applications. Of course, you'll probably discover new things on you road to creating your own applications.

Concerning data warehouses, you have discovered that indexing plays a major role in performance. As far as SQL Server goes, data warehousing offers nice features that can be dedicated to making your Decision Support Systems work more smoothly. These features include remote stored procedures, INSERT...SELECT statements, replication, and of course the CUBE statement. With CUBE and ROLLUP, you can prepare multidimensional data cubes with only one query.

In an OLTP application, response time and overall throughput play the best role. With optimizer and lock hints, you can modify the behavior of queries and increase performances dramatically. You also discovered the tools to solve and handle blocking and deadlocking problems.

At the end, you were granted few hints about creating the impossible: both applications with only one database. You have between your hands all the necessary knowledge to create brilliant OLTP or DSS applications with SQL Server.

IN THIS PART

VI
PART

Appendixes

The System Tables of the Master Database

IN THIS APPENDIX

You cannot develop applications on SQL Server 6.5 without a good knowledge of the system tables. This appendix gives you a quick reference for the system tables of the master database. I chose a logical and non-alphabetical order for the tables, grouping them as login, database, and system-wide tables.

Generally, system tables are not directly queried, but are accessed or modified with a stored procedure. After the description of each table, I give you the main stored procedures used to query or modify this table, with a quick explanation of each.

> **NOTE**
>
> To see more extensive definitions, syntax, and examples of the stored procedures listed here, refer to Appendix C, "System Stored and Extended Stored Procedures Quick Reference."

Login Tables

Two tables are in charge of the login into SQL Server: `syslogins` and `sysremotelogins`.

syslogins

`syslogins` contains one row for each valid user account. When you first install SQL Server, this table contains four accounts:

- `sa`. The system administrator. The associated password is NULL, so change it if you want a secure system.
- `probe`. This account is used by the Windows NT performance monitor and should not be deleted.
- `repl_subscriber`. Account used by the subscription process.
- `repl_publisher`. Account used by the publishing process.

Table A.1 lists the detailed information for the `syslogins` table.

Table A.1. syslogins table.

Column	Datatype	Description
suid	smallint	Server user ID
status	smallint	Reserved
accdate	datetime	Reserved
totcpu	int	Reserved
totio	int	Reserved
spacelimit	int	Reserved

Column	Datatype	Description
timelimit	int	Reserved
resultlimit	int	Reserved
dbname	varchar(30)	Name of user's default database when connection is established
name	varchar(30)	Login ID of user
password	varchar(30)	Password of user (encrypted if not NULL)
language	varchar(30)	User's default language (NULL for us_english)

Stored Procedures

sp_addalias

sp_addlogin

sp_addremotelogin

sp_adduser

sp_changedbowner

sp_defaultdb

sp_defaultlanguage

sp_droplogin

sp_helpdb

sp_helpuser

sp_password

sysremotelogins

sysremotelogins contains a row for each user who's authorized to execute remote stored procedures on this SQL Server. sysremotelogins is used with sysservers to define who is authorized to log into the remote server.

NOTE

The remote login only has to be defined on the remote server, but both servers have to be defined as remotes for each other.

Table A.2 lists the detailed information for the sysremotelogins table.

Table A.2. sysremotelogins table.

Column	Datatype	Description
remoteserverid	smallint	Remote server ID
remoteusername	varchar(30)	User's login name on the local server
suid	smallint	Remote server user ID
status	smallint	Bitmap of options

The descriptions I've given to the columns are different from the ones you've seen elsewhere. For me, the remote server is the one containing the stored procedure to run, and therefore the one on which to declare the remote logins. The local server is the server from which the remote procedure is called.

Stored Procedures

    sp_addremotelogin

    sp_addsubscriber

    sp_dropremotelogin

    sp_dropserver

    sp_dropsubscriber

    sp_remoteoption

Database Tables

The database tables are in charge of the space management. That is, the location of devices and the location of databases on devices.

sysdevices

sysdevices contains one row for each device. This table stores the reference information for dump devices (tape, disk, and so on) and for database devices. When you install SQL Server, sysdevices contains three database device entries, Master, MDSBData, and MSDBLog, and three dump devices, diskdump, diskettedumpa, and diskettedumpb.

> **WARNING**
>
> Never use the diskdump device for your backup. This device is called the "bit bucket." If you dump a database or a log in that device, the dump is lost.

Table A.3 lists the detail information for the sysdevices table.

The System Tables of the Master Database

763

APPENDIX A

A

THE SYSTEM
TABLES OF THE
MASTER DATABASE

Table A.3. sysdevices table.

Column	Datatype	Description
low	int	First virtual page number on a database device (not used for dump devices)
high	int	Last virtual page number on a database device (not used for dump devices)
status	smallint	Bitmap indicating the type of device: 1: Default disk 2: Physical disk 4: Logical disk 8: Skip header 16: Dump device 32: Serial writes 64: Device mirrored 128: Reads mirrored (reserved) 256: Half-mirror only (reserved) 512: Mirror enabled 4096: Read Only 8192: Deferred
cntrltype	smallint	Controller type: 0: Non CD-ROM database device 2: Disk dump device 3–4: Diskette dump device 5: Tape dump device 6: Named pipe device
name	varchar(30)	Logical name of the dump device or database device
phyname	varchar(127)	Name of the physical device
mirrorname	varchar(127)	Name of the mirror device
stripeset	varchar(30)	Reserved for future use

You probably noticed that the virtual device number has no associated columns. This is due to the fact that the vdevno is the last byte of the high or low word value. For example, msdbdata as a low value of 2130706432 (hex 7F 00 00 00). So its vdevno equals 7F (127), and the device starts at the virtual address 0.

Stored Procedures

```
sp_addsegment

sp_addumpdevice

sp_coalesce_fragments
```

```
sp_configure

sp_dbinstall

sp_dbremove

sp_devoption

sp_diskdefault

sp_dropdevice

sp_dropsegment

sp_extendsegment

sp_helpdb

sp_helpdevice

sp_helplog

sp_helpsegment

sp_logdevice
```

sysdatabases

sysdatabases contains one entry for each database created on the system. Table A.4 lists the detailed information for the sysdatabases table.

Table A.4. sysdatabases table.

Column	Datatype	Description
name	varchar(30)	Name of the database
dbid	smallint	Database ID
suid	smallint	Server user ID of database owner
mode	smallint	Used internally for locking a database while it is being created
status	smallint	Status bits, some of which can be set by the user with the sp_dboption system stored procedure (read only, dbo use only, single user, and so on):
		2: Database is in transition
		4: Select into/bulkcopy
		8: Trunc. log on chkpt
		16: No chkpt on recovery
		32: Crashed while the database was being loaded; instructs recovery not to proceed
		64: Database not recovered yet
		128: Database is in recovery

Column	Datatype	Description
		256: Database is suspect; cannot be opened or used in its present state
		512: Database is offline
		1024: Read only
		2048: DBO use only
		4096: Single user
		8192: Database being checkpointed
		16384: ANSI null default
		-32768: Emergency mode
version	smallint	Internal version number of the SQL Server code with which the database was created
logptr	int	Pointer to the transaction log
crdate	datetime	Creation date
dumptrdate	datetime	Date of the last DUMP TRANSACTION
category	int	Used for publication and subscription databases

TIP

Like all the system tables, sysdatabases should not be updated manually. But I have had some experiences where a suspect database (status = 255) could be accessed by simply modifying its status bit. This operation seems to work without danger.

Stored Procedures

sp_addlogin

sp_addpublication

sp_changearticle

sp_changedbowner

sp_changepublication

sp_databases

sp_dboption

sp_defaultdb

sp_devoption

sp_dropdevice

sp_droplogin

sp_helpdb

sp_logdevice

sp_renamedb

sp_spaceused

sp_tables

sysusages

sysusages contains one entry for each database fragment. When a database is created or altered, the system looks for available fragments (allocation units) in the referenced devices and reserves them for that database. Table A.5 lists the detailed information for the sysuses table.

Table A.5. sysusages table.

Column	Datatype	Description
dbid	smallint	Database ID
segmap	int	Bitmap of possible segment assignments: 1: System segment 2: Default segment 4: Log segment Other values: user-defined segments
lstart	int	First logical page number
size	int	Number of contiguous logical 2KB pages
vstart	int	Starting virtual page number

In order to know which device a database (or fragment) is on, the system compares the vstart value with low and high values of sysdevices. If the vstart value is between low and high, the fragment in question belongs to that device.

Stored Procedures

sp_addsegment

sp_dropsegment

sp_helpsegment

sp_databases

sp_extendsegment

sp_logdevice

sp_dbinstall

sp_helpdb

```
sp_dbremove

sp_devoption

sp_helplog

sp_spaceused

sp_dropdevice
```

System-Wide Tables

System-wide tables are in charge of the overall configuration of SQL Server, or are in charge on what's happening on the server but are not dedicated to a particular user or database.

syscharsets

syscharsets contains one entry for each character set and sort order defined on the server. All the available character sets and sort orders are stored, but only one is referenced in the configuration options of SQL Server for use. Table A.6 lists the detailed information for the syscharsets table.

Table A.6. syscharsets table.

Column	Datatype	Description
type	smallint	Type of entity this row represents. 1001 is a character set, 2001 is a sort order.
id	tinyint	Unique ID for the character set or sort order. Note that sort orders and character sets cannot share the same ID number. ID numbers 0 through 200 are reserved.
csid	tinyint	Unused for the character set. ID of the character set if the row represents the associated sort order.
status	smallint	Internal system status information bits.
name	varchar(30)	Unique name for the character set or sort order.
description	varchar(255)	Description of the features of the character set or sort order.
definition	image	Internal definition of the character set or sort order.

Stored Procedures

```
sp_helpsort
```

sysconfigures

sysconfigures contains one entry for each configurable option. This table is loaded at the start of SQL Server with the contents of the configuration block (the first four 2KB pages of the master device). Table A.7 lists the detailed information for the sysconfigures table.

Table A.7. sysconfigures table.

Column	Datatype	Description
config	smallint	Configuration variable number
value	int	User-modifiable value for the variable
comment	varchar(255)	Explanation of the configuration option
status	smallint	Bitmap indicating the status for the option: 1: Dynamic (The variable takes effect when the RECONFIGURE statement is executed) 2: Advanced (The variable is displayed only when the Show Advanced option is set)

The contents of the sysconfigures table are written back in the configuration block when the RECONFIGURE statement is run.

Stored Procedures

sp_configure (remember to run RECONFIGURE [WITH OVERRIDE] after sp_configure)

syscurconfigs

syscurconfigs, like sysconfigures, contains one entry for each configuration option. This table contains the running values of these options. This table is a pseudo-table because it does not exist on the disk but is created when a user or process queries it.

Its structure is identical to that of sysconfigures.

When you update a static option (one that won't take effect until SQL Server is restarted), its value is written in sysconfigures but does not appear in syscurconfigs.

Stored Procedures

sp_configure (remember to run RECONFIGURE [WITH OVERRIDE] after sp_configure).

syslanguages

syslanguages contains one entry for each language installed on SQL Server (except for U.S. English, the default language). Table A.8 lists the detailed information for the syslanguages table.

Table A.8. syslanguages table.

Column	*Datatype*	*Description*
langid	smallint	Unique language ID
dateformat	char(3)	Date order (for example, dmy)
datefirst	tinyint	First day of the week: 1 for Monday, 2 for Tuesday, and so on, through 7 for Sunday
upgrade	int	SQL Server version of last upgrade for this language
nuame	varchar(30)	Official language name (for example, français), including diacritical marks
alias	varchar(30)	Alternate language name (for example, french)
months	varchar(251)	Comma-separated list of full-length month names, in order from January through December (20 characters max)
shortmonths	varchar(119)	Comma-separated list of short month names, in order from January through December (9 characters max)
days	varchar(216)	Comma-separated list of day names, in order from Monday through Sunday (30 characters max)

Stored Procedures

sp_configure (remember to run RECONFIGURE [WITH OVERRIDE] after sp_configure)

sp_droplanguage

sp_helplanguage

sp_setlangalias.

syslocks

syslocks contains one entry for each lock held on the system at the time the procedure is run. syslocks is a pseudo-table (like syscurconfigs) because it does not exist on disk and is created when it is queried. Table A.9 lists the detailed information for the syslocks table.

Table A.9. syslocks table.

Column	Datatype	Description
id	int	Table ID
dbid	smallint	Database ID
page	int	Page number
type	smallint	Type of lock: 1: Exclusive table lock 2: Shared table lock 3: Exclusive intent lock 4: Shared intent lock 5: Exclusive page lock 6: Shared page lock 7: Update page lock 8: Exclusive extent lock 9: Update extent lock 11: Next extent lock 12: Previous extent lock Any of the preceding lock types can appear with 256 added to them, indicating that the lock is blocking another user. For example: 257: Blocking exclusive table lock 265: Blocking update extent lock
spid	smallint	ID of process that holds the lock

Stored Procedures

sp_lock

sp_lock2 (same as sp_lock, but gives the table and owner names)

sysmessages

sysmessages contains all the warning, informational, and error messages in SQL Server. Another table has been added to the msdb database (sysservermessages) for system-wide messages.

Table A.10. syslanguages table.

Column	Datatype	Description
error	int	Unique error number
severity	smallint	Severity level of the error
dlevel	smallint	Reserved. For internal use only

Column	Datatype	Description
description	varchar(255)	Explanation of the error with placeholders for parameters
langid	smallint	Language

Stored Procedures

sp_addmessage

sp_droplanguage

sp_dropmessage.

sysprocesses

sysprocesses contains one row for each process running or idle on SQL Server. This is a pseudo-table built on-the-fly if queried (like syscurconfigs and syslocks). Table A.11 lists the detailed information for the sysprocesses table.

Table A.11. sysprocesses table.

Column	Datatype	Description
spid	smallint	Process ID
kpid	smallint	Windows NT thread ID
status	char(10)	Process ID status (runnable, sleeping, and so on)
suid	smallint	Server user ID of user who executed command
hostname	char(10)	Name of workstation
program_name	char(16)	Name of application program
hostprocess	char(8)	Workstation process ID number
cmd	char(16)	Command currently being executed
cpu	int	Cumulative CPU time for process
physical_io	int	Cumulative disk reads and writes for process
memusage	int	Number of 2KB pages of the procedure cache that are currently allocated to the process
blocked	smallint	Process ID of blocking process, if any
waittype	binary	Reserved
dbid	smallint	Database ID
uid	smallint	ID of user who executed command

continues

Table A.11. continued

Column	Datatype	Description
gid	smallint	Group ID of user who executed command
login_time	char(8)	The time at which a client process logged into the server; for system processes, the time at which SQL Server startup occurred
last_batch	char(8)	The last time a client process executed a remote stored procedure call or an EXECUTE statement; for system processes, the time at which SQL Server startup occurred
nt_domain	char(30)	The Windows NT domain for the client (if using integrated security) or a trusted connection
nt_username	char(30)	The Windows NT username for the process (if using integrated security) or a trusted connection
net_address	char(12)	The assigned unique identifier for the network interface card on each user's workstation
net_library	char(12)	The client's network library name

stored procedures

sp_dboption

sp_who

sp_who2(same as sp_who, plus information on CPU time used, disk I/O used, and ProgramName)

sysservers

sysservers contains one entry for each remote server on which remote stored procedures can be executed. Remember that to execute remote stored procedures, you have to declare remote logins on the remote server. Table A.12 lists the detailed information for the sysservers table.

Table A.12. sysservers table.

Column	Datatype	Description
srvid	smallint	ID number (for local use only) of the remote server
srvstatus	smallint	Bitmap of options 0: Local server 1: Remote server (rpc) 2: Publisher

The System Tables of the Master Database

APPENDIX A

773

A

THE SYSTEM
TABLES OF THE
MASTER DATABASE

Column	Datatype	Description
		4: Subscriber
		8: Distributor
		16: Distribution publisher
		32: Data Source Name server
		64: Fallback server
srvname	varchar(30)	Name of the server
srvnetname	varchar(32)	Netbios name of the server, if it is not compliant with identifier rules
topologyx	int	Used by the SQL Enterprise Manager server topology diagram
topologyy	int	Used by the SQL Enterprise Manager server topology diagram

Stored Procedures

sp_addpublisher

sp_addremotelogin

sp_addserver

sp_addsubscriber

sp_addsubscription

sp_changesubscriber

sp_changesubscription

sp_changesubstatus

sp_droppublisher

sp_dropremotelogin

sp_dropserver

sp_dropsubscriber

sp_dropsubscription

sp_enumfullsubscribers

sp_helparticle

sp_helpdistributor

sp_helppublication

sp_helpremotelogin

sp_helpserver

sp_helpsubscriberinfo

```
sp_helpsubscription

sp_remoteoption

sp_serveroption

sp_setnetname

sp_subscribe

sp_unsubscribe
```

Special Tables

The master database contains special system tables that aren't identified as system tables (they have a U type in the sysobjects table), but are used as such by specific procedures or by ODBC. These tables are not documented and should not be updated manually:

- spt_datatype_info_ext
- spt_datatype_info
- spt_server_info
- helpsql
- spt_committab
- spt_monitor
- spt_values
- spt_fallback_db
- spt_fallback_dev
- spt_fallback_usg

The names are generally self-explanatory. Some of these special tables should become system tables in the next version of SQL Server.

The System Tables of All Databases

APPENDIX B

The 18 system tables of the model database are copied in each new database. In fact, the whole content of the model database is copied to new databases. If you add new objects (tables, views, stored procedures, users, and so on), they will be copied as well.

These 18 tables represent all the necessary information to self-manage each database. You find explanations about these 18 tables in this appendix, plus stored procedures used to query or to update them, and special undocumented gifts for some.

Object Tables

The object tables contains all necessary information to manage user and system tables, views, stored procedures, user-defined datatypes, default, rules, constraints, triggers, and indexes.

syscolumns

syscolumns contains one row for each table, each view column, and each stored procedure parameter.

Table B.1. syscolumns table.

Column	Datatype	Description
id	int	ID of the table/view to which this column belongs or of the stored procedure to which the parameter is associated.
number	smallint	Procedure number. Used when some procedures have the same name, and are identified by a number (0 for nonprocedure entries).
colid	tinyint	Column ID.
status	tinyint	Bitmap used to describe a property of the column or the parameter:
		8: The column allows NULL values.
		16: ANSI_PADDING was set during creation of a varchar or a varbinary column. Trailing blanks are preserved when varchar data is updated or inserted; trailing zeroes are preserved when varbinary data is updated or inserted.
		32: A varchar or a varbinary column is a fixed-length datatype that accepts NULLS. varchar data is padded with blanks to the maximum length, and varbinary data is padded with zeroes.
		64: OUTPUT parameter.
		128: Identity column.

Column	Datatype	Description
type	tinyint	Physical storage type (copied from systypes).
length	tinyint	Physical length of data (copied from systypes or supplied by the user).
offset	smallint	Offset of this column into the row; if negative, variable-length column.
usertype	smallint	User type ID (copied from systypes).
cdefault	int	ID of the stored procedure that generates the default value for this column.
domain	int	ID of the stored procedure that contains the rule for this column.
name	varchar(30)	Column name.
printfmt	varchar(255)	Reserved.
prec	tinyint	Level of precision for this column.
scale	tinyint	Scale for this column.

Stored Procedure

sp_articlecolumn

sp_bindefault

sp_bindrule

sp_column_privileges

sp_columns

sp_droptype

sp_fkeys

sp_help

sp_helparticle

sp_helparticlecolumns

sp_helprotect

sp_pkeys

sp_rename

sp_special_columns

sp_sproc_columns

sp_statistics

sp_tables

sp_unbindefault

sp_unbindrule

syscomments

syscomments contains one or more entries for each stored procedure, trigger, view, rule, CHECK constraint, and DEFAULT constraint. This table contains the source code of each object. The text column contains the code and is 255 characters long. If the code is longer than 255 characters (this is often the case for stored procedures and triggers), the code spans on more than one line.

Table B.2. syscomments table.

Column	Datatype	Description
id	int	Object ID to which the code belongs.
number	smallint	Number of the procedure, if it is grouped (0 for nonprocedure entries).
colid	tinyint	Row sequence number for code longer than 255 characters.
texttype	smallint	1: User-supplied comment—users can add entries describing an object or column.
		2: System-supplied code for views, rules, defaults, triggers, and stored procedures.
		4: Encrypted code for procedures, triggers, and views.
language	smallint	Reserved.
text	varchar(255)	SQL definition code.

Be careful not to get confused about the differences between syscomments and sysprocedures.

Stored Procedure

```
sp_helpconstraint
sp_helpextendedproc
sp_helptext
```

sysconstraints

sysconstraints is only a mapping table and a list of constraints, but does not contain any code or other table reference. This table is linked with syscomments for CHECK and DEFAULT constraints code, with sysreferences for FOREIGN KEY constraints, and with sysindexes for PRIMARY KEY and UNIQUE constraints.

Table B.3. sysconstraints table.

Column	Datatype	Description
constid	int	Constraint ID
id	int	ID of the table that owns the constraint
colid	tinyint	ID of the column on which the constraint is defined (0 if table constraint)
spare1	tinyint	Reserved
status	int	1: PRIMARY KEY 2: UNIQUE 3: FOREIGN KEY 4: CHECK 5: DEFAULT 16: Column-level constraint 32: Table-level constraint
actions	int	Reserved
error	int	Reserved

sysdepends

sysdepends describes functional dependencies between stored procedures, views, and tables. It contains one row for each stored procedure, view, and table referenced by a stored procedure, view, or trigger.

Table B.4. sysdepends table.

Column	Datatype	Description
id	int	Object ID
number	smallint	Number of the procedure, if it is grouped (0 for nonprocedure entries)
depid	int	Dependent object ID
depnumber	smallint	Number of the dependent procedure, if it is grouped (0 for nonprocedure entries)
depdbid	smallint	Reserved
depsiteid	smallint	Reserved
status	smallint	Internal status information
selall	bit	On, if the object is used in a SELECT * statement
resultobj	bit	On, if the object is being updated
readobj	bit	On, if the object is being read

Stored Procedures

sp_depends

sp_rename

sysindexes

sysindexes contains one row for each index, for each table that does not have a clustered index, and for each table that has text and image fields. The entry is created by the CREATE INDEX statement and the PRIMARY KEY and UNIQUE constraint creation.

Table B.5. sysindexes table.

Column	Datatype	Description
name	varchar(30)	Name of table for indid = 0 or 255; otherwise, name of index.
id	int	ID of table to which the index belongs (if indid<>0 and <>255; otherwise, ID of the table).
indid	smallint	ID of index: 0: Table 1: Clustered index >1: Nonclustered index 255: Entry for tables that have text or image data
dpages	int	For indid=0 or indid=1, dpages is the number of used data pages. For indid=255, 0. Otherwise, dpages is the number of leaf-level index pages.
reserved	int	For indid=0 or indid=1, it is the number of pages allocated for all indexes on the table and for data pages. For indid=255, it is the number of pages allocated for text or image data. Otherwise, it is the number of pages allocated only for this index.
used	int	For indid=0 or indid=1, it is the number of pages used for all indexes on the table and for data pages. For indid=255, it is the number of pages used for text or image data. Otherwise, it is the number of pages used only for this index.
rows	int	For indid>=0, data-level row count. For indid=255, it is set to 0.
first	int	Pointer to first data or leaf page.

Column	Datatype	Description
root	int	For indid>=1 and <255, pointer to the root page of the index. For indid=0 or indid=255, pointer to the last page.
distribution	int	Pointer to distribution page (if entry is an index).
OrigFillFactor	tinyint	The original fillfactor value used to create the index. This value is never updated, but is used by DBCC REINDEX for reindexation purposes.
segment	smallint	Number of segment used by this object.
status	smallint	System-status information:
		1: IGNORE_DUP_KEY
		2: Unique index
		4: IGNORE_DUP_ROW
		16: Clustered index
		64: ALLOW_DUP_ROW
		2048: PRIMARY KEY constraint index
		4096: UNIQUE constraint index
rowpage	smallint	Maximum count of rows per page.
minlen	smallint	Minimum size of a row.
maxlen	smallint	Maximum size of a row.
maxirow	smallint	Maximum size of a nonleaf index row.
keycnt	smallint	Number of keys.
keys1	varbinary(255)	Description of key columns (if entry is an index).
keys2	varbinary(255)	Description of key columns (if entry is an index).
soid	tinyint	Sort order ID that the index was created with. 0 if there is no character data in the keys.
csid	tinyint	Character set ID that the index was created with. 0 if there is no character data in the keys.
UpdateStamp	varbinary	This column is used for internal synchronization of changes to row and page counts.

This table is used to store statistics information.

Stored Procedures

sp_dropsegment

sp_fkeys

sp_helpconstraint

sp_helpindex

sp_helplog

sp_helpsegment

sp_pkeys

sp_placeobject

sp_rename

sp_spaceused

sp_special_columns

sp_statistics

syskeys

syskeys is kept for backward compatibility, and is no longer used by SQL Server 6.x.

sysobjects

sysobjects contains one row for each object of the database. These objects are: tables, views, default, rules, triggers, CHECK constraint, DEFAULT constraint, FOREIGN KEY constraint, and PRIMARY KEY constraint.

Table B.6. sysobjects table.

Column	Datatype	Description
name	varchar(30)	Object name
id	int	Object ID
uid	smallint	User ID of the owner
type	char(2)	Object type:
		C: CHECK constraint
		D: Default or DEFAULT constraint
		F: FOREIGN KEY constraint
		K: PRIMARY KEY or UNIQUE constraint
		P: Stored procedure
		R: Rule
		RF: Replication stored procedure
		S: System table
		TR: Trigger

Column	Datatype	Description
		U: User table
		V: View
		X: Extended stored procedure
userstat	smallint	Reserved
sysstat	smallint	Internal-status information
indexdel	smallint	Index delete count (incremented if an index is deleted)
Schema_ver	smallint	Number of changes in the schema of the object (incremented if a rule or default is added)
refdate	datetime	Reserved
crdate	datetime	Creation date
version	datetime	Reserved
deltrig	int	Stored-procedure ID of the delete trigger
instrig	int	Stored-procedure ID of the insert trigger
updtrig	int	Stored-procedure ID of the update trigger
seltrig	int	Reserved
category	int	Used for publication, constraints, and identity
cache	smallint	Reserved

B

THE SYSTEM
TABLES OF ALL
DATABASES

Stored Procedure

sp_addarticle

sp_bindefault

sp_bindrule

sp_changearticle

sp_changesubstatus

sp_column_privileges

sp_columns

sp_depends

sp_droparticle

sp_dropgroup

sp_droptype

sp_dropuser

sp_fkeys

```
sp_help

sp_helparticle

sp_helpconstraint

sp_helpextendedproc

sp_helprotect

sp_pkeys

sp_placeobject

sp_rename

sp_replica

sp_spaceused

sp_sproc_columns

sp_statistics

sp_stored_procedures

sp_table_privileges

sp_tables

sp_unbindefault

sp_unbindrule
```

Viewing the Content of an Object Page

It is possible to view the content of a table/index page with the non-documented DBCC PAGE procedure. In case of corruption or deadlocks, it is sometimes useful to detect the content of a specific page, or to view the forward and backward links to other pages.

The DBCC TRACEON(3604) procedure is necessary if you want to view the result. Remember to disable this trace flag with DBCC TRACEOFF(3604) once you are finished with it.

```
DBCC TRACEON(3604)

DBCC PAGE (dbid, pagenum[, printopt][, cache][, log_virt])
```

This statement shows the content or the header of a data page. The following list describes the various parts of the statement:

dbid	Database ID
pagenum	Page number
printopt	0: Header (default); 1: Page content one row at a time; 2: Page content
cache	0: reads the page from disk; 1: reads the page from cache (default)
log_virt	0: pagenum is a virtual page; 1: pagenum is a logical page (default)

sysprocedures

sysprocedures contains the query tree or query plan of each stored procedure, default, rule, view, trigger, CHECK constraint, and DEFAULT constraint. Since the query tree is stored in binary format, it cannot be read by a query and doesn't appear in the structure of the table.

Table B.7. sysprocedures table.

Column	Datatype	Description
type	smallint	Object type: 1: Plan 2: Tree
id	int	Object ID
sequence	smallint	Sequence number if more than one row is needed to store the query tree
status	smallint	Internal system status
number	smallint	Number of the procedure, if it is grouped (0 for nonprocedure entries)

Stored Procedures

sp_sproc_columns: Displays column information for a specific stored procedure.

sp_stored_procedures: Displays a list of stored procedures.

sysreferences

sysreferences contains the referenced columns of a foreign key. This table is used to enforce referential integrity.

Table B.8. sysreferences table.

Column	Datatype	Description
constid	int	Constraint ID
fkeyid	int	ID of referencing table
fkeydbid	smallint	Reserved
rkeyid	int	ID of referenced table
rkeydbid	smallint	Reserved
rkeyindid	smallint	Reserved
keycnt	smallint	Number of columns in key
fkey1 to fkey16	tinyint	Column ID of referencing column
rkey1 to rkey16	tinyint	Column ID of referenced column

Stored Procedures

```
sp_fkeys

sp_helpconstraint
```

systypes

systypes contains one row for each system datatype and for each user-defined datatypes.

Table B.9. systypes table.

Column	Datatype	Description
uid	smallint	User ID of the creator.
usertype	smallint	User type ID.
variable	bit	1: Variable-length datatype 0: Other types.
allownulls	bit	Indicates the nullability of this datatype. This nullability is overridden by the one specified in the CREATE TABLE or ALTER TABLE statement.
type	tinyint	Physical storage datatype.
length	tinyint	Physical length of datatype.
tdefault	int	ID of stored procedure that generates the default value of this datatype.
domain	int	ID of stored procedure that contains integrity checks for this datatype. The name of this column has nothing to do with Windows NT domains.
name	varchar(30)	Name of the datatype.
printfmt	varchar(255)	Reserved.
prec	tinyint	Precision.
scale	tinyint	Scale (function of the precision).

Stored Procedures

```
sp_addtype

sp_bindefault

sp_bindrule

sp_columns

sp_datatype_info

sp_droptype
```

```
sp_dropuser

sp_help

sp_rename

sp_special_columns

sp_sproc_columns

sp_unbindefault

sp_unbindrule
```

User, Group, and Security Tables

The database security is managed by the database and stored in the three following tables.

sysalternates

sysalternates contains a row for each alias name mapped to a SQL Server login account. The alias is used to impersonate a user and take profit of its rights. For example, it is possible to alias the developers of an application on the DBO to avoid ownership chains.

Table B.10. sysalternates table.

Column	Datatype	Description
suid	smallint	Server user ID
altsuid	smallint	Server user ID of the user to whom the suid is mapped

As you can see, that table is a mapping table between two login user IDs stored in the master..syslogins table. The user mapped has no database user ID, but use the database user ID of the login account to whom it is mapped.

Stored Procedures

```
sp_addalias

sp_adduser

sp_changedbowner

sp_dropalias

sp_droplogin

sp_dropuser

sp_helpuser
```

sysprotects

sysprotects contains one row for each granted or revoked user rights. By default, if a right is not granted for a user, or a group, or public, the user has no right. This table contains the right for individual users, groups, and public.

Table B.11. sysprotects table.

Column	Datatype	Description
id	int	ID of object to which this permission applies (taken from sysobjects)
uid	smallint	ID of user or group to which this permission applies (taken from sysusers)
action	tinyint	One of the following permissions: 26: REFERENCES 193: SELECT 195: INSERT 196: DELETE 197: UPDATE 198: CREATE TABLE 203: CREATE DATABASE 207: CREATE VIEW 222: CREATE PROCEDURE 224: EXECUTE 228: DUMP DATABASE 233: CREATE DEFAULT 235: DUMP TRANSACTION 236: CREATE RULE
protecttype	tinyint	Type of the protection: 204: GRANT WITH GRANT 205: GRANT 206: REVOKE
columns	varbinary(32)	Bitmap of columns to which this SELECT or UPDATE permission applies Bit 0: Columns Bit 1: Permission applies to that column NULL means no information
grantor	smallint	The user ID of the user who issued the GRANT or REVOKE permission

Stored Procedures

    sp_column_privileges

    sp_dropgroup

    sp_dropuser

    sp_helprotect

    sp_stored_procedures

    sp_table_privileges

    sp_tables

sysusers

sysusers contains one row for each database user, group, and for public.

Table B.12. sysusers table.

Column	Datatype	Description
suid	smallint	Server user ID (copied from syslogins). 1: sa; -1: guest; -2: public. Groups have negative suid, and individuals have mapped suid.
uid	smallint	User ID, unique in this database. 1: dbo.
gid	smallint	Group ID to which this user belongs. uid = - gid: this entry is a group; 0: public.
name	varchar(30)	Unique username or group name.
environ	varchar(255)	Reserved.

Stored Procedures

    sp_addalias

    sp_addgroup

    sp_adduser

    sp_changedbowner

    sp_changegroup

    sp_column_privileges

    sp_dboption

    sp_depends

    sp_dropgroup

    sp_droplogin

```
sp_droptype

sp_dropuser

sp_helparticle

sp_helpgroup

sp_helprotect

sp_helpuser

sp_stored_procedures

sp_table_privileges

sp_tables
```

Replication Tables

The replication appeared with SQL 6.x. As for all the new enhancements, the management is done with system tables. The three following tables manage SQL Server replication, but note that all the replication tasks are managed and stored in systasks.

sysarticles

sysarticles contains one row for each published article on the publication server. That table has all the necessary information concerning publishing operations.

Table B.13. sysarticles table.

Column	Datatype	Description
artid	int	Identity column, unique ID number for the article
columns	varbinary(32)	Columns published in the table
creation_script	varchar(127)	Schema script of the article
del_cmd	varchar(255)	Command to execute upon delete, or else built from the log entry
description	varchar(255)	Comments for the article
dest_table	varchar(30)	Name of the destination table
filter	int	Stored procedure ID, used for horizontal partitioning
filter_clause	text	WHERE clause of the article, used for horizontal filtering
ins_cmd	varchar(255)	Command to execute upon insert, or else built from the log entry

Column	Datatype	Description
name	varchar(30)	Unique name of the article
objid	int	Published table object ID
pubid	int	ID of the publication to which the article belongs
pre_creation_cmd		tinyint Command for dropping, deleting, or truncating, to run before the creation of the table:
		0: None
		1: Drop
		2: Delete
		3: Truncate
status	tinyint	Bitmap used to describe a property of the column or the parameter:
		8: Column allows NULL values
		64: Parameter is an OUTPUT parameter
		128: Identity column
sync_objid	int	The ID of the table or view that represents the article definition
type	tinyint	Type of article:
		1: Log-based article
		3: Log-based article with manual filter
		5: Log-based article with manual view
		7: Log-based article with manual filter and manual view
upd_cmd	varchar(255)	Command to execute upon update, or else built from the log entry

Stored Procedures

```
sp_addarticle
sp_addsubscription
sp_articlecolumn
sp_changearticle
sp_changesubscription
sp_changesubstatus
sp_droparticle
sp_droppublication
```

```
sp_dropsubscription

sp_enumfullsubscribers

sp_helparticle

sp_helparticlecolumns

sp_helppublication

sp_helpsubscription

sp_subscribe

sp_unsubscribe
```

syspublications

syspublications contains one row for each declared publication. This table is linked to the sysarticles table to find the articles belonging to a publication.

Table B.14. syspublications table.

Column	Datatype	Description
description	varchar(255)	Comments
name	varchar(30)	Unique name of the publication
pubid	int	Identity column, publication ID number
repl_freq	tinyint	Type of replication 0: Transaction based 1: Scheduled table refresh
restricted	bit	Security option for the publication 1: Restricted 0: Unrestricted (default)
status	tinyint	Log based status 0: Log-based (default) 1: Not log-based
sync_method	tinyint	Type of synchronization method 0: Native bcp 1: Character-based bcp
taskid	int	Associated scheduled task ID

Stored Procedures

```
sp_addarticle

sp_addpublication

sp_addsubscription

sp_articlecolumn
```

```
sp_changearticle

sp_changepublication

sp_changesubscription

sp_changesubstatus

sp_dboption

sp_droparticle

sp_droppublication

sp_droparticle

sp_droppublication

sp_dropsubscription

sp_enumfullsubscribers

sp_helparticle

sp_helparticlecolumns

sp_helppublication

sp_helpsubscription

sp_subscribe

sp_unsubscribe
```

syssubscriptions

syssubscriptions contains one row for each subscription on the subscriber.

Table B.15. syssubscriptions table.

Column	Datatype	Description
artid	int	Subscribed article ID
srvid	smallint	Subscription server ID
dest_db	varchar(30)	Name of the destination database
status	tinyint	Status: 0: Inactive 1: Subscribed 2: Active
sync_type	tinyint	Type of synchronization: 0: Manual 1: Automatic 2: None
timestamp	timestamp	Initial time of subscription

Stored Procedures

```
sp_addsubscription

sp_changesubscription

sp_changesubstatus

sp_droparticle

sp_droppublication

sp_dropsubscription

sp_enumfullsubscribers

sp_helparticle

sp_helppublication

sp_helpsubscription

sp_subscribe

sp_unsubscribe
```

Other Tables

You find all the other tables created in each database in the following sections. Among these, the syslogs table is probably the most important.

syslogs

syslogs is the database's transaction log. This table is not user-updatable. That table can be read, but you discover this information is not really directly useful.

Table B.16. syslogs table.

Column	Datatype	Description
xactid	binary(6)	Transaction ID
op	tinyint	Update-operation number

Stored Procedure

There is no stored procedure querying that table, the following stored procedures are the ones displaying information about the transaction log, but not what's inside.

```
sp_helplog

sp_logdevice
```

Displaying the Log

If you run the two previous commands in a ISQL/w window, you obtain each entry of the log with an almost user-friendly look. The DBCC LOG statement is undocumented.

```
DBCC TRACEON (3604)

DBCC LOG
```

syssegments

syssegments contains one entry for each segment on your database. By default, the syssegment table contains three entries: system segment, default segment, and log segment.

Table B.17. syssegments table.

Column	Datatype	Description
segment	smallint	Segment ID
name	varchar(30)	Segment name
status	smallint	Default segment

Stored Procedures

sp_addsegment

sp_dropsegment

sp_extendsegment

sp_helpdb

sp_helpindex

sp_helpsegment

sp_placeobject

System Stored and Extended Stored Procedures Quick Reference

Microsoft provides a variety of system stored procedures. These are summarized in Table C.1.

Table C.1. System stored procedures.

Stored procedure	*Description*
sp_addalias	Maps one user's attributes to another.
sp_addextendedproc	Used to register the name of a new extended stored procedure.
sp_addgroup	Adds a new group to the current database.
sp_addlogin	Creates a login account for a new user to SQL Server.
sp_addmessage	Creates a new message in the system sysmessages table.
sp_addremotelogin	Adds a new remote login ID for access to a remote server.
sp_addsegment	Defines a segment name for a database device.
sp_addserver	Creates a server name of a local or remote database.
sp_addtype	Creates a user-defined datatype.
sp_addumpdevice	Adds a dump device to SQL Server.
sp_adduser	Creates a new user account in the current database.
sp_altermessage	Changes whether a message is written to the Windows NT event log.
sp_bindefault	Creates a default bound to a column or user-defined datatype.
sp_bindrule	Creates a rule bound to a column or user-defined datatype.
sp_certify_removable	Verifies that a database can be safely removed for distribution to removable media.
sp_changedbowner	Transfers ownership of the database to the new owner specified.
sp_changegroup	Adds an existing user to the group.
sp_configure	Allows you to change or display the system configuration.
sp_create_removable	Creates a removable media database.
sp_dbinstall	Used to install a database.
sp_dboption	Used to change or display database options.
sp_dbremove	Removes a database and the associated devices.
sp_defaultdb	Assigns a default database to the user when the user first logs into SQL Server.

Stored procedure	Description
sp_defaultlanguage	Allows you to change the default language of an individual user.
sp_depends	Shows dependencies of a database object.
sp_devoptions	Changes or displays the device status.
sp_diskdefault	Sets default location where database is stored.
sp_dropalias	Removes alias established by sp_addalias.
sp_dropdevice	Removes database device.
sp_dropextendproc	Removes an extended stored procedure.
sp_dropgroup	Removes a group from a database. All users must be dropped from the group first.
sp_droplanguage	Removes the language specified from the server.
sp_droplogin	Deletes SQL Server login ID.
sp_dropmessage	Removes a specified error message.
sp_dropremotelogin	Deletes the remote user login ID specified.
sp_dropsegment	Deletes or unmaps the segment from a database device.
sp_dropserver	Deletes the server from a list of known servers.
sp_dropuser	Deletes the user from the database.
sp_droptype	Deletes the user-defined datatype from the system.
sp_extendsegment	Allows you to associate a segment with another database device.
sp_help	Displays information about a server or a database object, such as a table or view.
sp_helpconstraint	Returns a list of all constraint types.
sp_helpdb	Returns information about a specific database.
sp_helpdevice	Returns information about a specific database device.
sp_helpextendedproc	Returns information on extended stored procedures and the associated name of the dynamic-link library.
sp_helpgroup	Returns information on a specific group.
sp_helpindex	Returns information on indexes of a table.
sp_helplanguage	Returns information on a specific language.
sp_helplog	Returns information on the device name that contains the first page of the log in the current database.

C

STORED
PROCEDURE QUICK
REFERENCE

continues

Table C.1. continued

Stored procedure	Description
sp_helpremotelogin	Returns information about a specific remote user login ID.
sp_helpprotect	Returns the permissions of a user or group for a database object.
sp_helpsegment	Returns information on all segments or a specific segment in the current database.
sp_helpserver	Returns information on a specific server.
sp_helpsort	Returns information on the default sort order and character set.
sp_helpsql	Returns information on SQL statements, procedures, and additional special topics.
sp_helpstartup	Returns a listing of all stored procedures that are automatically started when the server starts.
sp_helptext	Returns the text that was used to create the object, such as a table, trigger, or view.
sp_helpuser	Returns information about a specific user.
sp_lock	Returns information on locks.
sp_logdevice	Places the transaction log on a separate database device.
sp_makestartup	Creates an auto-executable stored procedure when the SQL Server is started.
sp_monitor	Returns statistics on an SQL Server.
sp_password	Changes the password for a specific user ID.
sp_placeobject	Allocates space for future expansion of a table or index.
sp_processmail	Processes incoming mail using extended stored procedures.
sp_recompile	This stored procedure will recompile all triggers or stored procedures the next time the table is accessed.
sp_remoteoption	Changes or displays information for options for logging onto a remote server.
sp_rename	Renames an object created by the user.
sp_renamedb	Renames a database.
sp_serveroption	Sets the type of SQL Server desired.
sp_setlangalias	Creates an alias for an alternate language.
sp_spaceused	Returns the amount of disk space used.

Stored procedure	Description
sp_unbindefault	Removes a column default or a user-defined datatype default.
sp_unbindrule	Removes a column or a user-defined datatype rule.
sp_unmakestartup	Stops specified stored procedure from auto-executing.
sp_who	Returns information on users and processes currently running on the SQL Server.

I will briefly discuss the syntax and purpose of some of the stored procedures as a quick reference guide.

sp_addgroup

This system stored procedure creates a group to organize your users. This makes administrative tasks easier because it can automatically assign the default permissions to the user inherited from the group. Typical groups can be sales, marketing, or accounting, or can even be regional or by company. The syntax is

sp_addgroup *groupname*

The *groupname* is the name of the group desired.

sp_addlogin

This system stored procedure creates a login ID in order to access SQL Server. The syntax is

sp_addlogin *loginid,[password],[defaultdatabase],[defaultlanguage]*

Interestingly enough, the only required parameter is the *loginid*, which must start with an alphabetic character. The *password* should be assigned with a ideal minimum length of eight characters. You should ensure that the *defaultdatabase* exists. Finally, the *defaultlanguage* parameter is available to change the language seen by the end user.

sp_adduser

This system stored procedure creates a user ID for accessing SQL Server databases. The syntax is

sp_adduser *loginid,[username],[groupname]*

The *loginid* is the ID created when sp_addlogin is used. You cannot add a user to the database if the user does not have a login ID. The *username* is the name to identify the user. If not specified, the *loginid* becomes the default. The *groupname* is also optional to assign this user to a specific group.

sp_changegroup

This system stored procedure changes the group where the user belongs. The syntax is

sp_changegroup *new_group,username*

The *new_group* is the new group the user is being assigned. The *username* is the username assigned to the user in the current database.

sp_dropgroup

This system stored procedure removes the group entirely. However, if there are members of this group, you cannot delete this group until you perform sp_changegroup on all of the members. The syntax is

sp_dropgroup *groupname*

The *groupname* is the name of the group to permanently remove.

sp_droplogin

This system stored procedure removes the login ID of a specific user. The syntax is

sp_droplogin *loginID*

The *loginID* is the login ID of the user to permanently remove.

sp_dropuser

This system stored procedure removes the user ID from the current database. The syntax is

sp_dropuser *username*

The *username* is the user ID of the user to permanently remove.

sp_password

This system stored procedure changes the user's password. The syntax is

sp_password *oldpw,newpw,[loginid]*

The *oldpw* is the current user's password, and the *newpw* is what the new password will be. The optional *loginid* can only be used by a systems administrator to change the password of any user. However, if the user forgets her current password, only the system administrator can create a new password by substituting the NULL value for the old password.

sp_who

This system stored procedure displays the status of the current users of the system and what they are doing in the system. The syntax is

sp_who *[loginid¦spid]*

If no parameters are specified, you will receive a status of all users and processes. Otherwise, you can specify an optional *loginid* or *spid*, which locates a specific process for output to the console.

Using Stored Procedures for Assistance Acquiring Information

The following procedures will provide you with help when dealing with SQL Server: `sp_help`, `sp_helpconstraint`, `sp_helpdb`, `sp_helpgroup`, `sp_helprotect`, `sp_helpserver`, `sp_helpsort`, `sp_helpsql`, `sp_helpstartup`, `sp_helptext`, and `sp_helpuser`.

sp_help

This stored procedure provides detailed information on a database object. The syntax for `sp_help` is

```
sp_help [objectname]
```

By using `sp_help` with no parameters, you will see a list of all database objects in the current database:

```
sp_help
```

The output from this command would be enough to fill a chapter. However, it provides you with the Object Name, Object Owner, and Object Type. From the master database, you could try

```
sp_help sp_help
```

Your output would be

```
Name            Owner         Type                  When_created
- - - - - - - - - - - - - - - - - - - - - - - - - - - - - - - - - - - - - - - - - - -
sp_help         dbo           stored procedure        Apr 3 1996  3:42AM

Data_located_on_segment
- - - - - - - - - - - - - - -
not applicable

Parameter_name        Type          Length Prec Scale Param_order
- - - - - - - - - - - - - - - - -  - - - - - - - - - - - - - - - - - - - - - - - - - - -
@objname              varchar          92     92   (null)1
```

This provides all the information you need to understand `sp_help`. To get more information on a table, you could try

```
sp_help syslogins
```

Your output would be

```
Name            Owner         Type                  When_created
- - - - - - - - - - - - - - - - - - - - - - - - - - - - - - - - - - - - - - - - - -
syslogins       dbo           system table            Apr 3 1996  3:38AM
```

C

STORED PROCEDURE QUICK REFERENCE

```
Data_located_on_segment
----------------------------
system


Column_name    Type      Length Prec  Scale Nullable
----------------------------------------------------
suid           smallint    2      5      0    no
status         smallint    2      5      0    no
accdate        datetime    8                  no
totcpu         int         4     10      0    no
totio          int         4     10      0    no
spacelimit     int         4     10      0    no
timelimit      int         4     10      0    no
resultlimit    int         4     10      0    no
dbname         sysname    30                  yes
name           sysname    30                  no
password       sysname    30                  yes
language       varchar    30                  yes
Identity       Seed         Increment
No identity column defined.      (null)              (null)


index_name          index_description              index_keys
---------------------------------------------------------------
syslogins      clustered, unique located on system     suid
ncsyslogins    nonclustered, unique located on system  name
```

No constraints have been defined for this object.
No foreign keys reference this table.

Now you have the complete table layout and can query the table accordingly. I use this extensively when making changes to existing applications in order to recall the column names, format, and so on. Other people tend to make changes without documenting them, unfortunately.

sp_helpconstraint

This stored procedure provides a list of all table constraints. The syntax for sp_helpconstraint is

sp_constraint *tablename*

The *tablename* parameter is the name of the table desired. An example would be

sp_helpconstraint store

The output from this query would be

```
Object Name
---------------------------------------------------------------
store


constraint_type     constraint_name   status_enabled status_for_
    replication constraint_keys
PRIMARY KEY (clustered)   PK__store__StoreID__7CA47C3F   (n/a)(n/a) StoreID
UNIQUE (non-clustered)    stname                         (n/a)(n/a) StoreName,
    Address, City, State
```

```
Table is referenced by
-----------------------------------------------------
master.dbo.inventory: FK__inventory__Store__0AF29B96
master.dbo.salesall: FK__salesall__StoreI__16644E42
master.dbo.salesmw: FK__salesmw__StoreID__0DCF0841
master.dbo.salesne: FK__salesne__StoreID__119F9925
```

This table was created in Chapter 2, "Using Advanced Data Manipulation Language." As you can see, there are two constraints of a primary key and a secondary unique key. If you were having problems adding a record because it was a duplicate, this could quickly show why you are getting the error messages. The most common problem is with defaults set in the front-end systems, such as those created with Visual Basic.

sp_helpdb

This stored procedure provides a list of all databases or information on a specific database. The syntax for sp_helpdb is

```
sp_helpdb [databasename]
```

Running the procedure with no parameters returns summary information on all databases. The following example specifies the master database:

```
sp_helpdb master
```

The output from this query is

```
name   db_size        owner    dbid    created      status
-------------------------------------------------------------
master    17.00 MB sa     1      Apr  3 1996 trunc. log on chkpt

device_fragments             size          usage
-------------------------------------------------------
master                       3.00 MB data and log
master                      14.00 MB data and log

device                       segment
-------------------------------------------------------
master                       default
master                       logsegment
master                       system
```

This is useful for maintaining enough DASD for the databases, as well as monitoring the size of databases for abnormal increases.

sp_helpgroup

This stored procedure displays information about a specific group or lists a summary of all available groups. The syntax for sp_helpgroup is

```
sp_helpgroup [groupname]
```

Running the procedure with no parameters returns summary information on all available groups. Specifying the group name returns information regarding the group, such as permissions and members. This is very useful as a quick administrative utility.

sp_helprotect

This stored procedure displays permissions for a specific object, and even down to the user level. The syntax for `sp_helprotect` is

```
sp_helprotect [objectname,username]
```

If no parameter is supplied, you will receive a summary of all database objects. Specifying the object, or optionally the username, returns the corresponding permissions. The following example specifies the `syslogins` table:

```
sp_helprotect syslogins
```

The output from this query is

```
Owner Object    Grantee Grantor ProtectType Action Column
---- --------- ------- ------- ----------- ------ ----------
dbo   syslogins public  dbo     Grant       Select (New)
dbo   syslogins public  dbo     Grant       Select suid
dbo   syslogins public  dbo     Grant       Select status
dbo   syslogins public  dbo     Grant       Select accdate
dbo   syslogins public  dbo     Grant       Select totcpu
dbo   syslogins public  dbo     Grant       Select totio
dbo   syslogins public  dbo     Grant       Select spacelimit
dbo   syslogins public  dbo     Grant       Select timelimit
dbo   syslogins public  dbo     Grant       Select resultlimit
dbo   syslogins public  dbo     Grant       Select dbname
dbo   syslogins public  dbo     Grant       Select name
dbo   syslogins public  dbo     Grant       Select language

(12 row(s) affected)
```

sp_helpserver

This stored procedure displays information on one or all available SQL Servers. The syntax for `sp_helpserver` is

```
sp_helpserver [servername]
```

If no parameter is supplied, you will receive a summary of all available SQL Servers. Specifying the server name returns information for that specific server, including the type of SQL Server such as remote, subscription, and so on.

sp_helpsort

Ever have problems in how your SQL reports are sorting? This stored procedure displays information on the method SQL Server uses to sort. The syntax for `sp_helpsort` is

```
sp_helpsort
```

Running this displays the current character set, the sort order, and the actual order of the characters. Again, if someone changed the sort order, this could cause problems in output.

sp_helpsql

This command is very useful if you do not have access to any SQL books, the SQL Server online books are not installed, and you need a description and syntax of a particular function or stored procedure. This stored procedure returns text-based descriptions along with the syntax for almost every SQL statement available. The format is

```
sp_helpsql ["topic"]
```

If no topic is specified, this stored procedures provides you with sample topics. Quotes are necessary if you need to search for more than one word, such as "Create Table". The following example demonstrates finding information on the INSERT statement:

```
sp_helpsql "insert"
```

You will notice the quotations around the topic. If no quotes surround this topic, SQL Server will think that you are trying to use the INSERT statement and will display the appropriate error message. The output from the preceding statement produces

```
Transact-SQL Syntax Help
  INSERT Statement
  Adds a new row to a table or a view, which is optionally
  returned from a stored procedure.

  INSERT [INTO]
      {<table_name> ¦ <view_name>} [(<column_list>)]
  {DEFAULT VALUES ¦ <values_list> ¦ <select_statement> }
  EXECute {<procedure_name> ¦ @<procedure_name_var>}
  [[@<parameter_name> =] {<value>¦ @<variable> [OUTPUT] ¦ DEFAULT }
  [,[@<parameter_name> =] {<value>¦ @<variable> [OUTPUT] ¦ DEFAULT}]...]
```

sp_helpstartup

This stored procedure displays information on which stored procedures execute automatically when the SQL Server is started. The syntax for sp_helpstartup is

```
sp_helpstartup
```

No parameters are required. A list is returned of these procedures. Again, this is another powerful administrative tool for seeing what processes are launched when the SQL Server is started.

sp_helptext

This stored procedure provides text help associated with an object such as a trigger, stored procedure, view, or a rule, provided the object contains help text. The syntax for sp_helptext is

```
sp_helptext objectname
```

This is great for a documentation tool. For instance, you could use this on a trigger to see its purpose.

NOTE

If the stored procedure, trigger, or view was created with the ENCRYPTION option, the displayed text will be the garbled (encrypted) representation.

sp_helpuser

This stored procedure lists all users or provides information for a specific user. The syntax for sp_helpuser is

sp_helpuser *[username]*

This is yet another administrative tool for verifying information on a specific user or simply listing the available usernames in the system.

Extended Stored Procedures

The built-in extended stored procedures are summarized in Table C.2.

Table C.2. SQL Server built-in extended stored procedures.

Stored Procedure	Description
xp_cmdshell	Allows you full access to all of the operating system commands.
xp_deletemail	Deletes a message from the SQL Server inbox.
xp_enumgroups	Lists all groups in the specified Windows NT domain name.
xp_findnextmessage	Grabs the next message ID to allow the message to be read.
xp_grantlogin	Allows you to add SQL Server access to a Windows NT user.
xp_logevent	Sends error message to Windows NT log.
xp_loginconfig	Displays login security parameters of the Windows NT server.
xp_logininfo	Displays login information for one or all accounts on the system.
xp_msver	Returns information on the version of SQL Server, and also the server environment.
xp_readmail	Reads a message specified by the message ID.
xp_revokelogin	Removes login privileges to the SQL Server.

Stored Procedure	Description
xp_sendmail	Allows you to send mail, including attachments, to the user specified.
xp_sprintf	Formats output of a string for up to 50 variables of type string (%s). Similar to C programming language sprintf.
xp_sscanf	Reads only strings into an argument. Similar to C scanf.
xp_startmail	Starts the mail session if it's not automatically configured to start when the server starts.
xp_stopmail	Stops the current mail session.

Common Error Codes

This appendix lists many common error messages you will receive, the text output by SQL Server to describe the error, and what the errors could really mean since the descriptions are not always clear. Error messages will show %[letter], where [letter] represents a variable output in an error message. For example, %s would represent a string value, and %d would represent a decimal value.

Error Message #103

Text Output: The identifier that starts with %S_MSG is too long. Maximum length is %d.

Explanation of Error: You have attempted to assign a value a name greater than the maximum length. The SQL is

```
CREATE TABLE myuser(
    Addressaddressaddressadderssaddress          varchar(40))
```

This code will generate this error because the column name is too long. So will

```
select addressaddressaddressaddressaddress from myusers;
```

Error Message #105

Text Output: Unclosed quote before the character string %s.

Explanation of Error: You are missing a quote around a character string, usually above the line with the error message. For instance, you might type policy" instead of "policy".

Error Message #109

Text Output: There are more columns in the INSERT statement than values specified in the VALUES clause. The number of values in the VALUES clause must match the number of columns specified in the INSERT statement.

Explanation of Error: You have too few values for the number of columns you have specified when inserting values.

Error Message #110

Text Output: There are fewer columns in the INSERT statement than values specified in the VALUES clause. The number of values in the VALUES clause must match the number of columns specified in the INSERT statement.

Explanation of Error: You have too many values for the number of columns you have specified when inserting values.

Error Message #113

Text Output: Missing end comment mark */.

Explanation of Error: You forgot to end your comments with `*/`, or you made a typing error such as `/*` or `/`.

Error Message #137

Text Output: Must declare variable `%s`.

Explanation of Error: You have not declared the variable, or you tried to access a local variable as a global variable, which is unacceptable.

Error Message #156

Text Output: Incorrect syntax near the keyword `%s`.

Explanation of Error: This can be a result of improper formatting of a command, or misspelling the keyword. An example would be `CREATE PORC tim ...`

Error Message #170

Text Output: Incorrect syntax near `%s`.

Explanation of Error: This usually means that a keyword is misspelled or two words have run together. It also appears when you are trying to use functions on a line that uses `EXEC`.

Error Message #174

Text Output: The function `%s` requires `%d` arguments.

Explanation of Error: This means that too few or too many arguments were used with a function. Use the online help, or better yet use `sp_sqlhelp` to get the list of parameters required for the function.

Error Message #201

Text Output: Procedure `%s` expects parameter `%s`, which was not supplied.

Explanation of Error: If no default parameters are specified within the procedure, you will get this error when missing one or more parameters of a stored procedure.

Error Message #206

Text Output: Operand type clash: `%s` null is incompatible with `%s`.

Explanation of Error: This error could be a result of attempting to convert function output to string value without using `CONVERT`, such as using `STR(GETDATE())`. You will receive this error message when trying to perform one set of operations with an operator that is incompatible with a datatype.

Error Message #207

Text Output: Invalid column name %s.

Explanation of Error: You attempted to select a column and entered a column name incorrectly. Use `sp_help` `tablename` to get a list of all columns in the table quickly.

Error Message #208

Text Output: Invalid object name %s.

Explanation of Error: The object name you are referencing does not exist, or you need to reference the owner name of the object.

Error Message #225

Text Output: Cannot run query—referenced object (name %s) dropped during query optimization.

Explanation of Error: An object, such as an index, trigger, stored procedure, and so on, was added or removed during optimization of a table and can no longer be found by the query.

Error Message #229

Text Output: %s permission denied on object %s, database %s, owner %s.

Explanation of Error: You have not been granted privileges to that object, such as trying to access a system stored procedure without the appropriate privileges, like `xp_cmdshell`.

Error Message #230

Text Output: %s permission denied on column %s of object %s, database %s, owner %s.

Explanation of Error: You may not have full rights to a table. Or you may have only certain rights to certain columns in a table, and the column you selected is not one of them. You usually get this error if you try to select data from the systems tables and you are not the system administrator.

Error Message #235

Text Output: Cannot convert CHAR value to MONEY. The CHAR value has incorrect syntax.

Explanation of Error: This usually occurs when spaces or symbols in the character string are not allowed to convert to MONEY. Could also occur if you are dynamically creating the character string and the output does not comply to MONEY conversion.

Error Message #241

Text Output: Syntax error converting DATETIME from character string.

Explanation of Error: This usually is a result of a typing error when keying in a date in any of the acceptable date/time formats, or trying to assign a string value to a date/time value when the string is improperly formatted.

Error Message #257

Text Output: Implicit conversion from datatype %s to %s is not allowed. Use the CONVERT function to run this query.

Explanation of Error: This occurs when you're attempting to use SQL Server to automatically convert a datatype to another datatype and the conversion is not supported. One acceptable alternative for most cases is to use the CONVERT function.

Error Message #259

Text Output: Ad hoc updates to system catalogs not enabled. System Administrator must reconfigure system to allow this.

Explanation of Error: This occurs when you attempt to change system variables without using system stored procedures and the allow updates parameter has not been changed to a value of 1. Do not do this, because there is always another method! Chapter 6, "Effective Use of Stored Procedures as an Administrative Tool," demonstrates a query that caused this error and an alternate method to produce the same results.

Error Message #268

Text Output: You can't run SELECT INTO in this database. Please check with the Database Owner.

Explanation of Error: This occurs when you attempt to use the SELECT INTO statement to enter records into a table and the select into/bulkcopy option is disabled. This process does not allow logged transactions, so you may want to consider using INSERT...SELECT. If you must use SELECT INTO, which does work faster, use the sp_dboption stored procedure to set select into/bulkcopy to TRUE.

Error Message #284

Text Output: Rules may not be bound to TEXT or IMAGE datatypes.

Explanation of Error: TEXT and IMAGE datatypes do not allow the use of rules. If you are attempting to place a rule on TEXT content, you may consider changing the field value to a string datatype and bind the rule on this column.

Error Message #308

Text Output: Index %s on table %s (specified in the FROM clause) does not exist.

Explanation of Error: This can be caused by removing the index from the table or typing the index name incorrectly in the query. Also, verify that the correct table has been specified.

Error Message #404

Text Output: Too many ANDs or ORs in expression (limit %d per expression level). Try splitting query or limiting ANDs and ORs.

Explanation of Error: Although the maximum number of ANDs and ORs is 250, I have actually witnessed someone attempting to use more than the number allowed when selecting certain IDs from a large table.

> **NOTE**
>
> I do not agree with the Text Output solution. The ideal solution is to create a table, whether temporary or permanent, that stores the IDs to select, and then use this table to select data from the main table.

Error Message #511

Text Output: Updated or inserted row is bigger than maximum size (%d bytes) allowed for this table.

Explanation of Error: Attempting to insert data into a row of a table that is larger than the number of bytes allowed. Can occur when transferring data from one table to another with different column sizes.

Error Message #515

Text Output: Attempt to insert the value NULL into column %s, table%s; column does not allow nulls. %s fails.

Explanation of Error: This occurs when a NULL value is being inserted into a column in which NULL values are not allowed. One common oversight is to have a stored procedure that adds data to a table. If the stored procedure accepts input values, NULL is not tested, and you manipulate data with additional stored procedures. This could cause quite a few problems just with one input parameter.

Error Message #544

Text Output: Attempting to insert explicit value for identity column in table %s when IDENTITY_INSERT is set to OFF.

Explanation of Error: Using identity allows you to generate a column that auto-increments from a starting seed value. If `IDENTITY_INSERT` is set to `OFF` and you want to modify or insert the auto-increment value, use `SET IDENTITY_INSERT` `tablename` `ON`.

Error Message #601

Text Output: Descriptor for system table `%Id` in database `%d` not found in the descriptor hash table.

Explanation of Error: Although this message may not be as common, I have received it more often than needed. This error occurs when the same systems table is read into memory a second time due to poor memory management. The two tables have an obvious conflict, so the information is not accessible from SQL Server. The system tables are read and managed in memory; therefore, the problem must be fixed by shutting down the SQL Server and possibly even rebooting the machine. If the problem persists, you need to make sure your hardware is properly configured.

Error Message #602

Text Output: Could not find row in `Sysindexes` for `dbid %d`, object `%Id`, index `%d`. Run `DBCC CHECKTABLE on Sysindexes`.

Explanation of Error: This is the result of trying to retrieve a row of data from a table that may have been dropped. If the table hasn't been dropped, and it is properly indexed, you may have corrupted indexes. Run several DBCC type checks on the table to locate any errors.

Error Message #603

Text Output: There are not enough system session descriptors available to run this query. The maximum number available to a process is `%d`. Split query and rerun.

Explanation of Error: When you're referencing tables in very complex queries, information about the objects is loaded into memory for faster access. If you attempt to join/use too many tables, you will get this error. One way to get around this is to change the number of open objects with the `sp_configure` stored procedure. The alternative method is to rewrite the query with fewer joins/tables selected, or perhaps write temporary results into a temporary table.

Error Message #605

Text Output: Attempt to fetch logical page `%ld` in database `%s` belongs to object `%s`, not to object `%s`.

Explanation of Error: SQL Server generates this message when it detects database corruption. One or both objects are corrupted. Use the `DBCC CHECKDB` statement to see which database is corrupted. A possible cause of this is running SQL Server using the FAT operating system. I highly recommend using NTFS, and if this problem does occur, you will most likely have to restore to the last known good backup.

Error Message #606

Text Output: Error %d encountered while reading without locking, command is terminated.

Explanation of Error: In multi-user systems, if you are not careful with placing locks on transactions, you will get this error message. For instance, if you are trying to access a record being updated, added, or inserted by another connection, and the transaction is not locked, you will receive this error message. I recommend implementing locks on all transactions to prevent errors or data corruption.

Error Message #614

Text Output: A row on page %Id was accessed that has an illegal length of %d in database %s.

Explanation of Error: This is usually a result of corrupted data in one or more rows on a page. The root cause could be a result of hardware corruption or loading or importing data from another database. The best solution is to load the database from the last known good save and run DBCC CHECKDB against the database.

Error Message #624

Text Output: Attempt to retrieve row from page via RID failed because the requested RID has a higher number than the last RID on the page. %S_RID.%S_PAGE.

Explanation of Error: This error can be a result of accessing data that points to a ROW ID while other users are updating data at the same time. It can also mean that the table's indexes are corrupt, but this is less frequently the true cause behind the error. Run DBCC CHECKDB to make sure that the database is truly not corrupted.

Error Message #625

Text Output: Could not retrieve row from logical page %Id via RID because the entry in the offset table (=%d) for that RID (=%d) is less than or equal to 0.

Explanation of Error: This error is almost always a result of database corruption, possibly even problems with the hardware. Certain SCSI cards with on-board memory and write-back caches, if not properly flushed, could lead to data corruption. You may need to turn off write caching enabled on the controller.

Error Message #701

Text Output: There is insufficient system memory to run this query.

Explanation of Error: Occurs when the procedure cache is too low to execute the query, trigger, function, stored procedure, and so on. Either increase the memory allocation with sp_configure, or create smaller procedures, queries, and so on. In a multi-user environment, set this value relatively high. In addition, make sure the Windows NT machine SQL Server has plenty of memory (at least 256MB).

Error Message #1007

Text Output: Column or parameter #%d: — specified column precision %d is greater than the maximum precision of %d.

Explanation of Error: Attempting to exceed the precision of SQL Server. SQL Server goes out to 28 places. Other products, such as Dataease or Visual Basic, carry out the precision much farther. You can round off to 28 places to match SQL Server, or you can specify /p when starting SQL Server to increase the precision. You will see a performance hit, however, so it is typically better to round off than to increase the precision.

Error Message #1023

Text Output: Invalid parameter %d specified for datepart.

Explanation of Error: One of the parameters specified is invalid. Specifying the parameters in the wrong order or making a typing error usually causes this problem.

Error Message #1204

Text Output: SQL Server has run out of LOCKS. Re-run your command when there are fewer active users, or ask your System Administrator to reconfigure SQL Server with more LOCKS.

Explanation of Error: The number of available locks is too small for the process to execute. Use sp_configure to increase the number of available locks. Additionally, you could run the process with no users logged into the system (no locks are required), or run smaller increments of a process (such as reducing the range when updating data in a table).

Error Message #1205

Text Output: Your server command (process id#%d) was deadlocked with another process and has been chosen as deadlock victim. Re-run your command.

Explanation of Error: This occurs when two processes attempt to access the same resource. The process with the fastest execution time will run, and the second process will need to be run again. This error does not stop batch processing.

Error Message #1505

Text Output: Create unique index aborted on duplicate key. Primary key is %S_KEY

Explanation of Error: This occurs if you attempt to create a unique index on a table containing data that would cause the uniqueness to be violated. Fix the duplicate data and then re-index the table. An example would be a table with social security numbers. Ideally, there should be one person entered with a given social security number. However, if you do have more than one entry with an SSN of 355-68-9898, this error will be raised. Search the data and delete the duplicate record.

Error Message #1508

Text Output: Create index aborted on duplicate rows. Primary key is %S_KEY.

Explanation of Error: This error occurs when you're attempting to create a clustered index and duplicated data in the table violates the unique settings. You can either change the data in the table or set ALLOW_DUP_ROW to ON to allow for duplicate values (however, the latter is definitely not recommended).

Error Message #1510

Text Output: Sort failed: Out of space or locks in database %.*s.

Explanation of Error: This error usually occurs as a result of creating an index and running out of storage space. This error can also occur if you are updating or adding an index on a large table and there are not enough locks available. You can increase storage, increase the number of locks with sp_configure, or create the index when no one else is logged into the SQL Server.

Error Message #1521

Text Output: Sort failed because a table in tempdb used for the processing of the query had a bad data page count. Tempdb should not have been damaged.

Explanation of Error: Complex queries that are output to temporary tables that sort on non-indexed fields can cause this problem. Re-index the selected tables and re-execute the queries.

Error Message #1530

Text Output: Create index with sorted_data was aborted because of row out of order. Primary key of first out of order row is %S_KEY.

Explanation of Error: This is caused when you attempt to create a sorted index on a table column where data is stored out of sequence. You can create the index with the sorted data option either not specified or set to OFF, or you can copy the data sequentially into a temporary table and then reload the table with the data sorted properly.

Error Message #1601

Text Output: No resources available to start %s process. Use sp_configure to increase the number of user connections.

Explanation of Error: When you're launching processes from the server, each process uses a connection. The default is 15 available connections, which even a single user can quickly exhaust. Use sp_configure to increase the connections to a more reasonable value, depending upon your office size.

Error Message #1608

Text Output: A network error was encountered while sending results to the front end. Check the SQL Server errorlog for more information.

Explanation of Error: This error occurs when SQL Server attempts to send information back to the front end to complete a request, and there is no response from the front end. Common reasons are that there were network problems, the front-end computer locked up, or the application was abnormally terminated.

Error Message #1702

Text Output: Create table failed because column %s in table %s exceeds the maximum of 250 columns.

Explanation of Error: Although it seems rare to create a table with more than 250 columns, you could possibly exceed this number when creating a dynamic temporary table. If this occurs, review the normalization and output requirements to see if the data can be broken into two or more tables.

Error Message #1803

Text Output: CREATE DATABASE failed. Could not allocate enough disk space for a new database on the disks named in the command. Total space allocated must be at least %d Mbytes (%ld 2048-byte pages) to accommodate copy of Model Database.

Explanation of Error: Occurs when you run out of storage when creating a database. Free up disk space and try the process again.

Error Message #1814

Text Output: Problem creating Temporary Database - if out of space, please extend and reboot. If some other problem, please contact Technical Support.

Explanation of Error: Occurs when you run out of memory or space on a device when creating a temporary table. Create a new device with a minimum of 2MB and run the process again.

Error Message #1902

Text Output: Cannot create more than one clustered index on table %s. Drop the existing clustered index %s before creating another.

Explanation of Error: You can have only one clustered index per table. Either make this index non-clustered, or drop the clustered index and re-create it.

Error Message #1903

Text Output: %d is the maximum allowable size of an index. Composite index specified is %d bytes.

Explanation of Error: This error occurs if the total number of bytes for all columns in the index exceeds 255 bytes. You have several options, such as removing columns from the index, creating alternate indexes, or changing the length of one or more columns.

Error Message #1904

Text Output: Cannot specify more than %d column names for index key list. %d specified.

Explanation of Error: This error occurs if the concatenated index has more than 16 columns. Make sure that the table has been normalized properly, or perhaps combine two of the columns into one concatenated column. An example is using two separate columns to create a part number, such as combining BK for part type and 109 for part number to make BK109. You can then use SUBSTRING to extract the separate values.

Error Message #2601

Text Output: Attempt to insert duplicate key row in object %x with unique index %s.

Explanation of Error: You will receive this error when attempting to enter a duplicate record in a table with unique indexes. If the unique key of the row should be duplicated, you will need to drop the index and re-create your new unique key after you have reviewed your normalization of the table. An example of improper index usage occurred when interfacing a cash register to a sales database. If a person purchased more than one of the same item, the unique key was set to reject the extra purchase but didn't bother to increase the total number of items purchased.

Error Message #2615

Text Output: Attempt to insert duplicate row in table %s with index %s in database %s. Could drop and recreate index with ignore duprow or allow duprow.

Explanation of Error: Occurs when you're attempting to enter a duplicate record in a table with clustered indexes. If you drop the table and re-create it with ALLOW_DUP_ROW specified for the table, this should solve your problems.

Error Message #2714

Text Output: There is already an object named %s in the database.

Explanation of Error: The object name exists in the current database. You could drop and then re-create the object (if your intent is to replace the object), create the object in another database, or rename the object.

Error Message #2715

Text Output: Column or parameter #1: Can't find type %s.

Explanation of Error: This is caused when you assign a user-defined datatype that no longer exists or misspell the name of a system datatype.

Error Message #2729

Text Output: Object %s group number 1 already exists in the database. Choose another procedure name.

Explanation of Error: There's already a stored procedure with the name you are using. Either change the name or use the DROP PROC statement to remove the old procedure.

Error Message #2751

Text Output: Column or parameter #%d: -- specified column scale %d is greater than the specified precision of %d.

Explanation of Error: Occurs when the scale of the column is greater than the precision assigned to the table.

Error Message #2812

Text Output: Stored procedure %s not found.

Explanation of Error: Either the stored procedure has been deleted or its name was incorrectly typed in the query.

Error Message #3101

Text Output: Database in use. System Administrator must have exclusive use of database to run load.

Explanation of Error: You are attempting to load a database when users are logged into the database.

Error Message #3105

Text Output: Data on dump will not fit into current database. Need %ld Mbyte database.

Explanation of Error: You are attempting to load a larger database into a smaller database. You should increase the size of the database that is to receive the load.

Error Message #3604

Text Output: Duplicate key was ignored.

Explanation of Error: Message occurs when you're trying to insert a duplicate row into a series of transactions. Either fix the row or change the key to allow the row to be inserted.

Error Message #3606

Text Output: Arithmetic overflow occurred.

Explanation of Error: This always occurs when you're assigning a value too large for the datatype, such as assigning 9121212193833 to an integer datatype. Always test values before saving. If the field needs to store the number, change the datatype. Another common problem is the creation of a loop that doesn't exit because a new condition occurred that was not taken into account by the programmer, continuing a calculation until the overflow error occurs.

Error Message #5701

Text Output: Changed database context to %s.

Explanation of Error: This error occurs when the current database context has been changed back to master by the execution of the CHECKUPG.EXE utility.

Error Message #5808

Text Output: Do not recommend ad hoc updates to system catalogues, use override option to force this configuration.

Explanation of Error: If allow updates is set to 0, you can change this value with sp_configure and then run RECONFIGURE. However, as seen in Chapter 6, "Effective Use of Stored Procedures as an Administrative Tool," there are many alternative ways to accomplish a goal without removing this restriction. If you remove it, anyone with proper permissions could alter the system tables!

Error Message #5813

Text Output: Unable to run with specified memory size of %ld. Please see the System Administration Guide for more information on how to calculate this number.

Explanation of Error: This occurs when you're attempting to reconfigure the database with RECONFIGURE. This process calculates the internal memory requirements for SQL Server to allow for the changed items. In the rare cases when RECONFIGURE does not cause this error, SQL Server will not reboot after being shut down.

Error Message #8101

Text Output: An explicit value for the identity column in table %s can only be specified when a column list is used and IDENTITY_INSERT is ON.

Explanation of Error: You are attempting to insert a value into an identity column. If you must add values and bypass the auto-increment (such as to reuse old numbers), make sure IDENTITY_INSERT is set to ON with the SET command.

Error Message #8102

Text Output: Illegal attempt to update identity column %s.

Explanation of Error: This occurs when you attempt to update a value into an identity column. If you must update values and bypass the auto-increment (such as to reuse old numbers), you will need to copy the data into a temporary table, change the value(s), and reload the data into the original table.

Error Message #8106

Text Output: Table %s does not have the identity property, unable to perform SET operation.

Explanation of Error: You've attempted to set the value of an identity column to ON in a table that does not contain an identity column.

Error Message #8146

Text Output: Procedure %s has no parameters and arguments were supplied.

Explanation of Error: You passed parameters to a procedure that does not accept parameters.

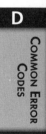

I
INDEX